2016 Edition

Federal-State Court Directory

**Federal Judges • Clerks of Court • Court Librarians
Probation Officers • Federal Prosecutors
Federal Public Defenders • Court Enforcement**

LEADERSHIP DIRECTORIES, INC.

www.leadershipdirectories.com
info@leadershipdirectories.com

New York Office
1407 Broadway, Suite 318
New York, NY 10018
(212) 627-4140
Fax (212) 645-0931

Washington, DC Office
1667 K Street, NW, Suite 801
Washington, DC 20006
(202) 347-7757
Fax (202) 628-3430

Leadership Directories, Inc.
FEDERAL-STATE COURT DIRECTORY

2016 Edition

Brian Beth, *Content Manager*

William W. Cressey, *Chairman of the Board*
Gretchen Teichgraeber, *President and Chief Executive Officer*
James M. Petrie, *Secretary*

Sales, Marketing, and Customer Service
Tom Silver, *Senior Vice President, Sales and Marketing*
Imogene Akins Hutchinson, *Vice President, Brand Development*
Jacqueline Johnson, *Fulfillment Manager*
Michele Anderson; Laurie Consoli; Anne Marie Del Vecchio; Heather Donegal; Ed Faas; Melissa Kaus; Jack Levengard; Jim Marcus; William Schneider; Nancy Scholem; Judy Smith; Wanda Speight-Bridgers

Products and Content
Sue Healy, *Senior Vice President, Products and Content*
Tom Zurla, *Assistant Vice President, Content*
Carmela Makabali, *Senior Director, Content and Database Management*
Harris Beringer, *Product Manager*
Dave Marmon, *Senior Product Specialist*
Gareth Sparks, *Manager, Content Development and Quality*

Information Technology
Brian F. Hanley, *Chief Information Officer*
Jill McLoughlin, *Project Leader/DBA*
Rabeya Khandaker, *Senior Software Engineer*
Cynthia Cordova, *Network Administrator*

Administration and Finance
James Gee, *Vice President for Administration and Treasurer*
Shai Tzach, *Controller*
Diane Calogrides, *Office Assistant (NY)*
Elvis A. Perez

The *Federal-State Court Directory* is published annually by Leadership Directories, Inc., 1407 Broadway, Suite 318, New York, NY 10018.
For additional information, including details about other Leadership Directories, Inc. publications, please call (212) 627-4140.

Leadership Directories
www.leadershipdirectories.com

Federal-State Court Directory

**Federal Judges • Clerks of Court • Court Librarians
Probation Officers • Federal Prosecutors
Federal Public Defenders • Court Enforcement**

Basic Structure of the U.S. Court System

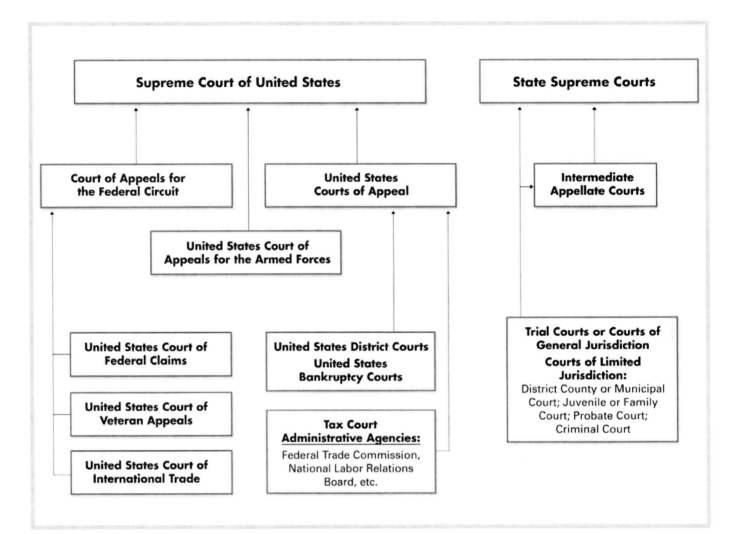

Table of Contents

(continued on next page)

Table of Contents—continued

Table of Contents—continued

Introduction

Leadership Directories is proud to present the completely updated 2016 edition of the *Federal–State Court Directory.*

This edition of the *Federal-State Court Directory*, we saw far fewer newly confirmed and sworn-in judges. After winning back the U.S. Senate in November 2014, Republicans have brought back the usual pace for confirming judicial nominations. As a result of fewer vacancies being filled, the judicial vacancy count has grown along with the number of pending nominees.

In the first eight months of 2015, a total of five new Article III judges were confirmed and sworn in. The appellate courts saw only Kara Farnandez Stoll be confirmed to the United States Court of Appeals for the Federal Circuit. District courts saw only four new judges.

At press time for this 2016 edition, there are 67 judicial vacancies throughout U.S. Federal Courts, with 28 nominees still pending review by the Senate. By comparison, on the day we published the 2015 edition, there were a total of 58 judicial vacancies throughout the U.S. Federal Courts.

The Federal–State Court Directory Content Overview
The *Federal–State Court Directory* is a comprehensive and easy–to–use guide to the U.S. federal and state judicial systems and their operations, including detailed and fully updated listings for courts, judges, administration, librarians, clerks, and federal and state enforcement officials.

The Federal–State Court Directory Section-by-Section
Below is a breakdown of the 2016 *Federal–State Court Directory*, with a detailed description of each section of the directory.

Introduction
• A detailed table of contents for sections and federal courts, so you can quickly flip to the page of the directory you need
• A chart of the U.S. Court System
• An historical record of the Justices of the U.S. Supreme Court
• A list of recent judicial nominations and confirmations
• A list of recent judicial vacancies

(continued on next page)

The Federal–State Court Directory Section-by-Section—continued

U.S. Supreme Court
- Address, phone, fax, and website for the Supreme Court
- The nine Supreme Court Justices with dates each began service, presidential appointment, and state from which they were appointed
- Clerk of the Court with full name, exact title, and complete contact information including email

Special Courts
- Address, phone, fax, and website for the U.S. Courts of Limited Jurisdiction, including the US Court of Federal Claims, US Court of International Trade, US Court of Appeals for the Armed Forces, US Court of Appeals for Veterans Claims, Alien Terrorist Removal Court, US Tax Court, and the Judicial Panel on Multidistrict Litigation
- The complete roster of judges for each court, with dates each began service, presidential appointment, and detailed contact information including email
- Clerks for each court, plus other key staff such as Chief Special Master, Executive Officer, and Panel Executive, with full name, exact title, and complete contact information including email

U.S. Courts of Appeals
- Address, phone, fax, and website for the eleven Circuit Courts of Appeals, plus the Federal Circuit and DC Circuit, and the newly added Bankruptcy Appellate Panels
- The complete roster of judges for each court, with dates each began service, presidential appointment, and detailed contact information including email
- Staff for each court, including Circuit Executive, Circuit Clerk, Circuit Mediator, and Circuit Librarian, with full name, exact title, and complete contact information including email

U.S. District Courts
- Address, phone, fax, website, circuit, and jurisdictional area for all 94 District Courts in the 50 U.S. states, the District of Columbia, the Commonwealth of Puerto Rico, and the territories of Guam, the U.S. Virgin Islands, and the Northern Mariana Islands
- The complete roster of judges for each court, with dates each began service, presidential appointment (when applicable), and detailed contact information including email
- Staff for each court, including Clerk and Chief Probation Officer, with full name, exact title, and complete contact information including email
- Each District's U.S. Attorney, with full name, exact title, and complete contact details including email
- Each District's Federal Public Defender, with full name, exact title, and complete contact information including email

Federal Districts—Divisions, Counties, and Court House Locations
- An overview of each federal district listing the court's website, counties within the district, and location and phone number for each holding court (civil session)

The Federal–State Court Directory Section-by-Section—continued

U.S. (Bankruptcy) Trustees
• Address, phone, fax, and website for each of the 21 regional offices of the U.S. Trustee Program, plus address, phone and fax for each of the 66 field offices
• U.S. Trustees for each region and Assistant U.S. Trustees at each field office with full name, exact title, and detailed contact information including email

Federal Administrative Law Judges
• Chief Federal Administrative Law Judges at major federal agencies listed with full name, exact title, address, phone, and email

Alternative Dispute Resolution—Selected Organizations
• Organizations involved in dispute resolution with name, address, phone, fax, and website

Federal and State Bar Associations
• Contact information, including address, phone, fax, and website for the American Bar Association and each state's bar association

State Courts
• A hierarchical visualization of the state court structure distinguishing trial level from appellate level, with clear indication of the route of appeal
• Description of case jurisdiction, trial types, and number of judges for each court within the state system
• Chief Justice and Supreme Court Justices
• Clerk of the Supreme Court, with name, address and phone
• State Court System website
• Court Administrative Director, with name, address and phone
• State Website and State Capitol phone
• Governor, Attorney General, and Secretary of State, each listed with name, address and phone
• Head of Vital Statistics, with name, address and phone

Name Index
• An index listing each person in the directory, with the page on which to find them

Thank you for purchasing the 2016 edition of *Federal–State Court Directory*. We invite you to visit our website or call us to provide comments, learn more about Leadership Directories' various publications, or to find out more about the companion book to *Federal–State Court Directory*, the *Directory of State Court Clerks and County Courthouses*. We also send our sincere appreciation to the countless contacts within courts, judges' chambers, and federal offices who assist us on a continuous basis by providing updated information for our directories.

How to Use the **Federal-State Court Directory**

Federal Courts

To the right is a sample of a page from the U.S. District Courts section. Use this guide to help you understand the layout of information on these pages.

See corresponding numbers on example.

1 Court Name
The official name of the Federal Court.

2 Contact Information
Address, telephone, PACER and other court information access numbers, and Internet address.

3 Court Details
Number of Judgeships in Court, Number of current vacancies (if any), Circuit (when applicable) and Areas Covered (when applicable).

4 Judges
Lists Judges with Began Service Date, name of President who appointed them (when applicable), phone, email, and address (if different from address listed at main court). Please note room numbers or other address details may be included aside the Judge's name when that information should be added to the main court address.

5 Court Staff
Lists court staff with phone, email, and address (if different from address listed at main court). Please note room numbers or other address details may be included aside the person's name when that information should be added to the main court address.

6 Bankruptcy Courts
Judges and staff for bankruptcy courts, listed exactly like main courts.

7 U.S. Attorney
In U.S. District Courts only, the U.S. Attorney for the District is listed with full contact details.

8 Federal Public Defender
In U.S. District Courts only, the Federal Public Defender for the District is listed with full contact details.

(continued on next page)

State Courts

To the right is a sample of a page from the State Courts section. Use this guide to help you understand the layout of information on these pages.

See corresponding numbers on example.

1 Listing begins with the state name.

2 The Chief Justice of the State Supreme Court.

3 Justices of the State Supreme Court are listed in alphabetical order.

4 Supreme Court Clerk with full contact details

5 Website for State court system

6 Main court administrator with exact title and full contact details

7 Governor with full contact details

8 State website and main capitol phone

9 State Attorney General with full contact details

10 Secretary of State with full contact details

11 Head of state vital statistics with exact title and full contact details

12 Structural chart of state court system

13 Guide for reading state court chart, indicating appellate level, trial level, and route of appeal

Judicial Nominations

U.S. Courts of Appeals

Name	Title	Court	Nominated	Confirmed
Felipe Restrepo	Circuit Judge	Third Circuit	1/7/2015	
Kara Farnandez Stoll	Circuit Judge	Federal Circuit	1/7/2015	7/7/2015

U.S. District Courts

Name	Title	Court	Nominated	Confirmed
Stephen R. Bough	District Judge	Western District of Missouri	1/16/2014	12/29/2014
Mark A. Kearney	District Judge	Eastern District of Pennsylvania	6/16/2014	12/4/2014
Joseph F. Leeson Jr.	District Judge	Eastern District of Pennsylvania	6/16/2014	12/4/2014
David J. Hale	District Judge	Western District of Kentucky	6/19/2014	12/4/2014
Greg N. Stivers	District Judge	Western District of Kentucky	6/19/2014	12/4/2014
Madeline Arleo	District Judge	District of New Jersey	6/26/2014	11/20/2014
Amos Mazzant	District Judge	Eastern District of Texas	6/26/2014	12/16/2014
Robert William Schroeder III	District Judge	Eastern District of Texas	6/26/2014	12/16/2014
Robert Lee Pitman	District Judge	Western District of Texas	6/26/2014	12/16/2014
Amit Priyavadan Mehta	District Judge	District of Columbia	7/31/2014	12/16/2014
Allison Dale Burroughs	District Judge	District of Massachusetts	7/31/2014	12/16/2014
John Robert Blakey	District Judge	Northern District of Illinois	8/5/2014	12/16/2014
Jorge L. Alonso	District Judge	Northern District of Illinois	8/5/2014	12/16/2014
Haywood Stirling Gilliam	District Judge	Northern District of California	8/18/2014	12/16/2014
Jill Parrish	District Judge	District of Utah	1/7/2015	5/21/2015
Joan Azrack	District Judge	Eastern District of New York	9/18/2014	12/16/2014
Loretta Copeland Biggs	District Judge	Middle District of North Carolina	9/18/2014	12/16/2014
George Hanks	District Judge	Southern District of Texas	1/7/2015	4/20/2015
Al Bennett	District Judge	Southern District of Texas	1/7/2015	4/13/2015
Rolando Olvera	District Judge	Southern District of Texas	1/7/2015	5/21/2015
Elizabeth K. Dillon	District Judge	Western District of Virginia	9/18/2014	12/16/2014
Dale Drozd	District Judge	Eastern District of California	1/7/2015	
LaShann Moutique DeArcy Hall	District Judge	Eastern District of New York	1/7/2015	
Ann M. Donnelly	District Judge	Eastern District of New York	1/7/2015	
Travis Randall McDonough	District Judge	Eastern District of Tennessee	1/7/2015	
Roseann A. Ketchmark	District Judge	Western District of Missouri	1/7/2015	
Lawrence Joseph Vilardo	District Judge	Western District of New York	2/4/2015	
Waverly D. Crenshaw Jr.	District Judge	Middle District of Tennessee	2/4/2015	
Julien Xavier Neals	District Judge	District of New Jersey	2/26/2015	
Mary Barzee Flores	District Judge	Southern District of Florida	2/26/2015	
John Michael Vazquez	District Judge	District of New Jersey	3/26/2015	
Paula Xinis	District Judge	District of Maryland	3/26/2015	
Wilhelmina Wright	District Judge	District of Minnesota	4/15/2015	
Edward L. Stanton	District Judge	Western District of Tennessee	5/21/2015	
Robert F. Rossiter	District Judge	District of Nebraska	6/11/2015	
Brian R. Martinotti	District Judge	District of New Jersey	6/11/2015	
Mark A. Young	District Judge	Central District of California	7/16/2015	
Leonard T. Strand	District Judge	Northern District of Iowa	7/21/2015	
Susan Paradise Baxter	District Judge	Western District of Pennsylvania	7/31/2015	
Inga S. Bernstein	District Judge	District of Massachusetts	7/31/2015	
Gary Richard Brown	District Judge	Eastern District of New York	7/31/2015	
Robert John Coville	District Judge	Western District of Pennsylvania	7/31/2015	

(continued on next page)

Judicial Nominations—continued

U.S. District Courts—continued

Name	Title	Court	Nominated	Confirmed
Marilyn Jean Horan	District Judge	Western District of Pennsylvania	7/31/2015	
Dax Eric Lopez	District Judge	Northern District of Georgia	7/31/2015	
John Milton Young	District Judge	Eastern District of Pennsylvania	7/31/2015	
Brenda K. Sannes	District Judge	Northern District of New York	5/8/2014	
Victor Allen Bolden	District Judge	District of Connecticut	6/16/2014	
Wendy Beetlestone	District Judge	Eastern District of Pennsylvania	6/16/2014	

Courts of Limited Jurisdiction

Name	Title	Court	Nominated	Confirmed
Nancy B. Firestone	Judge	U.S. Court of Federal Claims	1/7/2015	
Thomas L. Halkowski	Judge	U.S. Court of Federal Claims	1/7/2015	
Jeri Kaylene Somers	Judge	U.S. Court of Federal Claims	1/7/2015	
Patricia M. McCarthy	Judge	U.S. Court of Federal Claims	1/7/2015	
Armando Omar Bonilla	Judge	U.S. Court of Federal Claims	1/7/2015	
Lydia Kay Griggsby	Judge	U.S. Court of Federal Claims	4/10/2014	12/4/2014
Jeanne E. Davidson	Judge	United States Court of International Trade	1/7/2015	
Elizabeth J. Drake	Judge	United States Court of International Trade	7/31/2015	
Gary Stephen Katzmann	Judge	United States Court of International Trade	7/31/2015	
Jennifer Choe Groves	Judge	United States Court of International Trade	7/31/2015	
Elizabeth Ann Copeland	Judge	United States Tax Court	5/1/2015	

Judicial Vacancies

Special Courts

Court	Number of Vacancies
U.S. Court of Federal Claims	5
U.S. Court of International Trade	4

U.S. Courts of Appeals

Court	Number of Vacancies
U.S. Court of Appeals for the Eleventh Circuit	1
U.S. Court of Appeals for the Seventh Circuit	2
U.S. Court of Appeals for the Fifth Circuit	2
U.S. Court of Appeals for the Eighth Circuit	1
U.S. Court of Appeals for the Sixth Circuit	1
U.S. Court of Appeals for the Third Circuit	2

U.S. District Courts

Court	Number of Vacancies
U.S. District Court for the Middle District of Alabama	2
U.S. District Court for the Northern District of Alabama	2
U.S. District Court for the Central District of California	1
U.S. District Court for the Eastern District of California	1
U.S. District Court for the Middle District of Florida	2
U.S. District Court for the Southern District of Florida	1
U.S. District Court for the Northern District of Georgia	1
U.S. District Court for the District of Idaho	1
U.S. Bankruptcy Court for the Central District of Illinois	2
U.S. District Court for the Southern District of Indiana	1
U.S. District Court for the Northern District of Iowa	1
U.S. District Court for the Southern District of Iowa	1
U.S. District Court for the District of Kansas	1
U.S. District Court for the Eastern District of Kentucky	1
U.S. District Court for the Western District of Kentucky	1
U.S. Bankruptcy Court for the Eastern District of Kentucky	1
U.S. District Court for the Eastern District of Louisiana	1
U.S. District Court for the Western District of Louisiana	1
U.S. District Court for the District of Maryland	1
U.S. District Court for the District of Massachusetts	1
U.S. District Court for the District of Minnesota	1
U.S. District Court for the District of Nebraska	1
U.S. District Court for the District of New Jersey	4
U.S. District Court for the Eastern District of New York	3
U.S. District Court for the Southern District of New York	1
U.S. District Court for the Western District of New York	2
U.S. District Court for the Eastern District of North Carolina	1
U.S. Bankruptcy Court for the Western District of North Carolina	1
U.S. District Court for the Western District of Oklahoma	3
U.S. District Court for the Eastern District of Pennsylvania	1
U.S. District Court for the Western District of Pennsylvania	3
U.S. Bankruptcy Court for the Western District of Pennsylvania	2
U.S. District Court for the District of South Carolina	2

(continued on next page)

Judicial Vacancies—continued

U.S. District Courts

Court	Number of Vacancies
U.S. Bankruptcy Court for the District of South Dakota	1
U.S. District Court for the Eastern District of Tennessee	1
U.S. District Court for the Middle District of Tennessee	1
U.S. District Court for the Western District of Tennessee	1
U.S. District Court for the Eastern District of Texas	2
U.S. District Court for the Northern District of Texas	2
U.S. District Court for the Southern District of Texas	2
U.S. Bankruptcy Court for the Southern District of Texas	1
U.S. Bankruptcy Court for the Western District of Texas	1
U.S. District Court for the District of Utah	1

Members of the Supreme Court of the United States 1789 - 2015

	Date of Birth	State App't From	Appointed by President	Judicial Oath Taken	Age at Taking Oath	Date Service Terminated	Service Terminated by	Years of Service	Age at Termination	Age at Death
Chief Justices										
Jay, John	02/12/1745	NY	Washington	10/19/1789	44	06/29/1795	Resigned	5	49	83
Rutledge, John	09/1739	SC	Washington	08/12/1795	55	12/15/1795	Rejected	0	56	60
Ellsworth, Oliver	04/29/1745	CT.	Washington	03/08/1796	50	12/15/1800	Resigned	4	55	62
Marshall, John	09/22/1755	VA	Adams, John	02/04/1801	45	07/06/1835	Death	34	79	79
Taney, Roger Brooke	03/17/1777	MD	Jackson	03/28/1836	59	10/12/1864	Death	28	87	87
Chase, Salmon Portland	01/13/1808	OH	Lincoln	12/15/1864	56	05/07/1873	Death	8	65	65
Waite, Morrison Remick	11/29/1816	OH	Grant	03/04/1874	57	03/23/1888	Death	14	71	71
Fuller, Melville Weston	02/11/1833	IL	Cleveland	10/08/1888	55	07/04/1910	Death	21	77	77
White, Edward Douglas	11/03/1845	LA	Taft	12/19/1910	65	05/19/1921	Death	10	75	75
Taft, William Howard	09/15/1857	CT	Harding	07/11/1921	63	02/03/1930	Retired	8	72	72
Hughes, Charles Evans	04/11/1862	NY	Hoover	02/24/1930	67	06/30/1941	Retired	11	79	86
Stone, Harlan Fiske	10/11/1872	NY	Roosevelt, F.	07/03/1941	68	04/22/1946	Death	4	73	73
Vinson, Fred Moore	01/22/1890	KY	Truman	06/24/1946	56	09/08/1953	Death	7	63	63
Warren, Earl	03/19/1891	CA	Eisenhower	10/05/1953	62	06/23/1969	Retired	15	78	83
Burger, Warren Earl	09/17/1907	VA	Nixon	06/23/1969	61	06/17/1986	Retired	17	79	87
Rehnquist, William H.	10/01/1924	AZ	Reagan	09/26/1986	61	09/03/2005	Death	19	81	81
Roberts, John G. Jr.	01/27/1955	MD	Bush 2	09/29/2005	50					
Associate Justices										
Rutledge, John	09/1739	SC	Washington	05/12/1790	50	03/05/1791	Resigned	1	51	60
Cushing, William	03/01/1732	MA	Washington	02/02/1790	57	09/13/1810	Death	20	78	78
Wilson, James	09/14/1742	PA	Washington	10/05/1789	47	08/21/1798	Death	8	55	55
Blair, John	1732	VA	Washington	02/02/1790	58	01/27/1796	Resigned	5	64	68
Iredell, James	10/05/1751	NC	Washington	05/12/1790	38	10/20/1799	Death	9	48	48
Johnson, Thomas	11/04/1732	MD	Washington	08/06/1792	59	02/01/1793	Resigned	0	60	86
Paterson, William	12/24/1745	NJ	Washington	03/11/1793	47	09/09/1806	Death	13	60	60
Chase, Samuel	04/17/1741	MD	Washington	02/04/1796	54	06/19/1811	Death	15	70	70
Washington, Bushrod	06/05/1762	VA	Adams, John	02/04/1799	36	11/26/1829	Death	30	67	67
Moore, Alfred	05/21/1755	NC	Adams, John	04/21/1800	45	01/26/1804	Resigned	3	48	55
Johnson, William	12/27/1771	SC	Jefferson	05/07/1804	32	08/04/1834	Death	30	62	62
Livingston, Henry Brockholst	11/25/1757	KY	Jefferson	01/20/1807	49	03/18/1823	Death	16	65	65
Todd, Thomas	01/23/1765	KY	Jefferson	05/04/1807	42	02/07/1826	Death	18	81	61
Duvall, Gabriel	12/06/1752	MD	Madison	11/23/1811	58	01/14/1835	Resigned	23	82	91
Story, Joseph	09/18/1779	MA	Madison	02/03/1812	32	09/10/1845	Death	33	65	65
Thompson, Smith	01/17/1768	NY	Monroe	09/01/1823	55	12/18/1843	Death	20	75	75
Trimble, Robert	1777	KY	Adams, J.Q.	06/16/1826	49	08/25/1828	Death	2	51	51
McLean, John	03/11/1785	OH	Jackson	01/11/1830	44	04/04/1861	Death	31	76	76
Baldwin, Henry	01/14/1780	PA	Jackson	01/18/1830	50	04/21/1844	Death	14	64	64
Wayne, James Moore	1790	GA	Jackson	01/14/1835	45	07/05/1667	Death	32	77	77
Barbour, Philip Pendleton	05/25/1783	VA	Jackson	05/12/1836	52	02/25/1941	Death	4	57	57
Catron, John	1786	TN	Van Buren	05/01/1837	51	05/30/1865	Death	28	79	79
McKinley. John	05/01/1780	AL	Van Buren	01/09/1838	57	07/19/1852	Death	14	72	72
Daniel, Peter Vivian	04/24/1784	VA	Van Buren	01/10/1842	57	05/31/1860	Death	18	76	76
Nelson, Samuel	11/10/1792	NY	Tyler	02/27/1845	52	11/28/1872	Retired	27	80	81
Woodbury, Levi	12/22/1789	NH	Polk	09/23/1845	55	09/04/1851	Death	5	61	61
Grier, Robert Cooper	03/05/1794	PA	Polk	08/10/1846	52	01/31/1870	Retired	23	75	76
Curtis, Benjamin Robbins	11/04/1809	MA	Fillmore	10/10/1851	41	09/30/1857	Resigned	5	47	64
Campbell, John Archibald	06/24/1811	AL	Pierce	04/11/1853	41	04/30/1861	Resigned	8	49	77
Clifford, Nathan	08/18/1803	ME	Buchanan	01/21/1858	54	07/25/1881	Death	23	77	77
Swayne, Noah Haynes	12/07/1804	OH	Lincoln	01/27/1862	57	01/24/1881	Retired	18	76	79
Miller, Samuel Freeman	04/05/1816	IO	Lincoln	07/21/1862	46	09/13/1890	Death	28	74	74
Davis, David	03/09/1815	IL	Lincoln	12/10/1862	47	03/04/1877	Resigned	14	61	71
Field, Stephen Johnson	11/04/1816	CA	Lincoln	05/20/1863	46	12/01/1897	Retired	34	81	82
Strong, William	05/06/1808	PA	Grant	03/14/1870	61	12/14/1880	Retired	10	72	87
Bradley, Joseph	03/14/1813	NJ	Grant	03/23/1870	57	01/22/1892	Death	21	78	78
Hunt, Ward	06/14/1810	NY	Grant	01/09/1873	62	01/27/1882	Disabled	9	71	75
Harlan, John Marshall	06/01/1833	KY	Hayes	12/10/1877	44	10/14/1911	Death	33	78	78
Woods, William Burnham	08/03/1824	GA	Hayes	01/05/1881	56	05/14/1887	Death	6	62	62
Matthew, Stanley	07/21/1824	OH	Garfield	05/17/1881	56	03/22/1889	Death	7	64	64
Gray, Horace	03/24/1828	MA	Arthur	01/09/1882	53	09/15/1902	Death	20	74	74

Members of the Supreme Court of the United States 1789 - 2015

	Date of Birth	State App't From	Appointed by President	Judicial Oath Taken	Age at Taking Oath	Date Service Terminated	Service Terminated by	Years of Service	Age at Termination	Age at Death
Associate Justices *(continued)*										
Blatchtord, Samuel	03/09/1820	NY	Arthur	04/03/1882	62	07/07/1893	Death	11	73	73
Lamar, Lucius Quintus C.	09/17/1825	MS	Cleveland	01/18/1888	62	01/23/1893	Death	5	67	67
Brewer, David Josiah	06/20/1837	KS	Harrison	01/06/1890	52	05/28/1910	Death	20	72	72
Brown, Henry Billings	03/02/1836	MI	Harrison	01/05/1891	54	05/28/1906	Retired	15	70	77
Shiras, George Jr.	01/26/1832	PA	Harrison	10/10/1892	60	02/23/1903	Retired	10	71	92
Jackson, Howell Edmunds	04/08/1832	TN	Harrison	03/04/1893	60	08/08/1895	Death	2	63	63
White, Edward Douglas	11/03/1845	LA	Cleveland	03/12/1894	48	12/18/1910	Promoted	16	65	75
Peckham, Rufus Wheeler	11/08/1838	NY	Cleveland	01/06/1886	57	10/24/1909	Death	13	70	70
McKenna, Joseph	08/10/1843	CA	McKinley	01/26/1898	54	01/05/1925	Retired	26	81	83
Holmes, Oliver Wendell	03/08/1841	MA	Roosevelt, T.	12/08/1902	61	01/12/1932	Retired	29	90	93
Day, William Rufus	04/17/1849	OH	Roosevelt, T.	03/02/1903	53	11/13/1922	Retired	19	73	74
Moody, William Henry	12/23/1853	MA	Roosevelt, T.	12/17/1906	52	11/20/1910	Disabled	3	56	63
Lurton, Horace Harmon	02/26/1844	TN	Taft	01/03/1910	65	07/12/1914	Death	4	70	70
Hughes, Charles Evans	04/11/1862	NY	Taft	10/10/1910	48	06/10/1916	Resigned	5	54	86
Van Devanter, Willis	04/17/1859	WY	Taft	01/03/1911	51	06/02/1937	Retired	26	78	81
Lamar, Joseph Rucker	10/14/1857	GA	Taft	01/03/1911	53	01/02/1916	Death	4	58	58
Pitney, Mahlon	02/05/1858	NJ	Taft	03/18/1912	54	12/31/1922	Disabled	10	64	66
McReynolds, James Clark	02/03/1862	TN	Wilson	10/12/1914	52	01/31/1941	Retired	26	78	84
Brandeis, Louis Dembitz	11/13/1856	MA	Wilson	06/05/1916	59	02/13/1939	Retired	22	82	84
Clark, John Hessin	09/18/1857	OH	Wilson	10/09/1916	59	09/18/1922	Resigned	5	65	87
Sutherland, George	03/25/1862	UT	Harding	10/02/1922	60	01/17/1938	Retired	15	75	80
Butler, Pierce	03/17/1866	MN	Handing	01/02/1923	56	11/16/1939	Death	16	73	73
Sanford, Edward Terry	07/23/1865	TN	Harding	02/19/1923	57	03/08/1930	Death	7	64	64
Stone, Harlan Fiske	10/11/1872	NY	Coolidge	03/02/1925	52	07/02/1941	Promoted	16	68	73
Roberts, Owen Josephus	05/02/1875	PA	Hoover	06/02/1930	55	07/31/1945	Resigned	15	70	80
Cardozo, Benjamin Nathan	05/24/1870	NY	Hoover	03/14/1932	61	07/09/1938	Death	6	68	68
Black, Hugo Lafayette	02/27/1886	AL	Roosevelt, F.	08/19/1937	51	09/17/1971	Retired	34	85	85
Reed, Stanley Forman	12/31/1884	KY	Roosevelt, F.	01/31/1938	53	02/25/1957	Retired	19	72	95
Frankfurter, Felix	11/15/1882	MA	Roosevelt, F.	01/30/1939	56	08/28/1962	Retired	23	79	82
Douglas, William Orville	10/16/1898	CT	Roosevelt, F.	04/17/1939	40	11/12/1975	Retired	36	77	81
Murphy, Frank	04/13/1890	MI	Roosevelt, F.	02/05/1940	49	07/19/1949	Death	9	59	59
Byrnes, James Francis	05/02/1879	SC	Roosevelt, F	07/08/1941	62	10/03/1942	Retired	1	63	92
Jackson, Roberl Houghwout	02/13/1892	NY	Roosevelt, F.	07/11/1941	49	10/09/1954	Death	13	62	62
Rutledge, Wiley Blount	07/29/1894	IA	Roosevelt, F.	02/15/1943	48	09/10/1949	Death	6	55	55
Burton, Harold Hitz	06/22/1888	OH	Truman	10/01/1945	57	10/13/1958	Retired	13	70	76
Clark, Thomas Campbell	09/23/1899	TX	Truman	08/24/1949	49	06/12/1967	Retired	17	67	77
Minton, Sherman	10/20/1890	IN	Truman	10/12/1949	58	10/15/1956	Retired	7	65	74
Harlan, John Marshall	05/20/1899	NY	Eisenhower	03/28/1955	55	09/23/1971	Retired	16	72	72
Brennan, William J., Jr.	04/25/1906	NJ	Eisenhower	10/16/1956	50	07/20/1990	Retired	33	84	91
Whittaker, Charles Evans	02/22/1901	MO	Eisenhower	03/25/1957	56	03/31/1962	Disabled	5	61	72
Stewart, Potter	01/23/1915	OH	Eisenhower	10/14/1958	43	07/03/1981	Retired	23	66	70
White, Byron Raymond	06/08/1917	CO.	Kennedy	04/16/1962	44	06/28/1993	Retired	31	76	84
Goldberg, Arthur Joseph	08/08/1908	IL	Kennedy	10/01/1962	54	07/25/1965	Resigned	2	56	80
Fortas, Abe	06/19/1910	TN	Johnson, L.	10/01/1965	55	05/14/1969	Resigned	3	58	71
Marshall, Thurgood	07/02/1908	NY	Johnson, L.	10/02/1967	59	10/02/1991	Retired	24	83	84
Blackmun, Harry A.	11/12/1908	MN	Nixon	06/09/1970	61	06/30/1994	Retired	24	86	90
Rehnquist, William H.	10/01/1924	AZ	Nixon	01/07/1972	48	09/26/1986	Retired	14	61	81
Powell, Lewis F., Jr.	09/19/1907	VA	Nixon	01/07/1972	64	06/26/1987	Resigned	15	80	90
Stevens, John Paul	04/20/1920	IlL	Ford	12/19/1975	55	06/30/2010	Retired	34	90	
O'Connor, Sandra Day	03/26/1930	AZ	Reagan	09/25/1981	51	01/31/2006	Resigned	25	76	
Scalia, Antonin	03/11/1936	VA	Reagan	09/26/1986	50					
Kennedy, Anthony M.	07/23/1936	CA	Reagan	02/18/1988	51					
Souter, David H.	09/17/1939	NH	Bush 1	10/09/1990	51	06/30/2009	Retired	19	69	
Thomas, Clarence	06/23/1948	VA	Bush 1	10/23/1991	43					
Ginsburg, Ruth Bader	03/15/1933	NY	Clinton	08/10/1993	60					
Breyer, Stephen Gerald	08/15/1938	MA	Clinton	08/04/1994	56					
Roberts, John G. Jr.	01/27/1955	MD	Bush 2	10/03/2005	50					
Alito, Samuel A. Jr.	04/01/1950	NJ	Bush 2	01/31/2006	56					
Sotomayor, Sonia	06/25/1954	NY	Obarna	08/06/2009	55					
Kagan, Elena	04/28/1960	MA	Obama	08/07/2010	50					

U.S. Supreme Court

Supreme Court of the United States [SCOTUS]

U.S. Supreme Court Building, One First Street, NE,
Washington, DC 20543
Tel: (202) 479-3000 Tel: (202) 479-3211 (Public Information)
Tel: (202) 479-3175 (Library)
Tel: (202) 479-3360 (Opinion Announcements)
Tel: (202) 479-3030 (Visitor Information) Fax: (202) 479-2962
Internet: www.supremecourt.gov

Number of Judgeships: 9

The Supreme Court of the United States is the only court mandated by the Constitution and is the court of last resort. The Supreme Court has original jurisdiction over all disputes involving foreign ministers and interstate disputes, and disputes between the federal and state governments. The Court has jurisdiction of cases originating from any other court if the case involves constitutional issues, federal laws or maritime treaties and laws. The Supreme Court may affirm, modify, reverse or remand a decision of a lower court. The Supreme Court is comprised of the Chief Justice and eight associate justices, who are appointed for life by the President and confirmed by the Senate. Among his or her responsibilities, each Justice is assigned to serve as "Circuit Justice" for one or more of the United States Judicial Circuits. The Court holds one term annually, commencing on the first Monday in October.

Judges

Chief Justice **John G. Roberts, Jr.** . . . . (202) 479-3000
   Began Service: October 3, 2005
   Appointed By: President George W. Bush
   State Appointed From: Maryland
Associate Justice **Antonin Scalia** . . . . (202) 479-3000
   Began Service: September 26, 1986
   Appointed By: President Ronald Reagan
   State Appointed From: Virginia
Associate Justice **Anthony M. Kennedy** . . . . (202) 479-3000
   Began Service: February 18, 1988
   Appointed By: President Ronald Reagan
   State Appointed From: California
Associate Justice **Clarence Thomas** . . . . (202) 479-3000
   Began Service: October 23, 1991
   Appointed By: President George H.W. Bush
   State Appointed From: Georgia
Associate Justice **Ruth Bader Ginsburg** . . . . (202) 479-3000
   Began Service: August 10, 1993
   Appointed By: President William J. Clinton
   State Appointed From: New York
Associate Justice **Stephen G. Breyer** . . . . (202) 479-3000
   Began Service: August 3, 1994
   Appointed By: President William J. Clinton
   State Appointed From: Massachusetts
Associate Justice **Samuel A. Alito, Jr.** . . . . (202) 479-3000
   Began Service: January 31, 2006
   Appointed By: President George W. Bush
   State Appointed From: New Jersey
Associate Justice **Sonia Sotomayor** . . . . (202) 479-3000
   Began Service: August 8, 2009
   Appointed By: President Barack Obama
   State Appointed From: New York
Associate Justice **Elena Kagan** . . . . (202) 479-3000
   Began Service: August 7, 2010
   Appointed By: President Barack Obama
   State Appointed From: Massachusetts

Court Staff

Clerk of the Court **Scott S. Harris** . . . . (202) 479-3011
   E-mail: sharris@supremecourt.gov

Special Courts

United States Courts of Limited Jurisdiction

The United States Courts of Limited Jurisdiction are a special set of federal courts that hear cases based on specific subject matters the court is charged with by jurisdiction as outlined by the U.S constitution or provided by the U.S. Congress. Each court has authority over any case that involves subject matter in its charged jurisdiction. Most cases heard by these courts involve taxes, patents, international trade, members of the armed forces, and money claims against the U.S. government.

United States Court of Federal Claims [COFC]

National Courts Building, 717 Madison Place, NW,
Washington, DC 20439
Tel: (202) 357-6400
Internet: www.uscfc.uscourts.gov

Number of Judgeships: 16

Number of Vacancies: 5

The United States Court of Federal Claims, formerly known as the United States Claims Court, has jurisdiction over claims seeking money judgments against the United States. A claim must be founded upon the United States Constitution; an act of Congress; the regulation of an executive department; an express or implied-in-fact contract with the United States, or damages, liquidated or unliquidated, in cases not sounding in tort. Appeals are to the United States Court of Appeals for the Federal Circuit. All judges on the court are appointed by the President, with Senate consent, for 15-year terms. The chief judge is selected by the President to serve until the age of seventy or until another chief judge is chosen. Retirees may serve as senior judges on assigned cases.

Judges

Chief Judge **Patricia E. Campbell-Smith** . . . . (202) 357-6400
  Began Service: September 19, 2013
  Appointed By: President Barack Obama
  E-mail: patricia_campbell-smith@ao.uscourts.gov

Judge **Marian Blank Horn** . . . . (202) 357-6580
  Began Service: April 14, 1986
  Appointed By: President Ronald Reagan
  E-mail: Marian_Horn@ao.uscourts.gov

Judge **Lawrence J. Block** . . . . (202) 357-6508
  Began Service: October 2, 2002
  Appointed By: President George W. Bush
  E-mail: larry_block@ao.uscourts.gov

Judge **Susan G. Braden** Suite 702 . . . . (202) 357-6516
  Began Service: July 14, 2003
  Appointed By: President George W. Bush
  E-mail: susan_braden@ao.uscourts.gov

Judge **Mary Ellen Coster Williams** . . . . (202) 357-6660
  Began Service: July 21, 2003
  Appointed By: President George W. Bush
  E-mail: maryellen_williams@ao.uscourts.gov

Judge **Charles F. Lettow** . . . . (202) 357-6588
  Began Service: July 22, 2003
  Appointed By: President George W. Bush
  E-mail: charles_lettow@ao.uscourts.gov

Judge **Victor J. Wolski** . . . . (202) 357-6668
  Began Service: July 24, 2003
  Appointed By: President George W. Bush
  E-mail: victor_wolski@ao.uscourts.gov

Judge **Thomas Craig Wheeler** . . . . (202) 357-6596
  Began Service: November 28, 2005
  Appointed By: President George W. Bush
  E-mail: thomas_wheeler@ao.uscourts.gov

Judge **Margaret Mary Sweeney** . . . . (202) 357-6644
  Began Service: December 14, 2005
  Appointed By: President George W. Bush
  E-mail: margaret_sweeney@ao.uscourts.gov

United States Court of Federal Claims [COFC] *continued*

Judge **Elaine D. Kaplan** . . . . (202) 357-6400
  Began Service: November 1, 2013
  Appointed By: President Barack Obama
  E-mail: elaine_kaplan@ao.uscourts.gov

Judge **Lydia Kay Griggsby** . . . . (202) 357-6400
  Began Service: 2014
  Appointed By: President Barack Obama

Senior Judge **James F. Merow** . . . . (202) 357-6612
  Began Service: October 1, 1982
  Appointed By: President Ronald Reagan
  National Courts Building, 717 Madison Place, NW,
  Suite 601, Washington, DC 20005
  E-mail: james_merow@ao.uscourts.gov

Senior Judge **Eric G. Bruggink** . . . . (202) 357-6524
  Began Service: April 15, 1986
  Appointed By: President Ronald Reagan
  E-mail: eric_bruggink@ao.uscourts.gov

Senior Judge **John P. Wiese** . . . . (202) 357-6652
  Began Service: October 14, 1986
  Appointed By: President Ronald Reagan
  E-mail: john_wiese@ao.uscourts.gov

Senior Judge **Lynn J. Bush** . . . . (202) 357-6532
  Began Service: October 26, 1998
  Appointed By: President William J. Clinton
  E-mail: lynn_bush@ao.uscourts.gov

Senior Judge **Edward J. Damich** . . . . (202) 357-6483
  Began Service: October 22, 1998
  Appointed By: President William J. Clinton
  E-mail: Damich_Chambers@ao.uscourts.gov

Senior Judge **Nancy B. Firestone** . . . . (202) 357-6540
  Note: On January 7, 2015, President Obama
  nominated Nancy Firestone to be Judge for another
  term on the United States Court of Federal Claims.
  Began Service: December 4, 1998
  Appointed By: President William J. Clinton
  E-mail: nancy_firestone@ao.uscourts.gov

Court Staff

Clerk of Court **Hazel C. Keahey** . . . . (202) 357-6400 ext. 6411
  E-mail: hazel_keahey@ao.uscourts.gov

Chief Special Master **Col Denise K. Vowell** . . . . (202) 357-6354
  1440 New York Avenue, NW,
  Washington, DC 20005
  E-mail: denise_vowell@ao.uscourts.gov

United States Court of International Trade

One Federal Plaza, New York, NY 10278-0001
Tel: (212) 264-2800 Tel: (212) 264-2814 (General Info)
Fax: (212) 264-1085
E-mail: webmaster@cit.uscourts.gov
Internet: www.cit.uscourts.gov

Number of Judgeships: 9

Number of Vacancies: 4

The United States Court of International Trade is an Article III court with exclusive nationwide jurisdiction over civil actions against the United States, its agencies and officers. Its jurisdiction also includes certain civil actions brought by the United States, arising out of import transactions and the administration and enforcement of the federal customs and international trade laws. The Court reviews administrative decisions of the Bureau of Customs and Border Protection involving the tariff laws of the United States, including the classification and valuation of imported merchandise. The Court hears judicial challenges to determinations by the United States Department of Commerce and the United States International Trade Commission pertaining to the antidumping and countervailing duty laws. In addition, the Court reviews decisions by the Secretary of Labor, Commerce or Agriculture certifying workers, businesses or agricultural commodity procedures respectively eligible for assistance due to economic injury caused by import competition. The Court also possesses exclusive jurisdiction of actions brought by the United States to: (1) recover civil penalties for fraud, gross negligence or negligence in the entry of imported merchandise; (2) recover upon a bond relating to the importation of merchandise; or (3) recover customs duties. Judges are appointed by the President and confirmed by the Senate. These are Article III judgeships to which members are appointed for life, pending good behavior. Cases are determined by a single judge. Cases raising a constitutional issue or cases with broad significant implications may be assigned by the chief judge to a three-judge panel. Appeals from the Court of International Trade are heard by the United States Court of Appeals for the Federal Circuit. The Court is located in New York City, but sessions may be held anywhere within the United States. The Court is also authorized to hold hearings in foreign countries.

Judges

Chief Judge **Timothy C. Stanceu** . . . . (212) 264-2923
   Began Service: April 15, 2003
   Appointed By: President George W. Bush
Judge **Delissa A. Ridgway** . . . . (212) 264-5480
   Began Service: May 29, 1998
   Appointed By: President William J. Clinton
Judge **Leo M. Gordon** . . . . (212) 264-1611
   Began Service: March 16, 2006
   Appointed By: President George W. Bush
Judge **Mark A. Barnett** . . . . (212) 264-1628
   Began Service: 2013
   Appointed By: President Barack Obama
Judge **Claire R. Kelly** . . . . (212) 264-1611
   Began Service: 2013
   Appointed By: President Barack Obama
Senior Judge **Gregory W. Carman** . . . . (212) 264-2842
   Began Service: March 1983
   Appointed By: President Ronald Reagan
Senior Judge **Jane A. Restani** . . . . (212) 264-3668
   Began Service: 1983
   Appointed By: President Ronald Reagan
Senior Judge **Thomas J. Aquilino, Jr.** . . . . (212) 264-1611
   Began Service: May 2, 1985
   Appointed By: President Ronald Reagan
Senior Judge **Nicholas Tsoucalas** Suite 660 . . . . (212) 264-2918
   Began Service: June 6, 1986
   Appointed By: President Ronald Reagan
Senior Judge **R. Kenton Musgrave** . . . . (212) 264-2819
   Began Service: November 13, 1987
   Appointed By: President Ronald Reagan
Senior Judge **Richard W. Goldberg** . . . . (212) 264-9741
   Began Service: March 23, 1991
   Appointed By: President George H.W. Bush

United States Court of International Trade *continued*

Senior Judge **Donald C. Pogue** . . . . (212) 264-2126
   Began Service: August 1995
   Appointed By: President William J. Clinton
Senior Judge **Judith M. Barzilay** . . . . (212) 264-5420
   Began Service: June 3, 1998
   Appointed By: President William J. Clinton
Senior Judge **Richard K. Eaton** . . . . (212) 264-2900
   Began Service: January 3, 2000
   Appointed By: President William J. Clinton

Court Staff

Clerk of Court **Tina Potuto Kimble** . . . . (212) 264-2908
   E-mail: tina_kimble@cit.uscourts.gov

United States Court of Appeals for the Armed Forces [USCAAF]

450 E Street, NW, Washington, DC 20442-0001
Tel: (202) 761-1448 Tel: (202) 761-1452 (Docket Room Phone)
Fax: (202) 761-4672
Internet: www.armfor.uscourts.gov

Number of Judgeships: 5

The United States Court of Appeals for the Armed Forces, formerly known as the Court of Military Appeals, hears matters of law under the Uniform Code of Military Justice involving an officer, the death penalty, a sentence of one year or more imprisonment or dismissal, a dishonorable discharge or bad conduct discharge certified by the service's Judge Advocate General or the General Counsel of the Department of Transportation acting for the Coast Guard. The court's jurisdiction is worldwide. Appeals to this court come in response to court-martials in the Army, Navy-Marine Corps, Air Force and Coast Guard Courts of Criminal Appeals. Its decisions prior to 1984 were final, however now rulings can be appealed to the Supreme Court of the United States for review. The Washington, DC-based court is exclusively an appellate criminal court consisting of five civilian judges appointed to 15-year terms by the President with Senate confirmation.

Judges

Chief Judge **James E. Baker** . . . . (202) 761-1459
   Began Service: September 19, 2000
   Appointed By: President William J. Clinton
Associate Judge **Charles E. "Chip" Erdmann II** . . . . (202) 761-1458
   Began Service: October 15, 2002
   Appointed By: President George W. Bush
   E-mail: chip.erdmann@armfor.uscourts.gov
Associate Judge **Scott W. Stucky** . . . . (202) 761-1461
   Began Service: December 20, 2006
   Appointed By: President George W. Bush
   E-mail: scott.stucky@armfor.uscourts.gov
Associate Judge **Margaret A. Ryan** . . . . (202) 761-5214
   Began Service: December 20, 2006
   Appointed By: President George W. Bush
   E-mail: margaret.ryan@armfor.uscourts.gov
Associate Judge **Kevin A. Ohlson** . . . . (202) 761-1448
   Began Service: November 1, 2013
   Appointed By: President Barack Obama
Senior Judge **H. F. "Sparky" Gierke** . . . . (202) 761-5207
   Began Service: November 20, 1991
   Appointed By: President George H.W. Bush
Senior Judge **Susan Jean Crawford** . . . . (202) 761-5207
   Began Service: November 19, 1991
   Appointed By: President George H.W. Bush
Senior Judge **Eugene R. Sullivan** . . . . (301) 320-5964
   Began Service: October 1, 1986
   Appointed By: President Ronald Reagan
Senior Judge **Walter T. Cox III** . . . . (202) 761-5207
   Began Service: September 6, 1984
   Appointed By: President Ronald Reagan

United States Court of Appeals for the Armed Forces [USCAAF]
continued

Senior Judge **Andrew S. Effron** . . . .(202) 761-5207
  Began Service: 1996
  Appointed By: President William J. Clinton
  E-mail: andrew.effron@armfor.uscourts.gov

Court Staff
Clerk **William A. "Bill" DeCicco** . . . . (202) 761-1448
  E-mail: Bill.DeCicco@armfor.uscourts.gov

United States Court of Appeals for Veterans Claims

625 Indiana Avenue, NW, Suite 900, Washington, DC 20004-2950
Tel: (202) 501-5970 Fax: (202) 501-5848

Number of Judgeships: 9

Created in 1988, this Court consisting of a chief judge and eight associate judges has exclusive jurisdiction to review final decisions of the Board of Veterans Appeals, an administrative arm of the Department of Veterans Affairs. Cases involve reviewing the Board's determination of entitlement or disability benefits. The rulings can be appealed to the United States Court of Appeals for the Federal Circuit. The Court of Appeals for Veterans Claims is independent and does not come under the purview of the Judicial Conference of the United States or the Administrative Office of the United States Courts. The President appoints a chief judge and between two and six judges. The appointments are for 15-year terms and subject to Senate confirmation.

Judges
Chief Judge **Bruce E. Kasold** . . . .(202) 501-5870
  Began Service: December 31, 2003
  Appointed By: President George W. Bush
  E-mail: bkasold@uscourts.cavc.gov
Judge **Lawrence B. Hagel** . . . . (202) 501-5862
  Began Service: December 2003
  Appointed By: President George W. Bush
  E-mail: lhagel@uscourts.cavc.gov
Judge **William A. Moorman** . . . . (202) 501-5882
  Began Service: 2004
  Appointed By: President George W. Bush
  E-mail: wmoorman@uscourts.cavc.gov
Judge **Alan G. Lance, Sr.** . . . .(202) 501-5887
  Began Service: 2004
  Appointed By: President George W. Bush
  E-mail: alance@uscourts.cavc.gov
Judge **Robert N. Davis** . . . .(202) 501-5863
  Began Service: 2004
  Appointed By: President George W. Bush
  E-mail: rdavis@uscourts.cavc.gov
Judge **Mary J. Schoelen** . . . . (202) 501-5867
  Began Service: 2004
  Appointed By: President George W. Bush
  E-mail: mschoelen@uscourts.cavc.gov
Judge **BG Coral Wong Pietsch** . . . . (202) 501-5970
  Began Service: 2012
  Appointed By: President Barack Obama
Judge **Margaret "Meg" Bartley** . . . . (202) 501-5970
  Began Service: 2012
  Appointed By: President Barack Obama
  E-mail: mbartley@uscourts.cavc.gov
Judge **William S. Greenberg** . . . . (202) 501-5970
  Began Service: December 28, 2012
  Appointed By: President Barack Obama

Court Staff
Clerk of Court and Executive Officer
  COL Gregory O. Block . . . .(202) 501-5980
  E-mail: gblock@uscourts.cavc.gov

Alien Terrorist Removal Court

E. Barrett Prettyman U.S. Courthouse, 333 Constitution Avenue, NW, Washington, DC 20001
Tel: (202) 354-3050 Fax: (202) 354-3023

Number of Judgeships: 5

The Alien Terrorist Removal Court was created by the Antiterrorism and Effective Death Penalty Act of 1996. The court has the authority to conduct all proceedings to determine whether an alien should be removed from the United States on the grounds of being a terrorist. Applications for removal proceedings are brought by the Attorney General of the United States after being initiated and investigated by the Department of Justice. Decisions made by this court can be appealed to the United States Court of Appeals for the District of Columbia. The court is made up of five district court judges from five judicial circuits. The judges are appointed for five year terms by the Chief Justice of the United States. Judges may be redesignated by the Chief Justice.

Judges
Chief Judge **James C. Cacheris** . . . . (703) 299-2110
  Began Service: 1981
  Appointed By: President Ronald Reagan
Senior Judge **David Dudley Dowd, Jr.** . . . . (330) 252-6034
  Began Service: October 8, 1982
  Appointed By: President Ronald Reagan
Senior Judge **William C. O'Kelley** . . . . (404) 215-1530
  Began Service: October 23, 1970
  Appointed By: President Richard M. Nixon
Senior Judge **Michael A. Telesca** . . . . (585) 613-4060
  Began Service: 1982
  Appointed By: President Ronald Reagan
Senior Judge **Harold Albert Baker** . . . . (202) 354-3050
  Appointed By: President Jimmy Carter

Court Staff
Clerk of Court **Angela D. Caesar** . . . . (202) 354-3050

United States Tax Court

400 Second Street, NW, Washington, DC 20217
Tel: (202) 521-0700
Internet: www.ustaxcourt.gov

Number of Judgeships: 15

The United States Tax Court exercises jurisdiction as provided in title 26 of the U.S. code over matters involving Federal taxation, providing a forum in which taxpayers may dispute determinations made by the Internal Revenue Service. Upon receiving a notice of deficiency in tax from the IRS, taxpayers have a choice of three federal forums in which they can obtain a judicial determination of their rights. They may pay the tax and file a claim with the IRS for a refund. If the claim is disallowed, they may then file suit for a refund in a U.S. District Court or the U.S Court of Federal Claims. If they do not wish to pay the tax beforehand, they may litigate the matter in the U.S. Tax Court. The court is composed of 19 judges appointed to 15-year terms by the President with the advice and consent of the Senate; senior judges; and special trial judges (appointed by the Chief Judge and authorized by statute to decide particular categories of cases). Court proceedings take place on the record and are open to the public. Decisions by the court, except those issued in small tax cases, are generally appealable to the United States Courts of Appeals serving the geographic area in which the individual taxpayer resides or the corporate taxpayer has its principle place of business.

Judges
Chief Judge **Michael B. Thornton** . . . .(202) 521-0777
  Began Service: March 8, 1998
  Appointed By: President William J. Clinton

(continued on next page)

United States Tax Court *continued*

Judge **John O. Colvin** . . . . (202) 521-0662
  Began Service: 1988
  Appointed By: President Ronald Reagan
  E-mail: jcolvin@ustaxcourt.gov

Judge **Maurice B. Foley** . . . . (202) 521-0681
  Began Service: April 9, 1995
  Appointed By: President William J. Clinton
  E-mail: jfoley@ustaxcourt.gov

Judge **Joseph H. Gale** . . . . (202) 521-0688
  Began Service: February 6, 1996
  Appointed By: President William J. Clinton
  E-mail: jgale@ustaxcourt.gov

Judge **Joseph Robert Goeke** Room 410 . . . . (202) 521-0690
  Began Service: April 22, 2003
  Appointed By: President George W. Bush
  E-mail: jgoeke@ustaxcourt.gov

Judge **David D. Gustafson** . . . . (202) 521-0850
  Began Service: July 29, 2008
  Appointed By: President George W. Bush

Judge **James S. Halpern** . . . . (202) 521-0707
  Began Service: July 3, 1990
  Appointed By: President George H.W. Bush
  E-mail: jhalpern@ustaxcourt.gov

Judge **Mark van Dyke Holmes** . . . . (202) 521-0714
  Began Service: June 30, 2003
  Appointed By: President George W. Bush
  E-mail: jholmes@ustaxcourt.gov

Judge **Kathleen M. "Kathy" Kerrigan** . . . . (202) 521-0750
  Began Service: May 8, 2012
  Appointed By: President Barack Obama

Judge **Richard T. Morrison** . . . . (202) 521-0853
  Began Service: August 29, 2008
  Appointed By: President George W. Bush

Judge **Elizabeth Crewson Paris** . . . . (202) 521-0839
  Began Service: July 30, 2008
  Appointed By: President George W. Bush

Judge **Juan F. Vasquez** Room 406 . . . . (202) 521-0778
  Began Service: May 1, 1995
  Appointed By: President William J. Clinton
  E-mail: jvasquez@ustaxcourt.gov

Judge **Albert G. Lauber** . . . . (202) 521-0785
  Began Service: January 31, 2013
  Appointed By: President Barack Obama

Judge **Ronald Lee Buch** . . . . (202) 521-0810
  Began Service: January 14, 2013
  Appointed By: President Barack Obama

Judge **Joseph W. Nega** . . . . (202) 521-0640
  Began Service: 2013
  Appointed By: President Barack Obama

Judge **L. Paige Marvel** . . . . (202) 521-0740
  Note: On November 20, 2014, the Senate confirmed
  L. Paige Marvel for another term as Judge on the
  United States Tax Court.
  Began Service: April 6, 1998
  Appointed By: President Barack Obama
  E-mail: jmarvel@ustaxcourt.gov

Judge **Tamara W. Ashford** . . . . (202) 521-0700
  Began Service: 2014
  Appointed By: President Barack Obama

Judge **Cary Douglas Pugh** . . . . (202) 521-0824
  Began Service: 2014
  Appointed By: President Barack Obama

Senior Judge (recalled) **Harry Allen Haines** . . . . (202) 521-0699
  Began Service: April 22, 2003
  Appointed By: President George W. Bush

Senior Judge **Herbert L. Chabot** . . . . (202) 521-0644
  Began Service: April 3, 1978
  Appointed By: President Jimmy Carter

Senior Judge (recalled) **Howard A. Dawson, Jr.** . . . . (202) 521-0670
  Began Service: August 21, 1962
  Appointed By: President John F. Kennedy

Senior Judge (recalled) **Julian I. Jacobs** . . . . (202) 521-0720
  Began Service: March 30, 1984
  Appointed By: President Ronald Reagan
  E-mail: jjacobs@ustaxcourt.gov

United States Tax Court *continued*

Senior Judge **Robert P. Ruwe** . . . . (202) 521-0751
  Began Service: November 20, 1987
  Appointed By: President Ronald Reagan

Senior Judge **Laurence J. Whalen** Room 331 . . . . (202) 521-0792
  Began Service: November 23, 1987
  Appointed By: President Ronald Reagan

Senior Judge (recalled) **Joel Gerber** . . . . (202) 521-0699
  Began Service: June 18, 1984
  Appointed By: President Ronald Reagan
  E-mail: jgerber@ustaxcourt.gov

Senior Judge (recalled) **David Laro** . . . . (202) 521-0738
  Began Service: November 2, 1992
  Appointed By: President George H.W. Bush
  E-mail: jlaro@ustaxcourt.gov

Senior Judge (recalled) **Carolyn P. Chiechi** . . . . (202) 521-0650
  Began Service: October 1, 1992
  Appointed By: President George H.W. Bush

Senior Judge (recalled) **Stephen J. Swift** . . . . (202) 521-0700
  Began Service: August 16, 1983
  Appointed By: President Ronald Reagan

Senior Judge (recalled) **Thomas B. Wells** . . . . (202) 521-0790
  Began Service: October 13, 1986
  Appointed By: President Ronald Reagan

Senior Judge (recalled) **Mary Ann Cohen** . . . . (202) 521-0655
  Began Service: September 24, 1982
  Appointed By: President Ronald Reagan

Senior Judge (recalled) **Robert A. Wherry, Jr.** Room
413 . . . . (202) 521-0800
  Began Service: April 23, 2003
  Appointed By: President George W. Bush
  E-mail: jwherry@ustaxcourt.gov

Chief Special Trial Judge **Peter J. Panuthos** . . . . (202) 521-4707
  Began Service: June 13, 1983

Special Trial Judge **Robert N. Armen, Jr.** . . . . (202) 521-4711
  Began Service: 1993

Special Trial Judge **Lewis R. Carluzzo** . . . . (202) 521-3339
  Began Service: 1994

Special Trial Judge **Daniel A. Guy, Jr.** . . . . (202) 521-3370
  Began Service: May 31, 2012

Court Staff

Clerk of Court **Robert Di Trolio** . . . . (202) 521-4600
  E-mail: rditrolio@ustaxcourt.gov

Judicial Panel on Multidistrict Litigation

Thurgood Marshall Federal Judiciary Building, One Columbus Circle, NE, Room G-255 North Lobby, Washington, DC 20002-8004
Tel: (202) 502-2800 Fax: (202) 502-2888
Internet: www.jpml.uscourts.gov

Number of Judgeships: 7

The panel of seven federal circuit and district judges has the power to temporarily transfer to a single district court civil actions pending in different districts that involve one or more common questions of fact. The Chief Justice of the United States Supreme Court appoints the judges from different circuits to serve seven-year terms.

Judges

Chair **Sarah S. Vance** . . . . (504) 589-7595
  500 Poydras Street, Room C255,
  New Orleans, LA 00000

Judge **Marjorie O. Rendell** . . . . (215) 597-3015
  601 Market Street, Room 21613,
  Philadelphia, PA 19106-1598

Judge **Charles R. Breyer** . . . . (415) 522-2062

Judge **Lewis A. Kaplan** . . . . (212) 805-0216

Judge **Ellen Segal Huvelle** . . . . (202) 354-3230

Judge **R. David Proctor** . . . . (205) 278-1980

Judicial Panel on Multidistrict Litigation *continued*

Judge **Catherine D. Perry**..........................(314) 244-7520
  111 South Tenth, Room 14.182,
  St. Louis, MO 63102

Court Staff

Clerk of the Panel **Jeffery N. Lüthi**..................(202) 502-2800
Panel Executive **Thomasenia P. "Tommie" Duncan**.....(202) 502-2800
  Began Service: September 13, 2010

U.S. Courts of Appeals

United States Courts of Appeals

The intermediate appellate courts in the federal judicial system are the courts of appeals. There are eleven circuit courts of appeals plus the District of Columbia Circuit and the Federal Circuit. The Court of Appeals for the Federal Circuit is a specialized appellate court with national jurisdiction, hearing certain appeals (mainly patent appeals) from all of the U.S. district courts. The Federal Circuit also has jurisdiction over appeals from the U.S. Court of Federal Claims, the U.S. Court of International Trade, the U.S. Court of Appeals for Veterans Claims, United States Trademark Trial and Appeal Board, United States Board of Patent Appeals and Interferences, Boards of Contract Appeals, and the U.S. Merit Systems Protection Board. The eleven circuit courts plus the District of Columbia Circuit have appellate jurisdiction over U.S. district courts within its federal circuit (excluding patents) and selected federal agencies. A disappointed party in a district court usually has the right to have the case reviewed in the court of appeals for the circuit. Appeals court judges are appointed for life by the President with the advice and consent of the Senate. Each court of appeals consists of six or more judges, depending on the caseload of the court. The judge who has served on the court the longest and who is under 65 years of age is designated as the chief judge and performs administrative duties in addition to hearing cases.

United States Court of Appeals for the Federal Circuit

Howard T. Markey National Courts Building, 717 Madison Place, NW, Washington, DC 20439
Tel: (202) 275-8000 Tel: (202) 275-8031 (Electronic Opinions Data)
Tel: (202) 275-8030 (Electronic Opinions Voice) Fax: (202) 275-9678
Internet: http://www.cafc.uscourts.gov

Number of Judgeships: 12

Supreme Court Justice: Chief Justice John G. Roberts Jr.

The United States Court of Appeals for the Federal Circuit handles cases by subject matter without regard to the region. The Court hears all appeals for the United States Court of Federal Claims, the United States Court of International Trade and the United States Court of Veterans Appeals. The Federal Circuit hears appeals from United States District Courts in patent cases, cases involving energy regulation and economic stabilization as well as appeals from a variety of administrative proceedings. Established in 1982, the Washington, DC-based Federal Circuit possesses national jurisdiction as a result of the merger between the Appellate Division of the former United States Court of Claims and the United States Court of Customs and Patent Appeals.

Judges
Chief Judge **Sharon Prost** . . . . (202) 275-8700
  Began Service: October 2001
  Appointed By: President George W. Bush
Circuit Judge **Pauline Newman** . . . . (202) 275-8540
  Began Service: May 7, 1984
  Appointed By: President Ronald Reagan
Circuit Judge **Alan D. Lourie** . . . . (202) 275-8580
  Began Service: April 11, 1990
  Appointed By: President George H.W. Bush
Circuit Judge **Timothy B. Dyk** . . . . (202) 275-8680
  Began Service: June 9, 2000
  Appointed By: President William J. Clinton
Circuit Judge **Kimberly Ann Moore** . . . . (202) 275-8720
  Began Service: September 2006
  Appointed By: President George W. Bush
Circuit Judge **Kathleen M. O'Malley** . . . . (202) 275-8740
  Began Service: December 27, 2010
  Appointed By: President Barack Obama
Circuit Judge **Jimmie V. Reyna** . . . . (202) 275-8000
  Began Service: April 7, 2011
  Appointed By: President Barack Obama

United States Court of Appeals for the Federal Circuit *continued*
Circuit Judge **Evan Jonathan Wallach** . . . . (202) 275-8640
  Began Service: November 18, 2011
  Appointed By: President Barack Obama
Circuit Judge **Richard Gary Taranto** . . . . (202) 275-8800
  Began Service: March 15, 2013
  Appointed By: President Barack Obama
Circuit Judge **Raymond T. "Ray" Chen** . . . . (202) 275-8000
  Began Service: August 5, 2013
  Appointed By: President Barack Obama
Circuit Judge **Todd M. Hughes** . . . . (202) 275-8000
  Began Service: September 30, 2013
  Appointed By: President Barack Obama
Circuit Judge **Kara Farnandez Stoll** . . . . (202) 275-8000
  Began Service: July 17, 2015
  Appointed By: President Barack Obama
Senior Judge **S. Jay Plager** . . . . (202) 275-8940
  Began Service: November 11, 1989
  Appointed By: President George H.W. Bush
Senior Judge **Raymond C. Clevenger III** . . . . (202) 275-8950
  Began Service: May 3, 1990
  Appointed By: President George H.W. Bush
Senior Judge **Alvin Anthony Schall** . . . . (202) 275-8960
  Began Service: August 1992
  Appointed By: President George H.W. Bush
Senior Judge **Haldane Robert Mayer** . . . . (202) 275-8560
  Began Service: June 19, 1987
  Appointed By: President Ronald Reagan
Senior Judge **Richard Linn** . . . . (202) 275-8660
  Began Service: 2000
  Appointed By: President William J. Clinton
Senior Judge **William C. Bryson** . . . . (202) 275-8620
  Began Service: October 7, 1994
  Appointed By: President William J. Clinton

Court Staff
Circuit Executive/Clerk of the Court **Daniel O'Toole** . . . . . (202) 275-8001
Chief Circuit Mediator **James Amend** . . . . (202) 275-8121
  E-mail: amendj@cafc.uscourts.gov
Librarian **Patricia M. McDermott** . . . . (202) 275-8400
  E-mail: mcdermottp@cafc.uscourts.gov

United States Court of Appeals for the First Circuit

John Joseph Moakley U.S. Courthouse, 1 Courthouse Way, Boston, MA 02210-3945
Tel: (617) 748-9057 (General Info)
Tel: (617) 748-4640 (Electronic Opinions & Dockets Data)
Tel: (617) 748-9567 (Records Room) Fax: (617) 748-4081
Internet: www.ca1.uscourts.gov

Number of Judgeships: 6

Supreme Court Justice: Associate Justice Stephen G. Breyer

Areas Covered: Maine, Massachusetts, New Hampshire, Rhode Island and Puerto Rico

Judges
Chief Judge **Jeffrey R. Howard** . . . . (603) 225-1525
  Began Service: May 3, 2002
  Appointed By: President George W. Bush
Circuit Judge **Sandra L. Lynch** . . . . (617) 748-9014
  Began Service: May 1, 1995
  Appointed By: President William J. Clinton
  John Joseph Moakley U.S. Courthouse,
  One Courthouse Way, Suite 8710,
  Boston, MA 02210
  E-mail: sandra_lynch@ca1.uscourts.gov
Circuit Judge **Juan R. Torruella** . . . . (787) 977-6146
  Began Service: 1984
  Appointed By: President Ronald Reagan

(continued on next page)

United States Court of Appeals for the First Circuit *continued*

Circuit Judge **Ojetta Rogeriee Thompson** . . . . (401) 272-2960
  Began Service: April 1, 2010
  Appointed By: President Barack Obama
  John Joseph Moakley United States Courthouse,
  One Courthouse Way, Suite 6612,
  Boston, MA 02210

Circuit Judge **William J. Kayatta, Jr.** . . . . (207) 699-3600
  Began Service: March 8, 2013
  Appointed By: President Barack Obama
  E-mail: william_kayatta@ca1.uscourts.gov

Circuit Judge **David Jeremiah Barron** . . . . (617) 749-9057
  Began Service: May 23, 2014
  Appointed By: President Barack Obama

Senior Judge **Norman H. Stahl** . . . . (617) 748-4596
  Began Service: August 3, 1992
  Appointed By: President George H.W. Bush
  John Joseph Moakley U.S. Courthouse,
  One Courthouse Way, Suite 8730,
  Boston, MA 02210
  E-mail: norman_stahl@ca1.uscourts.gov

Senior Judge **Bruce M. Selya** . . . . (401) 752-7140
  Began Service: November 24, 1986
  Appointed By: President Ronald Reagan
  E-mail: bruce_selya@ca1.uscourts.gov

Senior Judge **Kermit V. Lipez** . . . . (207) 822-0455
  Began Service: July 1, 1998
  Appointed By: President William J. Clinton
  E-mail: kermit_lipez@ca1.uscourts.gov

Senior Judge **Michael Boudin** . . . . (617) 748-4431
  Began Service: May 26, 1992
  Appointed By: President George H.W. Bush
  John Joseph Moakley U.S. Courthouse,
  One Courthouse Way, Suite 8612,
  Boston, MA 02210
  E-mail: michael_boudin@ca1.uscourts.gov

Court Staff

Circuit Executive **Susan Goldberg** . . . . (617) 748-9614
  E-mail: susan_goldberg@ca1.uscourts.gov
Clerk of Court **Margaret Carter** . . . . (617) 748-9057
  E-mail: margaret_carter@ca1.uscourts.gov
Circuit Librarian **Susan C. Sullivan** . . . . (617) 748-9343
  E-mail: susan_sullivan@ca1.uscourts.gov
Settlement Counsel **Patrick King** . . . . (617) 748-9339

United States Bankruptcy Appellate Panel for the First Circuit

1 Courthouse Way, Suite 910, Boston, MA 02210-3945
Tel: (617) 748-9650 Fax: (617) 748-9659
Internet: www.bap1.uscourts.gov

Number of Judgeships: 12

Judges

Chief Bankruptcy Judge **Joan N. Feeney** . . . . (617) 748-6631
  Began Service: 1992
Bankruptcy Judge **William C. Hillman** . . . . (617) 748-5300
  Began Service: August 13, 1991
  E-mail: Judge_William_Hillman@mab.uscourts.gov
Bankruptcy Judge **Enrique S. Lamoutte** . . . . (787) 977-6030
  Began Service: November 1986
  U.S. Post Office and Courthouse Building,
  300 Recinto Sur Street, Suite 251,
  Old San Juan, PR 00901
  E-mail: Enrique_S._Lamoutte@prb.uscourts.gov
Bankruptcy Judge **Henry Jack Boroff** . . . . (413) 785-6860
  Began Service: 1993
  E-mail: henry.boroff@mab.uscourts.gov
Bankruptcy Judge **J. Michael Deasy** . . . . (603) 222-2640
  1000 Elm Street, Suite 1001,
  Manchester, NH 03101

United States Bankruptcy Appellate Panel for the First Circuit *continued*

Bankruptcy Judge **Brian K. Tester** . . . . (787) 977-6040
  Began Service: 2006
  Jose V. Toledo Federal Building and U.S.
  Courthouse, 300 Recinto Sur Street, Suite 245,
  San Juan, PR 00901
Bankruptcy Judge **Frank J. Bailey** . . . . (617) 748-9650
  Began Service: 2010
Bankruptcy Judge **Mildred Caban Flores** . . . . (787) 977-6020
  Jose V. Toledo Federal Building and U.S.
  Courthouse, 300 Recinto Sur Street, Courtroom 3,
  Old San Juan, PR 00901
Bankruptcy Judge **Melvin S. Hoffman** . . . . (508) 770-8927
Bankruptcy Judge **Edward A. Godoy** . . . . (787) 977-6074
Bankruptcy Judge **Diane Finkle** . . . . (401) 626-3060
  380 Westminster Mall, Room 619,
  Providence, RI 02903
Bankruptcy Judge **Bruce A. Harwood** . . . . (866) 222-8029
Bankruptcy Judge **Peter G. Cary** . . . . (207) 780-3482

Court Staff

Clerk **Mary P. Sharon** . . . . (617) 748-9650
Career Law Clerk **Gwen May** . . . . (617) 748-9650

United States Court of Appeals for the Second Circuit

Thurgood Marshall Courthouse, 40 Foley Square, New York, NY 10007
Tel: (212) 857-8500 Tel: (212) 857-8585 (Clerk's Office)
Tel: (212) 857-8544 (Agency Appeals)
Tel: (212) 851-8603 (Admissions) Tel: (212) 857-8595 (Calendar)
Tel: (212) 857-8560 (Case Closing) Tel: (212) 857-8551 (Case Initiation)
Tel: (212) 857-8576 (Civil Appeals)
Tel: (212) 857-8515 (Criminal Appeals)
Tel: (212) 857-8620 (Records) Fax: (212) 857-8710
Internet: www.ca2.uscourts.gov

Number of Judgeships: 13

Supreme Court Justice: Associate Justice Ruth Bader Ginsburg

Areas Covered: Connecticut, New York and Vermont

Judges

Chief Judge **Robert Allen Katzmann** Room 301 . . . . (212) 857-2180
  Began Service: July 14, 1999
  Appointed By: President William J. Clinton
  E-mail: robert_katzmann@ca2.uscourts.gov
Circuit Judge **Dennis Jacobs** . . . . (212) 857-2150
  Began Service: December 8, 1992
  Appointed By: President George H.W. Bush
  E-mail: dennis_jacobs@ca2.uscourts.gov
Circuit Judge **José A. Cabranes** . . . . (203) 867-8782
  Began Service: August 12, 1994   Tel: (347) 394-1890
  Appointed By: President William J. Clinton   (New York Office
  E-mail: jose_cabranes@ca2.uscourts.gov   Contact)
Circuit Judge **Rosemary Shankman Pooler** . . . . (315) 448-0420
  Began Service: June 9, 1998
  Appointed By: President William J. Clinton
  E-mail: rosemary_pooler@ca2.uscourts.gov
Circuit Judge **Reena Raggi** . . . . (718) 613-2490
  Began Service: October 7, 2002
  Appointed By: President George W. Bush
  E-mail: reena_raggi@ca2.uscourts.gov
Circuit Judge **Richard C. Wesley** . . . . (585) 243-7910
  Began Service: 2003
  Appointed By: President George W. Bush
  E-mail: richard_wesley@ca2.uscourts.gov
Circuit Judge **Peter W. Hall** . . . . (802) 775-3712
  Began Service: July 7, 2004
  Appointed By: President George W. Bush
  E-mail: peter_hall@ca2.uscourts.gov

United States Court of Appeals for the Second Circuit *continued*

Circuit Judge **Debra Ann Livingston** . . . . (212) 857-8500
  Began Service: May 17, 2007
  Appointed By: President George W. Bush
  E-mail: debra_livingston@ca2.uscourts.gov

Circuit Judge **Gerard E. Lynch** . . . . (212) 857-2320
  Began Service: September 21, 2009
  Appointed By: President Barack Obama
  E-mail: ca02_gelchambers@ca2.uscourts.gov

Circuit Judge **Denny Chin** . . . . (212) 857-8500
  Began Service: April 26, 2010
  Appointed By: President Barack Obama
  E-mail: denny_chin@ca2.uscourts.gov

Circuit Judge **Raymond Joseph Lohier, Jr.** Room 730 . . . (212) 857-8500
  Began Service: January 3, 2011
  Appointed By: President Barack Obama
  E-mail: raymond_lohier@ca2.uscourts.gov

Circuit Judge **Susan Laura Carney** . . . . (212) 857-8500
  Began Service: June 21, 2011
  Appointed By: President Barack Obama
  E-mail: susan_carney@ca2.uscourts.gov

Circuit Judge **Christopher F. Droney** . . . . (860) 240-2635
  Began Service: March 12, 2012
  Appointed By: President Barack Obama
  E-mail: christopher_droney@ca2.uscourts.gov

Senior Judge **Robert D. Sack** . . . . (212) 857-2140
  Began Service: August 6, 1998
  Appointed By: President William J. Clinton
  E-mail: robert_sack@ca2.uscourts.gov

Senior Judge **Barrington D. Parker, Jr.** . . . . (212) 857-2211
  Began Service: October 10, 2001
  Appointed By: President George W. Bush
  E-mail: ca02_bdpchambers@ca2.uscourts.gov

Senior Judge **Jon O. Newman** . . . . (860) 240-3260
  Began Service: June 25, 1979
  Appointed By: President Jimmy Carter
  E-mail: jon_newman@ca2.uscourts.gov

Senior Judge **Ralph K. Winter** . . . . (203) 782-3682
  Began Service: January 5, 1982
  Appointed By: President Ronald Reagan
  E-mail: ralph_winter@ca2.uscourts.gov

Senior Judge **Amalya Lyle Kearse** . . . . (212) 857-2250
  Began Service: June 1979
  Appointed By: President Jimmy Carter
  E-mail: ca02_alkchambers@ca2.uscourts.gov

Senior Judge **Pierre N. Leval** U.S. Courthouse, Room
  1901 . . . . (212) 857-2310
  Began Service: 1993
  Appointed By: President William J. Clinton
  E-mail: ca02_pnlchambers@ca2.uscourts.gov

Senior Judge **John M. Walker, Jr.** . . . . (203) 773-2181
  Began Service: 1989
  Appointed By: President George H.W. Bush
  E-mail: john_walker@ca2.uscourts.gov

Senior Judge **Chester J. Straub** . . . . (212) 857-8500
  Began Service: June 3, 1998
  Appointed By: President William J. Clinton
  E-mail: chester_straub@ca2.uscourts.gov

Senior Judge **Guido Calabresi** . . . . (203) 773-2291
  Began Service: September 16, 1994
  Appointed By: President William J. Clinton
  E-mail: guido_calabresi@ca2.uscourts.gov

Court Staff

Circuit Executive **Karen Greve Milton** . . . . (212) 857-8700
  E-mail: karen_milton@ca2.uscourts.gov

Clerk of the Court **Catherine O'Hagan Wolfe** . . . . (212) 857-8585
  E-mail: catherine_wolfe@ca2.uscourts.gov

Legal Affairs Director **(Vacant)** . . . . (212) 857-8800

Circuit Librarian **Luis Lopez** . . . . (212) 857-8990
  E-mail: luis_lopez@ca2.uscourts.gov

United States Court of Appeals for the Third Circuit

U.S. Courthouse, 601 Market Street, Philadelphia, PA 19106
Tel: (215) 597-0718
Tel: (215) 597-7371 (Electronic Opinions & Dockets Data)
Fax: (215) 597-8656
Internet: www.ca3.uscourts.gov

Number of Judgeships: 14

Number of Vacancies: 2

Supreme Court Justice: Associate Justice Samuel A. Alito Jr.

Areas Covered: Delaware, New Jersey, Pennsylvania and the Virgin Islands

Judges

Chief Judge **Theodore A. McKee** Room 20614 . . . . (215) 597-9601
  Began Service: June 20, 1994
  Appointed By: President William J. Clinton
  E-mail: chambers_of_judge_theodore_
  mckee@ca3.uscourts.gov

Circuit Judge **Thomas L. Ambro** . . . . (302) 573-6500
  Began Service: June 19, 2000
  Appointed By: President William J. Clinton
  E-mail: judge_thomas_ambro@ca3.uscourts.gov

Circuit Judge **Julio M. Fuentes** . . . . (973) 645-3831
  Began Service: May 15, 2000
  Appointed By: President William J. Clinton
  Martin Luther King, Jr. Federal Building & U.S.
  Courthouse, 50 Walnut Street, Room 5032,
  Newark, NJ 07102
  E-mail: chambers_of_judge_julio_
  fuentes@ca3.uscourts.gov

Circuit Judge **D. Brooks Smith** . . . . (814) 693-0570
  Began Service: September 23, 2002
  Appointed By: President George W. Bush
  Allegheny Professional Center,
  1798 Old Route 220 North, Suite 203,
  Duncansville, PA 16635

Circuit Judge **D. Michael Fisher** . . . . (412) 208-7320
  Began Service: December 11, 2003
  Appointed By: President George W. Bush
  U.S. Courthouse, 700 Grant Street, Room 5360,
  Pittsburgh, PA 15219-1906
  E-mail: chambers_of_judge_d_michael_
  fisher@ca3.uscourts.gov

Circuit Judge **Michael A. Chagares** . . . . (973) 368-6486
  Began Service: April 24, 2006
  Appointed By: President George W. Bush
  E-mail: chambers_of_judge_michael_
  chagares@ca3.uscourts.gov

Circuit Judge **Kent A. Jordan** . . . . (302) 573-6001
  Began Service: December 2006
  Appointed By: President George W. Bush
  E-mail: chambers_of_judge_kent_
  jordan@ca3.uscourts.gov

Circuit Judge **Thomas Michael Hardiman** . . . . (412) 208-7440
  Began Service: April 2007
  Appointed By: President George W. Bush
  U.S. Post Office & Courthouse,
  700 Grant Street, Suite 2270,
  Pittsburgh, PA 15219
  E-mail: chambers_of_judge_thomas_
  hardiman@ca3.uscourts.gov

Circuit Judge **Joseph A. Greenaway, Jr.** . . . . (973) 622-4828
  Began Service: February 12, 2010
  Appointed By: President Barack Obama
  Frank R. Lautenberg U.S. Post Office & Courthouse,
  Room 411, Newark, NJ 07101-0999

Circuit Judge **Thomas I. Vanaskie** . . . . (570) 207-5720
  Began Service: April 28, 2010
  Appointed By: President Barack Obama
  E-mail: judge_vanaskie@ca3.uscourts.gov

(continued on next page)

United States Court of Appeals for the Third Circuit *continued*

Circuit Judge **Patty Shwartz** . . . . (973) 645-6596
 Began Service: April 10, 2013
 Appointed By: President Barack Obama
 E-mail: chambers_of_judge_patty_
 shwartz@ca3.uscourts.gov

Circuit Judge **Cheryl Ann Krause** . . . . (215) 597-0718
 Began Service: July 9, 2014
 Appointed By: President Barack Obama
 E-mail: chambers_of_judge_cheryl_ann_
 krause@ca3.uscourts.gov

Senior Judge **Leonard I. Garth** Room 20613 . . . . (973) 645-6521
 Began Service: 1973   Tel: (215) 597-3925
 Appointed By: President Richard M. Nixon   (Philadelphia
 Martin Luther King, Jr. Federal Building & U.S.   Chambers)
 Courthouse, 50 Walnut Street, Room 5040,
 Newark, NJ 07102
 E-mail: chambers_of_judge_leonard_
 garth@ca3.uscourts.gov

Senior Judge **Dolores K. Sloviter** Room 18614 . . . . (215) 597-1588
 Began Service: 1979
 Appointed By: President Jimmy Carter
 E-mail: Chambers_of_Judge_Dolores_
 Sloviter@ca3.uscourts.gov

Senior Judge **Walter K. Stapleton** . . . . (302) 573-6165
 Began Service: May 1985
 Appointed By: President Ronald Reagan
 U.S. Courthouse, 844 King Street, Lockbox 33,
 Wilmington, DE 19801
 E-mail: chambers_of_judge_walter_
 stapleton@ca3.uscourts.gov

Senior Judge **Morton I. Greenberg** . . . . (609) 989-0436
 Began Service: June 18, 1987
 Appointed By: President Ronald Reagan
 U.S. Courthouse, 402 East State Street, Room 219,
 Trenton, NJ 08608
 E-mail: chambers_of_judge_morton_
 greenberg@ca3.uscourts.gov

Senior Judge **Anthony J. Scirica** Room 22614 . . . . (215) 597-2399
 Began Service: September 11, 1987
 Appointed By: President Ronald Reagan
 E-mail: anthony_scirica@ca3.uscourts.gov

Senior Judge **Robert E. Cowen** . . . . (609) 989-2188
 Began Service: November 1987
 Appointed By: President Ronald Reagan
 U.S. Courthouse, 402 East State Street, Room 207,
 Trenton, NJ 08608-1507
 E-mail: chambers_of_judge_robert_
 cowen@ca3.uscourts.gov

Senior Judge **The Honorable Richard L. Nygaard** . . . . . . (814) 464-9640
 Began Service: November 1988
 Appointed By: President Ronald Reagan
 17 South Park Row, Suite B - 230,
 Erie, PA 16501
 E-mail: chambers_of_judge_richard_
 nygaard@ca3.uscourts.gov

Senior Judge **Jane R. Roth** U. S. Courthouse, Room
 18316 . . . . (215) 597-7803
 Began Service: July 22, 1991
 Appointed By: President George H.W. Bush
 E-mail: chambers_of_judge_jane_
 roth@ca3.uscourts.gov

Senior Judge **Maryanne Trump Barry** . . . . (973) 645-2133
 Began Service: September 13, 1999
 Appointed By: President William J. Clinton
 E-mail: chambers_of_judge_maryanne_trump_
 barry@ca3.uscourts.gov

Senior Judge **Franklin S. Van Antwerpen** . . . . (215) 597-0718

Senior Judge **Marjorie O. Rendell** . . . . (215) 597-3015
 Began Service: November 21, 1997
 Appointed By: President William J. Clinton
 U.S. Courthouse, 601 Market Street, Room 21613,
 Philadelphia, PA 19106-1598
 E-mail: Chambers_of_Judge_Marjorie_
 Rendell@ca3.uscourts.gov

United States Court of Appeals for the Third Circuit *continued*

Court Staff

Circuit Executive **Margaret A. Wiegand** . . . . (215) 597-0718
 E-mail: margaret_wiegand@ca3.uscourts.gov

Clerk of Court **Marcia M. Waldron** . . . . (215) 597-2995
 E-mail: marcia_waldron@ca3.uscourts.gov

Circuit Librarian **Judith F. Ambler** . . . . (267) 299-4301
 E-mail: judith_ambler@ca3.uscourts.gov

Chief Circuit Mediator **Joseph A. Torregrossa** . . . . (267) 299-4130
 E-mail: joseph_torregrossa@ca3.uscourts.gov

United States Court of Appeals for the Fourth Circuit

Lewis F. Powell, Jr. U.S. Courthouse, 1100 East Main Street,
Suite 501, Richmond, VA 23219
Tel: (804) 916-2184
Tel: (804) 771-2028 (Electronic Opinions & Docket Data)
Fax: (804) 916-2188
Internet: www.ca4.uscourts.gov

Number of Judgeships: 15

Supreme Court Justice: Chief Justice John G. Roberts Jr.

Areas Covered: Maryland, North Carolina, South Carolina, Virginia and
West Virginia

Judges

Chief Judge **William B. Traxler, Jr.** . . . . (864) 241-2730
 Began Service: October 21, 1998
 Appointed By: President William J. Clinton
 300 East Washington Street, Suite 222,
 Greenville, SC 29601
 E-mail: wbt@ca4.uscourts.gov

Circuit Judge **J. Harvie Wilkinson III** . . . . (434) 296-7063
 Began Service: August 13, 1984
 Appointed By: President Ronald Reagan
 255 West Main Street, Room 230,
 Charlottesville, VA 22902
 E-mail: JHW@ca4.uscourts.gov

Circuit Judge **Paul V. Niemeyer** . . . . (410) 962-4210
 Began Service: 1990
 Appointed By: President George H.W. Bush
 E-mail: pvn@ca4.uscourts.gov

Circuit Judge **Diana Gribbon Motz** . . . . (410) 962-3606
 Began Service: June 1994
 Appointed By: President William J. Clinton
 U.S. Courthouse, 101 West Lombard Street,
 Room 920, Baltimore, MD 21201
 E-mail: dgm@ca4.uscourts.gov

Circuit Judge **Robert B. King** . . . . (304) 347-3533
 Began Service: October 23, 1998
 Appointed By: President William J. Clinton
 Robert C. Byrd U.S. Courthouse,
 300 Virginia Street East, Suite 7602,
 Charleston, WV 25301
 E-mail: RBK@ca4.uscourts.gov

Circuit Judge **Roger Lee Gregory** . . . . (804) 916-2607
 Began Service: January 18, 2001
 Appointed By: President William J. Clinton
 Lewis F. Powell, Jr. U.S. Courthouse,
 1000 East Main Street, Suite 212,
 Richmond, VA 23219-3517
 E-mail: rlg@ca4.uscourts.gov

Circuit Judge **Dennis W. Shedd** . . . . (803) 732-8250
 Began Service: December 10, 2002
 Appointed By: President George W. Bush
 E-mail: dennis_shedd@ca4.uscourts.gov

Circuit Judge **Allyson Kay Duncan** . . . . (919) 782-2554
 Began Service: August 15, 2003
 Appointed By: President George W. Bush
 4140 Parklake Avenue, Suite 520,
 Raleigh, NC 27612
 E-mail: akd@ca4.uscourts.gov

United States Court of Appeals for the Fourth Circuit *continued*

Circuit Judge **G. Steven Agee** Lewis F. Powell, Jr. U.S.
Courthouse Annex . . . . (540) 378-5066
Began Service: July 2, 2008
Appointed By: President George W. Bush
E-mail: gsa@ca4.uscourts.gov

Circuit Judge **Barbara Milano Keenan** Lewis F. Powell
Jr. U.S. Courthouse . . . . (703) 518-8180
Began Service: March 9, 2010
Appointed By: President Barack Obama
E-mail: bmk@ca4.uscourts.gov

Circuit Judge **James Andrew Wynn, Jr.** Lewis F.
Powell Jr. U.S. Courthouse . . . . (804) 916-2700
Began Service: August 10, 2010
Appointed By: President Barack Obama
E-mail: JAW@ca4.uscourts.gov

Circuit Judge **Albert Diaz** Lewis F. Powell Jr. U.S.
Courthouse . . . . (704) 333-8025
Began Service: December 22, 2010
Appointed By: President Barack Obama
E-mail: albert_diaz@ca4.uscourts.gov

Circuit Judge **Henry F. Floyd** Lewis F. Powell Jr. U.S.
Courthouse . . . . (864) 591-5300
Began Service: October 5, 2011
Appointed By: President Barack Obama
E-mail: henry_floyd@ca4.uscourts.gov

Circuit Judge **Stephanie Dawn Thacker** . . . . (304) 347-3516
Began Service: May 29, 2012
Appointed By: President Barack Obama
E-mail: sdt@ca4.uscourts.gov

Circuit Judge **Pamela A. Harris** . . . . (804) 416-2184
Began Service: July 29, 2014
Appointed By: President Barack Obama

Senior Judge **Clyde H. Hamilton** . . . . (803) 765-5461
Began Service: July 22, 1991
Appointed By: President George H.W. Bush
Bank of America Plaza, 1901 Main Street,
Compartment 704, Suite 1250,
Columbia, SC 29201

Senior Judge **Andre M. Davis** . . . . (410) 962-0801
Began Service: November 12, 2009
Appointed By: President Barack Obama
E-mail: AMD@ca4.uscourts.gov

Court Staff

Circuit Executive **Samuel W. Phillips** . . . . (804) 916-2184
E-mail: samuel_phillips@ca4.uscourts.gov

Circuit Clerk **Patricia S. Connor** . . . . (804) 916-2706

Chief Circuit Mediator **Thomas F. "Tom" Ball** . . . . (434) 589-1480
17 Brassie Terrace, Palmyra, VA 22963
E-mail: tom_ball@ca4.uscourts.gov

Circuit Librarian **Elaine Woodward** . . . . (804) 916-2319
E-mail: elaine_woodward@ca4.uscourts.gov

United States Court of Appeals for the Fifth Circuit

John Minor Wisdom U.S. Court of Appeals Building, 600 Camp Street, Room 100, New Orleans, LA 70130-3425
Tel: (504) 310-7700
Internet: www.ca5.uscourts.gov

Number of Judgeships: 17

Number of Vacancies: 2

Supreme Court Justice: Associate Justice Antonin Scalia

Areas Covered: Louisiana, Mississippi and Texas

Judges

Chief Judge **Carl Edmund Stewart** . . . . (318) 676-3765
Began Service: May 9, 1994
Appointed By: President William J. Clinton
U.S. Courthouse, 300 Fannin Street, Suite 5226,
Shreveport, LA 71101
E-mail: carl_stewart@ca5.uscourts.gov

Circuit Judge **E. Grady Jolly** . . . . (601) 608-4745
Began Service: August 2, 1982
Appointed By: President Ronald Reagan
501 Court Street, Suite 3850,
Jackson, MS 39201

Circuit Judge **W. Eugene Davis** . . . . (337) 593-5280
Began Service: 1983
Appointed By: President Ronald Reagan
800 Lafayette Street, Suite 5100,
Lafayette, LA 70501

Circuit Judge **Edith Hollan Jones** . . . . (713) 250-5484
Began Service: 1985
Appointed By: President Ronald Reagan
E-mail: edith_jones@ca5.uscourts.gov

Circuit Judge **Jerry E. Smith** . . . . (713) 250-5101
Began Service: January 7, 1988
Appointed By: President Ronald Reagan
E-mail: jerry_smith@ca5.uscourts.gov

Circuit Judge **James L. Dennis** . . . . (504) 310-8000
Began Service: October 2, 1995
Appointed By: President William J. Clinton
John Minor Wisdom U.S. Court of Appeals
Building, 600 Camp Street, Room 219,
New Orleans, LA 70130
E-mail: james_dennis@ca5.uscourts.gov

Circuit Judge **Edith Brown Clement** . . . . (504) 310-8068
Began Service: December 27, 2001
Appointed By: President George W. Bush
John Minor Wisdom U.S. Court of Appeals
Building, 600 Camp Street, Room 200,
New Orleans, LA 70130
E-mail: edith_clement@ca5.uscourts.gov

Circuit Judge **Edward Charles Prado** . . . . (504) 310-8311 (New Orleans)
Began Service: May 14, 2003   Tel: (210) 472-4060
Appointed By: President George W. Bush   (San Antonio)
755 East Mulberry Avenue, Room 350,
San Antonio, TX 78212
E-mail: edward_prado@ca5.uscourts.gov

Circuit Judge **Priscilla R. Owen** . . . . (512) 916-5167
Began Service: June 3, 2005
Appointed By: President George W. Bush
Homer Thornberry Judicial Building,
903 San Jacinto Boulevard, Room 434,
Austin, TX 78701-2450
E-mail: priscilla_owen@ca5.uscourts.gov

Circuit Judge **Jennifer Walker Elrod** . . . . (713) 250-7590
Began Service: October 2007
Appointed By: President George W. Bush
515 Rusk Street, Room 12014,
Houston, TX 77002-2600
E-mail: jennifer_elrod@ca5.uscourts.gov

Circuit Judge **Leslie H. Southwick** . . . . (601) 608-4760
Began Service: October 2007
Appointed By: President George W. Bush
501 East Court Street, Suite 3750,
Jackson, MS 39201
E-mail: leslie_southwick@ca5.uscourts.gov

(continued on next page)

United States Court of Appeals for the Fifth Circuit *continued*

Circuit Judge **Catharina Haynes** . . . . (214) 753-2750
  Began Service: April 22, 2008
  Appointed By: President George W. Bush
  1100 Commerce Street, Room 1452,
  Dallas, TX 75242
  E-mail: catharina_haynes@ca5.uscourts.gov

Circuit Judge **James E. Graves, Jr.** . . . . (601) 608-4775
  Began Service: February 17, 2011
  Appointed By: President Barack Obama
  501 East Court Street, Suite 3550,
  Jackson, MS 39201
  E-mail: james_graves@ca5.uscourts.gov

Circuit Judge **Stephen A. Higginson** . . . . (504) 310-8228
  Began Service: November 2, 2011
  Appointed By: President Barack Obama
  E-mail: stephen_higginson@ca5.uscourts.gov

Circuit Judge **Gregg Jeffrey Costa** . . . . (713) 250-5030
  Began Service: June 2, 2014
  Appointed By: President Barack Obama
  515 Rusk Street, Room 4627,
  Houston, TX 77002-2694
  E-mail: gregg_costa@ca5.uscourts.gov

Senior Judge **Thomas M. Reavley** . . . . (713) 250-5185
  Began Service: 1979
  Appointed By: President Jimmy Carter
  515 Rusk Street, Room 11009,
  Houston, TX 77002-2605
  E-mail: tmr@ca5.uscourts.gov

Senior Judge **Patrick E. Higginbotham** . . . . (512) 916-5723
  Began Service: August 3, 1982
  Appointed By: President Ronald Reagan
  E-mail: patrick_higginbotham@ca5.uscourts.gov

Senior Judge **John M. Duhé, Jr.** . . . . (504) 310-7777
  Began Service: October 17, 1988
  Appointed By: President Ronald Reagan

Senior Judge **Jacques L. Wiener, Jr.** . . . . (504) 310-8098
  Began Service: May 25, 1990
  Appointed By: President George H.W. Bush
  John Minor Wisdom U.S. Court of Appeals
  Building, 600 Camp Street, Room 244,
  New Orleans, LA 70130
  E-mail: jacques_wiener@ca5.uscourts.gov

Senior Judge **Rhesa H. Barksdale** . . . . (601) 608-4730
  Began Service: May 12, 1990
  Appointed By: President George H.W. Bush
  501 East Court Street, Suite 3.800,
  Jackson, MS 39201
  E-mail: rhesa_barksdale@ca5.uscourts.gov

Senior Judge **Fortunato P. Benavides** . . . . (512) 916-5796
  Began Service: 1994
  Appointed By: President William J. Clinton
  903 San Jacinto Boulevard, Room 450,
  Austin, TX 78701
  E-mail: fortunato_benavides@ca5.uscourts.gov

Senior Judge **Carolyn Dineen King** . . . . (713) 250-5750
  Began Service: July 13, 1979
  Appointed By: President Jimmy Carter

Court Staff

Circuit Executive **Paul Benjamin Anderson, Jr.** . . . . (504) 310-7777
Circuit Clerk **Lyle Cayce** . . . . (504) 310-7700
  E-mail: lyle_cayce@ca5.uscourts.gov
Senior Appellate Conference Attorney
  Joseph L. S. St. Amant . . . . (504) 310-7799
Circuit Librarian **Sue Creech** Room 106 . . . . (504) 310-7797
  E-mail: sue_creech@ca5.uscourts.gov

United States Court of Appeals for the Sixth Circuit

Potter Stewart U.S. Couthouse, 100 East Fifth Street, Room 540,
Cincinnati, OH 45202
Tel: (513) 564-7200
Tel: (513) 564-7000 (Electronic Opinions & Dockets Voice)
Tel: (513) 684-2842 (Electronic Opinions & Docket Data)
Fax: (513) 564-7210
Internet: www.ca6.uscourts.gov

Number of Judgeships: 16

Number of Vacancies: 1

Supreme Court Justice: Associate Justice Elena Kagan

Areas Covered: Kentucky, Michigan, Ohio and Tennessee

Judges

Chief Judge **R. Guy Cole, Jr.** . . . . (614) 719-3350
  Began Service: January 2, 1996
  Appointed By: President William J. Clinton
  U.S. Courthouse, 85 Marconi Boulevard, Suite 255,
  Columbus, OH 43215
  E-mail: ca06-Cole_Chambers@ca6.uscourts.gov

Circuit Judge **Alice M. Batchelder** . . . . (330) 764-6026
  Began Service: December 1991
  Appointed By: President George H.W. Bush
  Potter Stewart U.S. Courthouse,
  100 East Fifth Street, Room 532,
  Cincinnati, OH 45202-3988

Circuit Judge **Danny J. Boggs** . . . . (502) 625-3900
  Began Service: March 27, 1986
  Appointed By: President Ronald Reagan

Circuit Judge **Karen Nelson Moore** . . . . (216) 357-7290
  Began Service: March 29, 1995
  Appointed By: President William J. Clinton
  E-mail: ca06-Moore_Chambers@ca6.uscourts.gov

Circuit Judge **Eric Lee Clay** . . . . (313) 234-5260
  Began Service: August 15, 1997
  Appointed By: President William J. Clinton
  E-mail: eric_clay@ca6.uscourts.gov

Circuit Judge **Julia Smith Gibbons** . . . . (901) 495-1265
  Began Service: August 2, 2002
  Appointed By: President George W. Bush
  E-mail: julia_gibbons@ca6.uscourts.gov

Circuit Judge **John M. Rogers** . . . . (859) 233-2680
  Began Service: November 2002
  Appointed By: President George W. Bush
  Community Trust Bank Building,
  100 East Vine Street, Suite 400,
  Lexington, KY 40507-1442
  E-mail: john_rogers@ca6.uscourts.gov

Circuit Judge **Jeffrey S. Sutton** . . . . (614) 849-0134
  Began Service: May 5, 2003
  Appointed By: President George W. Bush
  E-mail: jeffrey_sutton@ca6.uscourts.gov

Circuit Judge **Deborah L. Cook** . . . . (330) 252-6248
  Began Service: May 7, 2003
  Appointed By: President George W. Bush
  U.S. Courthouse, Two South Main Street, Suite 433,
  Akron, OH 44308
  E-mail: deborah_cook@ca6.uscourts.gov

Circuit Judge **David William McKeague** . . . . (513) 564-7200
  Began Service: July 22, 2005
  Appointed By: President George W. Bush

Circuit Judge **Richard Allen Griffin** . . . . (231) 929-3190
  Began Service: June 26, 2005
  Appointed By: President George W. Bush
  13919 South West Bayshore Drive, Suite 208,
  Traverse City, MI 49684
  E-mail: richard_griffin@ca6.uscourts.gov

Circuit Judge **Raymond Michael Kethledge** . . . . (513) 564-7200
  Began Service: July 11, 2008
  Appointed By: President George W. Bush
  E-mail: raymond_kethledge@ca6.uscourts.gov

United States Court of Appeals for the Sixth Circuit *continued*

Circuit Judge **Helene Nita White** . . . . (313) 226-0003
  Began Service: August 12, 2008
  Appointed By: President George W. Bush
  E-mail: helene_white@ca6.uscourts.gov

Circuit Judge **Jane Branstetter Stranch** . . . . (615) 695-4294
  Began Service: October 1, 2010
  Appointed By: President Barack Obama
  701 Broadway, Room 330,
  Nashville, TN 37203
  E-mail: jane_stranch@ca6.uscourts.gov

Circuit Judge **Bernice B. Donald** Potter Stewart U.S.
  Courthouse . . . . (513) 564-7200
  Began Service: October 20, 2011
  Appointed By: President Barack Obama
  E-mail: bernice_donald@ca6.uscourts.gov

Senior Judge **Damon Jerome Keith** . . . . (313) 234-5245
  Began Service: October 1977
  Appointed By: President Jimmy Carter
  E-mail: damon_keith@ca6.uscourts.gov

Senior Judge **Gilbert S. Merritt** . . . . (615) 736-5957
  Began Service: November 18, 1977
  Appointed By: President Jimmy Carter

Senior Judge **Ralph Bright Guy, Jr.** . . . . (734) 741-2300
  Began Service: October 17, 1985
  Appointed By: President Ronald Reagan
  200 East Liberty Street, Room 226,
  Ann Arbor, MI 48104
  E-mail: ralph_guy@ca6.uscourts.gov

Senior Judge **Alan E. Norris** . . . . (614) 719-3330
  Began Service: 1986
  Appointed By: President Ronald Reagan
  E-mail: alan_norris@ca6.uscourts.gov

Senior Judge **Richard F. Suhrheinrich** . . . . (517) 377-1513
  Began Service: August 1990
  Appointed By: President George H.W. Bush
  E-mail: richard_suhrheinrich@ca6.uscourts.gov

Senior Judge **Eugene E. Siler, Jr.** . . . . (606) 877-7930
  Began Service: September 17, 1991
  Appointed By: President George H.W. Bush
  310 South Main Street, Suite 333,
  London, KY 40741

Senior Judge **Martha Craig Daughtrey** . . . . (513) 564-7000
  Began Service: November 22, 1993
  Appointed By: President William J. Clinton

Senior Judge **Ronald Lee Gilman** . . . . (901) 495-1575
  Began Service: November 21, 1997
  Appointed By: President William J. Clinton
  E-mail: ronald_gilman@ca6.uscourts.gov

Court Staff

Circuit Executive **Clarence G. Maddox** . . . . (513) 564-7200
  E-mail: clarence_maddox@ca6.uscourts.gov

Clerk of Court **Deborah S. Hunt** . . . . (513) 564-7000
  E-mail: deborah_hunt@ca6.uscourts.gov

Chief Circuit Mediator **Paul B. Calico** . . . . (513) 564-7330
  E-mail: paul_calico@ca6.uscourts.gov

Circuit Librarian **Owen Smith** . . . . (513) 564-7321
  E-mail: owen_smith@ca6.uscourts.gov

United States Bankruptcy Appellate Panel for the Sixth Circuit

540 Potter Stewart U.S. Courthouse, 100 East Fifth Street,
Cincinnati, OH 45202
Tel: (513) 564-7000 Fax: (513) 564-7098

Number of Judgeships: 6

Judges

Chief Bankruptcy Judge **C. Kathryn Preston** . . . (614) 469-6638 ext. 5795
Bankruptcy Judge **Marian F. Harrison** . . . . (615) 736-5589
  701 Broadway, Room 232,
  Nashville, TN 37203

United States Bankruptcy Appellate Panel for the Sixth Circuit *continued*

Bankruptcy Judge **Guy R. Humphrey** . . . . (937) 225-2863
Bankruptcy Judge **Joan A. Lloyd** . . . . (502) 627-5525
Bankruptcy Judge **Daniel S. Opperman** . . . . (989) 894-8850
Bankruptcy Judge **Paulette J. Delk** . . . . (901) 328-3552
  200 Jefferson Avenue, Suite 625,
  Memphis, TN 38103

Court Staff

Bankruptcy Appellate Panel Clerk **Deborah S. Hunt** . . . . . (513) 564-7000

United States Court of Appeals for the Seventh Circuit

U.S. Courthouse, 219 South Dearborn Street, Room 2722,
Chicago, IL 60604
Tel: (312) 435-5850
Internet: www.ca7.uscourts.gov

Number of Judgeships: 11

Number of Vacancies: 2

Supreme Court Justice: Associate Justice Elena Kagan

Areas Covered: Illinois, Indiana and Wisconsin

Judges

Chief Judge **Diane Pamela Wood** Room 2688 . . . . (312) 435-5521
  Began Service: July 24, 1995
  Appointed By: President William J. Clinton
  E-mail: dwood@ca7.uscourts.gov

Circuit Judge **Richard A. Posner** Room 2788 . . . . (312) 435-5806
  Began Service: December 4, 1981
  Appointed By: President Ronald Reagan
  E-mail: richard_posner@ca7.uscourts.gov

Circuit Judge **Joel M. Flaum** Room 2702 . . . . (312) 435-5626
  Began Service: June 1, 1983
  Appointed By: President Ronald Reagan
  E-mail: joel_flaum@ca7.uscourts.gov

Circuit Judge **Frank H. Easterbrook** Room 274 . . . . (312) 435-5808
  Began Service: 1985
  Appointed By: President Ronald Reagan
  E-mail: frank_easterbrook@ca7.uscourts.gov

Circuit Judge **Michael S. Kanne** Room 2744H . . . . (765) 420-6200
  Began Service: May 20, 1987   Tel: (312) 435-5764
  Appointed By: President Ronald Reagan   (Illinois Chambers)
  E-mail: michael_kanne@ca7.uscourts.gov

Circuit Judge **Ilana Diamond Rovner** Room 2774 . . . . (312) 435-5608
  Began Service: August 17, 1992
  Appointed By: President George H.W. Bush
  E-mail: ilana_rovner@ca7.uscourts.gov

Circuit Judge **Ann Claire Williams** 2722 U.S.
  Courthouse, Room 2602 . . . . (312) 435-5532
  Began Service: November 15, 1999
  Appointed By: President William J. Clinton
  E-mail: ann_c_williams@ca7.uscourts.gov

Circuit Judge **Diane S. Sykes** . . . . (414) 727-6988
  Began Service: July 4, 2004
  Appointed By: President George W. Bush
  E-mail: chambers_of_judge_sykes@ca7.uscourts.gov

Circuit Judge **David F. Hamilton** . . . . (317) 229-3640
  Began Service: November 2009
  Appointed By: President Barack Obama
  E-mail: david_hamilton@ca7.uscourts.gov

Senior Judge **William J. Bauer** Room 2754 . . . . (312) 435-5810
  Began Service: 1974
  Appointed By: President Gerald Ford
  E-mail: chambers_of_judge_bauer@ca7.uscourts.gov

(continued on next page)

United States Court of Appeals for the Seventh Circuit *continued*

Senior Judge **Richard D. Cudahy** . . . . (312) 435-5825
Note: Judge Cudahy's chambers will close effective
September 30, 2015.
Began Service: 1979
Appointed By: President Jimmy Carter
U.S. Courthouse, 219 South Dearborn Street,
Room 2648, Chicago, IL 60604-1813
E-mail: richard_cudahy@ca7.uscourts.gov

Senior Judge **Kenneth F. Ripple** . . . . (574) 246-8150
Began Service: June 10, 1985   Tel: (312) 435-5510
Appointed By: President Ronald Reagan   (Chicago Office)
E-mail: chambers_of_judge_
ripple@ca7.uscourts.gov

Senior Judge **Daniel A. Manion** . . . .(574) 246-8060
Began Service: 1986
Appointed By: President Ronald Reagan
E-mail: daniel_manion@ca7.uscourts.gov

Senior Judge **John Daniel Tinder** . . . . (317) 229-3680
Began Service: December 21, 2007   Tel: (312) 435-5820
Appointed By: President George W. Bush   (Chicago Office)
Birch Bayh Federal Building and United States
Courthouse, 46 East Ohio Street, Room 256,
Indianapolis, IN 46204
E-mail: jdt@ca7.uscourts.gov

Court Staff

Circuit Executive **Collins T. Fitzpatrick** . . . .(312) 435-5803
E-mail: collins_fitzpatrick@ca7.uscourts.gov
Circuit Clerk **Gino J. Agnello** . . . . (312) 435-5850
E-mail: gino_agnello@ca7.uscourts.gov
Senior Conference Attorney **Joel N. Shapiro** Room
1120 . . . . (312) 435-6883
E-mail: joel_shapiro@ca7.uscourts.gov
Circuit Librarian **Gretchen Van Dam** Room 1637 . . . . . . (312) 435-5660

United States Court of Appeals for the Eighth Circuit

Thomas F. Eagleton U.S. Courthouse, 111 South Tenth Street,
Suite 24.327, St. Louis, MO 63102
Tel: (314) 244-2400 Tel: (314) 244-2479 (Electronic Opinions Data)
Fax: (314) 244-2405
Internet: www.ca8.uscourts.gov

Number of Judgeships: 11

Number of Vacancies: 1

Supreme Court Justice: Associate Justice Samuel A. Alito Jr.

Areas Covered: Arkansas, Iowa, Minnesota, Missouri, Nebraska, North Dakota and South Dakota

Judges

Chief Judge **William Jay Riley** . . . . (402) 661-7575
Began Service: August 16, 2001
Appointed By: President George W. Bush
Roman L. Hruska Courthouse,
111 South 18th Plaza, Suite 4303,
Omaha, NE 68102-1322
E-mail: william_riley@ca8.uscourts.gov

Circuit Judge **James B. Loken** . . . .(612) 664-5810
Began Service: 1991
Appointed By: President George H.W. Bush
U.S. Courthouse, 300 South Fourth Street, 11W,
Minneapolis, MN 55415

Circuit Judge **Roger L. Wollman** . . . . (605) 330-6680
Began Service: September 6, 1985
Appointed By: President Ronald Reagan
E-mail: roger_wollman@ca8.uscourts.gov

United States Court of Appeals for the Eighth Circuit *continued*

Circuit Judge **Diana E. Murphy** . . . . (612) 664-5820
Began Service: October 11, 1994
Appointed By: President William J. Clinton
U.S. Courthouse, 300 South Fourth Street, 11E,
Minneapolis, MN 55415-2249
E-mail: Judge_Diana_Murphy@ca8.uscourts.gov

Circuit Judge **Lavenski R. Smith** . . . .(501) 324-7310
Began Service: July 19, 2002
Appointed By: President George W. Bush
Richard Sheppard Arnold U.S. Courthouse,
600 West Capitol Avenue, Suite A502,
Little Rock, AR 72201

Circuit Judge **Steven M. Colloton** . . . . (515) 284-6356
Began Service: September 30, 2003   Tel: (515) 284-6356
Appointed By: President George W. Bush
110 East Court Avenue, Suite 461,
Des Moines, IA 50309
110 East Court Avenue, Suite 461,
Des Moines, IA 50309

Circuit Judge **Raymond W. Gruender III** . . . . (314) 244-2820
Began Service: June 28, 2004
Appointed By: President George W. Bush
111 South Tenth Street, Suite 23.365,
St. Louis, MO 63102-1116

Circuit Judge **Duane Benton** . . . . (816) 512-5815
Began Service: July 8, 2004
Appointed By: President George W. Bush
400 East Ninth Street, Suite 1020,
Kansas City, MO 64106
E-mail: duane_benton@ca8.uscourts.gov

Circuit Judge **Bobby E. Shepherd** . . . . (870) 863-3173
Began Service: October 2006
Appointed By: President George W. Bush

Circuit Judge **Jane Kelly** . . . .(319) 423-6110
Began Service: April 25, 2013
Appointed By: President Barack Obama
E-mail: jane_kelly@ca8.uscourts.gov

Senior Judge **Myron H. Bright** . . . .(701) 297-7260
Began Service: 1968
Appointed By: President Lyndon B. Johnson
E-mail: judge_myron_bright@ca8.uscourts.gov

Senior Judge **Pasco M. Bowman II** . . . .(816) 512-5800
Began Service: August 1, 1983
Appointed By: President Ronald Reagan

Senior Judge **C. Arlen Beam** . . . . (402) 437-1600
Began Service: November 9, 1987
Appointed By: President Ronald Reagan

Senior Judge **Michael J. Melloy** . . . . (319) 423-6080
Began Service: February 26, 2002
Appointed By: President George W. Bush
E-mail: michael_melloy@ca8.uscourts.gov

Senior Judge **Kermit Edward Bye** . . . . (701) 297-7270
Began Service: April 22, 2000
Appointed By: President William J. Clinton
Quentin N. Burdick U.S. Courthouse,
655 North First Avenue, Chambers 330,
Fargo, ND 58102-4952

Court Staff

Circuit Executive **Millie Adams** . . . .(314) 244-2600
E-mail: millie_adams@ca8.uscourts.gov
Clerk of Court **Michael E. Gans** . . . . (314) 244-2400
E-mail: michael_gans@ca8.uscourts.gov
Circuit Librarian **Eric W. Brust** U.S. Courthouse, Room
22.300 . . . .(314) 244-2665
Chief Settlement Director **John H. Martin** . . . . (312) 244-2499

United States Bankruptcy Appellate Panel for the Eighth Circuit

Thomas F. Eagleton U.S. Courthouse, 111 South Tenth Street,
Suite 24.306, St. Louis, MO 63102
Tel: (314) 244-2430 Fax: (314) 244-2780
Internet: www.ca8.uscourts.gov

Number of Judgeships: 6

Judges
Chief Bankruptcy Judge **Arthur Federman** . . . .(816) 512-1910
  Began Service: December 18, 1989
  E-mail: arthur.federman@mow.uscourts.gov
Bankruptcy Judge **Robert J. Kressel** . . . .(612) 664-5250
  Began Service: 1996
  U.S. Courthouse, 300 South Fourth Street, 8 W,
  Minneapolis, MN 55415
Bankruptcy Judge **Barry S. Schermer** . . . .(314) 244-4500
  Began Service: 1997
Bankruptcy Judge **Thomas L. Saladino** . . . .(402) 661-7444
  Began Service: 2009
Bankruptcy Judge **Charles L. Nail, Jr.** . . . .(605) 945-4490
  Federal Building, 225 South Pierre Street,
  Room 211, Pierre, SD 57501
Bankruptcy Judge **Anita L. Shodeen** . . . . (515) 284-6118
  U.S. Courthouse Annex, 110 East Court Avenue,
  Room 300, Des Moines, IA 50309
  E-mail: anita_shodeen@iasb.uscourts.gov

Court Staff
Bankruptcy Appellate Panel Clerk **Michael E. Gans** . . . . . (314) 244-2430
  E-mail: michael_gans@ca8.uscourts.gov

United States Court of Appeals for the Ninth Circuit

James R. Browning U.S. Courthouse, 95 Seventh Street,
San Francisco, CA 94103-1526
P.O. Box 193939, San Francisco, CA 94119-3939
Tel: (415) 355-8000 (General Information)
Tel: (415) 355-7830 (Docketing-Civil)
Tel: (415) 355-7840 (Docketing-Criminal)
Tel: (415) 355-7900 (Mediation)
Internet: www.ca9.uscourts.gov

Number of Judgeships: 29

Supreme Court Justice: Associate Justice Anthony M. Kennedy

Areas Covered: Alaska, Arizona, California, Guam, Hawaii, Idaho, Montana, Nevada, Northern Mariana Islands, Oregon and Washington

Judges
Chief Judge **Sidney R. Thomas** . . . . (406) 373-3200
  Began Service: March 11, 1996
  Appointed By: President William J. Clinton
  E-mail: judge_sr_thomas@ca9.uscourts.gov
Circuit Judge **Alex Kozinski** . . . .(626) 229-7150
  Began Service: November 7, 1985
  Appointed By: President Ronald Reagan
  E-mail: kozinski@usc.edu
Circuit Judge **Harry Pregerson** . . . . (818) 710-7791
  Began Service: 1979
  Appointed By: President Jimmy Carter
  21800 Oxnard Street, Suite 1140,
  Woodland Hills, CA 91367-3633
  E-mail: harry_pregerson@ca9.uscourts.gov
Circuit Judge **Stephen Reinhardt** . . . .(213) 894-3639
  Began Service: 1980
  Appointed By: President Jimmy Carter
  E-mail: Judge_Reinhardt@ca9.uscourts.gov

United States Court of Appeals for the Ninth Circuit *continued*

Circuit Judge **Diarmuid F. O'Scannlain** . . . . (503) 833-5380
  Began Service: September 26, 1986
  Appointed By: President Ronald Reagan
  The Pioneer Courthouse, 700 SW 6th Avenue,
  Suite 313, Portland, OR 97204-1396
  E-mail: diarmuid_o'scannlain@ca9.uscourts.gov
Circuit Judge **Barry G. Silverman** . . . .(602) 322-7330
  Began Service: February 1998
  Appointed By: President William J. Clinton
  E-mail: judge_silverman@ca9.uscourts.gov
Circuit Judge **Susan P. Graber** . . . .(503) 833-5360
  Began Service: April 1, 1998
  Appointed By: President William J. Clinton
  E-mail: susan_graber@ca9.uscourts.gov
Circuit Judge **M. Margaret McKeown** . . . . (619) 557-5300
  Began Service: May 28, 1998
  Appointed By: President William J. Clinton
  401 West A Street, Suite 2000,
  San Diego, CA 92101-7908
  E-mail: judge_mckeown@ca9.uscourts.gov
Circuit Judge **Kim McLane Wardlaw** . . . . (626) 229-7130
  Began Service: August 3, 1998
  Appointed By: President William J. Clinton
  U.S. Court of Appeals Building,
  125 South Grand Avenue, Suite 500,
  Pasadena, CA 91105
  E-mail: judge_wardlaw@ca9.uscourts.gov
Circuit Judge **William A. Fletcher** . . . .(415) 355-8140
  Began Service: January 31, 1999
  Appointed By: President William J. Clinton
  E-mail: judge_w_fletcher@ca9.uscourts.gov
Circuit Judge **Ronald Murray Gould** . . . . (206) 224-2280
  Began Service: January 3, 2000
  Appointed By: President William J. Clinton
  E-mail: ronald_gould@ca9.uscourts.gov
Circuit Judge **Richard A. Paez** . . . .(626) 229-7180
  Began Service: March 14, 2000
  Appointed By: President William J. Clinton
  E-mail: richard_paez@ca9.uscourts.gov
Circuit Judge **Marsha S. Berzon** . . . .(415) 355-8160
  Began Service: March 21, 2000
  Appointed By: President William J. Clinton
  E-mail: marsha_berzon@ca9.uscourts.gov
Circuit Judge **Richard C. Tallman** . . . .(206) 224-2250
  Began Service: May 24, 2000
  Appointed By: President William J. Clinton
  William K. Nakamura U.S. Courthouse,
  1010 5th Avenue, Room 902,
  Seattle, WA 98104
  E-mail: judge_tallman@ca9.uscourts.gov
Circuit Judge **Johnnie B. Rawlinson** . . . . (702) 464-5670
  Began Service: July 21, 2000
  Appointed By: President William J. Clinton
  Lloyd D. George U.S. Courthouse,
  333 Las Vegas Boulevard South, Room 7072,
  Las Vegas, NV 89101
  E-mail: judge_rawlinson@ca9.uscourts.gov
Circuit Judge **Richard R. Clifton** . . . .(808) 522-7474
  Began Service: August 5, 2002
  Appointed By: President George W. Bush
  999 Bishop Street, Suite 2010,
  Honolulu, HI 96813
  E-mail: judge_clifton@ca9.uscourts.gov
Circuit Judge **Jay S. Bybee** . . . .(702) 464-5650
  Began Service: March 28, 2003
  Appointed By: President George W. Bush
  E-mail: jay_bybee@ca9.uscourts.gov
Circuit Judge **Consuelo Maria Callahan** . . . . (916) 930-4160
  Began Service: 2003
  Appointed By: President George W. Bush
  501 I Street, Room 12-700,
  Sacramento, CA 95814
  E-mail: consuelo_callahan@ca9.uscourts.gov
Circuit Judge **Carlos T. Bea** . . . .(415) 355-8180
  Began Service: October 2003
  Appointed By: President George W. Bush
  E-mail: judge_bea@ca9.uscourts.gov

(continued on next page)

United States Court of Appeals for the Ninth Circuit *continued*

Circuit Judge **Milan D. Smith, Jr.** . . . .(310) 607-4020
  Began Service: June 2006
  Appointed By: President George W. Bush
  222 North Sepulveda Boulevard, Room 2325,
  El Segundo, CA 90245
  E-mail: milan_smith@ca9.uscourts.gov

Circuit Judge **Sandra Segal Ikuta** . . . .(626) 229-7339
  Began Service: June 2006
  Appointed By: President George W. Bush
  E-mail: judge_ikuta@ca9.uscourts.gov

Circuit Judge **Norman Randy Smith** . . . . (208) 478-4140
  Began Service: March 19, 2007
  Appointed By: President George W. Bush
  E-mail: judge_smith@ca9.uscourts.gov

Circuit Judge **Mary Helen Murguia** . . . . (602) 322-7580
  Began Service: January 4, 2011
  Appointed By: President Barack Obama
  E-mail: mary_murguia@ca9.uscourts.gov

Circuit Judge **Morgan B. Christen** . . . .(907) 677-6295
  Began Service: January 11, 2012
  Appointed By: President Barack Obama
  E-mail: morgan_christen@ca9.uscourts.gov

Circuit Judge **Jacqueline H. Nguyen** . . . . (626) 229-7242
  Began Service: 2012
  Appointed By: President Barack Obama
  E-mail: jacqueline_nguyen@ca9.uscourts.gov

Circuit Judge **Paul J. Watford** . . . .(626) 229-7300
  Began Service: June 1, 2012
  Appointed By: President Barack Obama
  E-mail: paul_watford@ca9.uscourts.gov

Circuit Judge **Andrew D. Hurwitz** . . . .(602) 322-7690
  Began Service: 2012
  Appointed By: President Barack Obama
  E-mail: andrew_hurwitz@ca9.uscourts.gov

Circuit Judge **John B. Owens** . . . .(619) 557-6400
  Began Service: April 25, 2014
  Appointed By: President Barack Obama
  E-mail: john_owens@ca9.uscourts.gov

Circuit Judge **Michelle T. Friedland** . . . . (415) 355-8000
  Began Service: 2014
  Appointed By: President Barack Obama
  E-mail: michelle_friedland@ca9.uscourts.gov

Senior Judge **Alfred T. Goodwin** . . . .(626) 229-7100
  Began Service: 1972
  Appointed By: President Richard M. Nixon
  E-mail: alfred_goodwin@ca9.uscourts.gov

Senior Judge **J. Clifford Wallace** . . . .(619) 557-6114
  Began Service: 1972
  Appointed By: President Richard M. Nixon
  E-mail: Judge_Wallace@ca9.uscourts.gov

Senior Judge **Procter Hug, Jr.** . . . .(775) 686-5949
  Began Service: September 16, 1977
  Appointed By: President Jimmy Carter
  E-mail: judge_hug@ca9.uscourts.gov

Senior Judge **Mary M. Schroeder** . . . .(602) 322-7320
  Began Service: October 1979
  Appointed By: President Jimmy Carter
  Sandra Day O'Connor U.S. Courthouse,
  401 West Washington Street, SPC 54, Suite 610,
  Phoenix, AZ 85003-2156
  E-mail: judge_schroeder@ca9.uscourts.gov

Senior Judge **Jerome Farris** . . . .(206) 224-2260
  Began Service: October 16, 1979
  Appointed By: President Jimmy Carter
  1010 Fifth Avenue, Room 1030,
  Seattle, WA 98104
  E-mail: jerome_farris@ca9.uscourts.gov

Senior Judge **Dorothy Wright Nelson** . . . . (626) 229-7400
  Began Service: 1980
  Appointed By: President Jimmy Carter
  Richard H. Chambers U.S. Court of Appeals Federal
  Building, 125 South Grand Avenue, Suite 303,
  Pasadena, CA 91105-1652
  E-mail: dorothy_nelson@ca9.uscourts.gov

United States Court of Appeals for the Ninth Circuit *continued*

Senior Judge **William C. Canby, Jr.** . . . . (602) 322-7300
  Began Service: 1980
  Appointed By: President Jimmy Carter
  Sandra Day O'Connor U.S. Courthouse,
  401 West Washington Street, SPC 55, Room 612,
  Phoenix, AZ 85003-2156
  E-mail: william_canby@ca9.uscourts.gov

Senior Judge **John T. Noonan, Jr.** . . . .(415) 355-8130
  Began Service: January 16, 1986
  Appointed By: President Ronald Reagan
  E-mail: judge_noonan@ca9.uscourts.gov

Senior Judge **Edward Leavy** . . . . (503) 833-5350
  Began Service: March 23, 1987
  Appointed By: President Ronald Reagan
  700 Southwest Sixth Avenue, Suite 226,
  Portland, OR 97204
  E-mail: judge_leavy@ca9.uscourts.gov

Senior Judge **Stephen S. Trott** . . . . (208) 334-1612
  Began Service: April 1988
  Appointed By: President Ronald Reagan
  U.S. Courthouse, 550 West Fort Street, Room 667,
  Boise, ID 83724-0040
  E-mail: judge_trott@ca9.uscourts.gov

Senior Judge **Ferdinand Francis Fernandez** . . . . (626) 229-7121
  Began Service: 1989
  Appointed By: President George H.W. Bush
  E-mail: ferdinand_fernandez@ca9.uscourts.gov

Senior Judge **Andrew J. Kleinfeld** . . . .(907) 456-0564
  Began Service: September 16, 1991
  Appointed By: President George H.W. Bush
  Courthouse Square, 250 Cushman Street, Suite 3 A,
  Fairbanks, AK 99701-4665
  E-mail: judge_kleinfeld@ca9.uscourts.gov

Senior Judge **Michael Daly Hawkins** . . . . (602) 322-7310
  Began Service: 1994
  Appointed By: President William J. Clinton
  Sandra Day O'Connor U.S. Courthouse,
  401 West Washington Street, SPC 47, Suite 510,
  Phoenix, AZ 85003-2151
  E-mail: judge_hawkins@ca9.uscourts.gov

Senior Judge **A. Wallace Tashima** . . . .(626) 229-7373
  Began Service: 1995
  Appointed By: President William J. Clinton
  E-mail: judge_tashima@ca9.uscourts.gov

Senior Judge **Raymond C. Fisher** . . . .(626) 229-7110
  Began Service: October 29, 1999
  Appointed By: President William J. Clinton
  Richard H. Chambers U.S. Court of Appeals
  Building, 125 South Grand Avenue, Suite 400,
  Pasadena, CA 91105
  E-mail: raymond_fisher@ca9.uscourts.gov

Court Staff

Circuit and Court of Appeals Executive
Cathy A. Catterson . . . .(415) 355-8800
  E-mail: cathy_catterson@ca9.uscourts.gov

Clerk of the Court **Molly C. Dwyer** . . . .(415) 355-8000
  E-mail: molly_dwyer@ca9.uscourts.gov

Chief Circuit Mediator **Claudia Bernard** . . . .(415) 355-7900
  E-mail: claudia_bernard@ca9.uscourts.gov

Circuit Librarian **Eric Wade** . . . . (415) 355-8650

United States Bankruptcy Appellate Panel for the Ninth Circuit

U.S. Courthouse, 125 South Grand Avenue, Pasadena, CA 91105
Tel: (626) 229-7225 Fax: (626) 229-7475
Internet: www.ca9.uscourts.gov/bap

Number of Judgeships: 6

Judges

Chief Judge of the Bankruptcy Appellate Panel
Randall L. Dunn .... (503) 326-4175
  Began Service: 2006
  1001 SW Fifth Avenue, Room 700,
  Portland, OR 97204
Bankruptcy Judge **Jim D. Pappas** .... (208) 334-9571
  Began Service: 2010
Bankruptcy Judge **Meredith A. Jury** .... (951) 774-1043
  Began Service: 2007
Bankruptcy Judge **Ralph B. Kirscher** .... (406) 782-3338
  Began Service: 1999
  400 North Main Street, Room 215,
  Butte, MT 59701
Bankruptcy Judge **Laura S. Taylor** .... (626) 229-7225
Bankruptcy Judge **Frank L. Kurtz** .... (509) 576-6122

Court Staff

Bankruptcy Appellate Panel Clerk **Susan M. Spraul** ..... (626) 229-7220

United States Court of Appeals for the Tenth Circuit

Byron White U.S. Courthouse, 1823 Stout Street, Denver, CO 80257
Tel: (303) 844-3157
Tel: (303) 844-5682 (Electronic Opinions and Dockets Data)
Fax: (303) 844-2540
Internet: www.ca10.uscourts.gov

Number of Judgeships: 12

Supreme Court Justice: Associate Justice Sonia Sotomayor

Areas Covered: Colorado, Kansas, New Mexico, Oklahoma, Utah and Wyoming

Judges

Chief Judge **Mary Beck Briscoe** .... (785) 843-4067
  Began Service: May 31, 1995
  Appointed By: President William J. Clinton
  645 Massachusetts, Suite 400,
  Lawrence, KS 66044
Circuit Judge **Paul J. Kelly** .... (505) 988-6541
  Began Service: April 14, 1992
  Appointed By: President George H.W. Bush
Circuit Judge **Carlos F. Lucero** .... (303) 844-2200
  Began Service: July 22, 1995
  Appointed By: President William J. Clinton
  E-mail: Carlos_F_Lucero@ca10.uscourts.gov
Circuit Judge **Harris L Hartz** .... (505) 843-6196
  Began Service: December 2001
  Appointed By: President George W. Bush
  201 Third Street NW, Suite 1870,
  Albuquerque, NM 87102
Circuit Judge **Timothy M. Tymkovich** Room 102 G ...... (303) 335-3300
  Began Service: June 19, 2003
  Appointed By: President George W. Bush
  E-mail: timothy_m_tymkovich@ca10.uscourts.gov
Circuit Judge **Jerome A. Holmes** .... (405) 609-5480
  Began Service: August 2006
  Appointed By: President George W. Bush
  215 Dean A. McGee Avenue, Room 315,
  Oklahoma City, OK 73102
  E-mail: jerome_a_holmes@ca10.uscourts.gov

United States Court of Appeals for the Tenth Circuit *continued*

Circuit Judge **Neil M. Gorsuch** .... (303) 335-2800
  Began Service: August 2006
  Appointed By: President George W. Bush
Circuit Judge **Scott M. Matheson, Jr.** .... (801) 524-5145
  Began Service: January 6, 2011
  Appointed By: President Barack Obama
  125 South State Street, Suite 5402,
  Salt Lake City, UT 84138
  E-mail: scott_matheson@ca10.uscourts.gov
Circuit Judge **Robert E. Bacharach** .... (405) 609-5320
  Began Service: March 1, 2013
  Appointed By: President Barack Obama
Circuit Judge **Gregory Alan Phillips** .... (303) 844-3157
  Began Service: July 22, 2013
  Appointed By: President Barack Obama
Circuit Judge **Carolyn B. McHugh** .... (801) 401-8150
  Began Service: March 17, 2014
  Appointed By: President Barack Obama
  E-mail: carolyn_mchugh@ca10.uscourts.gov
Circuit Judge **Nancy L. Moritz** .... (303) 844-3157
  Began Service: July 29, 2014
  Appointed By: President Barack Obama
  E-mail: nancy_moritz@ca10.uscourts.gov
Senior Judge **Monroe G. McKay** .... (801) 524-5252
  Began Service: December 1, 1977
  Appointed By: President Jimmy Carter
Senior Judge **John C. Porfilio** .... (303) 844-3157
  Began Service: May 14, 1985
  Appointed By: President Ronald Reagan
Senior Judge **Stephen H. Anderson** .... (801) 524-6950
  Began Service: November 1985
  Appointed By: President Ronald Reagan
  E-mail: stephen_h_anderson@ca10.uscourts.gov
Senior Judge **Bobby R. Baldock** .... (575) 625-2388
  Began Service: 1985
  Appointed By: President Ronald Reagan
Senior Judge **Stephanie K. Seymour** .... (918) 699-4745
  Began Service: November 16, 1979
  Appointed By: President Jimmy Carter
Senior Judge **David Milton Ebel** Room 109L .... (303) 844-3800
  Began Service: July 1988
  Appointed By: President Ronald Reagan
  E-mail: David_M_Ebel@ca10.uscourts.gov
Senior Judge **Michael R. Murphy** .... (801) 524-5955
  Began Service: October 5, 1995
  Appointed By: President William J. Clinton
  E-mail: Judge_Michael_R_
  Murphy@ca10.uscourts.gov
Senior Judge **Terrence L. O'Brien** .... (307) 433-2400
  Began Service: April 23, 2002
  Appointed By: President George W. Bush
  2120 Carey Avenue, Room 2107,
  Cheyenne, WY 82001
  E-mail: terrence_l_obrien@ca10.uscourts.gov

Court Staff

Circuit Executive **David Tighe** .... (303) 844-2067
  E-mail: dave_tighe@ca10.uscourts.gov
Clerk of the Court **Elizabeth A. "Betsy" Shumaker** .... (303) 844-3157
  E-mail: Betsy_Shumaker@ca10.uscourts.gov
Chief Circuit Mediator **David W. Aemmer** .... (303) 844-6017
  E-mail: david_aemmer@ca10.uscourts.gov
Circuit Librarian **Madeline R. Cohen** .... (303) 844-3591
  1929 Stout Street, 4th Floor,
  Denver, CO 80294
  E-mail: madeline_cohen@ca10.uscourts.gov

United States Bankruptcy Appellate Panel for the Tenth Circuit

Byron White U.S. Courthouse, 1823 Stout Street, Denver, CO 80257
Tel: (303) 335-2900 Fax: (303) 335-2999
E-mail: 10th_circuit_bap@ca10.uscourts.gov
Internet: www.bap10.uscourts.gov

Number of Judgeships: 9

Judges

Chief Bankruptcy Judge **William T. Thurman** . . . . (801) 524-6572
  Began Service: May 6, 2008
Bankruptcy Judge **Tom R. Cornish** . . . . (918) 549-7205
  Began Service: February 7, 1996
Bankruptcy Judge **Terrence L. Michael** . . . . (918) 699-4065
  Began Service: June 9, 1997
Bankruptcy Judge **Robert E. Nugent** . . . . (316) 315-4150
  Began Service: 2007
Bankruptcy Judge **Janice Miller Karlin** . . . . (785) 338-5950
  Began Service: June 2008
Bankruptcy Judge **Michael E. Romero** . . . . (720) 904-7413
  Began Service: March 30, 2009
Bankruptcy Judge **Dale L. Somers** . . . . (785) 338-5960
  Began Service: 2011
  444 South East Quincy Street, Room 225,
  Topeka, KS 66683
Bankruptcy Judge **Robert H. Jacobvitz** . . . . (505) 348-2545
  Began Service: November 8, 2012
Bankruptcy Judge **Sarah A. Hall** . . . . (405) 609-5660

Court Staff

Bankruptcy Appellate Panel Clerk **Blaine F. Bates** . . . . (303) 335-2900

United States Court of Appeals for the Eleventh Circuit

Elbert P. Tuttle U.S. Court of Appeals Building, 56 NW Forsyth Street,
Atlanta, GA 30303
Tel: (404) 335-6100
Internet: www.ca11.uscourts.gov

Number of Judgeships: 12

Number of Vacancies: 1

Supreme Court Justice: Associate Justice Clarence Thomas

Areas Covered: Alabama, Florida and Georgia

Judges

Chief Judge **Edward Carnes** . . . . (334) 954-3580
  Began Service: October 2, 1992
  Appointed By: President George H.W. Bush
Circuit Judge **Gerald Bard Tjoflat** . . . . (904) 301-5670
  Began Service: November 21, 1975
  Appointed By: President Gerald Ford
  E-mail: gerald_tjoflat@ca11.uscourts.gov
Circuit Judge **Frank M. Hull** . . . . (404) 335-6550
  Began Service: October 3, 1997
  Appointed By: President William J. Clinton
  E-mail: frank_hull@ca11.uscourts.gov
Circuit Judge **Stanley Marcus** . . . . (305) 536-4841
  Began Service: November 24, 1997
  Appointed By: President William J. Clinton
  99 NE Fourth Street, Room 1235,
  Miami, FL 33132
  E-mail: stanley_marcus@ca11.uscourts.gov
Circuit Judge **Charles Reginald Wilson** . . . . (813) 301-5650
  Began Service: September 30, 1999
  Appointed By: President William J. Clinton
  Sam M. Gibbons Courthouse,
  801 North Florida Avenue, Suite 16-B,
  Tampa, FL 33602
  E-mail: charles_wilson@ca11.uscourts.gov

United States Court of Appeals for the Eleventh Circuit *continued*

Circuit Judge **William Holcombe "Bill" Pryor, Jr.** . . . . . . (205) 278-2030
  Began Service: February 20, 2004
  Appointed By: President George W. Bush
  1729 Fifth Avenue North, Suite 900,
  Birmingham, AL 35203
Circuit Judge **Beverly Baldwin Martin** . . . . (404) 335-6630
  Began Service: January 28, 2010
  Appointed By: President Barack Obama
Circuit Judge **Adalberto José Jordán** . . . . (305) 523-5560
  Began Service: 2012
  Appointed By: President Barack Obama
  E-mail: adalberto_jordan@ca11.uscourts.gov
Circuit Judge **Robin S. Rosenbaum** . . . . (954) 769-5670
  Began Service: June 3, 2014
  Appointed By: President Barack Obama
Circuit Judge **Julie E. Carnes** . . . . (404) 335-6100
  Began Service: July 31, 2014
  Appointed By: President Barack Obama
  E-mail: julie_carnes@ca11.uscourts.gov
Circuit Judge **Jill A. Pryor** . . . . (404) 335-6100
  Began Service: October 6, 2014
  Appointed By: President Barack Obama
Senior Judge **James C. Hill** . . . . (904) 301-6630
  Began Service: May 1976
  Appointed By: President Gerald Ford
  US Courthouse, 300 North Hogan Street,
  Suite 14-400, Jacksonville, FL 32202-4258
  E-mail: james_hill@ca11.uscourts.gov
Senior Judge **Peter T. Fay** . . . . (305) 579-4390
  Began Service: 1976
  Appointed By: President Gerald Ford
  Federal Justice Building, 99 NE Fourth Street,
  Room 1255, Miami, FL 33132
Senior Judge **Phyllis A. Kravitch** . . . . (404) 335-6300
  Began Service: April 10, 1979
  Appointed By: President Jimmy Carter
  56 Forsyth Street, Room 202,
  Atlanta, GA 30303
  E-mail: phyllis_kravitch@ca11.uscourts.gov
Senior Judge **R. Lanier Anderson III** . . . . (478) 752-8101
  Began Service: August 1979
  Appointed By: President Jimmy Carter
  475 Mulberry Street, Room 302,
  Macon, GA 31201
Senior Judge **J. L. Edmondson** Room 416 . . . . (404) 335-6230
  Began Service: June 9, 1986
  Appointed By: President Ronald Reagan
Senior Judge **Emmett Ripley Cox** . . . . (251) 690-2055
  Began Service: 1988
  Appointed By: President Ronald Reagan
  113 St. Joseph Street, Room 433,
  Mobile, AL 36602
  E-mail: emmett_cox@ca11.uscourts.gov
Senior Judge **Joel F. Dubina** . . . . (334) 954-3560
  Began Service: 1990
  Appointed By: President George H.W. Bush
  E-mail: joel_dubina@ca11.uscourts.gov
Senior Judge **Susan Harrell Black** . . . . (904) 301-5610
  Began Service: August 12, 1992
  Appointed By: President George H.W. Bush
  300 North Hogan Street, Suite 14-150,
  Jacksonville, FL 32202-4258
  E-mail: Susan_Black@ca11.uscourts.gov

Court Staff

Circuit Executive **COL James P. Gerstenlauer** . . . . (404) 335-6535
  E-mail: james_gerstenlauer@ca11.uscourts.gov
Clerk of the Court **Donald J. Mincher** . . . . (404) 335-6100
  E-mail: donald_mincher@ca11.uscourts.gov
Chief Circuit Mediator (Acting) **Caleb Davies** . . . . (404) 335-6260
  E-mail: caleb_davies@ca11.uscourts.gov
Circuit Librarian **Elaine P. Fenton** . . . . (404) 335-6500
  E-mail: elaine_fenton@ca11.uscourts.gov

United States Court of Appeals for the District of Columbia Circuit

E. Barrett Prettyman U.S. Courthouse, 333 Constitution Avenue, NW, Washington, DC 20001-2866
Tel: (202) 216-7000 Tel: (202) 216-7300 (Clerk's Office)
Tel: (202) 216-7312 (Calendar) Tel: (202) 216-7280 (Intake)
Tel: (202) 273-0926 (Appellate Case Voice Information)
Tel: (202) 216-7296 (Electronic Opinions Voice) Fax: (202) 273-0988
Internet: www.cadc.uscourts.gov

Number of Judgeships: 11

Supreme Court Justice: Chief Justice John G. Roberts Jr.

Judges

Chief Judge **Merrick B. Garland** . . . . (202) 216-7460
  Began Service: April 9, 1997   Tel: (202) 208-2449
  Appointed By: President William J. Clinton
  E-mail: merrick_garland@cadc.uscourts.gov
Circuit Judge **Karen LeCraft Henderson** . . . . (202) 216-7370
  Began Service: July 11, 1990
  Appointed By: President George H.W. Bush
  E. Barrett Prettyman U.S. Courthouse,
  333 Constitution Avenue, NW, Room 3118,
  Washington, DC 20001
  E-mail: karen_henderson@cadc.uscourts.gov
Circuit Judge **Judith W. Rogers** William B. Bryant
  Annex, Room 5907 . . . . (202) 216-7260
  Began Service: March 21, 1994
  Appointed By: President William J. Clinton
  E-mail: judith_rogers@cadc.uscourts.gov
Circuit Judge **David S. Tatel** . . . . (202) 216-7160
  Began Service: October 11, 1994
  Appointed By: President William J. Clinton
  E-mail: dtatel@cadc.uscourts.gov
Circuit Judge **Janice Rogers Brown** . . . . (202) 216-7220
  Began Service: July 1, 2005
  Appointed By: President George W. Bush
  E-mail: janice_brown@cadc.uscourts.gov
Circuit Judge **Thomas B. Griffith** . . . . (202) 216-7170
  Began Service: June 29, 2005
  Appointed By: President George W. Bush
  E-mail: Thomas_Griffith@cadc.uscourts.gov
Circuit Judge **Brett M. Kavanaugh** . . . . (202) 216-7180
  Began Service: May 30, 2006
  Appointed By: President George W. Bush
  E. Barrett Prettyman U.S. Courthouse,
  333 Constitution Avenue, NW, Room 3004,
  Washington, DC 20001
  E-mail: brett_kavanaugh@cadc.uscourts.gov
Circuit Judge **Srikanth "Sri" Srinivasan** . . . . (202) 216-7080
  Began Service: June 17, 2013
  Appointed By: President Barack Obama
  E-mail: srikanth_srinivasan@cadc.uscourts.gov
Circuit Judge **Patricia Ann Millett** . . . . (202) 216-7110
  Began Service: February 28, 2014
  Appointed By: President Barack Obama
  E-mail: patricia_millett@cadc.uscourts.gov
Circuit Judge **Cornelia T. L. "Nina" Pillard** . . . . (202) 216-7120
  Began Service: December 18, 2013
  Appointed By: President Barack Obama
  E-mail: cornelia_pillard@cadc.uscourts.gov
Circuit Judge **Robert Leon Wilkins** . . . . (202) 216-7240
  Began Service: January 24, 2014
  Appointed By: President Barack Obama
  E-mail: rwilkins@cadc.uscourts.gov
Senior Judge **Douglas H. Ginsburg** . . . . (202) 216-7190
  Began Service: October 14, 1986
  Appointed By: President Ronald Reagan
  E. Barrett Prettyman U.S. Courthouse,
  333 Constitution Avenue, NW, Room 5128,
  Washington, DC 20001
  E-mail: douglas_ginsburg@cadc.uscourts.gov
Senior Judge **David Bryan Sentelle** . . . . (202) 216-7330
  Began Service: October 19, 1987
  Appointed By: President Ronald Reagan
  E-mail: david_sentelle@cadc.uscourts.gov

United States Court of Appeals for the District of Columbia Circuit
continued

Senior Judge **Laurence H. Silberman** Room 3500 . . . . (202) 216-7353
  Began Service: November 1, 1985
  Appointed By: President Ronald Reagan
  E-mail: lsilberman@cadc.uscourts.gov
Senior Judge **Stephen F. Williams** Room 3700 . . . . (202) 216-7210
  Began Service: 1986
  Appointed By: President Ronald Reagan
  E-mail: sfwilliams@cadc.uscourts.gov
Senior Judge **Harry T. Edwards** . . . . (202) 216-7380
  Began Service: February 20, 1980
  Appointed By: President Jimmy Carter
  E. Barrett Prettyman U.S. Courthouse,
  333 Constitution Avenue, NW, Room 5500,
  Washington, DC 20001-2805
  E-mail: hedwards@cadc.uscourts.gov
Senior Judge **A. Raymond Randolph** Room 5010 . . . . (202) 216-7425
  Began Service: July 20, 1990
  Appointed By: President George H.W. Bush
  E-mail: raymond_randolph@cadc.uscourts.gov

Court Staff

Circuit Executive **Elizabeth H. "Betsy" Paret** . . . . (202) 216-7340
  E-mail: elizabeth_paret@cadc.uscourts.gov
Circuit Clerk **Mark J. Langer** . . . . (202) 216-7300
  E-mail: mark_langer@cadc.uscourts.gov
Legal Division Director **Martha J. Tomich** . . . . (202) 216-7500
  E-mail: martha_tomich@cadc.uscourts.gov
Chief Circuit Mediator **Amy Wind** . . . . (202) 216-7350
  E-mail: amy_wind@cadc.uscourts.gov
Circuit Librarian **Patricia Michalowskij** . . . . (202) 216-7400
  E-mail: patricia_michalowskij@cadc.uscourts.gov

U.S. District Courts

United States District Courts

Most federal cases are initially tried and decided in the United States District Courts, the federal courts of general trial jurisdiction. There are 94 courts in the 50 states, the District of Columbia, the Commonwealth of Puerto Rico, and the territories of Guam, the United States Virgin Islands, and the Northern Mariana Islands. Listed in this section for each district court are: U.S. District Court Staff, U.S. District Court judges and staff, U.S. Magistrate judges and staff, U.S. Senior judges and staff, and U.S. Bankruptcy judges and staff. The jurisdiction of the district courts extends to cases involving the U.S. constitution or federal laws, the U.S. government, or controversies between states or between the U.S. and foreign governments. The courts also hear cases involving citizens of different states, or between U. S. citizens and citizens from another country. With the exception of the territorial courts, all district court judges are appointed for life by the President with the advice and consent of the Senate. In each district, the judge who has served on the court the longest and who is under 65 years of age is designated as the chief judge. The chief judge has administrative duties in addition to a caseload. Within each district, the United States Bankruptcy Court hears and decides petitions of individuals and businesses seeking relief from bankruptcy. Bankruptcy judges are appointed by the court of appeals for a term of 14 years. The judges of each district appoint one or more magistrate judges, who discharge many of the ancillary duties of the district judges.

The district-by-district listings include both "active" and "senior" federal judges. Active Judges are listed by date of appointment. Senior judges are listed in the order in which they assumed senior status. Under current rules, an appellate or district court judge with 15 years of active service may "retire on salary" or assume "senior status" at age 65. A sliding scale makes judges with a minimum of 10 years of service eligible at age 70. Federal judges cannot be required to retire or take senior status when they become eligible, because they have life tenure under Article III of the Constitution, which is why they are called "Article III" judges. Those who take senior status continue to hear cases, though at a reduced level.

U.S. Magistrate judges play an important role in the federal litigation process. In civil cases it is not uncommon for magistrate judges to conduct almost all pretrial proceedings, preparing the case for trial before the assigned district judge. There are both full-time and part-time magistrate judge positions, and these positions are assigned to the district courts according to caseload criteria. A full-time magistrate judge serves a term of eight years; a part-time magistrate judge's term is four years.

United States District Court for the Middle District of Alabama

Frank M. Johnson, Jr. Federal Building & U.S. Courthouse,
One Church Street, Suite B - 110, Montgomery, AL 36104
P.O. Box 711, Montgomery, AL 36101
Tel: (334) 954-3600
Internet: www.almd.uscourts.gov

Number of Judgeships: 3

Number of Vacancies: 2

Circuit: Eleventh

Areas Covered: Counties of Autauga, Barbour, Bullock, Butler, Chambers, Chilton, Coffee, Coosa, Covington, Crenshaw, Dale, Elmore, Geneva, Henry, Houston, Lee, Lowndes, Macon, Montgomery, Pike, Randolph, Russell and Tallapoosa

Judges

Chief Judge **W. Keith Watkins** Room 300-E . . . . (334) 954-3760
  Began Service: January 12, 2006
  Appointed By: President George W. Bush
Senior Judge **Truman M. Hobbs** D-300 . . . . (334) 954-3750
  Began Service: April 14, 1980
  Appointed By: President Jimmy Carter
Senior Judge **W. Harold Albritton III** . . . . (334) 954-3710
  Began Service: May 1991
  Appointed By: President George H.W. Bush

United States District Court for the Middle District of Alabama *continued*

Senior Judge **Myron H. Thompson** . . . . (334) 954-3650
  Began Service: September 29, 1980
  Appointed By: President Jimmy Carter
  E-mail: myron_thompson@almd.uscourts.gov
Chief Magistrate Judge **Susan Russ Walker** Suite
  501-B . . . . (334) 954-3670
  Began Service: April 2008
  E-mail: susan_walker@almd.uscourts.gov
Magistrate Judge **Wallace Capel, Jr.** Room 501-A . . . . (334) 954-3730
  Began Service: December 2006
  E-mail: wallace_capel@almd.uscourts.gov
Magistrate Judge **Charles S. Coody** Frank M. Johnson,
  Jr. Federal Courthouse Annex, Room 401-B . . . . (334) 954-3700
  Began Service: May 1, 1987
Magistrate Judge **Terry F. Moorer** Frank M. Johnson, Jr.
  Federal Courthouse Annex, A-401 . . . . (334) 954-3740
  Began Service: January 2007
  E-mail: terry_moorer@almd.uscourts.gov
Magistrate Judge (recalled) **Paul W. Greene** . . . . (334) 954-3960

Court Staff

District Clerk **Debra P. "Debbie" Hackett** . . . . (334) 954-3600
  E-mail: Debbie_Hackett@almd.uscourts.gov
Chief Probation Officer **Dwayne Spurlock** . . . . (334) 954-3226
  P.O. Box 39, Montgomery, AL 36102

United States Bankruptcy Court for the Middle District of Alabama

One Church Street, Montgomery, AL 36104
Tel: (334) 954-3800   Fax: (334) 954-3819
Tel: (866) 222-8029 (Voice Case Information System VCIS)
Internet: www.almb.uscourts.gov

Number of Judgeships: 2

Judges

Chief Bankruptcy Judge **William R. Sawyer** . . . . (334) 954-3880
  Began Service: May 24, 1999
Bankruptcy Judge **Dwight H. Williams, Jr.** 4th Floor . . . . (334) 954-3890
  Began Service: October 1999
  E-mail: DHW@almb.uscourts.gov

Court Staff

Clerk of the Court **Juan-Carlos Guerrero** . . . . (334) 954-3800
  E-mail: jc_guerrero@almb.uscourts.gov

U.S. Attorney

Alabama - Middle District
131 Clayton Street, Montgomery, AL 36104
P.O. Box 197, Montgomery, AL 36101-0197
Tel: (334) 223-7280   Fax: (334) 223-7560

U.S. Attorney **George Lamar Beck, Jr.** . . . . (334) 223-7280
  E-mail: george.beck@usdoj.gov

Federal Public Defender

Middle District of Alabama Federal Defenders Program, Inc.
817 South Court Street, Montgomery, AL 36104
Tel: (334) 834-2099   Fax: (334) 834-0353

Executive Director **Christine A. Freeman** . . . . (334) 834-2099
  E-mail: cfreeman@almfd.org

United States District Court for the Northern District of Alabama

Hugo L. Black U.S. Courthouse, 1729 Fifth Avenue North,
Birmingham, AL 35203-2040
Tel: (205) 278-1700
Internet: www.alnd.uscourts.gov

Number of Judgeships: 8

Number of Vacancies: 2

Circuit: Eleventh

Areas Covered: Counties of Bibb, Blount, Calhoun, Cherokee, Clay, Cleburne, Colbert, Cullman, DeKalb, Etowah, Fayette, Franklin, Greene, Jackson, Jefferson, Lamar, Lauderdale, Lawrence, Limestone, Madison, Marion, Marshall, Morgan, Pickens, Shelby, St. Clair, Sumter, Talladega, Tuscaloosa, Walker and Winston

Judges

Chief Judge **Karon O. Bowdre** . . . .(205) 278-1800
  Began Service: November 8, 2001
  Appointed By: President George W. Bush
  E-mail: karon_bowdre@alnd.uscourts.gov

District Judge **R. David Proctor** . . . .(205) 278-1980
  Began Service: September 24, 2003
  Appointed By: President George W. Bush
  E-mail: proctor_chambers@alnd.uscourts.gov

District Judge **L. Scott Coogler** . . . .(205) 561-1670
  Began Service: June 3, 2003
  Appointed By: President George W. Bush
  2005 University Boulevard, Room 2300,
  Tuscaloosa, AL 35401

District Judge **Virginia Emerson Hopkins** . . . .(205) 278-1950
  Began Service: June 2004
  Appointed By: President George W. Bush
  Hugo L. Black U.S. Courthouse,
  1729 Fifth Avenue North, Suite 619,
  Birmingham, AL 35203
  E-mail: hopkins_chambers@alnd.uscourts.gov

District Judge **Abdul K. Kallon** . . . . (205) 278-1850
  Began Service: February 1, 2010
  Appointed By: President Barack Obama
  E-mail: abdul_kallon@alnd.uscourts.gov

District Judge **Madeline H. Haikala** . . . . (205) 278-1700
  Began Service: October 21, 2013
  Appointed By: President Barack Obama
  E-mail: madeline_haikala@alnd.uscourts.gov

Senior Judge **James Hughes Hancock** . . . .(205) 278-1840
  Began Service: 1973
  Appointed By: President Richard M. Nixon
  Hugo L. Black U.S. Courthouse,
  1729 Fifth Avenue North, Room 681,
  Birmingham, AL 35203
  E-mail: james_hancock@alnd.uscourts.gov

Senior Judge **William M. Acker, Jr.** . . . .(205) 278-1880
  Began Service: September 1982
  Appointed By: President Ronald Reagan
  Hugo L. Black U.S. Courthouse,
  1729 Fifth Avenue North, Room 481,
  Birmingham, AL 35203
  E-mail: William_Acker@alnd.uscourts.gov

Senior Judge **Inge P. Johnson** . . . .(256) 760-2061
  Began Service: October 23, 1998
  Appointed By: President William J. Clinton
  E-mail: inge_johnson@alnd.uscourts.gov

Senior Judge **C. Lynwood Smith, Jr.** . . . . (256) 533-9490
  Began Service: January 4, 1996
  Appointed By: President William J. Clinton

Senior Judge **Sharon Lovelace Blackburn** . . . .(205) 278-1810
  Began Service: July 8, 1991
  Appointed By: President George H.W. Bush
  Hugo L. Black U.S. Courthouse,
  1729 Fifth Avenue North, Room 882,
  Birmingham, AL 35203
  E-mail: sharon_blackburn@alnd.uscourts.gov

United States District Court for the Northern District of Alabama
continued

Chief Magistrate Judge **John E. Ott** . . . . (205) 278-1920
  Began Service: April 6, 1998
  E-mail: John_Ott@alnd.uscourts.gov

Magistrate Judge **Terry Michael Putnam** . . . . (205) 278-1900
  Began Service: February 9, 1987
  Hugo L. Black U.S. Courthouse,
  1729 Fifth Avenue North, Room 361,
  Birmingham, AL 35203

Magistrate Judge **John H. England III** . . . .(205) 278-1700
  Began Service: 2013
  E-mail: john_england@alnd.uscourts.gov

Magistrate Judge **Harwell G. Davis III** . . . .(256) 539-7705
  Began Service: March 19, 1998
  E-mail: harwell_davis@alnd.uscourts.gov

Magistrate Judge **Staci G. Cornelius** . . . .(205) 278-1930
  Began Service: 2014

Court Staff

District Court Clerk **Sharon N. Harris** . . . . (205) 278-1700
  E-mail: sharon_harris@alnd.uscourts.gov

Chief Probation Officer **David A. Russell** . . . .(205) 716-2900

United States Bankruptcy Court for the Northern District of Alabama

1800 Fifth Avenue North, Birmingham, AL 35203
Tel: (205) 714-4000 Tel: (877) 466-0795 (Toll Free)
Tel: (205) 254-7337 (Voice Case Information System VCIS)
Fax: (205) 714-3941
Internet: www.alnb.uscourts.gov

Number of Judgeships: 6

Judges

Chief Bankruptcy Judge **Thomas B. Bennett** . . . .(205) 714-3880
  Began Service: June 5, 1995
  E-mail: Thomas_Bennett@alnb.uscourts.gov

Bankruptcy Judge **Tamara O. Mitchell** . . . . (205) 714-3850
  Began Service: January 4, 1992

Bankruptcy Judge **James J. Robinson** . . . .(256) 741-1500
  Began Service: February 2006
  1129 Noble Street, Room 117,
  Anniston, AL 36201

Bankruptcy Judge **Jennifer H. Hudson** . . . .(205) 561-1623

Bankruptcy Judge **Clifton R. Jessup, Jr.** . . . .(256) 340-2700
  Began Service: 2015

Court Staff

Clerk of Court **Scott W. Ford** . . . .(205) 714-4001
  E-mail: scott_ford@alnb.uscourts.gov

U.S. Attorney

Alabama - Northern District
1801 Fourth Avenue North, Birmingham, AL 35203-2101
Tel: (205) 244-2001 Fax: (205) 244-2183

U.S. Attorney **Joyce White Vance** . . . . (205) 244-2001
  E-mail: joyce.vance@usdoj.gov

Federal Public Defender

Alabama Northern Federal Public Defender
505 20th Street North, Room 1425, Birmingham, AL 35203-2605
Tel: (205) 208-7170

Federal Public Defender **Kevin Butler** . . . .(205) 208-7170
  E-mail: kevin.butler@fd.org

United States District Court for the Southern District of Alabama
U.S. Courthouse, 113 St. Joseph Street, Mobile, AL 36602-3621
Tel: (251) 690-2371 Fax: (251) 694-4297
Internet: www.alsd.uscourts.gov

Number of Judgeships: 3

Circuit: Eleventh

Areas Covered: Counties of Baldwin, Choctaw, Clarke, Conecuh, Dallas, Escambia, Hale, Marengo, Mobile, Monroe, Perry, Washington and Wilcox

Judges
Chief Judge **William H. Steele** . . . . (251) 690-3239
  Began Service: March 14, 2003
  Appointed By: President George W. Bush
  E-mail: william_steele@alsd.uscourts.gov
District Judge **Callie V. S. "Ginny" Granade** . . . . (251) 690-3133
  Began Service: February 20, 2002
  Appointed By: President George W. Bush
  E-mail: ginny_granade@alsd.uscourts.gov
District Judge **Kristi K. DuBose** . . . . (251) 690-2020
  Began Service: December 28, 2005
  Appointed By: President George W. Bush
  E-mail: kristi_dubose@alsd.uscourts.gov
Senior Judge **Charles R. Butler, Jr.** . . . . (251) 690-2175
  Began Service: November 1, 1988
  Appointed By: President Ronald Reagan
  E-mail: charles_butler@alsd.uscourts.gov
Magistrate Judge **William E. Cassady** . . . . (251) 690-2345
  Began Service: 1985
  U.S. Courthouse, 113 St. Joseph Street, Room 306,
  Mobile, AL 36602
  E-mail: william_cassady@alsd.uscourts.gov
Magistrate Judge **Bert W. Milling, Jr.** . . . . (251) 690-3202
  Began Service: 1986
  E-mail: bert_milling@alsd.uscourts.gov
Magistrate Judge **Sonja Faye Bivins** . . . . (251) 694-4545
  Began Service: February 2, 2004
  E-mail: sonja_bivins@alsd.uscourts.gov
Magistrate Judge **Katherine P. Nelson** . . . . (251) 690-3200
  Began Service: June 2009
  E-mail: katherine_nelson@alsd.uscourts.gov

Court Staff
Clerk **Charles R. "Chuck" Diard, Jr.** . . . . (251) 690-2371
  E-mail: chuck_diard@alsd.uscourts.gov
Chief Probation Officer **Jennifer Childress** . . . . (251) 441-6800
  201 St. Michael Street, Second Floor,
  Mobile, AL 36602
  E-mail: jennifer_childress@alsp.uscourts.gov

United States Bankruptcy Court for the Southern District of Alabama
201 St. Louis Street, Mobile, AL 36602
Tel: (251) 441-5391 Tel: (251) 441-5638 (PACER)
Tel: (251) 441-5637 (Voice Case Information System VCIS)
Internet: www.alsb.uscourts.gov

Number of Judgeships: 2

Judges
Chief Bankruptcy Judge **William S. Shulman** . . . . (251) 441-5625
  Began Service: 1996
  E-mail: william_shulman@alsb.uscourts.gov

Court Staff
Clerk of Court **Leonard N. Maldonado** . . . .(251) 441-5391 ext. 4103
  E-mail: leonard_maldonado@alsb.uscourts.gov

United States Bankruptcy Court for the Southern District of Alabama
continued

Bankruptcy Administrator (Acting) **Mark Zimlich** . . . . (251) 441-5433
  P.O. Box 3083, Mobile, AL 36602

U.S. Attorney
Alabama - Southern District
Renaissance Riverview Plaza Office Building, 63 South Royal Street,
Suite 600, Mobile, AL 36602
Tel: (251) 441-5845 Fax: (251) 441-5277

U.S. Attorney **Kenyen Ray Brown** . . . . (251) 441-5845
  E-mail: kenyen.brown@usdoj.gov

Federal Public Defender
Southern District of Alabama Federal Defenders, Inc.
11 North Water Street, Mobile, AL 11290
Tel: (251) 433-0910 Tel: (251) 434-5711 (Collect Calls)
Fax: (251) 433-0686

Executive Director **Carlos Williams** . . . .(251) 433-0910
  E-mail: carlos_williams@federaldefender.org

United States District Court for the District of Alaska
Federal Building & U.S. Courthouse, 222 West Seventh Avenue, #4,
Anchorage, AK 99513-7564
Tel: (907) 677-6100 Tel: (866) 243-3814 (Toll Free)
Fax: (907) 677-6180
Internet: www.akd.uscourts.gov

Number of Judgeships: 3

Circuit: Ninth

Judges
Chief Judge **Ralph R. Beistline** . . . . (907) 677-6257
  Began Service: May 19, 2002
  Appointed By: President George W. Bush
  E-mail: ralph_beistline@akd.uscourts.gov
District Judge **Timothy Mark Burgess** . . . .(866) 243-3814 (Toll Free)
  Began Service: January 2006   Tel: (907) 677-6203
  Appointed By: President George W. Bush
District Judge **Sharon L. Gleason** . . . . (907) 677-6253
  Began Service: January 4, 2012
  Appointed By: President Barack Obama
Senior Judge **John W. Sedwick** . . . . (907) 677-6251
  Began Service: October 15, 1992
  Appointed By: President George H.W. Bush
  E-mail: john_sedwick@akd.uscourts.gov
Senior Judge **James K. Singleton, Jr.** . . . . (907) 677-6250
  Began Service: May 14, 1990
  Appointed By: President George H.W. Bush
Senior Judge **H. Russel Holland** . . . . (907) 677-6252
  Began Service: 1984
  Appointed By: President Ronald Reagan
Chief Magistrate Judge **Deborah M. Smith** . . . . (907) 677-6256
  Began Service: February 2007   Tel: (866) 243-3814
                                    (Toll Free)
Magistrate Judge (Part-Time) **Scott A. Oravec** . . . .(907) 451-5795
  Began Service: 2009
  E-mail: scott_oravec@akd.uscourts.gov
Magistrate Judge (Part-Time) **Leslie Longenbaugh** . . . . . .(907) 321-3402
  Began Service: February 2007
  U.S. Courthouse, 709 West Ninth Street, Room 979,
  Juneau, AK 99802
Magistrate Judge (Part-Time) **Kevin McCoy** . . . . (907) 677-6100

(continued on next page)

United States District Court for the **District of Alaska** *continued*

Court Staff

Clerk of the Court **Marvel Hansbraugh** . . . . (907) 677-6100
  E-mail: marvel_hansbraugh@akd.uscourts.gov
Chief Probation Officer **Karen Brewer** . . . . (907) 271-5492

United States Bankruptcy Court for the District of Alaska

605 West Fourth Avenue, Room 138, Anchorage, AK 99501-2296
Tel: (907) 271-2655 Tel: (800) 859-8059 (Toll Free within Alaska)
Tel: (907) 271-2695 (PACER)
Tel: (866) 222-8029 (Voice Case Information System VCIS)
Fax: (907) 271-2645
Internet: www.akb.uscourts.gov

Number of Judgeships: 2

Judges

Bankruptcy Judge **Gary Allan Spraker** . . . . (907) 271-2667
  Began Service: 2012
Bankruptcy Judge (recalled) **Herbert A. Ross** . . . . (907) 271-2630
  Began Service: 2007
  605 West 4th Avenue, Room 138,
  Anchorage, AK 99501-2253
  E-mail: herb_ross@akb.uscourts.gov

Court Staff

Clerk of the Court **Jan S. Ostrovsky** . . . . (907) 271-4000
  E-mail: jan_ostrovsky@akb.uscourts.gov

U.S. Attorney

Alaska District
Federal Building and U.S. Courthouse, 222 West Seventh Avenue, #9,
Room 253, Anchorage, AK 99513-7567
Tel: (907) 271-5071 Fax: (907) 271-3224

U.S. Attorney **Karen Louise Loeffler** . . . . (907) 271-5071
  E-mail: karen.loeffler@usdoj.gov

Federal Public Defender

Federal Public Defender for Alaska
601 West Fifth Avenue, Suite 800, Anchorage, AK 99501
Tel: (907) 646-3400 Fax: (907) 646-3480

Federal Public Defender **Richard Curtner III** . . . . (907) 646-3400

United States District Court for the District of Arizona

Sandra Day O'Connor U.S. Courthouse, 401 West Washington Street,
Room 130, Phoenix, AZ 85003
Tel: (602) 322-7200 Tel: (602) 514-7113 (PACER)
Internet: www.azd.uscourts.gov

Number of Judgeships: 13
Circuit: Ninth

Judges

Chief Judge **Raner C. Collins** . . . . (520) 205-4540
  Began Service: August 19, 1998
  Appointed By: President William J. Clinton
  405 West Congress Street, Suite 5190,
  Tucson, AZ 85701-5061
  E-mail: Raner_Collins@azd.uscourts.gov

United States District Court for the **District of Arizona** *continued*

District Judge **Susan R. Bolton** . . . . (602) 322-7570
  Began Service: October 2000
  Appointed By: President William J. Clinton
  Sandra Day O'Connor U.S. Courthouse,
  401 West Washington Street, SPC 50, Suite 522,
  Phoenix, AZ 85003
  E-mail: susan_bolton@azd.uscourts.gov
District Judge **Cindy K. Jorgenson** . . . . (520) 205-4550
  Began Service: March 15, 2002
  Appointed By: President George W. Bush
  Evo A. DeConcini U.S. Courthouse,
  405 West Congress Street, Suite 5180,
  Tucson, AZ 85701-5052
  E-mail: cindy_jorgenson@azd.uscourts.gov
District Judge **David G. Campbell** Suite 623 . . . . (602) 322-7645
  Began Service: July 3, 2003
  Appointed By: President George W. Bush
  E-mail: david_campbell@azd.uscourts.gov
District Judge **Neil V. Wake** SPC 52, Suite 524 . . . . (602) 322-7640
  Began Service: March 15, 2004
  Appointed By: President George W. Bush
  E-mail: neil_wake@azd.uscourts.gov
District Judge **G. Murray Snow** . . . . (602) 322-7650
  Began Service: November 7, 2008
  Appointed By: President George W. Bush
  Sandra Day O'Connor U.S. Courthouse,
  401 West Washington Street, SPC 80, Suite 622,
  Phoenix, AZ 85003-2156
District Judge **Jennifer C. Guerin Zipps** . . . . (520) 205-4610
  Began Service: October 5, 2011
  Appointed By: President Barack Obama
  Evo A. DeConcini U.S. Courthouse,
  405 West Congress Street, Suite 5170,
  Tucson, AZ 85701-5061
District Judge **Diane J. Humetewa** Suite 625 . . . . (602) 322-7600
  Began Service: May 16, 2014
  Appointed By: President Barack Obama
  E-mail: diane_humetewa@azd.uscourts.gov
District Judge **Steven Paul Logan** Suite 521 . . . . (602) 322-7550
  Began Service: May 16, 2014
  Appointed By: President Barack Obama
  E-mail: steven_logan@azd.uscourts.gov
District Judge **John Joseph Tuchi** Suite 525 . . . . (602) 322-7660
  Began Service: May 16, 2014
  Appointed By: President Barack Obama
  E-mail: john_tuchi@azd.uscourts.gov
District Judge **Rosemary Márquez** . . . . (520) 205-4620
  Began Service: May 19, 2014
  Appointed By: President Barack Obama
  405 West Congress Street, Suite 5160,
  Tucson, AZ 85701-5061
  E-mail: rosemary_marquez@azd.uscourts.gov
District Judge **Douglas L. Rayes** Suite 526. . . . . (602) 322-7530
  Began Service: May 28, 2014
  Appointed By: President Barack Obama
  E-mail: douglas_rayes@azd.uscourts.gov
District Judge **James Alan Soto** . . . . (520) 205-4510
  Began Service: June 9, 2014
  Appointed By: President Barack Obama
  405 West Congress Street, Suite 6160,
  Tucson, AZ 85701-5061
  E-mail: james_soto@azd.uscourts.gov
Senior Judge **Stephen M. McNamee** . . . . (602) 322-7555
  Began Service: June 8, 1990
  Appointed By: President George H.W. Bush
  Sandra Day O'Connor U.S. Courthouse,
  401 West Washington Street, SPC 60, Suite 625,
  Phoenix, AZ 85003-2158
  E-mail: Stephen_McNamee@azd.uscourts.gov
Senior Judge **Paul G. Rosenblatt** . . . . (602) 322-7510
  Began Service: 1984
  Appointed By: President Ronald Reagan
  Sandra Day O'Connor U.S. Courthouse,
  401 West Washington Street, SPC 56, Suite 621,
  Phoenix, AZ 85003-2156
  E-mail: paul_rosenblatt@azd.uscourts.gov

United States District Court for the District of Arizona *continued*

Senior Judge **Frank R. Zapata** . . . . (520) 205-4530
  Began Service: August 2, 1994
  Appointed By: President William J. Clinton
  Evo A. DeConcini U.S. Courthouse,
  405 West Congress Street, Suite 5160,
  Tucson, AZ 85701-5050

Senior Judge **David C. Bury** . . . . (520) 205-4560
  Began Service: March 29, 2002
  Appointed By: President George W. Bush
  Evo A. Deconcini U.S. Courthouse,
  405 West Congress, Suite 6170,
  Tucson, AZ 85701-5065
  E-mail: david_bury@azd.uscourts.gov

Senior Judge **Frederick J. Martone** . . . . (602) 322-7590
  Began Service: January 30, 2002
  Appointed By: President George W. Bush
  401 West Washington Street, SPC 62, Suite 526,
  Phoenix, AZ 85003
  E-mail: frederick_martone@azd.uscourts.gov

Senior Judge **James A. Teilborg** Suite 523 . . . . (602) 322-7560
  Began Service: October 17, 2000
  Appointed By: President William J. Clinton
  E-mail: teilborg_chambers@azd.uscourts.gov

Senior Judge **Roslyn O. Silver** Suite 624 . . . . (602) 322-7520
  Began Service: October 14, 1994
  Appointed By: President William J. Clinton
  E-mail: Roslyn_Silver@azd.uscourts.gov

Magistrate Judge **Bernardo P. Velasco** . . . . (520) 205-4630
  Began Service: September 29, 2000
  Evo A. DeConcini U.S. Courthouse,
  405 West Congress Street, Suite 5650,
  Tucson, AZ 85701-5054
  E-mail: bernardo_velasco@azd.uscourts.gov

Magistrate Judge **David K. Duncan** . . . . (602) 322-7630
  Began Service: June 14, 2001
  Sandra Day O'Connor U.S. Courthouse,
  401 West Washington Street, SPC 14, Suite 325,
  Phoenix, AZ 85003-2120
  E-mail: david_duncan@azd.uscourts.gov

Magistrate Judge **Charles R. Pyle** . . . . (520) 205-4650
  Began Service: June 28, 2002
  Evo A. DeConcini U.S. Courthouse,
  405 West Congress Street, Suite 5660,
  Tucson, AZ 85701-5055
  E-mail: charles_pyle@azd.uscourts.gov

Magistrate Judge **Jacqueline J. Rateau** . . . . (520) 205-4232
  Began Service: July 11, 2001
  Evo A. DeConcini U.S. Courthouse,
  405 West Congress Street, Suite 6650,
  Tucson, AZ 85701-5063
  E-mail: jacqueline_marshall@azd.uscourts.gov

Magistrate Judge **Michelle H. Burns** . . . . (602) 322-7610
  Began Service: February 2007
  Sandra Day O'Connor U.S. Courthouse,
  401 West Washington Street, SPC 12, Suite 323,
  Phoenix, AZ 85003-2120
  E-mail: michelle_burns@azd.uscourts.gov

Magistrate Judge **D. Thomas Ferraro** . . . . (520) 205-4590
  Began Service: December 31, 2008
  404 West Congress Street, Suitee 6660,
  Tucson, AZ 85701-5065

Magistrate Judge **Bridget S. Bade** Suite 321 . . . . (602) 322-7680
  Began Service: September 2012
  E-mail: bridget_bade@azd.uscourts.gov

Magistrate Judge **Leslie A. Bowman** . . . . (520) 205-4500
  Evo A. DeConcini U.S. Courthouse,
  405 West Congress Street, Suite 3170,
  Tucson, AZ 85701-5061
  E-mail: leslie_bowman@azd.uscourts.gov

Magistrate Judge **Bruce G. Macdonald** . . . . (520) 205-4520
  405 West Congress Street, Suite 3180,
  Tucson, AZ 85701-5061
  E-mail: bruce_macdonald@azd.uscourts.gov

Magistrate Judge **Eric M. Markovich** . . . . (520) 205-4600

Magistrate Judge **Eileen S. Willett** Suite 321 . . . . (602) 322-7620
  Began Service: 2014

Magistrate Judge **John Z. Boyle** Suite 321 . . . . (602) 322-7670
  Began Service: 2014

United States District Court for the District of Arizona *continued*

Magistrate Judge (Part-Time) **James F. Metcalf** . . . . (928) 329-4766
  Began Service: June 24, 2009
  E-mail: james_metcalf@azd.uscourts.gov

Magistrate Judge (Part-Time) **John A. Buttrick** . . . . (928) 329-4766

Court Staff
Clerk of the Court and District Court Executive
  Brian Karth . . . . (602) 322-7100
  E-mail: brian_karth@azd.uscourts.gov
Chief U.S. Pretrial Services Officer **David L. Martin** . . . . . (520) 205-4394
  E-mail: david_martin@azd.uscourts.gov
Chief U.S. Probation Officer **Mario Moreno** O'Connor
  U.S. Courthouse, Suite 160 . . . . (602) 322-7400
  E-mail: mario_moreno@azd.uscourts.gov

United States Bankruptcy Court for the District of Arizona
230 North 1st Avenue, Suite 101, Phoenix, AZ 85003
Tel: (602) 682-4000 (Phoenix)
Tel: (520) 202-7500 (Tucson) Tel: (928) 783-2288 (Yuma)
Tel: (888) 549-5336 (Voice Case Information System VCIS)
Internet: www.azb.uscourts.gov

Number of Judgeships: 8

Judges
Chief Bankruptcy Judge **Daniel P. Collins** . . . . (602) 682-4224
  230 North First Avenue, Suite 101,
  Phoenix, AZ 85003-1706
Bankruptcy Judge **George B. Nielsen, Jr.** . . . . (602) 682-4164
  Began Service: 1983
  230 North First Avenue, Suite 101,
  Phoenix, AZ 85003-1706
  E-mail: george_nielsen@azb.uscourts.gov
Bankruptcy Judge **Eddward P. Ballinger, Jr.** . . . . (602) 682-4184
  230 North First Avenue, Suite 101,
  Phoenix, AZ 85003-1706
Bankruptcy Judge **Brenda Moody Whinery** . . . . (602) 682-4268
Bankruptcy Judge **Madeleine C. Wanslee** . . . . (602) 682-4244
  Began Service: 2014
Bankruptcy Judge **Paul Sala** . . . . (602) 682-4146
  Began Service: 2014
Bankruptcy Judge **Brenda K. Martin** . . . . (602) 682-4264
Bankruptcy Judge **Scott H. Gan** . . . . (520) 202-7964
Bankruptcy Judge (recalled) **Eileen W. Hollowell** . . . . (520) 202-7964

Court Staff
Clerk of Court **George D. Prentice II** . . . . (602) 682-4024

U.S. Attorney
Arizona District
Two Renaissance Square, 40 North Central Avenue, Suite 1200,
Phoenix, AZ 85004-4408
Tel: (602) 514-7500 Fax: (602) 514-7693

U.S. Attorney **John S. Leonardo** . . . . (602) 514-7518
  E-mail: john.leonardo@usdoj.gov

Federal Public Defender
Federal Public Defender District of Arizona
850 West Adams Street, Suite 201, Phoenix, AZ 85007-2730
Tel: (602) 382-2700 Fax: (602) 382-2800

Federal Public Defender **Jon Sands** . . . . (602) 382-2700
  E-mail: jon.sands@fd.org

United States District Court for the Eastern District of Arkansas

U.S. Courthouse, 500 West Capitol Avenue, Room A-149,
Little Rock, AR 72201-3325
Tel: (501) 604-5351 Tel: (501) 604-5300 (General Info)
Tel: (501) 324-6190 (Civil Cases PACER) Fax: (501) 604-5321
Internet: www.are.uscourts.gov

Number of Judgeships: 5

Circuit: Eighth

Areas Covered: Counties of Arkansas, Chicot, Clay, Cleburne, Cleveland, Conway, Craighead, Crittenden, Cross, Dallas, Desha, Drew, Faulkner, Fulton, Grant, Greene, Independence, Izard, Jackson, Jefferson, Lawrence, Lee, Lincoln, Lonoke, Mississippi, Monroe, Perry, Phillips, Poinsett, Pope, Prairie, Pulaski, Randolph, Saline, Sharp, St. Francis, Stone, Van Buren, White, Woodruff and Yell

Judges

Chief Judge **Brian Stacy Miller** . . . .(501) 604-5400
  Began Service: June 27, 2008
  Appointed By: President George W. Bush
  U.S. Courthouse, 600 West Capitol Avenue,
  Room D258, Little Rock, AR 72201
  E-mail: brian_miller@ared.uscourts.gov
District Judge **Leon Holmes** Room D-469 . . . .(501) 604-5380
  Began Service: July 19, 2004
  Appointed By: President George W. Bush
  E-mail: Leon_Holmes@ared.uscourts.gov
District Judge **Denzil Price Marshall** . . . .(501) 604-5410
  Began Service: May 14, 2010
  Appointed By: President Barack Obama
  600 West Capitol Avenue, B155,
  Little Rock, AR 72201
  E-mail: price_marshall@ared.uscourts.gov
District Judge **Kristine Gerhard Baker** Room D444 . . . . . .(501) 604-5420
  Began Service: October 19, 2012
  Appointed By: President Barack Obama
  E-mail: kgbchambers@ared.uscourts.gov
District Judge **James Maxwell Moody, Jr.** . . . .(501) 604-5157
  Began Service: March 10, 2014
  Appointed By: President Barack Obama
  E-mail: jmmchambers@ared.uscourts.gov
Senior Judge **Garnett Thomas Eisele** . . . .(501) 604-5160
  Began Service: August 1970
  Appointed By: President Richard M. Nixon
  U.S. Courthouse, 500 West Capitol Avenue,
  Room C 244, Little Rock, AR 72201
Senior Judge **Billy Roy Wilson** . . . .(501) 604-5140
  Began Service: October 1, 1993
  Appointed By: President William J. Clinton
  600 West Capitol Avenue, Room A403,
  Little Rock, AR 72201
  E-mail: william_wilson@ared.uscourts.gov
Senior Judge **Susan Webber Wright** . . . .(501) 604-5100
  Began Service: May 11, 1990
  Appointed By: President George H.W. Bush
  U.S. Courthouse, 500 West Capitol Avenue,
  Room 157D, Little Rock, AR 72201
Chief Magistrate Judge **J. Thomas Ray** Room D-144 . . . . .(501) 604-5230
  Began Service: June 28, 2000
  E-mail: Thomas_Ray@ared.uscourts.gov
Magistrate Judge **Beth Deere** Suite C 150 . . . .(501) 604-5110
  Began Service: January 8, 2007
  E-mail: beth_deere@ared.uscourts.gov
Magistrate Judge **Joe Volpe** . . . .(501) 604-5190
  Began Service: July 30, 2009
  500 West Capitol, Room D245,
  Little Rock, AR 72201
  E-mail: joe_volpe@ared.uscourts.gov
Magistrate Judge **Jerome T. Kearney** . . . .(501) 604-5170
  Began Service: April 2010
  E-mail: jerome_kearney@ared.uscourts.gov
Magistrate Judge (recalled) **Jerry W. Cavaneau** . . . .(501) 604-5200
  Began Service: January 7, 1991
  500 West Capitol, Suite C163,
  Little Rock, AR 72201-3325

United States District Court for the Eastern District of Arkansas
continued

Magistrate Judge **Patricia Sievers "Tricia" Harris** . . . .(501) 604-5180
  Began Service: 2015

Court Staff

Clerk of Court **James W. McCormack** . . . .(501) 604-5351
  600 West Capitol Avenue, Room A149,
  Little Rock, AR 72201
  E-mail: james_mccormack@ared.uscourts.gov
Chief U.S. Probation Officer
  G. Edward "Eddie" Towe . . . .(501) 604-5240

United States Bankruptcy Court for the Eastern District of Arkansas

300 West Second Street, Little Rock, AR 72201
Tel: (501) 918-5500 Tel: (800) 676-6856 (Toll Free PACER)
Tel: (866) 222-8029 (Voice Case Information System McVCIS)
Fax: (501) 918-5520
Internet: www.arb.uscourts.gov

Number of Judgeships: 3

Judges

Chief Bankruptcy Judge **Richard D. Taylor** . . . .(501) 918-5620
  Began Service: January 2010
  E-mail: rick_taylor@areb.uscourts.gov
Bankruptcy Judge **Audrey R. Evans** . . . .(501) 918-5660
  Began Service: February 19, 2002
  E-mail: audrey_evans@areb.uscourts.gov
Bankruptcy Judge **Ben T. Barry** . . . .(479) 582-9801
  Began Service: April 2007
Bankruptcy Judge **Phyllis M. Jones** . . . .(501) 918-5640

Court Staff

Bankruptcy Clerk **Jean Rolfs** . . . .(501) 918-5506
  E-mail: jean_rolfs@areb.uscourts.gov

U.S. Attorney

Arkansas - Eastern District
Metropolitan National Bank Building, 425 West Capitol Avenue,
Suite 500, Little Rock, AR 72201
P.O. Box 1229, Little Rock, AR 72203-1229
Tel: (501) 340-2600 Fax: (501) 340-2728

U.S. Attorney **Christopher R. "Chris" Thyer** . . . .(501) 340-2600
  E-mail: chris.thyer@usdoj.gov

Federal Public Defender

Arkansas Eastern Federal Public Defender
Victory Building, 1401 West Capitol Avenue, Suite 490,
Little Rock, AR 72201
Tel: (501) 324-6113 Fax: (501) 624-6128

Federal Public Defender **Jenniffer Morris Horan** . . . .(501) 324-6113
  E-mail: jenniffer.horan@fd.org

United States District Court for the Western District of Arkansas

Isaac C. Parker Federal Building, 30 South Sixth Street, Room 1038,
Fort Smith, AR 72901-2437
Tel: (479) 783-6833 Tel: (479) 783-6833 (PACER Registration)
Tel: (479) 783-3538 (PACER) Fax: (479) 783-6308
Internet: www.arwd.uscourts.gov

Number of Judgeships: 3

Circuit: Eighth

Areas Covered: Counties of Ashley, Baxter, Benton, Boone, Bradley, Calhoun, Carroll, Clark, Columbia, Crawford, Franklin, Garland, Hempstead, Hot Spring, Howard, Johnson, Lafayette, Little River, Logan, Madison, Marion, Miller, Montgomery, Nevada, Newton, Ouachita, Pike, Polk, Scott, Searcy, Sebastian, Sevier, Union and Washington

Judges

Chief Judge **Paul Kinloch Holmes III** Room 317 . . . . (479) 783-1466
Began Service: February 14, 2011
Appointed By: President Barack Obama
E-mail: PKHinfo@arwd.uscourts.gov
District Judge **Susan Owens Hickey** . . . . (870) 862-1303
Began Service: October 25, 2011
Appointed By: President Barack Obama
101 South Jackson Avenue, Room 219,
El Dorado, AR 71730-6133
District Judge **Timothy L. Brooks** . . . . (479) 695-4460
Began Service: March 7, 2014
Appointed By: President Barack Obama
35 East Mountain Street, Room 559,
Fayetteville, AR 72701
Senior Judge **Robert T. Dawson** . . . . (479) 783-2898
Began Service: May 7, 1998
Appointed By: President William J. Clinton
Isaac C. Parker Federal Building,
30 South Sixth Street, Room 1015A,
Fort Smith, AR 72901
E-mail: robert_dawson@arwd.uscourts.gov
Senior Judge **Harry F. Barnes** . . . . (870) 862-1303
Began Service: November 22, 1993
Appointed By: President William J. Clinton
219 U.S. Post Office & Courthouse,
101 South Jackson Avenue, Room 210,
El Dorado, AR 71730-6133
E-mail: harry_barnes@arwd.uscourts.gov
Magistrate Judge **James R. Marschewski** . . . . (479) 783-7045
Began Service: 2010
E-mail: james_marschewski@arwd.uscourts.gov
Magistrate Judge **Barry A. Bryant** . . . . (870) 773-2005
Began Service: March 2007
United States Courthouse and Post Office,
500 North State Line Avenue, Room 202,
Texarkana, TX 75504
E-mail: barry_bryant@arwd.uscourts.gov
Magistrate Judge **Erin Setser** . . . . (479) 251-1946
Began Service: 2009
35 East Mountain, Suite 559, Suite 213,
Fayetteville, AR 72701
E-mail: erin_setser@arwd.uscourts.gov
Magistrate Judge **Mark E. Ford** . . . . (479) 783-7045
E-mail: mark_ford@arwd.uscourts.gov

Court Staff

Clerk of Court **Christopher R. Johnson** . . . . (479) 783-6833
E-mail: chris_johnson@arwd.uscourts.gov
Chief Probation Officer **Scott Thibodeaux** Room 1064 . . . (479) 783-8050

United States Bankruptcy Court for the Western District of Arkansas

35 East Mountain Street, Room 316, Fayetteville, AR 72701
Tel: (479) 582-9800 Tel: (800) 676-6856 (Toll Free Pacer)
Tel: (501) 918-5555 (Voice Case Information System VCIS)
Tel: (866) 222-8029 (Voice Case Information System McVCIS)
Fax: (479) 582-9825
Internet: www.arb.uscourts.gov

Number of Judgeships: 3

Judges

Chief Bankruptcy Judge **Richard D. Taylor** . . . . (501) 918-5620
Began Service: January 2010
E-mail: rick_taylor@areb.uscourts.gov
Bankruptcy Judge **Audrey R. Evans** . . . . (501) 918-5660
Began Service: February 19, 2002
Bankruptcy Judge **Ben T. Barry** . . . . (479) 582-9801
Began Service: April 26, 2007

Court Staff

Bankruptcy Clerk **Jean Rolfs** . . . . (501) 918-5506
E-mail: jean_rolfs@areb.uscourts.gov

U.S. Attorney

Arkansas - Western District
414 Parker Street, Fort Smith, AR 72901
Tel: (479) 783-5125 Fax: (479) 783-0578 Fax: (479) 785-2442

U.S. Attorney (Acting) **Kenneth P. "Kenny" Elser** . . . . . . (479) 783-5125

Federal Public Defender

Arkansas Western Federal Public Defender
3739 North Steele Boulevard, Suite 280, Fayetteville, AR 72703
Tel: (479) 442-2306 Fax: (479) 443-1904

Federal Public Defender **Bruce D. Eddy** . . . . (479) 442-2306
E-mail: bruce.eddy@fd.org

United States District Court for the Central District of California

312 North Spring Street, Los Angeles, CA 90012
Tel: (213) 894-1565 Tel: (213) 894-2215
Tel: (213) 894-3625 (Civil Cases PACER)
Tel: (213) 894-3535 (Intake) Fax: (213) 894-6860
Internet: www.cacd.uscourts.gov

Number of Judgeships: 28

Number of Vacancies: 1

Circuit: Ninth

Areas Covered: Counties of Los Angeles, Orange, Riverside, San Bernardino, San Luis Obispo, Santa Barbara and Ventura

Judges

Chief Judge **George H. King** . . . . (213) 894-5766
Began Service: July 3, 1995
Appointed By: President William J. Clinton
Edward R. Roybal Federal Building,
255 East Temple Street, Suite 660,
Los Angeles, CA 90012
E-mail: george_king@cacd.uscourts.gov
District Judge **Manuel L. Real** . . . . (213) 894-5267
Began Service: November 13, 1966
Appointed By: President Lyndon B. Johnson
E-mail: manuel_real@cacd.uscourts.gov

(continued on next page)

United States District Court for the Central District of California
continued

District Judge **Stephen V. Wilson** U.S. Courthouse,
Room 217J ....(213) 894-4327
  Began Service: 1985
  Appointed By: President Ronald Reagan
  E-mail: stephen_wilson@cacd.uscourts.gov

District Judge **Dean D. Pregerson** ....(213) 894-3913
  Began Service: August 1, 1996
  Appointed By: President William J. Clinton
  E-mail: dean_pregerson@cacd.uscourts.gov

District Judge **Fernando M. Olguin** ....(213) 894-5105
  Began Service: 2012
  Appointed By: President Barack Obama
  312 North Spring Street, Fifth Floor, Room 22,
  Los Angeles, CA 90012-8533
  E-mail: fernando_olguin@cacd.uscourts.gov

District Judge **Christina A. Snyder** U.S. Courthouse,
Courtroom 5 ....(213) 894-8551
  Began Service: November 24, 1997
  Appointed By: President William J. Clinton
  E-mail: christina_snyder@cacd.uscourts.gov

District Judge **Margaret M. Morrow** ....(213) 894-2949
  Began Service: March 8, 1998
  Appointed By: President William J. Clinton
  255 East Temple Street, Suite 770,
  Los Angeles, CA 90012-3332
  E-mail: margaret_morrow@cacd.uscourts.gov

District Judge **David O. Carter** ....(714) 338-4543
  Began Service: October 22, 1998
  Appointed By: President William J. Clinton
  E-mail: david_carter@cacd.uscourts.gov

District Judge **Jesus G. Bernal** ....(951) 328-4410
  Began Service: January 4, 2013
  Appointed By: President Barack Obama
  E-mail: jesus_bernal@cacd.uscourts.gov

District Judge **Virginia A. Phillips** ....(951) 328-4420
  Began Service: December 30, 1999
  Appointed By: President William J. Clinton
  3470 Twelfth Street, Room 280,
  Riverside, CA 92501
  E-mail: virginia_phillips@cacd.uscourts.gov

District Judge **Percy Anderson** ....(213) 894-5774
  Began Service: May 1, 2002
  Appointed By: President George W. Bush
  E-mail: percy_anderson@cacd.uscourts.gov

District Judge **R. Gary Klausner** ....(213) 894-3938
  Began Service: December 4, 2002
  Appointed By: President George W. Bush
  E-mail: gary_klausner@cacd.uscourts.gov

District Judge **S. James Otero** U.S. Courthouse, Suite
244-P ....(213) 894-4806
  Began Service: February 28, 2003
  Appointed By: President George W. Bush
  E-mail: sjo_chambers@cacd.uscourts.gov

District Judge **James V. Selna** ....(714) 338-2841
  Began Service: April 30, 2003
  Appointed By: President George W. Bush
  E-mail: james_selna@cacd.uscourts.gov

District Judge **Cormac J. Carney** ....(714) 338-4720
  Began Service: April 30, 2003
  Appointed By: President George W. Bush
  E-mail: cormac_carney@cacd.uscourts.gov

District Judge **Dale S. Fischer** ....(213) 894-7115
  Began Service: November 18, 2003
  Appointed By: President George W. Bush
  E-mail: Dale_Fischer@cacd.uscourts.gov

District Judge **Andrew J. Guilford** ....(714) 338-4757
  Began Service: June 2006
  Appointed By: President George W. Bush
  E-mail: andrew_guilford@cacd.uscourts.gov

District Judge **Philip S. Gutierrez** ....(213) 894-8899
  Began Service: February 2007
  Appointed By: President George W. Bush
  255 East Temple Street, Room 880,
  Los Angeles, CA 90012
  E-mail: philip_gutierrez@cacd.uscourts.gov

United States District Court for the Central District of California
continued

District Judge **Otis D. Wright II** ....(213) 894-8266
  Began Service: April 17, 2007
  Appointed By: President George W. Bush
  E-mail: otis_wright@cacd.uscourts.gov

District Judge **George H. Wu** ....(213) 894-0191
  Began Service: April 17, 2007
  Appointed By: President George W. Bush
  E-mail: george_wu@cacd.uscourts.gov

District Judge **Dolly M. Gee** ....(213) 894-5452
  Began Service: January 4, 2010
  Appointed By: President Barack Obama
  E-mail: dolly_gee@cacd.uscourts.gov

District Judge **Josephine Staton Tucker** ....(714) 338-4738
  Began Service: August 2, 2010
  Appointed By: President Barack Obama
  E-mail: josephine_tucker@cacd.uscourts.gov

District Judge **John A. Kronstadt** ....(213) 894-2156
  Began Service: April 25, 2011
  Appointed By: President Barack Obama
  E-mail: john_kronstadt@cacd.uscourts.gov

District Judge **Michael Walter Fitzgerald** ....(213) 894-1565
  Began Service: 2012
  Appointed By: President Barack Obama
  E-mail: michael_fitzgerald@cacd.uscourts.gov

District Judge **John F. Walter** ....(213) 894-5396
  Began Service: May 1, 2002
  Appointed By: President George W. Bush
  E-mail: john_walter@cacd.uscourts.gov

District Judge **Beverly Reid O'Connell** ....(213) 894-5283
  Began Service: April 30, 2013
  Appointed By: President Barack Obama

District Judge **André Birotte, Jr.** ....(213) 894-2833
  Began Service: August 3, 2014
  Appointed By: President Barack Obama
  E-mail: ab_chambers@cacd.uscourts.gov

Senior Judge **Terry J. Hatter, Jr.** ....(213) 894-5746
  Began Service: February 1, 1980
  Appointed By: President Jimmy Carter
  E-mail: terry_hatter@cacd.uscourts.gov

Senior Judge **Consuelo B. Marshall** ....(213) 894-6314
  Began Service: September 30, 1980
  Appointed By: President Jimmy Carter
  E-mail: consuelo_marshall@cacd.uscourts.gov

Senior Judge **William D. Keller** ....(213) 894-2659
  Began Service: 1984
  Appointed By: President Ronald Reagan
  E-mail: william_keller@cacd.uscourts.gov

Senior Judge **Ronald S. W. Lew** ....(213) 894-3508
  Began Service: May 7, 1987
  Appointed By: President Ronald Reagan
  E-mail: ronald_lew@cacd.uscourts.gov

Senior Judge **Robert James Timlin** Room 233 ....(213) 894-5275
  Began Service: October 18, 1994
  Appointed By: President William J. Clinton
  E-mail: robert_timlin@cacd.uscourts.gov

Senior Judge **Valerie Baker Fairbank** ....(213) 894-0066
  Began Service: February 16, 2007
  Appointed By: President George W. Bush
  E-mail: valerie_fairbank@cacd.uscourts.gov

Chief Magistrate Judge **Suzanne H. Segal** U.S.
Courthouse, 3rd Floor, Courtroom 23 ....(213) 894-1420
  Began Service: July 31, 2002
  E-mail: suzanne_segal@cacd.uscourts.gov

Magistrate Judge **Charles F. Eick** U.S. Courthouse,
Room 342 ....(213) 894-2964
  Began Service: 1988
  E-mail: charles_eick@cacd.uscourts.gov

Magistrate Judge **Andrew J. Wistrich** ....(213) 894-2523
  Began Service: March 30, 1994
  E-mail: andrew_wistrich@cacd.uscourts.gov

Magistrate Judge **Robert N. Block** ....(714) 338-4754
  Began Service: 1995
  E-mail: robert_block@cacd.uscourts.gov

Magistrate Judge **Carla M. Woehrle** ....(213) 894-4904
  Began Service: June 10, 1996
  E-mail: carla_woehrle@cacd.uscourts.gov

United States District Court for the Central District of California
continued

Magistrate Judge **Arthur Nakazato** . . . . (714) 338-4756
  Began Service: August 13, 1996
  E-mail: arthur_nakazato@cacd.uscourts.gov

Magistrate Judge **Margaret A. Nagle** . . . . (213) 894-8540
  Began Service: 1997
  E-mail: margaret_nagle@cacd.uscourts.gov

Magistrate Judge **Patrick J. Walsh** U.S. Courthouse,
  Room 323 . . . . (213) 894-5722
  Began Service: July 18, 2001
  E-mail: patrick_walsh@cacd.uscourts.gov

Magistrate Judge **Paul L. Abrams** U.S. Courthouse, 9th
  Floor . . . . (213) 894-7103
  Began Service: 2002
  E-mail: paul_abrams@cacd.uscourts.gov

Magistrate Judge **Jacqueline Chooljian** . . . . (213) 894-2921
  Began Service: January 13, 2006
  E-mail: jacqueline_chooljian@cacd.uscourts.gov

Magistrate Judge **Frederick F. Mumm** . . . . (213) 894-3046
  Began Service: 2006
  E-mail: frederick_mumm@cacd.uscourts.gov

Magistrate Judge **Alicia G. Rosenberg** . . . . (213) 894-5419
  Began Service: March 2007
  E-mail: alicia_rosenberg@cacd.uscourts.gov

Magistrate Judge **David T. Bristow** . . . . (951) 328-4466
  Began Service: October 2009
  E-mail: david_bristow@cacd.uscourts.gov

Magistrate Judge **John E. McDermott** . . . . (213) 894-0216
  Began Service: July 2009
  E-mail: john_mcdermott@cacd.uscourts.gov

Magistrate Judge **Vijay C. "Jay" Gandhi** . . . . (714) 338-4776
  Began Service: April 2010
  E-mail: jay_gandhi@cacd.uscourts.gov

Magistrate Judge **Michael R. Wilner** . . . . (213) 894-5496
  Began Service: April 1, 2011
  E-mail: michael_wilner@cacd.uscourts.gov

Magistrate Judge **Sheri Pym** . . . . (951) 328-4467
  Began Service: April 15, 2011
  E-mail: sheri_pym@cacd.uscourts.gov

Magistrate Judge **Jean P. Rosenbluth** . . . . (213) 894-5369
  E-mail: jean_rosenbluth@cacd.uscourts.gov

Magistrate Judge **Kenly Kiya Kato** . . . . (951) 328-4463
  Began Service: July 1, 2014

Magistrate Judge **Louise A. LaMothe** . . . . (213) 894-3787
  255 East Temple Street, Suite 181-L,
  Los Angeles, CA 90012

Magistrate Judge **Douglas F. McCormick** . . . . (714) 338-4755
  E-mail: DFM_Chambers@cacd.uscourts.gov

Magistrate Judge **Alka Sagar** . . . . (213) 894-4583

Magistrate Judge **Rozella A. Oliver** . . . . (213) 894-3922
  Began Service: 2015

Magistrate Judge **Alexander F. MacKinnon** . . . . (213) 894-4583
  Began Service: 2015

Court Staff

District Court Executive and Clerk of the Court
  (Acting) **Kiry Gray** . . . . (213) 894-1565
  E-mail: kiry_gray@cacd.uscourts.gov
Chief of Pretrial Services Officer **George M. Walker**
  Room 754 . . . . (213) 894-4727
Chief Probation Officer **Michelle Carey** . . . . (213) 894-3600

United States Bankruptcy Court for the Central District of California

Edward R. Roybal Federal Building and Courthouse, 255 East Temple Street, Room 940, Los Angeles, CA 90012
Tel: (213) 894-3118 (Los Angeles General Information)
Tel: (951) 774-1000 (Riverside General Information)
Tel: (714) 338-5300 (Santa Ana General Information)
Tel: (805) 884-4800 (Santa Barbara General Information)
Tel: (818) 587-2900 (San Fernando Valley General Information)
Tel: (213) 894-4111 (Voice Case Information System VCIS)
Tel: (866) 522-6053 (Voice Case Information System VCIS)
Internet: www.cacb.uscourts.gov

Number of Judgeships: 24

Judges

Chief Bankruptcy Judge **Sheri Bluebond** Edward R.
  Roybal Federal Building, Suite 1482 . . . . (213) 894-8980
  Began Service: February 1, 2001
  E-mail: sheri_bluebond@cacb.uscourts.gov

Bankruptcy Judge **Peter H. Carroll** Edward R. Roybal
  Federal Building, Room 1468 . . . . (213) 894-6343
  Began Service: August 1, 2002
  E-mail: peter_carroll@cacb.uscourts.gov

Bankruptcy Judge **Barry Russell** Edward R. Roybal
  Federal Building, Suite 1660 . . . . (213) 894-6091
  Began Service: September 1974
  E-mail: barry_russell@cacb.uscourts.gov

Bankruptcy Judge **Robert N. Kwan** Suite 1682 . . . . (213) 894-2775
  Began Service: February 2007
  E-mail: robert_kwan@cacb.uscourts.gov

Bankruptcy Judge **Robin L. Riblet** . . . . (805) 884-4825

Bankruptcy Judge **Alan M. Ahart** . . . . (818) 587-2836
  Began Service: April 1988
  21041 Burbank Boulevard, Suite 342,
  Woodland Hills, CA 91367
  E-mail: alan_ahart@cacb.uscourts.gov

Bankruptcy Judge **Ernest M. Robles** . . . . (213) 894-1522
  Began Service: June 12, 1993
  E-mail: ernest_robles@cacb.uscourts.gov

Bankruptcy Judge **Thomas B. Donovan** Room 1352 . . . . . (213) 894-3728
  Began Service: March 21, 1994
  E-mail: thomas_donovan@cacb.uscourts.gov

Bankruptcy Judge **Erithe A. Smith** . . . . (714) 338-5440
  Began Service: May 2, 1994
  411 West Fourth Street, Suite 5033,
  Santa Ana, CA 92701
  E-mail: erithe_smith@cacb.uscourts.gov

Bankruptcy Judge **Meredith A. Jury** . . . . (951) 774-1043
  Began Service: November 24, 1997
  3420 12th Street, Room 301,
  Riverside, CA 92501
  E-mail: meredith_jury@cacb.uscourts.gov

Bankruptcy Judge **Maureen A. Tighe** . . . . (818) 587-2806
  Began Service: November 2003
  E-mail: maureen_tighe@cacb.uscourts.gov

Bankruptcy Judge **Theodor C. Albert** . . . . (714) 338-5430
  Began Service: June 2005
  411 West Fourth Street, Suite 5073,
  Santa Ana, CA 92701-4593
  E-mail: theodor_albert@cacb.uscourts.gov

Bankruptcy Judge **Richard M. Neiter** Suite 1652 . . . . (213) 894-4080
  Began Service: February 8, 2006
  E-mail: richard_neiter@cacb.uscourts.gov

Bankruptcy Judge **Victoria S. Kaufman** . . . . (818) 587-2823
  Began Service: May 2006
  San Fernando Valley Courthouse,
  21041 Burbank Boulevard, Suite 354,
  Woodland Hills, CA 91367

Bankruptcy Judge **Catherine E. Bauer** . . . . (714) 338-5450
  Began Service: 2010
  E-mail: catherine_bauer@cacb.uscourts.gov

Bankruptcy Judge **Deborah J. Saltzman** . . . . (951) 774-1026
  Began Service: 2010
  E-mail: deborah_saltzman@cacb.uscourts.gov

(continued on next page)

United States Bankruptcy Court for the Central District of California
continued

Bankruptcy Judge **Vincent P. Zurzolo** Room 1360 . . . . (213) 894-3755
Began Service: April 18, 1988
E-mail: vincent_zurzolo@cacb.uscourts.gov
Bankruptcy Judge **Sandra R. Klein** Edward R. Roybal
Federal Building, Suite 1582 . . . .(213) 894-7741
Began Service: April 22, 2011
E-mail: sandra_klein@cacb.uscourts.gov
Bankruptcy Judge **Wayne Johnson** . . . .(951) 774-1031
Began Service: February 28, 2011
E-mail: wayne_johnson@cacb.uscourts.gov
Bankruptcy Judge **Mark S. Wallace** . . . .(714) 338-5470
Began Service: January 20, 2011
411 West Fourth Street, Suite 6113,
Santa Ana, CA 92701-4593
E-mail: mark_wallace@cacb.uscourts.gov
Bankruptcy Judge **Neil Bason** . . . . (213) 894-6098
Began Service: October 24, 2011
E-mail: neil_bason@cacb.uscourts.gov
Bankruptcy Judge **Julia W. Brand** . . . .(213) 894-6080
Began Service: 2011
Bankruptcy Judge **Mark D. Houle** . . . . (951) 774-1021
Began Service: February 17, 2012
3420 -12th Street, Suite 302,
Riverside, CA 92501-3819
E-mail: mark_houle@cacb.uscourts.gov
Bankruptcy Judge **Martin R. Barash** . . . .(818) 587-2836
Began Service: 2015
21041 Burbank Boulevard, Suite 342,
Woodland Hills, CA 91367
Bankruptcy Judge (recalled) **Geraldine Mund** . . . . (818) 587-2840
Began Service: February 1984
21041 Burbank Boulevard, Suite 342,
Woodland Hills, CA 91367
E-mail: geraldine_mund@cacb.uscourts.gov

Court Staff
Executive Officer/Clerk of Court
Kathleen J. "Kathy" Campbell . . . .(213) 894-6244
E-mail: kathy_campbell@cacb.uscourts.gov

U.S. Attorney
California - Central District
312 North Spring Street, Suite 1200, Los Angeles, CA 90012
Tel: (213) 894-2400 (Main Line) Tel: (213) 894-2434
Fax: (213) 894-0141

U.S. Attorney **Eileen M. Decker** . . . . (213) 894-2434
E-mail: eileen.decker@usdoj.gov

Federal Public Defender
Office of the Federal Public Defender for the Central District of California
321 East Second Street, Los Angeles, CA 90012
Tel: (213) 894-2854 Fax: (213) 894-0081

Federal Public Defender **Hilary Petashner** . . . . (213) 894-2854

United States District Court for the Eastern District of California
Robert T. Matsui United States Courthouse, 501 I Street,
Sacramento, CA 95814
Tel: (916) 930-4000 Tel: (916) 498-6567 (PACER)
Tel: (800) 530-7680 (Toll Free Pacer)
Internet: www.caed.uscourts.gov

Number of Judgeships: 6

Number of Vacancies: 1

Circuit: Ninth

Areas Covered: Counties of Alpine, Amador, Butte, Calaveras, Colusa, El Dorado, Fresno, Glenn, Inyo, Kern, Kings, Lassen, Madera, Mariposa, Merced, Modoc, Mono, Nevada, Placer, Plumas, Sacramento, San Joaquin, Shasta, Sierra, Siskiyou, Solano, Stanislaus, Sutter, Tehama, Trinity, Tulare, Tuolumne, Yolo and Yuba

Judges
Chief Judge **Morrison C. England, Jr.** Suite 14-230 . . . . . .(916) 930-4205
Began Service: August 2, 2002
Appointed By: President George W. Bush
E-mail: mengland@caed.uscourts.gov
District Judge **Lawrence J. O'Neill** . . . .(559) 499-5680
Began Service: February 2, 2007
Appointed By: President George W. Bush
Robert E. Coyle U.S. Courthouse,
2500 Tulare Street, Suite 7701,
Fresno, CA 93721
E-mail: loneill@caed.uscourts.gov
District Judge **John A. Mendez** . . . .(916) 930-4250
Began Service: 2008
Began Service: April 17, 2008
Appointed By: President George W. Bush
E-mail: jmendez@caed.uscourts.gov
District Judge **Kimberly J. Mueller** . . . .(916) 930-4260
Began Service: December 21, 2010
Appointed By: President Barack Obama
E-mail: kmueller@caed.uscourts.gov
District Judge **Troy L. Nunley** . . . . (916) 930-4163
Began Service: 2013
Appointed By: President Barack Obama
E-mail: tnunley@caed.uscourts.gov
Senior Judge **William B. Shubb** . . . . (916) 930-4230
Began Service: October 29, 1990
Appointed By: President George H.W. Bush
E-mail: wshubb@justice.com
Senior Judge **Garland E. Burrell, Jr.** . . . .(916) 930-4115
Began Service: March 3, 1992
Appointed By: President George H.W. Bush
E-mail: gburrell@caed.uscourts.gov
Senior Judge **Anthony W. Ishii** . . . .(559) 499-5660
Began Service: October 14, 1997
Appointed By: President William J. Clinton
Robert E. Coyle U.S. Courthouse,
2500 Tulare Street, Eighth Floor, Suite 1501,
Fresno, CA 93721
E-mail: aishii@caed.uscourts.gov
Chief Magistrate Judge **Dale A. Drozd** Room 8-240 . . . . . .(916) 930-4210
Began Service: September 15, 1997
E-mail: dale_drozd@caed.uscourts.gov
Magistrate Judge **Sandra M. Snyder** . . . .(559) 499-5690
Began Service: May 3, 1993
Robert E. Coyle U.S. Courthouse,
2500 Tulare Street, Suite 6801,
Fresno, CA 93721
E-mail: ssnyder@caed.uscourts.gov
Magistrate Judge **Gregory G. Hollows** . . . .(916) 930-4195
Began Service: March 1990
E-mail: ghollows@caed.uscourts.gov
Magistrate Judge **Dennis L. Beck** . . . .(559) 499-5670
Began Service: March 14, 1990
Robert E. Coyle U.S. Courthouse,
2500 Tulane Street, Room 6601,
Fresno, CA 93721
E-mail: dennis_beck@caed.uscourts.gov

United States District Court for the Eastern District of California
continued

Magistrate Judge **Gary S. Austin** . . . .(559) 499-5962
  Began Service: October 12, 2007
  Robert E. Coyle U.S. Courthouse,
  2500 Tulare Street, Sixth Floor, Suite 1501,
  Fresno, CA 93721
  E-mail: gaustin@caed.uscourts.gov

Magistrate Judge **Craig M. Kellison** . . . . (530) 246-5416
  Began Service: October 1, 1988
  E-mail: ckellison@caed.uscourts.gov

Magistrate Judge **Edmund F. Brennan** Room 4-200 . . . . . . (916) 930-4170
  Began Service: August 21, 2006
  E-mail: ebrennan@caed.uscourts.gov

Magistrate Judge **Jennifer Thurston** . . . .(661) 326-6620
  Began Service: 2009
  510 19th Street, Suite 200,
  Bakersfield, CA 93301
  E-mail: jthurston@caed.uscourts.gov

Magistrate Judge **Kendall J. Newman** . . . . (916) 930-4187
  Began Service: 2010
  E-mail: knewman@caed.uscourts.gov

Magistrate Judge **Barbara A. McAuliffe** . . . . (559) 499-5788
  Began Service: 2011
  E-mail: bmcauliffe@caed.uscourts.gov

Magistrate Judge **Carolyn K. Delaney** . . . . (916) 930-4004
  Began Service: 2011
  E-mail: cdelaney@caed.uscourts.gov

Magistrate Judge **Sheila K. Oberto** . . . . (559) 499-5975
  Began Service: 2011
  E-mail: soberto@caed.uscourts.gov

Magistrate Judge **Stanley A. Boone** . . . . (559) 499-5672
  E-mail: sboone@caed.uscourts.gov

Magistrate Judge **Michael J. Seng** . . . . (209) 372-0320
  Began Service: May 2010
  E-mail: mseng@caed.uscourts.gov

Magistrate Judge **Allison Claire** . . . .(916) 930-4199
  Began Service: November 19, 2012
  E-mail: aclaire@caed.uscourts.gov

Court Staff

Clerk of the Court **Marianne Matherly** Room 4-200 . . . . . (916) 930-4000
  E-mail: mmatherly@caed.uscourts.gov
Chief Probation Officer **Richard A. Ertola** Suite 2-500 . . . .(916) 930-4300
Chief of Pretrial Services **Gina Fauboin** . . . .(916) 930-4350

United States Bankruptcy Court for the Eastern District of California

Robert T. Matsui United States Courthouse, 501 I Street, Room 3-200,
Sacramento, CA 95814-2322
Tel: (916) 930-4400
Internet: www.caeb.uscourts.gov

Number of Judgeships: 7

Judges

Chief Bankruptcy Judge **Christopher M. Klein** . . . . (916) 930-4510
  Began Service: February 1988
  E-mail: christopher_klein@caeb.uscourts.gov

Bankruptcy Judge **Michael S. McManus** . . . . (916) 930-4540
  Began Service: January 11, 1994
  U.S. Courthouse, 501 I Street, Room 3-200,
  Sacramento, CA 95814
  E-mail: michael_mcmanus@caeb.uscourts.gov

Bankruptcy Judge **W. Richard Lee** . . . .(559) 499-5870
  Began Service: January 17, 2001
  Robert E. Coyle U.S. Courthouse,
  2500 Tulare Street, Suite 2501,
  Fresno, CA 93721
  E-mail: richard_lee@caeb.uscourts.gov

Bankruptcy Judge **Robert S. Bardwil** . . . . (916) 930-4400
  Began Service: July 6, 2005
  E-mail: robert_bardwil@caeb.uscourts.gov

United States Bankruptcy Court for the Eastern District of California
continued

Bankruptcy Judge **Ronald H. Sargis** . . . .(209) 521-5160
  Began Service: 2010
  1200 I Street, Suite 4, Modesto, CA 95354
  E-mail: ronald_sargis@caeb.uscourts.gov

Bankruptcy Judge **Fredrick E. Clement** . . . .(559) 499-5860
  E-mail: fredrick_clement@caeb.uscourts.gov

Bankruptcy Judge **Christopher D. Jaime** . . . . (916) 930-4421
  Began Service: January 5, 2015
  501 I Street, Suite 3-200, Sacramento, CA 95814

Bankruptcy Judge (recalled) **David E. Russell** . . . . (916) 930-4502
  Began Service: November 3, 1986
  Robert T. Matsui United States
  Courthouse, 501 I Street, Suite 3-200,
  Sacramento, CA 95814
  E-mail: david_russell@caeb.uscourts.gov

Bankruptcy Judge (recalled) **Philip H. Brandt** . . . . (916) 930-4400
  Note: Judge Brandt also serves in the United States
  Bankruptcy Court for the Western District of
  Washington.
  501 I Street, Suite 3-200, Sacramento, CA 95814

Bankruptcy Judge (recalled) **Whitney Rimel** . . . . (559) 499-5800
  2500 Tulare Street, Suite 2501,
  Fresno, CA 93721

Court Staff

Clerk **Wayne Blackwelder** . . . .(916) 930-4400
  E-mail: wayne_blackwelder@caeb.uscourts.gov

U.S. Attorney

California - Eastern District
501 I Street, Suite 10-100, Sacramento, CA 95814
Tel: (916) 554-2700   TTY: (916) 554-2124   Fax: (916) 554-2900

U.S. Attorney
  Benjamin Alden Belknap "Ben" Wagner . . . .(916) 554-2730
  E-mail: ben.wagner@usdoj.gov

Federal Public Defender

Office of the Federal Defender for the Eastern District of California
801 I Street, Third Floor, Sacramento, CA 95814
2300 Tulare Street, Suite 330, Fresno, CA 93721 (Fresno Office)
Tel: (916) 498-5700   Tel: (559) 487-5561 (Fresno)   Fax: (916) 498-5710
Fax: (559) 487-5950 (Fresno)

Federal Public Defender **Heather E. Williams** . . . . (916) 498-5700
  E-mail: heather.williams@fd.org

United States District Court for the Northern District of California

Federal Building, 450 Golden Gate Avenue, 16th Floor,
San Francisco, CA 94102
P.O. Box 36060, San Francisco, CA 94102
Tel: (415) 522-2000 Tel: (415) 522-2144 (PACER)
Fax: (415) 522-3605
Internet: www.cand.uscourts.gov

Number of Judgeships: 15

Circuit: Ninth

Areas Covered: Counties of Alameda, Contra Costa, Del Norte, Humboldt, Lake, Marin, Mendocino, Monterey, Napa, San Benito, San Francisco, San Mateo, Santa Clara, Santa Cruz and Sonoma

Judges

Chief Judge **Phyllis J. Hamilton** . . . . (510) 637-3530
  Began Service: July 7, 2000
  Appointed By: President William J. Clinton
  Oakland Courthouse, 1301 Clay Street, Room 3,
  Oakland, CA 94612
  E-mail: phyllis_hamilton@cand.uscourts.gov

District Judge **Jeremy D. Fogel** . . . . (408) 535-5426
  Began Service: March 31, 1998
  Appointed By: President William J. Clinton
  E-mail: jeremy_fogel@cand.uscourts.gov

District Judge **William Alsup** . . . . (415) 522-3684
  Began Service: August 17, 1999
  Appointed By: President William J. Clinton
  E-mail: william_alsup@cand.uscourts.gov

District Judge **Jeffrey S. White** 19th, Courtroom 11 . . . . . . (510) 637-1820
  Began Service: January 2, 2003
  Appointed By: President George W. Bush
  E-mail: jeffrey_white@cand.uscourts.gov

District Judge **Richard Seeborg** . . . . (415) 522-2123
  Began Service: January 4, 2010
  Appointed By: President Barack Obama
  E-mail: richard_seeborg@cand.uscourts.gov

District Judge **Lucy H. Koh** . . . . (408) 535-5357
  Began Service: June 11, 2010
  Appointed By: President Barack Obama
  E-mail: lucy_koh@cand.uscourts.gov

District Judge **Edward J. Davila** . . . . (408) 535-5356
  Began Service: March 4, 2011
  Appointed By: President Barack Obama
  E-mail: edward_davila@cand.uscourts.gov

District Judge **Edward Milton Chen** . . . . (415) 522-2034
  Began Service: May 17, 2011
  Appointed By: President Barack Obama
  E-mail: edward_chen@cand.uscourts.gov

District Judge **Yvonne Gonzalez Rogers** . . . . (510) 637-3540
  Began Service: November 21, 2011
  Appointed By: President Barack Obama
  1301 Clay Street, 400 South,
  Oakland, CA 94612
  E-mail: ygrcrd@cand.uscourts.gov

District Judge **Jon S. Tigar** . . . . (415) 522-2036
  Began Service: January 18, 2013
  Appointed By: President Barack Obama
  E-mail: jon_tigar@cand.uscourts.gov

District Judge **William Horsley Orrick III** . . . . (415) 522-2077
  Began Service: August 1, 2013
  Appointed By: President Barack Obama
  E-mail: william_orrick@cand.uscourts.gov

District Judge **James Donato** . . . . (415) 522-2066
  Began Service: March 21, 2014
  Appointed By: President Barack Obama
  E-mail: james_donato@cand.uscourts.gov

District Judge **Beth Labson Freeman** . . . . (408) 535-5381
  Began Service: February 28, 2014
  Appointed By: President Barack Obama
  E-mail: beth_freeman@cand.uscourts.gov

United States District Court for the Northern District of California
continued

District Judge **Vince Girdhari Chhabria** . . . . (415) 522-2000
  Began Service: March 7, 2014
  Appointed By: President Barack Obama
  E-mail: vince_chhabria@cand.uscourts.gov

District Judge **Haywood Stirling Gilliam, Jr.** . . . . (415) 522-2039
  Began Service: December 19, 2014
  Appointed By: President Barack Obama

Senior Judge **Samuel Conti** . . . . (415) 522-4080
  Began Service: 1970
  Appointed By: President Richard M. Nixon
  E-mail: samuel_conti@cand.uscourts.gov

Senior Judge **Thelton E. Henderson** 19th Floor,
  Courtroom 12 . . . . (415) 522-2047
  Began Service: 1980
  Appointed By: President Jimmy Carter
  E-mail: thelton_henderson@cand.uscourts.gov

Senior Judge **Saundra Brown Armstrong** . . . . (510) 879-3550
  Began Service: June 21, 1991
  Appointed By: President George H.W. Bush
  Ronald V. Dellums Federal Building,
  1301 Clay Street, Suite 400 South,
  Oakland, CA 94612-5212
  E-mail: saundra_armstrong@cand.uscourts.gov

Senior Judge **Ronald M. Whyte** . . . . (408) 535-5331
  Began Service: February 10, 1992
  Appointed By: President George H.W. Bush
  E-mail: ronald_whyte@cand.uscourts.gov

Senior Judge **Maxine M. Chesney** . . . . (415) 522-2041
  Began Service: 1995
  Appointed By: President William J. Clinton
  E-mail: maxine_chesney@cand.uscourts.gov

Senior Judge **Charles R. Breyer** . . . . (415) 522-2062
  Began Service: January 1, 1998
  Appointed By: President William J. Clinton
  E-mail: charles_breyer@cand.uscourts.gov

Senior Judge **Susan Yvonne Illston** . . . . (415) 522-2028
  Began Service: June 2, 1995
  Appointed By: President William J. Clinton

Senior Judge **Claudia A. Wilken** . . . . (510) 637-3542
  Began Service: December 1993
  Appointed By: President William J. Clinton
  Ronald V. Dellums Federal Building,
  1301 Clay Street, 4th Floor, Suite 400 South,
  Oakland, CA 94612-5212
  E-mail: claudia_wilken@cand.uscourts.gov

Chief Magistrate Judge **Joseph C. Spero** . . . . (415) 522-3691
  Began Service: March 13, 1999

Magistrate Judge **Elizabeth D. Laporte** . . . . (415) 522-3694
  Began Service: April 4, 1998

Magistrate Judge **Maria-Elena James** . . . . (415) 522-4698
  Began Service: October 11, 1994
  E-mail: maria-elena_james@cand.uscourts.gov

Magistrate Judge **Howard R. Lloyd** . . . . (408) 535-5411
  Began Service: June 4, 2002
  E-mail: howard_lloyd@cand.uscourts.gov

Magistrate Judge **Nandor J. Vadas** . . . . (707) 445-3612
  Began Service: June 18, 2004
  E-mail: nandor_vadas@cand.uscourts.gov

Magistrate Judge **Laurel Beeler** . . . . (415) 522-3140
  Began Service: 2009
  E-mail: laurel_beeler@cand.uscourts.gov

Magistrate Judge **Donna M. Ryu** . . . . (510) 637-3639
  Began Service: 2010
  1301 Clay Street, Room 400 South,
  Oakland, CA 94612

Magistrate Judge **Paul S. Grewal** . . . . (408) 535-5378
  Began Service: December 1, 2010
  E-mail: paul_grewal@cand.uscourts.gov

Magistrate Judge **Jacqueline Scott Corley** . . . . (415) 522-2015
  Began Service: 2011

Magistrate Judge **Nathanael Cousins** . . . . (415) 522-2039
  Began Service: July 5, 2011

Magistrate Judge **Kandis A. Westmore** . . . . (510) 637-3525
  Began Service: February 21, 2012
  E-mail: kandis_westmore@cand.uscourts.gov

United States District Court for the Northern District of California
continued

Court Staff
Clerk of Court **Richard W. Wieking** . . . . (415) 522-2000
 Note: Clerk of Court Rich Wieking will retire
 effective September 1, 2015.
 E-mail: richard_wieking@cand.uscourts.gov
Chief Probation Officer **Yador Harrell** . . . . (415) 436-7540
 P.O. Box 36057, San Francisco, CA 94102
Chief Pretrial Services Officer **Roy Saenz** . . . . (415) 436-7500
 P.O. Box 36108, San Francisco, CA 94102

United States Bankruptcy Court for the Northern District of California
1300 Clay Street, 20th Floor, Oakland, CA 94612
P.O. Box 7341, San Francisco, CA 94120-7341
Tel: (415) 268-2300
Tel: (888) 457-0604 (Voice Case Information System VCIS)
Fax: (415) 268-2303
Internet: pacer.canb.uscourts.gov

Number of Judgeships: 9

Judges
Chief Bankruptcy Judge **Roger L. Efremsky** Suite 300 . . . (510) 879-3540
 Began Service: August 2006
 E-mail: roger_efremsky@canb.uscourts.gov
Bankruptcy Judge **Alan Jaroslovsky** . . . . (707) 547-5900
 Began Service: January 1, 1987
 E-mail: alan_jaroslovsky@canb.uscourts.gov
Bankruptcy Judge **Thomas E. Carlson** . . . . (415) 268-2360
 Began Service: September 23, 1985
 235 Pine Street, 19th Floor,
 San Francisco, CA 94104-7341
 E-mail: thomas_carlson@canb.uscourts.gov
Bankruptcy Judge **Arthur S. Weissbrodt** . . . . (408) 278-7575
 Began Service: December 1989
 U.S. Courthouse, 280 South First Street,
 Room 3035, San Jose, CA 95113-3099
 E-mail: arthur_weissbrodt@canb.uscourts.gov
Bankruptcy Judge **Dennis Montali** . . . . (415) 268-2320
 Began Service: April 23, 1993
 235 Pine Street, 22nd Floor,
 San Francisco, CA 94104
 E-mail: dennis_montali@canb.uscourts.gov
Bankruptcy Judge **Charles Daniel Novack** Suite 215 . . . . . (510) 879-3525
 Began Service: 2010
 E-mail: charles_novack@canb.uscourts.gov
Bankruptcy Judge **Stephen L. Johnson** . . . . (408) 278-7515
 Began Service: 2010
 280 South First Street, Room 3035,
 San Jose, CA 95113
 E-mail: stephen_johnson@canb.uscourts.gov
Bankruptcy Judge **William J. Lafferty** . . . . (510) 879-3530
 Began Service: April 20, 2011
 E-mail: william_lafferty@canb.uscourts.gov
Bankruptcy Judge **M. Elaine Hammond** . . . . (408) 278-7538
 Began Service: 2012
 280 South First Street, Room 3035,
 San Jose, CA 95113
Bankruptcy Judge **Hannah Blumenstiel** . . . . (415) 268-2455
 E-mail: hannah_blumenstiel@canb.uscourts.gov

Court Staff
Clerk of Court **Edward "Eddy" Emmons** . . . . (415) 268-2300

United States Bankruptcy Court for the Northern District of California
continued

U.S. Attorney
California - Northern District
U.S. Courthouse, 450 Golden Gate Avenue, 11th Floor,
San Francisco, CA 94102
Tel: (415) 436-7200 TTY: (415) 436-7221 Fax: (415) 436-7234

U.S. Attorney **Melinda L. Haag** . . . . (415) 436-6938
 E-mail: melinda.haag@usdoj.gov

Federal Public Defender
Office of the Federal Public Defender-Northern District of California
450 Golden Gate Avenue, Box 36106, Room 19-6884,
San Francisco, CA 94102 (San Francisco Office)
555 - Twelfth Street, Sixth Floor, Suite 650, Oakland, CA 94607-3627
(Oakland Office)
160 West Santa Clara Street, Suite 575, San Jose, CA 95113
Tel: (415) 436-7700 Tel: (510) 637-3500 (Oakland)
Tel: (408) 291-7753 (San Jose) Fax: (415) 436-7706
Fax: (510) 637-3507 (Oakland) Fax: (408) 291-7399 (San Jose)

Federal Public Defender **Steven Kalar** . . . . (415) 436-7700
 E-mail: steven.kalar@fd.org

United States District Court for the Southern District of California
333 West Broadway, Suite 420, San Diego, CA 92101
Tel: (619) 557-5600 Tel: (800) 676-6856 (PACER Information)
Tel: (619) 557-5176 (Juror Information Recording)
Tel: (800) 998-9035 (Toll Free Juror Information) Fax: (619) 702-9900
Internet: www.casd.uscourts.gov

Number of Judgeships: 13

Circuit: Ninth

Areas Covered: Counties of Imperial and San Diego

Judges
Chief Judge **Barry Ted Moskowitz** Suite 1580 . . . . (619) 557-5583
 Began Service: January 2, 1996
 Appointed By: President William J. Clinton
District Judge **Marilyn L. Huff** . . . . (619) 557-6016
 Began Service: May 14, 1991
 Appointed By: President George H.W. Bush
 Edward J. Schwartz United States
 Courthouse, 940 Front Street, Suite 5135,
 San Diego, CA 92101-8913
District Judge **Larry Alan Burns** James M. Carter and
 Judith N. Keep US Courthouse, Suite 1410 . . . . (619) 557-5874
 Began Service: September 29, 2003
 Appointed By: President George W. Bush
District Judge **Dana M. Sabraw** James M. Carter and
 Judith N. Keep US Courthouse, Suite 1310 . . . . (619) 557-6262
 Began Service: September 29, 2003
 Appointed By: President George W. Bush
 E-mail: dana_sabraw@casd.uscourts.gov
District Judge **William Q. Hayes** . . . . (619) 557-6420
 Began Service: October 8, 2003
 Appointed By: President George W. Bush
 940 Front Street, 4th Floor, Suite 4135,
 San Diego, CA 92101
District Judge **John A. Houston** James M. Carter and
 Judith N. Keep US Courthouse, Suite 1380 . . . . (619) 557-5716
 Began Service: October 9, 2003
 Appointed By: President George W. Bush
 E-mail: john_houston@casd.uscourts.gov
District Judge **Roger T. Benitez** . . . . (619) 446-3589
 Began Service: June 2004
 Appointed By: President George W. Bush
 E-mail: roger_benitez@casd.uscourts.gov

(continued on next page)

United States District Court for the Southern District of California
continued

District Judge **Janis L. Sammartino** . . . . (619) 557-5542
  Began Service: September 21, 2007
  Appointed By: President George W. Bush

District Judge **Michael M. Anello** . . . . (619) 557-5960
  Began Service: October 10, 2008
  Appointed By: President George W. Bush
  221 West Broadway, Suite 3130,
  San Diego, CA 92101-8909
  E-mail: michael_anello@casd.uscourts.gov

District Judge **Anthony J. Battaglia** . . . . (619) 557-3446
  Began Service: March 10, 2011
  Appointed By: President Barack Obama
  221 West Broadway, Courtroom 2A,
  San Diego, CA 92101-8909

District Judge **Cathy Ann Bencivengo** . . . . (619) 557-5600
  Began Service: 2012
  Appointed By: President Barack Obama

District Judge **Gonzalo P. Curiel** . . . . (619) 557-5600
  Began Service: 2012
  Appointed By: President Barack Obama
  221 West Broadway, Suite 2190,
  San Diego, CA 92101
  E-mail: gonzalo_curiel@casd.uscourts.gov

District Judge **Cynthia Ann Bashant** . . . . (619) 321-0256
  Began Service: May 8, 2014
  Appointed By: President Barack Obama
  221 West Broadway, Suite 4145,
  San Diego, CA 92101-8900
  E-mail: cynthia_bashant@casd.uscourts.gov

Senior Judge **Gordon Thompson, Jr.** . . . . (619) 557-6480
  Began Service: October 16, 1970
  Appointed By: President Richard M. Nixon
  U.S. Courthouse, 221 West Broadway,
  3rd Floor, Room 3195, San Diego, CA 92101-8975
  E-mail: gordon_thompson@casd.uscourts.gov

Senior Judge **William B. Enright** . . . . (619) 557-5537
  Began Service: July 14, 1972
  Appointed By: President Richard M. Nixon
  221 West Broadway, Suite 5195,
  San Diego, CA 92101-8976

Senior Judge **Jeffrey T. Miller** . . . . (619) 557-6627
  Began Service: May 1997
  Appointed By: President William J. Clinton
  U.S. Courthouse, 940 Front Street,
  5th Floor, Suite 5190, San Diego, CA 92101-8906
  E-mail: jeffrey_miller@casd.uscourts.gov

Senior Judge **Thomas J. Whelan** . . . . (619) 557-6625
  Began Service: November 5, 1998
  Appointed By: President William J. Clinton
  U.S. Courthouse, 940 Front Street,
  3rd Floor, Suite 3155, San Diego, CA 92101

Senior Judge **M. James Lorenz** . . . . (619) 557-7669
  Began Service: October 5, 1999
  Appointed By: President William J. Clinton
  U.S. Courthouse, 940 Front Street,
  5th Floor, Room 5145, San Diego, CA 92101-8911

Presiding Magistrate Judge **Nita L. Stormes** . . . . (619) 557-5391
  Began Service: January 2000
  U.S. Courthouse, 940 Front Street,
  1st Floor, Room 1101, San Diego, CA 92101-8910

Magistrate Judge **Ruben B. Brooks** . . . . (619) 557-3404
  Began Service: September 2, 1993

Magistrate Judge **Jan M. Adler** . . . . (619) 557-5585
  Began Service: July 8, 2003
  Edward J. Schwartz U.S. Courthouse,
  221 West Broadway, Suite 2140,
  San Diego, CA 92101-8909
  E-mail: Jan_Adler@casd.uscourts.gov

Magistrate Judge **Barbara L. Major** 11th Floor, Suite
  1110 . . . . (619) 557-7372
  Began Service: January 2004
  E-mail: barbara_major@casd.uscourts.gov

Magistrate Judge **Peter C. Lewis** . . . . (760) 339-4248
  Began Service: June 28, 2004
  2003 West Adams Avenue, Suite 220,
  El Centro, CA 92243

United States District Court for the Southern District of California
continued

Magistrate Judge **William V. Gallo** . . . . (619) 557-6384
  Began Service: October 15, 2009

Magistrate Judge **Bernard G. Skomal** . . . . (619) 557-2993
  Began Service: 2010
  James M. Carter and Judith N. Keep US
  Courthouse, 333 West Broadway, Suite 1280,
  San Diego, CA 92101-8900

Magistrate Judge **David H. Bartick** . . . . (619) 557-5383
  Began Service: April 2, 2012
  U.S. Courthouse, 221 West Broadway, Suite 5140,
  San Diego, CA 92101-8909

Magistrate Judge **Karen Shichman Crawford** . . . . (619) 446-3964
  221 West Broadway, 10th Floor, Suite 1010,
  San Diego, CA 92101-8900

Magistrate Judge **Mitchell D. Dembin** . . . . (619) 446-3972

Court Staff

Clerk of Court (Acting) **John Morrill** . . . . (619) 557-6348
  E-mail: john_morrill@casd.uscourts.gov

Chief Pretrial Services Officer **Lori A. Garofalo** . . . . (619) 557-7610
  101 W. Broadway, Ste. 505,
  San Diego, CA 92243

Chief Probation Officer **David J. Sultzbaugh** . . . . (619) 557-6617
  101 West Broadway, Suite 700,
  San Diego, CA 92101-7991

United States Bankruptcy Court for the Southern District of California

Jacob W. Weinberger U.S. Courthouse, 325 West F Street,
San Diego, CA 92101-6991
Tel: (619) 557-5620   Tel: (210) 301-6440 (PACER)
Tel: (800) 676-6856 (Toll Free PACER)
Tel: (866) 222-8029 (Voice Case Information System VCIS)
Fax: (619) 557-5536
Internet: www.casb.uscourts.gov

Number of Judgeships: 4

Judges

Chief Bankruptcy Judge **Laura S. Taylor** Room 129 . . . . . . (619) 557-6580
  Began Service: January 2008
  E-mail: laura_taylor@casb.uscourts.gov

Bankruptcy Judge **Louise DeCarl Adler** . . . . (619) 557-5661
  Began Service: March 5, 1984
  E-mail: louise_adler@casb.uscourts.gov

Bankruptcy Judge **Margaret M. Mann** . . . . (619) 557-5848
  Began Service: April 2010
  E-mail: margaret_mann@casb.uscourts.gov

Bankruptcy Judge **Christopher B. Latham** Room 318 . . . . (619) 557-7570

Court Staff

Bankruptcy Clerk **Barry K. Lander** . . . . (619) 557-6582
  E-mail: barry_lander@casb.uscourts.gov

U.S. Attorney

California - Southern District
Federal Office Building, 880 Front Street, Room 6293,
San Diego, CA 92101-8893
Tel: (619) 557-5610   Fax: (619) 546-0620

U.S. Attorney **Laura E. Duffy** . . . . (619) 546-5690
  E-mail: laura.duffy@usdoj.gov

United States Bankruptcy Court for the Southern District of California *continued*

Federal Public Defender

Federal Defenders of San Diego Inc. [FDSDI]
225 Broadway, Suite 900, San Diego, CA 92101
1122 State Street, Suite E, El Centro, CA 92243 (El Centro Office)
Tel: (619) 234-8467 Tel: (760) 335-3510 (El Centro)
Fax: (619) 687-2666 Fax: (760) 335-3610 (El Centro)

Executive Director **Reuben C. Cahn** . . . . (619) 234-8467
    E-mail: reuben.cahn@fd.org

United States District Court for the District of Colorado

Alfred A. Arraj U.S. Courthouse, 901 19th Street, Denver, CO 80294
Tel: (303) 844-3433 Tel: (303) 844-3454 (PACER)
Internet: www.cod.uscourts.gov

Number of Judgeships: 7

Circuit: Tenth

Judges

Chief Judge **Marcia S. Krieger** Room A-105 . . . . (303) 335-2289
    Began Service: March 1, 2002
    Appointed By: President George W. Bush
    E-mail: marcia_krieger@cod.uscourts.gov
District Judge **Robert E. Blackburn** Room A1041 . . . . (303) 335-2350
    Began Service: March 8, 2002
    Appointed By: President George W. Bush
District Judge **Christine M. Arguello** Room A638 . . . . (303) 335-2174
    Began Service: October 21, 2008
    Appointed By: President George W. Bush
    E-mail: arguello_chambers@cod.uscourts.gov
District Judge **Philip A. Brimmer** Room A601 . . . . (303) 335-2794
    Began Service: October 14, 2008
    Appointed By: President George W. Bush
    E-mail: brimmer_chambers@cod.uscourts.gov
District Judge **William J. Martinez** Alfred A. Arraj
    United States Courthouse, Room A841 . . . . (303) 335-2805
    Began Service: January 10, 2011
    Appointed By: President Barack Obama
District Judge **Richard Brooke Jackson** Room A738 . . . . . (303) 844-4694
    Began Service: September 16, 2011
    Appointed By: President Barack Obama
District Judge **Raymond P. Moore** Room A601 . . . . (303) 335-2784
    Began Service: April 30, 2013
    Appointed By: President Barack Obama
Senior Judge **Richard Paul Matsch** . . . . (303) 844-4627
    Began Service: 1974
    Appointed By: President Richard M. Nixon
Senior Judge **John Lawrence Kane** . . . . (303) 844-6118
    Began Service: 1977
    Appointed By: President Jimmy Carter
    Alfred A. Arraj U.S. Courthouse,
    901 19th Street, Room A838,
    Denver, CO 80294-3589
    E-mail: john_l_kane@cod.uscourts.gov
Senior Judge **Lewis Thornton Babcock** C450 . . . . (303) 844-2527
    Began Service: November 21, 1988
    Appointed By: President Ronald Reagan
Senior Judge **Wiley Y. Daniel** Room A1038 . . . . (303) 335-2170
    Began Service: September 1, 1995
    Appointed By: President William J. Clinton
    E-mail: daniel_chambers@cod.uscourts.gov
Magistrate Judge **Michael J. Watanabe** . . . . (303) 844-2403
    Began Service: February 12, 1999
    Alfred A. Arraj U.S. Courthouse,
    901 19th Street, Suite A532,
    Denver, CO 80294-3589

United States District Court for the District of Colorado *continued*

Magistrate Judge **Craig B. Shaffer** . . . . (303) 844-2117
    Began Service: January 18, 2001
    Alfred A. Arraj U.S. Courthouse,
    901 19th Street, Room A432,
    Denver, CO 80294-3589
    E-mail: shaffer_chambers@cod.uscourts.gov
Magistrate Judge **Michael E. Hegarty** . . . . (303) 844-4507
    Began Service: February 15, 2006
    901 19th Street, Room A542,
    Denver, CO 80294
Magistrate Judge **Kristen L. Mix** . . . . (303) 335-2770
    Began Service: August 2007
    1929 Stout Street, Room C253,
    Denver, CO 80294
    E-mail: mix_chambers@cod.uscourts.gov
Magistrate Judge **Kathleen M. Tafoya** . . . . (303) 335-2780
    Began Service: January 2008
    1929 Stout Street, Suite C251,
    Denver, CO 80294
Magistrate Judge **Gordon P. Gallagher** . . . . (970) 241-8932
Magistrate Judge **Nina Y. Wang** . . . . (303) 335-2600
Magistrate Judge (Part-Time) **David L. West** . . . . (970) 259-0542
    Began Service: 2004
    U.S. Courthouse/Federal Building,
    103 Sheppard Drive, Suite 202,
    Durango, CO 81303

Court Staff

Clerk of the Court **Col Jeffrey P. Colwell** . . . . (303) 844-3433
Chief Probation Officer **Lavetra S. Castles** . . . . (303) 844-5424
    1929 Stout St., Denver, CO 80294

United States Bankruptcy Court for the District of Colorado

U.S. Custom House, 721 19th Street, Denver, CO 80202-2508
Tel: (720) 904-7300
Tel: (303) 844-0267 (Voice Case Information System VCIS)
Internet: www.cob.uscourts.gov

Number of Judgeships: 5

Judges

Chief Bankruptcy Judge **Michael E. Romero** . . . . (720) 904-7413
    Began Service: December 22, 2003
    E-mail: michael_romero@cob.uscourts.gov
Bankruptcy Judge **Howard R. Tallman** . . . . (720) 904-7438
    Began Service: December 2002
    E-mail: howard_tallman@cob.uscourts.gov
Bankruptcy Judge **Sidney B. Brooks** . . . . (720) 904-7338
    Began Service: 1988
Bankruptcy Judge **Elizabeth E. Brown** . . . . (720) 904-7346
    Began Service: April 16, 2001
    E-mail: elizabeth_brown@cob.uscourts.gov
Bankruptcy Judge **Thomas B. McNamara** . . . . (720) 904-7310

Court Staff

Clerk of Court **Kenneth S. Gardner** . . . . (720) 904-7300

U.S. Attorney

Colorado District
1225 - 17th Street, Suite 700, Denver, CO 80202
Tel: (303) 454-0100 Fax: (303) 454-0400

U.S. Attorney **John F. Walsh** . . . . (303) 454-0100
    E-mail: john.walsh@usdoj.gov

(continued on next page)

United States Bankruptcy Court for the **District of Colorado** *continued*

Federal Public Defender

Colorado and Wyoming Federal Public Defender
633 Seventeenth Street, Suite 1000, Denver, CO 80202
214 West Lincolnway, Suite 31A, Cheyenne, WY 82001
Tel: (303) 294-7002 (Denver) Tel: (307) 772-2781 (Cheyenne)
Fax: (303) 294-1192 (Denver) Fax: (307) 772-2788 (Cheyenne)

Federal Public Defender **Virginia L. Grady** . . . . (303) 294-7002
  E-mail: virginia.grady@fd.org

United States District Court for the District of Connecticut

U.S. Courthouse, 141 Church Street, New Haven, CT 06510
Tel: (203) 773-2140 Tel: (203) 773-2451 (PACER)
Fax: (203) 773-2334
Internet: www.ctd.uscourts.gov

Number of Judgeships: 8

Circuit: Second

Judges

Chief Judge **Janet C. Hall** . . . . (203) 773-2428
  Began Service: October 14, 1997
  Appointed By: President William J. Clinton
  E-mail: janet_hall@ctd.uscourts.gov
District Judge **Alvin W. Thompson** . . . . (860) 240-3224
  Began Service: October 11, 1994
  Appointed By: President William J. Clinton
  U.S. Courthouse, 450 Main Street, Suite 240,
  Hartford, CT 06103
  E-mail: alvin_thompson@ctd.uscourts.gov
District Judge **Robert N. Chatigny** . . . . (860) 240-3659
  Began Service: 1994
  Appointed By: President William J. Clinton
District Judge **Stefan R. Underhill** . . . . (203) 579-5714
  Began Service: September 1, 1999
  Appointed By: President William J. Clinton
  915 Lafayette Boulevard, Suite 411,
  Bridgeport, CT 06604
  E-mail: stefan_underhill@ctd.uscourts.gov
District Judge **Vanessa Lynne Bryant** . . . . (860) 240-3123
  Began Service: April 2, 2007
  Appointed By: President George W. Bush
  450 Main Street, Room 320,
  Hartford, CT 06103
  E-mail: vanessa_bryant@ctd.uscourts.gov
District Judge **Michael P. Shea** . . . . (203) 773-2140
  Began Service: December 31, 2012
  Appointed By: President Barack Obama
  E-mail: michael_shea@ctd.uscourts.gov
District Judge **Jeffrey Alker Meyer** . . . . (203) 579-5554
  Began Service: February 25, 2014   Tel: (203) 579-5681
  Appointed By: President Barack Obama
  915 Lafayette Boulevard, Suite 335,
  Bridgeport, CT 06604
District Judge **Victor Allen Bolden** . . . . (203) 579-5562
  Began Service: January 7, 2015
  Appointed By: President Barack Obama
  915 Lafayette Boulevard, Suite 335,
  Bridgeport, CT 06604
Senior Judge **Alfred Vincent Covello** . . . . (860) 240-3218
  Began Service: September 2, 1992
  Appointed By: President George H.W. Bush
  E-mail: alfred_covello@ctd.uscourts.gov
Senior Judge **Warren W. Eginton** . . . . (203) 579-5819
  Began Service: 1979
  Appointed By: President Jimmy Carter
  915 Lafayette Boulevard, Suite 335,
  Bridgeport, CT 06604-4765
  E-mail: warren_eginton@ctd.uscourts.gov

United States District Court for the **District of Connecticut** *continued*

Senior Judge **Dominic J. Squatrito** . . . . (860) 240-3873
  Began Service: October 6, 1994
  Appointed By: President William J. Clinton
  U.S. Courthouse, 450 Main Street, Suite 108,
  Hartford, CT 06103
  E-mail: dominic_squatrito@ctd.uscourts.gov
Senior Judge **Janet Bond Arterton** . . . . (203) 773-2456
  Began Service: May 15, 1995
  Appointed By: President William J. Clinton
  E-mail: janet_arterton@ctd.uscourts.gov
Magistrate Judge **Joan G. Margolis** . . . . (203) 773-2350
  Began Service: February 4, 1985
  U.S. Courthouse, 141 Church Street, Room 303,
  New Haven, CT 06510-2030
  E-mail: joan_margolis@ctd.uscourts.gov
Magistrate Judge **Donna F. Martinez** . . . . (860) 240-3605
  Began Service: February 8, 1994
  450 Main Street, Room 262,
  Hartford, CT 06103
  E-mail: donna_martinez@ctd.uscourts.gov
Magistrate Judge **William I. Garfinkel** . . . . (203) 579-5593
  Began Service: November 22, 1996
  915 Lafayette Boulevard, Suite 429,
  Bridgeport, CT 06604
  E-mail: william_garfinkel@ctd.uscourts.gov
Magistrate Judge **Sarah A. L. Merriam** . . . . (203) 773-2022
  Began Service: 2015

Court Staff

District Clerk **Robin D. Tabora** . . . . (203) 773-2140
  E-mail: robin_tabora@ctd.uscourts.gov
Chief Probation Officer **Edward Scott Chinn** . . . . (203) 773-2100

United States Bankruptcy Court for the District of Connecticut

U.S. Courthouse, 450 Main Street, Hartford, CT 06103
Tel: (860) 240-3675 Tel: (203) 240-3570 (PACER)
Tel: (203) 240-3345 (Voice Case Information System VCIS)
Tel: (800) 800-5113 (Toll Free Voice Case Information System VCIS)
Fax: (860) 240-3595
Internet: www.ctb.uscourts.gov

Number of Judgeships: 3

Judges

Chief Bankruptcy Judge **Julie A. Manning** . . . . (203) 773-2717
Bankruptcy Judge **Alan H. W. Shiff** . . . . (203) 579-5806
  Began Service: 1981
  915 Lafayette Boulevard, Room 104,
  Bridgeport, CT 06604
  E-mail: Alan_H_W_Shiff@ctb.uscourts.gov
Bankruptcy Judge **Ann M. Nevins** . . . . (860) 240-3176

Court Staff

Clerk of the Court **Gary M. Gfeller** . . . . (860) 240-3845
  E-mail: gary_gfeller@ctb.uscourts.gov

U.S. Attorney

Connecticut District
Connecticut Financial Center, 157 Church Street, 23rd Floor,
New Haven, CT 06510
Tel: (203) 821-3700 Fax: (203) 773-5376

U.S. Attorney **Deirdre M. Daly** . . . . (203) 821-3700
  E-mail: deirdre.daly@usdoj.gov

United States Bankruptcy Court for the **District of Connecticut** *continued*

Federal Public Defender

Federal Public Defender District of Connecticut
10 Columbus Boulevard, Floor 6, Hartford, CT 06106-1976
265 Church Street, Suite 702, New Haven, CT 06510-7005
Tel: (860) 493-6260 (Hartford) Tel: (203) 498-4200 (New Haven)
Fax: (860) 493-6269 (Hartford) Fax: (203) 498-4207 (New Haven)

Federal Public Defender **Terence S. Ward** . . . . (860) 493-6260
    E-mail: terence.ward@fd.org

United States District Court for the District of Delaware

J. Caleb Boggs Federal Building, 844 North King Street,
Wilmington, DE 19801
Tel: (302) 573-6170 Tel: (302) 573-6395 (PACER)
Internet: www.ded.uscourts.gov

Number of Judgeships: 4

Circuit: Third

Judges

Chief Judge **Leonard P. Stark** . . . . (302) 573-4571
    Began Service: August 16, 2010
    Appointed By: President Barack Obama
    844 North King Street, Unit 26, Room 6100,
    Wilmington, DE 19801-3556
    E-mail: judge_leonard_stark@ded.uscourts.gov
District Judge **Gregory M. Sleet** . . . . (302) 573-6470
    Began Service: September 28, 1998
    Appointed By: President William J. Clinton
    J. Caleb Boggs Federal Building,
    844 North King Street, Lockbox 19, Room 4324,
    Wilmington, DE 19801
    E-mail: judge_gregory_sleet@ded.uscourts.gov
District Judge **Sue L. Robinson** . . . .(302) 573-6310
    Began Service: 1991
    Appointed By: President George H.W. Bush
    J. Caleb Boggs Federal Building,
    844 North King Street, Unit 31, Room 4124,
    Wilmington, DE 19801
District Judge **Richard G. Andrews** Unit 9, Room 6325 . . .(302) 573-4581
    Began Service: February 13, 2012
    Appointed By: President Barack Obama
    E-mail: judge_richard_andrews@ded.uscourts.gov
Magistrate Judge **Mary Pat Thynge** Unit 8 . . . .(302) 573-6173
    Began Service: June 17, 1992
Magistrate Judge **Christopher J. Burke** . . . . (302) 573-4591
    Began Service: August 4, 2011
    844 North King Street, Room 6100,
    Wilmington, DE 19801-3555
    E-mail: judge_christopher_burke@ded.uscourts.gov
Magistrate Judge **Sherry R. Fallon** . . . . (302) 573-4551
    Began Service: April 25, 2012
    E-mail: judge_sherry_fallon@ded.uscourts.gov

Court Staff

Clerk of the Court **John A. Cerino** Room 4209 . . . . (302) 573-6170
    E-mail: john_cerino@ded.uscourts.gov
Chief Probation Officer **(Vacant)** . . . . (302) 252-2950
    824 Market Street, Unit 39,
    Wilmington, DE 19801

United States Bankruptcy Court for the District of Delaware

824 Market Street, Wilmington, DE 19801
Tel: (302) 252-2900 Tel: (800) 676-6856 (Toll Free PACER)
Tel: (302) 252-2560 (Voice Case Information System VCIS)
E-mail: helpdesk@deb.uscourts.gov
Internet: www.deb.uscourts.gov

Number of Judgeships: 6

Judges

Chief Bankruptcy Judge **Brendan L. Shannon** . . . .(302) 252-2915
    Began Service: 2006
Bankruptcy Judge **Kevin Gross** . . . . (302) 252-2913
    Began Service: 2006
Bankruptcy Judge **Kevin J. Carey** . . . . (302) 252-2927
    Began Service: December 9, 2005
Bankruptcy Judge **Mary F. Walrath** . . . .(302) 252-2929
    Began Service: 1998
Bankruptcy Judge **Christopher S. Sontchi** . . . .(302) 252-2888
    Began Service: 2006
Bankruptcy Judge **Laurie Selber Silverstein** . . . . (302) 252-2925

Court Staff

Clerk of Court **David D. Bird** . . . .(302) 252-2900
    E-mail: david_bird@deb.uscourts.gov

U.S. Attorney

Delaware District
1007 Orange Street, Suite 700, Wilmington, DE 19801
P.O. Box 2046, Wilmington, DE 19899-2046
Tel: (302) 573-6277 Fax: (302) 573-6220

U.S. Attorney **Charles M. Oberly III** . . . . (302) 573-6277
    E-mail: charles.oberly@usdoj.gov

Federal Public Defender

Federal Public Defender District of Delaware
800 King Street, Suite 200, Wilmington, DE 19801
Tel: (302) 573-6010 Tel: (877) 444-8244 (Toll Free)
Fax: (302) 573-6041

Federal Public Defender **Edson A. Bostic** . . . .(302) 573-6010
    E-mail: edson.bostic@fd.org

United States District Court for the Middle District of Florida

U.S. Courthouse & Federal Building, 401 West Central Boulevard, Suite 1200, Orlando, FL 32801
Tel: (407) 835-4200 Tel: (800) 676-6856 (Toll Free PACER)
Fax: (407) 835-4207
Internet: www.flmd.uscourts.gov

Number of Judgeships: 15

Number of Vacancies: 2

Circuit: Eleventh

Areas Covered: Counties of Baker, Bradford, Brevard, Charlotte, Citrus, Clay, Collier, Columbia, DeSoto, Duval, Flagler, Glades, Hamilton, Hardee, Hendry, Hernando, Hillsborough, Lake, Lee, Manatee, Marion, Nassau, Orange, Osceola, Pasco, Pinellas, Polk, Putnam, Sarasota, Seminole, St. Johns, Sumter, Suwannee, Union and Volusia

Judges

Chief Judge **Steven D. Merryday** . . . . (813) 301-5001
Began Service: March 16, 1992
Appointed By: President George H.W. Bush
E-mail: steven_merryday@flmd.uscourts.gov

District Judge **Elizabeth A. Kovachevich** . . . . (813) 301-5730
Began Service: 1982
Appointed By: President Ronald Reagan
E-mail: elizabeth_kovachevich@flmd.uscourts.gov

District Judge **James D. Whittemore** . . . . (813) 301-5880
Began Service: May 27, 2000
Appointed By: President William J. Clinton
Sam M. Gibbons U.S. Courthouse,
801 North Florida Avenue, Suite 13-B,
Tampa, FL 33602
E-mail: james_whittemore@flmd.uscourts.gov

District Judge **Timothy J. Corrigan** . . . . (904) 549-1300
Began Service: September 14, 2002
Appointed By: President George W. Bush
E-mail: timothy_corrigan@flmd.uscourts.gov

District Judge **Virginia M. Hernandez Covington** . . . . . . (813) 301-5340
Began Service: September 10, 2004
Appointed By: President George W. Bush
E-mail: virginia_covington@flmd.uscourts.gov

District Judge **Marcia Morales Howard** . . . . (904) 301-6750
Began Service: February 2007
Appointed By: President George W. Bush
E-mail: marcia_howard@flmd.uscourts.gov

District Judge **Mary Stenson Scriven** . . . . (813) 301-5710
Began Service: September 30, 2008
Appointed By: President George W. Bush
E-mail: mary_scriven@flmd.uscourts.gov

District Judge **Charlene Edwards Honeywell** . . . . (407) 835-3840
Began Service: November 2009
Appointed By: President Barack Obama
E-mail: charlene_honeywell@flmd.uscourts.gov

District Judge **Roy Bale Dalton, Jr.** . . . . (407) 835-2590
Began Service: May 4, 2011
Appointed By: President Barack Obama
E-mail: chambers_flmd_dalton@flmd.uscourts.gov

District Judge **Sheri Polster Chappell** . . . . (239) 461-2060
Began Service: May 28, 2013
Appointed By: President Barack Obama
E-mail: sheri_chappell@flmd.uscourts.gov

District Judge **Brian J. Davis** . . . . (904) 301-6625
Began Service: December 30, 2013
Appointed By: President Barack Obama
E-mail: brian_davis@flmd.uscourts.gov

District Judge **Paul G. Byron** . . . . (407) 835-4321
Began Service: June 27, 2014
Appointed By: President Barack Obama
E-mail: chambers_flmd_byron@flmd.uscourts.gov

District Judge **Carlos Eduardo Mendoza** . . . . (407) 835-4310
Began Service: 2014
Appointed By: President Barack Obama
E-mail: carlos_mendoza@flmd.uscourts.gov

United States District Court for the Middle District of Florida *continued*

Senior Judge **Henry Lee Adams, Jr.** . . . . (904) 549-1930
Began Service: December 10, 1993
Appointed By: President William J. Clinton
U.S. Courthouse, 300 North Hogan Street,
Suite 11-200, Jacksonville, FL 32202-4245
E-mail: henry_adams@flmd.uscourts.gov

Senior Judge **William J. Castagna** . . . . (813) 301-5935
Began Service: July 24, 1979
Appointed By: President Jimmy Carter
801 North Florida Avenue, Chambers 7A,
Tampa, FL 33602-3800
E-mail: william_castagna@flmd.uscourts.gov

Senior Judge **William Terrell Hodges** . . . . (352) 690-6907
Began Service: 1971
Appointed By: President Richard M. Nixon

Senior Judge **George Kendall Sharp** . . . . (407) 835-4260
Began Service: 1983
Appointed By: President Ronald Reagan

Senior Judge **Harvey E. Schlesinger** . . . . (904) 549-1990
Began Service: July 2, 1991
Appointed By: President George H.W. Bush
U.S. Courthouse, 300 North Hogan Street,
Suite 11-150, Jacksonville, FL 32202-4246
E-mail: harvey_schlesinger@flmd.uscourts.gov

Senior Judge **Patricia C. Fawsett** . . . . (407) 835-4250
Began Service: 1986
Appointed By: President Ronald Reagan
E-mail: patricia_fawsett@flmd.uscourts.gov

Senior Judge **Susan Cawthon Bucklew** . . . . (813) 301-5858
Began Service: December 1993
Appointed By: President William J. Clinton
Sam M. Gibbons U.S. Courthouse,
801 North Florida Avenue, Suite 1430,
Tampa, FL 33602
E-mail: susan_bucklew@flmd.uscourts.gov

Senior Judge **Richard Alan Lazzara** . . . . (813) 301-5350
Began Service: November 1, 1997
Appointed By: President William J. Clinton
E-mail: richard_lazzara@flmd.uscourts.gov

Senior Judge **Gregory A. Presnell** . . . . (407) 835-4301
Began Service: August 2, 2000
Appointed By: President William J. Clinton
401 West Central Boulevard, Suite 5750,
Orlando, FL 32801-0575

Senior Judge **John Antoon II** . . . . (407) 835-4334
Began Service: June 2, 2000
Appointed By: President William J. Clinton
E-mail: chambers_flmd_antoon@flmd.uscourts.gov

Senior Judge **John E. Steele** . . . . (239) 461-2140
Began Service: July 28, 2000
Appointed By: President William J. Clinton
U.S. Courthouse & Federal Building,
2110 First Street, Suite 6-109,
Fort Myers, FL 33901
E-mail: chambers_flmd_steele@flmd.uscourts.gov

Senior Judge **James S. Moody, Jr.** . . . . (813) 301-5680
Began Service: 2000
Appointed By: President William J. Clinton
Sam M. Gibbons U.S. Courthouse,
801 North Florida Avenue, Suite 17,
Tampa, FL 33602

Senior Judge **Anne C. Conway** Suite 6750 . . . . (407) 835-4270
Began Service: 1992
Appointed By: President George H.W. Bush
E-mail: anne_conway@flmd.uscourts.gov

Magistrate Judge **Thomas G. Wilson** . . . . (813) 301-5588
Began Service: April 6, 1979
E-mail: thomas_wilson@flmd.uscourts.gov

Magistrate Judge **Elizabeth A. Jenkins** . . . . (813) 301-5774
Began Service: 1985
E-mail: elizabeth_jenkins@flmd.uscourts.gov

Magistrate Judge **David A. Baker** . . . . (407) 835-4290
Began Service: December 13, 1991
401 West Central Boulevard, Suite 6550,
Orlando, FL 32801-0655
E-mail: david_baker@flmd.uscourts.gov

United States District Court for the Middle District of Florida *continued*

Magistrate Judge **Thomas B. McCoun III** . . . . (813) 301-5550
  Began Service: February 1, 1994
  E-mail: thomas_mccoun@flmd.uscourts.gov

Magistrate Judge **The Honorable Mark A. Pizzo** . . . . (813) 301-5011
  Began Service: May 22, 1995
  E-mail: mark_pizzo@flmd.uscourts.gov

Magistrate Judge **Karla Rae Spaulding** . . . . (407) 835-4320
  Began Service: December 29, 1997
  E-mail: chambers_flmd_
  spaulding@flmd.uscourts.gov

Magistrate Judge **Douglas N. Frazier** . . . . (239) 461-2120
  Began Service: January 8, 2000
  U.S. Courthouse and Federal Building,
  2110 First Street, Room 5-181,
  Fort Myers, FL 33901
  E-mail: douglas_frazier@flmd.uscourts.gov

Magistrate Judge **Monte C. Richardson** . . . . (904) 301-6740
  Began Service: June 2, 2003
  300 North Hogan Street, Suite 5-411,
  Jacksonville, FL 32202-4242
  E-mail: monte_richardson@flmd.uscourts.gov

Magistrate Judge **James R. Klindt** . . . . (904) 360-1520
  Began Service: October 2007
  United States Courthouse, 300 North Hogan Street,
  Room 5-111, Jacksonville, FL 32202-4242
  E-mail: james_klindt@flmd.uscourts.gov

Magistrate Judge **Gregory J. Kelly** . . . . (407) 835-3855
  Began Service: January 2008
  U.S. Courthouse & Federal Building,
  401 West Central Boulevard, Suite 5550,
  Orlando, FL 32801-0120

Magistrate Judge **Anthony E. Porcelli** . . . . (813) 301-5540
  Began Service: 2009
  801 North Florida Avenue, Room 1034,
  Tampa, FL 33602-3899
  E-mail: anthony_porcelli@flmd.uscourts.gov

Magistrate Judge **Joel B. Toomey** . . . . (904) 549-1960
  Began Service: July 6, 2010
  E-mail: joel_toomey@flmd.uscourts.gov

Magistrate Judge **Thomas B. Smith** Suite337 . . . . (407) 835-4305
  Began Service: 2011
  E-mail: thomas_smith@flmd.uscourts.gov

Magistrate Judge **Philip R. Lammens** . . . . (352) 369-4869
  E-mail: philip_lammens@flmd.uscourts.gov

Magistrate Judge **Patricia Barksdale** . . . . (904) 549-1950
  Began Service: 2013

Magistrate Judge **Carol Mirando** . . . . (239) 461-2170
  Began Service: 2014

Magistrate Judge **Julie S. Sneed** . . . . (813) 301-5260
  Began Service: 2015

Court Staff

Clerk of Court **Sheryl L. Loesch** . . . . (407) 835-4222
  E-mail: sheryl_loesch@flmd.uscourts.gov

Chief Probation Officer **Joseph Collins** . . . . (813) 301-5600
  U.S. Probation Office, 501 E. Polk Street,
  Room 3955, Tampa, FL 33602-3945

Chief Pretrial Services Officer
  Shelia Arrington Jacoby . . . . (407) 835-3950
  Fairwinds Bank Building,
  135 West Central Boulevard, Suite 740,
  Orlando, FL 32801

United States Bankruptcy Court for the Middle District of Florida

400 West Washington Street, Suite 5100, Orlando, FL 32801
Tel: (407) 237-8000
Tel: (866) 222-8029 (Voice Case Information System VCIS)
Internet: www.flmb.uscourts.gov

Number of Judgeships: 9

Judges

Chief Bankruptcy Judge **Karen S. Jennemann** Suite
  6100 . . . . (407) 237-8110
  Began Service: November 1993
  E-mail: karen_jennemann@flmb.uscourts.gov

Bankruptcy Judge **Paul M. Glenn** . . . . (904) 301-6550
  Began Service: November 24, 1993
  300 North Hogan Street, Suite 4-204,
  Jacksonville, FL 32202-4242

Bankruptcy Judge **Jerry A. Funk** . . . . (904) 301-6560
  Began Service: November 3, 1993
  300 North Hogan Street, Suite 4-104,
  Jacksonville, FL 32202-4254

Bankruptcy Judge **Michael G. Williamson** . . . . (813) 301-5520
  Began Service: March 1, 2000
  Sam M. Gibbons U.S. Courthouse,
  801 North Florida Avenue, Suite 840,
  Tampa, FL 33602-3899
  E-mail: mwilliamson@flmb.uscourts.gov

Bankruptcy Judge **K. Rodney May** . . . . (813) 301-5200
  Began Service: December 2003

Bankruptcy Judge **Catherine Peek McEwen** . . . . (813) 301-5082
  Began Service: 2005
  Sam M. Gibbons U.S. Courthouse,
  801 North Florida Avenue, Suite 555,
  Tampa, FL 33602-3899

Bankruptcy Judge **Caryl E. Delano** . . . . (813) 301-5190
  Began Service: 2008
  Sam M. Gibbons U.S. Courthouse,
  801 North Florida Avenue, Suite 555,
  Tampa, FL 33602-3899

Bankruptcy Judge **Cynthia C. "Cyndi" Jackson** . . . . (407) 237-8141
  Began Service: June 24, 2013

Bankruptcy Judge (recalled) **Arthur B. Briskman** Suite
  950 . . . . (407) 237-8121

Court Staff

Clerk of the Court **LeeAnn Bennett** . . . . (407) 237-8080
  E-mail: leeann_bennett@flmb.uscourts.gov

U.S. Attorney

Florida - Middle District
Park Tower, 400 North Tampa Street, Suite 3200, Tampa, FL 33602
Tel: (813) 274-6000   Fax: (813) 274-6358

U.S. Attorney **Arthur Lee Bentley** . . . . (813) 274-6000
  E-mail: lee.bentley@usdoj.gov

(continued on next page)

United States Bankruptcy Court for the Middle District of Florida *continued*

Federal Public Defender

Office of the Federal Public Defender Middle District of Florida
Park Tower, 400 North Tampa Street, Suite 2700, Tampa, FL 33602
Seaside Plaza, 201 South Orange Avenue, Orlando, FL 32801
201 SW Second Street, Suite 102, Ocala, FL 34471
BB&T Tower, 200 West Forsyth Street, Jacksonville, FL 32202
Kress Building, 1514 Broadway, Fort Myers, FL 33901
Tel: (813) 228-2715 (Tampa) Tel: (407) 648-6338 (Orlando)
Tel: (352) 351-9157 (Ocala) Tel: (904) 232-3039 (Jacksonville)
Tel: (239) 334-0397 (Fort Myers) Fax: (813) 228-2562 (Tampa)
Fax: (407) 648-6095 (Orlando) Fax: (352) 351-9162 (Ocala)
Fax: (904) 232-1937 (Jacksonville) Fax: (239) 334-4109 (Fort Myers)

Federal Public Defender **Donna Lee Elm** . . . . (813) 228-2715
  E-mail: donna_elm@fd.org

United States District Court for the Northern District of Florida

U.S. Courthouse, 111 North Adams Street, Tallahassee, FL 32301
Tel: (850) 521-3501 Fax: (850) 521-3656
Internet: www.flnd.uscourts.gov

Number of Judgeships: 4

Circuit: Eleventh

Areas Covered: Counties of Alachua, Bay, Calhoun, Dixie, Escambia, Franklin, Gadsden, Gilchrist, Gulf, Holmes, Jackson, Jefferson, Lafayette, Leon, Levy, Liberty, Madison, Okaloosa, Santa Rosa, Taylor, Wakulla, Walton and Washington

Judges

Chief Judge **M. Casey Rodgers** . . . . (850) 435-8448
  Began Service: November 24, 2003
  Appointed By: President George W. Bush
  E-mail: casey_rodgers@flnd.uscourts.gov
District Judge **Robert Lewis Hinkle** . . . . (850) 521-3601
  Began Service: August 6, 1996
  Appointed By: President William J. Clinton
  E-mail: robert_hinkle@flnd.uscourts.gov
District Judge **John Richard Smoak, Jr.** . . . . (850) 785-9761
  Began Service: November 7, 2005
  Appointed By: President George W. Bush
  E-mail: richard_smoak@flnd.uscourts.gov
District Judge **Mark E. Walker** . . . . (850) 521-3631
  Began Service: December 7, 2012
  Appointed By: President Barack Obama
Senior Judge **William H. Stafford, Jr.** . . . . (850) 521-3611
  Began Service: May 30, 1975
  Appointed By: President Gerald Ford
  E-mail: william_stafford@flnd.uscourts.gov
Senior Judge **Maurice M. Paul** . . . . (352) 380-2415
  Began Service: 1982
  Appointed By: President Ronald Reagan
  E-mail: maurice_paul@flnd.uscourts.gov
Senior Judge **Lacey A. Collier** . . . . (850) 444-0174
  Began Service: November 20, 1991
  Appointed By: President George H.W. Bush
  E-mail: lacey_collier@flnd.uscourts.gov
Senior Judge **Roger Vinson** . . . . (850) 435-8444
  Began Service: 1983
  Appointed By: President Ronald Reagan
  E-mail: roger_vinson@flnd.uscourts.gov
Magistrate Judge **Charles Stampelos** . . . . (850) 521-3621
  Began Service: 2012
  E-mail: charles_stampelos@flnd.uscourts.gov
Magistrate Judge **Elizabeth M. Timothy** . . . . (850) 437-6823
  Began Service: June 10, 2004
  E-mail: elizabeth_timothy@flnd.uscourts.gov

United States District Court for the Northern District of Florida *continued*

Magistrate Judge **Gary R. Jones** . . . . (352) 380-2746
  Began Service: September 13, 2010
  401 SE First Avenue, Suite 383,
  Gainesville, FL 32601
  E-mail: gary_r_jones@flnd.uscourts.gov
Magistrate Judge **Charles J. Kahn, Jr.** . . . . (850) 470-3090
  Began Service: March 4, 2011
  E-mail: charles_kahn@flnd.uscourts.gov
Magistrate Judge (part-time) **Larry A. Bodiford** . . . . (850) 763-0723
  Began Service: 1985
  E-mail: larry_bodiford@flnd.uscourts.gov

Court Staff

Clerk of Court **Jessica J. Lyublanovits** . . . . (850) 435-8440
  E-mail: jessica_lyublanovits@flnd.uscourts.gov
Chief Probation Officer **Mark Cook** Suite 100 . . . . (850) 521-3551

United States Bankruptcy Court for the Northern District of Florida

110 East Park Avenue, Suite 100, Tallahassee, FL 32301
Tel: (850) 521-5001 (Tallahassee) Tel: (866) 639-4615 (All Divisions)
Tel: (888) 765-1751 (Voice Case Information System VCIS)
Fax: (850) 521-5004
Internet: www.flnb.uscourts.gov

Number of Judgeships: 1

Judges

Bankruptcy Judge **Karen K. Specie** . . . . (850) 521-5031
  Began Service: July 25, 2012

Court Staff

Fax: (850) 521-5004

Clerk of Court **Traci Abrams** . . . . (850) 521-5001
  E-mail: traci_abrams@flnb.uscourts.gov

U.S. Attorney

Florida - Northern District
111 North Adams Street, 4th Floor, Tallahassee, FL 32301
Tel: (850) 942-8430 Fax: (850) 942-8429

U.S. Attorney **Pamela Cothran Marsh** . . . . (850) 942-8430
  E-mail: pamela.marsh@usdoj.gov

Federal Public Defender

Office of the Federal Public Defender Northern District of Florida
City Centre, 227 North Bronough Street, Suite 4200,
Tallahassee, FL 32301
Blount Building, 3 West Garden Street, Suite 200, Pensacola, FL 32502
101 SE Second Place, Suite 112, Gainesville, FL 32601
30 West Government Street, Panama City, FL 32401
Tel: (850) 942-8818 (Tallahassee) Tel: (850) 432-1418 (Pensacola)
Tel: (352) 373-5823 (Gainesville) Tel: (850) 769-8580 (Panama City)
Fax: (850) 942-8809 (Tallahassee) Fax: (850) 434-3855 (Pensacola)
Fax: (352) 373-7644 (Gainesville) Fax: (850) 769-8581 (Panama City)

Federal Public Defender **Randolph P. Murrell** . . . . (850) 942-8818
  E-mail: randolph.murrell@fpd-fln.org

United States District Court for the Southern District of Florida

U.S. Courthouse, 400 North Miami Avenue, Miami, FL 33128
Tel: (305) 523-5100 Tel: (305) 536-7265 (PACER)
Internet: www.flsd.uscourts.gov

Number of Judgeships: 18

Number of Vacancies: 1

Circuit: Eleventh

Areas Covered: Counties of Broward, Dade, Highlands, Indian River, Martin, Miami-Dade, Monroe, Okeechobee, Palm Beach and St. Lucie

Judges

Chief Judge **K. Michael Moore** Wilkie D. Ferguson
Federal Courthouse, Room 13-1 . . . . (305) 523-5160
Began Service: February 10, 1992
Appointed By: President George H.W. Bush
E-mail: moore@flsd.uscourts.gov

District Judge **William J. Zloch** . . . . (954) 769-5480
Began Service: November 1985
Appointed By: President Ronald Reagan
U.S. Courthouse, 299 East Broward Boulevard,
Room 202B, Fort Lauderdale, FL 33301
E-mail: zloch@flsd.uscourts.gov

District Judge **Federico A. Moreno** Wilkie D. Ferguson
Courthouse, Room 13-3 . . . . (305) 523-5110
Began Service: 1990
Appointed By: President George H.W. Bush
E-mail: moreno@flsd.uscourts.gov

District Judge **Ursula Ungaro** . . . . (305) 523-5550
Began Service: 1992
Appointed By: President George H.W. Bush

District Judge **Joan A. Lenard** Room 12-1 . . . . (305) 523-5500
Began Service: March 1, 1996
Appointed By: President William J. Clinton
E-mail: lenard@flsd.uscourts.gov

District Judge **Donald M. Middlebrooks** . . . . (561) 514-3720
Began Service: July 28, 1997
Appointed By: President William J. Clinton
U.S. Courthouse, 701 Clematis Street, Room 257,
West Palm Beach, FL 33401
E-mail: middlebrooks@flsd.uscourts.gov

District Judge **William P. Dimitrouleas** . . . . (954) 769-5650
Began Service: June 1, 1998
Appointed By: President William J. Clinton
U.S. Courthouse, 299 East Broward Boulevard,
Room 205F, Fort Lauderdale, FL 33301
E-mail: dimitrouleas@flsd.uscourts.gov

District Judge **Kenneth A. Marra** . . . . (561) 514-3760
Began Service: September 16, 2002
Appointed By: President George W. Bush
701 Clematis Street, Room 316,
West Palm Beach, FL 33401
E-mail: marra@flsd.uscourts.gov

District Judge **Jose E. Martinez** . . . . (305) 523-5590
Began Service: September 17, 2002
Appointed By: President George W. Bush
400 North Miami Avenue, Room 10-1,
Miami, FL 33128-1807
E-mail: martinez@flsd.uscourts.gov

District Judge **Cecilia Maria Altonaga** Federal
Courthouse Square, Room 12-2 . . . . (305) 523-5510
Began Service: May 2003
Appointed By: President George W. Bush
E-mail: cecilia_altonaga@flsd.uscourts.gov

District Judge **James I. Cohn** . . . . (954) 769-5490
Began Service: August 5, 2003
Appointed By: President George W. Bush
299 East Broward Boulevard, Room 203,
Fort Lauderdale, FL 33301
E-mail: cohn@flsd.uscourts.gov

District Judge **Marcia G. Cooke** . . . . (305) 523-5150
Began Service: May 18, 2004
Appointed By: President George W. Bush
E-mail: marcia_cooke@flsd.uscourts.gov

United States District Court for the Southern District of Florida *continued*

District Judge **Kathleen Mary Williams** . . . . (305) 523-5540
Began Service: August 8, 2011
Appointed By: President Barack Obama
E-mail: kathleen_williams@flsd.uscourts.gov

District Judge **Robert N. Scola, Jr.** . . . . (305) 523-5140
Began Service: October 20, 2011
Appointed By: President Barack Obama
E-mail: scola@flsd.uscourts.gov

District Judge **Darrin P. Gayles** Room 10-2 . . . . (305) 523-5170
Began Service: June 19, 2014
Appointed By: President Barack Obama
E-mail: darrin_gayles@flsd.uscourts.gov

District Judge **Beth Bloom** . . . . (954) 769-5680
Began Service: June 25, 2014
Appointed By: President Barack Obama
299 East Broward Boulevard, Room 207,
Fort Lauderdale, FL 33301
E-mail: Bloom@flsd.uscourts.gov

District Judge **Robin L. Rosenberg** . . . . (772) 467-2340
Began Service: July 24, 2014
Appointed By: President Barack Obama
E-mail: robin_rosenberg@flsd.uscourts.gov

Senior Judge **James Lawrence King** . . . . (305) 523-5000
Began Service: October 30, 1970
Appointed By: President Richard M. Nixon
James Lawrence King Federal Justice Building,
99 NE Fourth Street, Room 1127,
Miami, FL 33132
E-mail: king@flsd.uscourts.gov

Senior Judge **Jose A. Gonzalez, Jr.** . . . . (954) 769-5560
Began Service: July 28, 1978
Appointed By: President Jimmy Carter
E-mail: gonzalez@flsd.uscourts.gov

Senior Judge **Kenneth L. Ryskamp** . . . . (561) 803-3420
Began Service: 1986
Appointed By: President Ronald Reagan
Paul G. Rogers Federal Building,
701 Clematis Street, Room 416,
West Palm Beach, FL 33401
E-mail: ryskamp@flsd.uscourts.gov

Senior Judge **Daniel T. K. Hurley** . . . . (561) 803-3450
Began Service: April 1, 1994
Appointed By: President William J. Clinton
U.S. Courthouse, 701 Clematis Street, Room 352,
West Palm Beach, FL 33401-5196
E-mail: hurley@flsd.uscourts.gov

Senior Judge **Paul C. Huck** Room 13-2 . . . . (305) 523-5520
Began Service: August 5, 2000
Appointed By: President William J. Clinton
E-mail: huck@flsd.uscourts.gov

Senior Judge **Patricia A. Seitz** Courtroom 11-4 . . . . (305) 523-5530
Began Service: November 16, 1998
Appointed By: President William J. Clinton
E-mail: seitz@flsd.uscourts.gov

Senior Judge **Donald L. Graham** Wilkie D. Ferguson Jr.
US Courthouse, Chambers 13-4 . . . . (305) 523-5130
Began Service: October 1991
Appointed By: President George H.W. Bush
E-mail: graham@flsd.uscourts.gov

Chief Magistrate Judge **Frank J. Lynch, Jr.** . . . . (772) 467-2320
Began Service: April 1, 1995
E-mail: frank_lynch@flsd.uscourts.gov

Magistrate Judge **Barry S. Seltzer** . . . . (954) 769-5450
Began Service: 2012
E-mail: seltzer@flsd.uscourts.gov

Magistrate Judge **William C. Turnoff** . . . . (305) 523-5710
Began Service: 1986
E-mail: turnoff@flsd.uscourts.gov

Magistrate Judge **Lurana S. Snow** . . . . (954) 769-5460
Began Service: 1986
299 East Broward Boulevard, Room 204,
Fort Lauderdale, FL 33301
E-mail: snow@flsd.uscourts.gov

Magistrate Judge **Andrea M. Simonton** . . . . (305) 523-5930
Began Service: April 1, 1999
E-mail: simonton@flsd.uscourts.gov

(continued on next page)

United States District Court for the Southern District of Florida
continued

Magistrate Judge **John J. O'Sullivan** . . . . (305) 523-5920
   Began Service: April 1, 1999
   E-mail: osullivan@flsd.uscourts.gov
Magistrate Judge **Patrick A. White** . . . . (305) 523-5780
   Began Service: April 2003
   E-mail: white@flsd.uscourts.gov
Magistrate Judge **James M. Hopkins** . . . . (561) 514-3710
   Began Service: October 2003
   701 Clematis Street, Room 331,
   West Palm Beach, FL 33401
   E-mail: james_hopkins@flsd.uscourts.gov
Magistrate Judge **Edwin G. Torres** . . . .(305) 523-5750
   Began Service: 2003
   E-mail: torres@flsd.uscourts.gov
Magistrate Judge **Chris M. McAliley** . . . . (305) 523-5890
   Began Service: March 25, 2004
   301 North Miami Avenue, Room 105,
   Miami, FL 33128
   E-mail: chris_mcaliley@flsd.uscourts.gov
Magistrate Judge **Jonathan Goodman** . . . . (305) 523-5720
   Began Service: 2010
   E-mail: jonathan_goodman@flsd.uscourts.gov
Magistrate Judge **Dave Lee Brannon** . . . . (561) 803-3470
   Began Service: 2012
   E-mail: dave_brannon@flsd.uscourts.gov
Magistrate Judge **Alicia Otazo-Reyes** . . . . (305) 523-5740
   Began Service: 2012
Magistrate Judge **William Matthewman** . . . . (561) 803-3440
   Began Service: 2012
   E-mail: william_matthewman@flsd.uscourts.gov
Magistrate Judge **Barry L. Garber** . . . . (305) 523-5730
   Began Service: September 13, 1991
   U.S. Courthouse, 99 NE 4th Street, Room 1061,
   Miami, FL 33132
   E-mail: garber@flsd.uscourts.gov
Magistrate Judge **Patrick M. Hunt** . . . . (954) 769-5470
   Began Service: 2014
   299 East Broward Boulevard, Room 205E,
   Fort Lauderdale, FL 33301
Magistrate Judge **Alicia O. Valle** . . . . (954) 769-5750
   Began Service: 2014
Magistrate Judge (recalled) **Peter R. Palermo** . . . .(305) 523-5760
   Began Service: January 1, 1971
   James Lawrence King Federal Justice
   Building, 99 NE 4th Street, Room 1067,
   Miami, FL 33132
   E-mail: palermo@flsd.uscourts.gov

Court Staff
Clerk of Court **Steven M. Larimore** . . . . (305) 523-5001
   E-mail: steven_larimore@flsd.uscourts.gov
Chief Probation Officer **Reginald D. Michael** . . . .(305) 523-5300
   301 North Miami Avenue, Room 315,
   Miami, FL 33128

United States Bankruptcy Court for the Southern District of Florida
Claude Pepper Federal Building, 51 SW First Avenue, Room 1510,
Miami, FL 33130-1669
Tel: (305) 714-1800
Tel: (305) 536-5979 (Voice Case Information System VCIS)
Tel: (305) 536-5696 (Voice Case Information System VCIS)
Tel: (800) 473-0226 (Toll Free Voice Case Information System VCIS)
Tel: (800) 676-6856 (Toll Free PACER Registration)
Fax: (305) 714-1801
Internet: www.flsb.uscourts.gov

Number of Judgeships: 7

Judges
Chief Bankruptcy Judge **Paul G. Hyman, Jr.** . . . . (561) 514-4109
   Began Service: October 4, 1993
   E-mail: paul_hyman@flsb.uscourts.gov
Bankruptcy Judge **Robert A. Mark** . . . . (305) 714-1760
   Began Service: 1990
   301 North Miami Avenue, Room 417,
   Miami, FL 33128
   E-mail: robert_mark@flsb.uscourts.gov
Bankruptcy Judge **A. Jay Cristol** . . . . (305) 714-1770
   Began Service: April 1985
   E-mail: a_jay_cristol@flsb.uscourts.gov
Bankruptcy Judge **Raymond B. Ray** . . . . (954) 769-5760
   Began Service: November 9, 1993
   112 U.S. Courthouse, 299 East Broward Boulevard,
   Room 306, Fort Lauderdale, FL 33301
Bankruptcy Judge **Laurel M. Isicoff** . . . .(305) 714-1750
   Began Service: 2006
   300 North Miami Avenue, Room 817,
   Miami, FL 33128
Bankruptcy Judge **John K. Olson** . . . . (954) 769-5772
   299 East Broward Boulevard, Room 303,
   Fort Lauderdale, FL 33301
   E-mail: jko_chambers@flsb.uscourts.gov
Bankruptcy Judge **Erik B. Kimball** . . . . (561) 514-4140
   Began Service: 2010

Court Staff
Clerk of Court **Joseph "Joe" Falzone** . . . . (305) 714-1800

U.S. Attorney
Florida - Southern District
99 NE Fourth Street, Suite 800, Miami, FL 33132
Tel: (305) 961-9001   Fax: (305) 530-7679

U.S. Attorney **Wifredo A. "Willy" Ferrer** . . . . (305) 961-9001
   E-mail: wifredo.ferrer@usdoj.gov

Federal Public Defender
Office of the Federal Public Defender for the Southern District of Florida
150 West Flagler Street, Suite 1700, Miami, FL 13313-1556
One East Broward Boulevard, Suite 1100, Fort Lauderdale, FL 33301
450 Australian Avenue South, Suite 500,
West Palm Beach, FL 33401-5040
109 North Second Street, Fort Pierce, FL 34950
Tel: (305) 530-7000 (Miami) Tel: (954) 356-7436 (Fort Lauderdale)
Tel: (561) 833-6288 (West Palm Beach)
Tel: (772) 489-2123 (Fort Pierce) Fax: (305) 536-4559 (Miami)
Fax: (954) 356-7556 (Fort Lauderdale)
Fax: (561) 833-0368 (West Palm Beach)
Fax: (772) 489-3997 (Fort Pierce)

Federal Public Defender **Michael Caruso** . . . . (305) 536-6900
   E-mail: michael_caruso@fls.fd.org

United States District Court for the Middle District of Georgia

William Augustus Bootle U.S. Courthouse, 475 Mulberry Street, Macon, GA 31201
P.O. Box 128, Macon, GA 31202
Tel: (478) 752-3497 Tel: (478) 752-8170 (PACER)
Fax: (478) 752-3496
Internet: www.gamd.uscourts.gov

Number of Judgeships: 4

Circuit: Eleventh

Areas Covered: Counties of Baker, Baldwin, Ben Hill, Berrien, Bibb, Bleckley, Brooks, Butts, Calhoun, Chattahoochee, Clarke, Clay, Clinch, Colquitt, Cook, Crawford, Crisp, Decatur, Dooly, Dougherty, Early, Echols, Elbert, Franklin, Grady, Greene, Hancock, Harris, Hart, Houston, Irwin, Jasper, Jones, Lamar, Lanier, Lee, Lowndes, Macon, Madison, Marion, Miller, Mitchell, Monroe, Morgan, Muscogee, Oconee, Oglethorpe, Peach, Pulaski, Putnam, Quitman, Randolph, Schley, Seminole, Stewart, Sumter, Talbot, Taylor, Terrell, Thomas, Tift, Turner, Twiggs, Upson, Walton, Washington, Webster, Wilcox, Wilkenson and Worth

Judges

Chief Judge **Clay D. Land** . . . . (706) 649-7812
  Began Service: December 28, 2001
  Appointed By: President George W. Bush
District Judge **C. Ashley Royal** . . . . (478) 752-3445
  Began Service: December 28, 2001
  Appointed By: President George W. Bush
  E-mail: ashley_royal@gamd.uscourts.gov
District Judge **Marc Thomas Treadwell** . . . . (478) 752-0717
  Began Service: June 25, 2010
  Appointed By: President Barack Obama
  E-mail: marc_treadwell@gamd.uscourts.gov
District Judge **Leslie J. Abrams** . . . . (229) 431-2510
  Began Service: 2014
  Appointed By: President Barack Obama
Senior Judge **Hugh Lawson** . . . . (478) 752-3591
  Began Service: December 29, 1995
  Appointed By: President William J. Clinton
  E-mail: Hugh_Lawson@gamd.uscourts.gov
Senior Judge **W. Louis Sands** . . . . (229) 430-8553
  Began Service: May 1994
  Appointed By: President William J. Clinton
Magistrate Judge **Thomas Q. Langstaff** . . . . (229) 903-1312
  Began Service: June 2010
  E-mail: thomas_langstaff@gamd.uscourts.gov
Magistrate Judge **M. Stephen Hyles** . . . . (706) 649-7860
  Began Service: 2010
Magistrate Judge **Charles H. Weigle** . . . . (478) 752-0730
  Began Service: October 19, 2010

Court Staff

Clerk of Court **David Bunt** . . . . (478) 752-0711
Chief Probation Officer **Ellen S. Moore** . . . . (478) 752-8106
  431 Walnut St., Macon, GA 31201
  P.O. Box 1736, Macon, GA 31202-1736

United States Bankruptcy Court for the Middle District of Georgia

433 Cherry Street, Macon, GA 31201
P.O. Box 1957, Macon, GA 31202
Tel: (478) 752-3506 Tel: (800) 546-7343 (Toll Free PACER)
Tel: (478) 752-8183 (Voice Case Information System VCIS)
Tel: (800) 211-3015 (Toll Free Voice Case Information System VCIS)
Fax: (478) 752-8157
Internet: www.gamb.uscourts.gov

Number of Judgeships: 3

Judges

Chief Bankruptcy Judge **James P. Smith** . . . . (478) 752-3506
  Began Service: 2010
  E-mail: james_smith@gamb.uscourts.gov
Bankruptcy Judge **John T. Laney III** . . . . (706) 596-7150
  Began Service: October 1, 1986
  One Arsenal Place, 901 Front Avenue, Room 309,
  Columbus, GA 31901
  E-mail: john_laney@gamb.uscourts.gov
Bankruptcy Judge **Austin E. Carter** . . . . (478) 749-6880
  Began Service: May 20, 2014
  E-mail: austin_carter@gamb.uscourts.gov

Court Staff

Bankruptcy Clerk **Kyle George** . . . . (478) 749-6842

U.S. Attorney

Georgia - Middle District
300 Mulberry Street, Suite 400, Macon, GA 31201
P.O. Box 1702, Macon, GA 31202-1702
Tel: (478) 752-3511 Fax: (478) 621-2655
Fax: (478) 621-2667 (Administration) Fax: (478) 621-2679 (Personnel)

U.S. Attorney **Michael J. Moore** . . . . (478) 621-2600
  E-mail: michael.j.moore@usdoj.gov

Federal Public Defender

Federal Defenders of the Middle District of Georgia, Inc.
440 Martin Luther King Jr. Boulevard, Suite 400, Macon, GA 31201
P.O. Box 996, Macon, GA 31202
323 Pine Avenue, Suite 400, Albany, GA 31701
233 Twelfth Street, Suite 400, Columbus, GA 31901
Tel: (478) 743-4747 (Macon) Tel: (229) 435-6162 (Albany)
Tel: (706) 358-0030 (Columbus) Fax: (478) 207-3419 (Macon)
Fax: (229) 435-4085 (Albany) Fax: (706) 358-0029 (Columbus)

Federal Public Defender (Interim)
  Christina L. "Tina" Hunt . . . . (478) 743-4747
  E-mail: tina_hunt@fd.org

United States District Court for the Northern District of Georgia

U.S. Courthouse, 75 Spring Street, SW, Room 2211,
Atlanta, GA 30303-3309
Tel: (404) 215-1600
Tel: (404) 215-1655 (Civil and Criminal Case Information)
Tel: (404) 215-1300 (District Executive)
Tel: (404) 215-1635 (Filing and Fee Information)
Tel: (404) 215-1640 (Jury Information)
Internet: www.gand.uscourts.gov

Number of Judgeships: 11

Number of Vacancies: 1

Circuit: Eleventh

Areas Covered: Counties of Banks, Barrow, Bartow, Carroll, Catoosa, Chattooga, Cherokee, Clayton, Cobb, Coweta, Dade, Dawson, DeKalb, Douglas, Fannin, Fayette, Floyd, Forsyth, Fulton, Gilmer, Gordon, Gwinnett, Habersham, Hall, Haralson, Heard, Henry, Jackson, Lumpkin, Meriwether, Murray, Newton, Paulding, Pickens, Pike, Polk, Rabun, Rockdale, Spalding, Stephens, Towns, Troup, Union, Walker, White and Whitfield

Judges

Chief Judge **Thomas W. Thrash, Jr.** Room 2188 . . . . (404) 215-1550
Began Service: August 15, 1997
Appointed By: President William J. Clinton
E-mail: Thomas_W_Thrash@gand.uscourts.gov
District Judge **Harold L. Murphy** . . . .(706) 378-4080
Began Service: August 9, 1977
Appointed By: President Jimmy Carter
600 East First Street, Room 311,
Rome, GA 30161
District Judge **Richard W. Story** . . . . (404) 215-1350
Began Service: 1998
Appointed By: President William J. Clinton
U.S. Courthouse, 75 Spring Street, SW,
Room 2121, Atlanta, GA 30303-3361
District Judge **William S. Duffey, Jr.** Suite 1721 . . . . (404) 215-1480
Began Service: July 1, 2004
Appointed By: President George W. Bush
E-mail: william_s_duffey@gand.uscourts.gov
District Judge **Timothy C. Batten, Sr.** . . . . (404) 215-1420
Began Service: April 2006
Appointed By: President George W. Bush
U.S. Courthouse, 75 Spring Street, SW,
Room 1756, Atlanta, GA 30303-3361
E-mail: timothy_c_batten@gand.uscourts.gov
District Judge **Steven CarMichael Jones** Room 1967 . . . . (404) 215-1228
Began Service: March 4, 2011
Appointed By: President Barack Obama
District Judge **Amy Mil Totenberg** Room 2388 . . . .(404) 215-1438
Began Service: March 4, 2011
Appointed By: President Barack Obama
E-mail: amy_totenberg@gand.uscourts.gov
District Judge **Leigh Martin May** Room 2167 . . . . (404) 215-1510
Began Service: 2014
Appointed By: President Barack Obama
District Judge **Eleanor Louise Ross** Room 1788 . . . . (404) 215-1520
Began Service: 2014
Appointed By: President Barack Obama
District Judge **Mark Howard Cohen** Room 1909 . . . . (404) 215-1310
Began Service: 2014
Appointed By: President Barack Obama
Senior Judge **Orinda D. Evans** . . . . (404) 215-1490
Began Service: August 1979
Appointed By: President Jimmy Carter
U.S. Courthouse, 75 Spring Street, SW,
Room 1988, Atlanta, GA 30303
Senior Judge **William C. O'Kelley** Room 1942 . . . . (404) 215-1530
Began Service: October 23, 1970
Appointed By: President Richard M. Nixon

United States District Court for the Northern District of Georgia
continued

Senior Judge **Marvin H. Shoob** . . . .(404) 215-1470
Began Service: 1979
Appointed By: President Jimmy Carter
U.S. Courthouse, 75 Spring Street, SW,
Room 1767, Atlanta, GA 30303-3361
Senior Judge **Willis B. Hunt, Jr.** Room 1756 . . . .(404) 215-1450
Began Service: July 1, 1995
Appointed By: President William J. Clinton
E-mail: willis_b_hunt@gand.uscourts.gov
Senior Judge **Clarence Cooper** Room 1701 . . . .(404) 215-1390
Began Service: May 9, 1994
Appointed By: President William J. Clinton
E-mail: clarence_cooper@gand.uscourts.gov
Senior Judge **Charles A. Pannell, Jr.** . . . .(404) 215-1580
Began Service: December 1, 1999
Appointed By: President William J. Clinton
Magistrate Judge **Janet F. King** . . . . (404) 215-1385
Began Service: October 20, 1998
U.S. Courthouse, 75 Spring Street, SW, Suite 2007,
Atlanta, GA 30303-3361
E-mail: janet_f_king@gand.uscourts.gov
Magistrate Judge **Gerrilyn G. Brill** . . . .(404) 215-1365
Began Service: January 1995
E-mail: gerrilyn_brill@gand.uscourts.gov
Magistrate Judge **Linda T. Walker** . . . .(404) 215-1370
Began Service: January 3, 2000
U.S. Courthouse, 75 Spring Street, SW,
Room 1856, Atlanta, GA 30303
Magistrate Judge **Alan J. Baverman** Room 1885 . . . . (404) 215-1395
Began Service: February 1, 2001
E-mail: alan_j_baverman@gand.uscourts.gov
Magistrate Judge **Walter E. Johnson** . . . . (706) 378-4090
Began Service: March 18, 2002
600 East First Street, Room 212,
Rome, GA 30161-3187
Magistrate Judge **J. Clay Fuller** . . . . (678) 450-2790
121 Spring Street, SE, Suite 106,
Gainesville, GA 30501
Magistrate Judge **Russell G. Vineyard** . . . . (404) 215-1375
Began Service: October 23, 2006
U.S. Courthouse, 75 Spring Street, SW,
Room 2027, Atlanta, GA 30303
Magistrate Judge **Justin S. Anand** Room 1909 . . . .(404) 215-1440
Magistrate Judge **Catherine M. Salinas** Suite 1807 . . . . . . (404) 215-1380
Began Service: 2015

Court Staff

District Court Executive and Clerk of Court
James N. Hatten . . . .(404) 215-1610
E-mail: james_hatten@gand.uscourts.gov
Chief Probation Officer **Thomas Bishop** Russell
Federal Building, Suite 900 . . . .(404) 215-1950

United States Bankruptcy Court for the Northern District of Georgia

U.S. Courthouse, 75 Spring Street, SW, Room 1340,
Atlanta, GA 30303-3367
Tel: (404) 215-1000 Tel: (404) 730-3264 (PACER)
Tel: (800) 676-6856 (Toll Free PACER)
Tel: (404) 730-2867 (Voice Case Information System VCIS)
Tel: (404) 730-2866 (Voice Case Information System VCIS)
Fax: (404) 730-2216
Internet: www.ganb.uscourts.gov

Number of Judgeships: 9

Judges

Chief Bankruptcy Judge **C. Ray Mullins** . . . . (404) 215-1002
  Began Service: February 29, 2000
  U.S. Courthouse, 75 Spring Street, SW,
  Room 1270, Atlanta, GA 30303
  E-mail: ray_mullins@ganb.uscourts.gov
Bankruptcy Judge **Walter Homer Drake, Jr.** . . . . (678) 423-3080
  Began Service: September 1, 1964
  E-mail: Homer_Drake@ganb.uscourts.gov
Bankruptcy Judge **Margaret H. Murphy** Room 1290 . . . . . (404) 215-1006
  Began Service: October 19, 1987
  E-mail: margaret_murphy@ganb.uscourts.gov
Bankruptcy Judge **Barbara Ellis-Monro** . . . . (404) 215-1030
  Began Service: 2012
  U.S. Courthouse, 75 Spring Street, SW,
  Room 1431, Atlanta, GA 30303-3309
Bankruptcy Judge **Paul W. Bonapfel** . . . . (404) 215-1018
  Began Service: April 10, 2002
  U.S. Courthouse, 75 Spring Street, SW,
  Room 1492, Atlanta, GA 30303
  E-mail: paul_bonapfel@ganb.uscourts.gov
Bankruptcy Judge **Mary Grace Diehl** . . . . (404) 215-1202
  Began Service: February 23, 2004
  75 Spring Street, SW, Room 1215,
  Atlanta, GA 30303
  E-mail: mgdchambers@ganb.uscourts.gov
Bankruptcy Judge **Wendy L. Hagenau** . . . . (404) 215-1190
  Began Service: 2010
  E-mail: wendy_hagenau@ganb.uscourts.gov
Bankruptcy Judge **James R. Sacca** . . . . (404) 215-1790
  Began Service: October 21, 2010
  75 Spring Street, SW, Room 1481,
  Atlanta, GA 30303-3309
  E-mail: jrschambers@ganb.uscourts.gov
Bankruptcy Judge **Paul M. Baisier** . . . . (404) 215-1010

Court Staff

Clerk of Court **M. Regina Thomas** . . . . (404) 215-1000
  E-mail: regina_thomas@ganb.uscourts.gov

U.S. Attorney

Georgia - Northern District
Richard B. Russell Federal Building, 75 Spring Street, NW,
Suite 600, Atlanta, GA 30303-3309
Tel: (404) 581-6000 Fax: (404) 581-6181

U.S. Attorney (Acting) **John A. Horn** . . . . (404) 581-6000
  E-mail: john.horn@usdoj.gov

Federal Public Defender

The Federal Defender Program, Inc.
1500 The Centenniel Tower, 101 Marietta Street, Atlanta, GA 30303
Tel: (404) 688-7530 Fax: (404) 688-0768

Executive Director **Stephanie Kearns** . . . . (404) 688-7530
  E-mail: stephanie.kearns@fd.org

United States District Court for the Southern District of Georgia

P.O. Box 8286, Savannah, GA 31412
125 Bull Street, Room 306, Savannah, GA 31401
Tel: (912) 650-4020 Tel: (912) 650-4042 (PACER)
Fax: (912) 650-4029
Internet: www.gasd.uscourts.gov

Number of Judgeships: 3

Circuit: Eleventh

Areas Covered: Counties of Appling, Atkinson, Bacon, Brantley, Bryan, Bulloch, Burke, Camden, Candler, Charlton, Chatham, Coffee, Columbia, Dodge, Effingham, Emanuel, Evans, Glascock, Glynn, Jeff Davis, Jefferson, Jenkins, Johnson, Laurens, Liberty, Lincoln, Long, McDuffie, McIntosh, Montgomery, Pierce, Richmond, Screven, Taliaferro, Tattnall, Telfair, Toombs, Treutlen, Ware, Warren, Wayne, Wheeler and Wilkes

Judges

Chief Judge **Lisa Godbey Wood** . . . . (912) 262-2600
  Began Service: February 2007
  Appointed By: President George W. Bush
  801 Gloucester Street, Suite 220,
  Brunswick, GA 31520
  E-mail: lisa_wood@gas.uscourts.gov
District Judge **William T. Moore, Jr.** . . . . (912) 650-4173
  Began Service: October 31, 1994
  Appointed By: President William J. Clinton
District Judge **James Randal Hall** . . . . (706) 823-6460
  Began Service: May 1, 2008
  Appointed By: President George W. Bush
Senior Judge **Dudley H. Bowen, Jr.** . . . . (706) 849-4440
  Began Service: December 5, 1979
  Appointed By: President Jimmy Carter
  E-mail: dudley_bowen@gas.uscourts.gov
Magistrate Judge **G. R. Smith** . . . . (912) 650-4180
  Began Service: 1988
Magistrate Judge **James E. Graham** . . . . (912) 280-1360
  Note: Judge Graham has retired but will remain
  active until his term in expires in February 2016.
  Began Service: 1987
  E-mail: James_Graham@gas.uscourts.gov
Magistrate Judge **Brian K. Epps** . . . . (706) 849-4404
Magistrate Judge **R. Stan Baker** . . . . (912) 280-1334

Court Staff

Clerk of Court **Scott L. Poff** . . . . (912) 650-4031
  E-mail: scott_poff@gas.uscourts.gov
Chief Probation Officer **Richard A. Long** Room 237 . . . . . (912) 650-4150
  P.O. Box 8165, Savannah, GA 31412
  E-mail: richard_long@gas.uscourts.gov

United States Bankruptcy Court for the Southern District of Georgia

U.S. Courthouse, 125 Bull Street, Savannah, GA 31401
P.O. Box 8347, Savannah, GA 31412
Tel: (912) 650-4100
Internet: www.gasb.uscourts.gov

Number of Judgeships: 3

Judges

Chief Bankruptcy Judge **Susan D. Barrett** . . . . (706) 849-4478
  Began Service: March 2006
Bankruptcy Judge **Edward J. Coleman III** . . . . (912) 650-4100
Bankruptcy Judge **Lamar W. Davis, Jr.** Room 240 . . . . (912) 650-4109
  Began Service: 1986
Bankruptcy Judge **John S. Dalis** . . . . (912) 280-1376

(continued on next page)

United States Bankruptcy Court for the Southern District of Georgia *continued*

Court Staff
Bankruptcy Clerk **Lucinda B. Rauback** . . . .(912) 650-4105
  E-mail: lucinda_rauback@gas.uscourts.gov

U.S. Attorney
Georgia - Southern District
22 Barnard Street, Suite 300, Savannah, GA 31401
P.O. Box 8970, Savannah, GA 31412
Tel: (912) 652-4422 Fax: (912) 652-4388

U.S. Attorney **Edward J. Tarver** . . . . (912) 652-4422
  E-mail: edward.tarver@usdoj.gov

Federal Public Defender
Note: There is no federal public defender for the Southern District of
Georgia. Inquiries should be directed to the Federal Public Defender for
the Northern District of Georgia at (404) 688-7530.

United States District Court for the District of Hawaii
U.S. Courthouse, 300 Ala Moana Boulevard, Honolulu, HI 96850
Tel: (808) 541-1300 Fax: (808) 541-1303
Internet: www.hid.uscourts.gov

Number of Judgeships: 4

Circuit: Ninth

Judges
Chief Judge **Susan Oki Mollway** . . . . (808) 541-1720
  Began Service: June 23, 1998
  Appointed By: President William J. Clinton
  U.S. Courthouse, 300 Ala Moana Boulevard,
  Room C409, Honolulu, HI 96850-0409
  E-mail: susan_mollway@hid.uscourts.gov
District Judge **J. Michael Seabright** Room C-435 . . . . (808) 541-1804
  Began Service: May 17, 2005
  Appointed By: President George W. Bush
District Judge **Leslie E. Kobayashi** C-423 . . . .(808) 541-1331
  Began Service: December 22, 2010
  Appointed By: President Barack Obama
  E-mail: leslie_kobayashi@hid.uscourts.gov
District Judge **Derrick Kahala Watson** . . . . (808) 541-1470
  Began Service: May 6, 2013
  Appointed By: President Barack Obama
Senior Judge **Helen Gillmor** . . . .(808) 541-3502
  Began Service: 1994
  Appointed By: President William J. Clinton
  E-mail: helen_gillmor@hid.uscourts.gov
Senior Judge **Alan C. Kay** C-415 . . . . (808) 541-1904
  Began Service: 1987
  Appointed By: President Ronald Reagan
  E-mail: alan_kay@hid.uscourts.gov
Senior Judge **David Alan Ezra** . . . . (210) 472-5870
  Note: Senior Judge Ezra is sitting by designation in
  the United States District Court for the Western
  District of Texas.
Magistrate Judge **Barry M. Kurren** . . . . (808) 541-1306
  Began Service: March 1992
  E-mail: Barry_Kurren@hid.uscourts.gov
Magistrate Judge **Kevin S. C. Chang** . . . .(808) 541-1308
  Began Service: December 2000
  E-mail: Kevin_Chang@hid.uscourts.gov
Magistrate Judge **Richard L. Puglisi** . . . . (808) 541-1900
  Began Service: 2011

United States District Court for the District of Hawaii *continued*

Court Staff
District Clerk **Sue Beitia** . . . . (808) 541-1300
  E-mail: sue_beitia@hid.uscourts.gov
Chief Probation Officer **Felix Mata** Room 2-300 . . . .(808) 541-1283
Chief Pretrial Services Officer **Carol M. Miyashiro**
  Room 7-222 . . . . (808) 541-3412

United States Bankruptcy Court for the District of Hawaii
1132 Bishop Street, Suite 250L, Honolulu, HI 96813
Tel: (808) 522-8100
Tel: (866) 222-8029 (Voice Case Information System VCIS)
Fax: (808) 522-8120
Internet: www.hib.uscourts.gov

Number of Judgeships: 1

Judges
Chief Bankruptcy Judge **Robert J. Faris** . . . .(808) 522-8111
  Began Service: February 14, 2002
  E-mail: Robert_Faris@hib.uscourts.gov
Bankruptcy Judge (recalled) **Lloyd King** . . . .(808) 522-8111
  Began Service: 2008

Court Staff
Clerk of Court **Michael B. Dowling** . . . . (808) 522-8115
  E-mail: michael_dowling@hib.uscourts.gov

U.S. Attorney
Hawaii District
300 Ala Moana Boulevard, Room 6-100, Honolulu, HI 96850
Tel: (808) 541-2850 Fax: (808) 541-2958

U.S. Attorney **Florence T. Nakakuni** . . . .(808) 541-2850
  E-mail: florence.nakakuni@usdoj.gov

Federal Public Defender
Office of the Federal Public Defender
Prince Kuhio Federal Building, 300 Ala Moana Boulevard,
Suite 7-104, Honolulu, HI 96850-0001
Tel: (808) 541-2521 Fax: (808) 541-3545

Federal Public Defender **Peter C. Wolff, Jr.** . . . . (808) 541-2521
  E-mail: peter.wolff@fd.org

United States District Court for the District of Idaho
James A. McClure Federal Building & U.S. Courthouse, 550 West Fort
Street, Room 400, Boise, ID 83724
Tel: (208) 334-1361 Tel: (866) 496-1250 (Toll Free)
Fax: (208) 334-9362
Internet: www.id.uscourts.gov

Number of Judgeships: 2

Number of Vacancies: 1

Circuit: Ninth

Judges
Chief Judge **B. Lynn Winmill** 6th Floor . . . .(208) 334-9145
  Began Service: August 16, 1995
  Appointed By: President William J. Clinton

United States District Court for the District of Idaho *continued*

Chief Magistrate Judge **Candy W. Dale** . . . . (208) 334-9111
  Began Service: March 30, 2008
  Appointed By: President George W. Bush
  E-mail: candy_dale@id.uscourts.gov
Magistrate Judge **Ronald E. Bush** . . . . (208) 334-9150
  Began Service: September 2008
  E-mail: ronald_bush@id.uscourts.gov
Magistrate Judge **Mikel H. Williams** . . . . (208) 334-9330
  Began Service: 1984
  E-mail: mikel_williams@id.uscourts.gov
Magistrate Judge **Larry M. Boyle** Room 518 . . . . (208) 334-9010
  Began Service: 1992
  E-mail: larry_boyle@id.uscourts.gov
Senior Judge **Edward J. Lodge** . . . . (208) 334-9270
  Began Service: 1989
  Appointed By: President George H.W. Bush
  E-mail: edward_lodge@id.uscourts.gov

Court Staff

Clerk of Court **Elizabeth A. "Libby" Smith** . . . . (208) 334-1361
Chief Probation Officer **Jeffrey S. Thomason** . . . . (208) 334-1630
  E-mail: jeffrey_thomason@idp.uscourts.gov

United States Bankruptcy Court for the District of Idaho

James A. McClure Federal Building & U.S. Courthouse, 550 West Fort
Street, Boise, ID 83724
Tel: (208) 334-1074
Tel: (208) 334-9386 (Voice Case Information System VCIS)
Fax: (208) 334-9362
Internet: www.id.uscourts.gov

Number of Judgeships: 2

Judges

Chief Bankruptcy Judge **Terry L. Myers** . . . . (208) 334-9341
  Began Service: August 1, 1998
  E-mail: Terry_Myers@id.uscourts.gov
Bankruptcy Judge **Jim D. Pappas** . . . . (208) 334-9571
  Began Service: 2010
  E-mail: jim_pappas@id.uscourts.gov

Court Staff

Clerk of Court **Elizabeth A. "Libby" Smith** . . . . (208) 334-1361

U.S. Attorney

Idaho District
Washington Group Plaza IV, 800 E. Park Boulevard, Suite 600,
Boise, ID 83712-7788
Tel: (208) 334-1211 Fax: (208) 334-9375

U.S. Attorney **Wendy J. Olson** . . . . (208) 334-1211 (Boise)
  E-mail: wendy.olson@usdoj.gov

Federal Public Defender

Federal Defender Services of Idaho, Inc.
702 West Idaho, Suite 1000, Boise, ID 83702
757 North Seventh Avenue, Pocatello, ID 83201
Tel: (208) 331-5500 Tel: (208) 478-2046 (Pocatello)
Fax: (208) 331-5525 Fax: (208) 478-6698 (Pocatello)

Federal Public Defender **Samuel Richard Rubin** . . . . (208) 331-5500

United States District Court for the Central District of Illinois

U.S. Courthouse, 600 East Monroe Street, Room 151,
Springfield, IL 62701
Tel: (217) 492-4020 Tel: (217) 492-4997 (PACER)
Fax: (217) 492-4028
Internet: www.ilcd.uscourts.gov

Number of Judgeships: 4

Circuit: Seventh

Areas Covered: Counties of Adams, Brown, Bureau, Cass, Champaign,
Christian, Coles, De Witt, Douglas, Edgar, Ford, Fulton, Greene, Hancock,
Henderson, Henry, Iroquois, Kankakee, Knox, Livingston, Logan, Macon,
Macoupin, Marshall, Mason, McDonough, McLean, Menard, Mercer,
Montgomery, Morgan, Moultrie, Peoria, Piatt, Pike, Putnam, Rock Island,
Sangamon, Schuyler, Scott, Shelby, Stark, Tazewell, Vermilion, Warren
and Woodford

Judges

Chief District Judge **James E. Shadid** . . . . (309) 671-4227
  Began Service: March 11, 2011
  Appointed By: President Barack Obama
  E-mail: james_shadid@ilcd.uscourts.gov
District Judge **Sue E. Myerscough** Room 319 . . . . (217) 492-4000
  Began Service: March 14, 2011
  Appointed By: President Barack Obama
District Judge **Sara Lynn Darrow** . . . . (309) 793-5779
  Began Service: August 11, 2011
  Appointed By: President Barack Obama
  E-mail: sara_darrow@ilcd.uscourts.gov
District Judge **Colin Stirling Bruce** . . . . (217) 974-7510
  Began Service: 2013
  Appointed By: President Barack Obama
  201 South Vine Street, Suite 318,
  Urbana, IL 61802-3348
Senior Judge **Joe Billy McDade** . . . . (309) 671-7821
  Began Service: December 13, 1991
  Appointed By: President George H.W. Bush
Senior Judge **Michael M. Mihm** . . . . (309) 671-7113
  Began Service: August 22, 1982
  Appointed By: President Ronald Reagan
  Federal Building, 100 NE Monroe Street,
  Room 112, Peoria, IL 61602
  E-mail: michael_mihm@ilcd.uscourts.gov
Senior Judge **Harold Albert Baker** . . . . (217) 373-5835
  Began Service: 1978
  Appointed By: President Jimmy Carter
  201 South Vine Street, Room 338,
  Urbana, IL 61802-3348
  E-mail: harold_baker@ilcd.uscourts.gov
Senior Judge **Richard Mills** . . . . (217) 492-4340
  Began Service: August 27, 1985
  Appointed By: President Ronald Reagan
  U.S. Courthouse, 600 East Monroe Street,
  Room 117, Springfield, IL 62701-1659
  E-mail: Judge_Mills@ilcd.uscourts.gov
Magistrate Judge **David G. Bernthal** . . . . (217) 373-5839
  Began Service: May 1, 1995
  E-mail: david_bernthal@ilcd.uscourts.gov
Magistrate Judge **Jonathan E. Hawley** . . . . (309) 671-7140
  100 NE Monroe Street, Room 211,
  Peoria, IL 61602
Magistrate Judge **Thomas Schanzle-Haskins** Room
  124 . . . . (217) 492-4396
Magistrate Judge **Eric I. Long** . . . . (217) 373-5839
  Began Service: 2015

Court Staff

Clerk of the Court **Kenneth A. Wells** . . . . (217) 492-4707
  E-mail: ken_wells@ilcd.uscourts.gov
Chief Probation Officer **Douglas Heuermann** . . . . (309) 671-7031

United States Bankruptcy Court for the Central District of Illinois

226 U.S. Courthouse, 600 East Monroe Street, Springfield, IL 62701
Tel: (217) 492-4551 Tel: (217) 492-4260 (PACER)
Tel: (217) 492-4550 (Voice Case Information System VCIS)
Tel: (800) 827-9005 (Toll Free Voice Case Information System VCIS)
Fax: (217) 492-4556
Internet: www.ilcb.uscourts.gov

Number of Judgeships: 5

Number of Vacancies: 2

Judges

Chief Bankruptcy Judge **Mary P. Gorman** . . . .(217) 492-4567
  Began Service: 2006
Bankruptcy Judge **Thomas L. Perkins** . . . . (309) 671-7075
  Began Service: July 2000
  E-mail: thomas_perkins@ilcb.uscourts.gov
Bankruptcy Judge (recalled) **William V. Altenberger** . . . . (309) 671-7290
  Began Service: June 20, 2000

Court Staff

Clerk of Court **Khadijia Thomas** . . . .(217) 492-4551

U.S. Attorney

Illinois - Central District
318 South Sixth Street, Springfield, IL 62701-1806
Tel: (217) 492-4450 Fax: (217) 492-4512

U.S. Attorney **James A. "Jim" Lewis** . . . . (217) 492-4450
  E-mail: jim.lewis2@usdoj.gov

Federal Public Defender

Federal Public Defender for the Central District of Illinois
401 Main Street, Suite 1500, Peoria, IL 61602
600 East Adams Street, Second Floor, Springfield, IL 62701
300 West Main Street, Urbana, IL 61802
Tel: (309) 671-7891 (Peoria) Tel: (217) 592-5070 (Springfield)
Tel: (217) 373-0666 (Urbana) Fax: (309) 671-7898 (Peoria)
Fax: (217) 492-5077 (Springfield) Fax: (217) 373-0667 (Urbana)

Federal Public Defender **Thomas W. Patton** . . . . (309) 671-7891

United States District Court for the Northern District of Illinois

Everett McKinley Dirksen U.S. Courthouse, 219 South Dearborn Street, Chicago, IL 60604
Tel: (312) 435-5670 Tel: (312) 408-7777 (PACER)
Fax: (312) 554-8512 Fax: (312) 554-8674
Internet: www.ilnd.uscourts.gov

Number of Judgeships: 22

Circuit: Seventh

Areas Covered: Counties of Boone, Carroll, Cook, DeKalb, DuPage, Grundy, Jo Daviess, Kane, Kendall, La Salle, Lake, Lee, McHenry, Ogle, Stephenson, Whiteside, Will and Winnebago

Judges

Chief Judge **Ruben Castillo** Room 2548 . . . . (312) 435-5600
  Began Service: May 9, 1994
  Appointed By: President William J. Clinton
  E-mail: ruben_castillo@ilnd.uscourts.gov
District Judge **Charles Ronald Norgle, Sr.** Room 2346 . . . (312) 435-5634
  Began Service: October 1984
  Appointed By: President Ronald Reagan
  E-mail: charles_norgle@ilnd.uscourts.gov

United States District Court for the Northern District of Illinois *continued*

District Judge **James B. Zagel** Room 2588 . . . .(312) 435-5713
  Began Service: 1987
  Appointed By: President Ronald Reagan
  E-mail: james_zagel@ilnd.uscourts.gov
District Judge **Rebecca R. Pallmeyer** . . . . (312) 435-5636
  Began Service: October 21, 1998
  Appointed By: President William J. Clinton
  Everett McKinley Dirksen U.S. Courthouse,
  219 South Dearborn Street, Room 2146,
  Chicago, IL 60604-1702
  E-mail: rebecca_pallmeyer@ilnd.uscourts.gov
District Judge **Matthew F. Kennelly** Suite 2188 . . . .(312) 435-5618
  Began Service: June 22, 1999
  Appointed By: President William J. Clinton
  E-mail: matthew_kennelly@ilnd.uscourts.gov
District Judge **Ronald A. Guzman** Room 1278 . . . .(312) 435-5363
  Began Service: November 16, 1999
  Appointed By: President William J. Clinton
  E-mail: ronald_guzman@ilnd.uscourts.gov
District Judge **John W. Darrah** Room 1288 . . . .(312) 435-5619
  Began Service: September 1, 2000
  Appointed By: President William J. Clinton
District Judge **Amy J. St. Eve** Room 1260 . . . . (312) 435-5686
  Began Service: August 30, 2002
  Appointed By: President George W. Bush
  E-mail: amy_st_eve@ilnd.uscourts.gov
District Judge **Samuel Der-Yeghiayan** Room 1988 . . . .(312) 435-5675
  Began Service: August 4, 2003
  Appointed By: President George W. Bush
  E-mail: samuel_der-yeghiayan@ilnd.uscourts.gov
District Judge **Virginia M. Kendall** Room 2378 . . . .(312) 435-5692
  Began Service: December 30, 2005
  Appointed By: President George W. Bush
  E-mail: virginia_kendall@ilnd.uscourts.gov
District Judge **Frederick J. Kapala** . . . . (815) 987-4357
  Began Service: May 10, 2007
  Appointed By: President George W. Bush
  327 South Church Street, Room 6300,
  Rockford, IL 61101
  E-mail: frederick_kapala@ilnd.uscourts.gov
District Judge **Robert M. "Bob" Dow, Jr.** Room 1919 . . . (312) 435-5668
  Began Service: December 5, 2007
  Appointed By: President George W. Bush
  E-mail: robert_dow@ilnd.uscourts.gov
District Judge **Gary Feinerman** Room 2156 . . . . (312) 435-5627
  Began Service: September 13, 2010
  Appointed By: President Barack Obama
  E-mail: gary_feinerman@ilnd.uscourts.gov
District Judge **Sharon Johnson Coleman** Room 1460 . . . (312) 435-6885
  Began Service: September 7, 2010
  Appointed By: President Barack Obama
District Judge **Edmond E-Min Chang** Room 2178 . . . .(312) 435-5795
  Began Service: December 20, 2010
  Appointed By: President Barack Obama
  E-mail: edmond_chang@ilnd.uscourts.gov
District Judge **John Z. Lee** Room 1262 . . . .(312) 435-5670
  Began Service: 2012
  Appointed By: President Barack Obama
  E-mail: john_lee@ilnd.uscourts.gov
District Judge **John J. "Jay" Tharp, Jr.** Room 1478 . . . . . (312) 435-5861
  Began Service: June 26, 2012
  Appointed By: President Barack Obama
  E-mail: john_tharp@ilnd.uscourts.gov
District Judge **Thomas M. Durkin** Room 1764 . . . .(312) 435-5840
  Began Service: January 14, 2013
  Appointed By: President Barack Obama
  E-mail: thomas_durkin@ilnd.uscourts.gov
District Judge **Sara Lee Ellis** . . . . (312) 435-5560
  Began Service: 2013
  Appointed By: President Barack Obama
  E-mail: sara_ellis@ilnd.uscourts.gov
District Judge **Andrea Robin Wood** Room 1764 . . . . (312) 435-5582
  Began Service: 2013
  Appointed By: President Barack Obama
  E-mail: andrea_wood@ilnd.uscourts.gov

United States District Court for the Northern District of Illinois *continued*

District Judge **Manish S. Shah** Room 1778 . . . . (312) 435-5649
Began Service: May 1, 2014
Appointed By: President Barack Obama
E-mail: manish_shah@ilnd.uscourts.gov

District Judge **Jorge Luis Alonso** Room 1756 . . . . (312) 435-6044
Began Service: December 19, 2014
Appointed By: President Barack Obama

District Judge **John Robert Blakey** Room 1046 . . . . (312) 435-6058
Began Service: December 19, 2014
Appointed By: President Barack Obama

Senior Judge **Elaine E. Bucklo** Room 1446 . . . . (312) 435-7611
Began Service: October 11, 1994
Appointed By: President William J. Clinton
E-mail: elaine_bucklo@ilnd.uscourts.gov

Senior Judge **Robert W. Gettleman** Room 1788 . . . . (312) 435-5543
Began Service: October 11, 1994
Appointed By: President William J. Clinton
E-mail: robert_gettleman@ilnd.uscourts.gov

Senior Judge **Marvin E. Aspen** Room 2578 . . . .(312) 435-5696
Began Service: July 24, 1979
Appointed By: President Jimmy Carter
E-mail: marvin_aspen@ilnd.uscourts.gov

Senior Judge **Milton I. Shadur** Room 2388 . . . . (312) 435-5766
Began Service: June 1980
Appointed By: President Jimmy Carter
E-mail: milton_shadur@ilnd.uscourts.gov

Senior Judge **William T. Hart** Room 2502 . . . . (312) 435-5776
Began Service: May 1, 1982
Appointed By: President Ronald Reagan
E-mail: william_hart@ilnd.uscourts.gov

Senior Judge **Harry D. Leinenweber** Room 1946 . . . . (312) 435-7612
Began Service: January 17, 1986
Appointed By: President Ronald Reagan
E-mail: harry_leinenweber@ilnd.uscourts.gov

Senior Judge **Charles P. Kocoras** Room 2560 . . . . (312) 435-6872
Began Service: November 24, 1980
Appointed By: President Jimmy Carter
E-mail: charles_kocoras@ilnd.uscourts.gov

Senior Judge **Philip G. Reinhard** . . . .(815) 987-4480
Began Service: February 12, 1992
Appointed By: President George H.W. Bush
E-mail: philip_reinhard@ilnd.uscourts.gov

Senior Judge **Joan B. Gottschall** Suite 2356 . . . .(312) 435-5640
Began Service: September 3, 1996
Appointed By: President William J. Clinton
E-mail: joan_gottschall@ilnd.uscourts.gov

Senior Judge **Joan Humphrey Lefkow** . . . .(312) 435-5832
Began Service: September 1, 2000
Appointed By: President William J. Clinton
Everett McKinley Dirksen U.S. Courthouse,
219 South Dearborn Street, Room 1956,
Chicago, IL 60604-1952
E-mail: joan_lefkow@ilnd.uscourts.gov

Senior Judge **George M. Marovich** Room 1874 . . . . (312) 435-5590
Began Service: 1988
Appointed By: President Ronald Reagan
E-mail: george_marovich@ilnd.uscourts.gov

Presiding Magistrate Judge **Geraldine Soat Brown**
Suite 1822 . . . .(312) 435-5612
Began Service: June 19, 2000

Magistrate Judge **Sidney I. Schenkier** . . . . (312) 435-5609
Began Service: October 30, 1998
Everett McKinley Dirksen U.S. Courthouse,
219 South Dearborn Street, Room 1846,
Chicago, IL 60604-1976
E-mail: sidney_schenkier@ilnd.uscourts.gov

Magistrate Judge **Michael T. Mason** Room 2270 . . . . (312) 435-5610
Began Service: September 29, 2001

Magistrate Judge **Jeffrey Cole** Room 1088 . . . .(312) 435-5601
Began Service: May 6, 2005
E-mail: jeffrey_cole@ilnd.uscourts.gov

Magistrate Judge **Maria G. Valdez** . . . .(312) 435-5690
Began Service: 2005
Everett McKinley Dirksen U.S. Courthouse,
219 South Dearborn Street, Room 1058,
Chicago, IL 60604-1702
E-mail: maria_valdez@ilnd.uscourts.gov

United States District Court for the Northern District of Illinois *continued*

Magistrate Judge **Susan E. Cox** Chamber 1068 . . . .(312) 435-5615
Began Service: August 27, 2007

Magistrate Judge **Sheila M. Finnegan** Room 2206 . . . .(312) 435-5657
Began Service: 2010
E-mail: sheila_finnegan@ilnd.uscourts.gov

Magistrate Judge **Young B. Kim** Room 1000 . . . . (312) 408-5168
Began Service: May 7, 2010

Magistrate Judge **Jeffrey T. Gilbert** Room 1366 . . . . (312) 435-5672
Began Service: May 7, 2010
E-mail: jeffrey_gilbert@ilnd.uscourts.gov

Magistrate Judge **Daniel G. Martin** . . . . (312) 435-5354

Magistrate Judge **Mary M. Rowland** . . . .(312) 435-5358

Magistrate Judge **Iain D. Johnston** . . . . (815) 987-4255

Court Staff

Clerk **Thomas G. Bruton** . . . .(312) 435-6860
E-mail: thomas_bruton@ilnd.uscourts.gov

Chief Pretrial Services Officer **Ann Marie Carey** . . . . (312) 435-5793

Chief Probation Officer **Kristine Phillips** . . . . (312) 435-5700

United States Bankruptcy Court for the Northern District of Illinois

Everett McKinley Dirksen U.S. Courthouse, 219 South Dearborn Street, Chicago, IL 60604-1702
U.S. Bankruptcy Court, 327 South Church Street, Rockford, IL 61101
Tel: (312) 408-5101 (Chicago PACER)
Tel: (866) 222-8029 (Chicago and Rockford McVCIS)
Tel: (312) 408-5000 (Customer Service)
Tel: (815) 987-4489 (Rockford PACER)
Tel: (888) 541-1078 (Toll Free PACER for Chicago)
Tel: (888) 293-3701 (Toll Free PACER for Rockford)
Internet: www.ilnb.uscourts.gov

Number of Judgeships: 11

Judges

Chief Bankruptcy Judge **Bruce W. Black** . . . . (312) 435-6867
Began Service: August 13, 2001
Everett McKinley Dirksen U.S. Courthouse,
219 South Dearborn Street, Room 756,
Chicago, IL 60604
E-mail: bruce_black@ilnb.uscourts.gov

Bankruptcy Judge **Eugene R. Wedoff** . . . . (312) 435-5644
Began Service: September 16, 1987
Everett McKinley Dirksen U.S. Courthouse,
219 South Dearborn Street, Room 748,
Chicago, IL 60604
E-mail: eugene_wedoff@ilnb.uscourts.gov

Bankruptcy Judge **Jack B. Schmetterer** . . . . (312) 435-5654
Began Service: May 9, 1985
Everett McKinley Dirksen U.S. Courthouse,
219 South Dearborn Street, Room 600,
Chicago, IL 60604
E-mail: jack_schmetterer@ilnb.uscourts.gov

Bankruptcy Judge **Carol A. Doyle** . . . . (312) 435-6010
Began Service: July 26, 1999
Everett McKinley Dirksen U.S. Courthouse,
219 South Dearborn Street, Room 738,
Chicago, IL 60604
E-mail: carol_doyle@ilnb.uscourts.gov

Bankruptcy Judge **Pamela S. Hollis** . . . . (312) 435-5534
Began Service: January 27, 2003
Everett McKinley Dirksen U.S. Courthouse,
219 South Dearborn Street, Chambers 648,
Chicago, IL 60604
E-mail: pamela_hollis@ilnb.uscourts.gov

Bankruptcy Judge **A. Benjamin Goldgar** Room 638 . . . . . (312) 435-5642
Began Service: February 3, 2003
E-mail: ABenjamin_Goldgar@ilnb.uscourts.gov

Bankruptcy Judge **Jacqueline P. Cox** Chambers 676 . . . . . .(312) 435-5679
Began Service: February 3, 2003
E-mail: Jacqueline_Cox@ilnb.uscourts.gov

(continued on next page)

United States Bankruptcy Court for the Northern District of Illinois *continued*

Bankruptcy Judge **Donald R. Cassling** . . . . (312) 435-6056
  Began Service: 2012
  Everett McKinley Dirksen U.S. Courthouse,
  219 South Dearborn Street, Room 656,
  Chicago, IL 60604
  E-mail: donald_cassling@ilnb.uscourts.gov

Bankruptcy Judge **Janet S. Baer** . . . .(312) 435-6054
  Began Service: 2012
  Everett McKinley Dirksen U.S. Courthouse,
  219 South Dearborn Street, Room 662,
  Chicago, IL 60604

Bankruptcy Judge **Timothy A. Barnes** . . . . (312) 435-5646
  Began Service: 2012
  Everett McKinley Dirksen U.S. Courthouse,
  219 South Dearborn Street, Room 668,
  Chicago, IL 60604

Bankruptcy Judge **Thomas M. Lynch** . . . . (815) 987-4366

Court Staff

Clerk of Court **Jeffrey P. Allsteadt** . . . . (312) 435-6036
  E-mail: jeffrey_allsteadt@ilnb.uscourts.gov

U.S. Attorney

Illinois - Northern District
Dirksen Federal Building, 219 South Dearborn Street, 5th Floor,
Chicago, IL 60604
Tel: (312) 353-5300 Fax: (312) 353-2067

U.S. Attorney **Zachary Thomas Fardon** . . . .(312) 353-5300
  E-mail: zachary.fardon@usdoj.gov

Federal Public Defender

Illinois Federal Defender Program, Inc.
55 East Monroe Street, Suite 2800, Chicago, IL 60603
202 West State Street, Suite 600, Rockford, IL 61101
Tel: (312) 621-8300 (Chicago) Tel: (815) 961-0800 (Rockford)
Fax: (312) 621-8399 (Chicago) Fax: (815) 961-0813 (Rockford)

Executive Director **Carol A. Brook** . . . . (312) 621-8300
  E-mail: carol.brook@fd.org

United States District Court for the Southern District of Illinois

Melvin Price Federal Courthouse, 750 Missouri Avenue,
East St. Louis, IL 62201
Benton Federal Building and U.S. Courthouse, 301 West Main Street,
Benton, IL 62812 (Divisional Office)
Tel: (618) 482-9371 Tel: (618) 439-7760 (Benton)
Tel: (866) 867-3169 (CM/ECF East St. Louis)
Tel: (866) 222-2104 (CM/ECF Benton)
Tel: (800) 676-6856 (PACER) Fax: (618) 482-9383
Internet: www.ilsd.uscourts.gov

Number of Judgeships: 4

Circuit: Seventh

Areas Covered: Counties of Alexander, Bond, Calhoun, Clark, Clay,
Clinton, Crawford, Cumberland, Edwards, Effingham, Fayette, Franklin,
Gallatin, Hamilton, Hardin, Jackson, Jasper, Jefferson, Jersey, Johnson,
Lawrence, Madison, Marion, Massac, Monroe, Perry, Pope, Pulaski,
Randolph, Richland, Saline, Saint Clair, Union, Wabash, Washington,
Wayne, White and Williamson

Judges

Chief Judge **Michael J. Reagan** Room 220 . . . .(618) 482-9225
  Began Service: October 23, 2000
  Appointed By: President William J. Clinton

United States District Court for the Southern District of Illinois *continued*

District Judge **David R. Herndon** . . . .(618) 482-9077
  Began Service: November 16, 1998
  Appointed By: President William J. Clinton
  E-mail: judge_herndon@ilsd.uscourts.gov

District Judge **Nancy J. Rosenstengel** . . . . (618) 482-9172
  Began Service: May 19, 2014
  Appointed By: President Barack Obama
  E-mail: nancy_rosenstengel@ilsd.uscourts.gov

District Judge **Staci Michelle Yandle** . . . . (618) 439-7740
  Began Service: June 19, 2014
  Appointed By: President Barack Obama

Magistrate Judge **Philip M. Frazier** . . . . (618) 439-7750
  Began Service: 1987

Magistrate Judge **Donald G. Wilkerson** . . . . (618) 482-9380
  Began Service: January 4, 2005

Magistrate Judge **Stephen C. Williams** . . . .(618) 482-9467
  Began Service: 2011

Magistrate Judge **Clifford J. Proud** . . . . (618) 482-9006
  Began Service: February 28, 1994

Senior Judge **J. Phil Gilbert** . . . .(618) 439-7720
  Began Service: October 1, 1992
  Appointed By: President George H.W. Bush

Court Staff

Clerk of Court (Acting) **Justine Flanagan** . . . . (618) 482-9172
  E-mail: justine_flanagan@ilsd.uscourts.gov

Chief Probation Officer **John M. Koechner** . . . . (618) 439-4828

United States Bankruptcy Court for the Southern District of Illinois

Melvin Price Federal Courthouse, 750 Missouri Avenue,
East St. Louis, IL 62201
Tel: (618) 482-9400 Tel: (618) 482-9114 (PACER)
Tel: (618) 482-9365 (Voice Case Information System VCIS)
Tel: (800) 726-5622 (Toll Free Voice Case Information System VCIS)
Tel: (618) 425-2200 (Benton Divisional Office)
Internet: www.ilsb.uscourts.gov

Number of Judgeships: 1

Judges

Bankruptcy Judge **Laura K. Grandy** . . . . (618) 482-9401
  Began Service: 2010
  E-mail: laura_grandy@ilsb.uscourts.gov

Bankruptcy Judge (visiting) **William V. Altenberger** . . . . .(309) 671-7290
  Began Service: May 2000

Court Staff

Bankruptcy Clerk **Donna N. Beyersdorfer** . . . .(618) 482-9427
  E-mail: donna_beyersdorfer@ilsb.uscourts.gov

U.S. Attorney

Illinois - Southern District
Nine Executive Drive, Fairview Heights, IL 62208
Tel: (618) 628-3700 Fax: (618) 628-3730

U.S. Attorney **Stephen R. Wigginton** . . . . (618) 628-3700
  E-mail: stephen.wigginton@usdoj.gov

United States Bankruptcy Court for the Southern District of Illinois
continued

Federal Public Defender

Office of the Federal Public Defender for the Southern District of Illinois
650 Missouri Avenue, Suite G10A, East St. Louis, IL 62201
401 West Main Street, Benton, IL 62812
Tel: (618) 482-9050 (East St. Louis) Tel: (618) 435-2552 (Benton)
Fax: (618) 482-9057 (East St. Louis) Fax: (618) 435-2447 (Benton)

Federal Public Defender **Phillip J. Kavanaugh** . . . .(618) 482-9050
    E-mail: phillip.kavanaugh@fd.org

United States District Court for the Northern District of Indiana

Robert A. Grant U.S. Courthouse, 204 South Main Street,
Room 102, South Bend, IN 46601-2119
Tel: (574) 246-8000 Tel: (800) 371-8843 (Toll Free PACER)
Fax: (574) 246-8002
Internet: www.innd.uscourts.gov

Number of Judgeships: 5

Circuit: Seventh

Judges

Chief Judge **Philip P. Simon** . . . . (219) 852-6740
    Began Service: March 31, 2003
    Appointed By: President George W. Bush
    5400 Federal Plaza, Suite 4400,
    Hammond, IN 46320-1840
    E-mail: simon_chambers@innd.uscourts.gov
District Judge **Robert L. Miller, Jr.** . . . . (574) 246-8080
    Began Service: January 1986
    Appointed By: President Ronald Reagan
    Robert A. Grant U.S. Courthouse,
    204 South Main Street, Room 325,
    South Bend, IN 46601
    E-mail: robert_miller@innd.uscourts.gov
District Judge **Theresa L. Springmann** . . . . (260) 423-3050
    Began Service: June 24, 2003
    Appointed By: President George W. Bush
    E-mail: theresa_springmann@innd.uscourts.gov
District Judge **Joseph S. Van Bokkelen** . . . .(219) 852-6720
    Began Service: July 20, 2007
    Appointed By: President George W. Bush
    5400 Federal Plaza, Suite 4200,
    Hammond, IN 46320-1840
    E-mail: joseph_vanbokkelen@innd.uscourts.gov
District Judge **Jon E. DeGuilio** . . . . (574) 246-8170
    Began Service: May 20, 2010
    Appointed By: President Barack Obama
    Robert A. Grant U.S. Courthouse,
    204 South Main Street, Room 124,
    South Bend, IN 46601
    E-mail: jon_deguilio@innd.uscourts.gov
Senior Judge **William C. Lee** . . . . (260) 423-3030
    Began Service: August 19, 1981
    Appointed By: President Ronald Reagan
    E-mail: william_lee@innd.uscourts.gov
Senior Judge **James T. Moody** . . . . (219) 852-3460
    Began Service: February 24, 1982
    Appointed By: President Ronald Reagan
    5400 Federal Plaza, Suite 4100,
    Hammond, IN 46320
    E-mail: moody_chambers@innd.uscourts.gov
Senior Judge **Rudy Lozano** . . . . (219) 852-3600
    Began Service: March 1988
    Appointed By: President Ronald Reagan
    5400 Federal Plaza, Suite 4300,
    Hammond, IN 46320
    E-mail: rudy_lozano@innd.uscourts.gov

United States District Court for the Northern District of Indiana
continued

Magistrate Judge **Christopher A. Nuechterlein** . . . .(574) 246-8100
    Began Service: January 10, 2000
    Robert A. Grant U.S. Courthouse,
    204 South Main Street, Room 201,
    South Bend, IN 46601
Magistrate Judge **Paul R. Cherry** . . . . (219) 852-6700
    Began Service: October 1, 2003
    5400 Federal Plaza, Suite 3500,
    Hammond, IN 46320-1840
    E-mail: cherry_chambers@innd.uscourts.gov
Magistrate Judge **John E. Martin** . . . . (219) 852-6610
    5400 Federal Plaza, Suite 3700,
    Hammond, IN 46320-1840
    E-mail: john_martin@innd.uscourts.gov
Magistrate Judge **Susan L. Collins** . . . . (260) 423-3042
    1300 South Harrison Street, Suite 1130,
    Fort Wayne, IN 46802
Magistrate Judge **Andrew P. Rodovich** . . . . (219) 852-6600
    5400 Federal Plaza, Suite 3400,
    Hammond, IN 46320-1840

Court Staff

Clerk of Court **Robert N. Trgovich** . . . . (574) 246-8000
    E-mail: robert_trgovich@innd.uscourts.gov
Chief Probation Officer **Derek Plants** . . . . (219) 852-3620
    5400 Federal Plaza, Hammond, IN 46320-1840
    E-mail: derek_plants@innd.uscourts.gov

United States Bankruptcy Court for the Northern District of Indiana

Robert K. Rodibaugh U.S. Courthouse, 401 South Michigan Street,
South Bend, IN 46601
Tel: (574) 968-2100
Tel: (574) 968-2275 (Voice Case Information System VCIS)
Tel: (800) 755-8393 (Toll Free Voice Case Information System VCIS)
Fax: (574) 968-2231
Internet: www.innb.uscourts.gov

Number of Judgeships: 3

Judges

Chief Bankruptcy Judge **Robert E. Grant** . . . .(260) 426-2455
    Began Service: August 17, 1987
    E-mail: robert_grant@innb.uscourts.gov
Bankruptcy Judge **Harry C. Dees, Jr.** Room 234 . . . .(574) 968-2280
    Began Service: October 1, 1986
Bankruptcy Judge **J. Philip Klingeberger** . . . .(219) 852-3575
    Began Service: June 16, 2003
    5400 Federal Plaza, Suite 3800,
    Hammond, IN 46320-1840
Bankruptcy Judge (recalled) **Kent Lindquist** . . . .(219) 852-3550
    Began Service: May 1985
    5400 Federal Plaza, Suite 3600,
    Hammond, IN 46320-1859
    E-mail: kent_lindquist@innb.uscourts.gov

Court Staff

Clerk of the Court **Christopher M. DeToro** . . . . (574) 968-2100
    E-mail: christopher_detoro@innb.uscourts.gov

U.S. Attorney

Illinois - Northern District
Dirksen Federal Building, 219 South Dearborn Street, 5th Floor,
Chicago, IL 60604
Tel: (312) 353-5300 Fax: (312) 353-2067

U.S. Attorney **Zachary Thomas Fardon** . . . .(312) 353-5300
    E-mail: zachary.fardon@usdoj.gov

(continued on next page)

United States Bankruptcy Court for the Northern District of Indiana
continued

Federal Public Defender

Northern District of Indiana Federal Community Defenders, Inc.
31 East Sibley Street, Hammond, IN 46320
1300 South Harrison Street, Fort Wayne, IN 45802
227 South Main Street, Suite 100, South Bend, IN 46601
Tel: (219) 937-8020 (Hammond) Tel: (260) 422-9940 (Fort Wayne)
Tel: (574) 245-7393 (South Bend) Fax: (219) 937-8021 (Hammond)
Fax: (260) 422-9954 (Fort Wayne) Fax: (574) 245-7394 (South Bend)

Executive Director **Jerome T. "Jerry" Flynn** . . . . (219) 937-8020

United States District Court for the Southern District of Indiana

U.S. Courthouse, 46 East Ohio Street, Indianapolis, IN 46204
Tel: (317) 229-3700 Fax: (317) 229-3959
Internet: www.insd.uscourts.gov

Number of Judgeships: 5

Number of Vacancies: 1

Circuit: Seventh

Judges
Chief Judge **Richard L. Young** . . . . (812) 434-6444
  Began Service: March 25, 1998
  Appointed By: President William J. Clinton
  U.S. Courthouse,
  101 NW Martin Luther King Jr. Boulevard,
  Room 310, Evansville, IN 47708
  E-mail: rly@insd.uscourts.gov
District Judge **William T. Lawrence** Room 204 . . . . (317) 229-3610
  Began Service: June 26, 2008
  Appointed By: President George W. Bush
  E-mail: william_lawrence@insd.uscourts.gov
District Judge **Jane E. Magnus-Stinson** Room 304 . . . . . . (317) 229-3670
  Began Service: June 14, 2010
  Appointed By: President Barack Obama
District Judge **Tanya Walton Pratt** Room 524 . . . . (317) 229-3984
  Began Service: June 25, 2010
  Appointed By: President Barack Obama
  E-mail: tanya_pratt@insd.uscourts.gov
Senior Judge **Larry J. McKinney** Room 361 . . . . (317) 229-3650
  Began Service: 1987
  Appointed By: President Ronald Reagan
  E-mail: larry_mckinney@insd.uscourts.gov
Senior Judge **Sarah Evans Barker** Room 210 . . . . (317) 229-3600
  Began Service: March 30, 1984
  Appointed By: President Ronald Reagan
Magistrate Judge **William G. Hussmann, Jr.** . . . . (812) 434-6430
  Began Service: April 4, 1988
  101 NW Martin Luther King Boulevard, Room 328,
  Evansville, IN 47708-1951
Magistrate Judge **Tim A. Baker** Room 234 . . . . (317) 229-3660
  Began Service: October 1, 2001
  E-mail: mjbaker@insd.uscourts.gov
Magistrate Judge **Debra McVicker Lynch** Room 277 . . . . . (317) 229-3630
  Began Service: October 24, 2008
Magistrate Judge **Mark J. Dinsmore** Room 257 . . . . (317) 229-3901
  Began Service: December 17, 2010   Tel: (317) 229-3664
  E-mail: mark_dinsmore@insd.uscourts.gov
Magistrate Judge **Denise K. LaRue** Room 243 . . . . (317) 229-3930
  Began Service: May 24, 2011
  E-mail: denise_larue@insd.uscourts.gov
Magistrate Judge (Part-Time) **Craig M. McKee** . . . . (812) 232-4311
  Began Service: August 23, 2007

Court Staff
Clerk of Court **Laura A. Briggs** . . . . (317) 229-3700
  E-mail: laura_briggs@insd.uscourts.gov

United States District Court for the Southern District of Indiana
continued

Chief Probation Officer **Dwight T. Wharton** Room 101 . . . (317) 229-3750
  E-mail: dwight_wharton@insp.uscourts.gov

United States Bankruptcy Court for the Southern District of Indiana

U.S. Courthouse, 46 East Ohio Street, Room 116, Indianapolis, IN 46204
P.O. Box 44978, Indianapolis, IN 46244
Tel: (317) 229-3800
Tel: (317) 229-3888 (Voice Case Information System VCIS)
Fax: (317) 229-3801
Internet: www.insb.uscourts.gov

Number of Judgeships: 4

Judges
Chief Bankruptcy Judge **Robyn Lynn Moberley** . . . . (317) 229-3880
  Began Service: November 1, 2012
Bankruptcy Judge **Basil H. Lorch III** . . . . (812) 542-4570
  Began Service: April 14, 1992
  E-mail: basil_lorch@insb.uscourts.gov
Magistrate Judge **James M. Carr** . . . . (317) 229-3833
Bankruptcy Judge **Jeffrey J. Graham** . . . . (317) 229-3800

Court Staff
Clerk of Court **Kevin P. Dempsey** . . . . (317) 229-3800

U.S. Attorney
Indiana - Southern District
10 West Market Street, Suite 2100, Indianapolis, IN 46204
Tel: (317) 226-6333 Fax: (317) 226-6125 (Criminal)
Fax: (317) 226-5027 (Civil)

U.S. Attorney (Acting) **Joshua J. Minkler** . . . . (317) 226-6333

Federal Public Defender
Indiana Federal Community Defender, Inc.
111 Monument Circle, Suite 752, Indianapolis, IN 46204-5173
Tel: (317) 383-3520 Fax: (317) 383-3525

Executive Director **Monica Foster** . . . . (317) 383-3520
  E-mail: monica.foster@fd.org

United States District Court for the Northern District of Iowa

111 Seventh Avenue SE, Cedar Rapids, IA 52401-2101
Tel: (319) 286-2300 Fax: (319) 286-2301
Internet: www.iand.uscourts.gov

Number of Judgeships: 2

Number of Vacancies: 1

Circuit: Eighth

Areas Covered: Counties of Allamakee, Benton, Black Hawk, Bremer, Buchanan, Buena Vista, Butler, Calhoun, Carroll, Cedar, Cerro Gordo, Cherokee, Chickasaw, Clay, Clayton, Crawford, Delaware, Dickinson, Dubuque, Emmet, Fayette, Floyd, Franklin, Grundy, Hamilton, Hancock, Hardin, Howard, Humboldt, Ida, Iowa, Jackson, Jones, Kossuth, Linn, Lyon, Mitchell, Monona, O'Brien, Osceola, Palo Alto, Plymouth, Pocahontas, Sac, Sioux, Tama, Webster, Winnebago, Winneshiek, Woodbury, Worth and Wright

Judges

Chief District Judge **Linda R. Reade** . . . . (319) 286-2330
  Began Service: November 26, 2002
  Appointed By: President George W. Bush
  E-mail: Linda_Reade@iand.uscourts.gov
Senior Judge **Mark W. Bennett** . . . . (712) 233-3909
  Began Service: August 26, 1994
  Appointed By: President William J. Clinton
  E-mail: mark_bennett@iand.uscourts.gov
Senior Judge **Edward J. McManus** . . . . (319) 286-2350
  Began Service: 1962
  Appointed By: President John F. Kennedy
  E-mail: edward_mcmanus@iand.uscourts.gov
Chief Magistrate Judge **Jon S. Scoles** . . . . (319) 286-2340
  Began Service: 2012
  E-mail: jon_scoles@iand.uscourts.gov
Magistrate Judge **Leonard Terry "Len" Strand** . . . . (712) 233-3921
  Began Service: 2012
  320 Sixth Street, Room 104,
  Sioux City, IA 51102
  E-mail: leonard_strand@iand.uscourts.gov

Court Staff

Clerk of Court **Robert L. Phelps II** . . . . (319) 286-2300
  E-mail: robert_phelps@iand.uscourts.gov
Chief Probation Officer **John Zielke** . . . . (319) 286-2386

United States Bankruptcy Court for the Northern District of Iowa

111 Seventh Avenue SE, Box 15, Cedar Rapids, IA 52401-2101
P.O. Box 74890, Cedar Rapids, IA 52407-4890
Tel: (319) 286-2200 Tel: (800) 676-6856 (Toll Free PACER)
Tel: (866) 222-8029 (Toll Free Voice Case Information System VCIS)
Fax: (319) 286-2280
Internet: www.ianb.uscourts.gov

Number of Judgeships: 2

Judges

Chief Bankruptcy Judge **Thad J. Collins** . . . . (319) 286-2230
  Began Service: March 29, 2010
  E-mail: thad_collins@ianb.uscourts.gov

Court Staff

Bankruptcy Clerk **Jean Hekel** . . . . (319) 286-2200
  E-mail: jean_hekel@ianb.uscourts.gov

United States Bankruptcy Court for the Northern District of Iowa
continued

U.S. Attorney

Iowa - Northern District
111 7th Avenue SE, Box 1, Cedar Rapids, IA 52401
Tel: (319) 363-6333 TTY: (319) 286-9258 Fax: (319) 363-1990

U.S. Attorney **Kevin W. Techau** . . . . (319) 363-6333
  E-mail: kevin.techau@usdoj.gov

Federal Public Defender

Northern and Southern District of Iowa Federal Public Defender
400 Locust Street, Suite 340, Des Moines, IA 50309
320 Third Street SE, Cedar Rapids, IA 52401
101 West Second Street, Suite 401, Davenport, IA 52801
701 Pierce Street, Suite 400, Sioux City, IA 51101
Tel: (515) 309-9610 (Des Moines) Tel: (319) 363-9540 (Cedar Rapids)
Tel: (563) 322-8931 (Davenport) Tel: (712) 252-4158 (Sioux City)
Fax: (515) 309-9625 (Des Moines) Fax: (319) 363-9542 (Cedar Rapids)
Fax: (563) 383-0052 (Davenport) Fax: (712) 252-4194 (Sioux City)

Federal Public Defender **James F. "Jim" Whalen** . . . . (515) 309-9610

United States District Court for the Southern District of Iowa

U.S. Courthouse, 123 East Walnut Street, Des Moines, IA 50309
P.O. Box 9344, Des Moines, IA 50306-9344
Tel: (515) 284-6248
Internet: www.iasd.uscourts.gov

Number of Judgeships: 3

Number of Vacancies: 1

Circuit: Eighth

Areas Covered: Counties of Adair, Adams, Appanoose, Audubon, Boone, Cass, Clarke, Clinton, Dallas, Davis, Decatur, Des Moines, Fremont, Greene, Guthrie, Harrison, Henry, Jasper, Jefferson, Johnson, Keokuk, Lee, Louisa, Lucas, Madison, Mahaska, Marion, Marshall, Mills, Monroe, Montgomery, Muscatine, Page, Polk, Pottawattamie, Poweshiek, Ringgold, Scott, Shelby, Story, Taylor, Union, Van Buren, Wapello, Warren, Washington and Wayne

Judges

Chief Judge **John A. Jarvey** . . . . (563) 884-7727
  Began Service: March 2007
  Appointed By: President George W. Bush
  E-mail: john_jarvey@iasd.uscourts.gov
District Judge **Stephanie M. Rose** Room 420 . . . . (515) 284-6248
  Began Service: November 13, 2012
  Appointed By: President Barack Obama
  E-mail: stephanie_rose@iasd.uscourts.gov
Senior Judge **Harold D. Vietor** Room 485 . . . . (515) 284-6237
  Began Service: 1979
  Appointed By: President Jimmy Carter
  E-mail: harold_vietor@iasd.uscourts.gov
Senior Judge **Charles R. Wolle** . . . . (515) 284-6289
  Began Service: August 1987
  Appointed By: President Ronald Reagan
  110 East Court Avenue, Room 403,
  Des Moines, IA 50309
  E-mail: charles_wolle@iasd.uscourts.gov
Senior Judge **Ronald E. Longstaff** Room 115 . . . . (515) 284-6235
  Began Service: November 5, 1991
  Appointed By: President George H.W. Bush
  E-mail: ronald_longstaff@iasd.uscourts.gov
Senior Judge **Robert W. "Bob" Pratt** Room 221 . . . . (515) 284-6254
  Began Service: July 1, 1997
  Appointed By: President William J. Clinton
  E-mail: Robert_Pratt@iasd.uscourts.gov

(continued on next page)

United States District Court for the Southern District of Iowa *continued*

Senior Judge **James E. Gritzner** . . . . (515) 284-6291
  Began Service: February 19, 2002
  Appointed By: President George W. Bush
  E-mail: nancy_harris@iasd.uscourts.gov
Chief Magistrate Judge **Celeste F. Bremer** . . . . (515) 284-6200
  Began Service: January 1, 1990
  U.S. Courthouse, 123 East Walnut Street, Suite 435,
  Des Moines, IA 50309-2036
  E-mail: celeste_bremer@iasd.uscourts.gov
Magistrate Judge **Helen Adams** . . . . (515) 284-6217
  E-mail: helen_adams@iasd.uscourts.gov
Magistrate Judge **Ross A. Walters** Suite 440 . . . . (515) 284-6217
  Began Service: 1994
  E-mail: ross_a_walters@iasd.uscourts.gov
Magistrate Judge **Stephen B. Jackson, Jr.** . . . . (563) 884-7601
  Began Service: 2015

Court Staff

Clerk of Court **Marjorie E. Krahn** . . . . (515) 323-2865
  E-mail: Marge_Krahn@iasd.uscourts.gov
Chief Probation Officer **Michael J. Elbert** . . . . (515) 284-6207

United States Bankruptcy Court for the Southern District of Iowa

U.S. Courthouse Annex, 110 East Court Avenue, Suite 300,
Des Moines, IA 50309
Tel: (515) 284-6230 Tel: (800) 597-5917 (Toll Free PACER)
Tel: (866) 222-8029 (Toll Free Voice Case Information System VCIS)
Fax: (515) 284-6404
E-mail: bankruptcy_court@iasb.uscourts.gov
Internet: www.iasb.uscourts.gov

Number of Judgeships: 2

Judges

Chief Bankruptcy Judge **Anita L. Shodeen** Room 300 . . . . (515) 284-6118
  Began Service: August 26, 2009
  E-mail: anita_shodeen@iasb.uscourts.gov
Bankruptcy Judge **Lee M. Jackwig** . . . . (515) 284-6229
  Began Service: November 3, 1986
  U.S. Courthouse Annex, 110 East Court Avenue,
  Suite 443, Des Moines, IA 50309-2050
  E-mail: lee_jackwig@iasb.uscourts.gov

Court Staff

Clerk of the Court **Virginia L. Satterstrom** . . . . (515) 284-6230 ext. 2843
  E-mail: ginny_satterstrom@iasb.uscourts.gov

U.S. Attorney

Iowa - Southern District
U.S. Courthouse Annex, 110 East Court Avenue, Suite 286,
Des Moines, IA 50309-2053
Tel: (515) 473-9300 Fax: (515) 473-9298

U.S. Attorney **Nicholas A. Klinefeldt** . . . . (515) 473-9300

United States Bankruptcy Court for the Southern District of Iowa
continued

Federal Public Defender

Northern and Southern District of Iowa Federal Public Defender
400 Locust Street, Suite 340, Des Moines, IA 50309
320 Third Street SE, Cedar Rapids, IA 52401
101 West Second Street, Suite 401, Davenport, IA 52801
701 Pierce Street, Suite 400, Sioux City, IA 51101
Tel: (515) 309-9610 (Des Moines) Tel: (319) 363-9540 (Cedar Rapids)
Tel: (563) 322-8931 (Davenport) Tel: (712) 252-4158 (Sioux City)
Fax: (515) 309-9625 (Des Moines) Fax: (319) 363-9542 (Cedar Rapids)
Fax: (563) 383-0052 (Davenport) Fax: (712) 252-4194 (Sioux City)

Federal Public Defender **James F. "Jim" Whalen** . . . . (515) 309-9610

United States District Court for the District of Kansas

Robert J. Dole U.S. Courthouse, 500 State Avenue,
Kansas City, KS 66101
Tel: (913) 735-2200 Fax: (913) 735-2201
Internet: www.ksd.uscourts.gov

Number of Judgeships: 6

Number of Vacancies: 1

Circuit: Tenth

Judges

Chief Judge **J. Thomas "Tom" Marten** . . . . (316) 315-4300
  Began Service: January 5, 1996
  Appointed By: President William J. Clinton
  U.S. Courthouse, 401 North Market Street,
  Room 232, Wichita, KS 67202
  E-mail: judge_marten@ksd.uscourts.gov
District Judge **Carlos Murguia** Room 537 . . . . (913) 735-2340
  Began Service: September 23, 1999
  Appointed By: President William J. Clinton
District Judge **Julie A. Robinson** . . . . (913) 735-2360
  Began Service: December 14, 2001
  Appointed By: President George W. Bush
  500 State Avenue, Suite 511,
  Topeka, KS 66683-3502
District Judge **Eric F. Melgren** . . . . (316) 315-4320
  Began Service: October 9, 2008
  Appointed By: President George W. Bush
  401 North Market, Suite 414,
  Wichita, KS 67202
  E-mail: ksd_melgren_chambers@ksd.uscourts.gov
District Judge **Daniel D. Crabtree** . . . . (785) 338-5340
  Began Service: May 13, 2014
  Appointed By: President Barack Obama
Senior Judge **Sam A. Crow** . . . . (785) 338-5360
  Began Service: December 10, 1981
  Appointed By: President Ronald Reagan
  444 SE Quincy Street, Room 430,
  Topeka, KS 66683
Senior Judge **Monti L. Belot** . . . . (316) 315-4340
  Note: Judge Belot will retire effective September
  2015.
  Began Service: 1991
  Appointed By: President George H.W. Bush
  U.S. Courthouse, 401 North Market Street,
  Room 111, Wichita, KS 67202
Senior Judge **John Watson Lungstrum** Suite 517 . . . . (913) 735-2320
  Began Service: 1991
  Appointed By: President George H.W. Bush
  E-mail: ksd_lungstrum_chambers@ksd.uscourts.gov

United States District Court for the District of Kansas *continued*

Senior Judge **Kathryn Hoefer Vratil** . . . . (913) 735-2300
  Began Service: October 30, 1992
  Appointed By: President George H.W. Bush
  Robert J. Dole U.S. Courthouse,
  500 State Avenue, Suite 529,
  Kansas City, KS 66101-2435
  E-mail: ksd_vratil_chambers@ksd.uscourts.gov
Chief Magistrate Judge **James P. O'Hara** Suite 219 . . . . . . (913) 735-2280
  Began Service: April 17, 2000
  E-mail: ksd_ohara_chambers@ksd.uscourts.gov
Magistrate Judge **Karen M. Humphreys** . . . . (316) 315-4360
  Began Service: 1993
  U.S. Courthouse, 401 North Market Street,
  Suite 322, Wichita, KS 67202
  E-mail: ksd_humphreys_
  chambers@ksd.uscourts.gov
Magistrate Judge **Gerald L. Rushfelt** . . . . (913) 735-2270
  Began Service: September 9, 1985
  Robert J. Dole U.S. Courthouse,
  500 State Avenue, Suite 628,
  Kansas City, KS 66101-2428
  E-mail: KSD_Rushfelt_chambers@ksd.uscourts.gov
Magistrate Judge **K. Gary Sebelius** . . . . (785) 338-5480
  Began Service: February 21, 2003
  U.S. Courthouse, 444 SE Quincy Street, Suite 475,
  Topeka, KS 66683
  E-mail: ksd_sebelius_chambers@ksd.uscourts.gov
Magistrate Judge **Kenneth G. Gale** . . . . (316) 315-4380
  Began Service: August 2, 2010
  United States District Court,
  401 North Market Street, Suite 403,
  Wichita, KS 67202
Magistrate Judge **Teresa J. James** Suite 208 . . . . (913) 735-2260
  E-mail: ksd_james_chambers@ksd.uscourts.gov
Magistrate Judge **David J. Waxse** . . . . (913) 735-2290
  Began Service: October 4, 1999
  Robert J. Dole U.S. Courthouse,
  500 State Avenue, Suite 630,
  Kansas City, KS 66101-2428
  E-mail: ksd_waxse_chambers@ksd.uscourts.gov
Magistrate Judge (recalled) **Donald W. Bostwick** . . . . (316) 315-4270
  U.S. Courthouse, 401 North Market Street,
  Suite 403, Wichita, KS 67202

Court Staff
Clerk of Court **Timothy O'Brien** . . . . (913) 735-2200
Chief Probation Officer **Ronald G. Schweer** . . . . (913) 735-2424
  E-mail: ronald_schweer@ksd.uscourts.gov

United States Bankruptcy Court for the District of Kansas
167 U.S. Courthouse, 401 North Market Street, Wichita, KS 67202
Tel: (316) 315-4110
Tel: (316) 315-4101 (Voice Case Information System VCIS)
Tel: (800) 827-9028 (Toll Free Voice Case Information System VCIS)
Fax: (316) 315-4111
Internet: www.ksb.uscourts.gov

Number of Judgeships: 4

Judges
Chief Bankruptcy Judge **Robert E. Nugent** . . . . (316) 315-4150
  Began Service: June 14, 2000
  E-mail: Judge_Nugent@ksb.uscourts.gov
Bankruptcy Judge **Janice Miller Karlin** . . . . (785) 338-5950
  Began Service: October 17, 2002
  U.S. Courthouse, 444 SE Quincy Street, Suite 240,
  Topeka, KS 66683
Bankruptcy Judge **Dale L. Somers** . . . . (785) 338-5960
  Began Service: 2010
  444 SE Quincy Street, Room 225,
  Topeka, KS 66683

United States Bankruptcy Court for the District of Kansas *continued*

Bankruptcy Judge **Robert D. Berger** . . . . (913) 735-2150
  Began Service: 2003
  500 State Avenue, Room 161,
  Kansas City, KS 66101

Court Staff
Fax: (316) 315-4111

Clerk of Court **David D. Zimmerman** . . . . (316) 315-4180

U.S. Attorney
Kansas District
1200 Epic Center, 301 North Main Street, Wichita, KS 67202
Tel: (316) 269-6481 Fax: (316) 269-6484

U.S. Attorney **Barry R. Grissom** . . . . (913) 551-6730
  E-mail: barry.grissom@usdoj.gov

Federal Public Defender
Office of the Federal Public Defender for the District of Kansas
301 North Main Street, Room 850, Wichita, KS 67202
Robert J. Dole U.S. Courthouse, 500 State Avenue, Room 201,
Kansas City, KS 66101
424 South Kansas Avenue, Room 205, Topeka, KS 66603
Tel: (316) 269-6445 (Wichita) Tel: (913) 551-6712 (Kansas City)
Tel: (785) 232-9829 (Topeka) Fax: (316) 269-6175 (Wichita)
Fax: (913) 551-6562 (Kansas City) Fax: (785) 232-9886 (Topeka)

Federal Public Defender **Melody Brannon Evans** . . . . (316) 269-6445
  E-mail: melody.evans@fd.org

United States District Court for the Eastern District of Kentucky
U.S. Courthouse, 101 Barr Street, Lexington, KY 40507
Tel: (859) 233-2503 Tel: (800) 676-6856 (PACER)
Fax: (859) 233-2470
Internet: www.kyed.uscourts.gov

Number of Judgeships: 6

Number of Vacancies: 1

Circuit: Sixth

Areas Covered: Counties of Anderson, Bath, Bell, Boone, Bourbon, Boyd, Boyle, Bracken, Breathitt, Campbell, Carroll, Carter, Clark, Clay, Elliott, Estill, Fayette, Fleming, Floyd, Franklin, Gallatin, Garrard, Grant, Greenup, Harlan, Harrison, Henry, Jackson, Jessamine, Johnson, Kenton, Knott, Knox, Laurel, Lawrence, Lee, Leslie, Letcher, Lewis, Lincoln, Madison, Magoffin, Martin, Mason, McCreary, Menifee, Mercer, Montgomery, Morgan, Nicholas, Owen, Owsley, Pendleton, Perry, Pike, Powell, Pulaski, Robertson, Rockcastle, Rowan, Scott, Shelby, Trimble, Wayne, Whitley, Wolfe and Woodford

Judges
Chief Judge **Karen K. Caldwell** . . . . (859) 233-2828
  Began Service: November 13, 2001
  Appointed By: President George W. Bush
  E-mail: karen.caldwell@kyed.uscourts.gov
District Judge **Danny C. Reeves** . . . . (859) 233-2453
  Began Service: December 31, 2001
  Appointed By: President George W. Bush
  101 Barr Street, Room 136,
  Lexington, KY 40601
  E-mail: reeves_chambers@kyed.uscourts.gov

(continued on next page)

United States District Court for the Eastern District of Kentucky
continued

District Judge **David L. Bunning** . . . . (859) 392-7907
  Began Service: February 21, 2002
  Appointed By: President George W. Bush
  35 West Fifth Street, Room 410,
  Covington, KY 41012
  E-mail: david_bunning@kyed.uscourts.gov
District Judge **Gregory F. Van Tatenhove** . . . . (606) 877-7950
  Began Service: January 6, 2006
  Appointed By: President George W. Bush
District Judge **Amul R. Thapar** . . . . (513) 684-3711
  Began Service: January 4, 2008   Tel: (606) 877-7966
  Appointed By: President George W. Bush
Senior Judge **William O. Bertelsman** . . . . (859) 392-7900
  Began Service: November 29, 1979
  Appointed By: President Jimmy Carter
  U.S. Courthouse, 35 West Fifth Street, Suite 505,
  Covington, KY 41011
Senior Judge **Henry Rupert Wilhoit, Jr.** . . . . (606) 329-2592
  Began Service: 1981
  Appointed By: President Ronald Reagan
  Federal Building, 110 Main Street, Suite 320,
  Pikeville, KY 41501
Senior Judge **Joseph M. Hood** . . . . (859) 233-2415
  Began Service: May 1, 1990
  Appointed By: President George H.W. Bush
Magistrate Judge **Robert E. Wier** Room 417 . . . . (859) 233-2697
  Began Service: September 2006
Magistrate Judge **Edward B. Atkins** . . . . (606) 877-7956
  Began Service: August 2006
Magistrate Judge **Candace J. Smith** . . . . (859) 392-7903
  Began Service: 2010
  35 West Fifth Street, Suite 375,
  Covington, KY 41011
  E-mail: candace_smith@kyed.uscourts.gov
Magistrate Judge **Hanly A. Ingram** . . . . (606) 877-7940
  Began Service: October 1, 2010
  310 South Main Street, Suite 351,
  London, KY 40741
  E-mail: hanly_ingram@kyed.uscourts.gov
Magistrate Judge (recalled) **J. Gregory Wehrman** . . . . (859) 392-7909
  Began Service: January 1992
  35 West Fifth Street, Room 310,
  Covington, KY 41011
  E-mail: wehrman_chambers@kyed.uscourts.gov

Court Staff
Clerk of Court **Robert R. Carr** . . . . (859) 233-2503
Chief Probation Officer **Rozel L. Hollingsworth** . . . . (859) 233-2646

United States Bankruptcy Court for the Eastern District of Kentucky
Community Trust Bank Building, 100 East Vine Street, Suite 200,
Lexington, KY 40507
P.O. Box 1111, Lexington, KY 40588-1111
Tel: (859) 233-2608
Tel: (866) 222-8029 (Voice Case Information System VCIS)
Tel: (800) 998-2650 (Toll Free Voice Case Information System VCIS)
Internet: www.kyeb.uscourts.gov

Number of Judgeships: 3
Number of Vacancies: 1

Judges
Chief Bankruptcy Judge **Tracey N. Wise** . . . . (859) 233-2465
  Began Service: 2012
  E-mail: tracey_wise@kyeb.uscourts.gov
Bankruptcy Judge **Gregory R. "Greg" Schaaf** . . . . (859) 233-2814
  E-mail: gregory_schaaf@kyeb.uscourts.gov
Bankruptcy Judge (recalled) **Joe Lee** 2nd Floor . . . . (859) 233-2814
  Began Service: September 1, 1961
  E-mail: joe_lee@kyeb.uscourts.gov

United States Bankruptcy Court for the Eastern District of Kentucky
continued

Court Staff
Clerk of Court **Jerry D. Truitt** . . . . (859) 233-2608
  E-mail: jerry_truitt@kyeb.uscourts.gov

U.S. Attorney
Kentucky - Eastern District
260 West Vine Street, Suite 300, Lexington, KY 40507
Tel: (859) 233-2661   Fax: (859) 233-2666

U.S. Attorney **Kerry B. Harvey** . . . . (859) 233-2661
  E-mail: kerry.harvey@usdoj.gov

Federal Public Defender
Note: There is no federal public defender for the eastern district of
Kentucky. Inquiries should be directed to the Federal Public Defender for
the Western District of Kentucky at (502) 584-0525.

United States District Court for the Western District of Kentucky
Gene Snyder U.S. Courthouse, 601 West Broadway, Room 106,
Louisville, KY 40202-2249
Tel: (502) 625-3500   Tel: (800) 676-6856 (PACER)
Fax: (502) 625-3880
Internet: www.kywd.uscourts.gov

Number of Judgeships: 4
Number of Vacancies: 1
Circuit: Sixth

Areas Covered: Counties of Adair, Allen, Ballard, Barren, Breckinridge,
Bullitt, Butler, Caldwell, Calloway, Carlisle, Casey, Christian, Clinton,
Crittenden, Cumberland, Daviess, Edmonson, Fulton, Graves, Grayson,
Green, Hancock, Hardin, Hart, Henderson, Hickman, Hopkins, Jefferson,
Larue, Livingston, Logan, Lyon, Marion, Marshall, McCracken, McLean,
Meade, Metcalfe, Monroe, Muhlenberg, Nelson, Ohio, Oldham, Russell,
Simpson, Spencer, Taylor, Todd, Trigg, Union, Warren, Washington and
Webster

Judges
Chief Judge **Joseph H. McKinley, Jr.** . . . . (270) 689-4430
  Began Service: August 25, 1995
  Appointed By: President William J. Clinton
District Judge **David J. Hale** Room 202 . . . . (502) 625-3640
  Began Service: December 10, 2014
  Appointed By: President Barack Obama
District Judge **Gregory N. Stivers** . . . . (270) 393-2440
  Began Service: December 5, 2014
  Appointed By: President Barack Obama
  241 E. Main St., Room 207,
  Bowling Green, KY 42101-2175
Senior Judge **Charles R. Simpson III** . . . . (502) 625-3600
  Began Service: October 15, 1986
  Appointed By: President Ronald Reagan
  Gene Snyder U.S. Courthouse,
  601 West Broadway, Room 247,
  Louisville, KY 40202
Senior Judge **Thomas B. Russell** . . . . (270) 415-6430
  Began Service: October 11, 1994
  Appointed By: President William J. Clinton
  Federal Building, 501 Broadway,
  1st Floor, Room 121, Paducah, KY 42001
Magistrate Judge **Lanny King** . . . . (270) 415-6470
  Began Service: November 14, 2011
  U.S. Courthouse, 501 Broadway, Room 330,
  Paducah, KY 42001
  E-mail: judge_king_chambers@kywd.uscourts.gov

United States District Court for the Western District of Kentucky
continued

Magistrate Judge **Dave Whalin** Room 200 . . . . (502) 625-3830
  Began Service: July 26, 2004
  E-mail: dwhalin@kywd.uscourts.gov
Magistrate Judge **H. Brent Brennenstuhl** . . . . (270) 393-2425
  Began Service: 2012
  241 E. Main St., Room 207,
  Bowling Green, KY 42101-2175
Magistrate Judge **Colin Lindsay** . . . . (502) 625-3660

Court Staff
Clerk of Court **Vanessa L. Armstrong** . . . . (502) 625-3522
  E-mail: vanessa_armstrong@kywd.uscourts.gov
Chief Probation Officer **Kathryn B. Jarvis** . . . . (502) 681-1000
  Gene Snyder U.S. Courthouse,
  601 W. Broadway, Room 400,
  Louisville, KY 40202-2277

United States Bankruptcy Court for the Western District of Kentucky
Gene Snyder U.S. Courthouse, 601 West Broadway, Suite 450,
Louisville, KY 40202-2264
Tel: (502) 627-5700   Tel: (502) 627-5800 (Administrative Office)
Fax: (502) 627-5710
Internet: www.kywb.uscourts.gov

Number of Judgeships: 3

Judges
Chief Bankruptcy Judge **Thomas H. Fulton** Suite 528 . . . . (502) 627-5550
  Began Service: December 6, 2002
Bankruptcy Judge **Joan A. Lloyd** . . . . (502) 627-5525
  Began Service: December 22, 1999
  Gene Snyder U.S. Courthouse,
  601 West Broadway, Room 541,
  Louisville, KY 40202
  E-mail: joan_lloyd@kywb.uscourts.gov
Bankruptcy Judge **Alan C. Stout** . . . . (502) 627-5575
  Began Service: October 25, 2011
  Gene Snyder U.S. Courthouse,
  601 West Broadway, Suite 533,
  Louisville, KY 40202-2249
  E-mail: alan_stout@kywb.uscourts.gov

Court Staff
Clerk of Court **Diane S. Robl** . . . . (502) 627-5700
  E-mail: diane_robl@kywb.uscourts.gov

U.S. Attorney
Kentucky - Western District
717 West Broadway, Louisville, KY 40202
Tel: (502) 582-5911   Fax: (502) 582-5097

U.S. Attorney (Acting) **John E. Kuhn, Jr.** . . . . (502) 582-5911
  E-mail: john.kuhn@usdoj.gov

Federal Public Defender
Western Kentucky Federal Community Defender, Inc.
629 South Fourth Avenue, Louisville, KY 40202
Tel: (502) 584-0525   Fax: (502) 584-2808

Executive Director **Scott Wendelsdorf** . . . . (502) 584-0525
  E-mail: scott.wendelsdorf@fd.org

United States District Court for the Eastern District of Louisiana
U.S. Courthouse, 500 Poydras Street, Room C-151,
New Orleans, LA 70130
Tel: (504) 589-7600   Tel: (504) 589-7650 (Clerk's office)
Tel: (800) 676-6856 (PACER)   Fax: (504) 589-7697
Internet: www.laed.uscourts.gov

Number of Judgeships: 12

Number of Vacancies: 1

Circuit: Fifth

Areas Covered: Parishes of Assumption, Jefferson, Lafourche, Orleans, Plaquemines, St. Bernard, St. Charles, St. James, St. John the Baptist, St. Tammany, Tangipahoa, Terrebonne and Washington

Judges
Chief Judge **Sarah S. Vance** Room C255 . . . . (504) 589-7595
  Began Service: September 29, 1994
  Appointed By: President William J. Clinton
  E-mail: sarah_vance@laed.uscourts.gov
District Judge **Helen Ginger Berrigan** Room C556 . . . . . . (504) 589-7515
  Began Service: March 1994
  Appointed By: President William J. Clinton
District Judge **Martin L. C. Feldman** C555 . . . . (504) 589-7550
  Began Service: 1983
  Appointed By: President Ronald Reagan
  E-mail: martin_feldman@laed.uscourts.gov
District Judge **Eldon E. Fallon** Room C-456 . . . . (504) 589-7545
  Began Service: June 26, 1995
  Appointed By: President William J. Clinton
  E-mail: eldon_fallon@laed.uscourts.gov
District Judge **Carl J. Barbier** Room C256 . . . . (504) 589-7525
  Began Service: October 12, 1998
  Appointed By: President William J. Clinton
  E-mail: Barbier@laed.uscourts.gov
District Judge **Kurt D. Engelhardt** Room C-367 . . . . (504) 589-7645
  Began Service: December 14, 2001
  Appointed By: President George W. Bush
  E-mail: kurt_engelhardt@laed.uscourts.gov
District Judge **Jay C. Zainey** Room C455 . . . . (504) 589-7590
  Began Service: February 19, 2002
  Appointed By: President George W. Bush
  E-mail: jay_zainey@laed.uscourts.gov
District Judge **Lance M. Africk** Room C405 . . . . (504) 589-7605
  Began Service: April 17, 2002
  Appointed By: President George W. Bush
  E-mail: lance_africk@laed.uscourts.gov
District Judge **Nannette Jolivette-Brown** Room C205 . . . (504) 589-7505
  Began Service: October 4, 2011
  Appointed By: President Barack Obama
District Judge **Jane Margaret Triche Milazzo** Room
C206 . . . . (504) 589-7585
  Began Service: October 12, 2011
  Appointed By: President Barack Obama
District Judge **Susie Morgan** Room C322 . . . . (504) 589-7535
  Began Service: June 29, 2012
  Appointed By: President Barack Obama
Senior Judge **Stanwood R. Duval, Jr.** Room C-368 . . . . . . (504) 589-7540
  Began Service: October 31, 1994
  Appointed By: President William J. Clinton
  E-mail: stanwood_duval@laed.uscourts.gov
Senior Judge **Mary Ann Vial Lemmon** Room C406 . . . . . . (504) 589-7565
  Began Service: July 26, 1996
  Appointed By: President William J. Clinton
  E-mail: mary_ann_lemmon@laed.uscourts.gov
Senior Judge **Ivan L.R. Lemelle** Room C525 . . . . (504) 589-7555
  Began Service: April 13, 1998
  Appointed By: President William J. Clinton
  E-mail: ivan_lemelle@laed.uscourts.gov
Chief Magistrate Judge **Joseph C. Wilkinson, Jr.**
Room B409 . . . . (504) 589-7630
  Began Service: March 27, 1995
Magistrate Judge **Sally Shushan** Room B-345 . . . . (504) 589-7620
  Began Service: February 1, 1999
  E-mail: sally_shushan@laed.uscourts.gov

(continued on next page)

United States District Court for the Eastern District of Louisiana
continued

Magistrate Judge **Karen Wells Roby** Room B-437 . . . . (504) 589-7615
  Began Service: February 1999
  E-mail: karen_roby@laed.uscourts.gov
Magistrate Judge **Daniel E. Knowles III** Room B335 . . . . . (504) 589-7575
  Began Service: January 6, 2003
  E-mail: daniel_knowles@laed.uscourts.gov
Magistrate Judge **Michael B. North** B419 . . . . (504) 589-7610

Court Staff
Clerk of Court **William W. Blevins** . . . . (504) 589-7650
  E-mail: william_blevins@laed.uscourts.gov
Chief Probation Officer **Kito Bess** . . . . (504) 589-3200
  Hale Boggs Federal Building,
  500 Poydras Street, Room 505,
  New Orleans, LA 70130-3321
Chief Pretrial Services Officer **Harold Schlumbrecht**
  Room 614 . . . . (504) 589-7900

United States Bankruptcy Court for the Eastern District of Louisiana
Hale Boggs Federal Building, 500 Poydras Street, Suite B601,
New Orleans, LA 70130
Tel: (504) 589-7878 Tel: (504) 589-6761 (PACER)
Tel: (504) 589-3951 (Voice Case Information System VCIS)
Tel: (866) 222-8029 (Toll Free Voice Case Information System VCIS)
Internet: www.laeb.uscourts.gov

Number of Judgeships: 2

Judges
Chief Bankruptcy Judge **Elizabeth W. Magner** Suite
  B-741B . . . . (504) 589-7800
  Began Service: 2012
  E-mail: elizabeth_magner@laeb.uscourts.gov
Bankruptcy Judge (recalled) **Jerry A. Brown** . . . . (504) 589-7810
  Began Service: August 27, 1992
  Hale Boggs Federal Building,
  500 Poydras Street, Suite B-741A,
  New Orleans, LA 70130-3310
  E-mail: jerry_brown@laeb.uscourts.gov

Court Staff
Clerk of the Court **Sheila Booth** . . . . (504) 589-7878

U.S. Attorney
Louisiana - Eastern District
650 Poydras Street, Suite 1600, New Orleans, LA 70130
Tel: (504) 680-3000 Fax: (504) 589-4510

U.S. Attorney **Kenneth Allen Polite, Jr.** . . . . (504) 680-3078
  E-mail: kenneth.a.polite@usdoj.gov

Federal Public Defender
Office of the Federal Public Defender - Eastern District of Louisiana
Hale Boggs Federal Building, 500 Poydras Street, Room 318,
New Orleans, LA 70130
Tel: (504) 589-7930 Fax: (504) 589-2556

Federal Public Defender **Claude Kelly** . . . . (504) 589-7930
  E-mail: claude.kelly@fd.org

United States District Court for the Middle District of Louisiana
Russell B. Long Federal Building, 777 Florida Street, Suite 139,
Baton Rouge, LA 70801-1712
Tel: (225) 389-3500 Tel: (800) 676-6856 (PACER)
Fax: (225) 389-3501
Internet: www.lamd.uscourts.gov

Number of Judgeships: 3

Circuit: Fifth

Areas Covered: Parishes of Ascension, East Baton Rouge, East Feliciana, Iberville, Livingston, Pointe Coupee, St. Helena, West Baton Rouge and West Feliciana

Judges
Chief District Judge **Brian A. Jackson** Suite 375 . . . . (225) 389-3692
  Began Service: June 18, 2010
  Appointed By: President Barack Obama
District Judge **Shelly Deckert Dick** Suite 301 . . . . (225) 389-3634
  Began Service: May 15, 2013
  Appointed By: President Barack Obama
  E-mail: shelly_dick@lamd.uscourts.gov
District Judge **John W. deGravelles** Suite 313 . . . . (225) 389-3568
  Began Service: July 23, 2014
  Appointed By: President Barack Obama
  E-mail: john_degravelles@lamd.uscourts.gov
Senior Judge **James J. Brady** . . . . (225) 389-4030
  Began Service: May 29, 2000
  Appointed By: President William J. Clinton
  Russell B. Long Federal Building,
  777 Florida Street, Suite 369,
  Baton Rouge, LA 70801
  E-mail: James_Brady@lamd.uscourts.gov
Magistrate Judge **Stephen C. Riedlinger** . . . . (225) 389-3584
  Note: Judge Riedlinger will retire effective
  December 31, 2015.
  Began Service: May 29, 1986
  Russell B. Long Federal Building,
  777 Florida Street, Room 260,
  Baton Rouge, LA 70801-1764
Magistrate Judge **Richard L. Bourgeois, Jr.** Suite 278 . . . . (225) 389-3602
  Began Service: February 21, 2013

Court Staff
District Clerk **Michael L. McConnell** . . . . (225) 389-3500
Chief Probation Officer **Clarence P. Bambo** Room 161 . . . (225) 389-3600
  E-mail: clarence_bambo@lamd.uscourts.gov

United States Bankruptcy Court for the Middle District of Louisiana
U.S. Courthouse, 707 Florida Street, Room 119, Baton Rouge, LA 70801
Tel: (225) 346-3333
Tel: (225) 382-2175 (Voice Case Information System VCIS)
Fax: (225) 346-3334
Internet: www.lamb.uscourts.gov

Number of Judgeships: 1

Judges
Bankruptcy Judge **Douglas D. Dodd** Room 236 . . . . (225) 346-3335
  Began Service: May 2, 2002
  E-mail: douglas_dodd@lamb.uscourts.gov

Court Staff
Bankruptcy Clerk **Monica Menier** . . . . (225) 346-3333
  E-mail: monica_menier@lamb.uscourts.gov

United States Bankruptcy Court for the Middle District of Louisiana
continued

U.S. Attorney

Louisiana - Middle District
Russell B. Long Federal Building, 777 Florida Street, Suite 208,
Baton Rouge, LA 70801-1717
Tel: (225) 389-0443   Fax: (225) 389-0561

U.S. Attorney **James Walter Green** . . . . (225) 389-0443

Federal Public Defender

**Office of the Federal Public Defender for the Middle and
Western Districts of Louisiana**
102 Versailles Boulevard, Suite 816, Lafayette, LA 70501
300 Fannin Street, Suite 2199, Shreveport, LA 71101
707 Florida Boulevard, Suite 303, Baton Rouge, LA 70801
Tel: (337) 262-6336 (Lafayette)   Tel: (318) 676-3310 (Shreveport)
Tel: (225) 382-2118 (Baton Rouge)   Fax: (337) 262-6605 (Lafayette)
Fax: (318) 676-3313 (Shreveport)   Fax: (225) 382-2119 (Baton Rouge)

Federal Public Defender **Rebecca L. Hudsmith** . . . . (337) 262-6336
   E-mail: rebecca.hudsmith@fd.org

United States District Court for the Western District of Louisiana

U.S. Courthouse, 300 Fannin Street, Room 1167,
Shreveport, LA 71101-3083
Tel: (318) 676-4273   Tel: (318) 676-3957 (PACER)
Fax: (318) 676-3962
Internet: www.lawd.uscourts.gov

Number of Judgeships: 7

Number of Vacancies: 1

Circuit: Fifth

Areas Covered: Parishes of Acadia, Allen, Avoyelles, Beauregard, Bienville, Bossier, Caddo, Calcasieu, Caldwell, Cameron, Catahoula, Claiborne, Concordia, De Soto, East Carroll, Evangeline, Franklin, Grant, Iberia, Jackson, Jefferson Davis, Lafayette, La Salle, Lincoln, Madison, Morehouse, Natchitoches, Ouachita, Rapides, Red River, Richland, Sabine, St. Landry, St. Martin, St. Mary, Tensas, Union, Vermilion, Vernon, Webster, West Carroll and Winn

Judges

Chief Judge **Dee D. Drell** . . . . (318) 473-7420
   Began Service: May 9, 2003
   Appointed By: President George W. Bush
   Federal Building, 515 Murray Street, Room 233,
   Alexandria, LA 71301
   E-mail: dee_drell@lawd.uscourts.gov
District Judge **Robert G. James** . . . . (318) 322-6230
   Began Service: October 31, 1998
   Appointed By: President William J. Clinton
   E-mail: robert_james@lawd.uscourts.gov
District Judge **Rebecca F. Doherty** . . . . (337) 593-5050
   Began Service: November 18, 1991
   Appointed By: President George H.W. Bush
   E-mail: rebecca_doherty@lawd.uscourts.gov
District Judge **S. Maurice Hicks, Jr.** Suite 5101 . . . . (318) 676-3055
   Began Service: June 12, 2003
   Appointed By: President George W. Bush
   E-mail: maury_hicks@lawd.uscourts.gov
District Judge **Patricia Head Minaldi** . . . . (337) 437-3880
   Began Service: June 16, 2003
   Appointed By: President George W. Bush
   611 Broad Street, Suite 328,
   Lake Charles, LA 70601
   E-mail: patricia_minaldi@lawd.uscourts.gov

United States District Court for the Western District of Louisiana
continued

District Judge **Elizabeth Erny Foote** Suite 4300 . . . . (318) 934-4780
   Began Service: September 10, 2010
   Appointed By: President Barack Obama
   E-mail: elizabeth_foote@lawd.uscourts.gov
Senior Judge **Donald E. Walter** . . . . (318) 676-3175
   Began Service: July 15, 1985
   Appointed By: President Ronald Reagan
   U.S. Courthouse, 300 Fannin Street, Suite 4200,
   Shreveport, LA 71101
   E-mail: donald_walter@lawd.uscourts.gov
Senior Judge **James T. Trimble, Jr.** . . . . (337) 437-3884
   Began Service: September 12, 1991
   Appointed By: President George H.W. Bush
   Edwin F. Hunter Jr. Federal Building,
   611 Broad Street, Room 237,
   Lake Charles, LA 70601
Senior Judge **Tom Stagg** . . . . (318) 676-3260
   Began Service: April 1974
   Appointed By: President Richard M. Nixon
   U.S. Courthouse, 300 Fannin Street, Room 4100,
   Shreveport, LA 71101-3091
   E-mail: tom_stagg@lawd.uscourts.gov
Senior Judge **Richard T. Haik, Sr.** . . . . (337) 593-5100
   Began Service: June 14, 1991
   Appointed By: President George H.W. Bush
   U.S. Courthouse, 800 Lafayette Street, Suite 4200,
   Lafayette, LA 70501
   E-mail: richard_haik@lawd.uscourts.gov
Magistrate Judge **James D. Kirk** . . . . (318) 473-7510
   Began Service: December 15, 1997
   Federal Building, 515 Murray Street, Room 331,
   Alexandria, LA 71301
Magistrate Judge **C. Michael Hill** . . . . (337) 593-5160
   Began Service: July 30, 2001
   U.S. Courthouse, 800 Lafayette Street, Suite 3400,
   Lafayette, LA 70501
   E-mail: c_michael_hill@lawd.uscourts.gov
Magistrate Judge **Mark L. Hornsby** . . . . (318) 676-3265
   Began Service: January 14, 2005
   U.S. Courthouse, 300 Fannin Street, Suite 1148,
   Shreveport, LA 71101-3087
   E-mail: mark_hornsby@lawd.uscourts.gov
Magistrate Judge **Karen L. Hayes** . . . . (318) 388-6036
   Began Service: June 26, 1997
Magistrate Judge **Kathleen Kay** . . . . (337) 437-3874
   Began Service: December 2007
   U.S. Courthouse, 611 Broad Street, Suite 209,
   Lake Charles, LA 70601
   E-mail: kathleen_kay@lawd.uscourts.gov
Magistrate Judge **Patrick J. Hanna** . . . . (337) 593-5140
   Began Service: December 2009
   800 Lafayette Street, Suite 3500,
   Lafayette, LA 70501
   E-mail: patrick_hanna@lawd.uscourts.gov

Court Staff

Clerk of Court **Tony R. Moore** . . . . (318) 676-4273
   Began Service: 2009
Chief Probation Officer **Lisa Johnson** . . . . (337) 262-6615
   800 Lafayette St., Suite 2400,
   Lafayette, LA 70501-6936

United States Bankruptcy Court for the Western District of Louisiana

U.S. Courthouse, 300 Fannin Street, Suite 2201, Shreveport, LA 71101
Tel: (318) 676-4267 Tel: (318) 676-4235 (PACER)
Tel: (888) 523-1976 (Toll Free PACER)
Tel: (318) 676-4234 (Voice Case Information System VCIS)
Tel: (800) 326-4026 (Toll Free Voice Case Information System VCIS)
Internet: www.lawb.uscourts.gov

Number of Judgeships: 3

Judges

Chief Bankruptcy Judge **Robert R. Summerhays** . . . . (337) 262-6383
  Began Service: October 2006
  214 Jefferson Street, Suite 120,
  Lafayette, LA 70501-7050
  E-mail: robert_summerhays@lawb.uscourts.gov
Bankruptcy Judge **Henley A. Hunter** . . . . (318) 443-8083
  Began Service: July 31, 1987
  300 Jackson Street, Suite 201,
  Alexandria, LA 71301-8357
  E-mail: Henley_Hunter@lawb.uscourts.gov
Bankruptcy Judge **Jeffrey P. Norman** . . . . (318) 676-4269

Court Staff

Bankruptcy Clerk **Edward A. Takara** . . . .(318) 676-4267

U.S. Attorney

Louisiana - Western District
300 Fannin Street, Suite 3201, Shreveport, LA 71101-3068
Tel: (318) 676-3600 TTY: (318) 676-3680 Fax: (318) 676-3641
Fax: (318) 676-3654

U.S. Attorney **Stephanie A. Finley** . . . .(337) 262-6618
  E-mail: stephanie.finley@usdoj.gov

Federal Public Defender

Office of the Federal Public Defender for the Middle and Western Districts of Louisiana
102 Versailles Boulevard, Suite 816, Lafayette, LA 70501
300 Fannin Street, Suite 2199, Shreveport, LA 71101
707 Florida Boulevard, Suite 303, Baton Rouge, LA 70801
Tel: (337) 262-6336 (Lafayette) Tel: (318) 676-3310 (Shreveport)
Tel: (225) 382-2118 (Baton Rouge) Fax: (337) 262-6605 (Lafayette)
Fax: (318) 676-3313 (Shreveport) Fax: (225) 382-2119 (Baton Rouge)

Federal Public Defender **Rebecca L. Hudsmith** . . . . (337) 262-6336
  E-mail: rebecca.hudsmith@fd.org

United States District Court for the District of Maine

156 Federal Street, Portland, ME 04101
Tel: (207) 780-3356 Tel: (800) 260-9774 (Toll Free PACER)
Internet: www.med.uscourts.gov

Number of Judgeships: 3
Circuit: First

Judges

Chief Judge **Nancy Torresen** . . . . (207) 221-0028
  Began Service: May 4, 2012
  Appointed By: President Barack Obama
  E-mail: nancy_torresen@med.uscourts.gov
District Judge **John Alden Woodcock, Jr.** . . . .(207) 945-0549
  Began Service: February 2009
  Appointed By: President George W. Bush

United States District Court for the District of Maine *continued*

District Judge **Jon David Levy** . . . .(207) 780-3356
  Began Service: May 2, 2014
  Appointed By: President Barack Obama
  E-mail: jon_levy@med.uscourts.gov
Senior Judge **D. Brock Hornby** . . . . (207) 780-3280
  Began Service: 1990
  Appointed By: President George H.W. Bush
Senior Judge **George Z. Singal** . . . . (207) 780-3119
  Began Service: July 2000
  Appointed By: President William J. Clinton
Magistrate Judge **John C. Nivison** . . . . (207) 945-0315
  Began Service: January 27, 2014
  202 Harlow Street, Room 300,
  Bangor, ME 04401
  E-mail: jcn@med.uscourts.gov
Magistrate Judge **John Rich III** . . . .(207) 780-3360
  Began Service: April 2, 2008

Court Staff

Clerk of Court **Christa K. Berry** . . . .(207) 780-3356
  E-mail: christa@med.uscourts.gov
Chief Probation Officer **Karen Lee-Moody** Suite 305 . . . . .(207) 780-3358

United States Bankruptcy Court for the District of Maine

Edward T. Gignoux Courthouse, 156 Federal Street, Portland, ME 04101
Margaret Chase Smith Federal Building and Courthouse, 202 Harlow Street, Bangor, ME 04401
Tel: (207) 780-3482 Tel: (207) 945-0348 (Bangor Office)
Tel: (207) 780-3755 (Voice Case Information System VCIS)
Tel: (800) 650-7253 (Toll-Free Voice Case Information System VCIS)
Fax: (207) 780-3679 Fax: (207) 945-0304 (Bangor Office)
Internet: www.meb.uscourts.gov

Number of Judgeships: 2

Judges

Chief Bankruptcy Judge **Peter G. Cary** . . . . (207) 780-3482
Bankruptcy Judge
  Michael A. "Mike" Fagone . . . . (207) 945-0550 ext. 6490
  Began Service: 2015

Court Staff

Clerk of the Court **Alec Leddy** . . . .(207) 274-5965
  Began Service: November 13, 2006
  E-mail: alec_leddy@meb.uscourts.gov

U.S. Attorney

Maine District
East Tower, 100 Middle Street, 6th Floor, Portland, ME 04101
Tel: (207) 780-3257 TTY: (207) 780-3060 Fax: (207) 780-3304

U.S. Attorney **Thomas Edward Delahanty II** . . . . (207) 780-3257
  E-mail: thomas.delahanty@usdoj.gov

Federal Public Defender

Maine Federal Public Defender
One City Center, Second Floor, Portland, ME 04101
Key Plaza, 23 Water Street, Bangor, ME 04401
Tel: (207) 553-7070 (Portland) Tel: (207) 992-4111 (Bangor)
Fax: (207) 553-7017 (Portland) Fax: (207) 992-9190 (Bangor)

Federal Public Defender **David Beneman** . . . .(207) 553-7070
  E-mail: david.beneman@fd.org

United States District Court for the District of Maryland

U.S. Courthouse, 6500 Cherrywood Lane, Greenbelt, MD 20770
101 West Lombard Street, Baltimore, MD 21201
Tel: (410) 962-2600 (Baltimore)
Tel: (410) 962-1812 (Civil Cases PACER)
Tel: (301) 344-0660 (Greenbelt)
Internet: www.mdd.uscourts.gov

Number of Judgeships: 10

Number of Vacancies: 1

Circuit: Fourth

Judges
Chief Judge **Catherine C. Blake** U.S. Courthouse,
Room 7D . . . . (410) 962-3220
  Began Service: August 1995
  Appointed By: President William J. Clinton
  E-mail: mdd_ccbchambers@mdd.uscourts.gov
District Judge **William D. Quarles, Jr.** U.S. Courthouse,
Room 3A . . . . (410) 962-0946
  Began Service: March 24, 2003
  Appointed By: President George W. Bush
District Judge **Richard D. Bennett** U.S. Courthouse,
Chambers 5.D . . . . (410) 962-3190
  Began Service: April 29, 2003
  Appointed By: President George W. Bush
District Judge **James K. Bredar** . . . .(410) 962-0950
  Began Service: December 22, 2010
  Appointed By: President Barack Obama
District Judge **Ellen Lipton Hollander** . . . . (410) 962-0742
  Began Service: January 4, 2011
  Appointed By: President Barack Obama
District Judge **George L. Russell III** . . . . (410) 962-2600
  Began Service: May 24, 2012
  Appointed By: President Barack Obama
District Judge **Paul William Grimm** Room 8B . . . . (301) 344-0670
  Began Service: December 10, 2012
  Appointed By: President Barack Obama
District Judge **Theodore David Chuang** . . . .(301) 344-3982
  Began Service: May 2, 2014
  Appointed By: President Barack Obama
District Judge **George Jarrod Hazel** . . . . (301) 344-0637
  Began Service: May 2, 2014
  Appointed By: President Barack Obama
Senior Judge **William M. Nickerson** . . . . (410) 962-7810
  Began Service: 1990
  Appointed By: President George H.W. Bush
Senior Judge **Marvin Joseph Garbis** . . . . (410) 962-7700
  Began Service: 1989
  Appointed By: President George H.W. Bush
  U.S. Courthouse, 101 West Lombard Street,
  Room 530, Baltimore, MD 21201-2691
  E-mail: judge_garbis@mdd.uscourts.gov
Senior Judge **Peter J. Messitte** . . . . (301) 344-0632
  Began Service: October 20, 1993
  Appointed By: President William J. Clinton
Senior Judge **J. Frederick Motz** U.S. Courthouse, Room
510 . . . . (410) 962-0782
  Began Service: 1985
  Appointed By: President Ronald Reagan
  E-mail: judge_j_frederick_motz@mdd.uscourts.gov
Senior Judge **Roger W. Titus** Room 255A . . . . (301) 344-0052
  Began Service: November 2003
  Appointed By: President George W. Bush
  E-mail: judge_roger_titus@mdd.uscourts.gov
Senior Judge **Deborah K. Chasanow** . . . . (301) 344-0634
  Began Service: 1993
  Appointed By: President William J. Clinton
Chief Magistrate Judge **William G. Connelly** U.S.
Courthouse, Room 355A . . . .(301) 344-0627
  Began Service: March 31, 1995
  E-mail: Judge_Connelly@mdd.uscourts.gov
Magistrate Judge **Jillyn K. Schulze** . . . . (301) 344-0630
  Began Service: October 24, 1994

United States District Court for the District of Maryland *continued*
Magistrate Judge **Charles Bernard Day** 235A . . . . (301) 344-0393
  Began Service: February 18, 1997
Magistrate Judge **Beth P. Gesner** U.S. Courthouse,
Room 7C . . . . (410) 962-4288
  Began Service: May 1999
Magistrate Judge **Thomas M. DiGirolamo** . . . . (301) 344-0080
  Began Service: June 30, 2004
  E-mail: judge_digirolamo@mdd.uscourts.gov
Magistrate Judge **Stephanie A. Gallagher** . . . . (410) 962-7780
  Began Service: April 19, 2011
Magistrate Judge **J. Mark Coulson** . . . . (410) 962-2600
Magistrate Judge **Timothy J. Sullivan** . . . . (410) 962-4560
  Began Service: 2012
Magistrate Judge (Part-Time) **C. Bruce Anderson** . . . . (410) 749-7990
  Began Service: 2012

Court Staff
Clerk of Court **Felicia Cannon** . . . . (410) 962-2600
  E-mail: felicia_cannon@mdd.uscourts.gov
Chief U.S. Probation/Pretrial Officer **William F. Henry** . . . (410) 962-4740
  250 West Pratt Street, Suite 400,
  Baltimore, MD 21201

United States Bankruptcy Court for the District of Maryland

U.S. Courthouse, 101 West Lombard Street, Room 8305,
Baltimore, MD 21201
Tel: (410) 962-2688   Tel: (800) 676-6856 (Toll Free PACER)
Tel: (800) 829-0145 (Toll Free Voice Case Information System VCIS)
Internet: www.mdb.uscourts.gov

Number of Judgeships: 9

Judges
Chief Bankruptcy Judge **Nancy V. Alquist** 2A . . . . (410) 962-7479
  Began Service: 2012   Tel: (410) 962-7857
Bankruptcy Judge **James F. Schneider** Room 9442 . . . . . . (410) 962-2820
  Began Service: February 1, 1982
Bankruptcy Judge **Paul Mannes** . . . . (301) 344-8040
  Began Service: December 30, 1981
  U.S. Courthouse, 6500 Cherrywood Lane, 385A,
  Greenbelt, MD 20770
  E-mail: paul_mannes@mdb.uscourts.gov
Bankruptcy Judge **Thomas J. Catliota** . . . . (301) 344-3660
  Began Service: April 2006
  6500 Cherrywood Lane, Suite 365A,
  Greenbelt, MD 20770
  E-mail: judge_catliota@mdb.uscourts.gov
Bankruptcy Judge **Wendelin I. Lipp** . . . . (301) 344-3377
  Began Service: 2006
  6500 Cherrywood Lane, Room 365,
  Greenbelt, MD 20770
Bankruptcy Judge **Robert A. Gordon** . . . . (410) 962-4162
  Began Service: June 2006
Bankruptcy Judge **David E. Rice** . . . . (410) 962-4211
  Began Service: April 1, 2011
Bankruptcy Judge (recalled) **E. Stephen Derby** Room
9442 . . . . (410) 962-7801
  Began Service: December 9, 1987
Bankruptcy Judge (recalled) **Duncan W. Keir**
Chambers 1B . . . . (410) 962-3555
  Began Service: 2012

Court Staff
Clerk **Mark A. Neal** . . . . (410) 962-2688
(continued on next page)

United States Bankruptcy Court for the District of Maryland *continued*

U.S. Attorney

Maryland District
36 South Charles Street, 4th Floor, Baltimore, MD 21201
Tel: (410) 209-4800 Fax: (410) 962-3124 Fax: (410) 962-0122

U.S. Attorney **Rod J. Rosenstein** . . . . (410) 209-4800
E-mail: rod.rosenstein@usdoj.gov

Federal Public Defender

Office of the Federal Public Defender for the District of Maryland
Nations Bank Center Tower II, 100 South Charles Street, Ninth Floor, Baltimore, MD 21201-1201
Capitol Office Park 4, 6411 Ivy Lane, Room 710, Greenbelt, MD 20770
Tel: (410) 962-3962 (Baltimore) Fax: (410) 962-0872 (Baltimore)
Tel: (301) 344-0600 (Greenbelt) Fax: (301) 344-0019 (Greenbelt)

Federal Public Defender **James "Jim" Wyda** . . . . (410) 962-3962
E-mail: jim_wyda@fd.org

United States District Court for the District of Massachusetts

John Joseph Moakley U.S. Courthouse, One Courthouse Way, Suite 2300, Boston, MA 02210
Tel: (617) 748-9152 Fax: (617) 748-9096
Internet: www.mad.uscourts.gov

Number of Judgeships: 13

Number of Vacancies: 1

Circuit: First

Judges

Chief Judge **Patti B. Saris** Suite 8110 . . . . (617) 748-4141
Began Service: November 24, 1993
Appointed By: President William J. Clinton
E-mail: honorable_patti_saris@mad.uscourts.gov
District Judge **William G. Young** Suite 5710 . . . . (617) 748-9138
Began Service: 1985
Appointed By: President Ronald Reagan
E-mail: William_Young@mad.uscourts.gov
District Judge **Nathaniel M. Gorton** Suite 3110 . . . . (617) 748-9247
Began Service: October 27, 1992
Appointed By: President George H.W. Bush
E-mail: honorable_nathaniel_gorton@mad.uscourts.gov
District Judge **Richard G. Stearns** Suite 7130 . . . . (617) 748-9283
Began Service: January 5, 1994
Appointed By: President William J. Clinton
E-mail: honorable_richard_stearns@mad.uscourts.gov
District Judge **George A. O'Toole, Jr.** Suite 4730 . . . . (617) 748-9618
Began Service: July 10, 1995
Appointed By: President William J. Clinton
E-mail: george_otoole@mad.uscourts.gov
District Judge **F. Dennis Saylor IV** . . . . (617) 748-9212
Began Service: June 15, 2004
Appointed By: President George W. Bush
E-mail: dennis_saylor@mad.uscourts.gov
District Judge **Denise J. Casper** . . . . (617) 748-4829
Began Service: January 17, 2011
Appointed By: President Barack Obama
E-mail: denise_casper@mad.uscourts.gov
District Judge **Timothy S. Hillman** . . . . (508) 929-9904
Began Service: 2012
Appointed By: President Barack Obama
E-mail: honorable_timothy_hillman@mad.uscourts.gov

United States District Court for the District of Massachusetts *continued*

District Judge **Indira Talwani** . . . . (617) 748-9152
Began Service: May 12, 2014
Appointed By: President Barack Obama
E-mail: indira_talwani@mad.uscourts.gov
District Judge **Mark G. Mastroianni** . . . . (617) 785-6804
Began Service: June 1, 2014
Appointed By: President Barack Obama
District Judge **Leo T. Sorokin** . . . . (617) 748-4231
Began Service: 2014
Appointed By: President Barack Obama
District Judge **Allison Dale Burroughs** . . . . (617) 748-4232
Began Service: January 7, 2015
Appointed By: President Barack Obama
Senior Judge **Michael A. Ponsor** . . . . (413) 785-6824
Began Service: 1994
Appointed By: President William J. Clinton
E-mail: michael_ponsor@mad.uscourts.gov
Senior Judge **Mark L. Wolf** . . . . (617) 748-9272
Began Service: 1985
Appointed By: President Ronald Reagan
E-mail: mark_wolf@mad.uscourts.gov
Senior Judge **Joseph L. Tauro** . . . . (617) 748-9288
Began Service: 1972
Appointed By: President Richard M. Nixon
E-mail: honorable_joseph_tauro@mad.uscourts.gov
Senior Judge **Rya W. Zobel** . . . . (617) 748-9144
Began Service: 1979
Appointed By: President Jimmy Carter
John Joseph Moakley U.S. Courthouse,
One Courthouse Way, Suite 6110,
Boston, MA 02210-3008
E-mail: rya_zobel@mad.uscourts.gov
Senior Judge **Douglas P. Woodlock** Suite 4110 . . . . (617) 748-9293
Began Service: 1986
Appointed By: President Ronald Reagan
E-mail: honorable_douglas_woodlock@mad.uscourts.gov
Chief Magistrate Judge **Jennifer C. Boal** . . . . (617) 748-9238
Began Service: 2010
E-mail: jennifer_boal@mad.uscourts.gov
Magistrate Judge **Marianne B. Bowler** Suite 8420 . . . . (617) 748-9219
Began Service: May 7, 1990
E-mail: Honorable_Marianne_Bowler@mad.uscourts.gov
Magistrate Judge **Kenneth P. Neiman** . . . . (413) 785-6818
Began Service: January 5, 1995
U.S. Courthouse, 300 State Street, Suite 252,
Springfield, MA 01105
Magistrate Judge **Judith Gail Dein** Room 6420 . . . . (617) 748-4736
Began Service: July 2000
E-mail: judith_dein@mad.uscourts.gov
Magistrate Judge **David H. Hennessey** . . . . (508) 929-9905
Magistrate Judge **M. Page Kelley** . . . . (617) 748-9183
Magistrate Judge **Katherine A. "Katy" Robertson** . . . . . . (413) 785-6802
Magistrate Judge **Donald L. Cabell** . . . . (617) 748-9233
Magistrate Judge (recalled) **Jerome J. Niedermeier** . . . . . (617) 748-9155
Began Service: 2010
Magistrate Judge (recalled) **Robert B. Collings** . . . . (617) 748-9229
Began Service: 1982
John Joseph Moakley U.S. Courthouse,
One Courthouse Way, Suite 7420,
Boston, MA 02210-3008

Court Staff
Clerk of Court **Robert M. Farrell** . . . . (617) 748-9165
Chief Probation/Pretrial Officer **Christopher Maloney** . . . (617) 748-4200

United States Bankruptcy Court for the District of Massachusetts

John W. McCormack Post Office and Courthouse, 5 Post Office Square, Suite 1150, Boston, MA 02109-3945
Tel: (617) 748-5300 Tel: (617) 748-5350 (PACER)
Tel: (617) 748-5311 (PACER) Tel: (888) 201-3571 (Toll Free PACER)
Tel: (888) 201-3572 (Toll Free Voice Case Information System VCIS)
Tel: (508) 770-8900 (Worcester Divisional Office) Fax: (617) 748-5315
Fax: (508) 793-0189 (Worcester Divisional Office Intake Fax)
Internet: www.mab.uscourts.gov

Number of Judgeships: 5

Judges

Chief Bankruptcy Judge **Melvin S. Hoffman** . . . . (617) 748-5300
Bankruptcy Judge **Frank J. Bailey** . . . . (617) 748-5300
  Began Service: 2010
Bankruptcy Judge **Joan N. Feeney** . . . . (617) 748-6631
  Began Service: 1992
Bankruptcy Judge **William C. Hillman** . . . . (617) 748-5300
  Began Service: August 13, 1991
  E-mail: Judge_William_Hillman@mab.uscourts.gov
Bankruptcy Judge **Henry Jack Boroff** . . . . (413) 785-6860
  Began Service: 1993
  E-mail: henry.boroff@mab.uscourts.gov

Court Staff

Bankruptcy Clerk **James M. Lynch** . . . . (617) 748-5300
  E-mail: james_lynch@mab.uscourts.gov

U.S. Attorney

Massachusetts District
John Joseph Moakley U.S. Courthouse, One Courthouse Way,
Suite 9200, Boston, MA 02210
Tel: (617) 748-3100 Fax: (617) 748-3953

U.S. Attorney **Carmen Milagros Ortiz** . . . . (617) 748-3100
  E-mail: carmen.ortiz@usdoj.gov

Federal Public Defender

Federal Public Defender Office - District of Massachusetts, New Hampshire and Rhode Island
51 Sleeper Street, 5th Floor, Boston, MA 02210
The Ralph Pill Building, 22 Bridge Street, Third Floor,
Concord, NH 03301-4922
101 Weybosset Street, Third Floor, Providence, RI 02903
Tel: (317) 223-8061 (Boston) Tel: (603) 226-7360 (Concord)
Tel: (401) 528-4281 (Providence) Fax: (617) 223-8080 (Boston)
Fax: (603) 226-7358 (Concord) Fax: (401) 528-4284 (Providence)

Federal Public Defender **Miriam Conrad** . . . . (617) 223-8061
  E-mail: miriam.conrad@fd.org

United States District Court for the Eastern District of Michigan

Theodore Levin U.S. Courthouse, 231 West Lafayette Boulevard,
Detroit, MI 48226
Tel: (313) 234-5005 Tel: (313) 226-7249 (PACER)
Tel: (313) 961-4934 (PACER) Fax: (313) 234-5395
Internet: www.mied.uscourts.gov

Number of Judgeships: 15

Circuit: Sixth

Areas Covered: Counties of Alcona, Alpena, Arenac, Bay, Cheboygan, Clare, Crawford, Genesee, Gladwin, Gratiot, Huron, Iosco, Isabella, Jackson, Lapeer, Lenawee, Livingston, Macomb, Midland, Monroe, Montmorency, Oakland, Ogemaw, Oscoda, Otsego, Presque Isle, Roscommon, Saginaw, Sanilac, Shiawassee, St. Clair, Tuscola, Washtenaw and Wayne

Judges

Chief Judge **Gerald E. Rosen** Room 730 . . . . (313) 234-5135
  Began Service: 1990
  Appointed By: President George H.W. Bush
  E-mail: gerald_rosen@mied.uscourts.gov
District Judge **Denise Page Hood** Room 251 . . . . (313) 234-5165
  Began Service: June 11, 1994
  Appointed By: President William J. Clinton
District Judge **Victoria A. Roberts** Room 123 . . . . (313) 234-5230
  Began Service: August 11, 1998
  Appointed By: President William J. Clinton
  E-mail: Victoria_Roberts@mied.uscourts.gov
District Judge **Paul David Borman** Room 740 . . . . (313) 234-5120
  Began Service: September 2, 1994
  Appointed By: President William J. Clinton
  E-mail: paul_borman@mied.uscourts.gov
District Judge **David M. Lawson** Room 802 . . . . (313) 234-2660
  Began Service: August 4, 2000
  Appointed By: President William J. Clinton
  E-mail: David_Lawson@mied.uscourts.gov
District Judge **Sean F. Cox** Room 257 . . . . (313) 234-2650
  Began Service: June 2006
  Appointed By: President George W. Bush
  E-mail: sean_cox@mied.uscourts.gov
District Judge **Thomas L. Ludington** . . . . (989) 894-8810
  Began Service: June 30, 2006
  Appointed By: President George W. Bush
  E-mail: thomas_ludington@mied.uscourts.gov
District Judge **Stephen Joseph Murphy III** Room 235 . . . (313) 234-2680
  Began Service: July 2, 2008
  Appointed By: President George W. Bush
District Judge **Mark A. Goldsmith** . . . . (313) 234-5240
  Began Service: June 21, 2010   Tel: (313) 243-5368
  Appointed By: President Barack Obama
  E-mail: mark_goldsmith@mied.uscourts.gov
District Judge **Gershwin A. Drain** Room 123 . . . . (313) 234-5215
  Began Service: September 29, 2012
  Appointed By: President Barack Obama
  E-mail: gershwin_drain@mied.uscourts.gov
District Judge **Terrence G. Berg** . . . . (810) 341-9760
  Note: On Leave.
  Began Service: December 7, 2012
  Appointed By: President Barack Obama
  E-mail: terrence_berg@mied.uscourts.gov
District Judge **Judith Ellen Levy** . . . . (734) 887-4700
  Began Service: March 14, 2014
  Appointed By: President Barack Obama
  200 East Liberty Street, Suite 300,
  Ann Arbor, MI 48104
  E-mail: judith_levy@mied.uscourts.gov
District Judge **Laurie J. Michelson** 640 . . . . (313) 234-5095
  Began Service: March 14, 2014
  Appointed By: President Barack Obama
  E-mail: laurie_michelson@mied.uscourts.gov

(continued on next page)

United States District Court for the Eastern District of Michigan
continued

District Judge **Matthew Frederick Leitman** Room
1013 . . . . (313) 234-5125
 Began Service: March 14, 2014
 Appointed By: President Barack Obama
 E-mail: matthew_leitman@mied.uscourts.gov
District Judge **Linda Vivienne Parker** Room 619 . . . . (313) 234-5105
 Began Service: March 17, 2014
 Appointed By: President Barack Obama
 E-mail: linda_parker@mied.uscourts.gov
Senior Judge **Bernard A. Friedman** Room 100 . . . . (313) 234-5170
 Began Service: June 1, 1988
 Appointed By: President Ronald Reagan
 E-mail: bernard_friedman@mied.uscourts.gov
Senior Judge **Patrick J. Duggan** Room 867 . . . . (313) 234-5145
 Began Service: 1987
 Appointed By: President Ronald Reagan
 E-mail: patrick_duggan@mied.uscourts.gov
Senior Judge **John Corbett O'Meara** . . . . (734) 741-2106
 Began Service: October 4, 1994
 Appointed By: President William J. Clinton
 200 East Liberty Street, Suite 400,
 Ann Arbor, MI 48104
 E-mail: john_corbett_omeara@mied.uscourts.gov
Senior Judge **Avern Levin Cohn** . . . . (313) 234-5160
 Began Service: October 9, 1979
 Appointed By: President Jimmy Carter
 Theodore Levin U.S. Courthouse,
 231 West Lafayette Boulevard, Room 219,
 Detroit, MI 48226-2792
 E-mail: Avern_Cohn@mied.uscourts.gov
Senior Judge **Arthur J. Tarnow** Room 124 . . . . (313) 234-5180
 Began Service: May 26, 1998
 Appointed By: President William J. Clinton
 E-mail: arthur_tarnow@mied.uscourts.gov
Senior Judge **Nancy G. Edmunds** Room 851 . . . . (313) 234-5155
 Began Service: February 10, 1992
 Appointed By: President George H.W. Bush
 E-mail: nancy_edmunds@mied.uscourts.gov
Senior Judge **Marianne O. Battani** . . . . (313) 234-2625
 Began Service: June 9, 2000
 Appointed By: President William J. Clinton
 E-mail: marianne_battani@mied.uscourts.gov
Senior Judge **George Caram Steeh** . . . . (313) 234-5175
 Began Service: July 2, 1998
 Appointed By: President William J. Clinton
 Theodore Levin U.S. Courthouse,
 231 West Lafayette Boulevard, Room 238,
 Detroit, MI 48226-2788
 E-mail: george_caram_steeh@mied.uscourts.gov
Senior Judge **Robert Hardy Cleland** . . . . (313) 234-5525
 Began Service: June 19, 1990
 Appointed By: President George H.W. Bush
 E-mail: robert_cleland@mied.uscourts.gov
Magistrate Judge **R. Steven Whalen** Room 673 . . . . (313) 234-5115
 Began Service: September 11, 2002
Magistrate Judge **Mona K. Majzoub** Room 642 . . . . (313) 234-5205
 Began Service: January 6, 2004
 E-mail: mona_majzoub@mied.uscourts.gov
Magistrate Judge **Michael Hluchaniuk** . . . . (810) 341-7850
 Began Service: January 2008
 Federal Building and U.S. Courthouse,
 600 Church Street, Room 112,
 Flint, MI 48502
 E-mail: michael_hluchaniuk@mied.uscourts.gov
Magistrate Judge **David R. Grand** . . . . (734) 741-2485
 Began Service: November 1, 2011
 200 East Liberty Street, Suite 100,
 Ann Arbor, MI 48104
 E-mail: david_grand@mied.uscourts.gov
Magistrate Judge **Patricia T. Morris** . . . . (989) 894-8820
 1000 Washington Avenue, Room 323,
 Bay City, MI 48708
Magistrate Judge **Anthony P. Patti** . . . . (313) 234-5200
Magistrate Judge **Elizabeth Stafford** Room 619 . . . . (313) 234-5105

United States District Court for the Eastern District of Michigan
continued

Court Staff
Court Administrator and Clerk of the Court
 David J. Weaver . . . . (313) 234-5051
 E-mail: david_weaver@mied.uscourts.gov
Court Services Manager **Michael Kregear** . . . . (313) 234-5055
 E-mail: michael_kregear@mied.uscourts.gov
Chief Probation Officer **Philip Miller** . . . . (313) 234-5400
Chief Pretrial Services Officer **Alan Murray** . . . . (313) 234-5300

United States Bankruptcy Court for the Eastern District of Michigan
211 West Fort Street, Detroit, MI 48226
Tel: (313) 234-0068 Tel: (313) 234-0065 (General Info)
Tel: (313) 961-4934 (PACER)
Tel: (313) 961-4940 (Voice Case Information System VCIS)
Internet: www.mieb.uscourts.gov

Number of Judgeships: 5

Judges
Chief Bankruptcy Judge **Phillip J. Shefferly** Suite 1950 . . . (313) 234-0040
 Began Service: 2008
 E-mail: phillip_shefferly@mieb.uscourts.gov
Bankruptcy Judge **Marci B. McIvor** Suite 1850 . . . . (313) 234-0010
 Began Service: 2003
 E-mail: marci_mcivor@mieb.uscourts.gov
Bankruptcy Judge **Thomas J. Tucker** Suite 1900 . . . . (313) 234-0030
 Began Service: March 21, 2003
 E-mail: thomas_tucker@mieb.uscourts.gov
Bankruptcy Judge **Daniel S. Opperman** . . . . (989) 894-8850
 Began Service: July 2006
 E-mail: daniel_opperman@mieb.uscourts.gov
Bankruptcy Judge (recalled) **Walter Shapero** . . . . (313) 234-2640
 Began Service: July 15, 2002
 Theodore Levin Courthouse,
 231 West Lafayette Boulevard, Room 1029,
 Detroit, MI 48226
 E-mail: walter_shapero@mieb.uscourts.gov
Bankruptcy Judge **Mark A. Randon** Suite 1820 . . . . (313) 234-0026

Court Staff
Bankruptcy Clerk **Katherine B. Gullo** . . . . (313) 234-0065
 E-mail: katherine_gullo@mieb.uscourts.gov

U.S. Attorney
Michigan - Eastern District
211 West Fort Street, Suite 2001, Detroit, MI 48226-3211
Tel: (313) 226-9100 TTY: (313) 226-9560 Fax: (313) 226-4609

U.S. Attorney **Barbara L. McQuade** . . . . (313) 226-9100
 E-mail: barbara.mcquade@usdoj.gov

Federal Public Defender
Federal Defender Office for the Eastern District of Michigan
613 Abbott, Detroit, MI 48226
653 South Saginaw Street, Suite 105, Flint, MI 48502
Tel: (313) 967-5542 (Detroit) Tel: (810) 232-3600 (Flint)
Fax: (313) 962-0685 (Detroit) Fax: (810) 232-9434 (Flint)

Federal Public Defender **Miriam Seifer** . . . . (313) 967-5542

United States District Court for the Western District of Michigan

Federal Building, 110 Michigan Street, NW, Room 399,
Grand Rapids, MI 49503
Tel: (616) 456-2381 Tel: (616) 732-2765 (PACER)
Tel: (800) 547-6398 (Toll Free PACER) Fax: (616) 456-2066
Internet: www.miwd.uscourts.gov

Number of Judgeships: 5

Circuit: Sixth

Areas Covered: Counties of Alger, Allegan, Antrim, Baraga, Barry, Benzie, Berrien, Branch, Calhoun, Cass, Charlevoix, Chippewa, Clinton, Delta, Dickinson, Eaton, Emmet, Gogebic, Grand Traverse, Hillsdale, Houghton, Ingham, Ionia, Iron, Kalamazoo, Kalkaska, Kent, Keweenaw, Lake, Leelanau, Luce, Mackinac, Manistee, Marquette, Mason, Mecosta, Menominee, Missaukee, Montcalm, Muskegon, Newaygo, Oceana, Ontonagon, Osceola, Ottawa, Schoolcraft, St. Joseph, Van Buren and Wexford

Judges

Chief Judge **Paul Lewis Maloney** . . . . (269) 381-4741
    Began Service: July 18, 2007   Tel: (269) 381-4741
    Appointed By: President George W. Bush
    E-mail: paul_maloney@miwd.uscourts.gov
District Judge **Robert Holmes Bell** Room 602 . . . . (616) 456-2021
    Began Service: August 6, 1987
    Appointed By: President Ronald Reagan
District Judge **Robert James Jonker** Room 640 . . . . (616) 456-2551
    Began Service: July 18, 2007
    Appointed By: President George W. Bush
    E-mail: robert_jonker@miwd.uscourts.gov
District Judge **Janet T. Neff** Room 401 . . . . (616) 456-6774
    Began Service: August 2007
    Appointed By: President George W. Bush
    E-mail: janet_neff@miwd.uscourts.gov
Senior Judge **R. Allan Edgar** . . . . (906) 226-2084
    Began Service: May 16, 1985
    Appointed By: President Ronald Reagan
Senior Judge **Gordon J. Quist** Room 482 . . . . (616) 456-2253
    Began Service: August 28, 1992
    Appointed By: President George H.W. Bush
    E-mail: gordon_j_quist@miwd.uscourts.gov
Magistrate Judge **Hugh W. Brenneman, Jr.** Room 580 . . . (616) 456-2568
    Note: Until August 1, 2015.
    Began Service: April 1, 1980
    E-mail: hugh_brenneman@miwd.uscourts.gov
Magistrate Judge **Timothy P. Greeley** . . . . (906) 226-3854
    Began Service: January 11, 1988
    E-mail: timothy_greeley@miwd.uscourts.gov
Magistrate Judge **Ellen S. Carmody** Room 664 . . . . (616) 456-2528
    Began Service: October 11, 2000
    E-mail: ellen_carmody@miwd.uscourts.gov
Magistrate Judge **Phillip J. Green** Room 712 . . . . (616) 456-2309
Magistrate Judge **Ray Kent** . . . . (616) 456-2381

Court Staff

Clerk of the Court **Tracey Cordes** . . . . (616) 456-2381
    E-mail: tracey_cordes@miwd.uscourts.gov
Chief Probation Officer **Rebecca Howell** Room 137 . . . . . . (616) 456-2384

United States Bankruptcy Court for the Western District of Michigan

One Division Avenue, North, Room 200, Grand Rapids, MI 49503
Tel: (616) 456-2693 Tel: (800) 676-6856 (Toll Free PACER)
Tel: (866) 222-8029 (Toll Free Voice Case Information System VCIS)
Fax: (616) 456-2919
E-mail: clerk_miwb@miwb.uscourts.gov
Internet: www.miwb.uscourts.gov

Number of Judgeships: 3

Judges

Chief Bankruptcy Judge **Scott W. Dales** Room 210 . . . . . . (616) 456-2949
    Began Service: October 5, 2007
    E-mail: scott_dales@miwb.uscourts.gov

Court Staff

Clerk of Court **Daniel M. LaVille** . . . . (616) 456-2693
    E-mail: dan_laville@miwb.uscourts.gov

U.S. Attorney

Michigan - Western District
330 Ionia NW, Suite 501, Grand Rapids, MI 49503
P.O. Box 208, Grand Rapids, MI 49501-0208
Tel: (616) 456-2404 Fax: (616) 456-2408

U.S. Attorney **Patrick A. "Pat" Miles, Jr.** . . . . (616) 456-2404

Federal Public Defender

Federal Public Defender for Western Michigan
50 Louis Street NW, Suite 300, Grand Rapids, MI 49503
100 North Front Street, Suite 104, Marquette, MI 49855
Tel: (616) 742-7420 (Grand Rapids) Tel: (906) 226-3050 (Marquette)
Fax: (616) 742-7430 (Grand Rapids) Fax: (906) 226-3499 (Marquette)

Federal Public Defender (Interim) **Sharon Turek** . . . . (616) 742-7420

United States District Court for the District of Minnesota

U.S. Courthouse, 300 South Fourth Street, Room 202,
Minneapolis, MN 55415
Tel: (612) 664-5000 Tel: (612) 664-5170 (PACER)
Tel: (800) 818-8761 (Toll Free)
Internet: www.mnd.uscourts.gov

Number of Judgeships: 7

Number of Vacancies: 1

Circuit: Eighth

Judges

Chief Judge **John R. Tunheim** Suite 15E . . . . (612) 664-5080
    Began Service: December 29, 1995
    Appointed By: President William J. Clinton
District Judge **Ann D. Montgomery** . . . . (612) 664-5090
    Began Service: August 6, 1996
    Appointed By: President William J. Clinton
    U.S. Courthouse, 300 South Fourth Street,
    Room 13 West, Minneapolis, MN 55415-1320
    E-mail: ADMontgomery@mnd.uscourts.gov
District Judge **Donovan W. Frank** . . . . (651) 848-1290
    Began Service: November 2, 1998
    Appointed By: President William J. Clinton
    Warren E. Burger Federal Building and U.S.
    Courthouse, 316 North Robert Street, Suite 724,
    St. Paul, MN 55101
    E-mail: frank_chambers@mnd.uscourts.gov

(continued on next page)

United States District Court for the District of Minnesota *continued*

District Judge **Joan N. Ericksen** Suite 12 West . . . .(612) 664-5890
    Began Service: June 14, 2002
    Appointed By: President George W. Bush
    E-mail: joanericksen_chambers@mnd.uscourts.gov

District Judge **Patrick Joseph Schiltz** Suite 14 East . . . . . .(612) 664-5480
    Began Service: September 22, 2006
    Appointed By: President George W. Bush

District Judge **Susan Richard Nelson** . . . .(651) 848-1970
    Began Service: December 22, 2010
    Appointed By: President Barack Obama
    E-mail: nelson_chambers@mnd.uscourts.gov

Senior Judge **Donald D. Alsop** . . . . (651) 848-1170
    Began Service: December 20, 1974
    Appointed By: President Richard M. Nixon
    E-mail: ddalsop@mnd.uscourts.gov

Senior Judge **Paul A. Magnuson** . . . .(651) 848-1150
    Began Service: 1981
    Appointed By: President Ronald Reagan
    E-mail: PAMagnuson@mnd.uscourts.gov

Senior Judge **David S. Doty** . . . .(612) 664-5060
    Began Service: May 1987
    Appointed By: President Ronald Reagan

Senior Judge **Richard H. Kyle** . . . . (651) 848-1160
    Began Service: May 15, 1992
    Appointed By: President George H.W. Bush
    E-mail: RHKyle@mnd.uscourts.gov

Senior Judge **Michael J. Davis** Room 15 East . . . .(612) 664-5070
    Began Service: March 30, 1994
    Appointed By: President William J. Clinton
    E-mail: MJDavis@mnd.uscourts.gov

Magistrate Judge **Franklin L. Noel** Room 9 West . . . .(612) 664-5110
    Began Service: November 3, 1989

Magistrate Judge **Janie S. Mayeron** . . . .(651) 848-1190
    Began Service: February 7, 2003   Tel: (651) 848-1192
    E-mail: mayeron_chambers@mnd.uscourts.gov

Magistrate Judge **Jeffrey J. Keyes** . . . .(651) 848-1180
    Began Service: April 28, 2008
    E-mail: keyes_chambers@mnd.uscourts.gov

Magistrate Judge **Leo I. Brisbois** . . . .(218) 529-3520
    Began Service: 2010
    515 West First Street, Room 412,
    Duluth, MN 55802-1397

Magistrate Judge **Steven E. Rau** . . . .(651) 848-1620
    Began Service: 2011   Tel: (651) 848-1622
    Warren E. Burger Federal Courthouse,
    316 North Robert Street, Room 334,
    St. Paul, MN 55101
    E-mail: rau_chambers@mnd.uscourts.gov

Magistrate Judge **Tony N. Leung** . . . .(651) 848-1870
    Began Service: April 29, 2011
    E-mail: leung_chambers@mnd.uscourts.gov

Magistrate Judge **Hildy Bowbeer** . . . .(651) 848-1900
    316 North Robert Street, Room 632,
    St. Paul, MN 55101

Magistrate Judge **Becky R. Thorson** . . . .(651) 848-1210
    Began Service: December 2014

Magistrate Judge (Part-Time) **Jon T. Huseby** . . . .(218) 751-0399

Court Staff

Clerk of Court **Richard D. Sletten** . . . . (612) 664-5000
Chief Probation and Pretrial Officer **Kevin Lowry** . . . .(612) 664-5400

United States Bankruptcy Court for the District of Minnesota

U.S. Courthouse, 300 South Fourth Street, Room 301,
Minneapolis, MN 55415
Tel: (612) 664-5200
Tel: (866) 222-8029 (Toll Free Voice Case Information System)
Fax: (612) 664-5303
Internet: www.mnb.uscourts.gov

Number of Judgeships: 4

Judges

Chief Bankruptcy Judge **Gregory F. Kishel** . . . .(651) 848-1060
    Began Service: May 24, 1984
    E-mail: gregory_kishel@mnb.uscourts.gov

Bankruptcy Judge **Robert J. Kressel** Room 8W . . . .(612) 664-5250
    Began Service: December 6, 1982
    E-mail: robert_kressel@mnb.uscourts.gov

Bankruptcy Judge **Kathleen Hvass Sanberg** . . . .(612) 664-5280

Bankruptcy Judge **Katherine A. Constantine** . . . .(651) 848-1050
    Began Service: 2013
    Warren E. Burger Federal Building,
    316 North Robert Street, Room 206,
    St. Paul, MN 55101

Bankruptcy Judge **Michael E. Ridgway** . . . .(612) 664-5260

Court Staff

Clerk of Court **Lori Vosejpka** . . . .(612) 664-5200
    E-mail: lori_vosejpka@mnb.uscourts.gov

U.S. Attorney

Minnesota District

600 U.S. Courthouse, 300 South Fourth Street, Minneapolis, MN 55415
Tel: (612) 664-5600 Tel: (651) 848-1950 (St. Paul, MN Office)
Fax: (612) 664-5787

U.S. Attorney **Andrew Mark "Andy" Luger** . . . .(612) 664-5600
    E-mail: andrew.luger@usdoj.gov

Federal Public Defender

Office of the Federal Public Defender - District of Minnesota

300 South Fourth Street, Room 107, Minneapolis, MN 55415
Tel: (612) 664-5858 Fax: (612) 664-5850

Federal Public Defender **Katherian Roe** . . . .(612) 664-5858
    E-mail: katherian.roe@fd.org

United States District Court for the Northern District of Mississippi

Federal Building, 911 Jackson Avenue, Room 369, Oxford, MS 38655
Tel: (662) 234-1971 Tel: (662) 236-4706 (PACER)
Fax: (662) 236-5210
Internet: www.msnd.uscourts.gov

Number of Judgeships: 3

Circuit: Fifth

Areas Covered: Counties of Alcorn, Attala, Benton, Bolivar, Calhoun, Carroll, Chickasaw, Choctaw, Clay, Coahoma, DeSoto, Grenada, Humphreys, Itawamba, Lafayette, Lee, Leflore, Lowndes, Marshall, Monroe, Montgomery, Oktibbeha, Panola, Pontotoc, Prentiss, Quitman, Sunflower, Tallahatchie, Tate, Tippah, Tishomingo, Tunica, Union, Washington, Webster, Winston and Yalobusha

Judges

Chief Judge **Sharion Aycock** . . . . (662) 369-2628
  Began Service: October 26, 2007
  Appointed By: President George W. Bush
  301 West Commerce Street, Room 218,
  Aberdeen, MS 39730
  E-mail: sharion_aycock@msnd.uscourts.gov
District Judge **Michael P. Mills** . . . . (662) 234-1538
  Began Service: November 1, 2001
  Appointed By: President George W. Bush
  Federal Building, 911 Jackson Avenue, Room 335,
  Oxford, MS 38655-3622
  E-mail: judge_mills@msnd.uscourts.gov
District Judge **Debra M. Brown** . . . . (662) 335-4416
  Began Service: December 19, 2013
  Appointed By: President Barack Obama
  E-mail: judge_brown@msnd.uscourts.gov
Senior Judge **Neal B. Biggers** . . . . (662) 234-3401
  Began Service: 1984
  Appointed By: President Ronald Reagan
  Federal Building, 911 Jackson Avenue, Suite 388,
  Oxford, MS 38655-3622
  E-mail: neal_biggers@msnd.uscourts.gov
Senior Judge **Glen H. Davidson** . . . . (662) 369-6486
  Began Service: October 29, 1985
  Appointed By: President Ronald Reagan
  E-mail: glen_davidson@msnd.uscourts.gov
Magistrate Judge **S. Allan Alexander** Suite 242 . . . . (662) 281-3008
  Began Service: November 17, 1994
  E-mail: judge_alexander@msnd.uscourts.gov
Magistrate Judge **David A. Sanders** . . . . (662) 369-2138
  Began Service: July 2008
  E-mail: judge_sanders@msnd.uscourts.gov
Magistrate Judge **Jane M. Virden** . . . . (662) 335-9214
  Began Service: 2011
  305 Main Street, Room 329,
  Greenville, MS 38701
  E-mail: jane_virden@msnd.uscourts.gov

Court Staff

Clerk of Court **David Crews** . . . . (662) 234-1971
  E-mail: david_crews@msnd.uscourts.gov
Chief Probation Officer **Danny Ray McKittrick** . . . . (662) 234-2761

United States Bankruptcy Court for the Northern District of Mississippi

Thad Cochran United States Bankruptcy Courthouse, 703 Highway 145 North, Aberdeen, MS 39730
Tel: (662) 369-2596 Tel: (800) 676-6856 (PACER Subscription)
Tel: (800) 392-8653 (Voice Case Information System)
Internet: www.msnb.uscourts.gov

Number of Judgeships: 2

Judges

Chief Bankruptcy Judge **Jason D. Woodward** . . . . (662) 369-2624
  Began Service: 2013
Bankruptcy Judge **Neil P. Olack** . . . . (601) 608-4600
  Began Service: 2006

Court Staff

Clerk of Court **David J. Puddister** . . . . (662) 369-2596

U.S. Attorney

Mississippi - Northern District
900 Jefferson Avenue, Oxford, MS 38655-3608
Tel: (662) 234-3351 Fax: (662) 234-4818

U.S. Attorney **Felicia C. Adams** . . . . (662) 234-3351
  E-mail: felicia.adams@usdoj.gov

Federal Public Defender

Federal Public Defender, Northern and Southern District of Mississippi
200 South Lamar Street, Suite 200N, Jackson, MS 39201
2510 Fourteenth Street, Suite902, Gulfport, MS 39501
1200 Jefferson Avenue, Oxford, MS 39501
Tel: (601) 948-4284 (Jackson) Tel: (228) 865-1202 (Gulfport)
Tel: (662) 236-2889 (Oxford) Fax: (601) 948-5510 (Jackson)
Fax: (228) 867-1907 (Gulfport) Fax: (662) 234-0428 (Oxford)

Federal Public Defender **Dennis Joiner** . . . . (601) 948-4284
  E-mail: dennis.joiner@fd.org

United States District Court for the Southern District of Mississippi

316 James O. Eastland U.S. Courthouse, 245 East Capitol Street, Jackson, MS 39201
P.O. Box 23552, Jackson, MS 39225-3552
Tel: (601) 608-4000
Internet: www.mssd.uscourts.gov

Number of Judgeships: 6

Circuit: Fifth

Areas Covered: Counties of Adams, Amite, Claiborne, Clarke, Copiah, Covington, Forrest, Franklin, George, Greene, Hancock, Harrison, Hinds, Holmes, Issaquena, Jackson, Jasper, Jefferson, Jefferson Davis, Jones, Kemper, Lamar, Lauderdale, Lawrence, Leake, Lincoln, Madison, Marion, Neshoba, Newton, Noxubee, Pearl River, Perry, Pike, Rankin, Scott, Sharkey, Simpson, Smith, Stone, Walthall, Warren, Wayne, Wilkinson and Yazoo

Judges

Chief District Judge **Louis Guirola, Jr.** . . . . (228) 563-1767
  Began Service: March 22, 2004
  Appointed By: President George W. Bush
  2012 15th Street, Suite 814,
  Gulfport, MS 39501

(continued on next page)

United States District Court for the Southern District of Mississippi
continued

District Judge **The Honorable Keith Starrett** . . . . (601) 583-4422
  Began Service: January 1, 2005
  Appointed By: President George W. Bush
  701 North Main Street, Suite 228,
  Hattiesburg, MS 39401
  E-mail: keith_starrett@mssd.uscourts.gov

District Judge **Daniel Porter Jordan III** . . . . (601) 608-4120
  Began Service: August 7, 2006
  Appointed By: President George W. Bush
  2012 15th Street, Suite 5.750,
  Jackson, MS 39201

District Judge **Halil Suleyman Ozerden** . . . . (228) 679-1070
  Began Service: May 1, 2007
  Appointed By: President George W. Bush
  2012 15th Street, Suite 714,
  Gulfport, MS 39501
  E-mail: ozerden_chambers@mssd.uscourts.gov

District Judge **Henry T. Wingate** . . . . (601) 608-4100
  Began Service: October 1985
  Appointed By: President Ronald Reagan
  2012 15th Street, Suite 6.750,
  Jackson, MS 39201
  E-mail: henry_wingate@mssd.uscourts.gov

District Judge **Carlton W. Reeves** . . . . (601) 608-4140
  Began Service: December 30, 2010
  Appointed By: President Barack Obama
  2012 15th Street, Suite 5.550,
  Jackson, MS 39201
  E-mail: reeves_chambers@mssd.uscourts.gov

Senior Judge **Walter J. Gex III** . . . . (228) 563-1732
  Began Service: 1986
  Appointed By: President Ronald Reagan
  2012 15th Street, Suite 572,
  Gulfport, MS 39501
  E-mail: walter_gex@mssd.uscourts.gov

Senior Judge **William H. Barbour, Jr.** . . . . (601) 608-4400
  Began Service: April 1983
  Appointed By: President Ronald Reagan
  2012 15th Street, Suite 4.550,
  Jackson, MS 39201
  E-mail: william_barbour@mssd.uscourts.gov

Senior Judge **David C. Bramlette III** . . . . (601) 442-3006
  Began Service: December 1991   Tel: (601) 442-9324
  Appointed By: President George H.W. Bush   (Alternate number)
  E-mail: david_bramlette@mssd.uscourts.gov

Senior Judge **Tom Stewart Lee** . . . . (601) 608-4420
  Began Service: June 25, 1984
  Appointed By: President Ronald Reagan
  2012 15th Street, Suite 4.756,
  Jackson, MS 39201
  E-mail: Tom_Lee@mssd.uscourts.gov

Magistrate Judge **Robert H. Walker** . . . . (228) 563-1720
  Began Service: November 15, 2004
  2012 15th Street, Suite 870,
  Gulfport, MS 39501
  E-mail: robert_walker@mssd.uscourts.gov

Magistrate Judge **Michael T. Parker** . . . . (601) 544-9100
  Began Service: May 26, 2006
  701 North Main Street, Room 216,
  Hattiesburg, MS 39401

Magistrate Judge **Linda R. Anderson** . . . . (601) 608-4440
  Began Service: July 12, 2006
  2012 15th Street, Suiet 6.150,
  Jackson, MS 39201
  E-mail: linda_anderson@mssd.uscourts.gov

Magistrate Judge **F. Keith Ball** . . . . (601) 608-4460
  Began Service: January 2010
  2012 15th Street, Suite 5.150,
  Jackson, MS 39201
  E-mail: keith_ball@mssd.uscourts.gov

Magistrate Judge **John Gargiulo** . . . . (601) 608-4000
  Began Service: 2014

Court Staff

Clerk of Court **Arthur Johnston** . . . . (601) 608-4000

United States District Court for the Southern District of Mississippi
continued

Chief Probation Officer **Carolyn Romano** . . . . (601) 608-4900
  2012 15th Street, Suite 1.550,
  Jackson, MS 39201

United States Bankruptcy Court for the Southern District of Mississippi

2012 15th Street, Jackson, MS 39201
P.O. Box 2448, Jackson, MS 39225-2448
Tel: (601) 608-4600
Tel: (866) 222-8029 (Toll Free Voice Case Information System VCIS)
Internet: www.mssb.uscourts.gov

Number of Judgeships: 3

Judges

Chief Bankruptcy Judge **Neil P. Olack** . . . . (601) 608-4690
  Began Service: May 1, 2006
  E-mail: neil_olack@mssb.uscourts.gov

Bankruptcy Judge **Edward Ellington** Suite 2300 . . . . (601) 608-4670
  Began Service: January 15, 1986
  E-mail: edward_ellington@mssb.uscourts.gov

Bankruptcy Judge **Katharine M. Samson** Suite 244 . . . . . . (228) 563-1841
  Began Service: 2010
  E-mail: katharine_samson@mssb.uscourts.gov

Court Staff

Bankruptcy Clerk **Danny L. Miller** . . . . (601) 608-4600
  E-mail: danny_miller@mssb.uscourts.gov

U.S. Attorney

Mississippi - Southern District
501 East Court Street, Suite 4-430, Jackson, MS 39201
Tel: (601) 965-4480   Fax: (601) 965-4409

U.S. Attorney **Gregory Keith Davis** . . . . (601) 965-4480
  E-mail: gregory.davis@usdoj.gov

Federal Public Defender

Federal Public Defender, Northern and Southern District of Mississippi
200 South Lamar Street, Suite 200N, Jackson, MS 39201
2510 Fourteenth Street, Suite902, Gulfport, MS 39501
1200 Jefferson Avenue, Oxford, MS 39501
Tel: (601) 948-4284 (Jackson) Tel: (228) 865-1202 (Gulfport)
Tel: (662) 236-2889 (Oxford) Fax: (601) 948-5510 (Jackson)
Fax: (228) 867-1907 (Gulfport) Fax: (662) 234-0428 (Oxford)

Federal Public Defender **Dennis Joiner** . . . . (601) 948-4284
  E-mail: dennis.joiner@fd.org

United States District Court for the Eastern District of Missouri

Thomas F. Eagleton U.S. Courthouse, 111 South Tenth Street, Room 3.300, St. Louis, MO 63102
Tel: (314) 244-7900 Tel: (314) 244-7775 (PACER)
Fax: (314) 244-7909
Internet: www.moed.uscourts.gov

Number of Judgeships: 9

Circuit: Eighth

Areas Covered: Counties of Adair, Audrain, Bollinger, Butler, Cape Girardeau, Carter, Chariton, Clark, Crawford, Dent, Dunklin, Franklin, Gasconade, Iron, Jefferson, Knox, Lewis, Lincoln, Linn, Macon, Madison, Maries, Marion, Mississippi, Monroe, Montgomery, New Madrid, Pemiscot, Perry, Phelps, Pike, Ralls, Randolph, Reynolds, Ripley, Schuyler, Scotland, Scott, Shannon, Shelby, St. Charles, St. Francois, St. Louis, Ste. Genevieve, Stoddard, Warren, Washington and Wayne

Judges

Chief Judge **Catherine D. Perry** Room 14.182 . . . .(314) 244-7520
 Began Service: October 21, 1994   Tel: (314) 244-7520
 Appointed By: President William J. Clinton
 E-mail: catherine_perry@moed.uscourts.gov
District Judge **Carol E. Jackson** Suite 14.148 . . . . (314) 244-7540
 Began Service: October 15, 1992
 Appointed By: President George H.W. Bush
 E-mail: carol_jackson@moed.uscourts.gov
District Judge **Rodney W. Sippel** . . . . (314) 244-7430
 Began Service: January 27, 1998
 Appointed By: President William J. Clinton
 Thomas F. Eagleton U.S. Courthouse,
 111 South Tenth Street, Suite 16.182,
 St. Louis, MO 61302
 E-mail: rodney_sippel@moed.uscourts.gov
District Judge **Henry Edward Autrey** Suite 10.182 . . . .(314) 244-7450
 Began Service: September 16, 2002
 Appointed By: President George W. Bush
District Judge **Stephen N. Limbaugh, Jr.** . . . . (573) 331-8873
 Began Service: 2008
 Appointed By: President George W. Bush
 555 Independence Street, Suite 4000,
 Cape Girardeau, MO 63703
District Judge **Audrey Goldstein Fleissig** Suite 12.182 . . . (314) 244-7420
 Began Service: June 11, 2010
 Appointed By: President Barack Obama
 E-mail: audrey_fleissig@moed.uscourts.gov
District Judge **John A. Ross** Room 12.148 . . . . (314) 244-7560
 Began Service: November 2, 2011
 Appointed By: President Barack Obama
District Judge **Brian C. Wimes** . . . . (314) 244-7900
 Began Service: 2012
 Appointed By: President Barack Obama
District Judge **Ronnie L. White** Room 17.182 . . . .(314) 244-7580
 Appointed By: President Barack Obama
 E-mail: ronnie_white@moed.uscourts.gov
Senior Judge **Edward L. Filippine** . . . .(314) 244-7640
 Began Service: August 1977
 Appointed By: President Jimmy Carter
 E-mail: edward_filippine@moed.uscourts.gov
Senior Judge **E. Richard Webber, Jr.** Suite 8 South . . . . . . (314) 244-7460
 Began Service: December 26, 1995
 Appointed By: President William J. Clinton
 E-mail: Richard_Webber@moed.uscourts.gov
Senior Judge **Jean C. Hamilton** Room 16.148 . . . . (314) 244-7600
 Began Service: November 1990   Tel: (314) 244-7600
 Appointed By: President George H.W. Bush
 E-mail: jean_hamilton@moed.uscourts.gov
Senior Judge **Charles A. Shaw** Suite 8.148 . . . .(314) 244-7480
 Began Service: January 3, 1994
 Appointed By: President William J. Clinton
Chief Magistrate Judge **Thomas C. Mummert III** . . . . (314) 244-7510
 Began Service: May 15, 1995
 E-mail: thomas_mummert@moed.uscourts.gov

Magistrate Judge **David D. Noce** Suite 17.156 . . . .(314) 244-7630
 Began Service: October 1, 1976
 E-mail: david_noce@moed.uscourts.gov
Magistrate Judge **Nannette A. Baker** Suite 9.152 . . . .(314) 244-7470
 Began Service: February 3, 2011
 E-mail: nannette_baker@moed.uscourts.gov
Magistrate Judge **Shirley Padmore Mensah** Suite
 14.148 . . . .(314) 244-7490
 Began Service: 2012
 E-mail: shirley_mensah@moed.uscourts.gov
Magistrate Judge **Noelle C. Collins** . . . .(314) 246-7570
 E-mail: noelle_collins@moed.uscourts.gov
Magistrate Judge **John Bodenhausen** . . . . (314) 244-7900
Magistrate Judge **Abbie Crites-Leoni** . . . . (573) 331-8870

Court Staff

Clerk of Court **Gregory "Greg" Linhares** . . . . (314) 244-7890
 E-mail: greg_linhares@moed.uscourts.gov
Chief Probation Officer **Douglas W. Burris** . . . . (314) 244-6700
Chief Pretrial Services **Mark Reichert** . . . .(314) 244-7000

United States Bankruptcy Court for the Eastern District of Missouri

Thomas F. Eagleton U.S. Courthouse, 111 South Tenth Street, Room 4.380, St. Louis, MO 63102
Tel: (314) 244-4500 Tel: (314) 244-4601 (Clerk's office)
Tel: (800) 676-6856 (PACER)
Tel: (866) 222-8029 ext. 87 (McVIS) Fax: (314) 244-4990
Internet: www.moeb.uscourts.gov

Number of Judgeships: 3

Judges

Chief Bankruptcy Judge **Kathy A. Surratt-States** Suite
 7 North . . . .(314) 244-4541
 Began Service: March 17, 2003
 E-mail: kathy_surratt-states@ca8.uscourts.gov
Bankruptcy Judge **Barry S. Schermer** . . . .(314) 244-4531
 Began Service: 1986
Bankruptcy Judge **Charles E. Rendlen III** . . . .(314) 244-4511
 Began Service: May 2006

Court Staff

Clerk of Court **Dana C. McWay** . . . .(314) 244-4601
 E-mail: dana_mcway@ca8.uscourts.gov

U.S. Attorney

Missouri - Eastern District
Thomas F. Eagleton U.S. Courthouse, 111 South 10th Street, Room 20.333, St. Louis, MO 63102
Tel: (314) 539-2200 Fax: (314) 539-2309

U.S. Attorney **Richard G. Callahan** . . . .(314) 539-2200
 E-mail: richard.callahan@usdoj.gov

Federal Public Defender

Office of the Federal Public Defender, Eastern District of Missouri
1010 Market Street, St. Louis, MO 63101
325 Broadway Street, Second Floor, Cape Girardeau, MO 63702
Tel: (314) 241-1255 (St. Louis) Tel: (573) 339-0242 (Cape Girardeau)
Fax: (314) 421-3177 (St. Louis) Tel: (573) 339-0305 (Cape Girardeau)

Federal Public Defender **Lee T. Lawless** . . . .(314) 241-1255
 E-mail: lee.lawless@fd.org

United States District Court for the Western District of Missouri

Charles Evans Whittaker U.S. Courthouse, 400 East Ninth Street, Kansas City, MO 64106
Tel: (816) 512-5000 Fax: (816) 512-5078
Internet: www.mow.uscourts.gov
Internet: ecf.mowd.uscourts.gov (Electronic Case Filing)

Number of Judgeships: 6

Circuit: Eighth

Areas Covered: Counties of Andrew, Atchison, Barry, Barton, Bates, Benton, Boone, Buchanan, Caldwell, Callaway, Camden, Carroll, Cass, Cedar, Christian, Clay, Clinton, Cole, Cooper, Dade, Dallas, Daviess, DeKalb Douglas, Gentry, Greene, Grundy, Harrison, Henry, Hickory, Holt, Howard, Howell, Jackson, Jasper, Johnson, Laclede, Lafayette, Lawrence, Livingston, McDonald, Mercer, Miller, Moniteau, Morgan, Newton, Nodaway, Oregon, Osage, Ozark, Pettis, Platte, Polk, Pulaski, Putnam, Ray, Saline, St. Clair, Stone, Sullivan, Taney, Texas, Vernon, Webster, Worth and Wright

Judges

Chief Judge **David Gregory Kays** Room 8652 . . . . (816) 512-5600
  Began Service: June 19, 2008
  Appointed By: President George W. Bush
  E-mail: greg_kays@mow.uscourts.gov
District Judge **Gary A. Fenner** . . . . (816) 512-5660
  Began Service: July 26, 1996
  Appointed By: President William J. Clinton
  Charles Evans Whittaker U.S. Courthouse,
  400 East Ninth Street, Room 8452,
  Kansas City, MO 64106-2607
  E-mail: gary_fenner@mow.uscourts.gov
District Judge **Mary Elizabeth "Beth" Phillips** Room
  7452 . . . . (816) 512-5384
  Began Service: March 23, 2012
  Appointed By: President Barack Obama
District Judge **Brian C. Wimes** Room 7652 . . . . (816) 512-5391
  Began Service: 2012
  Appointed By: President Barack Obama
  E-mail: brian_wimes@mow.uscourts.gov
District Judge **M. Douglas Harpool** . . . . (417) 865-3741
  Began Service: March 28, 2014
  Appointed By: President Barack Obama
  222 North John Q. Hammons Parkway, Suite 3100,
  Springfield, MO 65806
District Judge **Stephen R. Bough** Room 7462 . . . . (816) 512-5370
  Began Service: 2014
  Appointed By: President Barack Obama
Senior Judge **Howard F. Sachs** Room 7462 . . . . (816) 512-5715
  Began Service: October 5, 1979
  Appointed By: President Jimmy Carter
  E-mail: howard_sachs@mow.uscourts.gov
Senior Judge **Dean Whipple** Room 8462 . . . . (816) 512-5615
  Began Service: December 1987
  Appointed By: President Ronald Reagan
  E-mail: dean_whipple@mow.uscourts.gov
Senior Judge **Ortrie D. Smith** Room 8552 . . . . (816) 512-5645
  Began Service: August 1995
  Appointed By: President William J. Clinton
  E-mail: ortrie_smith@mow.uscourts.gov
Senior Judge **Nanette Kay Laughrey** . . . . (573) 632-6623
  Began Service: August 26, 1996
  Appointed By: President William J. Clinton
  80 Lafayette Street, Room 4112,
  Jefferson City, MO 65101
  E-mail: nanette_laughrey@mow.uscourts.gov
Senior Judge **Fernando J. Gaitan, Jr.** Room 7552 . . . . (816) 512-5630
  Began Service: 1991
  Appointed By: President George H.W. Bush
  E-mail: fernando_gaitan@mow.uscourts.gov
Chief Magistrate Judge **Sarah Hays** . . . . (816) 512-5775
  Began Service: 1992
  E-mail: sarah_hays@mow.uscourts.gov

United States District Court for the Western District of Missouri
continued

Magistrate Judge **Robert E. Larsen** . . . . (816) 512-5760
  Began Service: May 24, 1991
  E-mail: robert_larsen@mow.uscourts.gov
Magistrate Judge **John T. Maughmer** Room 7662 . . . . (816) 512-5745
  Began Service: September 29, 1988
  E-mail: john_maughmer@mow.uscourts.gov
Magistrate Judge **Matt J. Whitworth** . . . . (573) 634-3418
  Began Service: January 24, 2010
  80 Lafayette Street, Suite 3114,
  Jefferson City, MO 65101
  E-mail: matt_whitworth@mow.uscourts.gov
Magistrate Judge **David P. Rush** . . . . (417) 865-3761
  222 N. John Q. Hammons Parkway, Suite 2000,
  Springfield, MO 65806
  E-mail: david_rush@mow.uscourts.gov

Court Staff

Clerk of Court/Court Executive **Ann Thompson** . . . . (816) 512-5000
  E-mail: ann_thompson@mow.uscourts.gov
Chief Probation/Pretrial Services Officer **Kevin F. Lyon** . . . (816) 512-1300
  E-mail: kevin_lyon@mow.uscourts.gov

United States Bankruptcy Court for the Western District of Missouri

Charles Evans Whittaker U.S. Courthouse, 400 East Ninth Street, Kansas City, MO 64106
Tel: (816) 512-1800
Tel: (816) 512-5110 (Voice Case Information System VCIS)
Tel: (888) 205-2527 (Toll Free Voice Case Information System VCIS)
Fax: (816) 512-1832
Internet: www.mow.uscourts.gov
Internet: ecf.mowb.uscourts.gov (Electronic Case Filing)

Number of Judgeships: 3

Judges

Chief Bankruptcy Judge **Dennis R. Dow** Room 6562 . . . . . (816) 512-1880
  Began Service: November 10, 2003
  E-mail: dennis_dow@mow.uscourts.gov
Chief Bankruptcy Judge **Arthur Federman** Room 6552 . . . (816) 512-1910
  Began Service: December 18, 1989
  E-mail: arthur.federman@mow.uscourts.gov

Court Staff

Court Executive **Ann Thompson** . . . . (816) 512-5000

U.S. Attorney

Missouri - Western District
Charles Evans Whittaker Courthouse, 400 East Ninth Street, Room 5510, Kansas City, MO 64106
Tel: (816) 426-3122 Fax: (816) 426-4210

U.S. Attorney **Angela Tammy Dickinson** . . . . (816) 426-3122

Federal Public Defender

Office of the Federal Public Defender Western District of Missouri
818 Grand, Suite 300, Kansas City, MO 64106
221 Bolivar Street, Suite 104, Jefferson City, MO 65101
901 St. Louis Street, Suite 801, Springfield, MO 65806
Tel: (816) 471-8282 (Kansas City) Tel: (573) 636-8747 (Jefferson City)
Tel: (417) 873-9022 (Springfield) Fax: (816) 471-8008 (Kansas City)
Fax: (573) 636-9161 (Jefferson City) Fax: (417) 973-9038 (Springfield)

Federal Public Defender **Madeleine Cardarella** . . . . (816) 471-8282

United States District Court for the District of Montana

Missouri River Courthouse, 125 Central Avenue West,
Great Falls, MT 59404
Tel: (406) 727-1922 Tel: (406) 452-9581 (Civil Cases PACER)
Tel: (800) 305-5235 (Toll Free Civil Cases PACER) Fax: (406) 727-7648

Number of Judgeships: 3

Circuit: Ninth

Judges

Chief Judge **Dana L. Christensen** . . . . (406) 829-7140
  Began Service: December 6, 2011
  Appointed By: President Barack Obama
District Judge **Brian Morris** . . . . (406) 727-8877
  Began Service: December 18, 2013
  Appointed By: President Barack Obama
District Judge **Susan P. Watters** . . . . (406) 727-2350
  Began Service: December 19, 2013
  Appointed By: President Barack Obama
Senior Judge **Charles C. Lovell** . . . . (406) 441-1350
  Began Service: April 1985
  Appointed By: President Ronald Reagan
  U.S. Courthouse, 901 Front Street, Suite 3100,
  Helena, MT 59626
  E-mail: charles_lovell@mtd.uscourts.gov
Senior Judge **Donald W. Molloy** . . . . (406) 542-7286
  Began Service: August 16, 1996
  Appointed By: President William J. Clinton
  E-mail: donald_molloy@mtd.uscourts.gov
Senior Judge **Sam E. Haddon** . . . . (406) 457-4910
  Began Service: July 26, 2001
  Appointed By: President George W. Bush
  Paul G. Hatfield Courthouse,
  901 Front Street, Suite 3100A,
  Helena, MT 59626
Magistrate Judge **Keith Strong** . . . . (406) 727-0028
  Began Service: January 2007
  E-mail: keith_strong@mtd.uscourts.gov
Magistrate Judge **Carolyn S. Ostby** . . . . (406) 247-7025
  Began Service: February 2002
  E-mail: Carolyn_Ostby@mtd.uscourts.gov
Magistrate Judge **Jeremiah C. Lynch** . . . . (406) 542-7280
  Began Service: June 10, 2006
Magistrate Judge **John T. Johnston** . . . . (406) 727-1922
Magistrate Judge (recalled) **Richard W. Anderson** . . . . . . (406) 247-7000
  Began Service: January 1, 1991
  James F. Battin United States Courthouse,
  2601 Second Avenue North, Room 1200,
  Billings, MT 59101
  E-mail: richard_anderson@mtd.uscourts.gov
Magistrate Judge (recalled) **Robert M. Holter** . . . . (406) 727-0028
  Began Service: January 21, 1988
  Began Service: January 3, 2003
  125 Central Avenue West, Suite 110,
  Great Falls, MT 59403-2386

Court Staff

Clerk of Court **Tyler Gilman** . . . . (406) 542-7260
  E-mail: tyler_gilman@mtd.uscourts.gov
Chief Probation Officer **Tom Holter** . . . . (406) 542-7105
  201 East Broadway, Missoula, MT 59802
  E-mail: tom_holter@mtp.uscourts.gov

United States Bankruptcy Court for the District of Montana

Federal Building, 400 North Main Street, Butte, MT 59701
Tel: (406) 497-1240
Internet: www.mtb.uscourts.gov

Number of Judgeships: 2

Judges

Bankruptcy Judge **Ralph B. Kirscher** Room 215 . . . . (406) 497-1240
  Began Service: November 18, 1999
  E-mail: ralph_kirscher@mtb.uscourts.gov

Court Staff

Clerk of Court **Bernard F. McCarthy** . . . . (406) 497-1243
  E-mail: Bernard_McCarthy@mtb.uscourts.gov

U.S. Attorney

Montana District
2601 Second Ave North, Suite 3200, Billings, MT 59101
Tel: (406) 657-6101 Fax: (406) 657-6989

U.S. Attorney **Michael W. Cotter** . . . . (406) 457-5120
  E-mail: michael.cotter@usdoj.gov

Federal Public Defender

Federal Defenders of Montana
104 Second Street South, Suite 301, Great Falls, MT 59401-3645
2702 Montana Avenue, Suite 101, Billings, MT 59101
50 West Fourteenth Street, Suite 300, Helena, MT 59601
Tel: (406) 727-5328 (Great Falls) Tel: (406) 259-2459 (Billings)
Tel: (406) 449-8381 (Helena) Fax: (406) 727-4329 (Great Falls)
Fax: (406) 259-2569 (Billings) Fax: (406) 449-5651 (Helena)

Federal Public Defender **Anthony Gallagher** . . . . (406) 727-5328
  E-mail: anthony_gallagher@fd.org

United States District Court for the District of Nebraska

Roman L. Hruska U.S. Courthouse, 111 South 18th Plaza,
Suite 1152, Omaha, NE 68102-1322
Tel: (402) 661-7350 Tel: (866) 220-4381 (Toll Free)
Fax: (402) 661-7387
Internet: www.ned.uscourts.gov

Number of Judgeships: 3

Number of Vacancies: 1

Circuit: Eighth

Judges

Chief Judge **Laurie Smith Camp** Suite 3210 . . . . (402) 661-7323
  Began Service: November 2, 2001
  Appointed By: President George W. Bush
  E-mail: laurie_smith_camp@ned.uscourts.gov
District Judge **John M. Gerrard** . . . . (402) 437-1660
  Began Service: February 5, 2012
  Appointed By: President Barack Obama
  E-mail: gerrard@ned.uscourts.gov
Senior Judge **Lyle E. Strom** Suite 3190 . . . . (402) 661-7320
  Began Service: November 1, 1985
  Appointed By: President Ronald Reagan
  E-mail: lyle_strom@ned.uscourts.gov
Senior Judge **Richard G. Kopf** . . . . (402) 437-1640
  Began Service: May 26, 1992
  Appointed By: President George H.W. Bush
  E-mail: richard_kopf@ned.uscourts.gov

(continued on next page)

United States District Court for the District of Nebraska *continued*

Senior Judge **Joseph F. "Joe" Bataillon** Suite 3259 . . . . . (402) 661-7302
  Began Service: October 1997
  Appointed By: President William J. Clinton
  E-mail: Bataillon@ned.uscourts.gov
Magistrate Judge **Thomas D. Thalken** Suite 2271 . . . . (402) 661-7343
  Began Service: January 4, 1993
  E-mail: thalken@ned.uscourts.gov
Magistrate Judge **F. A. Gossett III** . . . . (402) 661-7340
  Began Service: May 29, 2003
  111 South 18th Plaza, Suite 2210,
  Omaha, NE 68102
Magistrate Judge **Cheryl Renae Zwart** . . . . (402) 437-1670
  Began Service: January 15, 2010

Court Staff

Clerk of Court **Denise Lucks** . . . . (402) 661-7350
  E-mail: denise_lucks@ned.uscourts.gov
Chief Probation and Pretrial Services Officer
  Mary Lee Ranheim . . . . (402) 661-7555
  E-mail: mary_lee_ranheim@nep.uscourts.gov

United States Bankruptcy Court for the District of Nebraska

Roman L. Hruska U.S. Courthouse, 111 South 18th Plaza,
Suite 1125, Omaha, NE 68102
Tel: (402) 661-7444
Tel: (866) 222-8029 (Toll Free Voice Case Information System)
Fax: (402) 661-7492
Internet: www.neb.uscourts.gov

Number of Judgeships: 2

Judges

Chief Bankruptcy Judge **Thomas L. Saladino** . . . . (402) 661-7482
  Began Service: August 2006
  Roman L. Hruska U.S. Courthouse,
  111 South 18th Plaza, Suite 2144,
  Omaha, NE 68102-1322

Court Staff

Clerk **Diane L. Zech** . . . . (402) 661-7444
  E-mail: Diane_Zech@neb.uscourts.gov

U.S. Attorney

Nebraska District
1620 Dodge Street, Suite 1400, Omaha, NE 68102-1506
Tel: (800) 899-9124 Tel: (402) 661-3700 Fax: (402) 345-6958

U.S. Attorney **Deborah K. R. Gilg** . . . . (402) 661-3700
  E-mail: deborah.gilg@usdoj.gov

Federal Public Defender

Federal Public Defender - District of Nebraska
222 South 15th Street, Suite 300N, Omaha, NE 68102
100 Centennial Mall North, Room 112, Lincoln, NE 68508
Tel: (402) 221-7896 (Omaha) Tel: (402) 437-5871 (Lincoln)
Fax: (402) 221-7884 (Omaha) Fax: (402) 437-5874 (Lincoln)

Federal Public Defender **David R. Stickman** . . . . (402) 221-7896
  E-mail: david.stickman@fd.org

United States District Court for the District of Nevada

Lloyd D. George U.S. Courthouse, 333 Las Vegas Boulevard South,
Las Vegas, NV 89101
Tel: (702) 464-5400 Fax: (702) 464-5457
Internet: www.nvd.uscourts.gov

Number of Judgeships: 7

Circuit: Ninth

Judges

Chief Judge **Gloria M. Navarro** . . . . (702) 464-5490
  Began Service: May 25, 2010
  Appointed By: President Barack Obama
  E-mail: gloria_navarro@nvd.uscourts.gov
District Judge **Robert C. Jones** . . . . (775) 686-5670
  Began Service: November 30, 2003
  Appointed By: President George W. Bush
  U.S. Courthouse, 400 South Virginia Street,
  Suite 805, Reno, NV 89501
District Judge **James C. Mahan** . . . . (702) 464-5520
  Began Service: February 1, 2002
  Appointed By: President George W. Bush
  E-mail: James_Mahan@nvd.uscourts.gov
District Judge **Miranda Du** . . . . (775) 686-5919
  Began Service: June 18, 2012
  Appointed By: President Barack Obama
  E-mail: miranda_du@nvd.uscourts.gov
District Judge **Andrew Patrick Gordon** . . . . (702) 868-4940
  Began Service: April 15, 2013
  Appointed By: President Barack Obama
  E-mail: andrew_gordon@nvd.uscourts.gov
District Judge **Jennifer A. Dorsey** . . . . (702) 868-4960
  Began Service: July 9, 2013
  Appointed By: President Barack Obama
District Judge **Richard Franklin Boulware III** . . . . (702) 868-4970
  Began Service: June 10, 2014
  Appointed By: President Barack Obama
  E-mail: richard_boulware@nvd.uscourts.gov
Senior Judge **Lloyd D. George** Room 6073 . . . . (702) 464-5500
  Began Service: May 1984
  Appointed By: President Ronald Reagan
  E-mail: lloyd_george@nvd.uscourts.gov
Senior Judge **Howard D. McKibben** . . . . (775) 686-5880
  Began Service: October 12, 1984
  Appointed By: President Ronald Reagan
  Bruce R. Thompson U.S. Courthouse and Federal
  Building, 400 South Virginia Street, Room 607,
  Reno, NV 89501
  E-mail: howard_mckibben@nvd.uscourts.gov
Senior Judge **Roger L. Hunt** . . . . (702) 464-5530
  Began Service: May 26, 2000
  Appointed By: President William J. Clinton
  E-mail: roger_hunt@nvd.uscourts.gov
Senior Judge **Kent J. Dawson** Suite 4085 . . . . (702) 464-5560
  Began Service: July 17, 2000
  Appointed By: President William J. Clinton
  E-mail: kent_dawson@nvd.uscourts.gov
Senior Judge **Larry R. Hicks** . . . . (775) 686-5700
  Began Service: November 29, 2001
  Appointed By: President George W. Bush
  Bruce R. Thompson U.S. Courthouse,
  400 South Virginia Street, Suite 506,
  Reno, NV 89501
  E-mail: larry_hicks@nvd.uscourts.gov
Magistrate Judge **Valerie P. Cooke** . . . . (775) 686-5855
  Began Service: November 1, 1999
  Bruce R. Thompson U.S. Courthouse and Federal
  Building, 400 South Virginia Street, Suite 404,
  Reno, NV 89501
  E-mail: valerie_cooke@nvd.uscourts.gov
Magistrate Judge **Peggy A. Leen** . . . . (702) 464-5570
  Began Service: January 16, 2001
  E-mail: peggy_leen@nvd.uscourts.gov

United States District Court for the District of Nevada *continued*

Magistrate Judge **George W. Foley, Jr.** Suite 3099 . . . . (702) 464-5575
  Began Service: August 2005
  E-mail: george_foley@nvd.uscourts.gov
Magistrate Judge **Carl W. Hoffman** . . . . (702) 464-5580
  Began Service: 2011
Magistrate Judge **William G. Cobb** . . . . (775) 686-5858
  Began Service: 2011
  E-mail: william_cobb@nvd.uscourts.gov
Magistrate Judge **Vincent "Cam" Ferenbach** . . . . (702) 464-5540
  Began Service: October 2011
Magistrate Judge **Nancy Koppe** . . . . (702) 464-5550
  E-mail: nancy_koppe@nvd.uscourts.gov
Magistrate Judge (recalled) **Robert A. McQuaid, Jr.** . . . . . (775) 686-5654
  Began Service: April 15, 1996
  E-mail: bob_mcquaid@nvd.uscourts.gov

Court Staff

Clerk of the Court **Lance S. Wilson** . . . . (702) 464-5400
  E-mail: lance_wilson@nvd.uscourts.gov
Chief U.S. Probation Officer **Chad Boardman** . . . . (702) 527-7300
  300 Las Vegas Boulevard South, Suite 1100,
  Las Vegas, NV 89101
Chief Pretrial Services Officer **Shiela Adkins** Room
  1112 . . . . (702) 464-5630

United States Bankruptcy Court for the District of Nevada

Foley Federal Building, 300 Las Vegas Boulevard South, 4th Floor,
Las Vegas, NV 89101
Clifton Young Federal Building, 300 Booth Street, 1st Floor,
Reno, NV 89509
Tel: (702) 527-7000 Tel: (775) 326-2100
Tel: (866) 222-8029 (Toll Free Voice Case Information System VCIS)
Internet: www.nvb.uscourts.gov

Number of Judgeships: 4

Judges

Chief Bankruptcy Judge **Mike K. Nakagawa** . . . . (702) 527-7138
  Began Service: 2009
  E-mail: mike_nakagawa@nvb.uscourts.gov
Bankruptcy Judge **Gregg W. Zive** . . . . (775) 326-2100
  Began Service: January 23, 1995
  E-mail: gregg_zive@nvb.uscourts.gov
Bankruptcy Judge **Bruce T. Beesley** . . . . (702) 527-7000
Bankruptcy Judge **Laurel E. Davis** . . . . (702) 527-7030
Bankruptcy Judge **August B. Landis** . . . . (702) 527-7010
  Began Service: November 27, 2013

Court Staff

Clerk of Court **Mary A. Schott** . . . . (702) 527-7000
  E-mail: mary_schott@nvb.uscourts.gov

U.S. Attorney

Nevada District
333 Las Vegas Boulevard South, Suite 5000, Las Vegas, NV 89101
Tel: (702) 388-6336 Fax: (702) 388-6296

U.S. Attorney **Daniel G. Bogden** . . . . (702) 388-6336
  E-mail: daniel.bogden@usdoj.gov

United States Bankruptcy Court for the District of Nevada *continued*

Federal Public Defender

Office of the Federal Public Defender of Nevada
411 East Bonneville Road, Suite 250, Las Vegas, NV 89101
201 West Liberty Street, Suite 102, Reno, NV 89501
Tel: (712) 388-6577 (Las Vegas) Tel: (775) 321-8451 (Reno)
Fax: (702) 388-6261 (Las Vegas) Fax: (775) 784-5369 (Reno)

Federal Public Defender **R.L. Valladares** . . . . (702) 388-6577

United States District Court for the District of New Hampshire

Warren B. Rudman U.S. Courthouse, 55 Pleasant Street,
Concord, NH 03301
Tel: (603) 225-1423 Tel: (800) 361-7205 (Toll Free PACER)
Internet: www.nhd.uscourts.gov

Number of Judgeships: 3

Circuit: First

Judges

Chief Judge **Joseph N. Laplante, Jr.** 110 Warren B.
  Rudman U.S. Courthouse, Room 401 . . . . (603) 225-1423
  Began Service: December 28, 2007
  Appointed By: President George W. Bush
  E-mail: joseph_laplante@nhd.uscourts.gov
District Judge **Paul James Barbadoro** . . . . (603) 226-7303
  Began Service: November 17, 1992
  Appointed By: President George H.W. Bush
  E-mail: paul_barbadoro@nhd.uscourts.gov
District Judge **Landya Boyer McCafferty** . . . . (603) 225-1423
  Began Service: December 21, 2013
  Appointed By: President Barack Obama
Senior District Judge **Joseph A. DiClerico, Jr.** Room
  400 . . . . (603) 226-7746
  Began Service: September 11, 1992
  Appointed By: President George H.W. Bush
  E-mail: joseph_diclerico@nhd.uscourts.gov
Senior Judge **Steven James McAuliffe** . . . . (603) 225-1423
  Began Service: 1992
  Appointed By: President George H.W. Bush
  E-mail: steven_mcauliffe@nhd.uscourts.gov
Magistrate Judge **Andrea K. Johnstone** . . . . (603) 225-1441
  Began Service: 2014

Court Staff

Clerk of Court **Daniel Lynch** . . . . (603) 225-1477
  E-mail: daniel_lynch@nhd.uscourts.gov
Chief U.S. Probation Officer **Jonathan Hurtig** . . . . (603) 225-1599

United States Bankruptcy Court for the District of New Hampshire

1000 Elm Street, Suite 1001, Manchester, NH 03101-1708
Tel: (603) 222-2600
Tel: (866) 222-8029 (Voice Case Information System VCIS)
Tel: (800) 676-6856 (PACER Sign up) Fax: (603) 222-2697
Internet: www.nhb.uscourts.gov

Number of Judgeships: 2

Judges

Chief Bankruptcy Judge **Bruce A. Harwood** . . . . (866) 222-8029
Bankruptcy Judge **J. Michael Deasy** . . . . (603) 222-2640

Court Staff

Clerk of Court **Bonnie L. McAlary** . . . . (603) 222-2600

(continued on next page)

United States Bankruptcy Court for the District of New Hampshire
continued

U.S. Attorney

New Hampshire District
James C. Cleveland Federal Building, 53 Pleasant Street,
Concord, NH 03301-3904
Tel: (603) 225-1552 Fax: (603) 225-1470

U.S. Attorney (Acting) **Donald Feith**. . . . .(603) 225-1552
  E-mail: donald.feith@usdoj.gov

Federal Public Defender

Federal Public Defender Office - District of Massachusetts, New Hampshire and Rhode Island
51 Sleeper Street, 5th Floor, Boston, MA 02210
The Ralph Pill Building, 22 Bridge Street, Third Floor,
Concord, NH 03301-4922
101 Weybosset Street, Third Floor, Providence, RI 02903
Tel: (317) 223-8061 (Boston) Tel: (603) 226-7360 (Concord)
Tel: (401) 528-4281 (Providence) Fax: (617) 223-8080 (Boston)
Fax: (603) 226-7358 (Concord) Fax: (401) 528-4284 (Providence)

Federal Public Defender **Miriam Conrad**. . . . .(617) 223-8061
  E-mail: miriam.conrad@fd.org

United States District Court for the District of New Jersey

Martin Luther King, Jr. Federal Building & U.S. Courthouse,
50 Walnut Street, Room 4015, Newark, NJ 07101
P.O. Box 419, Newark, NJ 07101-0419
Tel: (973) 645-3730 Tel: (800) 676-6856 (Toll Free PACER)

Number of Judgeships: 17

Number of Vacancies: 4

Circuit: Third

Judges

Chief Judge **Jerome B. Simandle**. . . . .(856) 757-5167
  Began Service: 1992
  Appointed By: President George H.W. Bush
District Judge **Robert B. Kugler** . . . . (856) 757-5019
  Began Service: December 4, 2002
  Appointed By: President George W. Bush
  Mitchell H. Cohen U.S. Courthouse,
  One John F. Gerry Plaza, Room 6040,
  Camden, NJ 08101
  E-mail: chambers_of_judge_robert_
  kugler@njd.uscourts.gov
District Judge **Jose L. Linares** Martin Luther King, Jr.
  Federal Building and U.S. Courthouse, Room 5054 . . . . (973) 645-6042
  Began Service: December 3, 2002
  Appointed By: President George W. Bush
  E-mail: Chambers_of_Judge_Jose_
  Linares@njd.uscourts.gov
District Judge **Freda L. Wolfson** . . . . (609) 989-2182
  Began Service: December 4, 2002
  Appointed By: President George W. Bush
  Clarkson S. Fisher Federal Building and U.S.
  Courthouse, 402 East State Street, Room 5050,
  Trenton, NJ 08608
  E-mail: Freda_Wolfson@njd.uscourts.gov
District Judge **Susan D. Wigenton** . . . .(973) 645-5903
  Began Service: June 2006
  Appointed By: President George W. Bush
  Martin Luther King, Jr. Federal Building and
  U.S. Courthouse, 50 Walnut Street, Room 5060,
  Newark, NJ 07102
  E-mail: judge_susan_wigenton@njd.uscourts.gov
District Judge **Renée Marie Bumb** . . . . (856) 757-5020
  Began Service: June 2006
  Appointed By: President George W. Bush

United States District Court for the District of New Jersey *continued*

District Judge **Noel Lawrence Hillman** . . . .(856) 757-5057
  Began Service: June 2006
  Appointed By: President George W. Bush
  E-mail: noel_hillman@njd.uscourts.gov
District Judge **Peter G. Sheridan** . . . . (609) 989-0508
  Began Service: June 2006
  Appointed By: President George W. Bush
  Clarkson S. Fisher Building and United States
  Courthouse, 402 East State Street, Room 4E,
  Trenton, NJ 08608
  E-mail: judge_peter_sheridan@njd.uscourts.gov
District Judge **Claire C. Cecchi** Martin Luther King Jr.
  Federal Building & U.S. Courthouse . . . .(973) 645-6664
  Began Service: June 14, 2011
  Appointed By: President Barack Obama
  E-mail: judge_claire_cecchi@njd.uscourts.gov
District Judge **Esther Salas** Martin Luther King Jr.
  Federal Building and U.S. Courthouse, Room 5076 . . . . (973) 297-4887
  Began Service: June 14, 2011
  Appointed By: President Barack Obama
  E-mail: judge_esther_salas@njd.uscourts.gov
District Judge **Kevin McNulty** . . . .(973) 645-3493
  Began Service: 2012
  Appointed By: President Barack Obama
District Judge **Michael A. Shipp** . . . .(609) 989-2009
  Began Service: 2012
  Appointed By: President Barack Obama
  Clarkson S. Fisher Building and U.S. Courthouse,
  402 East State Street, Room 7W,
  Trenton, NJ 08608
District Judge **Madeline Cox Arleo**. . . . .(973) 645-3730
  Began Service: November 21, 2014
  Appointed By: President Barack Obama
Senior Judge **Dickinson R. Debevoise** . . . .(973) 645-6121
  Began Service: 1979
  Appointed By: President Jimmy Carter
  Martin Luther King, Jr. Federal Building and
  U.S. Courthouse, 50 Walnut Street, Room 5083,
  Newark, NJ 07102
Senior Judge **Joseph H. Rodriguez** . . . . (856) 757-5002
  Began Service: May 23, 1985
  Appointed By: President Ronald Reagan
Senior Judge **Anne E. Thompson** . . . .(609) 989-2123
  Began Service: 1979
  Appointed By: President Jimmy Carter
Senior Judge **Joseph E. Irenas** . . . .(856) 757-5223
  Began Service: April 13, 1992
  Appointed By: President George H.W. Bush
  U.S. Courthouse, 401 Market Street, Room 310,
  Camden, NJ 08101
Senior Judge **William H. Walls** . . . . (973) 645-2564
  Began Service: 1994
  Appointed By: President William J. Clinton
  E-mail: chambers_of_judge_william_
  walls@njd.uscourts.gov
Senior Judge **Mary L. Cooper** . . . . (609) 989-2105
  Began Service: March 1992
  Appointed By: President George H.W. Bush
  Clarkson S. Fisher Federal Building & U.S.
  Courthouse, 402 East State Street, Room 5000,
  Trenton, NJ 08608-1507
  E-mail: mary_cooper@njd.uscourts.gov
Senior Judge **Katharine S. Hayden** . . . .(973) 645-4611
  Began Service: October 14, 1997
  Appointed By: President William J. Clinton
Senior Judge **William J. Martini** Martin Luther King,
  Jr. Federal Building and U.S. Courthouse, Room 4069 . . . . .(973) 645-6340
  Began Service: November 19, 2002
  Appointed By: President George W. Bush
  E-mail: judge_william_martini@njd.uscourts.gov
Senior Judge **Stanley R. Chesler**. . . . .(973) 645-3136
  Began Service: December 4, 2002
  Appointed By: President George W. Bush
  E-mail: judge_stanley_chesler@njd.uscourts.gov

United States District Court for the District of New Jersey *continued*

Magistrate Judge **Mark Falk** . . . . (973) 645-3110
  Began Service: March 1, 2002
  U.S. Post Office and Courthouse,
  One Federal Square, Room 457,
  Newark, NJ 07102-3513
  E-mail: chambersofmagistratejudgemark_
  falk@njd.uscourts.gov
Magistrate Judge **Ann Marie Donio** . . . . (856) 757-5211
  Began Service: March 24, 2003
Magistrate Judge **Tonianne J. Bongiovanni** . . . . (609) 989-2040
  Began Service: April 14, 2003
  E-mail: tjb_orders@njd.uscourts.gov
Magistrate Judge **Joel Schneider** . . . . (856) 757-5446
  Began Service: October 2006
  2060 Mitchell H. Cohen US Courthouse,
  One John F. Gerry Plaza, Room 3C,
  Camden, NJ 08101
Magistrate Judge **Karen Williams** . . . . (856) 757-6843
  Began Service: May 1, 2009
Magistrate Judge **Douglas E. Arpert** . . . . (609) 989-2144
  Began Service: April 2009   Tel: (609) 989-2144
Magistrate Judge **Lois H. Goodman** . . . . (609) 989-2138
  Began Service: 2009   Tel: (609) 989-2138
  Clarkson S. Fisher Building and U.S. Courthouse,
  402 East State Street, Room 7E,
  Trenton, NJ 08608
Magistrate Judge **Michael A. Hammer, Jr.** . . . . (973) 776-7858
  Began Service: August 12, 2011
Magistrate Judge **Joseph A. Dickson** . . . . (973) 645-2580
  Began Service: 2010
Magistrate Judge **Cathy L. Waldor** . . . . (973) 776-7862
  Began Service: September 1, 2011
Magistrate Judge **Steven C. Mannion** . . . . (973) 645-3827
Magistrate Judge **James B. Clark III** . . . . (973) 776-7700
Magistrate Judge **Leda Dunn Wettre** . . . . (973) 645-3574
Magistrate Judge (Part-Time) **Anthony R. Mautone** . . . . . (973) 325-5900
  Began Service: October 12, 2000
  E-mail: Judge_Anthony_Mautone@njd.uscourts.gov

Court Staff
Clerk of the Court **William T. Walsh** . . . . (973) 645-3730
Chief Probation Officer **Wilfredo Torres** Room 1005 . . . . . (973) 645-4747
Chief Pretrial Services Officer **Christine A. Dozier**
  Room 1018 . . . . (973) 645-2230

United States Bankruptcy Court for the District of New Jersey
Martin Luther King, Jr. Federal Building & U.S. Courthouse,
50 Walnut Street, 3rd Floor, Newark, NJ 07102
P.O. Box 1352, Newark, NJ 17101-1352
Tel: (973) 645-4764 (Phone)   Tel: (800) 676-6856 (PACER)
Tel: (866) 222-8029 ext. 88 (Voice Case Information System VCIS)
Internet: www.njb.uscourts.gov

Number of Judgeships: 9

Judges
Chief Bankruptcy Judge **Kathryn C. Ferguson** . . . . (609) 858-9350
  Began Service: November 10, 1993
Bankruptcy Judge **Rosemary Gambardella** . . . . (973) 645-2326
  Began Service: May 3, 1985
Bankruptcy Judge **Michael B. Kaplan** . . . . (609) 989-9397
  Began Service: October 2006
Bankruptcy Judge **Christine M. Gravelle** . . . . (609) 858-9370
Bankruptcy Judge **Andrew B. Altenburg, Jr.** . . . . (856) 361-2321
Bankruptcy Judge **Vincent F. Papalia** . . . . (973) 368-1244

Court Staff
Clerk of Court **James J. Waldron** . . . . (973) 776-3460

United States Bankruptcy Court for the District of New Jersey *continued*

U.S. Attorney
New Jersey District
970 Broad Street, Suite 700, Newark, NJ 07102
Tel: (973) 645-2700 Fax: (973) 645-2702

U.S. Attorney **Paul Joseph Fishman** . . . . (973) 645-2700
  E-mail: paul.fishman@usdoj.gov

Federal Public Defender
Federal Public Defender's Office for the District of New Jersey
800-840 Cooper Street, Suite 350, Camden, NJ 08102-1155
1002 Broad Street, First Floor, Newark, NJ 07102
22 South Clinton Avenue, Station Plaza #4, Trenton, NJ 08609
Tel: (856) 757-5341 (Camden) Tel: (973) 645-6347 (Newark)
Tel: (609) 989-2160 (Trenton) Fax: (856) 757-5273 (Camden)
Fax: (973) 645-3101 (Newark) Fax: (609) 989-2153 (Trenton)

Federal Public Defender **Richard Coughlin** . . . . (856) 757-5341
  E-mail: richard.coughlin@fd.org

United States District Court for the District of New Mexico
333 Lomas Boulevard, NW, Albuquerque, NM 87102
Tel: (505) 348-2000 Fax: (505) 348-2028
Internet: www.nmcourt.fed.us/dcdocs

Number of Judgeships: 7

Circuit: Tenth

Judges
Chief District Judge **M. Christina Armijo** U.S.
  Courthouse, Suite 760 . . . . (505) 348-2310
  Began Service: November 15, 2001
  Appointed By: President George W. Bush
  E-mail: marmijo@nmcourt.fed.us
District Judge **Martha A. Vázquez** . . . . (505) 988-6330
  Began Service: 1993
  Appointed By: President William J. Clinton
  E-mail: vazquezchambers@nmcourt.fed.us
District Judge **William P. Johnson** U.S. Courthouse,
  Suite 640 . . . . (505) 348-2330
  Began Service: December 28, 2001
  Appointed By: President George W. Bush
  E-mail: wjohnson@nmcourt.fed.us
District Judge **James O. Browning** . . . . (505) 348-2280
  Began Service: August 6, 2003
  Appointed By: President George W. Bush
  333 Lomas Boulevard, Suite 660,
  Albuquerque, NM 87102
  E-mail: jbrowning@nmcourt.fed.us
District Judge **Robert C. Brack** . . . . (575) 528-1450
  Began Service: July 28, 2003
  Appointed By: President George W. Bush
  100 North Church Street, Suite 590,
  Las Cruces, NM 88001
  E-mail: Robert_Brack@nmcourt.fed.us
District Judge **Judith C. Herrera** Suite 710 . . . . (505) 348-2390
  Began Service: June 2004
  Appointed By: President George W. Bush
  E-mail: herrerachambers@nmcourt.fed.us
District Judge **Kenneth John Gonzales** . . . . (505) 348-2000
  Began Service: October 18, 2013
  Appointed By: President Barack Obama
Senior Judge **James A. Parker** . . . . (505) 348-2220
  Began Service: November 13, 1987
  Appointed By: President Ronald Reagan
  E-mail: jparker@nmcourt.fed.us
Senior Judge **C. LeRoy Hansen** . . . . (505) 348-2240
  Began Service: October 1992
  Appointed By: President George H.W. Bush

(continued on next page)

United States District Court for the District of New Mexico *continued*

Chief Magistrate Judge **Karen Ballard Molzen** . . . . (505) 348-2290
  Began Service: April 26, 1999
  U.S. Courthouse, 333 Lomas Boulevard, Suite 730,
  Albuquerque, NM 87102
  E-mail: kmolzen@nmcourt.fed.us
Magistrate Judge **Lourdes A. Martinez** . . . .(575) 528-1650
  Began Service: April 1, 2011
  100 North Church Street, Suite 540,
  Las Cruces, NM 88001
  E-mail: lmartinez@nmcourt.fed.us
Magistrate Judge **William P. Lynch** . . . . (575) 528-1660
  Began Service: 2005
  United States District Court,
  100 North Church Street, Suite 550,
  Las Cruces, NM 88001
  E-mail: wlynch@nmcourt.fed.us
Magistrate Judge **Carmen E. Garza** . . . .(575) 528-1670
  Began Service: August 25, 2006
  United States District Court,
  100 North Church Street, Suite 520,
  Las Cruces, NM 88001
  E-mail: garzaschambers@nmcourt.fed.us
Magistrate Judge **Gregory B. Wormuth** . . . . (575) 528-1460
  Began Service: 2009
  United States District Court,
  100 North Church Street, Suite 530,
  Las Cruces, NM 88001
  E-mail: gwormuth@nmcourt.fed.us
Magistrate Judge **Stephan M. Vidmar** . . . . (575) 528-1480
  Began Service: December 27, 2011
  United States District Court,
  100 North Church Street, Suite 510,
  Las Cruces, NM 88001
  E-mail: svidmar@nmcourt.fed.us
Magistrate Judge **Steven C. Yarbrough** . . . . (505) 348-2270
Magistrate Judge **Kirtan Khalsa** . . . . (505) 348-2340
  333 Lomas Boulevard, Suite 630,
  Albuquerque, NM 87102
  E-mail: kirtan_khalsa@nmcourt.fed.us
Magistrate Judge (recalled) **Lorenzo F. Garcia** U.S.
  Courthouse, Suite 680 . . . . (505) 348-2320
Magistrate Judge (Part-Time) **B. Paul Briones** . . . . (505) 955-8823
  E-mail: paul_briones@nmcourt.fed.us

Court Staff

Clerk of Court **Matthew J. Dykman** . . . . (505) 348-2000
  E-mail: mdykman@nmcourt.fed.us
Chief U.S. Probation Officer **Margaret Vigil** . . . .(505) 348-2600

United States Bankruptcy Court for the District of New Mexico

500 Gold Avenue, SW, Albuquerque, NM 87102
P.O. Box 546, Albuquerque, NM 87103-0546
Tel: (505) 348-2500 Tel: (866) 291-6805 (Toll Free)
Tel: (888) 435-7822 (Toll Free Voice Case Information System VCIS)
Tel: (888) 821-8813 (Toll Free PACER) Fax: (505) 348-2473
Internet: www.nmcourt.fed.us

Number of Judgeships: 2

Judges

Bankruptcy Judge **Robert H. Jacobvitz** . . . . (505) 348-2545
  Began Service: August 2009
  E-mail: robert_jacobvitz@nmcourt.fed.us
Bankruptcy Judge **David T. Thuma** . . . . (505) 348-2420
  Began Service: August 29, 2012

Court Staff

Clerk of the Court **Norman H. Meyer, Jr.** . . . . (505) 348-2450
  E-mail: norman_meyer@nmcourt.fed.us

United States Bankruptcy Court for the District of New Mexico
continued

U.S. Attorney

New Mexico District
201 Third Street, NW, Suite 900, Albuquerque, NM 87102
P.O. Box 607, Albuquerque, NM 87103-0607
Tel: (505) 346-7274 Fax: (505) 346-7296

U.S. Attorney **MAJ Damon Paul Martinez** . . . . (505) 346-7274
  E-mail: damon.martinez@usdoj.gov

Federal Public Defender

Federal Public Defender - District of New Mexico
111 Lomas Boulevard NW, Suite 501, Albuquerque, NM 87102
506 South Main, Suite 600, Las Cruces, NM 88001
Tel: (505) 346-2489 (Albuquerque) Tel: (575) 527-6930 (Las Cruces)
Tel: (877) 511-4686 (Toll Free Albuquerque)
Tel: (855) 527-6930 (Toll Free Las Cruces)
Fax: (505) 346-2494 (Albuquerque) Fax: (575) 527-6933 (Las Cruces)

Federal Public Defender **Stephen McCue** . . . .(505) 346-2489
  E-mail: stephen.mccue@fd.org

United States District Court for the Eastern District of New York

U.S. Courthouse, 225 Cadman Plaza East, Brooklyn, NY 11201
Tel: (718) 613-2600 Tel: (718) 330-7200 (PACER)
Fax: (718) 613-2333
Internet: www.nyed.uscourts.gov

Number of Judgeships: 15

Number of Vacancies: 3

Circuit: Second

Areas Covered: Counties of Kings, Nassau, Queens, Richmond and Suffolk

Judges

Chief District Judge **Carol Bagley Amon** . . . .(718) 613-2410
  Began Service: 1990
  Appointed By: President George H.W. Bush
  E-mail: carol_amon@nyed.uscourts.gov
District Judge **John Gleeson** . . . .(718) 613-2450
  Began Service: October 24, 1994
  Appointed By: President William J. Clinton
  E-mail: john_gleeson@nyed.uscourts.gov
District Judge **Dora Lizette Irizarry** Room 928S . . . . (718) 613-2150
  Began Service: August 30, 2004
  Appointed By: President George W. Bush
  E-mail: Dora_L_Irizarry@nyed.uscourts.gov
District Judge **Eric Nicholas Vitaliano** . . . . (718) 613-2130
  Began Service: December 30, 2005
  Appointed By: President George W. Bush
  E-mail: eric_vitaliano@nyed.uscourts.gov
District Judge **Joseph F. Bianco** . . . . (631) 712-5670
  Began Service: January 3, 2006
  Appointed By: President George W. Bush
  E-mail: joseph_bianco@nyed.uscourts.gov
District Judge **Brian M. Cogan** . . . . (718) 613-2230
  Began Service: June 2006
  Appointed By: President George W. Bush
  E-mail: brian_cogan@nyed.uscourts.gov
District Judge **Roslynn Renee Mauskopf** . . . .(718) 613-2210
  Began Service: October 2007
  Appointed By: President George W. Bush
  E-mail: roslynn_mauskopf@nyed.uscourts.gov
District Judge **Kiyo A. Matsumoto** . . . . (718) 613-2180
  Began Service: July 22, 2008
  Appointed By: President George W. Bush
  E-mail: kiyo_matsumoto@nyed.uscourts.gov

United States District Court for the Eastern District of New York
continued

District Judge **William F. Kuntz II** . . . . (718) 613-2200
   Began Service: October 4, 2011
   Appointed By: President Barack Obama
   E-mail: william_kuntz@nyed.uscourts.gov

District Judge **Margo Kitsy Brodie** . . . . (718) 613-2140
   Began Service: January 29, 2012
   Appointed By: President Barack Obama
   E-mail: margo_brodie@nyed.uscourts.gov

District Judge **Pamela Ki Mai Chen** . . . . (718) 613-2510
   Began Service: March 19, 2013
   Appointed By: President Barack Obama
   E-mail: chen_chambers@nyed.uscourts.gov

District Judge **Joan Marie Azrack** . . . . (718) 613-2530 (Brooklyn)
   Began Service: 2014   Tel: (631) 712-5600
   Appointed By: President Barack Obama   (Central Islip)
   E-mail: joan_azrack@nyed.uscourts.gov

Senior Judge **Jack B. Weinstein** . . . . (718) 613-2520
   Began Service: April 15, 1967
   Appointed By: President Lyndon B. Johnson
   E-mail: jack_weinstein@nyed.uscourts.gov

Senior Judge **Raymond J. Dearie** . . . . (718) 613-2430
   Began Service: March 21, 1986
   Appointed By: President Ronald Reagan
   E-mail: raymond_dearie@nyed.uscourts.gov

Senior Judge **I. Leo Glasser** . . . . (718) 613-2440
   Began Service: 1982
   Appointed By: President Ronald Reagan
   E-mail: leo_glasser@nyed.uscourts.gov

Senior Judge **Leonard D. Wexler** . . . . (631) 712-5640
   Began Service: 1983
   Appointed By: President Ronald Reagan
   E-mail: leonard_wexler@nyed.uscourts.gov

Senior Judge **Sterling Johnson, Jr.** . . . . (718) 613-2460
   Began Service: 1991
   Appointed By: President George H.W. Bush
   225 Cadman Plaza East, Room 720S,
   Brooklyn, NY 11201
   E-mail: sterling_johnson@nyed.uscourts.gov

Senior Judge **Arthur D. Spatt** . . . . (631) 712-5620
   Began Service: December 15, 1989
   Appointed By: President George H.W. Bush
   E-mail: arthur_spatt@nyed.uscourts.gov

Senior Judge **Denis R. Hurley** . . . . (631) 712-5650
   Began Service: December 1991
   Appointed By: President George H.W. Bush
   E-mail: denis_hurley@nyed.uscourts.gov

Senior Judge **Frederic Block** . . . . (718) 613-2420
   Began Service: 1994
   Appointed By: President William J. Clinton
   E-mail: frederic_block@nyed.uscourts.gov

Senior Judge **Edward R. Korman** . . . . (718) 613-2470
   Began Service: 1985
   Appointed By: President Ronald Reagan
   E-mail: edward_korman@nyed.uscourts.gov

Senior Judge **Nina Gershon** . . . . (718) 613-2650
   Began Service: 1996
   Appointed By: President William J. Clinton
   E-mail: nina_gershon@nyed.uscourts.gov

Senior Judge **Allyne R. Ross** Room 915 S . . . . (718) 613-2380
   Began Service: 1994
   Appointed By: President William J. Clinton
   E-mail: allyne_ross@nyed.uscourts.gov

Senior Judge **Joanna Seybert** . . . . (631) 712-5610
   Began Service: January 12, 1994
   Appointed By: President William J. Clinton
   Long Island Federal Courthouse,
   100 Federal Plaza, Room 1034,
   Central Islip, NY 11722-9014
   E-mail: joanna_seybert@nyed.uscourts.gov

Senior Judge **Nicholas G. Garaufis** . . . . (718) 613-2540
   Began Service: August 28, 2000
   Appointed By: President William J. Clinton
   E-mail: nicholas_garaufis@nyed.uscourts.gov

United States District Court for the Eastern District of New York
continued

Senior Judge **Sandra L. Townes** Room 905S . . . . (718) 613-2160
   Began Service: September 2004
   Appointed By: President George W. Bush
   E-mail: sandra_townes@nyed.uscourts.gov

Senior Judge **Sandra J. Feuerstein** . . . . (631) 712-5630
   Began Service: October 23, 2003
   Appointed By: President George W. Bush
   1014 Federal Plaza, Room 1024,
   Central Islip, NY 11722
   E-mail: sandra_feuerstein@nyed.uscourts.gov

Chief Magistrate Judge **Steven M. Gold** . . . . (718) 613-2560
   Began Service: February 23, 1993
   E-mail: steven_gold@nyed.uscourts.gov

Magistrate Judge **Marilyn D. Go** . . . . (718) 613-2550
   Began Service: March 10, 1993
   E-mail: marilyn_go@nyed.uscourts.gov

Magistrate Judge **Arlene Rosario Lindsay** . . . . (631) 712-5730
   Began Service: 1994
   E-mail: arlene_lindsay@nyed.uscourts.gov

Magistrate Judge **Roanne L. Mann** . . . . (718) 613-2350
   Began Service: March 2, 1994
   E-mail: roanne_mann@nyed.uscourts.gov

Magistrate Judge **Robert M. Levy** . . . . (718) 613-2340
   Began Service: March 20, 1995

Magistrate Judge **Viktor V. Pohorelsky** Room 1207-S . . . . (718) 613-2400
   Began Service: 1995
   E-mail: viktor_pohorelsky@nyed.uscourts.gov

Magistrate Judge **Cheryl L. Pollak** Room 1230 . . . . (718) 613-2360
   Began Service: November 1995
   E-mail: cheryl_pollak@nyed.uscourts.gov

Magistrate Judge **Lois Bloom** . . . . (718) 613-2170
   Began Service: May 18, 2001
   E-mail: lois_bloom@nyed.uscourts.gov

Magistrate Judge **James Orenstein** . . . . (718) 613-2110
   Began Service: 2004
   E-mail: james_orenstein@nyed.uscourts.gov

Magistrate Judge **Ramon E. Reyes, Jr.** . . . . (718) 613-2120
   Began Service: February 13, 2006
   E-mail: ramon_reyes@nyed.uscourts.gov

Magistrate Judge **Gary R. Brown** . . . . (631) 712-5700
   Began Service: 2011
   E-mail: gary_brown@nyed.uscourts.gov

Magistrate Judge **A. Kathleen Tomlinson** . . . . (631) 712-5760
   Began Service: February 24, 2006

Magistrate Judge **Vera M. Scanlon** Room 504N . . . . (718) 613-2300
   Began Service: August 14, 2012
   E-mail: scanlon_chambers@nyed.uscourts.gov

Magistrate Judge **Steven I. Locke** . . . . (631) 712-5724
   Began Service: 2014
   E-mail: steven_locke@nyed.uscourts.gov

Court Staff

Clerk of Court **Douglas C. Palmer** . . . . (718) 613-2270
   E-mail: douglas_palmer@nyed.uscourts.gov

Chief Pretrial Services Officer **Roberto Cordeiro** . . . . (718) 613-2570
   E-mail: roberto_cordeiro@nyept.uscourts.gov

Chief Probation Officer **Eileen Kelly** . . . . (347) 534-3501
   E-mail: eileen_kelly@nyep.uscourts.gov

United States Bankruptcy Court for the Eastern District of New York

271 Cadman Plaza East, Suite 1595, Brooklyn, NY 11201
Tel: (347) 394-1700
Tel: (800) 252-2537 (Toll Free Voice Case Information System VCIS)
Internet: www.nyeb.uscourts.gov
Internet: ecf.nyeb.uscourts.gov (PACER)

Number of Judgeships: 6

Judges

Chief Bankruptcy Judge **Carla Elizabeth Craig** . . . . (347) 394-1840
  Began Service: February 28, 2000
  271 Cadman Plaza East, Suite 1595,
  Brooklyn, NY 11201-1800
  E-mail: carla_craig@nyeb.uscourts.gov
Bankruptcy Judge **Elizabeth S. Stong** . . . . (347) 394-1862
  Began Service: September 2, 2003
  E-mail: elizabeth_stong@nyeb.uscourts.gov
Bankruptcy Judge **Alan S. Trust** . . . . (631) 712-5680
  Began Service: April 2, 2008
  Long Island Federal Court House,
  290 Federal Plaza, Room 960,
  Central Islip, NY 11722
  E-mail: alan_trust@nyeb.uscourts.gov
Bankruptcy Judge **Robert E. Grossman** . . . . (631) 712-5740
  Began Service: 2008
  290 Federal Plaza, Room 860,
  Central Islip, NY 11722
  E-mail: robert_grossman@nyeb.uscourts.gov
Bankruptcy Judge **Nancy Hershey Lord** . . . . (347) 394-1850
  Began Service: April 1, 2012
  E-mail: nancy_lord@nyeb.uscourts.gov
Bankruptcy Judge **Louis A. Scarcella** . . . . (631) 712-6278

Court Staff

Clerk of the Court **Robert A. Gavin, Jr.** . . . . (347) 394-1741
  E-mail: robert_gavin@nyeb.uscourts.gov   Tel: (631) 712-6281
                                                          (Central Islip)

U.S. Attorney

New York - Eastern District
271 Cadman Plaza East, Brooklyn, NY 11201
Tel: (718) 254-7000 Fax: (718) 254-6479

U.S. Attorney (Acting) **Kelly T. Currie** . . . . (718) 254-7000
  E-mail: kelly.currie@usdoj.gov

Federal Public Defender

Federal Defenders of New York, Inc.
52 Duane Street, Tenth Floor, New York, NY 10007-1226
147 Pierrepont Street, Sixteenth Floor, Brooklyn, NY 11201
Alfonse M. D'Amato United States Courthouse, Federal Plaza,
Room 460, Central Islip, NY 11722
Charles L. Brieant Jr. United States Courthouse, 300 Quarropas Street,
Room 260, White Plains, NY 10601-4150
Tel: (212) 417-8700 (New York) Tel: (718) 330-1200 (Brooklyn)
Tel: (631) 712-6500 (Central Islip) Tel: (914) 428-7124 (White Plains)
Fax: (212) 571-0392 (New York) Fax: (718) 855-0760 (Brooklyn)
Fax: (631) 712-6505 (Central Islip) Fax: (914) 997-6872 (White Plains)

Federal Public Defender **David E. Patton** . . . . (212) 417-8700
  E-mail: david.patton@fd.org

United States District Court for the Northern District of New York

Federal Building, 100 South Clinton Street, Syracuse, NY 13261
Tel: (315) 234-8500 Tel: (315) 448-0537 (PACER)
Tel: (800) 480-7525 (Toll Free PACER) Fax: (315) 234-8501
Internet: www.nynd.uscourts.gov

Number of Judgeships: 5

Circuit: Second

Areas Covered: Counties of Albany, Broome, Cayuga, Chenango, Clinton, Columbia, Cortland, Delaware, Essex, Franklin, Fulton, Greene, Hamilton, Herkimer, Jefferson, Lewis, Madison, Montgomery, Oneida, Onondaga, Oswego, Otsego, Rensselaer, Saratoga, Schenectady, Schoharie, St. Lawrence, Tioga, Tompkins, Ulster, Warren and Washington

Judges

Chief Judge **Gary L. Sharpe** . . . . (518) 257-1870
  Began Service: January 2004
  Appointed By: President George W. Bush
  E-mail: glsharpe@nynd.uscourts.gov
District Judge **David N. Hurd** . . . . (315) 793-9571
  Began Service: September 24, 1999
  Appointed By: President William J. Clinton
  U.S. Courthouse, 10 Broad Street, Room 300,
  Utica, NY 13501
  E-mail: david_hurd@nynd.uscourts.gov
District Judge **Glenn T. Suddaby** . . . . (315) 234-8580
  Began Service: September 5, 2008
  Appointed By: President George W. Bush
  E-mail: glenn_suddaby@nynd.uscourts.gov
District Judge **Mae A. D'Agostino** . . . . (518) 257-1880
  Began Service: September 19, 2011
  Appointed By: President Barack Obama
  E-mail: mae_dagostino@nynd.uscourts.gov
District Judge **Brenda K. Sannes** . . . . (315) 234-8500
  Began Service: 2014
  Appointed By: President Barack Obama
Senior Judge **Thomas J. McAvoy** . . . . (607) 773-2892
  Began Service: 1986
  Appointed By: President Ronald Reagan
  U.S. Courthouse, 15 Henry Street, Room 206,
  Binghamton, NY 13901
  E-mail: thomas_mcavoy@nynd.uscourts.gov
Senior Judge **Frederick J. Scullin, Jr.** . . . . (315) 234-8560
  Began Service: March 13, 1992
  Appointed By: President George H.W. Bush
  E-mail: FScullin@nynd.uscourts.gov
Senior Judge **Lawrence E. Kahn** . . . . (518) 257-1830
  Began Service: August 1, 1996
  Appointed By: President William J. Clinton
  E-mail: lawrence_kahn@nynd.uscourts.gov
Senior Judge **Norman A. Mordue** . . . . (315) 234-8570
  Began Service: December 4, 1998
  Appointed By: President William J. Clinton
  E-mail: norman_mordue@nynd.uscourts.gov
Magistrate Judge **David E. Peebles** . . . . (315) 234-8620
  Began Service: May 22, 2000
  E-mail: dpeebles@nynd.uscourts.gov
Magistrate Judge **Randolph F. Treece** . . . . (518) 257-1840
  Began Service: September 25, 2001
  James T. Foley U.S. Courthouse, 445 Broadway,
  Room 407, Albany, NY 12207-2936
  E-mail: randolph_treece@nynd.uscourts.gov
Magistrate Judge **Andrew T. Baxter** . . . . (315) 234-8603
  Began Service: January 2010
  E-mail: andrew_baxter@nynd.uscourts.gov
Magistrate Judge **Christian F. Hummel** . . . . (518) 257-1850
  E-mail: christian_hummel@nynd.uscourts.gov
Magistrate Judge **Therese Wiley Dancks** . . . . (315) 234-8500
  E-mail: therese_dancks@nynd.uscourts.gov
Magistrate Judge **Gary Favro** . . . . (315) 234-8500
  Began Service: 2014
  E-mail: gary_favro@nynd.uscourts.gov

United States District Court for the Northern District of New York
continued

Magistrate Judge (recalled)
William B. Mitchell Carter . . . . (315) 234-8500
Began Service: 2015

Court Staff
Clerk of Court **Lawrence K. Baerman** . . . . (315) 234-8516
Chief Probation Officer **Matthew L. Brown** . . . . (315) 234-8700

United States Bankruptcy Court for the Northern District of New York
James T. Foley Courthouse, 445 Broadway, Suite 330, Albany, NY 12207
Tel: (518) 257-1661 Tel: (518) 431-0175 (PACER)
Tel: (800) 390-8432 (Toll Free PACER)
Tel: (866) 222-8029 (Toll Free Voice Case Information System VCIS)
Fax: (518) 257-1648
Internet: www.nynb.uscourts.gov

Number of Judgeships: 3

Judges
Chief Bankruptcy Judge **Margaret Cangilos-Ruiz** . . . . (315) 295-1682
Began Service: February 2007
E-mail: margaret_cangilos-ruiz@nynb.uscourts.gov
Bankruptcy Judge **Robert E. Littlefield, Jr.** . . . . (518) 257-1668
Began Service: 2009
E-mail: robert_littlefield@nynb.uscourts.gov
Bankruptcy Judge **Diane Davis** . . . . (315) 793-8111
Began Service: March 6, 2009

Court Staff
Clerk **Kim F. Lefebvre** . . . . (518) 257-1661
E-mail: kim_lefebvre@nynb.uscourts.gov

U.S. Attorney
New York - Northern District
James M. Hanley Federal Building, 100 South Clinton Street,
Room 900, Syracuse, NY 13261-7198
P.O. Box 7198, Syracuse, NY 13261-7198
Tel: (315) 448-0672 Fax: (315) 448-0689

U.S. Attorney **Richard S. Hartunian** . . . . (518) 431-0247
E-mail: richard.hartunian@usdoj.gov

Federal Public Defender
Office of the Federal Public Defender Northern District of New York
Clinton Exchange Building, 4 Clinton Square Building, Third Floor,
Syracuse, NY 13202
39 North Pearl Street, Fifth Floor, Syracuse, NY 13202
Tel: (315) 701-0080 (Syracuse) Tel: (518) 436-1850 (Albany)
Fax: (315) 701-0081 (Syracuse) Fax: (518) 436-1780 (Albany)

Federal Public Defender **Lisa Peebles** . . . . (315) 701-0080
E-mail: lisa.peebles@fd.org

United States District Court for the Southern District of New York
Daniel Patrick Moynihan U.S. Courthouse, 40 Foley Square,
New York, NY 10007
Tel: (212) 805-0136 Tel: (212) 791-8050 (PACER)
Internet: www.nysd.uscourts.gov

Number of Judgeships: 28

Number of Vacancies: 1

Circuit: Second

Areas Covered: Counties of Bronx, Dutchess, New York, Orange, Putnam, Rockland, Sullivan and Westchester

Judges
Chief Judge **Loretta A. Preska** . . . . (212) 805-0240
Began Service: August 2, 1992
Appointed By: President George H.W. Bush
Daniel Patrick Moynihan U.S. Courthouse,
500 Pearl Street, Room 2220,
New York, NY 10007
E-mail: preskanysdchambers@nysd.uscourts.gov
District Judge **John G. Koeltl** . . . . (212) 805-0222
Began Service: 1994
Appointed By: President William J. Clinton
1030 Daniel Patrick Moynihan U.S.
Courthouse, 500 Pearl Street, Room 1030,
New York, NY 10007
E-mail: koeltlnysdchambers@nysd.uscourts.gov
District Judge **Colleen McMahon** . . . . (212) 805-6325
Began Service: October 26, 1998
Appointed By: President William J. Clinton
E-mail: colleen_mcmahon@nysd.uscourts.gov
District Judge **William H. Pauley III** . . . . (212) 805-6387
Began Service: October 28, 1998
Appointed By: President William J. Clinton
E-mail: William_Pauley@nysd.uscourts.gov
District Judge **George B. Daniels** . . . . (212) 805-6735
Began Service: April 17, 2000
Appointed By: President William J. Clinton
Daniel Patrick Moynihan U.S. Courthouse,
500 Pearl Street, Room 1310,
New York, NY 10007
E-mail: George_Daniels@nysd.uscourts.gov
District Judge **Laura Taylor Swain** . . . . (212) 805-0417
Began Service: August 31, 2000
Appointed By: President William J. Clinton
E-mail: swainnysdchambers@nysd.uscourts.gov
District Judge **P. Kevin Castel** . . . . (212) 805-0262
Began Service: November 4, 2003
Appointed By: President George W. Bush
E-mail: castelnysdchambers@nysd.uscourts.gov
District Judge **Kenneth M. Karas** . . . . (914) 390-4145
Began Service: October 2004
Appointed By: President George W. Bush
E-mail: karasnysdchambers@nysd.uscourts.gov
District Judge **Richard J. Sullivan** . . . . (212) 805-0264
Began Service: August 2007
Appointed By: President George W. Bush
E-mail: richard_sullivan@nysd.uscourts.gov
District Judge **Paul G. Gardephe** . . . . (212) 805-0224
Began Service: October 3, 2008
Appointed By: President George W. Bush
E-mail: gardephenysdchambers@nysd.uscourts.gov
District Judge **Cathy Seibel** . . . . (914) 390-4271
Began Service: July 30, 2008
Appointed By: President George W. Bush
300 Quarropas Street, Room 275,
White Plains, NY 10601-4150
E-mail: cathy_seibel@nysd.uscourts.gov
District Judge **Vincent L. Briccetti** . . . . (914) 390-4166
Began Service: April 21, 2011
Appointed By: President Barack Obama
300 Quarropas Street, Room 630,
White Plains, NY 10601-4150
E-mail: briccettinysdchambers@nysd.uscourts.gov

(continued on next page)

United States District Court for the Southern District of New York
continued

District Judge **J. Paul Oetken** . . . . (212) 805-0266
  Began Service: July 20, 2011
  Appointed By: President Barack Obama
  E-mail: oetkennysdchambers@nysd.uscourts.gov

District Judge **Paul A. Engelmayer** . . . . (212) 805-0268
  Began Service: July 27, 2011
  Appointed By: President Barack Obama
  E-mail: paul_engelmayer@nysd.uscourts.gov

District Judge **Alison J. Nathan** . . . . (212) 805-0278
  Began Service: October 17, 2011
  Appointed By: President Barack Obama
  E-mail: alison_nathan@nysd.uscourts.gov

District Judge **Katherine B. Forrest** . . . . (212) 805-0276
  Began Service: October 17, 2011
  Appointed By: President Barack Obama
  E-mail: katherine_forrest@nysd.uscourts.gov

District Judge **Andrew L. Carter, Jr.** . . . . (212) 805-0280
  Began Service: December 12, 2011
  Appointed By: President Barack Obama
  E-mail: andrew_carter@nysd.uscourts.gov

District Judge **Edgardo Ramos** . . . . (212) 805-0294
  Began Service: December 6, 2011
  Appointed By: President Barack Obama
  E-mail: edgardo_ramos@nysd.uscourts.gov

District Judge **Jesse M. Furman** . . . . (212) 805-0282
  Began Service: 2012
  Appointed By: President Barack Obama
  E-mail: jesse_furman@nysd.uscourts.gov

District Judge **Ronnie Abrams** . . . . (212) 805-0284
  Began Service: 2012
  Appointed By: President Barack Obama
  E-mail: ronnie_abrams@nysd.uscourts.gov

District Judge **Lorna G. Schofield** . . . . (212) 805-0288
  Began Service: March 28, 2013
  Appointed By: President Barack Obama
  E-mail: lorna_schofield@nysd.uscourts.gov

District Judge **Katherine Polk Failla** Room 618 . . . . (212) 805-0290
  Began Service: 2013
  Appointed By: President Barack Obama
  E-mail: faillanysdchambers@nysd.uscourts.gov

District Judge **Analisa Torres** . . . . (212) 805-0292
  Began Service: April 23, 2013
  Appointed By: President Barack Obama
  E-mail: analisa_torres@nysd.uscourts.gov

District Judge **Nelson Stephen Román** . . . . (914) 390-4177
  Began Service: May 13, 2013
  Appointed By: President Barack Obama
  E-mail: romannysdchambers@nysd.uscourts.gov

District Judge **Valerie E. Caproni** . . . . (212) 805-6350
  Began Service: 2013
  Appointed By: President Barack Obama
  E-mail: caproninysdchambers@nysd.uscourts.gov

District Judge **Vernon S. Broderick** . . . . (212) 805-6165
  Began Service: 2013
  Appointed By: President Barack Obama
  E-mail: brodericknysdchambers@nysd.uscourts.gov

District Judge **Gregory Howard Woods** . . . . (212) 805-0296
  Began Service: November 18, 2013
  Appointed By: President Barack Obama
  E-mail: gregory_woods@nysd.uscourts.gov

Senior Judge **Kimba M. Wood** . . . . (212) 805-0258
  Began Service: April 20, 1988
  Appointed By: President Ronald Reagan
  E-mail: woodnysdchambers@nysd.uscourts.gov

Senior Judge **Robert W. Sweet** . . . . (212) 805-0254
  Began Service: 1978
  Appointed By: President Jimmy Carter
  Daniel Patrick Moynihan U.S. Courthouse,
  500 Pearl Street, Room 1920,
  New York, NY 10007-1312
  E-mail: sweetnysdchambers@nysd.uscourts.gov

Senior Judge **John F. Keenan** . . . . (212) 805-0220
  Began Service: October 21, 1983
  Appointed By: President Ronald Reagan
  E-mail: john_f._keenan@nysd.uscourts.gov

United States District Court for the Southern District of New York
continued

Senior Judge **Miriam Goldman Cedarbaum** . . . . (212) 805-0198
  Began Service: March 27, 1986
  Appointed By: President Ronald Reagan
  Daniel Patrick Moynihan U.S. Courthouse,
  500 Pearl Street, Room 1330,
  New York, NY 10007-1312
  E-mail: cedarbaumnysdchambers@nysd.uscourts.gov

Senior Judge **Thomas P. Griesa** . . . . (212) 805-0210
  Began Service: 1972
  Appointed By: President Richard M. Nixon
  Daniel Patrick Moynihan U.S. Courthouse,
  500 Pearl Street, Room 1630,
  New York, NY 10007
  E-mail: thomas_griesa@nysd.uscourts.gov

Senior Judge **Kevin Thomas Duffy** . . . . (212) 805-6125
  Began Service: November 28, 1972
  Appointed By: President Richard M. Nixon
  500 Pearl Street, Room 2540,
  New York, NY 10007-1312
  E-mail: duffynysdchambers@nysd.uscourts.gov

Senior Judge **Charles Sherman Haight, Jr.** . . . . (203) 773-2052
  Began Service: May 3, 1976
  Appointed By: President Gerald Ford
  E-mail: haightnysdchambers@nysd.uscourts.gov

Senior Judge **Louis L. Stanton** . . . . (212) 805-0252
  Began Service: September 1985
  Appointed By: President Ronald Reagan
  E-mail: louis_stanton@nysd.uscourts.gov

Senior Judge **Sidney H. Stein** . . . . (212) 805-0192
  Began Service: May 1, 1995
  Appointed By: President William J. Clinton
  E-mail: sidney_h_stein@nysd.uscourts.gov

Senior Judge **Alvin K. Hellerstein** . . . . (212) 805-0152
  Began Service: November 30, 1998
  Appointed By: President William J. Clinton
  Daniel Patrick Moynihan U.S. Courthouse,
  500 Pearl Street, Room 1050,
  New York, NY 10007-1312
  E-mail: alvin_hellerstein@nysd.uscourts.gov

Senior Judge **Victor Marrero** Daniel Patrick Moynahan
  U.S. Courthouse, Room 660 . . . . (212) 805-6374
  Began Service: December 1, 1999
  Appointed By: President William J. Clinton
  E-mail: Victor_Marrero@nysd.uscourts.gov

Senior Judge **Jed S. Rakoff** . . . . (212) 805-0401
  Began Service: March 1, 1996
  Appointed By: President William J. Clinton
  E-mail: Jed_S_Rakoff@nysd.uscourts.gov

Senior Judge **Lewis A. Kaplan** . . . . (212) 805-0216
  Began Service: 1994
  Appointed By: President William J. Clinton
  E-mail: kaplannysdchambers@nysd.uscourts.gov

Senior Judge **Deborah A. Batts** . . . . (212) 805-0186
  Began Service: June 23, 1994
  Appointed By: President William J. Clinton
  E-mail: battsnysdchambers@nysd.uscourts.gov

Senior Judge **Shira A. Scheindlin** . . . . (212) 805-0246
  Began Service: November 14, 1994
  Appointed By: President William J. Clinton
  E-mail: Shira_A_Scheindlin@nysd.uscourts.gov

Senior Judge **Denise Cote** . . . . (212) 805-0202
  Began Service: August 11, 1994
  Appointed By: President William J. Clinton
  Daniel Patrick Moynihan U.S. Courthouse,
  500 Pearl Street, Room 1040,
  New York, NY 10007
  E-mail: cotenysdchambers@nysd.uscourts.gov

Senior Judge **Richard M. Berman** . . . . (212) 805-6715
  Began Service: November 23, 1998
  Appointed By: President William J. Clinton
  E-mail: richard_berman@nysd.uscourts.gov

Senior Judge **Naomi Reice Buchwald** . . . . (212) 805-0194
  Began Service: September 13, 1999
  Appointed By: President William J. Clinton
  E-mail: buchwaldnysdchambers@nysd.uscourts.gov

United States District Court for the Southern District of New York
continued

Senior Judge **Paul A. Crotty** . . . . (212) 805-6309
  Began Service: August 1, 2005
  Appointed By: President George W. Bush
  500 Pearl Street, Room 1350,
  New York, NY 10007-1312
  E-mail: crottynysdchambers@nysd.uscourts.gov

Chief Magistrate Judge **Frank Maas** . . . . (212) 805-6727
  Began Service: June 1999
  500 Pearl Street, Room 740,
  New York, NY 10007
  E-mail: Frank_Maas@nysd.uscourts.gov

Magistrate Judge **Kevin Nathaniel Fox** . . . . (212) 805-6705
  Began Service: October 2, 1997
  U.S. Courthouse, 40 Centre Street, Room 425,
  New York, NY 10007

Magistrate Judge **Henry B. Pitman** . . . . (212) 805-6105
  Began Service: July 8, 1996

Magistrate Judge **Lisa Margaret Smith** . . . . (914) 390-4130
  Began Service: March 20, 1995

Magistrate Judge **Andrew J. Peck** . . . . (212) 805-0036
  Began Service: February 27, 1995
  Daniel Patrick Moynihan U.S. Courthouse,
  500 Pearl Street, Room 1370,
  New York, NY 10007-1312

Magistrate Judge **Michael H. Dolinger** . . . . (212) 805-0204
  Began Service: March 12, 1984

Magistrate Judge **James Clark Francis IV** . . . . (212) 805-0206
  Began Service: October 28, 1985

Magistrate Judge **Ronald L. Ellis** . . . . (212) 805-0242
  Began Service: November 16, 1993
  Daniel Patrick Moynihan U.S. Courthouse,
  500 Pearl Street, Suite 1970,
  New York, NY 10007

Magistrate Judge **Debra Freeman** Room 1660 . . . . (212) 805-4250
  Began Service: March 2, 2001
  E-mail: debra_freeman@nysd.uscourts.gov

Magistrate Judge **Gabriel William Gorenstein** . . . . (212) 805-4260
  Began Service: March 2, 2001
  U.S. Courthouse, 40 Centre Street, Room 431,
  New York, NY 10007

Magistrate Judge **Paul E. Davison** . . . . (914) 390-4250
  Began Service: 2009

Magistrate Judge **James L. Cott** . . . . (212) 805-0250
  Began Service: 2009
  E-mail: james_cott@nysd.uscourts.gov

Magistrate Judge **Sarah Netburn** . . . . (212) 805-0286
  E-mail: netburn_NYSDChamber@nysd.uscourts.gov

Magistrate Judge **Judith C. McCarthy** . . . . (914) 390-4124
  Began Service: January 2014

Magistrate Judge (Part-Time) **Martin R. Goldberg** . . . . . . (845) 343-1130
  Began Service: 1992
  E-mail: Martin_R_Goldberg@nysd.uscourts.gov

Court Staff
Clerk of the Court **Ruby J. Krajick** . . . . (212) 805-0140
  E-mail: ruby_krajick@nysd.uscourts.gov

Chief Probation Officer **Michael Fitzpatrick** . . . (212) 805-0040 ext. 5141
  E-mail: michael_fitzpatrick@nysp.uscourts.gov

Chief Pretrial Services Officer **Arthur Penny** . . . . (212) 805-0015
  E-mail: art_penny@nyspt.uscourts.gov

United States Bankruptcy Court for the Southern District of New York

Alexander Hamilton Custom House, One Bowling Green,
New York, NY 10004-1408
Tel: (212) 668-2870 Tel: (212) 668-2896 (PACER)
Tel: (800) 676-6856 (Toll Free PACER)
Tel: (212) 668-2772 (Voice Case Information System VCIS)
Fax: (212) 668-2878
Internet: www.nysb.uscourts.gov

Number of Judgeships: 10

Judges
Chief Bankruptcy Judge **Cecelia G. Morris** . . . . (845) 452-4200
  Began Service: July 1, 2000
  E-mail: cecelia_morris@nysb.uscourts.gov

Bankruptcy Judge **Robert E. Gerber** . . . . (212) 668-5660
  Began Service: September 5, 2000
  E-mail: judge_gerber@nysb.uscourts.gov

Bankruptcy Judge **Robert Dale Drain** Room 632 . . . . (914) 390-4155
  Began Service: May 2002
  E-mail: RDD.Chambers@nysb.uscourts.gov

Bankruptcy Judge **Martin Glenn** Room 606 . . . . (212) 284-4551
  Began Service: November 2006
  E-mail: martin_glenn@nysb.uscourts.gov

Bankruptcy Judge **Sean H. Lane** . . . . (212) 668-5637
  Began Service: September 7, 2010
  E-mail: sean_lane@nysb.uscourts.gov

Bankruptcy Judge **Stuart M. Bernstein** . . . . (212) 668-2304
  Began Service: November 24, 1993
  Alexander Hamilton Custom House,
  One Bowling Green, Room 729,
  New York, NY 10004
  E-mail: judge_bernstein@nysb.uscourts.gov

Bankruptcy Judge **Shelley C. Chapman** . . . . (212) 668-2301
  Began Service: March 5, 2010

Bankruptcy Judge **James L. Garrity, Jr.** . . . . (212) 668-2870
  Began Service: 2015

Bankruptcy Judge **Michael E. Wiles** . . . . (212) 668-5663

Court Staff
Clerk of Court **Vito Genna** . . . . (212) 668-2870
  E-mail: vito_genna@nysb.uscourts.gov

U.S. Attorney
New York - Southern District
One St. Andrew's Plaza, New York, NY 10007
Tel: (212) 637-2200

U.S. Attorney **Preetinder "Preet" Bharara** . . . . (212) 637-1025

Federal Public Defender
Federal Defenders of New York, Inc.
52 Duane Street, Tenth Floor, New York, NY 10007-1226
147 Pierrepont Street, Sixteenth Floor, Brooklyn, NY 11201
Alfonse M. D'Amato United States Courthouse, Federal Plaza,
Room 460, Central Islip, NY 11722
Charles L. Brieant Jr. United States Courthouse, 300 Quarropas Street,
Room 260, White Plains, NY 10601-4150
Tel: (212) 417-8700 (New York) Tel: (718) 330-1200 (Brooklyn)
Tel: (631) 712-6500 (Central Islip) Tel: (914) 428-7124 (White Plains)
Fax: (212) 571-0392 (New York) Fax: (718) 855-0760 (Brooklyn)
Fax: (631) 712-6505 (Central Islip) Fax: (914) 997-6872 (White Plains)

Federal Public Defender **David E. Patton** . . . . (212) 417-8700
  E-mail: david.patton@fd.org

United States District Court for the Western District of New York

Robert H. Jackson U.S. Courthouse, 2 Niagara Square, Buffalo, NY 14202
Kenneth B. Keating Federal Building, 100 State Street,
Rochester, NY 14614 (Rochester Office)
Tel: (716) 551-1700 Fax: (716) 551-4850
Tel: (585) 613-4000 (Rochester Office phone number)
Internet: www.nywd.uscourts.gov

Number of Judgeships: 4

Number of Vacancies: 2

Circuit: Second

Areas Covered: Counties of Allegany, Cattaraugus, Chautauqua, Chemung, Erie, Genesee, Livingston, Monroe, Niagara, Ontario, Orleans, Schuyler, Seneca, Steuben, Wayne, Wyoming and Yates

Judges

Chief Judge **Frank Paul Geraci, Jr.** U.S. Courthouse,
Room 4230 . . . . (585) 613-4090
Began Service: March 22, 2013   Tel: (585) 613-4095
Appointed By: President Barack Obama
E-mail: frank_geraci@nywd.uscourts.gov

District Judge **Elizabeth A. Wolford** . . . . (585) 613-4320
Began Service: December 17, 2013
Appointed By: President Barack Obama
E-mail: elizabeth_wolford@nywd.uscourts.gov

Senior Judge **John T. Curtin** Room 774 . . . . (716) 551-1830
Began Service: December 23, 1967
Appointed By: President Lyndon B. Johnson
E-mail: john_curtin@nywd.uscourts.gov

Senior Judge **Michael A. Telesca** 2120 U.S. Courthouse . . . (585) 613-4060
Began Service: 1982   Tel: (585) 613-4060
Appointed By: President Ronald Reagan
E-mail: michael_telesca@nywd.uscourts.gov

Senior Judge **David G. Larimer** . . . . (585) 613-4040
Began Service: November 6, 1987
Appointed By: President Ronald Reagan
E-mail: david_larimer@nywd.uscourts.gov

Senior Judge **Charles J. Siragusa** . . . . (585) 613-4050
Began Service: December 15, 1997
Appointed By: President William J. Clinton
E-mail: charles_siragusa@nywd.uscourts.gov

Senior Judge **William M. Skretny** . . . . (716) 551-1820
Began Service: October 1, 1990
Appointed By: President George H.W. Bush
E-mail: william_skretny@nywd.uscourts.gov

Senior Judge **Richard J. Arcara** . . . . (716) 551-1810
Began Service: June 1, 1988
Appointed By: President Ronald Reagan
E-mail: richard_arcara@nywd.uscourts.gov

Magistrate Judge **Jonathan W. Feldman** . . . . (585) 613-4070
Began Service: November 1995
E-mail: jonathan_feldman@nywd.uscourts.gov

Magistrate Judge **H. Kenneth Schroeder, Jr.** . . . . (716) 551-1870
Began Service: June 1, 2000
Robert H. Jackson U.S. Courthouse,
2 Niagara Square, Room 593,
Buffalo, NY 14202-3498

Magistrate Judge **Marian W. Payson** . . . . (585) 613-4080
Began Service: April 14, 2003
E-mail: marian_payson@nywd.uscourts.gov

Magistrate Judge **Jeremiah J. McCarthy** . . . . (716) 551-1880
Began Service: April 13, 2007
E-mail: jeremiah_mccarthy@nywd.uscourts.gov

Magistrate Judge (recalled) **Leslie G. Foschio** Robert
H. Jackson United States Courthouse, Room 724 . . . . (716) 551-1850
Began Service: February 1, 1991
E-mail: leslie_foschio@nywd.uscourts.gov

Court Staff

Clerk of the Court **Michael J. Roemer** . . . . (716) 332-1700
E-mail: michael_roemer@nywd.uscourts.gov

United States District Court for the Western District of New York
continued

Chief U.S. Probation Officer
Anthony M. San Giacomo . . . . (716) 551-4241
E-mail: anthony_sangiacomo@nywd.uscourts.gov

United States Bankruptcy Court for the Western District of New York

Olympic Towers, 300 Pearl Street, Suite 250, Buffalo, NY 14202-2501
100 State Street, Rochester, NY 14614
Tel: (585) 613-4200 (Rochester) Tel: (716) 362-3200 (Buffalo)
Tel: (716) 362-3201 (Voice Case Information System VCIS)
Tel: (866) 222-8029 (Toll Free Voice Case Information System VCIS)
Internet: www.nywb.uscourts.gov

Number of Judgeships: 3

Judges

Chief Bankruptcy Judge **Carl L. Bucki** . . . . (716) 362-3281
Began Service: December 30, 1993
Olympic Towers, 300 Pearl Street, Suite 350,
Buffalo, NY 14202-2510

Bankruptcy Judge **Michael J. Kaplan** Suite 350 . . . . (716) 362-3271
Began Service: October 7, 1991

Bankruptcy Judge **Paul R. Warren** . . . . (585) 613-4250

Court Staff

Clerk of the Court **Lisa Bertino-Beaser** . . . . (716) 362-3200 (Buffalo)
Tel: (585) 613-4200
(Rochester)

U.S. Attorney

New York - Western District
138 Delaware Avenue, Buffalo, NY 14202
Tel: (716) 843-5700 Fax: (716) 551-3052

U.S. Attorney **William J. Hochul, Jr.** . . . . (716) 843-5700
E-mail: william.hochul@usdoj.gov

Federal Public Defender

Office of the Federal Public Defender Western District of New York
Olympic Towers, 300 Pearl Street, Suite 200, Buffalo, NY 14202
First Federal Plaza, 28 East Main Street, Suite 400, Rochester, NY 14614
Tel: (716) 551-3341 (Buffalo) Tel: (585) 263-6201 (Rochester)
Fax: (716) 551-3346 (Buffalo) Fax: (585) 263-5871 (Rochester)

Federal Public Defender **Marianne Mariano** . . . . (716) 551-3341
E-mail: marianne.mariano@fd.org

United States District Court for the Eastern District of North Carolina

Terry Sanford Federal Building, 310 New Bern Avenue,
Raleigh, NC 27601
P.O. Box 25670, Raleigh, NC 27611
Tel: (919) 645-1700 Tel: (919) 856-4768 (Civil Cases PACER)
Fax: (919) 645-1750
Internet: www.nced.uscourts.gov

Number of Judgeships: 4

Number of Vacancies: 1

Circuit: Fourth

Areas Covered: Counties of Beaufort, Bertie, Bladen, Brunswick, Camden, Chowan, Columbus, Craven, Cumberland, Currituck, Dare, Duplin, Edgecombe, Franklin, Gates, Granville, Greene, Halifax, Harnett, Hertford, Hyde, Johnson, Sones, Lenoir, Martin, Nash, New Hanover, Northampton, Onslow, Pamlico, Pasquotank, Pender, Perquimans, Pitt, Robeson, Sampson, Tyrrell, Vance, Wake, Warren, Washington, Wayne and Wilson

Judges

Chief Judge **James C. Dever III** . . . . (919) 645-6570
  Began Service: May 3, 2005
  Appointed By: President George W. Bush
  E-mail: james_dever@nced.uscourts.gov
District Judge **Terrence W. Boyle** . . . . (252) 338-4033
  Began Service: January 1, 1984
  Appointed By: President Ronald Reagan
  E-mail: terrence_boyle@nced.uscourts.gov
District Judge **Louise W. Flanagan** . . . . (252) 638-3068
  Began Service: July 21, 2003
  Appointed By: President George W. Bush
Senior Judge **W. Earl Britt** . . . . (919) 645-1745
  Began Service: 1980
  Appointed By: President Jimmy Carter
  E-mail: W_Earl_Britt@nced.uscourts.gov
Senior Judge **James C. Fox** . . . . (910) 815-4738
  Began Service: September 30, 1982
  Appointed By: President Ronald Reagan
  E-mail: james_fox@nced.uscourts.gov
Senior Judge **Malcolm J. Howard** . . . . (252) 830-4990
  Began Service: March 11, 1988
  Appointed By: President Ronald Reagan
  E-mail: malcolm_howard@nced.uscourts.gov
Magistrate Judge **James E. Gates** . . . . (919) 645-1790
  Began Service: 2006
  E-mail: james_gates@nced.uscourts.gov
Magistrate Judge **Robert B. Jones, Jr.** . . . . (910) 815-4663
  Began Service: October 12, 2007
  E-mail: robert_jones@nced.uscourts.gov
Magistrate Judge **Kimberly A. Swank** . . . . (252) 830-6009
Magistrate Judge **Robert T. Numbers II** . . . . (919) 645-1714

Court Staff

Clerk of Court **Julie Richards Johnston** . . . . (919) 645-1700
  E-mail: julie_richards@nced.uscourts.gov
Chief Probation Officer **James Corpening** . . . . (919) 861-8660

United States Bankruptcy Court for the Eastern District of North Carolina

150 Reade Circle, Greenville, NC 27858
Tel: (919) 856-4752
Tel: (866) 222-8029 (Voice Case Information System VCIS)
Internet: www.nceb.uscourts.gov

Number of Judgeships: 3

Judges

Bankruptcy Judge **Stephani Humrickhouse** . . . . (919) 856-4194
  Began Service: 2010
Bankruptcy Judge **David M. Warren** . . . . (919) 856-4033

Court Staff

Clerk of the Court **Stephanie J. Edmondson** . . . . (919) 856-4752
  E-mail: stephanie_edmondson@nceb.uscourts.gov

U.S. Attorney

North Carolina - Eastern District
Terry Sanford Federal Building and U.S. Courthouse, 310 New Bern Avenue, Suite 800, Raleigh, NC 27601-1461
Tel: (919) 856-4530 Fax: (919) 856-4487

U.S. Attorney **Thomas Gray Walker** . . . . (919) 856-4530
  E-mail: thomas.walker@usdoj.gov

Federal Public Defender

Office of the Federal Public Defender Eastern North Carolina
150 Fayetteville Street, Suite 450, Raleigh, NC 27601
Wachovia Building, 225 Green Street, Suite 218,
Fayetteville, NC 28301-5043
United States Courthouse, 201 South Evans Street, Suite 153,
Greenville, NC 28301
Tel: (919) 856-4236 (Raleigh) Tel: (910) 484-0179 (Fayetteville)
Tel: (252) 830-2620 (Greenville) Fax: (919) 856-4477 (Raleigh)
Fax: (910) 484-6496 (Fayetteville) Fax: (252) 830-2232 (Greenville)

Federal Public Defender **Thomas P. McNamara** . . . . (919) 856-4236
  E-mail: thomas.mcnamara@fd.org

United States District Court for the Middle District of North Carolina

324 West Market Street, Room 401, Greensboro, NC 27401
P.O. Box 2708, Greensboro, NC 27402
Tel: (336) 332-6000 Tel: (336) 332-6010 (PACER)
Fax: (336) 332-6060
Internet: www.ncmd.uscourts.gov

Number of Judgeships: 4

Circuit: Fourth

Areas Covered: Counties of Alamance, Cabarrus, Caswell, Chatham, Davidson, Davie, Durham, Forsyth, Guilford, Hoke, Lee, Montgomery, Moore, Orange, Person, Randolph, Richmond, Rockingham, Rowan, Scotland, Stanly, Stokes, Surry and Yadkin

Judges

Chief Judge **William Lindsay Osteen, Jr.** . . . . (336) 332-6090
  Began Service: September 19, 2007
  Appointed By: President George W. Bush
District Judge **Judge Thomas David Schroeder** . . . . (336) 734-2530
  Began Service: January 2008
  Appointed By: President George W. Bush
District Judge **Catherine C. Eagles** . . . . (336) 332-6070
  Began Service: December 23, 2010
  Appointed By: President Barack Obama

(continued on next page)

United States District Court for the Middle District of North Carolina
continued

District Judge **Loretta Copeland Biggs** . . . . (336) 726-2250
  Began Service: 2014
  Appointed By: President Barack Obama
Senior Judge **Norwood Carlton "Woody" Tilley, Jr.** . . . . (336) 332-6080
  Began Service: November 4, 1988
  Appointed By: President Ronald Reagan
Senior Judge **James A. Beaty, Jr.** . . . . (336) 734-2540
  Began Service: November 1, 1994
  Appointed By: President William J. Clinton
Magistrate Judge **L. Patrick Auld** . . . . (336) 332-6120
  Began Service: 2010
Magistrate Judge **Joi Peake** . . . . (336) 734-2520
  E-mail: joi_peake@ncmd.uscourts.gov
Magistrate Judge **Joe L. Webster** . . . . (919) 425-8900
                                                          Tel: (919) 425-8900

Court Staff

Clerk of Court **John Brubaker** . . . . (336) 332-6000
  E-mail: john_brubaker@ncmd.uscourts.gov
Chief Probation Officer **Melissa Alexander** . . . . (336) 333-5341
  101 South Edgeworth Street, Suite R312,
  Greensboro, NC 27402

United States Bankruptcy Court for the Middle District of North Carolina

101 South Edgeworth Street, Greensboro, NC 27401
P.O. Box 26100, Greensboro, NC 27402-6100
Tel: (336) 358-4000
Tel: (866) 222-8029 (Voice Case Information System VCIS)
Internet: www.ncmb.uscourts.gov

Number of Judgeships: 3

Judges

Chief Bankruptcy Judge **Catharine R. Aron** . . . . (336) 358-4150
  Began Service: July 24, 1995
Bankruptcy Judge **Benjamin A. Kahn** . . . . (336) 358-4018
Bankruptcy Judge **Lena M. James** . . . . (336) 397-7789

Court Staff

Clerk of Court **Reid Wilcox** . . . . (336) 358-4000

U.S. Attorney

North Carolina - Middle District
101 South Edgeworth Street, 4th Floor, Greensboro, NC 27401
Tel: (336) 333-5351   Fax: (336) 333-5438

U.S. Attorney **Ripley Eagles Rand** . . . . (336) 333-5351
  E-mail: ripley.rand@usdoj.gov

Federal Public Defender

Office of the Federal Public Defender Middle District of North Carolina
301 North Elm Street, Suite 410, Greensboro, NC 27401
Hirma H. Ward Federal Building and U.S. Courthouse, 251 North Main Street, Suite 849, Winston-Salem, NC 27101
Tel: (336) 333-5455 (Greensboro) Tel: (336) 631-5278 (Winston-Salem)
Fax: (336) 333-5463 (Greensboro) Fax: (336) 631-5280 (Winston-Salem)

Federal Public Defender **Louis C. Allen III** . . . . (336) 333-5455
  E-mail: louis.allen@fd.org

United States District Court for the Western District of North Carolina

Charles R. Jonas Federal Building, 401 West Trade Street,
Room 212, Charlotte, NC 28202
Tel: (704) 350-7400   Fax: (704) 344-6703
Internet: www.ncwd.uscourts.gov

Number of Judgeships: 5

Circuit: Fourth

Areas Covered: Counties of Alexander, Alleghany, Anson, Ashe, Avery, Buncombe, Burke, Caldwell, Catawba, Cherokee, Clay, Cleveland, Gaston, Graham, Haywood, Henderson, Iredell, Jackson, Lincoln, Macon, Madison, McDowell, Mecklenburg, Mitchell, Polk, Rutherford, Swain, Transylvania, Union, Watauga, Wilkes and Yancey

Judges

Chief Judge **Frank D. Whitney** Room 195 . . . . (704) 350-7480
  Began Service: July 2006
  Appointed By: President George W. Bush
  E-mail: frank_whitney@ncwd.uscourts.gov
District Judge **Robert J. Conrad, Jr.** Room 235 . . . . (704) 350-7460
  Began Service: June 3, 2005
  Appointed By: President George W. Bush
  E-mail: robert_conrad@ncwd.uscourts.gov
District Judge **Richard Lesley Voorhees** . . . . (704) 350-7442
  Began Service: October 28, 1988
  Appointed By: President Ronald Reagan
  E-mail: richard_voorhees@ncwd.uscourts.gov
District Judge **Martin Karl Reidinger** . . . . (828) 771-7260
  Began Service: September 17, 2007
  Appointed By: President George W. Bush
  E-mail: martin_reidinger@ncwd.uscourts.gov
District Judge **Max Oliver Cogburn, Jr.** . . . . (828) 771-7250
  Began Service: March 14, 2011
  Appointed By: President Barack Obama
  E-mail: max_cogburn@ncwd.uscourts.gov
Senior Judge **Graham C. Mullen** Room 230 . . . . (704) 350-7450
  Began Service: October 25, 1990
  Appointed By: President George H.W. Bush
  E-mail: Graham_Mullen@ncwd.uscourts.gov
Magistrate Judge **David C. Keesler** Room 238 . . . . (704) 350-7430
  Began Service: May 3, 2004
  E-mail: David_Keesler@ncwd.uscourts.gov
Magistrate Judge **David S. Cayer** . . . . (704) 350-7470
  Began Service: 2009
  E-mail: david_cayer@ncwd.uscourts.gov
Magistrate Judge **Dennis L. Howell** . . . . (828) 771-7240
  Began Service: October 5, 2004
  E-mail: dennis_howell@ncwd.uscourts.gov

Court Staff

Clerk of Court **Frank G. Johns** . . . . (704) 350-7413
Chief U.S. Probation Officer **Greg Forest** . . . . (704) 350-7608
  200 South College Street, Suite 1650,
  Charlotte, NC 28202-2005

United States Bankruptcy Court for the Western District of North Carolina

Charles R. Jonas Federal Building, 401 West Trade Street,
Suite 111, Charlotte, NC 28202
Tel: (704) 350-7500 Tel: (704) 344-6121 (PACER)
Tel: (704) 344-6311 (Voice Case Information System VCIS)
Fax: (704) 350-7503
E-mail: clerk@ncbankruptcy.org
Internet: www.ncwb.uscourts.gov

Number of Judgeships: 3
Number of Vacancies: 1

Judges

Chief Bankruptcy Judge **Laura Turner Beyer** . . . . (704) 350-7575
  Began Service: 2011
Bankruptcy Judge **J. Craig Whitley** . . . . (704) 350-7575
  Began Service: June 27, 1994
  Charles R. Jonas Federal Building,
  401 West Trade Street, Suite 111,
  Charlotte, NC 28202
  E-mail: craig_whitley@ncwb.uscourts.gov
Bankruptcy Judge (recalled) **George R. Hodges** . . . . (704) 350-7575
  Began Service: 2011

Court Staff

Clerk of Court **COL Steven T. Salata** . . . . (704) 350-7500

U.S. Attorney

North Carolina - Western District
Carillon Building, 227 West Trade Street, Suite 1650,
Charlotte, NC 28202
Tel: (704) 344-6222 Fax: (704) 277-0259

U.S. Attorney (Acting) **Jill Westmoreland Rose** . . . . (704) 344-6222
  E-mail: jill.rose@usdoj.gov

Federal Public Defender

Federal Defenders of Western North Carolina
129 West Trade Street, Room 300, Charlotte, NC 28202
One Page Avenue, Suite 210, Asheville, NC 28801
Tel: (704) 374-0720 (Charlotte) Tel: (828) 232-9992 (Asheville)
Fax: (704) 374-0722 (Charlotte) Fax: (828) 232-5575 (Asheville)

Executive Director **Ross Richardson** . . . . (704) 374-0720
  E-mail: ross.richardson@fd.org

United States District Court for the District of North Dakota

U.S. Courthouse, 220 East Rosser Avenue, Room 476,
Bismarck, ND 58501
P.O. Box 1193, Bismarck, ND 58502-1193
Tel: (701) 530-2300 Tel: (701) 530-2368 (PACER)
Fax: (701) 530-2312
Internet: www.ndd.uscourts.gov

Number of Judgeships: 2
Circuit: Eighth

Judges

Chief Judge **Ralph R. Erickson** . . . . (701) 297-7080
  Began Service: November 1, 2009
  Appointed By: President George W. Bush
  655 First Avenue North, Suite 410,
  Fargo, ND 58102
  E-mail: ralph_erickson@ndd.uscourts.gov

United States District Court for the District of North Dakota *continued*

District Judge **Daniel L. Hovland** Room 411 . . . . (701) 530-2320
  Began Service: November 26, 2002
  Appointed By: President George W. Bush
  E-mail: ndd_j-hovland@ndd.uscourts.gov
Magistrate Judge **Charles S. Miller, Jr.** Room 426 . . . . (701) 530-2340
  Began Service: November 2004
Magistrate Judge **Alice R. Senechal** . . . . (701) 297-7070
  Began Service: November 15, 1990
  E-mail: alice_senechal@ndd.uscourts.gov

Court Staff

Clerk of Court **Robert Ansley** . . . . (701) 530-2300
  E-mail: rob_ansley@ndd.uscourts.gov
Chief Probation Officer **Wade Warren** . . . . (701) 530-2400
  220 E. Rosser Avenue, Room 154,
  Bismarck, ND 58501

United States Bankruptcy Court for the District of North Dakota

Quentin N. Burdick U.S. Courthouse, 655 First Avenue North,
Suite 210, Fargo, ND 58102-4932
Tel: (701) 297-7100 Tel: (800) 676-6856 (PACER)
Tel: (866) 222-8029 (Voice Case Information System VCIS)
Fax: (701) 297-7105
Internet: www.ndb.uscourts.gov

Number of Judgeships: 1

Judges

Bankruptcy Judge **Shon Kaelberer Hastings** . . . . (701) 297-7140
  Began Service: September 13, 2011
  Appointed By: President Barack Obama

Court Staff

Clerk of Court **Dianne G. Schmitz** . . . . (701) 297-7100
  E-mail: dianne_schmitz@ndb.uscourts.gov

U.S. Attorney

North Dakota District
Quentin N. Burdick U.S. Courthouse, 655 First Avenue, North,
Suite 250, Fargo, ND 58102-4932
Tel: (701) 297-7400 Fax: (701) 297-7405

U.S. Attorney (Acting) **Christopher C. Myers** . . . . (701) 297-7400

Federal Public Defender

Federal Public Defender for the District of South Dakota and North Dakota
Pierre Professional Plaza, 124 South Euclid Avenue, Pierre, SD 57501
Federal Plaza, 324 North Third Street, Suite 1, Bismarck, ND 58501
Federal Square Building, 112 Roberts Street North, Suite 202,
Fargo, ND 58102
The Sweeney Building 703 Main Street, Second Floor,
Rapid City, SD 57001
200 West Tenth Street, Suite 200, Sioux Falls, SD 57104
Tel: (605) 224-0009 (Pierre) Tel: (701) 250-4500 (Bismarck)
Tel: (701) 239-5111 (Fargo) Tel: (605) 343-5110 (Rapid City)
Tel: (605) 330-4489 (Sioux Falls) Fax: (605) 224-0010 (Pierre)
Fax: (701) 250-4498 (Bismarck) Fax: (701) 239-5098 (Fargo)
Fax: (605) 343-1498 (Rapid City) Fax: (605) 330-4499 (Sioux Falls)

Federal Public Defender **Neil Fulton** . . . . (605) 224-0009
  E-mail: neil.fulton@fd.org

United States District Court for the Northern District of Ohio

801 West Superior Avenue, Cleveland, OH 44113-1830
Tel: (216) 357-7000 Fax: (216) 357-7040
Internet: www.ohnd.uscourts.gov

Number of Judgeships: 11

Circuit: Sixth

Areas Covered: Counties of Allen, Ashland, Ashtabula, Auglaize, Carroll, Columbiana, Crawford, Cuyahoga, Defiance, Erie, Fulton, Geauga, Hancock, Hardin, Henry, Holmes, Huron, Lake, Lorain, Lucas, Mahoning, Marion, Medina, Mercer, Ottawa, Paulding, Portage, Putnam, Richland, Sandusky, Seneca, Stark, Summit, Trumbull, Tuscarawas, Van Wert, Wayne, Williams, Wood and Wyandot

Judges

Chief Judge **Solomon Oliver, Jr.** . . . . (216) 357-7171
  Began Service: May 9, 1994
  Appointed By: President William J. Clinton
  E-mail: solomon_oliver@ohnd.uscourts.gov

District Judge **Donald C. Nugent** . . . . (216) 357-7160
  Began Service: June 30, 1995
  Appointed By: President William J. Clinton
  Carl B. Stokes U.S. Courthouse,
  801 West Superior Avenue, Room 15A,
  Cleveland, OH 44113-1842
  E-mail: donald_c_nugent@ohnd.uscourts.gov

District Judge **Patricia A. Gaughan** . . . . (216) 357-7210
  Began Service: January 17, 1996
  Appointed By: President William J. Clinton

District Judge **James S. Gwin** . . . . (216) 357-7112
  Began Service: November 10, 1997
  Appointed By: President William J. Clinton
  E-mail: james_gwin@ohnd.uscourts.gov

District Judge **Dan A. Polster** . . . . (216) 357-7190
  Began Service: August 10, 1998
  Appointed By: President William J. Clinton
  Carl B. Stokes U.S. Court House,
  801 West Superior Avenue, Room 18B,
  Cleveland, OH 44113-1837
  E-mail: Dan_Polster@ohnd.uscourts.gov

District Judge **John R. Adams** . . . . (330) 252-6070
  Began Service: February 12, 2003
  Appointed By: President George W. Bush
  E-mail: john_adams@ohnd.uscourts.gov

District Judge **Christopher A. Boyko** . . . . (216) 357-7151
  Began Service: January 4, 2005
  Appointed By: President George W. Bush
  E-mail: christopher_boyko@ohnd.uscourts.gov

District Judge **Jack Zouhary** . . . . (419) 213-5675
  Began Service: April 2006
  Appointed By: President George W. Bush
  E-mail: jack_zouhary@ohnd.uscourts.gov

District Judge **Sara Lioi** . . . . (330) 252-6060
  Began Service: March 2007
  Appointed By: President George W. Bush
  E-mail: sara_lioi@ohnd.uscourts.gov

District Judge **Benita Y. Pearson** . . . . (330) 884-7435
  Began Service: December 29, 2010
  Appointed By: President Barack Obama
  125 Market Street, Suite 313,
  Youngstown, OH 44503-1780
  E-mail: benita_pearson@ohnd.uscourts.gov

District Judge **Jeffrey J. Helmick** . . . . (419) 213-5690
  Began Service: June 19, 2012
  Appointed By: President Barack Obama
  1716 Spielbusch Avenue, Room 210,
  Toledo, OH 43604
  E-mail: jeffrey_helmick@ohnd.uscourts.gov

Senior Judge **David A. Katz** . . . . (419) 213-5710
  Began Service: October 21, 1994
  Appointed By: President William J. Clinton
  E-mail: david_a_katz@ohnd.uscourts.gov

Senior Judge **Lesley Wells** . . . . (216) 615-4480
  Began Service: February 1994
  Appointed By: President William J. Clinton
  E-mail: lesley_wells@ohnd.uscourts.gov

Senior Judge **James Gray Carr** . . . . (419) 213-5555
  Began Service: May 12, 1994
  Appointed By: President William J. Clinton
  U.S. Courthouse, 1716 Spielbusch Avenue,
  Suite 210, Toledo, OH 43604
  E-mail: james_g_carr@ohnd.uscourts.gov

Magistrate Judge **Nancy A. Vecchiarelli** . . . . (216) 357-7130
  Began Service: April 20, 1998
  E-mail: nancy_vecchiarelli@ohnd.uscourts.gov

Magistrate Judge **George J. Limbert** . . . . (330) 884-7460
  Began Service: November 8, 1999
  Thomas D. Lambros Federal Building & U.S.
  Courthouse, 125 Market Street, Room 229,
  Youngstown, OH 44503-1780
  E-mail: George_Limbert@ohnd.uscourts.gov

Magistrate Judge **William H. Baughman, Jr.** . . . . (216) 357-7220
  Began Service: February 15, 2000
  Carl B. Stokes U.S. Court House,
  801 West Superior Avenue, Suite 10-A,
  Cleveland, OH 44113-1846
  E-mail: william_baughman@ohnd.uscourts.gov

Magistrate Judge **Kenneth S. McHargh** . . . . (216) 357-7230
  Began Service: March 2004
  E-mail: kenneth_mchargh@ohnd.uscourts.gov

Magistrate Judge **Gregory A. White** . . . . (216) 357-7135
  Began Service: March 1, 2008

Magistrate Judge **James R. Knepp II** . . . . (419) 213-5570
  Began Service: July 30, 2010
  James M. Ashley and Thomas W.L. Ashley U.S.
  Courthouse, 1716 Spielbusch Avenue, Room 318,
  Toledo, OH 43604-1363
  E-mail: knepp_chambers@ohnd.uscourts.gov

Magistrate Judge **Kathleen Burke** . . . . (330) 252-6170
  Began Service: August 20, 2011   Tel: (330) 252-6175
  Two South Main Street, Room 480,
  Akron, OH 44308-1813
  E-mail: kathleen_burke@ohnd.uscourts.gov

Court Staff

Fax: (216) 357-7066

Clerk of Court **Geri M. Smith** . . . . (216) 357-7068
Chief Pre-Trial Services Officer and Probation Officer
  Burton Maroney . . . . (216) 357-7300

United States Bankruptcy Court for the Northern District of Ohio

Howard M. Metzenbaum U.S. Courthouse, 201 Superior Avenue,
Cleveland, OH 44114
Tel: (216) 615-4300 Tel: (800) 579-5735 (Toll Free PACER)
Tel: (866) 222-8029 (Toll Free Voice Case Information System VCIS)
Fax: (216) 615-4364
Internet: www.ohnb.uscourts.gov

Number of Judgeships: 8

Judges

Chief Bankruptcy Judge
  Patricia E. Morgenstern-Clarren . . . . (216) 615-4422
  Began Service: December 1, 1995
  E-mail: pat_morgenstern-clarren@ohnb.uscourts.gov

Bankruptcy Judge **Mary Ann Whipple** . . . . (419) 213-5621
  Began Service: May 1, 2001
  U.S. Courthouse, 1716 Spielbusch Avenue,
  Room 111, Toledo, OH 43604

Bankruptcy Judge **Russ Kendig** . . . . (330) 458-2440
  Began Service: February 28, 2001

United States Bankruptcy Court for the Northern District of Ohio
continued

Bankruptcy Judge **Arthur Isaac Harris** . . . . (216) 615-4405
  Began Service: October 7, 2002
  E-mail: arthur_harris@ohnb.uscourts.gov
Bankruptcy Judge **Kay Woods** . . . . (330) 742-0900
  Began Service: July 7, 2004
Bankruptcy Judge **Jessica E. Price Smith** . . . . (216) 615-4451
  Began Service: 2011
Bankruptcy Judge **John P. Gustafson** . . . . (419) 213-5631
Bankruptcy Judge **Alan M. Koschik** . . . . (330) 252-6130
  Two South Main Street, Suite 240,
  Akron, OH 44308
  E-mail: alan_koschik@ohnb.uscourts.gov

Court Staff
Clerk of Court **Kenneth J. Hirz** . . . . (216) 615-4300

U.S. Attorney
Ohio - Northern District
801 West Superior Avenue, Suite 400, Cleveland, OH 44113
Tel: (216) 622-3600 TTY: (216) 522-3086
Fax: (216) 522-3370 (Administrative Division)
Fax: (216) 522-7545 (Executive Division)
Fax: (216) 522-2806 (Law Enforcement Committee Coordinator)
Fax: (216) 522-7358 (Major Fraud and Corruption)
Fax: (216) 522-7499 (Organized Crime Drug Enforcement Task Force)

U.S. Attorney **Steven M. Dettelbach** . . . . (216) 622-3600

Federal Public Defender
Office of the Federal Public Defender Northern District of Ohio
Skylight Office Tower, 1660 West Second Street, Suite 750,
Cleveland, OH 44113
50 South Main Street, Room 700, Akron, OH 44308
617 Adams Street, Second Floor, Toledo, OH 43604
Tel: (216) 522-4856 (Cleveland) Tel: (330) 375-5739 (Akron)
Tel: (419) 259-7370 (Toledo) Fax: (216) 522-4321 (Cleveland)
Fax: (330) 375-5738 (Akron) Fax: (419) 259-7375 (Toledo)

Federal Public Defender **Dennis G. Terez** . . . . (216) 522-4856
  E-mail: dennis.terez@fd.org

United States District Court for the Southern District of Ohio
260 Joseph P. Kinneary U.S. Courthouse, 85 Marconi Boulevard,
Columbus, OH 43215
Tel: (614) 719-3000 Tel: (210) 301-6440 (PACER)
Tel: (800) 676-6856 (Toll Free PACER) Fax: (614) 719-3500
Internet: www.ohsd.uscourts.gov

Number of Judgeships: 8

Circuit: Sixth

Areas Covered: Counties of Adams, Athens, Belmont, Brown, Butler, Champaign, Clark, Clermont, Clinton, Coshocton, Darke, Delaware, Fairfield, Fayette, Franklin, Gallia, Greene, Guernsey, Hamilton, Harrison, Highland, Hocking, Jackson, Jefferson, Knox, Lawrence, Licking, Logan, Madison, Meigs, Miami, Monroe, Montgomery, Morgan, Morrow, Muskingum, Noble, Perry, Pickaway, Pike, Preble, Ross, Scioto, Shelby, Union, Vinton, Warren and Washington

Judges
Chief Judge **Edmund A. Sargus, Jr.** . . . . (614) 719-3240
  Began Service: August 23, 1996
  Appointed By: President William J. Clinton
  Joseph P. Kinneary U.S. Courthouse,
  85 Marconi Boulevard, Room 301,
  Columbus, OH 43215-2823
  E-mail: sargus_chambers@ohsd.uscourts.gov
District Judge **Susan J. Dlott** . . . . (513) 564-7630
  Began Service: December 29, 1995
  Appointed By: President William J. Clinton
  E-mail: susan_dlott@ohsd.uscourts.gov
District Judge **Algenon L. Marbley** Joseph P. Kinneary
  U.S. Courthouse, Room 319 . . . . (614) 719-3260
  Began Service: November 11, 1997
  Appointed By: President William J. Clinton
  E-mail: Algenon_Marbley@ohsd.uscourts.gov
District Judge **Thomas M. Rose** . . . . (937) 512-1600
  Began Service: June 21, 2002
  Appointed By: President George W. Bush
  Federal Building, 200 West Second Street,
  Room 910, Dayton, OH 45402
  E-mail: rose_chambers@ohsd.uscourts.gov
District Judge **Gregory L. Frost** Joseph P. Kinneary U.S.
  Courthouse, Room 169 . . . . (614) 719-3300
  Began Service: March 19, 2003
  Appointed By: President George W. Bush
  E-mail: greg_frost@ohsd.uscourts.gov
District Judge **Michael H. Watson** Joseph
  P. Kinneary Courthouse, Room 109 . . . . (614) 719-3280 (Columbus)
  Began Service: October 2004   Tel: (513) 564-7692
  Appointed By: President George W. Bush   (Cincinnati)
  Potter Stewart U.S. Courthouse,
  100 East Fifth Street, Room 815,
  Cincinnati, OH 45202-3905
  E-mail: watson_chambers@ohsd.uscourts.gov
District Judge **Michael R. Barrett** . . . . (513) 564-7660
  Began Service: May 2006
  Appointed By: President George W. Bush
  Potter Stewart U.S. Courthouse,
  100 East Fifth Street, Room 239,
  Cincinnati, OH 45202
District Judge **Timothy S. Black** . . . . (513) 564-7640
  Began Service: June 21, 2010   Tel: (937) 512-1620
  Appointed By: President Barack Obama
  Potter Stewart U.S. Courthouse,
  100 East Fifth Street, Room 815,
  Cincinnati, OH 45202
  Federal Building, 200 West Second Street,
  Room 902, Dayton, OH 45402
Senior Judge **Herman J. Weber** . . . . (513) 564-7600
  Began Service: 1985
  Appointed By: President Ronald Reagan
  E-mail: herman_weber@ohsd.uscourts.gov
Senior Judge **George C. Smith** Joseph P. Kinneary U.S.
  Courthouse, Room 101 . . . . (614) 719-3220
  Began Service: 1987
  Appointed By: President Ronald Reagan

(continued on next page)

United States District Court for the Southern District of Ohio *continued*

Senior Judge **James L. Graham** . . . . (614) 719-3200
  Began Service: 1986
  Appointed By: President Ronald Reagan
Senior Judge **Walter Herbert Rice** . . . . (937) 512-1500
  Began Service: June 4, 1980
  Appointed By: President Jimmy Carter
  E-mail: walter_rice@ohsd.uscourts.gov
Senior Judge **Sandra S. Beckwith** . . . . (513) 564-7610
  Began Service: February 21, 1992
  Appointed By: President George H.W. Bush
  Potter Stewart U.S. Courthouse,
  100 East Fifth Street, Suite 810,
  Cincinnati, OH 45202
  E-mail: Sandra_Beckwith@ohsd.uscourts.gov
Chief Magistrate Judge **Sharon L. Ovington** . . . . (937) 512-1570
  Began Service: October 28, 2002
  Federal Building, 200 West Second Street,
  Room 523, Dayton, OH 45402
  E-mail: sharon_ovington@ohsd.uscourts.gov
Magistrate Judge **Terence P. Kemp** Joseph P. Kinneary
  U.S. Courthouse, Room 172 . . . . (614) 719-3410
  Began Service: September 18, 1987
  E-mail: terry_kemp@ohsd.uscourts.gov
Magistrate Judge **Norah McCann King** . . . . (614) 719-3390
  Began Service: June 17, 1982
  E-mail: Norah_McCann_King@ohsd.uscourts.gov
Magistrate Judge **Michael R. Merz** . . . . (937) 512-1550
  Began Service: November 21, 1984
  Federal Building, 200 West Second Street,
  Room 501, Dayton, OH 45402
  E-mail: michael_merz@ohsd.uscourts.gov
Magistrate Judge **Elizabeth A. Deavers** Joseph P.
  Kinneary Courthouse, Room 208 . . . . (614) 719-3460
  Began Service: March 15, 2010
Magistrate Judge **Stephanie K. Bowman** . . . . (513) 564-7680
  Began Service: October 28, 2010
  Potter Stewart U.S. Courthouse,
  100 East Fifth Street, Room 706,
  Cincinnati, OH 45202
  E-mail: stephanie_bowman@ohsd.uscourts.gov
Magistrate Judge **Karen Litkovitz** . . . . (513) 564-7690
  Began Service: October 14, 2010
  Potter Stewart U.S. Courthouse,
  100 East Fifth Street, Room 716,
  Cincinnati, OH 45202
  E-mail: karen_litkovitz@ohsd.uscourts.gov
Magistrate Judge **Michael J. Newman** . . . . (937) 512-1640
  Began Service: July 25, 2011
  Federal Building, 200 West Second Street,
  Room 505, Dayton, OH 45402
  E-mail: michael_newman@ohsd.uscourts.gov
Magistrate Judge (recalled) **Mark R. Abel** . . . . (614) 719-3370
  Began Service: May 1, 1971
  Joseph P. Kinneary U.S. Courthouse,
  85 Marconi Boulevard, Room 208,
  Columbus, OH 43215-2823
  E-mail: Mark_Abel@ohsd.uscourts.gov

Court Staff
Clerk of Court **Richard W. Nagel** . . . . (614) 719-3000
Chief Pretrial Services Officer **Melanie Furry** Joseph P.
  Kenneary Courthouse, Room 512 . . . . (614) 719-3080
  Potter Stewart U.S. Courthouse,
  100 East Fifth Street, Suite 301,
  Cincinnati, OH 45202-3905
Chief Probation Officer **John Dierna** . . . . (513) 564-7575
  Potter Stewart U.S. Courthouse,
  100 East Fifth Street, Room 110,
  Cincinnati, OH 45202-3905

United States Bankruptcy Court for the Southern District of Ohio
221 East Fourth Street, Cincinnati, OH 45202-4133
170 North High Street, Columbus, OH 43215
120 West Third Street, Dayton, OH 45402
Tel: (614) 469-6638 Tel: (937) 225-7561 (PACER)
Tel: (800) 793-7003 (Toll Free PACER) Tel: (937) 225-2516 (Dayton)
Tel: (866) 222-8029 (Dayton & Cincinnati Toll Free VCIS)
Tel: (513) 684-2572 (Cincinnati)
Internet: www.ohsb.uscourts.gov

Number of Judgeships: 8

Judges
Chief Bankruptcy Judge **Jeffery P. Hopkins** . . . . (513) 684-2852
  Began Service: 1996
  Atrium Two, 221 East Fourth Street, Suite 800,
  Cincinnati, OH 45202
  E-mail: jeffery_hopkins@ohsb.uscourts.gov
Bankruptcy Judge **Charles M. Caldwell** . . . . (614) 469-6638 ext. 260
  Began Service: May 26, 1993
  E-mail: charles_caldwell@ohsb.uscourts.gov
Bankruptcy Judge **John E. Hoffman, Jr.** . . . . (614) 469-7704
  Began Service: February 25, 2000
  E-mail: john_hoffman@ohsb.uscourts.gov
Bankruptcy Judge **Lawrence S. Walter** . . . . (937) 225-2516 ext. 7684
  Began Service: 2003
Bankruptcy Judge **Beth A. Buchanan** . . . . (513) 684-2572 ext. 6725
  Began Service: May 10, 2011
  221 East Fourth Street, Atrium Two, Suite 800,
  Cincinnati, OH 45202
Bankruptcy Judge **C. Kathryn Preston** . . . . (614) 469-6638 ext. 5795
  Began Service: 2005
Bankruptcy Judge **Guy R. Humphrey** . . . . (937) 225-2516
  Began Service: October 2007
  E-mail: guy_humphrey@ohsb.uscourts.gov
Bankruptcy Judge (recalled)
  Burton Perlman . . . . (513) 684-2572 ext. 6944
  Began Service: 1976
  Atrium Two, 221 East Fourth Street, Suite 800,
  Cincinnati, OH 45202
  E-mail: Burton_Perlman@ohsb.uscourts.gov

Court Staff
Clerk of Court **Kenneth Jordan** . . . . (513) 684-2572 ext. 3201
  E-mail: kenneth_jordan@ohsb.uscourts.gov

U.S. Attorney
Ohio - Southern District
303 Marconi Boulevard, Suite 200, Columbus, OH 43215
Tel: (614) 469-5715 Fax: (614) 469-7769

U.S. Attorney **Carter M. Stewart** . . . . (614) 469-5715

Federal Public Defender
Federal Public Defender's Office Southern District of Ohio
10 West Broad Street, Suite 1020, Columbus, OH 43215
Chiquita Center, 250 East Fifth Street, Suite 350, Cincinnati, OH 45202
One Dayton Centre, One South Main Street, Suite 490,
Dayton, OH 45402
Tel: (614) 469-2999 (Columbus) Tel: (513) 929-4834 (Cincinnati)
Tel: (937) 225-7687 (Dayton) Fax: (614) 469-5999 (Columbus)
Fax: (513) 929-4842 (Cincinnati) Fax: (937) 225-7688 (Dayton)

Federal Public Defender **Dennis G. Terez** . . . . (614) 469-2999
  E-mail: dennis.terez@fd.org

United States District Court for the Eastern District of Oklahoma

U.S. Courthouse, 101 North Fifth Street, Room 208,
Muskogee, OK 74401
P.O. Box 607, Muskogee, OK 74402
Tel: (918) 684-7920 Fax: (918) 684-7902
Internet: www.oked.uscourts.gov

Number of Judgeships: 2

Circuit: Tenth

Areas Covered: Counties of Adair, Atoka, Bryan, Carter, Cherokee,
Choctaw, Coal, Haskell, Hughes, Johnson, Latimer, Le Flore, Love,
Marshall, McCurtain, McIntosh, Murray, Muskogee, Okfuskee, Okmulgee,
Pittsburg, Pontotoc, Pushmataha, Seminole, Sequoyah and Wagoner

Judges

Chief Judge **James Hardy Payne** . . . . (918) 684-7940
  Began Service: December 17, 2001
  Appointed By: President George W. Bush
  E-mail: james_payne@oked.uscourts.gov
District Judge **Ronald A. White** . . . .(918) 684-7965
  Began Service: October 6, 2003
  Appointed By: President George W. Bush
  E-mail: ronald_white@oked.uscourts.gov
Senior Judge **Frank H. Seay** . . . .(918) 684-7950
  Began Service: November 5, 1979
  Appointed By: President Jimmy Carter
  E-mail: frank_seay@oked.uscourts.gov
Magistrate Judge **Kimberly E. West** . . . . (918) 684-7930
  Began Service: March 15, 2002
  E-mail: kimberly_west@oked.uscourts.gov
Magistrate Judge **Steven P. Shreder** . . . . (918) 684-7960
  Began Service: 2003
  E-mail: steven_shreder@oked.uscourts.gov

Court Staff

Clerk **Patrick Keaney** . . . . (918) 684-7920
  Began Service: March 2013
  E-mail: pat_keaney@oked.uscourts.gov
Chief Probation and Pretrial Services Officer
  William H. Bliss, Jr. Room 118 . . . .(918) 687-2366
  P.O. Box 1645, Muskogee, OK 74401

United States Bankruptcy Court for the Eastern District of Oklahoma

111 West Fourth Street, Second Floor, Okmulgee, OK 74447
P.O. Box 1347, Okmulgee, OK 74447
Tel: (918) 549-7200
Tel: (877) 377-1221 (Voice Case Information System VCIS)
Fax: (918) 549-7248
Internet: www.okeb.uscourts.gov

Number of Judgeships: 1

Judges

Chief Bankruptcy Judge **Tom R. Cornish** . . . . (918) 549-7226
  Began Service: February 8, 1994

Court Staff

Clerk **Therese Buthod** . . . . (918) 549-7221
  E-mail: therese_buthod@okeb.uscourts.gov

United States Bankruptcy Court for the Eastern District of Oklahoma
continued

U.S. Attorney

Oklahoma - Eastern District
1200 West Okmulgee Street, Muskogee, OK 74401
Tel: (918) 684-5100 Fax: (918) 684-5130

U.S. Attorney **Mark Frederick Green** . . . . (918) 684-5100

Federal Public Defender

**Federal Public Defender for the Northern and Eastern Districts
of Oklahoma**
Williams Center Tower 1, One West Third Street, Suite 1225,
Tulsa, OK 74103
627 West Broadway, Muskogee, OK 74401
Tel: (918) 581-7656 (Tulsa) Tel: (918) 687-2430 (Muskogee)
Fax: (918) 581-7630 (Tulsa) Fax: (918) 687-2392 (Muskogee)

Federal Public Defender **Julia O'Connell** . . . . (918) 581-7656
  E-mail: julia_o'connell@fd.org

United States District Court for the Northern District of Oklahoma

U.S. Courthouse, 333 West Fourth Street, Room 411, Tulsa, OK 74103
Tel: (918) 699-4700 Tel: (918) 581-6903 (Civil Cases PACER)
Fax: (918) 699-4756
Internet: www.oknd.uscourts.gov

Number of Judgeships: 4

Circuit: Tenth

Areas Covered: Counties of Craig, Creek, Delaware, Mayes, Nowata,
Osage, Ottawa, Pawnee, Rogers, Tulsa and Washington

Judges

Chief Judge **Gregory Kent Frizzell** . . . . (918) 699-4781
  Began Service: February 2007
  Appointed By: President George W. Bush
District Judge **Claire V. Eagan** . . . . (918) 699-4795
  Began Service: October 25, 2001
  Appointed By: President George W. Bush
  E-mail: ceagan@oknd.uscourts.gov
District Judge **James Hardy Payne** . . . . (918) 699-4790
  Began Service: December 17, 2001
  Appointed By: President George W. Bush
District Judge **John E. Dowdell** . . . .(918) 699-4130
  Began Service: December 28, 2012
  Appointed By: President Barack Obama
Senior Judge **Terence C. "Terry" Kern** . . . . (918) 699-4770
  Began Service: June 9, 1994
  Appointed By: President William J. Clinton
  United States District Court, The Federal Building,
  224 South Boulder Avenue, Room 241,
  Tulsa, OK 74103
Magistrate Judge **F. H. McCarthy** . . . . (918) 699-4765
  Began Service: April 10, 1995
Magistrate Judge **Paul J. Cleary** . . . .(918) 699-4890
  Began Service: July 22, 2002
  U.S. Courthouse, 333 West Fourth Street,
  Room 411, Tulsa, OK 74103-3819
  E-mail: pcleary@oknd.uscourts.gov
Judge **T. Lane Wilson** . . . . (918) 699-4760
  Began Service: 2009
  333 West Fourth, Room 411,
  Tulsa, OK 74103

Court Staff

Clerk of the Court **Phil Lombardi** . . . . (918) 699-4700
  E-mail: phil_lombardi@oknd.uscourts.gov
Chief Probation Officer **Todd Gollihare** Room 3820 . . . . . . (918) 699-4800

United States Bankruptcy Court for the Northern District of Oklahoma

224 South Boulder Avenue, Room 105, Tulsa, OK 74103
Tel: (918) 699-4000
Tel: (918) 699-4001 (Voice Case Information System VCIS)
Tel: (866) 222-8029   Fax: (918) 699-4045
Internet: www.oknb.uscourts.gov

Number of Judgeships: 2

Judges

Chief Bankruptcy Judge **Terrence L. Michael** . . . . (918) 699-4065
  Began Service: June 9, 1997
  E-mail: terrence_michael@oknb.uscourts.gov
Bankruptcy Judge **Dana L. Rasure** . . . . (918) 699-4085
  Began Service: 1997
  E-mail: Dana_Rasure@oknb.uscourts.gov

Court Staff

Clerk of Court **Michael L. Williams** . . . . (918) 699-4000
  E-mail: michael_l_williams@oknb.uscourts.gov

U.S. Attorney

Oklahoma - Northern District
110 West Seventh Street, Suite 300, Tulsa, OK 74119
Tel: (918) 382-2700   Fax: (918) 560-7938

U.S. Attorney **Danny Chappelle Williams, Sr.** . . . . (918) 382-2700
  E-mail: danny.c.williams@usdoj.gov

Federal Public Defender

Federal Public Defender for the Northern and Eastern Districts of Oklahoma
Williams Center Tower 1, One West Third Street, Suite 1225,
Tulsa, OK 74103
627 West Broadway, Muskogee, OK 74401
Tel: (918) 581-7656 (Tulsa)   Tel: (918) 687-2430 (Muskogee)
Fax: (918) 581-7630 (Tulsa)   Fax: (918) 687-2392 (Muskogee)

Federal Public Defender **Julia O'Connell** . . . . (918) 581-7656
  E-mail: julia_o'connell@fd.org

United States District Court for the Western District of Oklahoma

U.S. Courthouse, 200 NW Fourth Street, Room 1210,
Oklahoma City, OK 73102
Tel: (405) 609-5000   Fax: (405) 609-5099
Internet: www.okwd.uscourts.gov

Number of Judgeships: 6

Number of Vacancies: 3

Circuit: Tenth

Areas Covered: Counties of Alfalfa, Beaver, Beckham, Blaine, Caddo, Canadian, Cimarron, Cleveland, Comanche, Cotton, Custer, Dewey, Ellis, Garfield, Garvin, Grady, Grant, Greer, Harmon, Harper, Jackson, Jefferson, Kay, Kingfisher, Kiowa, Lincoln, Logan, Major, McClain, Noble, Oklahoma, Payne, Pottawatomie, Roger Mills, Stephens, Texas, Tillman, Washita, Woods and Woodward

Judges

Chief Judge **Vicki Miles-LaGrange** Room 3301 . . . . (405) 609-5400
  Began Service: November 28, 1994
  Appointed By: President William J. Clinton

United States District Court for the Western District of Oklahoma
continued
District Judge **Joe Heaton** . . . . (405) 609-5600
  Began Service: December 13, 2001
  Appointed By: President George W. Bush
  U.S. Courthouse, 200 NW Fourth Street,
  Room 3108, Oklahoma City, OK 73102-3092
District Judge **Timothy D. DeGiusti** Room 5012 . . . . (405) 609-5120
  Began Service: August 9, 2007
  Appointed By: President George W. Bush
  E-mail: timothy_degiusti@okwd.uscourts.gov
Senior Judge **Lee R. West** . . . . (405) 609-5140
  Began Service: November 5, 1979
  Appointed By: President Jimmy Carter
Senior Judge **Tim Leonard** Room 4301 . . . . (405) 609-5300
  Began Service: August 1992
  Appointed By: President George H.W. Bush
Senior Judge **David L. Russell** Room 3309 . . . . (405) 609-5100
  Began Service: 1982
  Appointed By: President Ronald Reagan
Senior Judge **Robin J. Cauthron** Room 4001 . . . . (405) 609-5200
  Began Service: April 5, 1991
  Appointed By: President George H.W. Bush
Senior Judge **Stephen P. Friot** Room 3102 . . . . (405) 609-5500
  Began Service: November 19, 2001
  Appointed By: President George W. Bush
  E-mail: judge_stephen_friot@okwd.uscourts.gov
Magistrate Judge **Gary M. Purcell** Room 2006 . . . . (405) 609-5260
  Began Service: December 28, 1992
Magistrate Judge **Shon T. Erwin** . . . . (580) 355-6340
  Began Service: June 1, 1995
  U.S. Courthouse, 410 SW Fifth Street, Room 102,
  Lawton, OK 73501-4628
Magistrate Judge **Suzanne Mitchell** . . . . (405) 609-5220
  U.S. Courthouse, 200 Fourth Street NW,
  First Floor, Room 1301, Oklahoma City, OK 73102
Magistrate Judge **Charles B. Goodwin** First Floor,
  Room 1305 . . . . (405) 609-5440
  E-mail: charles_goodwin@okwd.uscourts.gov

Court Staff

Clerk of Court **Carmelita Reeder Shinn** . . . . (405) 609-5000
Chief Probation Officer **Steve Skinner** . . . . (405) 609-5800
  United States Probation Office,
  215 Dean A McGee, Room 201,
  Oklahoma City, OK 73102

United States Bankruptcy Court for the Western District of Oklahoma

Old Post Office Building, 215 Dean A. McGee Avenue,
Oklahoma City, OK 73102
Tel: (405) 609-5700
Tel: (866) 222-8029 ext. 13 (Voice Case Information System VCIS)

Number of Judgeships: 3

Judges

Chief Bankruptcy Judge **Sarah A. Hall** . . . . (405) 609-5660
  Began Service: 2012
Bankruptcy Judge **Janice Loyd** . . . . (405) 609-5678

Court Staff

Clerk of the Court **Grant E. Price** . . . . (405) 609-5700
  E-mail: grant_price@okwb.uscourts.gov

United States Bankruptcy Court for the Western District of Oklahoma
continued

U.S. Attorney

Oklahoma - Western District
Oklahoma Tower, 210 Park Avenue, Suite 400,
Oklahoma City, OK 73102-5602
Tel: (405) 553-8700 Fax: (405) 553-8888

U.S. Attorney **Sanford C. Coats** . . . . (405) 553-8720
E-mail: sandy.coats@usdoj.gov

Federal Public Defender

Federal Public Defender for the Western District of Oklahoma
Old Post Office Building, 215 Dean A. McGee Avenue, Room 109,
Oklahoma City, OK 73102
Tel: (405) 609-5930 Fax: (405) 609-5932

Federal Public Defender **Susan M. Otto** . . . . (405) 609-5930
E-mail: susan.otto@fd.org

United States District Court for the District of Oregon

Mark O. Hatfield U.S. Courthouse, 1000 SW Third Street,
Portland, OR 97204-2902
Tel: (503) 326-8000 Tel: (503) 326-8904 (PACER)
Fax: (503) 326-8010
Internet: www.ord.uscourts.gov

Number of Judgeships: 6

Circuit: Ninth

Judges

Chief Judge **Ann L. Aiken** . . . . (541) 431-4140
Began Service: February 4, 1998
Appointed By: President William J. Clinton
Wayne L. Morse U.S. Courthouse,
405 East Eighth Avenue, Suite 5500,
Eugene, OR 97401
E-mail: Ann_Aiken@ord.uscourts.gov

District Judge **Anna J. Brown** . . . . (503) 326-8350
Began Service: October 27, 1999
Appointed By: President William J. Clinton
Mark O. Hatfield U.S. Courthouse,
1000 SW Third Street, Room 1407,
Portland, OR 97204-2944
E-mail: anna_brown@ord.uscourts.gov

District Judge **Michael W. Mosman** . . . . (503) 326-8330
Began Service: October 3, 2003
Appointed By: President George W. Bush
1000 SW Third Avenue, Room 1615,
Portland, OR 97204
E-mail: michael_mosman@ord.uscourts.gov

District Judge **Marco A. Hernandez** . . . . (503) 326-8210
Began Service: February 9, 2011
Appointed By: President Barack Obama
E-mail: marco_hernandez@ord.uscourts.gov

District Judge **Michael H. Simon** . . . . (503) 326-8380
Began Service: June 22, 2011
Appointed By: President Barack Obama
Mark O. Hatfield U.S. Courthouse,
1000 SW Third Street, Room 1327,
Portland, OR 97204
E-mail: michael_simon@ord.uscourts.gov

District Judge **Michael J. McShane** . . . . (503) 431-4150
Began Service: June 3, 2013
Appointed By: President Barack Obama
405 East Eighth Avenue, Room 5700,
Eugene, OR 97401
E-mail: michael_mcshane@ord.uscourts.gov

United States District Court for the District of Oregon *continued*

Senior Judge **Owen M. Panner** . . . . (541) 608-8756
Began Service: February 20, 1980
Appointed By: President Jimmy Carter
E-mail: owen_panner@ord.uscourts.gov

Senior Judge **James A. Redden, Jr.** Room 1527 . . . . (503) 326-8370
Began Service: March 24, 1980
Appointed By: President Jimmy Carter
E-mail: james_redden@ord.uscourts.gov

Senior Judge **Malcolm F. Marsh** . . . . (503) 326-8360
Began Service: April 16, 1987
Appointed By: President Ronald Reagan
Mark O. Hatfield U.S. Courthouse,
1000 SW Third Avenue, Room 1507,
Portland, OR 97204-2902
E-mail: malcolm_marsh@ord.uscourts.gov

Senior Judge **Robert E. Jones** . . . . (503) 326-8340
Began Service: May 1990
Appointed By: President George H.W. Bush
Mark O. Hatfield U.S. Courthouse,
1000 SW Third Avenue, Room 1007,
Portland, OR 97204-2946
E-mail: robert_jones@ord.uscourts.gov

Senior Judge **Garr M. King** . . . . (503) 326-8230
Began Service: May 1, 1998
Appointed By: President William J. Clinton
Mark O. Hatfield U.S. Courthouse,
1000 SW Third Street, Room 907,
Portland, OR 97204-2939
E-mail: Garr_King@ord.uscourts.gov

Magistrate Judge **Thomas M. Coffin** . . . . (541) 431-4130
Began Service: February 5, 1992
Wayne L. Morse U.S. Courthouse,
405 East Eighth Avenue, Room 5300,
Eugene, OR 97401
E-mail: thomas_coffin@ord.uscourts.gov

Magistrate Judge **Janice M. Stewart** . . . . (503) 326-8260
Began Service: October 14, 1993
E-mail: janice_stewart@ord.uscourts.gov

Magistrate Judge **Dennis J. Hubel** . . . . (503) 326-8240
Began Service: January 1, 1998
E-mail: dennis_hubel@ord.uscourts.gov

Magistrate Judge **Paul J. Papak** Room 1027 . . . . (503) 326-8270
Began Service: September 19, 2005
E-mail: paul_papak@ord.uscourts.gov

Magistrate Judge **Mark D. Clarke** . . . . (541) 608-8750
Began Service: February 28, 2007
E-mail: rebecca_moore@ord.uscourts.gov

Magistrate Judge **John V. Acosta** . . . . (503) 326-8280
Began Service: March 5, 2008
E-mail: john_acosta@ord.uscourts.gov

Magistrate Judge **Stacie Bekcerman** . . . . (503) 326-8240
Began Service: 2015
1000 Southwest Third Avenue, Suite 927,
Portland, OR 97204-2944

Magistrate Judge (Part-Time) **Patricia Sullivan** . . . . (503) 326-8028
Began Service: September 2005
E-mail: patricia_sullivan@ord.uscourts.gov

Magistrate Judge (recalled) **John Jelderks** . . . . (503) 326-8310
Began Service: July 11, 1991
E-mail: john_jelderks@ord.uscourts.gov

Court Staff

Clerk of Court **Mary L. Moran** . . . . (503) 326-8091
E-mail: mary_moran@ord.uscourts.gov

Chief Probation Officer **(Vacant)** . . . . (503) 326-8601
340 U.S. Courthouse, 1000 SW Third Ave.,
Portland, OR 97204

United States Bankruptcy Court for the District of Oregon

1001 SW Fifth Avenue, Room 700, Portland, OR 97204
Tel: (503) 326-1500 Tel: (503) 326-5650 (PACER)
Tel: (503) 326-2249 (Voice Case Information System VCIS)
Tel: (866) 222-8029 (Voice Case Information System VCIS)
Tel: (800) 726-2227 (Toll Free Voice Case Information System VCIS)
Internet: www.orb.uscourts.gov

Number of Judgeships: 5

Judges

Chief Bankruptcy Judge **Frank R. Alley III** . . . . (541) 431-4055
  Began Service: January 1995
  Wayne L. Morse Federal Courthouse,
  405 East Eighth Avenue, Suite 2600,
  Eugene, OR 97401
  E-mail: frank_alley@orb.uscourts.gov
Bankruptcy Judge **Randall L. Dunn** . . . .(503) 326-1538
  Began Service: February 1, 1998
  E-mail: randall_dunn@orb.uscourts.gov
Bankruptcy Judge **Thomas Renn** . . . .(541) 431-5040
  Began Service: 2011
Bankruptcy Judge **Trish M. Brown** . . . . (503) 326-1592
  Began Service: December 3, 1999
  1001 SW Fifth Avenue, Room 700,
  Portland, OR 97204-1141
  E-mail: Trish_Brown@orb.uscourts.gov
Bankruptcy Judge **Peter C. McKittrick** . . . . (503) 326-1536

Court Staff

Clerk of the Court **Charlene M. Hiss** . . . . (503) 326-1500
  E-mail: charlene_hiss@orb.uscourts.gov

U.S. Attorney

Oregon District
Mark O. Hatfield U.S. Courthouse, 1000 SW Third Avenue,
Suite 600, Portland, OR 97204-2902
Tel: (503) 727-1000 Fax: (503) 727-1117

U.S. Attorney (Acting) **Bill J. Williams** . . . .(503) 727-1000

Federal Public Defender

Office of the Federal Public Defender District of Oregon
One Main Place, 101 South Main Street, Room 1700, Portland, OR 97204
859 Willamette Street, Room 200, Eugene, OR 97401
15 Newtown Road, Medford, OR 97501
Tel: (503) 326-2123 (Portland) Tel: (541) 465-6937 (Eugene)
Tel: (541) 776-3630 (Medford) Fax: (503) 326-5524 (Portland)
Fax: (541) 465-6975 (Eugene) Fax: (541) 776-3624 (Medford)

Federal Public Defender **Lisa Hay** . . . . (503) 326-2123

United States District Court for the Eastern District of Pennsylvania

U.S. Courthouse, 601 Market Street, Philadelphia, PA 19106-1741
Tel: (215) 597-7704 Fax: (215) 580-2164
Internet: www.paed.uscourts.gov
Internet: pacer.paed.uscourts.gov (PACER)

Number of Judgeships: 22

Number of Vacancies: 1

Circuit: Third

Areas Covered: Counties of Berks, Bucks, Chester, Delaware, Lancaster, Lehigh, Montgomery, Northampton and Philadelphia

Judges

Chief Judge **Petrese B. Tucker** Room 9613 . . . .(267) 299-7610
  Began Service: July 14, 2000
  Appointed By: President William J. Clinton
  E-mail: chambers_of_judge_petrese_b_
  tucker@paed.uscourts.gov
District Judge **Legrome D. Davis** . . . . (267) 299-7650
  Began Service: May 3, 2002
  Appointed By: President George W. Bush
  E-mail: Chambers_of_judge_legrome_
  davis@paed.uscourts.gov
District Judge **Cynthia M. Rufe** Room 12614 . . . . (267) 299-7490
  Began Service: June 10, 2002
  Appointed By: President George W. Bush
  E-mail: chambers_of_judge_cynthia_m_
  rufe@paed.uscourts.gov
District Judge **Timothy J. Savage** . . . .(267) 299-7480
  Began Service: August 19, 2002
  Appointed By: President George W. Bush
  U.S. Courthouse, 601 Market Street, Room 9614,
  Philadelphia, PA 19106
  E-mail: chambers_of_judge_timothy_j_
  savage@paed.uscourts.gov
District Judge **James Knoll Gardner** . . . . (610) 434-3457
  Began Service: November 27, 2002
  Appointed By: President George W. Bush
  Edward N. Cahn U.S. Courthouse and Federal
  Building, 504 West Hamilton Street, Suite 4701,
  Allentown, PA 18101
  E-mail: chambers_of_Judge_James_Knoll_
  Gardner@paed.uscourts.gov
District Judge **Gene E. K. Pratter** . . . . (267) 299-7350
  Began Service: June 18, 2004
  Appointed By: President George W. Bush
  United States Courthouse, 601 Market Street,
  Room 10613, Philadelphia, PA 19106-1752
  E-mail: Chambers_of_Judge_Gene_E_K_
  Pratter@paed.uscourts.gov
District Judge **Lawrence F. Stengel** . . . . (267) 299-7760
  Began Service: June 2004
  Appointed By: President George W. Bush
  601 Market Street, Room 3809,
  Philadelphia, PA 19106
District Judge **Paul S. Diamond** Room 6613 . . . .(267) 299-7730
  Began Service: June 22, 2004
  Appointed By: President George W. Bush
District Judge **Juan R. Sánchez** Room 11614 . . . .(267) 299-7780
  Began Service: June 2004
  Appointed By: President George W. Bush
District Judge **Joel H. Slomsky** . . . .(267) 299-7340
  Began Service: October 8, 2008
  Appointed By: President George W. Bush
  601 Market Street, Room 5614,
  Philadelphia, PA 19106
District Judge **C. Darnell Jones II** . . . .(267) 299-7750
  Began Service: October 30, 2008
  Appointed By: President George W. Bush
  601 Market Street, Room 5613,
  Philadelphia, PA 19106

United States District Court for the Eastern District of Pennsylvania
continued

District Judge **Mitchell S. Goldberg** . . . . (267) 299-7500
Began Service: November 3, 2008
Appointed By: President George W. Bush
601 Market Street, Room 7614,
Philadelphia, PA 19106

District Judge **Nitza I. Quiñones Alejandro** Suite 4000 . . . (267) 299-7460
Began Service: November 1, 2013
Appointed By: President Barack Obama

District Judge **Luis Felipe Restrepo** Room 8613 . . . . (267) 299-7690
Began Service: 2013
Appointed By: President Barack Obama

District Judge **Jeffrey L. Schmehl** . . . . (610) 320-5099
Began Service: September 27, 2013
Appointed By: President Barack Obama
400 Washington Street, Suite 401,
Reading, PA 19601
E-mail: chambers_of_judge_jeffrey_l_
schmehl@paed.uscourts.gov

District Judge **Gerald Austin McHugh, Jr.** Suite 5918 . . . . (267) 299-7301
Began Service: March 28, 2014
Appointed By: President Barack Obama
E-mail: chambers_of_judge_gerald_a_
mchugh@paed.uscourts.gov

District Judge **Edward G. Smith** . . . . (610) 391-7030
Began Service: March 31, 2014
Appointed By: President Barack Obama
E-mail: chambers_of_judge_edward_g_
smith@paed.uscourts.gov

District Judge **Wendy Beetlestone** Room 5918 . . . . (215) 597-7704
Began Service: December 21, 2014
Appointed By: President Barack Obama

District Judge **Mark A. Kearney** Room 5118 . . . . (215) 299-7688
Began Service: December 4, 2014
Appointed By: President Barack Obama

District Judge **Gerald J. "Jerry" Pappert** Room 4006 . . . . (215) 299-7537
Began Service: 2014
Appointed By: President Barack Obama

District Judge **Joseph F. Leeson, Jr.** . . . . (610) 391-7020
Began Service: December 5, 2014
Appointed By: President Barack Obama
504 West Hamilton Street, Suite 3401,
Allentown, PA 18101

Senior Judge **J. William Ditter, Jr.** . . . . (215) 597-9640
Began Service: December 2, 1970
Appointed By: President Richard M. Nixon

Senior Judge **Norma L. Shapiro** . . . . (215) 597-9141
Began Service: September 1978
Appointed By: President Jimmy Carter

Senior Judge **Thomas N. O'Neill, Jr.** . . . . (215) 597-2750
Began Service: August 30, 1983
Appointed By: President Ronald Reagan
E-mail: chambers_of_judge_thomas_
o'neill@paed.uscourts.gov

Senior Judge **Robert F. Kelly** . . . . (215) 597-0736
Began Service: 1987
Appointed By: President Ronald Reagan

Senior Judge **Jan E. DuBois** . . . . (215) 597-5579
Began Service: 1988
Appointed By: President Ronald Reagan
E-mail: chambers_of_judge_jan_e_
dubois@paed.uscourts.gov

Senior Judge **Ronald L. Buckwalter** . . . . (215) 597-3084
Began Service: April 20, 1990
Appointed By: President George H.W. Bush

Senior Judge **William H. Yohn, Jr.** . . . . (215) 597-4361
Began Service: September 23, 1991
Appointed By: President George H.W. Bush
E-mail: Chambers_of_Judge_William_H_
Yohn@paed.uscourts.gov

Senior Judge **Harvey Bartle III** . . . . (215) 597-2693
Began Service: September 23, 1991
Appointed By: President George H.W. Bush

United States District Court for the Eastern District of Pennsylvania
continued

Senior Judge **Stewart Dalzell** . . . . (215) 597-9773
Began Service: October 7, 1991
Appointed By: President George H.W. Bush
U.S. Courthouse, 601 Market Street, Room 15613,
Philadelphia, PA 19106-1705
E-mail: Chambers_of_Judge_Stewart_
Dalzell@paed.uscourts.gov

Senior Judge **John R. Padova** . . . . (215) 597-1178
Began Service: March 31, 1992
Appointed By: President George H.W. Bush
U.S. Courthouse, 601 Market Street, Room 17613,
Philadelphia, PA 19106

Senior Judge **J. Curtis Joyner** . . . . (215) 597-1537
Began Service: April 13, 1992
Appointed By: President George H.W. Bush
U.S. Courthouse, 601 Market Street, Room 17614,
Philadelphia, PA 19106
E-mail: Chambers_of_Judge_J_Curtis_
Joyner@paed.uscourts.gov

Senior Judge **Eduardo C. Robreno** . . . . (215) 597-4073
Began Service: July 27, 1992
Appointed By: President George H.W. Bush
U.S. Courthouse, 601 Market Street, Room 15614,
Philadelphia, PA 19106

Senior Judge **Anita B. Brody** . . . . (215) 597-3978
Began Service: 1992
Appointed By: President George H.W. Bush
E-mail: Chambers_of_Judge_Anita_B_
Brody@paed.uscourts.gov

Senior Judge **Berle M. Schiller** . . . . (267) 299-7620
Began Service: June 6, 2000
Appointed By: President William J. Clinton
U.S. Courthouse, 601 Market Street, Room 13613,
Philadelphia, PA 19106-1797

Senior Judge **Mary A. McLaughlin** . . . . (267) 299-7600
Began Service: May 31, 2000
Appointed By: President William J. Clinton
E-mail: Chambers_of_Judge_Mary_A_
McLaughlin@paed.uscourts.gov

Senior Judge **R. Barclay Surrick** . . . . (267) 299-7630
Began Service: July 14, 2000
Appointed By: President William J. Clinton

Senior Judge **Michael M. Baylson** . . . . (267) 299-7520
Began Service: July 12, 2002
Appointed By: President George W. Bush
E-mail: chambers_of_judge_michael_
baylson@paed.uscourts.gov

Chief Magistrate Judge **Carol Sandra Moore Wells** . . . . . (215) 597-7833
Began Service: June 3, 1996
E-mail: chambers_of_magistrate_judge_carol_
sandra_moore_wells@paed.uscourts.gov

Magistrate Judge **Thomas J. Rueter** . . . . (215) 597-0048
Began Service: February 22, 1994
U.S. Courthouse, 601 Market Street, Room 3000,
Philadelphia, PA 19106

Magistrate Judge **Linda K. Caracappa** . . . . (267) 299-7640
Began Service: November 17, 2000
U.S. Courthouse, 601 Market Street, Room 3042,
Philadelphia, PA 19106

Magistrate Judge **Timothy R. Rice** . . . . (267) 299-7660
Began Service: March 2005
U.S. Courthouse, 601 Market Street, Room 3029,
Philadelphia, PA 19106
E-mail: timothy_rice@paed.uscourts.gov

Magistrate Judge **David R. Strawbridge** . . . . (267) 299-7790
Began Service: April 26, 2005
601 Market Street, Room 3030,
Philadelphia, PA 19106
E-mail: Chambers_of_Magistrate_Judge_David_
Strawbridge@paed.uscourts.gov

Magistrate Judge **Henry S. Perkin** . . . . (610) 434-3823
Began Service: March 2, 2007
Edward N. Cahn U.S. Courthouse and Federal
Building, 504 West Hamilton Street, Suite 4401,
Allentown, PA 18101

(continued on next page)

United States District Court for the Eastern District of Pennsylvania
continued

Magistrate Judge **Elizabeth T. Hey** . . . . (267) 299-7670
  Began Service: April 2007
  Robert N.C. Nix Federal Building,
  900 Market Street, Suite 219,
  Philadelphia, PA 19107
Magistrate Judge **Lynne A. Sitarski** . . . . (267) 299-7810
  Began Service: October 29, 2007
  U. S. Courthouse, 601 Market Street, Room 3015,
  Philadelphia, PA 19106
Magistrate Judge **Jacob P. Hart** . . . . (215) 597-2733
  Began Service: November 17, 1997
  U.S. Courthouse, 601 Market Street, Room 3006,
  Philadelphia, PA 19106
  E-mail: Judge_Jacob_Hart@paed.uscourts.gov
Magistrate Judge **Marilyn Heffley** Room 4001 . . . .(267) 299-7420
Magistrate Judge **Richard A. Lloret** . . . .(267) 299-7410
  900 Market Street, Suite 219,
  Philadelphia, PA 19107-4299
Magistrate Judge (recalled) **M. Faith Angell** . . . .(215) 597-6079
  Began Service: May 14, 1990
  Robert N.C. Nix Building, 900 Market Street,
  Suite 211, Philadelphia, PA 19107
  E-mail: chambers_of_magistrate_judge_m_faith_
  angell@paed.uscourts.gov

Court Staff

Clerk of Court **Michael E. Kunz** . . . . (215) 597-7704
  E-mail: michael_kunz@paed.uscourts.gov
Chief Pretrial Services Officer **Karen D. McKim** . . . . (267) 299-4400
  600 Arch Street, Suite 4408,
  Philadelphia, PA 19106
Chief Probation Officer **Ronald DeCastro** . . . . (215) 597-7950
  600 Arch Street, Suite 2400,
  Philadelphia, PA 19106

United States Bankruptcy Court for the Eastern District of Pennsylvania

900 Market Street, Suite 400, Philadelphia, PA 19107-4299
Tel: (215) 408-4411 Tel: (215) 408-2800 (General Information)
Tel: (800) 676-6856 (PACER Registration)
Tel: (888) 584-5853 (VCIS) Fax: (215) 408-2992
Internet: www.paeb.uscourts.gov

Number of Judgeships: 6

Judges

Chief Bankruptcy Judge **Eric L. Frank** Suite 201 . . . .(215) 408-2970
  Began Service: February 2006
Bankruptcy Judge **Stephen Raslavich** . . . . (215) 408-2982
  Began Service: 1993
  900 Market Street, Suite 204,
  Philadelphia, PA 19107
Bankruptcy Judge **Richard E. Fehling** . . . .(610) 208-5040
  Began Service: February 2006
Bankruptcy Judge **Jean K. FitzSimon** Room 214 . . . . (215) 408-2891
  Began Service: June 2006
  E-mail: jean_fitzsimon@paeb.uscourts.gov
Bankruptcy Judge **Magdeline D. Coleman** Suite 214 . . . . .(215) 408-2978
  Began Service: 2010
Bankruptcy Judge **Ashely M. Chan** Suite 214 . . . .(215) 408-2830

Court Staff

Clerk of Court **Timothy B. McGrath** . . . . (215) 408-4411
  E-mail: timothy_mcgrath@paeb.uscourts.gov

United States Bankruptcy Court for the Eastern District of Pennsylvania
continued

U.S. Attorney

Pennsylvania - Eastern District
615 Chestnut Street, Suite 1250, Philadelphia, PA 19106
Tel: (215) 861-8200 Fax: (215) 861-8618

U.S. Attorney **Zane David Memeger** . . . . (215) 861-8200
  E-mail: zane.memeger@usdoj.gov

Federal Public Defender

Federal Community Defenders for the Eastern District of Pennsylvania
Curtis Center Building, 601 Walnut Street, Suite 540 West,
Philadelphia, PA 19106
Edward N. Cahn Federal Building and United States Courthouse,
504 West Hamilton Street, Room 3, Allentown, PA 18101-1502
Tel: (215) 928-1100 (Philadelphia) Tel: (610) 434-6316 (Allentown)
Fax: (215) 928-1112 (Philadelphia) Fax: (610) 434-7246 (Allentown)

Federal Public Defender **Leigh M. Skipper** . . . .(215) 928-1100
  E-mail: leigh.skipper@fd.org

United States District Court for the Middle District of Pennsylvania

U.S. Courthouse and Federal Office Building, 240 West Third Street,
Suite 218, Williamsport, PA 17701
P.O. Box 1148, Scranton, PA 18501
P.O. Box 983, Harrisburg, PA 17108
Tel: (570) 207-5600 (General Info) Tel: (570) 207-5680 (Clerk's office)
Fax: (570) 207-5689 Tel: (717) 221-3920 (Harrisburg Division)
Fax: (717) 221-3959 (Harrisburg Division)
Tel: (570) 323-6380 (Williamsport Division)
Fax: (570) 323-0636 (Williamsport Division)
E-mail: mdpacourt@pamd.uscourts.gov
Internet: www.pamd.uscourts.gov

Number of Judgeships: 6

Circuit: Third

Areas Covered: Counties of Adams, Bradford, Cameron, Carbon, Centre, Clinton, Columbia, Cumberland, Dauphin, Franklin, Fulton, Huntingdon, Juniata, Lackawanna, Lebanon, Luzerne, Lycoming, Mifflin, Monroe, Montour, Northumberland, Perry, Pike, Potter, Schuylkill, Snyder, Sullivan, Susquehanna, Tioga, Union, Wayne, Wyoming and York

Judges

Chief Judge **Christopher C. Conner** . . . . (717) 221-3945
  Began Service: August 2, 2002
  Appointed By: President George W. Bush
  Federal Building and U.S. Courthouse,
  228 Walnut Street, Room 930,
  Harrisburg, PA 17101
  E-mail: chambers_of_chief_judge_christopher_c_
  conner@pamd.uscourts.gov
District Judge **Yvette Kane** . . . . (717) 221-3920
  Began Service: October 27, 1998
  Appointed By: President William J. Clinton
District Judge **John E. Jones III** . . . . (717) 221-3986
  Began Service: August 2, 2002
  Appointed By: President George W. Bush
  E-mail: chambers_of_judge_john_e_
  jones@pamd.uscourts.gov
District Judge **Robert David Mariani** . . . . (570) 207-5750
  Began Service: October 19, 2011
  Appointed By: President Barack Obama
  E-mail: robert_mariani@pamd.uscourts.gov
District Judge **Malachy Edward Mannion** . . . . (570) 207-5760
  Began Service: December 28, 2012
  Appointed By: President Barack Obama

United States District Court for the Middle District of Pennsylvania
continued

District Judge **Matthew W. Brann** . . . . (570) 323-9772
  Began Service: February 24, 2013
  Appointed By: President Barack Obama
  E-mail: matthew_brann@pamd.uscourts.gov
Senior Judge **William J. Nealon, Jr.** . . . . (570) 207-5700
  Began Service: December 15, 1962
  Appointed By: President John F. Kennedy
Senior Judge **Richard P. Conaboy** . . . . (570) 207-5710
  Began Service: 1979
  Appointed By: President Jimmy Carter
  William J. Nealon Federal Building & U.S.
  Courthouse, 235 North Washington Avenue,
  Room 405, Scranton, PA 18501
Senior Judge **Sylvia H. Rambo** . . . . (717) 221-3960
  Began Service: August 8, 1979
  Appointed By: President Jimmy Carter
  E-mail: chambers_of_judge_sylvia_
  rambo@pamd.uscourts.gov
Senior Judge **William W. Caldwell** . . . . (717) 221-3970
  Began Service: 1982
  Appointed By: President Ronald Reagan
Senior Judge **Edwin M. Kosik** . . . . (570) 207-5730
  Began Service: July 15, 1986
  Appointed By: President Ronald Reagan
Senior Judge **A. Richard Caputo** . . . . (570) 831-2556
  Began Service: November 12, 1997
  Appointed By: President William J. Clinton
  Max Rosenn U.S. Courthouse,
  197 South Main Street, Suite 235,
  Wilkes Barre, PA 18701
Senior Judge **James M. Munley** . . . . (570) 207-5780
  Began Service: October 22, 1998
  Appointed By: President William J. Clinton
Magistrate Judge **Martin C. Carlson** . . . . (717) 614-4120
  Began Service: August 15, 2009
  E-mail: martin_carlson@pamd.uscourts.gov
Magistrate Judge **Susan E. Schwab** . . . . (717) 221-3980
  E-mail: susan_schwab@pamd.uscourts.gov
Magistrate Judge **Karoline Mehalchick** . . . . (570) 831-2570
  Began Service: September 7, 2013
  E-mail: magistrate_judge_
  mehalchick@pamd.uscourts.gov
Magistrate Judge **Joseph F. Saporito, Jr.** . . . . (570) 831-2570
  Began Service: April 17, 2015
Magistrate Judge **William I. Arbuckle III** . . . . (570) 323-9881
  Began Service: July 29, 2008
  E-mail: william_arbuckle@pamd.uscourts.gov

Court Staff

Clerk of Court **Maria Elkins** . . . . (570) 207-5680
  E-mail: maria_elkins@pamd.uscourts.gov
Chief Probation Officer **Drew Thompson** . . . . (570) 207-5840
  P.O. Box 191, Scranton, PA 18501
  235 North Washington Avenue, Room 107,
  Scranton, PA 18501-0191

United States Bankruptcy Court for the Middle District of Pennsylvania

274 Max Rosenn U.S. Courthouse, 197 South Main Street,
Wilkes Barre, PA 18701
Tel: (570) 831-2500   Fax: (570) 829-0249
Internet: www.pamb.uscourts.gov

Number of Judgeships: 3

Judges

Chief Bankruptcy Judge **Mary D. France** . . . . (717) 901-2845
  Began Service: March 3, 2003

United States Bankruptcy Court for the Middle District of Pennsylvania
continued

Bankruptcy Judge **John J. Thomas** Max Rosenn U.S.
  Courthouse, Suite 150 . . . . (570) 831-2531
  Began Service: January 10, 1992
  E-mail: chambers_of_judge_john_
  thomas@pamb.uscourts.gov
Bankruptcy Judge **Robert N. Opel** Suite 144 . . . . (570) 831-2536
  Began Service: September 2006

Court Staff

Clerk of Court **Terrence S. Miller** . . . . (717) 901-2816

U.S. Attorney

Pennsylvania - Middle District
Federal Building, 228 Walnut Street, Room 220,
Harrisburg, PA 17108-1754
Federal Building, P.O. Box 11754, Harrisburg, PA 17108-1754
Tel: (717) 221-4482   Fax: (717) 221-4582

U.S. Attorney **Peter J. Smith** . . . . (717) 221-4482

Federal Public Defender

Office of the Federal Public Defender Middle District of Pennsylvania
Chestnut Office Building, 100 Chestnut Street, Room 306,
Harrisburg, PA 17101
Lenahan and Dempsey Professional Building, 116 North Washington
Avenue, Room 2C, Scranton, PA 18503
Executive Plaza, 330 Pine Street, Room 302, Williamsport, PA 17701
Tel: (717) 782-2237 (Harrisburg)   Tel: (570) 343-6285 (Scranton)
Tel: (570) 323-9314 (Williamsport)   Fax: (717) 782-3881 (Harrisburg)
Fax: (570) 343-6285 (Scranton)   Fax: (570) 323-9836 (Williamsport)

Federal Public Defender **James V. Wade** . . . . (717) 782-2237

United States District Court for the Western District of Pennsylvania

U.S. Post Office & Courthouse, 700 Grant Street, Pittsburgh, PA 15219
Tel: (412) 208-7500   Fax: (412) 208-7530
Internet: www.pawd.uscourts.gov

Number of Judgeships: 10

Number of Vacancies: 3

Circuit: Third

Areas Covered: Counties of Allegheny, Armstrong, Beaver, Bedford, Blair, Butler, Cambria, Clarion, Clearfield, Crawford, Elk, Erie, Fayette, Forest, Greene, Indiana, Jefferson, Lawrence, McKean, Mercer, Somerset, Venango, Warren, Washington and Westmoreland

Judges

Chief Judge **Joy Flowers Conti** . . . . (412) 208-7330
  Began Service: August 30, 2002
  Appointed By: President George W. Bush
District Judge **David Stewart Cercone** U.S.
  Courthouse, Room 7270 . . . . (412) 208-7363
  Began Service: September 12, 2002
  Appointed By: President George W. Bush
District Judge **Arthur J. Schwab** U.S. Courthouse,
  Suite 7280 . . . . (412) 208-7423
  Began Service: January 1, 2003
  Appointed By: President George W. Bush
District Judge **Kim R. Gibson** . . . . (814) 533-4514
  Began Service: 2003
  Appointed By: President George W. Bush
  Penn Traffic Building Courtroom A,
  319 Washington Street, Room 104,
  Johnstown, PA 15901

(continued on next page)

United States District Court for the Western District of Pennsylvania
continued

District Judge **Nora Barry Fischer** . . . . (412) 208-7480
  Began Service: April 2007
  Appointed By: President George W. Bush
District Judge **Cathy Bissoon** . . . . (412) 208-7460
  Began Service: October 19, 2011
  Appointed By: President Barack Obama
District Judge **Mark R. Hornak** . . . . (412) 208-7433
  Began Service: 2011
  Appointed By: President Barack Obama
Senior Judge **Maurice B. Cohill, Jr.** Suite 8170 . . . . (814) 464-9620
  Began Service: June 1, 1976
  Appointed By: President Gerald Ford
  E-mail: judge_cohill@pawd.uscourts.gov
Senior Judge **Gustave Diamond** Suite 8270 . . . . (412) 208-7390
  Began Service: May 2, 1978
  Appointed By: President Jimmy Carter
  E-mail: judge_gustave_diamond@pawd.uscourts.gov
Senior Judge **Alan N. Bloch** Suite 8370 . . . . (412) 208-7360
  Began Service: November 21, 1979
  Appointed By: President Jimmy Carter
  E-mail: judge_alan_bloch@pawd.uscourts.gov
Senior Judge **Donetta W. Ambrose** . . . . (412) 208-7350
  Began Service: 1994
  Appointed By: President William J. Clinton
  U.S. Post Office & Courthouse,
  700 Grant Street, Suite 3280,
  Pittsburgh, PA 15219-1906
  E-mail: Judge_Donetta_
  Ambrose@pawd.uscourts.gov
Senior Judge **Terrence F. McVerry** . . . . (412) 208-7495
  Began Service: September 27, 2002
  Appointed By: President George W. Bush
Magistrate Judge **Susan Paradise Baxter** . . . . (814) 464-9630
  Began Service: January 29, 1995
  U.S. District Court, 17 South Park Row,
  Room A280, Erie, PA 16501
  E-mail: Judge_Susan_Baxter@pawd.uscourts.gov
Magistrate Judge **The Honorable Lisa Pupo Lenihan** . . . (412) 208-7370
  Began Service: April 2, 2004
  E-mail: judge_lisa_lenihan@pawd.uscourts.gov
Magistrate Judge **Maureen P. Kelly** Room 9280 . . . . (412) 208-7450
  Began Service: June 13, 2011
Magistrate Judge **Cynthia Reed Eddy** Suite 5380 . . . . (412) 208-7490
  Began Service: October 19, 2011
Magistrate Judge (Part-Time) **Keith A. Pesto** . . . . (814) 536-4342
  Began Service: March 1994
  E-mail: Judge_Keith_Pesto@pawd.uscourts.gov
Magistrate Judge (recalled) **Robert C. Mitchell** Suite
  9240 . . . . (412) 208-7470
  Began Service: February 17, 1972

Court Staff
Clerk of the Court **Robert V. Barth** . . . . (412) 208-7500
  E-mail: robert_barth@pawd.uscourts.gov
Chief U.S. Probation and Pretrial Services Officer
  Belinda M. Ashley Suite 3330 . . . . (412) 395-6907
  E-mail: belinda_ashley@pawp.uscourts.gov

United States Bankruptcy Court for the Western District of Pennsylvania
U.S. Steel Tower, 600 Grant Street, Suite 5414, Pittsburgh, PA 15219
Tel: (412) 644-2700 Tel: (800) 676-6856 (PACER)
Tel: (412) 355-3210 (Voice Case Information System VCIS)
Tel: (866) 299-8515 (Voice Case Information System VCIS)
Fax: (412) 644-6812
Internet: www.pawb.uscourts.gov

Number of Judgeships: 6

Number of Vacancies: 2

Judges
Chief Bankruptcy Judge **Jeffery A. Deller** . . . . (412) 644-4710
  Began Service: 2005
Bankruptcy Judge **Thomas P. Agresti** . . . . (814) 464-9760
  Began Service: April 2004
  U.S. Courthouse, 17 South Park Row, Room B250,
  Erie, PA 16501
Bankruptcy Judge **Carlota Bohm** . . . . (412) 644-4328
  Began Service: 2011
Bankruptcy Judge **Gregory L. Taddonio** . . . . (412) 644-3541

Court Staff
Clerk of the Court **Michael R. "Mike" Rhodes** . . . . (412) 644-2700
  E-mail: michael_rhodes@pawb.uscourts.gov

U.S. Attorney
Pennsylvania - Western District
U.S. Post Office and Courthouse Building, 700 Grant Street,
Suite 4000, Pittsburgh, PA 15219
Tel: (412) 644-3500 Fax: (412) 644-4549

U.S. Attorney **David J. Hickton** . . . . (412) 894-7325
  E-mail: david.hickton@usdoj.gov

Federal Public Defender
Office of the Federal Public Defender Western District of Pennsylvania
Liberty Center, 1001 Liberty Avenue, Room 1500,
Pittsburgh, PA 15222-3714
Renaissance Centre, 1001 State Street, Room 1111, Erie, PA 16501
Tel: (412) 644-6565 (Pittsburgh) Tel: (814) 455-8089 (Erie)
Fax: (412) 644-4594 (Pittsburgh) Fax: (814) 455-8624 (Erie)

Federal Public Defender **Lisa B. Freeland** . . . . (412) 644-6565
  E-mail: lisa.freeland@fd.org

United States District Court for the District of Rhode Island
Federal Building and U.S. Courthouse, One Exchange Terrace,
Providence, RI 02903-1720
Tel: (401) 752-7200 Tel: (401) 752-7262 (PACER)
Fax: (401) 752-7247
Internet: www.rid.uscourts.gov

Number of Judgeships: 3
Circuit: First

Judges
Chief Judge **William E. Smith** . . . . (401) 752-7120
  Began Service: December 9, 2002
  Appointed By: President George W. Bush

United States District Court for the District of Rhode Island *continued*

District Judge **Mary M. Lisi** . . . . (401) 752-7200
 Note: Judge Lisi will take senior status effective
 October 1, 2015.
 Began Service: June 13, 1994
 Appointed By: President William J. Clinton
District Judge **John J. McConnell, Jr.** . . . . (401) 752-7200
 Began Service: May 17, 2011
 Appointed By: President Barack Obama
Senior Judge **Ronald R. Lagueux** . . . . (401) 752-7060
 Began Service: September 4, 1986
 Appointed By: President Ronald Reagan
Magistrate Judge **Lincoln D. Almond** . . . . (401) 752-7224
 Began Service: September 2004
 E-mail: Mag_Judge_Almond@rid.uscourts.gov
Magistrate Judge **Patricia A. Sullivan** . . . . (401) 752-7080
 Began Service: October 1, 2012
Magistrate Judge (recalled) **Robert W. Lovegreen** . . . . . . (401) 752-7110
 Began Service: March 1993
 E-mail: Mag_Judge_Lovegreen@rid.uscourts.gov

Court Staff
Clerk of Court **David A. DiMarzio** . . . . (401) 752-7220
 E-mail: david_dimarzio@rid.uscourts.gov
Chief Probation Officer **Barry Weiner** . . . . (401) 752-7300
 Two Exchange Terrace, Third,
 Providence, RI 02903

United States Bankruptcy Court for the District of Rhode Island
The Federal Center, 380 Westminster Street, Providence, RI 02903
Tel: (401) 626-3100
Tel: (866) 222-8029 (Voice Case Information System VCIS)
Fax: (401) 626-3150
Internet: www.rib.uscourts.gov

Number of Judgeships: 1

Judges
Bankruptcy Judge **Diane Finkle** Room 619 . . . . (401) 626-3060

Court Staff
Fax: (401) 626-3150
E-mail: rib_helpdesk@rib.uscourts.gov

Clerk of the Court **Susan M. Thurston** . . . . (401) 626-3130
 E-mail: susan_thurston@rib.uscourts.gov

U.S. Attorney
Rhode Island District
50 Kennedy Plaza, 8th Floor, Providence, RI 02903
Tel: (401) 709-5000 Fax: (401) 709-5001

U.S. Attorney **Peter F. Neronha** . . . . (401) 709-5000
 E-mail: peter.neronha@usdoj.gov

United States Bankruptcy Court for the District of Rhode Island
continued

Federal Public Defender
Federal Public Defender Office - District of Massachusetts, New Hampshire and Rhode Island
51 Sleeper Street, 5th Floor, Boston, MA 02210
The Ralph Pill Building, 22 Bridge Street, Third Floor,
Concord, NH 03301-4922
101 Weybosset Street, Third Floor, Providence, RI 02903
Tel: (317) 223-8061 (Boston) Tel: (603) 226-7360 (Concord)
Tel: (401) 528-4281 (Providence) Fax: (617) 223-8080 (Boston)
Fax: (603) 226-7358 (Concord) Fax: (401) 528-4284 (Providence)

Federal Public Defender **Miriam Conrad** . . . . (617) 223-8061
 E-mail: miriam.conrad@fd.org

United States District Court for the District of South Carolina
901 Richland Street, Columbia, SC 29201-2431
Tel: (803) 765-5816 Tel: (803) 765-5871 (PACER)
Fax: (803) 765-5960
Internet: www.scd.uscourts.gov

Number of Judgeships: 10

Number of Vacancies: 2

Circuit: Fourth

Judges
Chief Judge **Terry L. Wooten** . . . . (803) 253-6420
 Began Service: December 3, 2001
 Appointed By: President George W. Bush
 E-mail: terry_wooten@scd.uscourts.gov
District Judge **David C. Norton** . . . . (843) 579-1450
 Began Service: July 13, 1990
 Appointed By: President George H.W. Bush
 E-mail: david_norton@scd.uscourts.gov
District Judge **Robert Bryan Harwell** . . . . (843) 676-3800
 Began Service: July 13, 2004
 Appointed By: President George W. Bush
 E-mail: harwell_ecf@scd.uscourts.gov
District Judge **J. Michelle Childs** . . . . (803) 253-3850
 Began Service: August 23, 2010
 Appointed By: President Barack Obama
 E-mail: michelle_childs@scd.uscourts.gov
District Judge **Richard Mark Gergel** . . . . (843) 579-2610
 Began Service: August 5, 2010
 Appointed By: President Barack Obama
 E-mail: richard_gergel@scd.uscourts.gov
District Judge **Timothy M. Cain** . . . . (864) 261-2030
 Began Service: September 26, 2011
 Appointed By: President Barack Obama
 E-mail: timothy_cain@scd.uscourts.gov
District Judge **Mary Geiger Lewis** . . . . (864) 591-5340
 Began Service: 2012
 Appointed By: President Barack Obama
 E-mail: lewis_ecf@scd.uscourts.gov
District Judge **Bruce H. Hendricks** . . . . (864) 239-5710
 Began Service: 2014
 Appointed By: President Barack Obama
 E-mail: bruce_hendricks@scd.uscourts.gov
Senior Judge **Henry M. Herlong, Jr.** . . . . (864) 241-2720
 Began Service: May 14, 1991
 Appointed By: President George H.W. Bush
 300 East Washington Street, Room 324,
 Greenville, SC 29601
 E-mail: henry_herlong@scd.uscourts.gov
Senior Judge **Patrick Michael Duffy** . . . . (843) 579-1460
 Began Service: December 1995
 Appointed By: President William J. Clinton
Senior Judge **Sol Blatt, Jr.** . . . . (843) 579-1470
 Began Service: July 1971
 Appointed By: President Richard M. Nixon
 E-mail: Sol_Blatt@scd.uscourts.gov

(continued on next page)

United States District Court for the District of South Carolina *continued*

Senior Judge **C. Weston Houck** ....(843) 579-1480
  Began Service: 1979
  Appointed By: President Jimmy Carter
Senior Judge **G. Ross Anderson, Jr.** ....(864) 226-9799
  Began Service: May 23, 1980
  Appointed By: President Jimmy Carter
Senior Judge **Margaret B. Seymour** ....(803) 765-5590
  Began Service: October 30, 1998   Tel: (803) 253-3397
  Appointed By: President William J. Clinton
  E-mail: margaret_seymour@scd.uscourts.gov
Senior Judge **Cameron McGowan Currie** ....(803) 253-3680
  Began Service: 1994
  Appointed By: President William J. Clinton
Senior Judge **Joseph F. Anderson, Jr.** ....(803) 765-5136
  Began Service: 1986
  Appointed By: President Ronald Reagan
  E-mail: joe_anderson@scd.uscourts.gov
Magistrate Judge **Bristow Marchant** ....(843) 579-2626
  Began Service: September 1, 1992
  E-mail: bristow_marchant@scd.uscourts.gov
Magistrate Judge **Thomas E. Rogers III** ....(843) 676-3805
  Began Service: May 8, 2002
  E-mail: thomas_rogers@scd.uscourts.gov
Magistrate Judge **Paige Jones Gossett** ....(803) 765-5498
  Began Service: January 30, 2009
  E-mail: gossett_ecf@scd.uscourts.gov
Magistrate Judge **Kevin F. McDonald** ....(864) 241-2740
  Began Service: 2010
  300 East Washington Street, Suite 300,
  Greenville, SC 29601
  E-mail: kevin_mcdonald@scd.uscourts.gov
Magistrate Judge **Shiva V. Hodges** ....(803) 253-6431
  Began Service: 2010
  E-mail: hodges_ecf@scd.uscourts.gov
Magistrate Judge **Jacquelyn D. Austin** ....(864) 241-2700
  Began Service: 2012
  E-mail: jacquelyn_austin@scd.uscourts.gov
Magistrate Judge **Kaymani West** ....(843) 292-5630
  Began Service: January 1, 2012
Magistrate Judge **Mary Gordon Baker** ....(843) 579-1440
Magistrate Judge (Part-Time)
  Robert L. Buchanan, Jr. ....(803) 649-2586 ext. 203
  Began Service: April 1, 1979
  E-mail: rlbuchananjr@atlanticbbn.net

Court Staff

Clerk of Court **Robin Blume** ....(803) 765-5816
  E-mail: robin_blume@scd.uscourts.gov
Chief Probation and Pretrial Officer **Dickie Brunson** .....(803) 253-3310
  1835 Assembly Street, Suite 611,
  Columbia, SC 29201

United States Bankruptcy Court for the District of South Carolina

J. Bratton Davis U.S. Bankruptcy Courthouse, 1100 Laurel Street,
Columbia, SC 29201-2423
Tel: (803) 765-5436 Tel: (866) 222-8029
Internet: http://ecf.scb.uscourts.gov (Electronic Case Files)

Number of Judgeships: 3

Judges

Chief Bankruptcy Judge **David R. Duncan** ....(803) 765-5657
  Began Service: May 2006
  E-mail: david_duncan@scb.uscourts.gov
Bankruptcy Judge **John E. Waites**....................(803) 253-3751
  Began Service: June 1994
  E-mail: john_waites@scb.uscourts.gov
Bankruptcy Judge **Helen Elizabeth Burris** ....(864) 591-5315
  Began Service: March 2006

United States Bankruptcy Court for the District of South Carolina *continued*

Court Staff

Clerk of Court **Laura A. Austin** ....(803) 765-5209
  E-mail: laura_austin@scb.uscourts.gov

U.S. Attorney

South Carolina District
Wells Fargo Building, 1441 Main Street, Suite 500, Columbia, SC 29201
Tel: (803) 929-3000 Fax: (803) 254-2912 Fax: (803) 254-2943
Fax: (803) 254-2889

U.S. Attorney **William N. "Bill" Nettles** ....(803) 929-3000

Federal Public Defender

Federal Public Defender for the District of South Carolina
BB&T Bank Building, 1901 Assembly Street, Suite 200,
Columbia, SC 29201
King and Queen Street Building, 145 King Street, Suite 325,
Charleston, SC 29401
McMillan Federal Building and U.S. Courthouse, 401 West Evans Street,
Suite 105, Florence, SC 29501
75 Beattie Place, Suite 950, Greenville, SC 29601
Tel: (803) 765-5070 (Columbia) Tel: (843) 727-4148 (Charleston)
Tel: (843) 662-1510 (Florence) Tel: (864) 235-8714 (Greenville)
Fax: (803) 765-5084 (Columbia) Fax: (843) 727-4179 (Charleston)
Fax: (843) 667-1355 (Florence) Fax: (864) 233-0188 (Greenville)

Federal Public Defender **Parks N. Small** ....(803) 765-5070
  E-mail: parks.small@fd.org

United States District Court for the District of South Dakota

128 U.S. Courthouse, 400 South Phillips Avenue, Sioux Falls, SD 57104
Tel: (605) 330-6600 Fax: (605) 330-6601
Internet: www.sdd.uscourts.gov

Number of Judgeships: 4

Circuit: Eighth

Judges

Chief Judge **Jeffrey Viken** ....(605) 399-6050
  Began Service: October 2009
  Appointed By: President Barack Obama
  United States Courthouse, 515 Ninth Street,
  Room 318, Rapid City, SD 57701
  E-mail: jeffrey_viken@sdd.uscourts.gov
District Judge **Karen E. Schreier** ....(605) 330-6670
  Began Service: August 13, 1999
  Appointed By: President William J. Clinton
  E-mail: karen_schreier@sdd.uscourts.gov
District Judge **Roberto A. Lange** ....(605) 945-4610
  Began Service: November 6, 2009
  Appointed By: President Barack Obama
  E-mail: roberto_lange@sdd.uscourts.gov
Senior Judge **Charles B. Kornmann** ....(605) 377-2600
  Began Service: May 1995
  Appointed By: President William J. Clinton
  12 Second Avenue SW, Suite 200,
  Aberdeen, SD 57401-4309
  E-mail: charles_kornmann@sdd.uscourts.gov
Senior Judge **John B. Jones** ....(605) 330-6640
  Began Service: December 5, 1981
  Appointed By: President Ronald Reagan
  400 South Phillips Avenue, Room 202,
  Sioux Falls, SD 57104-6851
Senior Judge **Lawrence L. Piersol** ....(605) 330-6640
  Began Service: December 11, 1993
  Appointed By: President William J. Clinton

United States District Court for the District of South Dakota *continued*

Magistrate Judge **Mark A. Moreno** . . . . (605) 945-4620
Began Service: February 1, 1993
Federal Building & Courthouse,
225 South Pierre Street, Room 419,
Pierre, SD 57501
E-mail: Mark_Moreno@sdd.uscourts.gov

Magistrate Judge **Veronica L. Duffy** . . . . (605) 330-6655
Began Service: June 2007
E-mail: veronica_duffy@sdd.uscourts.gov

Magistrate Judge **William D. Gerdes**. . . . .(605) 622-2100
Began Service: 2015
104 South Lincoln, Room 111,
Aberdeen, SD 57401

Court Staff

Clerk of Court **Joseph A. Haas**. . . . .(605) 330-6606
E-mail: Joe_Haas@sdd.uscourts.gov

Chief Probation and Pretrial Services Officer
John Bentley. . . . . (605) 977-8960
314 South Main Avenue, Sioux Falls, SD 57104

United States Bankruptcy Court for the District of South Dakota

104 U.S. Courthouse, 400 South Phillips Avenue,
Sioux Falls, SD 57104-6851
P.O. Box 5060, Sioux Falls, SD 57117-5060
Tel: (605) 357-2400
Tel: (800) 768-6218 (Voice Case Information System VCIS)
Fax: (605) 357-2401
Internet: www.sdb.uscourts.gov

Number of Judgeships: 2

Number of Vacancies: 1

Judges

Bankruptcy Judge **Charles L. Nail, Jr.**. . . . . (605) 945-4490
Began Service: 2006
Federal Building, 225 South Pierre Street,
Room 211, Pierre, SD 57501

Court Staff

Clerk of Court **Rick Entwistle**. . . . . (605) 357-2400

U.S. Attorney

South Dakota District
325 South First Avenue, Suite 300, Sioux Falls, SD 57104
P.O. Box 2638, Sioux Falls, SD 57101-2638
Tel: (605) 330-4400 Fax: (605) 330-4410

U.S. Attorney (Acting) **Randy Seiler**. . . . .(605) 330-4400
E-mail: randy.seiler@usdoj.gov

United States Bankruptcy Court for the District of South Dakota
continued

Federal Public Defender

Federal Public Defender for the District of South Dakota and North Dakota
Pierre Professional Plaza, 124 South Euclid Avenue, Pierre, SD 57501
Federal Plaza, 324 North Third Street, Suite 1, Bismarck, ND 58501
Federal Square Building, 112 Roberts Street North, Suite 202,
Fargo, ND 58102
The Sweeney Building 703 Main Street, Second Floor,
Rapid City, SD 57001
200 West Tenth Street, Suite 200, Sioux Falls, SD 57104
Tel: (605) 224-0009 (Pierre) Tel: (701) 250-4500 (Bismarck)
Tel: (701) 239-5111 (Fargo) Tel: (605) 343-5110 (Rapid City)
Tel: (605) 330-4489 (Sioux Falls) Fax: (605) 224-0010 (Pierre)
Fax: (701) 250-4498 (Bismarck) Fax: (701) 239-5098 (Fargo)
Fax: (605) 343-1498 (Rapid City) Fax: (605) 330-4499 (Sioux Falls)

Federal Public Defender **Neil Fulton** . . . . (605) 224-0009
E-mail: neil.fulton@fd.org

United States District Court for the Eastern District of Tennessee

Howard H. Baker, Jr. U.S. Courthouse, 800 Market Street,
Suite 130, Knoxville, TN 37902
Tel: (865) 545-4228 Fax: (865) 545-4247
Internet: www.tned.uscourts.gov

Number of Judgeships: 5

Number of Vacancies: 1

Circuit: Sixth

Areas Covered: Counties of Anderson, Bedford, Bledsoe, Blount, Bradley, Campbell, Carter, Claiborne, Cocke, Coffee, Franklin, Grainger, Greene, Grundy, Hamblen, Hamilton, Hancock, Hawkins, Jefferson, Johnson, Knox, Lincoln, Loudon, Marion, McMinn, Meigs, Monroe, Moore, Morgan, Polk, Rhea, Roane, Scott, Sequatchie, Sevier, Sullivan, Unicoi, Union, Van Buren, Warren and Washington

Judges

Chief Judge **Thomas A. Varlan** Suite 143 . . . .(865) 545-4762
Began Service: April 5, 2003
Appointed By: President George W. Bush
E-mail: varlan_chambers@tned.uscourts.gov

District Judge **J. Ronnie Greer** . . . . (423) 639-0063
Began Service: June 25, 2003
Appointed By: President George W. Bush
220 West Depot Street, Suite 405,
Greeneville, TN 37743
E-mail: ronnie_greer@tned.uscourts.gov

District Judge **Harry S. Mattice, Jr.** . . . . (423) 752-5200
Began Service: November 18, 2005
Appointed By: President George W. Bush
Joel W. Solomon Federal Building & US
Courthouse, 900 Georgia Avenue, Room 104,
Chattanooga, TN 37402

District Judge **Pamela L. Reeves** Suite 145 . . . .(865) 545-4255
Began Service: March 5, 2014
Appointed By: President Barack Obama

Senior Judge **Robert Leon Jordan** . . . . (865) 545-4224
Began Service: November 15, 1988
Appointed By: President Ronald Reagan
E-mail: leon_jordan@tned.uscourts.gov

Senior Judge **Curtis L. Collier** . . . . (423) 752-5287
Began Service: May 22, 1995
Appointed By: President William J. Clinton
900 Georgia Avenue, Room 317,
Chattanooga, TN 37402
E-mail: curtis_collier@tned.uscourts.gov

Magistrate Judge **Dennis H. Inman**. . . . . (423) 787-7400
Began Service: November 14, 1995
E-mail: dennis_inman@tned.uscourts.gov

(continued on next page)

United States District Court for the Eastern District of Tennessee
continued

Magistrate Judge **C. Clifford Shirley, Jr.** . . . . (865) 545-4260
  Began Service: February 13, 2002
  E-mail: clifford_shirley@tned.uscourts.gov
Magistrate Judge **H. Bruce Guyton** Suite 142 . . . . (865) 545-4260
  Began Service: June 25, 2003
  E-mail: bruce_guyton@tned.uscourts.gov
Magistrate Judge **Susan K. Lee** . . . . (423) 752-5230
  Began Service: April 25, 1988
  900 Georgia Avenue, Room 401,
  Chattanooga, TN 37402
  E-mail: susan_k_lee@tned.uscourts.gov
Magistrate Judge **Christopher H. Steger** . . . . (423) 752-5200
  Began Service: 2015

Court Staff
Clerk of the Court **Debra C. Poplin** . . . .(865) 545-4228
  E-mail: debbie_poplin@tned.uscourts.gov
Chief U.S. Probation Officer **Tony Anderson** Suite 311 . . . (865) 545-4001

United States Bankruptcy Court for the Eastern District of Tennessee

Howard H. Baker, Jr. U.S. Courthouse, 800 Market Street,
Suite 330, Knoxville, TN 37902
Tel: (865) 545-4279 Tel: (423) 752-5272 (VCIS)
Tel: (800) 767-1512 (Toll Free Voice Case Information System VCIS)
Fax: (865) 545-4271
Internet: www.tneb.uscourts.gov
Internet: http://pacer.tneb.uscourts.gov (Pacer)

Number of Judgeships: 4

Judges
Chief Bankruptcy Judge **Marcia Phillips Parsons** . . . . (423) 638-2264
  Began Service: November 23, 1993
Bankruptcy Judge **Shelley D. Rucker** . . . . (423) 752-5104
  Began Service: 2010
Bankruptcy Judge **Suzanne Bauknight** . . . . (865) 545-4284

Court Staff
Clerk of the Court **William T. Magill** . . . . (423) 787-0113

U.S. Attorney
Tennessee - Eastern District
800 Market Street, Suite 211, Knoxville, TN 37902
Tel: (865) 545-4167 Fax: (865) 545-4176

U.S. Attorney **William C. "Bill" Killian** . . . .(865) 545-4167

Federal Public Defender
Federal Defender Services of Eastern Tennessee, Inc [FDSET]
The Plaza Tower, 800 South Gay Street, Suite 2400,
Knoxville, TN 37929-9714
707 Georgia Avenue, Suite 203, Chattanooga, TN 37402
129 West Depot Street, Suite 1, Greeneville, TN 37743
Tel: (865) 637-7979 (Knoxville) Tel: (423) 756-4349 (Chattanooga)
Tel: (423) 636-1301 (Greeneville) Fax: (865) 637-7999 (Knoxville)
Fax: (423) 756-4345 (Chattanooga) Fax: (423) 636-1385 (Greeneville)

Federal Public Defender **Elizabeth Ford** . . . . (865) 637-7979
  E-mail: elizabeth.ford@fd.org

United States District Court for the Middle District of Tennessee

U.S. Courthouse, 801 Broadway, Nashville, TN 37203
Tel: (615) 736-5498 Tel: (615) 736-7164 (PACER)
Fax: (615) 736-7488
Internet: www.tnmd.uscourts.gov

Number of Judgeships: 4

Number of Vacancies: 1

Circuit: Sixth

Areas Covered: Counties of Cannon, Cheatham, Clay, Cumberland, Davidson, DeKalb, Dickson, Fentress, Giles, Hickman, Houston, Humphreys, Jackson, Lawrence, Lewis, Macon, Marshall, Maury, Montgomery, Overton, Pickett, Putnam, Robertson, Rutherford, Smith, Stewart, Sumner, Trousdale, Wayne, White, Williamson and Wilson

Judges
Chief Judge **Kevin Hunter Sharp** Room A820 . . . . (615) 736-2774
  Began Service: May 4, 2011
  Appointed By: President Barack Obama
  E-mail: kevin_sharp@tnmd.uscourts.gov
District Judge **Todd J. Campbell** Suite A820 . . . . (615) 736-5291
  Began Service: 1995
  Appointed By: President William J. Clinton
District Judge **Aleta Arthur Trauger** Room 825 . . . . (615) 736-7143
  Began Service: December 1, 1998
  Appointed By: President William J. Clinton
Senior Judge **John T. Nixon** Room 770 . . . . (615) 736-5778
  Began Service: 1980
  Appointed By: President Jimmy Carter
  E-mail: john_nixon@tnmd.uscourts.gov
Senior Judge **William J. Haynes, Jr.** . . . .(615) 736-7217
  Began Service: November 1999
  Appointed By: President William J. Clinton
Magistrate Judge **Juliet Griffin** Room 756 . . . . (615) 736-5164
  Began Service: 1995
  E-mail: juliet_griffin@tnmd.uscourts.gov
Magistrate Judge **E. Clifton Knowles** . . . . (615) 736-7344
  Began Service: 2000
  U.S. Courthouse, 801 Broadway, Suite 649,
  Nashville, TN 37203-3869
Magistrate Judge (recalled) **Joe B. Brown** . . . . (615) 736-2119
  Began Service: August 3, 1998
  E-mail: joe_b_brown@tnmd.uscourts.gov
Magistrate Judge **John S. Bryant** Room 797 . . . . (615) 736-5878
  Began Service: November 1999
  Appointed By: President William J. Clinton
  E-mail: john_bryant@tnmd.uscourts.gov

Court Staff
Clerk of Court **Keith Throckmorton** . . . . (615) 736-2364 ext. 3225
  E-mail: keith_throckmorton@tnmd.uscourts.gov
Chief U.S. Probation Officer **Robert W. Musser, Jr.** . . . . . (615) 736-5771

United States Bankruptcy Court for the Middle District of Tennessee

Customs House, 701 Broadway, Nashville, TN 37203
Tel: (615) 736-5584 (Clerk's Office)
Tel: (800) 676-6856 (PACER Service)
Tel: (615) 736-5577 (PACER Registration)
Tel: (615) 736-5584 (Voice Case Information Systems)
Fax: (615) 736-2305 (Admin) Fax: (615) 695-4980 (Intake)
E-mail: webmaster@tnmb.uscourts.gov
E-mail: pacer@psc.uscourts.gov
Internet: www.tnmb.uscourts.gov

Number of Judgeships: 3

Judges

Chief Bankruptcy Judge **Keith M. Lundin** . . . . (615) 736-5586
    Began Service: May 25, 1982
    E-mail: keith_lundin@tnmb.uscourts.gov
Bankruptcy Judge **Marian F. Harrison** Room 232 . . . . (615) 736-5589
    Began Service: December 21, 1999
    E-mail: marian_harrison@tnmb.uscourts.gov
Bankruptcy Judge **Randal S. Mashburn** . . . . (615) 736-5587
    Began Service: 2011

Court Staff

Clerk of the Court **Matthew T. Loughney** . . . . (615) 736-5590
    E-mail: matt_loughney@tnmb.uscourts.gov

U.S. Attorney

Tennessee - Middle District

110 Ninth Avenue South, Suite A-961, Nashville, TN 37203-3870
Tel: (615) 736-5151 Fax: (615) 736-5323

U.S. Attorney **David Rivera** . . . . (615) 736-5151
    E-mail: david.rivera@usdoj.gov

Federal Public Defender

Office of the Federal Public Defender Middle District of Tennessee

810 Broadway, Suite 200, Nashville, TN 37203
Tel: (615) 736-5047 Fax: (615) 736-5265

Federal Public Defender **Henry A. Martin** . . . . (615) 736-5047
    E-mail: henry_martin@fd.org

United States District Court for the Western District of Tennessee

242 Federal Building, 167 North Main Street, Memphis, TN 38103
Tel: (901) 495-1200 Tel: (901) 495-1259 (PACER)
Tel: (800) 407-4456 (Toll-free) Fax: (901) 495-1250
Internet: www.tnwd.uscourts.gov

Number of Judgeships: 5

Number of Vacancies: 1

Circuit: Sixth

Areas Covered: Counties of Benton, Carroll, Chester, Crockett, Decatur, Dyer, Fayette, Gibson, Hardeman, Hardin, Haywood, Henderson, Henry, Lake, Lauderdale, Madison, McNairy, Obion, Perry, Shelby, Tipton and Weakley

Judges

Chief Judge **J. Daniel Breen** . . . . (731) 421-9200
    Began Service: March 18, 2003
    Appointed By: President George W. Bush
    111 South Highland Avenue, Room 444,
    Jackson, TN 38301-6101
    E-mail: daniel_breen@tnwd.uscourts.gov
District Judge **Stanley Thomas Anderson** . . . . (901) 495-1495
    Began Service: May 21, 2008
    Appointed By: President George W. Bush
District Judge **John T. Fowlkes, Jr.** . . . . (901) 495-1326
    Began Service: August 9, 2012
    Appointed By: President Barack Obama
District Judge **Sheryl H. "Sheri" Lipman** . . . . (901) 495-1337
    Began Service: August 14, 2014
    Appointed By: President Barack Obama
    E-mail: ecf_judge_lipman@tnwd.uscourts.gov
Magistrate Judge **Diane K. Vescovo** . . . . (901) 495-1307
    Began Service: June 15, 1995
    E-mail: diane_vescovo@tnwd.uscourts.gov
Magistrate Judge **Tu M. Pham** . . . . (901) 495-1351
    Began Service: May 16, 2003
    Clifford Davis Federal Building,
    167 North Main Street, Courtroom 6 Room 338,
    Memphis, TN 38103-1814
    E-mail: tu_pham@tnwd.uscourts.gov
Magistrate Judge **Edward Glenn "Ed" Bryant** . . . . (731) 421-9200
    Began Service: December 15, 2008
    111 South Highland, Room 345,
    Jackson, TN 38301
Magistrate Judge **Charmiane G. Claxton** Room 357 . . . . . (901) 495-1326
    Began Service: May 29, 2009
    E-mail: charmiane_claxton@tnwd.uscourts.gov
Senior Judge **James Dale Todd** . . . . (731) 421-9222
    Began Service: July 11, 1985
    Appointed By: President Ronald Reagan
    U.S. Courthouse, 111 South Highland Avenue,
    Room 417, Jackson, TN 38301
    E-mail: james_todd@tnwd.uscourts.gov
Senior Judge **Jon P. McCalla** Room 1157 . . . . (901) 495-1200
    Began Service: 1992
    Appointed By: President George H.W. Bush
    E-mail: jon_mccalla@tnwd.uscourts.gov
Senior Judge **Samuel H. Mays, Jr.** . . . . (901) 495-1283
    Began Service: June 17, 2002
    Appointed By: President George W. Bush
    E-mail: samuel_mays@tnwd.uscourts.gov

Court Staff

Clerk of Court **Thomas M. Gould** . . . . (901) 495-1200
Chief Probation Officer **Alice Conley** Room 234 . . . . (901) 495-1400
    E-mail: alice_conley@tnwd.uscourts.gov
Chief Pretrial Services Officer **Carolyn Moore** Room
    459 . . . . (901) 495-1550
    E-mail: carolyn_moore@tnwd.uscourts.gov

United States Bankruptcy Court for the Western District of Tennessee

200 Jefferson Avenue, Suite 413, Memphis, TN 38103
Tel: (901) 328-3500 Tel: (800) 406-0190 (Toll Free PACER)
Tel: (901) 328-3617 (PACER)
Tel: (901) 328-3509 (Voice Case Information System VCIS)
Tel: (888) 381-4961 (Toll Free Voice Case Information System VCIS)
Internet: www.tnwb.uscourts.gov

Number of Judgeships: 4

Judges

Chief Bankruptcy Judge **David S. Kennedy** Suite 950 . . . . (901) 328-3522
  Began Service: November 24, 1980
Bankruptcy Judge **Jennie D. Latta** Suite 650 . . . . (901) 328-3542
  Began Service: March 6, 1997
  E-mail: jennie_d_latta@tnwb.uscourts.gov
Bankruptcy Judge **Paulette J. Delk** . . . .(901) 328-3534
  Began Service: July 2006
  Appointed By: President George W. Bush
Bankruptcy Judge **George W. Emerson, Jr.**. . . . .(901) 328-3614
  Began Service: July 2006
Bankruptcy Judge **Jimmy L. Croom** . . . . (731) 421-9314

Court Staff

Clerk of Court **Jed G. Weintraub** . . . .(901) 328-3500
  E-mail: jed_weintraub@tnwb.uscourts.gov

U.S. Attorney

Tennessee - Western District
Clifford Davis Federal Building, 167 North Main Street, Suite 800,
Memphis, TN 38103
Tel: (901) 544-4231 Fax: (901) 544-4230

U.S. Attorney **Edward L. "Ed" Stanton III** . . . . (901) 544-4231
  E-mail: edward.stanton@usdoj.gov

Federal Public Defender

Office of the Federal Public Defender Western District of Tennessee
One Memphis Place, 200 Jefferson Avenue, Suite 200, Jackson, TN 38103
Ed Jones Federal Building, 109 South Highland Avenue, Room 105,
Jackson, TN 38301
Tel: (901) 544-3895 (Memphis) Tel: (731) 427-2556 (Jackson)
Fax: (901) 544-4355 (Memphis) Fax: (731) 427-3052 (Jackson)

Federal Public Defender **Doris Randle-Holt** . . . . (901) 544-3895

United States District Court for the Eastern District of Texas

U.S. Courthouse, 211 West Ferguson Street, Room 106, Tyler, TX 75702
Tel: (903) 590-1000 Tel: (903) 531-9210 (PACER)
Fax: (903) 590-1015
Internet: www.txed.uscourts.gov

Number of Judgeships: 8

Number of Vacancies: 2

Circuit: Fifth

Areas Covered: Counties of Anderson, Angelina, Bowie, Camp, Cass, Cherokee, Collin, Cooke, Delta, Denton, Fannin, Franklin, Grayson, Gregg, Hardin, Harrison, Henderson, Hopkins, Houston, Jasper, Jefferson, Lamar, Liberty, Marion, Morris, Nacogdoches, Newton, Orange, Panola, Polk, Rains, Red River, Rusk, Sabine, San Augustine, Shelby, Smith, Titus, Trinity, Tyler, Upshur, Van Zandt and Wood

Judges

Chief Judge **Ron Clark** . . . . (409) 654-2800
  Began Service: November 22, 2002
  Appointed By: President George W. Bush
  300 Willow Street, Suite 221,
  Beaumont, TX 77701
  E-mail: ron_clark@txed.uscourts.gov
District Judge **Marcia Ann Cain Crone** . . . . (409) 654-2880
  Began Service: October 3, 2003
  Appointed By: President George W. Bush
  300 Willow Street, Suite 239,
  Beaumont, TX 77701
  E-mail: Marcia_Crone@txed.uscourts.gov
District Judge **Michael H. Schneider** Room 100 . . . .(903) 590-1091
  Began Service: September 2004
  Appointed By: President George W. Bush
  E-mail: michael_schneider@txed.uscourts.gov
District Judge **James Rodney Gilstrap** . . . . (903) 935-3868
  Began Service: December 15, 2011
  Appointed By: President Barack Obama
  U.S. Courthouse, 100 East Houston, Room 101,
  Marshall, TX 75670
District Judge **Amos L. Mazzant III** . . . . (903) 893-7008
  Began Service: December 19, 2014
  Appointed By: President Barack Obama
  E-mail: amos_mazzant@txed.uscourts.gov
District Judge **Robert William Schroeder III** . . . . (903) 794-4067
  Began Service: December 19, 2014
  Appointed By: President Barack Obama
Senior Judge **Thad Heartfield** . . . . (409) 654-2860
  Began Service: May 1, 1995
  Appointed By: President William J. Clinton
  E-mail: thad_heartfield@txed.uscourts.gov
Senior Judge **Richard A. Schell** . . . .(214) 872-4820
  Began Service: August 15, 1988
  Appointed By: President Ronald Reagan
  U.S. District Court, 7940 Preston Road, Suite 111,
  Plano, TX 75024
  E-mail: richard_schell@txed.uscourts.gov
Magistrate Judge **Caroline M. Craven** . . . .(903) 792-6424
  Began Service: May 26, 1998
  U.S. Courthouse, 500 State Line Avenue,
  Room 401, Box 2090, Texarkana, TX 75501
  E-mail: caroline_craven@txed.uscourts.gov
Magistrate Judge **Don D. Bush** . . . . (214) 872-4840
  Began Service: February 24, 2003
  E-mail: Don_Bush@txed.uscourts.gov
Magistrate Judge **Keith F. Giblin** . . . . (409) 654-2845
  Began Service: October 1, 2004
  300 Willow Street, Suite 118,
  Beaumont, TX 77701
  E-mail: keith_giblin@txed.uscourts.gov
Magistrate Judge **John D. Love** Room 210 . . . . (903) 590-1164
  Began Service: January 2, 2006
  E-mail: john_love@txed.uscourts.gov

United States District Court for the Eastern District of Texas *continued*

Magistrate Judge **Zachary J. Hawthorn** . . . . (409) 654-2815
   Began Service: August 2, 2011
   300 Willow Street, Suite 234,
   Beaumont, TX 77701
Magistrate Judge **Roy S. Payne** . . . . (903) 935-2498
   Began Service: December 28, 2011
   E-mail: roy_payne@txed.uscourts.gov
Magistrate Judge **Nicole Mitchell** Room 300 . . . .(903) 590-1077
   Began Service: August 16, 2013
   E-mail: nicole_mitchell@txed.uscourts.gov
Magistrate Judge **Christine A. Nowak** . . . . (903) 893-7667
   Began Service: 2015

Court Staff

Clerk of Court **David J. Maland** . . . . (903) 590-1000
   Note: Until September 3, 2015.
   William M. Steger Federal Building and U.S.
   Courthouse, 211 W Ferguson Street, Room 106,
   Tyler, TX 75702
   E-mail: david_maland@txed.uscourts.gov
Clerk of Court **David O'Toole** . . . . (903) 590-1000
   Note: Effective September 4, 2015.
   211 W Ferguson Street, Tyler, TX 75702
Chief Probation Officer **Shane Ferguson** . . . . (903) 590-1330
   1700 South Southeast Loop 323,
   Tyler, TX 75701

United States Bankruptcy Court for the Eastern District of Texas

110 North College, 9th Floor, Tyler, TX 75702
Tel: (903) 590-3200
Tel: (903) 590-3251 (Voice Case Information System VCIS)
Fax: (903) 590-3226
Internet: www.txeb.uscourts.gov

Number of Judgeships: 2

Judges

Chief Bankruptcy Judge **Brenda T. Rhoades** . . . . (972) 509-1250
   Began Service: September 1, 2003
   660 North Central Expressway, Room 300 A,
   Plano, TX 75074
   E-mail: brenda_rhoades@txeb.uscourts.gov
Bankruptcy Judge **Bill Parker** . . . . (903) 590-3240
   Began Service: October 30, 1998

Court Staff

Clerk of the Court **Jeanne B. Henderson** . . . . (903) 590-3200
   E-mail: jeanne_henderson@txeb.uscourts.gov

U.S. Attorney

Texas - Eastern District
Federal Building, 350 Magnolia Avenue, Suite 150, Beaumont, TX 77701
Tel: (409) 839-2538   Fax: (409) 839-2550

U.S. Attorney **John Malcolm Bales** . . . . (409) 839-2538

United States Bankruptcy Court for the Eastern District of Texas
continued

Federal Public Defender

Office of the Federal Public Defender, Eastern District of Texas
Plaza Tower, 110 North College Avenue, Suite 1122,
Tyler, TX 75702-7226
Sears Building, 350 Magnolia Street, Suite 117, Beaumont, TX 77701
7460 Warren Parkway, Room 270, Frisco, TX 75034
One Grand Centre, 14800 Teague Drive, Suite 204, Sherman, TX 75090
Tel: (903) 531-9233 (Tyler)   Tel: (409) 839-2608 (Beaumont)
Tel: (469) 362-8506 (Frisco)   Tel: (903) 892-4448 (Sherman)
Fax: (903) 531-9625 (Tyler)   Fax: (409) 839-2610 (Beaumont)
Fax: (469) 362-6010 (Frisco)   Fax: (903) 892-4448 (Sherman)

Federal Public Defender **G. Patrick Black** . . . . (903) 531-9233

United States District Court for the Northern District of Texas

U.S. Courthouse, 1100 Commerce Street, Room 1452, Dallas, TX 75242
Tel: (214) 753-2200   Tel: (800) 676-6856 (Toll Free PACER)
Fax: (214) 753-2266
Internet: www.txnd.uscourts.gov

Number of Judgeships: 12

Number of Vacancies: 2

Circuit: Fifth

Areas Covered: Counties of Archer, Armstrong, Bailey, Baylor, Borden, Briscoe, Brown, Callahan, Carson, Castro, Childress, Clay, Cochran, Coke, Coleman, Collingsworth, Comanche, Concho, Cottle, Crockett, Crosby, Dallam, Dallas, Dawson, Deaf Smith, Dickens, Donley, Eastland, Ellis, Erath, Fisher, Floyd, Foard, Gaines, Garza, Glasscock, Gray, Hale, Hall, Hansford, Hardeman, Hartley, Haskell, Hemphill, Hockley, Hood, Howard, Hunt, Hutchinson, Irion, Jack, Johnson, Jones, Kaufman, Kent, King, Knox, Lamb, Lipscomb, Lubbock, Lynn, Menard, Mills, Mitchell, Montague, Moore, Motley, Navarro, Nolan, Ochiltree, Oldham, Palo Pinto, Parker, Parmer, Potter, Randall, Reagan, Roberts, Rockwall, Runnels, Schleicher, Scurry, Shackelford, Sherman, Stephens, Sterling, Stonewall, Sutton, Swisher, Tarrant, Taylor, Terry, Throckmorton, Tom Green, Wheeler, Wichita, Wilbarger, Wise, Yoakum and Young

Judges

Chief Judge **Jorge A. Solis** Room 1654 . . . .(214) 753-2342
   Began Service: 1991
   Appointed By: President George H.W. Bush
District Judge **Sidney A. Fitzwater** . . . .(214) 753-2333
   Began Service: 1986
   Appointed By: President Ronald Reagan
   E-mail: judge_fitzwater@txnd.uscourts.gov
District Judge **Mary Lou Robinson** . . . .(806) 468-3822
   Began Service: 1979
   Appointed By: President Jimmy Carter
   205 East 5th Avenue, Room F13248,
   Amarillo, TX 79101
   E-mail: judge_robinson@txnd.uscourts.gov
District Judge **John H. McBryde** . . . .(817) 850-6650
   Began Service: 1990
   Appointed By: President George H.W. Bush
   E-mail: john_mcbryde@txnd.uscourts.gov
District Judge **Sam A. Lindsay** . . . . (214) 753-2365
   Began Service: September 1, 1998
   Appointed By: President William J. Clinton
   U.S. Courthouse, 1100 Commerce Street,
   Room 1544, Dallas, TX 75242-1003
   E-mail: judge_lindsay@txnd.uscourts.gov
District Judge **Barbara M. G. Lynn** Room 1572 . . . . (214) 753-2420
   Began Service: February 14, 2000
   Appointed By: President William J. Clinton
   E-mail: judge_lynn@txnd.uscourts.gov

(continued on next page)

United States District Court for the Northern District of Texas *continued*

District Judge **David C. Godbey** 13th Floor, Room
1358 .... (214) 753-2700
    Began Service: August 7, 2002
    Appointed By: President George W. Bush
    E-mail: judge_godbey@txnd.uscourts.gov
District Judge **Ed Kinkeade** .... (214) 753-2720
    Began Service: November 18, 2002
    Appointed By: President George W. Bush
    1100 Commerce Street, Room 1625,
    Dallas, TX 75242-1103
    E-mail: Judge_Kinkeade@txnd.uscourts.gov
District Judge **Jane J. Boyle** Room 1520 .... (214) 753-2740
    Began Service: June 2004
    Appointed By: President George W. Bush
    E-mail: boyle_clerk@txnd.uscourts.gov
District Judge **Reed Charles O'Connor** .... (817) 850-6788
    Began Service: November 2007
    Appointed By: President George W. Bush
    E-mail: judge_o'connor@txnd.uscourts.gov
Senior Judge **A. Joe Fish** Room 1528 .... (214) 753-2310
    Began Service: March 11, 1983
    Appointed By: President Ronald Reagan
Senior Judge **Terry R. Means** .... (817) 850-6670
    Began Service: November 5, 1991
    Appointed By: President George H.W. Bush
    U.S. Courthouse, 501 West Tenth Street, Room 502,
    Fort Worth, TX 76102
    E-mail: terry_means@txnd.uscourts.gov
Senior Judge **Sam R. Cummings** .... (806) 472-1922
    Began Service: December 11, 1987
    Appointed By: President Ronald Reagan
    E-mail: judge_cummings@txnd.uscourts.gov
Magistrate Judge **Clinton E. Averitte** .... (806) 468-3832
    Began Service: 1987
    Federal Building, 205 East Fifth Street, Room 326,
    Amarillo, TX 79101-1524
Magistrate Judge **Paul Stickney** .... (214) 753-2409
    Began Service: 1998
    E-mail: judge_stickney@txnd.uscourts.gov
Magistrate Judge **Nancy M. Koenig** .... (806) 472-1933
    Began Service: December 28, 1998
    E-mail: Judge_Koenig@txnd.uscourts.gov
Magistrate Judge **Irma Carrillo Ramirez** Room 1567 ..... (214) 753-2393
    Began Service: September 9, 2002
Magistrate Judge **Jeffrey L. Cureton** .... (817) 850-6690
    Began Service: 2010
    501 West Tenth Street, Room 520,
    Fort Worth, TX 76102
    E-mail: judge_cureton@txnd.uscourts.gov
Magistrate Judge **Renee H. Toliver** Room 1407 .... (214) 753-2385
Magistrate Judge **E. Scott Frost** .... (325) 677-6311
    341 Pine Street, Room 2313,
    Abilene, TX 79601
Magistrate Judge **David L. Horan** Room 1549 .... (214) 753-2400

Court Staff
Clerk of Court **Karen Mitchell** .... (214) 753-2201
    E-mail: karen_mitchell@txnd.uscourts.gov
Chief U.S. Probation and Pretrial Officer
    Mitsi Westendorff .... (214) 753-2506

United States Bankruptcy Court for the Northern District of Texas
1100 Commerce Street, Room 1254, Dallas, TX 75242-1496
Tel: (214) 753-2000 Tel: (800) 676-6856 (Toll Free PACER)
Tel: (866) 222-8029 (Voice Case Information System VCIS)
Fax: (214) 753-2038
Internet: www.txnb.uscourts.gov

Number of Judgeships: 6

Judges
Chief Bankruptcy Judge **Barbara J. Houser** .... (214) 753-2055
    Began Service: January 20, 2000
Bankruptcy Judge **Robert L. Jones** .... (806) 472-5020
    Began Service: April 2000
    1205 Texas Avenue, Room 312,
    Lubbock, TX 79401
Bankruptcy Judge **D. Michael Lynn** .... (817) 333-6020
    Began Service: September 18, 2001
    E-mail: Judge_DM_Lynn@txnb.uscourts.gov
Bankruptcy Judge **Harlin DeWayne "Cooter" Hale** ..... (214) 753-2016
    Began Service: November 1, 2002
Bankruptcy Judge **Russell F. Nelms** .... (817) 333-6025
    Began Service: November 22, 2004
    E-mail: Judge_Russell_Nelms@txnb.uscourts.gov
Bankruptcy Judge **Stacey G. C. Jernigan** .... (214) 753-2040
    Began Service: May 2006
    1100 Commerce Street, Room 1254,
    Dallas, TX 75242
    E-mail: sgj_settings@txnb.uscourts.gov

Court Staff
Clerk of Court **Tawana C. Marshall** .... (214) 753-2000
    E-mail: tawana_marshall@txnb.uscourts.gov

U.S. Attorney
Texas - Northern District
Earle Cabell Federal Building, 1100 Commerce Street, 3rd Floor,
Dallas, TX 75242-1699
Tel: (214) 659-8600 Fax: (214) 659-8806

U.S. Attorney (Acting) **John R. Parker** .... (214) 659-8600
    E-mail: john.parker@usdoj.gov

Federal Public Defender
Federal Public Defender Northern District of Texas
A. Maceo Smith Federal Building, 525 South Griffin Street,
Suite 629, Dallas, TX 75202
Amarillo National Bank Building, 500 South Taylor Street,
Suite 110, Amarillo, TX 79101-2442
Fritz G. Lanham Federal Building, 819 Taylor Street, Room 9A10,
Fort Worth, TX 76102
George H. Mahon Federal Building and U.S. Courthouse,
1205 Texas Avenue, Room 506, Lubbock, TX 79401
Tel: (214) 767-2746 (Dallas) Tel: (806) 324-2370 (Amarillo)
Tel: (817) 978-2753 (Fort Worth) Tel: (806) 472-7236 (Lubbock)
Fax: (214) 767-2886 (Dallas) Fax: (806) 324-2372 (Amarillo)
Fax: (817) 978-2757 (Fort Worth) Fax: (806) 472-7241 (Lubbock)

Federal Public Defender **Jason D. Hawkins** .... (214) 767-2746
    E-mail: jason.hawkins@fd.org

United States District Court for the Southern District of Texas

Bob Casey U.S. Courthouse, 515 Rusk Street, Houston, TX 77002
P.O. Box 61010, Houston, TX 77208
Tel: (713) 250-5500 Tel: (800) 676-6856 (Toll Free PACER)
Internet: www.txs.uscourts.gov

Number of Judgeships: 19

Number of Vacancies: 2

Circuit: Fifth

Areas Covered: Counties of Aransas, Austin, Bee, Brazoria, Brazos, Brooks, Calhoun, Cameron, Chambers, Colorado, DeWitt, Duval, Fayette, Fort Bend, Galveston, Goliad, Grimes, Harris, Hidalgo, Jackson, Jim Hogg, Jim Wells, Kenedy, Kleberg, La Salle, Lavaca, Live Oak, Madison, Matagorda, McMullen, Montgomery, Nueces, Refugio, San Jacinto, San Patricio, Starr, Victoria, Walker, Waller, Webb, Wharton, Willacy and Zapata

Judges

Chief Judge **Ricardo H. Hinojosa** . . . . (956) 618-8100
  Began Service: May 5, 1983
  Appointed By: President Ronald Reagan
  1701 West Business Highway 83, Suite 1028,
  McAllen, TX 78501
  E-mail: ricardo_hinojosa@txs.uscourts.gov

District Judge **Micaela Alvarez** . . . . (956) 928-8270
  Began Service: December 27, 2004
  Appointed By: President George W. Bush
  1701 West Business Highway 83, Suite 911,
  McAllen, TX 78501
  E-mail: micaela_alvarez@txs.uscourts.gov

District Judge **Randy Crane** . . . . (956) 618-8083
  Began Service: March 27, 2002   Tel: (956) 928-8273
  Appointed By: President George W. Bush
  Bentsen Tower, 1701 West Business Highway 83,
  Suite 928, McAllen, TX 78501
  E-mail: randy_crane@txs.uscourts.gov

District Judge **Keith Paty Ellison** Room 3716 . . . . (713) 250-5806
  Began Service: August 2, 1999
  Appointed By: President William J. Clinton
  E-mail: Keith_Ellison@txs.uscourts.gov

District Judge **Vanessa D. Gilmore** . . . . (713) 250-5931
  Began Service: 1994
  Appointed By: President William J. Clinton
  Bob Casey U.S. Courthouse,
  515 Rusk Avenue, Room 9513,
  Houston, TX 77002
  E-mail: vanessa_gilmore@txs.uscourts.gov

District Judge **Andrew S. Hanen** . . . . (956) 548-2591
  Began Service: June 6, 2002
  Appointed By: President George W. Bush
  600 East Harrison Street, Room 301,
  Brownsville, TX 78520-7114
  E-mail: andrew_hanen@txs.uscourts.gov

District Judge **Melinda Harmon** . . . . (713) 250-5194
  Began Service: 1989
  Appointed By: President George H.W. Bush
  Bob Casey U.S. Courthouse, 515 Rusk Avenue,
  Suite 9114, Houston, TX 77002
  E-mail: melinda_harmon@txs.uscourts.gov

District Judge **Lynn Nettleton Hughes** . . . . (713) 250-5900
  Began Service: December 17, 1985
  Appointed By: President Ronald Reagan

District Judge **Sim Lake** . . . . (713) 250-5177
  Began Service: September 2, 1988
  Appointed By: President Ronald Reagan
  Bob Casey U.S. Courthouse, 515 Rusk Street,
  Room 9535, Houston, TX 77002-2600
  E-mail: sim_lake@txs.uscourts.gov

District Judge **Gray Hampton Miller** . . . . (713) 250-5377
  Began Service: May 2006
  Appointed By: President George W. Bush
  515 Rusk Avenue, Room 9136,
  Houston, TX 77002
  E-mail: gray_miller@txs.uscourts.gov

United States District Court for the Southern District of Texas *continued*

District Judge **Lee H. Rosenthal** . . . . (713) 250-5980
  Began Service: 1992
  Appointed By: President George H.W. Bush
  E-mail: lee_rosenthal@txs.uscourts.gov

District Judge **Diana Saldaña** . . . . (956) 790-1381
  Began Service: February 11, 2011
  Appointed By: President Barack Obama
  1300 Victoria Street, Suite 2317,
  Laredo, TX 78040
  E-mail: diana_saldana@txs.uscourts.gov

District Judge **Nelva Gonzales Ramos** . . . . (361) 888-3142
  Began Service: September 27, 2011
  Appointed By: President Barack Obama

District Judge **Marina Garcia Marmolejo** . . . . (713) 250-5500
  Began Service: October 4, 2011   Tel: (800) 676-6856
  Appointed By: President Barack Obama
  E-mail: marina_marmolejo@txs.uscourts.gov

District Judge **Alfred H. Bennett** . . . . (713) 250-5849
  Began Service: April 22, 2015
  Appointed By: President Barack Obama

District Judge **George C. Hanks, Jr.** . . . . (713) 250-5500
  Began Service: April 23, 2015
  Appointed By: President Barack Obama

District Judge **Jose Rolando Olvera, Jr.** . . . . (956) 548-2595
  Began Service: 2015
  Appointed By: President Barack Obama

Senior Judge **George P. Kazen** . . . . (956) 726-2237
  Began Service: May 11, 1979
  Appointed By: President Jimmy Carter
  E-mail: George_Kazen@txs.uscourts.gov

Senior Judge **Hayden Head** . . . . (361) 888-3148
  Began Service: October 26, 1981
  Appointed By: President Ronald Reagan
  1133 North Shoreline Boulevard, Room 308,
  Corpus Christi, TX 78401
  E-mail: hayden_head@txs.uscourts.gov

Senior Judge **David Hittner** U.S. Courthouse, Room
  8509 . . . . (713) 250-5711
  Began Service: June 9, 1986
  Appointed By: President Ronald Reagan
  E-mail: David_Hittner@txs.uscourts.gov

Senior Judge **Ewing Werlein, Jr.** . . . . (713) 250-5920
  Began Service: May 22, 1992
  Appointed By: President George H.W. Bush
  E-mail: ewing_werlein@txs.uscourts.gov

Senior Judge **Janis Graham Jack** . . . . (361) 888-3525
  Began Service: March 14, 1994
  Appointed By: President William J. Clinton
  1133 North Shoreline Boulevard, Room 321,
  Corpus Christi, TX 78401
  E-mail: janis_jack@txs.uscourts.gov

Senior Judge **John D. Rainey** . . . . (361) 788-5030
  Began Service: May 28, 1990
  Appointed By: President George H.W. Bush
  E-mail: john_rainey@txs.uscourts.gov

Senior Judge **Kenneth M. Hoyt** . . . . (713) 250-5611
  Began Service: April 1988
  Appointed By: President Ronald Reagan
  Bob Casey U.S. Courthouse,
  515 Rusk Avenue, Room 11-144,
  Houston, TX 77002

Senior Judge **Hilda G. Tagle** . . . . (956) 548-2510
  Began Service: March 27, 1998
  Appointed By: President William J. Clinton
  Federal Building, 600 East Harrison Street,
  Room 306, Brownsville, TX 78520
  E-mail: hilda_tagle@txs.uscourts.gov

Senior Judge **Nancy Friedman Atlas** . . . . (713) 250-5990
  Began Service: August 22, 1995
  Appointed By: President William J. Clinton
  9015 Bob Casey U.S. Courthouse,
  515 Rusk Avenue, Suite 9015,
  Houston, TX 77002-2601
  E-mail: Nancy_Atlas@txs.uscourts.gov

(continued on next page)

United States District Court for the Southern District of Texas *continued*

Magistrate Judge **Frances H. Stacy** . . . .(713) 250-5681
Began Service: February 20, 1990
Bob Casey U.S. Courthouse,
515 Rusk Avenue, Room 7525,
Houston, TX 77002
E-mail: frances_stacy@txs.uscourts.gov

Magistrate Judge **Nancy K. Johnson** . . . . (713) 250-5375
Began Service: June 12, 1990

Magistrate Judge **John R. Froeschner** . . . . (409) 766-3729
Began Service: 1991
601 Rosenberg, Suite 704,
Galveston, TX 77550
E-mail: john_froeschner@txs.uscourts.gov

Magistrate Judge **Maryrose Milloy** . . . . (713) 250-5860
Began Service: October 1992

Magistrate Judge **Dorina Ramos** . . . . (956) 618-8060
Began Service: 1996
1701 West Business Highway 83, Suite 811,
McAllen, TX 78501
E-mail: dorina_ramos@txs.uscourts.gov

Magistrate Judge **B. Janice Ellington** . . . . (361) 888-3291
Began Service: November 14, 1996
1133 North Shoreline Boulevard, Room 312,
Corpus Christi, TX 78401

Magistrate Judge **Peter E. Ormsby** . . . . (956) 618-8080
Began Service: March 1, 2005
1701 West Business Highway 83, Suite 805,
McAllen, TX 78501
E-mail: peter_ormsby@txs.uscourts.gov

Magistrate Judge **Stephen Wm. Smith** . . . . (713) 250-5100
Began Service: July 22, 2004
E-mail: stephen_smith@txs.uscourts.gov

Magistrate Judge **J. Scott Hacker** . . . . (956) 790-1750
Began Service: October 17, 2008
Appointed By: President George W. Bush
United States Courthouse, 1300 Victoria Street,
Suite 2276, Laredo, TX 78040

Magistrate Judge **Ronald G. Morgan** . . . . (956) 548-2570
Began Service: May 2009

Magistrate Judge **Guillermo R. Garcia** . . . . (956) 723-3542
Began Service: May 21, 2010

Magistrate Judge **Ignacio Torteya III** . . . .(956) 548-2564
E-mail: ignacio_torteya@txs.uscourts.gov

Magistrate Judge **Jason B. Libby** . . . .(361) 888-3550
Began Service: 2013

Magistrate Judge **Diana Song Quiroga** . . . .(956) 726-2242
1300 Victoria Street, Suite 2276,
Laredo, TX 78040

Court Staff

Clerk of Court **David J. Bradley** . . . . (713) 250-5500
E-mail: david_bradley@txs.uscourts.gov
Chief U.S. Probation Officer (Acting) **Sean Harmon**
Suite 2301 . . . .(713) 250-5266
Chief Pretrial Services Officer **Alma A. Connor** Suite
6214 . . . . (713) 250-5218

United States Bankruptcy Court for the Southern District of Texas

Bob Casey U.S. Courthouse, 515 Rusk Avenue, Houston, TX 77002
Tel: (713) 250-5500 Tel: (713) 250-5046 (PACER)
Tel: (800) 998-9037 (Toll Free PACER)
Tel: (800) 745-4459 (Toll Free Voice Case Information System VCIS)
Tel: (713) 250-5049 (Voice Case Information System VCIS)
Internet: www.txs.uscourts.gov

Number of Judgeships: 6

Number of Vacancies: 1

Judges

Chief Bankruptcy Judge **David R. Jones** . . . . (713) 250-5713

United States Bankruptcy Court for the Southern District of Texas
continued

Bankruptcy Judge **Jeffery Bohm** . . . .(713) 250-5405
Began Service: 2004

Bankruptcy Judge **Marvin Isgur** . . . .(713) 250-5421
Began Service: June 1, 2009
515 Rusk Street, 4th Floor, Room 4636, Courtroom
404, Houston, TX 77002

Bankruptcy Judge **Karen Kennedy Brown** . . . .(713) 250-5250
Began Service: April 2, 1990

Bankruptcy Judge **Letitia Z. Paul** . . . .(713) 250-5410
Began Service: 1985

Bankruptcy Judge **Richard S. Schmidt** . . . .(361) 888-3207
Began Service: July 31, 1987
1133 North Shoreline Boulevard, Suite 221,
Corpus Christi, TX 78401
E-mail: richard_schmidt@txs.uscourts.gov

Court Staff

Clerk of Court **David J. Bradley** . . . .(713) 250-5500
E-mail: david_bradley@txs.uscourts.gov

U.S. Attorney

Texas - Southern District
1000 Louisiana Street, Suite 2300, Houston, TX 77002
P.O. Box 61129, Houston, TX 77208-1129
Tel: (713) 567-9000 Fax: (713) 718-3300

U.S. Attorney **Kenneth Magidson** . . . . (713) 567-9300
E-mail: ken.magidson@usdoj.gov

Federal Public Defender

Office of the Federal Public Defender, Southern District of Texas
The Lyric Center, 440 Louisiana Street, Room 1350,
Houston, TX 77002-1634
Federal Building and United States Courthouse, 600 East Harrison Street,
Room 102, Brownsville, TX 78520
Wilson Plaza, 606 North Carancahua Street, Room 401,
Corpus Christi, TX 78401
Mejia Building, 1202 Houston Street, Laredo, TX 78040-8014
Bentsen Tower, 1701 West Business Highway 83, Room 405,
McAllen, TX 78501
Tel: (713) 718-4600 (Houston) Tel: (956) 548-2573 (Brownsville)
Tel: (361) 888-3532 (Corpus Christi) Tel: (956) 753-5313 (Laredo)
Tel: (956) 630-2995 (McAllen) Fax: (713) 718-4610 (Houston)
Fax: (956) 548-2674 (Brownsville) Fax: (361) 888-3534 (Corpus Christi)
Fax: (956) 753-5317 (Laredo) Fax: (956) 631-8647 (McAllen)

Federal Public Defender **Majorie A. Myers** . . . .(713) 718-4600

United States District Court for the Western District of Texas

John H. Wood, Jr. Federal Courthouse, 655 East Cesar E. Chavez Boulevard, Suite G65, San Antonio, TX 78206-1198
Tel: (210) 472-6550 Tel: (210) 472-5241 (PACER)
Internet: www.txwd.uscourts.gov

Number of Judgeships: 13

Number of Vacancies: 1

Circuit: Fifth

Areas Covered: Counties of Andrews, Atascosa, Bandera, Bastrop, Bell, Bexar, Blanco, Bosque, Brewster, Burleson, Burnet, Caldwell, Comal, Coryell, Crane, Culberson, Dimmit, Ector, Edwards, El Paso, Falls, Freestone, Frio, Gillespie, Gonzales, Guadalupe, Hamilton, Hays, Hill, Hudspeth, Jeff Davis, Karnes, Kendall, Kerr, Kimble, Kinney, Lampasas, Lee, Leon, Limestone, Llano, Loving, Martin, Mason, Maverick, McCulloch, McLennan, Medina, Midland, Milam, Pecos, Presidio, Real, Reeves, Robertson, San Saba, Somervell, Terrell, Travis, Upton, Uvalde, Val Verde, Ward, Washington, Williamson, Wilson, Winkler and Zavalla

Judges

Chief Judge **Fred Biery** . . . . (210) 472-6505
  Began Service: March 14, 1994
  Appointed By: President William J. Clinton
  E-mail: Fred_Biery@txwd.uscourts.gov

District Judge **Walter S. Smith, Jr.** . . . . (254) 750-1519
  Began Service: October 6, 1984
  Appointed By: President Ronald Reagan
  U.S. Courthouse, 800 Franklin Avenue, Suite 301,
  Waco, TX 76701

District Judge **Sam Sparks** . . . . (512) 916-5230
  Began Service: December 7, 1991
  Appointed By: President George H.W. Bush
  501 West Fifth Street, Suite 4120,
  Austin, TX 78701-3822

District Judge **Orlando L. Garcia** . . . . (210) 472-6565
  Began Service: 1994
  Appointed By: President William J. Clinton

District Judge **Philip R. Martinez** . . . . (915) 534-6736
  Began Service: February 15, 2002
  Appointed By: President George W. Bush
  U.S. Courthouse, 525 Magoffin Avenue, Suite 661,
  El Paso, TX 79901
  E-mail: philip_martinez@txwd.uscourts.gov

District Judge **Alia Moses** . . . . (830) 703-2038
  Began Service: November 18, 2002
  Appointed By: President George W. Bush
  E-mail: alia_moses@txwd.uscourts.gov

District Judge **Xavier Rodriguez** . . . . (210) 472-6575
  Began Service: August 18, 2003
  Appointed By: President George W. Bush
  E-mail: xavier_rodriguez@txwd.uscourts.gov

District Judge **Lee Yeakel** . . . . (512) 916-5756
  Began Service: July 31, 2003
  Appointed By: President George W. Bush
  E-mail: lee_yeakel@txwd.uscourts.gov

District Judge **Frank Montalvo** . . . . (915) 534-6600
  Began Service: August 8, 2003
  Appointed By: President George W. Bush
  525 Magoffin Avenue, Courtroom 422,
  El Paso, TX 79901
  E-mail: frank_montalvo@txwd.uscourts.gov

District Judge **Kathleen Cardone** . . . . (915) 534-6740
  Began Service: July 29, 2003
  Appointed By: President George W. Bush
  E-mail: kathleen_cardone@txwd.uscourts.gov

District Judge **David Campos Guaderrama** . . . . (915) 534-6005
  Began Service: 2012
  Appointed By: President Barack Obama
  E-mail: david_guaderrama@txwd.uscourts.gov

District Judge **Robert Lee Pitman** . . . . (210) 472-6570
  Began Service: December 19, 2014
  Appointed By: President Barack Obama

United States District Court for the Western District of Texas *continued*

Senior Judge **Harry Lee Hudspeth** . . . . (512) 916-5837
  Began Service: November 1979
  Appointed By: President Jimmy Carter
  903 San Jacinto Boulevard, Suite 440,
  Austin, TX 78701-2452

Senior Judge **James Robertson Nowlin** . . . . (512) 916-5675
  Began Service: November 6, 1981
  Appointed By: President Ronald Reagan
  U.S. Courthouse, 501 West Fifth Street, Suite 6400,
  Austin, TX 78701

Senior Judge **David Briones** . . . . (915) 534-6744
  Began Service: October 17, 1994
  Appointed By: President William J. Clinton
  U.S. Courthouse, 525 Magoffin Avenue, Suite 761,
  El Paso, TX 79901
  E-mail: david_briones@txwd.uscourts.gov

Senior Judge **Robert A. Junell** . . . . (432) 686-4020
  Began Service: February 13, 2003
  Appointed By: President George W. Bush
  George H.W. Bush and George W. Bush U.S.
  Courthouse, 200 West Wall Street, Suite 301,
  Midland, TX 79701
  E-mail: rob_junell@txwd.uscourts.gov

Magistrate Judge **B. Dwight Goains** . . . . (432) 837-9740
  Began Service: 2007
  2450 North Highway 118, Suite 222,
  Alpine, TX 79830

Magistrate Judge **John W. Primomo** . . . . (210) 472-6357
  Began Service: July 18, 1988
  E-mail: john_primomo@txwd.uscourts.gov

Magistrate Judge **Miguel A. Torres** . . . . (915) 534-6732
  Began Service: 2013
  525 Magoffin Avenue, Room 751,
  El Paso, TX 79901
  E-mail: miguel_torres@txwd.uscourts.gov

Magistrate Judge **Pamela Ann Mathy** . . . . (210) 472-6350
  Began Service: June 8, 1998
  E-mail: pamela_mathy@txwd.uscourts.gov

Magistrate Judge **Andrew W. Austin** . . . . (512) 916-5744
  Began Service: November 22, 1999
  U.S. Courthouse, 501 West Fifth Street, Suite 4190,
  Austin, TX 78701

Magistrate Judge **Jeffrey C. Manske** . . . . (254) 750-1545
  Began Service: 2001
  E-mail: jeffrey_manske@txwd.uscourts.gov

Magistrate Judge **Victor Roberto Garcia** . . . . (830) 703-2170
  Began Service: May 14, 2003
  E-mail: victor_garcia@txwd.uscourts.gov

Magistrate Judge **Collis White** . . . . (830) 703-2050
  Began Service: 2009
  E-mail: collis_white@txwd.uscourts.gov

Magistrate Judge **Norbert J. Garney** . . . . (915) 534-6980
  Began Service: 2000
  E-mail: norbert_garney@txwd.uscourts.gov

Magistrate Judge **Robert F. Castañeda** . . . . (915) 534-6028
  Began Service: April 1, 2011
  525 Magoffin Avenue, Suite 651,
  El Paso, TX 79901
  E-mail: robert_castaneda@txwd.uscourts.gov

Magistrate Judge **Mark Lane** . . . . (512) 916-5679
  501 West Fifth Street, Suite 7400,
  Austin, TX 78701

Magistrate Judge **Anne T. Berton** . . . . (915) 834-0579

Magistrate Judge **David Counts** . . . . (432) 570-4439

Magistrate Judge **Henry J. Bemporad** . . . . (210) 472-6363

Court Staff

Clerk of Court **Jeannette J. Clack** . . . . (210) 472-4955

Chief Pretrial Services Officer **Charles Mason** . . . . (210) 472-4053
  727 East Cesar E. Chavez Boulevard, Suite 636,
  San Antonio, TX 78205

Chief U.S. Probation Officer **Joe Sanchez** . . . . (210) 472-6590
  727 East Cesar E. Chavez Boulevard,
  San Antonio, TX 78205
  E-mail: joe_sanchez@txwd.uscourts.gov

United States Bankruptcy Court for the Western District of Texas

615 East Houston Street, Suite 597, San Antonio, TX 78205
Tel: (210) 472-6720 Tel: (800) 676-6856 (PACER)
Tel: (210) 472-4023 (Voice Case Information System VCIS)
Tel: (888) 436-7477 (Voice Case Information System VCIS)
Fax: (210) 472-5196
Internet: www.txwb.uscourts.gov

Number of Judgeships: 4
Number of Vacancies: 1

Judges

Chief Bankruptcy Judge **Ronald B. King** . . . . (210) 472-6609
 Began Service: October 1, 1988
Bankruptcy Judge **Craig A. Gargotta** Hipolito F. Garcia
 Federal Building and U.S. Courthouse, Room 505 . . . . (210) 472-5181
 Began Service: October 2007
Bankruptcy Judge **H. Christopher Mott** . . . . (512) 916-5800
 Began Service: 2010
 Homer J. Thornberry Federal Judicial Building,
 903 San Jacinto Boulevard, Suite 326,
 Austin, TX 78701
Bankruptcy Judge **Tony M. Davis** . . . . (512) 916-5875
 903 San Jacinto Boulevard, Suite 332,
 Austin, TX 78701

Court Staff

Clerk of Court **Yvette M. Taylor** . . . . (210) 472-6720
 E-mail: yvette_taylor@txwb.uscourts.gov

U.S. Attorney

Texas - Western District
601 NW Loop 410, Suite 600, San Antonio, TX 78216
Tel: (210) 384-7100 Fax: (210) 384-7106

U.S. Attorney (Acting) **Richard L. Durbin, Jr.** . . . . (210) 384-7400

Federal Public Defender

Office of the Federal Public Defender, Western District of Texas
Federal Building, 727 East Cesar E. Chavez Boulevard, Suite B207,
San Antonio, TX 78206
108 North Tenth Street, Alpine, TX 79830
504 Lavaca Street, Suiet 960, Austin, TX 78701-2860
2205 Veterans Boulevard, Suite A-2, Del Rio, TX 78840-3120
Richard C. White Federal Building, 700 East San Antonio Avenue,
Suite D-401, El Paso, TX 79901
410 South Cedar Street, First Floor, Pecos, TX 79772
Tel: (210) 472-6700 (San Antonio) Tel: (432) 837-5598 (Alpine)
Tel: (512) 916-5025 (Austin) Tel: (830) 703-2040 (Del Rio)
Tel: (915) 534-6525 (El Paso) Tel: (432) 445-2024 (Pecos)
Fax: (210) 472-4454 (San Antonio) Fax: (432) 837-9023 (Alpine)
Fax: (512) 916-5035 (Austin) Fax: (830) 703-2047 (Del Rio)
Fax: (915) 534-6534 (El Paso) Fax: (432) 445-2204 (Pecos)

Federal Public Defender **Maureen Scott Franco** . . . . (210) 472-6700
 E-mail: maureen_franco@txw.fd.org

United States District Court for the District of Utah

U.S. Courthouse, 351 South West Temple, Room 1.100,
Salt Lake City, UT 84101
Tel: (801) 524-6100 Fax: (801) 526-1175
Internet: www.utd.uscourts.gov

Number of Judgeships: 5
Number of Vacancies: 1
Circuit: Tenth

Judges

Chief Judge **David Nuffer** Frank E. Moss U.S.
 Courthouse, Room 10.100 . . . . (801) 524-6100
 Began Service: May 28, 2012
 Appointed By: President Barack Obama
 E-mail: david_nuffer@utd.uscourts.gov
District Judge **Clark Waddoups** Room 9.420 . . . . (801) 524-4221
 Began Service: October 23, 2008
 Appointed By: President George W. Bush
 E-mail: clark_waddoups@utd.uscourts.gov
District Judge **Robert J. Shelby** Frank E. Moss U.S.
 Courthouse, Room 10.220 . . . . (801) 524-6100
 Began Service: September 25, 2012
 Appointed By: President Barack Obama
 E-mail: robert_shelby@utd.uscourts.gov
District Judge **Jill N. Parrish** . . . . (801) 524-6100
 Note: On May 22, 2015, the Senate confirmed Jill
 N. Parrish to be District Judge for the United States
 District Court for the District of Utah.
 Began Service: 2015
 Appointed By: President Barack Obama
Senior Judge **Bruce S. Jenkins** . . . . (801) 524-6507
 Began Service: 1978
 Appointed By: President Jimmy Carter
 E-mail: bruce_jenkins@utd.uscourts.gov
Senior Judge **Dale A. Kimball** . . . . (801) 524-6610
 Began Service: November 24, 1997
 Appointed By: President William J. Clinton
 E-mail: Dale_Kimball@utd.uscourts.gov
Senior Judge **David Sam** . . . . (801) 524-6190
 Began Service: 1985
 Appointed By: President Ronald Reagan
 E-mail: david_sam@utd.uscourts.gov
Senior Judge **Tena Campbell** Suite 9.220 . . . . (801) 524-6170
 Began Service: July 10, 1995
 Appointed By: President William J. Clinton
 E-mail: Tena_Campbell@utd.uscourts.gov
Senior Judge **Dee V. Benson** . . . . (801) 524-6160
 Began Service: 1991
 Appointed By: President George H.W. Bush
 Frank E. Moss U.S. Courthouse,
 350 South Main Street, Room 253,
 Salt Lake City, UT 84101
 E-mail: dee_benson@utd.uscourts.gov
Senior Judge **Ted Stewart** . . . . (801) 524-6617
 Began Service: December 1999
 Appointed By: President William J. Clinton
 Frank E. Moss U.S. Courthouse,
 350 South Main Street, Room 148,
 Salt Lake City, UT 84101
 E-mail: ted_stewart@utd.uscourts.gov
Chief Magistrate Judge **Brooke C. Wells** . . . . (801) 524-6422
 Began Service: June 4, 2003
 350 South Main Street, Room 431,
 Salt Lake City, UT 84101-2180
 E-mail: brooke_wells@utd.uscourts.gov
Magistrate Judge **Paul Michael Warner** Room 10.440 . . . . (801) 524-6620
 Began Service: 2006
 E-mail: paul_warner@utd.uscourts.gov
Magistrate Judge **Dustin B. Pead** Room 9.200 . . . . (801) 524-6155
 Began Service: 2012
 E-mail: utdecf_pead@utd.uscourts.gov
Magistrate Judge **Evelyn J. Furse** Room 10.200 . . . . (801) 524-6180
 E-mail: evelyn_furse@utd.uscourts.gov

United States District Court for the District of Utah *continued*

Magistrate Judge (Part-Time) **Robert T. Braithwaite** . . . . .(435) 656-7580
Began Service: May 7, 2003
206 West Tabernacle, Suite 225,
St. George, UT 84770
E-mail: robert_braithwaite@utd.uscourts.gov

Court Staff

Clerk of Court **D. Mark Jones** . . . .(801) 524-6100
  E-mail: mark_jones@utd.uscourts.gov
Chief Probation Officer **Dave Christenson** . . . .(801) 524-5176

United States Bankruptcy Court for the District of Utah

Frank E. Moss U.S. Courthouse, 350 South Main Street, Room 301,
Salt Lake City, UT 84101
Tel: (801) 524-6687 Tel: (800) 676-6856 (Toll Free PACER)
Tel: (866) 222-8029 (Toll Free Voice Case Information System VCIS)
Fax: (801) 524-4409
E-mail: bankruptcy_clerk@utb.uscourts.gov
Internet: www.utb.uscourts.gov

Number of Judgeships: 3

Judges

Chief Bankruptcy Judge **William T. Thurman** . . . . (801) 524-6572
Began Service: September 4, 2001
Frank E. Moss U.S. Courthouse,
350 South Main Street, Room 358,
Salt Lake City, UT 84101-2195
E-mail: william_thurman@utb.uscourts.gov
Bankruptcy Judge **R. Kimball Mosier** Room 365 . . . . (801) 524-6568
Began Service: February 2009
Bankruptcy Judge **Joel T. Marker** . . . . (801) 524-5749
Began Service: July 9, 2010
E-mail: joel_marker@utb.uscourts.gov

Court Staff

Clerk **David A. Sime** . . . . (801) 524-6565
  E-mail: david_sime@utb.uscourts.gov

U.S. Attorney

Utah District
185 South State Street, Suite 300, Salt Lake City, UT 84111-1506
Tel: (801) 524-5682 Fax: (801) 524-6924

U.S. Attorney **John W. Huber** . . . .(801) 325-3224
  E-mail: john.huber@usdoj.gov

Federal Public Defender

Office of the Federal Public Defender for the District of Utah
American Towers, 46 West Broadway, Suite 110,
Salt Lake City, UT 84101-2028
Tel: (801) 524-4010 Fax: (801) 524-4023

Federal Public Defender **Kathryn "Kathy" Nester** . . . . . . (801) 524-4010

United States District Court for the District of Vermont

U.S. Post Office & Courthouse, 11 Elmwood Avenue,
Burlington, VT 05401
P.O. Box 945, Burlington, VT 05402
204 Main Street, Room 201, Brattleboro, VT 05301
P.O. Box 998, Brattleboro, VT 05302-0998
151 West Street, Rutland, VT 05701
P.O. Box 607, Rutland, VT 05702-0607
Tel: (802) 951-6301 Tel: (802) 254-0250 (Brattleboro Office)
Tel: (802) 773-0245 (Rutland Office) Tel: (802) 951-6623 (PACER)
Internet: www.vtd.uscourts.gov

Number of Judgeships: 2
Circuit: Second

Judges

Chief Judge **Christina Reiss** . . . .(802) 951-6623
Began Service: January 8, 2010
Appointed By: President Barack Obama
E-mail: christina_reiss@vtd.uscourts.gov
District Judge **Geoffrey W. Crawford** . . . . (802) 951-6301
Began Service: August 4, 2014
Appointed By: President Barack Obama
Senior Judge **J. Garvan Murtha** . . . . (802) 258-4413
Began Service: May 26, 1995
Appointed By: President William J. Clinton
Senior Judge **William K. Sessions III** . . . . (802) 951-6350
Began Service: August 15, 1995
Appointed By: President William J. Clinton
E-mail: william_sessions@vtd.uscourts.gov
Magistrate Judge **John M. Conroy** . . . . (802) 951-6308
Began Service: January 2009
E-mail: john_conroy@vtd.uscourts.gov

Court Staff

Clerk of Court **Jeffrey S. Eaton** . . . . (802) 951-6301
Chief Probation Officer **Joseph McNamara** . . . .(802) 652-3000

United States Bankruptcy Court for the District of Vermont

U.S. Post Office and Courthouse, 151 West Street, Rutland, VT 05701
P.O. Box 6648, Rutland, VT 05702-6648
Tel: (802) 776-2000 Fax: (802) 776-2020
Internet: www.vtb.uscourts.gov

Number of Judgeships: 1

Judges

Bankruptcy Judge **Colleen A. Brown** . . . . (802) 776-2030
Began Service: April 10, 2000
E-mail: Colleen_Brown@vtb.uscourts.gov

Court Staff

Fax: (802) 776-2020

Clerk of Court **Thomas J. Hart** . . . .(802) 776-2000

U.S. Attorney

Vermont District
U.S. Federal Building, 11 Elmwood Avenue, 3rd Floor,
Burlington, VT 05401
P.O. Box 570, Burlington, VT 05402
Tel: (802) 951-6725 Fax: (802) 951-6540

U.S. Attorney **Eric Steven Miller** . . . .(802) 951-6725

(continued on next page)

United States Bankruptcy Court for the **District of Vermont** *continued*
Federal Public Defender
Office of the Federal Public Defender for the District of Vermont
Park Plaza, 126 College Street, Room 410, Burlington, VT 05401
Tel: (802) 862-6990 Fax: (802) 862-7836

Federal Public Defender **Michael L. Desautels** . . . . (802) 862-6990
   E-mail: michael.desautels@fd.org

United States District Court for the Eastern District of Virginia
Albert V. Bryan Sr. U.S. Courthouse, 401 Courthouse Square,
Alexandria, VA 22314-5798
Tel: (703) 299-2100 Tel: (800) 852-5186 (PACER)
Fax: (703) 299-2109
Internet: www.vaed.uscourts.gov

Number of Judgeships: 11

Circuit: Fourth

Areas Covered: Counties of Accomack, Amelia, Arlington, Brunswick, Caroline, Charles City, Chesterfield, Dinwiddie, Essex, Fairfax, Fauquier, Gloucester, Goochland, Greensville, Hanover, Henrico, Isle of Wight, James City, King and Queen, King George, King William, Lancaster, Loudoun, Lunenburg, Mathews, Mecklenburg, Middlesex, New Kent, Northampton, Northumberland, Nottoway, Powhatan, Prince Edward, Prince George, Prince William, Richmond, Southampton, Spotsylvania, Stafford, Surry, Sussex, Westmoreland and York

Judges
Chief Judge **Rebecca Beach Smith** . . . . (757) 222-7001
   Began Service: 1989
   Appointed By: President George H.W. Bush
   E-mail: rebecca_smith@vaed.uscourts.gov
District Judge **Leonie M. Brinkema** . . . . (703) 299-2116
   Began Service: October 21, 1993
   Appointed By: President William J. Clinton
District Judge **Raymond A. Jackson** . . . . (757) 222-7003
   Began Service: 1993
   Appointed By: President William J. Clinton
   E-mail: Raymond_Jackson@vaed.uscourts.gov
District Judge **Gerald Bruce Lee** . . . . (703) 299-2117
   Began Service: October 9, 1998
   Appointed By: President William J. Clinton
District Judge **Henry E. Hudson** . . . . (804) 916-2290
   Began Service: September 3, 2002
   Appointed By: President George W. Bush
   701 East Broad Street, Suite 6312,
   Richmond, VA 23219
   E-mail: henry_hudson@vaed.uscourts.gov
District Judge **Liam O'Grady** . . . . (703) 299-2121
   Began Service: September 21, 2007
   Appointed By: President George W. Bush
District Judge **Mark S. Davis** . . . . (757) 222-7014
   Began Service: June 23, 2008
   Appointed By: President George W. Bush
   United States Courthouse, 600 Granby Street,
   Room 132, Norfolk, VA 23510-2449
District Judge **Anthony John Trenga** . . . . (703) 299-2113
   Began Service: October 15, 2008
   Appointed By: President George W. Bush
   E-mail: anthony_trenga@vaed.uscourts.gov
District Judge **John A. Gibney, Jr.** . . . . (804) 916-2870
   Began Service: December 27, 2010
   Appointed By: President Barack Obama
   E-mail: john_gibney@vaed.uscourts.gov
District Judge **Arenda L. Wright Allen** . . . . (757) 222-7013
   Began Service: October 27, 2011
   Appointed By: President Barack Obama
District Judge **M. Hannah Lauck** . . . . (804) 916-2890
   Began Service: June 10, 2014
   Appointed By: President Barack Obama

United States District Court for the **Eastern District of Virginia** *continued*
Senior Judge **Claude M. Hilton** . . . . (703) 299-2112
   Began Service: July 11, 1985
   Appointed By: President Ronald Reagan
Senior Judge **Robert George Doumar** . . . . (757) 222-7006
   Began Service: 1982
   Appointed By: President Ronald Reagan
   E-mail: robert_doumar@vaed.uscourts.gov
Senior Judge **James C. Cacheris** . . . . (703) 299-2110
   Began Service: 1981
   Appointed By: President Ronald Reagan
Senior Judge **Henry Coke Morgan, Jr.** . . . . (757) 222-7111
   Began Service: May 1, 1992
   Appointed By: President George H.W. Bush
   E-mail: Henry_Morgan@vaed.uscourts.gov
Senior Judge **T. S. Ellis III** . . . . (703) 299-2114
   Began Service: 1987
   Appointed By: President Ronald Reagan
Senior Judge **Robert E. Payne** . . . . (804) 916-2260
   Began Service: May 13, 1992
   Appointed By: President George H.W. Bush
   E-mail: robert_payne@vaed.uscourts.gov
Senior Judge **James R. Spencer** . . . . (804) 916-2250
   Began Service: 1986
   Appointed By: President Ronald Reagan
   E-mail: james_spencer@vaed.uscourts.gov
Magistrate Judge **Tommy E. Miller** . . . . (757) 222-7007
   Note: Judge Miller will retire effective August 2015.
   Began Service: September 8, 1987
   E-mail: tommy_miller@vaed.uscourts.gov
Magistrate Judge **Theresa Carroll Buchanan** . . . . (703) 299-2120
   Began Service: September 12, 1996
Magistrate Judge **Douglas E. Miller** . . . . (757) 222-7012
   Began Service: February 2010
   E-mail: douglas_miller@vaed.uscourts.gov
Magistrate Judge **John F. Anderson** . . . . (703) 299-2118
   Began Service: January 22, 2008
   E-mail: john_anderson@vaed.uscourts.gov
Magistrate Judge **David J. Novak** . . . . (804) 916-2270
   Began Service: February 1, 2012
   E-mail: david_novak@vaed.uscourts.gov
Magistrate Judge **Ivan D. Davis** . . . . (703) 299-2119
   Began Service: 2008
   E-mail: ivan_davis@vaed.uscourts.gov
Magistrate Judge **Lawrence R. Leonard** . . . . (757) 222-7020
   E-mail: lawrence_leonard@vaed.uscourts.gov
Magistrate Judge **Roderick C. Young** . . . . (804) 916-2240
   Began Service: October 29, 2014
Magistrate Judge **Michael S. Nachmanoff** . . . . (703) 299-3367
Magistrate Judge **Thomas Rawles Jones, Jr.** . . . . (703) 299-2122
   Began Service: 1994
Magistrate Judge (recalled) **William T. Prince** . . . . (757) 222-7170
   Began Service: March 1, 1990   Tel: (757) 222-7008
   E-mail: william_prince@vaed.uscourts.gov

Court Staff
Clerk of Court **G. Fernando Galindo** . . . . (757) 222-7200
Chief Probation Officer **Mary Farashahi** . . . . (703) 222-7300

United States Bankruptcy Court for the Eastern District of Virginia

United States Bankruptcy Court, 701 East Broad Street,
Richmond, VA 23219
Tel: (804) 916-2400 Tel: (800) 676-6856 (Alexandria PACER)
Tel: (800) 676-6856 (Newport News PACER)
Tel: (800) 676-6856 (Richmond PACER)
Tel: (866) 222-8029 (Toll Free Voice Case Information System VCIS)
Fax: (804) 916-2498
Internet: www.vaeb.uscourts.gov

Number of Judgeships: 6

Judges

Chief Bankruptcy Judge **Stephen C. St. John** . . . .(757) 222-7480
  Began Service: 1995
Bankruptcy Judge **Robert G. Mayer** . . . . (703) 258-1280
  Began Service: October 15, 1999
  E-mail: Robert_Mayer@vaeb.uscourts.gov
Bankruptcy Judge **Kevin R. Huennekens** 5th Floor . . . . . . (804) 916-2455
  Began Service: September 2006
  E-mail: kevin_huennekens@vaeb.uscourts.gov
Bankruptcy Judge **Frank J. Santoro** . . . . (757) 222-7471
  Began Service: February 21, 2008
Bankruptcy Judge **Brian F. Kenney** . . . . (703) 258-1240
  Began Service: September 2011
Bankruptcy Judge **Keith L. Phillips** . . . .(804) 916-2461
  Began Service: 2013

Court Staff

Clerk of Court **William C. Redden** . . . . (804) 916-2490
  E-mail: william_redden@vaeb.uscourts.gov

U.S. Attorney

Virginia - Eastern District
2100 Jamieson Avenue, Alexandria, VA 22314-5794
Tel: (703) 299-3700 Fax: (703) 299-3983

U.S. Attorney (Acting) **Dana James Boente** . . . . (703) 299-3700
  E-mail: dana.boente@usdoj.gov

Federal Public Defender

Office of the Federal Public Defender for the Eastern District of Virginia
1650 King Street, Suite 500, Alexandria, VA 22314
Town Point Center, 150 Boush Street, Suite 403, Norfolk, VA 23510-1626
701 East Broad Street, Room 3600, Richmond, VA 23219
Tel: (703) 600-0800 (Alexandria) Tel: (757) 457-0800 (Norfolk)
Tel: (804) 343-0800 (Richmond) Fax: (703) 600-0880 (Alexandria)
Fax: (757) 457-0880 (Norfolk) Fax: (804) 648-5033 (Richmond)

Federal Public Defender **Geremy Kamens** . . . . (703) 600-0800
  E-mail: geremy.kamens@fd.org

United States District Court for the Western District of Virginia

Richard H. Poff Federal Building, 242 Franklin Road, SW,
Suite 540, Roanoke, VA 24011
Tel: (540) 857-5100 Fax: (540) 857-5110 Fax: (540) 857-5193
Internet: www.vawd.uscourts.gov

Number of Judgeships: 4

Circuit: Fourth

Areas Covered: Counties of Albemarle, Alleghany, Amherst, Appomattox, Augusta, Bath, Bedford, Bland, Botetourt, Bristol, Buchanan, Buckingham, Buena Vista, Campbell, Carroll, Charlotte, Charlottesville, Clarke, Covington, Craig, Culpeper, Cumberland, Danville, Dickenson, Floyd, Fluvanna, Franklin, Frederick, Galax, Giles, Grayson, Greene, Halifax, Harrisonburg, Henry, Highland, Lee, Lexington, Louisa, Lynchburg, Madison, Martinsville, Montgomery, Nelson, Norton, Orange, Page, Patrick, Pittsylvania, Pulaski, Radford, Rappahannock, Roanoke, Rockbridge, Rockingham, Russell, Salem, Scott, Shenandoah, Staunton, Smyth, Tazewell, Warren, Washington, Waynesboro, Winchester, Wise and Wythe

Judges

Chief Judge **Glen E. Conrad** . . . . (540) 857-5135
  Began Service: October 17, 2003
  Appointed By: President George W. Bush
  Richard H. Poff Federal Building,
  210 Franklin Road, SW, Room 206,
  Roanoke, VA 24011
District Judge **James P. Jones** . . . .(276) 628-4080
  Began Service: August 30, 1996
  Appointed By: President William J. Clinton
  E-mail: james_jones@vawd.uscourts.gov
District Judge **Michael F. Urbanski** . . . .(540) 857-5124
  Began Service: May 13, 2011
  Appointed By: President Barack Obama
  210 Franklin Road, SW, Suite 350,
  Roanoke, VA 24011
  E-mail: urbanski.ecf@vawd.uscourts.gov
District Judge **Elizabeth K. Dillon** . . . .(540) 857-5120
  Began Service: 2014
  Appointed By: President Barack Obama
Senior Judge **Jackson L. Kiser** . . . .(434) 799-8700
  Began Service: January 12, 1982
  Appointed By: President Ronald Reagan
  700 Main Street, Room 202,
  Danville, VA 24541
  E-mail: jackson_kiser@vawd.uscourts.gov
Senior Judge **Norman K. Moon** . . . .(434) 845-4891
  Began Service: November 25, 1997
  Appointed By: President William J. Clinton
Magistrate Judge **Pamela Meade Sargent** . . . . (276) 628-6021
  Began Service: December 1997
  E-mail: pamela_sargent@vawd.uscourts.gov
Magistrate Judge **Robert S. Ballou** . . . . (540) 857-5158
  Began Service: October 3, 2011
  Richard H. Poff Federal Building,
  210 Franklin Road, SW, Room 344,
  Roanoke, VA 24011-2214
  E-mail: robert_ballou@vawd.uscourts.gov
Magistrate Judge **Joel Hoppe** . . . .(540) 434-3181
  Began Service: 2014
  116 North Main Street, Room 314,
  Harrisonburg, VA 22802
Magistrate Judge (Part-Time) **James G. Welsh** . . . . (540) 434-3181
  Began Service: November 16, 2004
  E-mail: jamesw@vawd.uscourts.gov

Court Staff

Clerk of Court **Julia C. Dudley** . . . . (540) 857-5100
  E-mail: julie_dudley@vawd.uscourts.gov
Chief Probation Officer **Philip K. Williams** . . . .(540) 857-5180
  P.O. Box 1563, Roanoke, VA 24007

United States Bankruptcy Court for the Western District of Virginia

210 Church Avenue, SW, Room 200, Roanoke, VA 24011-0210
Tel: (540) 857-2391 Fax: (540) 857-2873
Internet: www.vawb.uscourts.gov

Number of Judgeships: 3

Judges

Chief Bankruptcy Judge **Rebecca B. Connelly** . . . . (540) 434-6747
  Began Service: 2012
Bankruptcy Judge **Paul M. Black** . . . . (540) 857-2394
  E-mail: paul_black@vawb.uscourts.gov

Court Staff

Clerk of the Court **John W. L. Craig II** . . . . (540) 857-2391

U.S. Attorney

Virginia - Western District
BB&T Building, 310 First Street, SW, Room 906, Roanoke, VA 24011
P.O. Box 1709, Roanoke, VA 24008-1709
Tel: (540) 857-2250 Fax: (540) 857-2614

U.S. Attorney (Acting) **Anthony P. Giorno** . . . . (540) 857-2878
  E-mail: anthony.giorno@usdoj.gov

Federal Public Defender

Office of the Federal Public Defender for the Western District of Virginia
First Campbell Square, 210 First Street SW, Suite 400,
Roanoke, VA 24011
201 Abingdon Place, Suite 201, Abingdon, VA 24211-5797
401 East Market Street, Suite 106, Charlottesville, VA 22902
Tel: (540) 777-0880 (Roanoke) Tel: (276) 619-6080 (Abingdon)
Tel: (434) 220-3380 (Charlottesville) Fax: (540) 777-0890 (Roanoke)
Fax: (276) 619-6090 (Abingdon) Fax: (434) 220-3390 (Charlottesville)

Federal Public Defender **Larry W. Shelton** . . . . (540) 777-0880
  E-mail: larry_shelton@fd.org

United States District Court for the Eastern District of Washington

Thomas S. Foley U.S. Courthouse, 920 West Riverside Avenue,
Room 840, Spokane, WA 99201-1493
P.O. Box 1493, Spokane, WA 99210-1493
Tel: (509) 458-3400 Fax: (509) 458-3420
Internet: www.waed.uscourts.gov

Number of Judgeships: 4

Circuit: Ninth

Areas Covered: Counties of Adams, Asotin, Benton, Chelan, Columbia, Douglas, Ferry, Franklin, Garfield, Grant, Kittitas, Klickitat, Lincoln, Okanogan, Pend Oreille, Spokane, Stevens, Walla Walla, Whitman and Yakima

Judges

Chief Judge **Rosanna Malouf Peterson** . . . . (509) 458-5260
  Began Service: January 26, 2010
  Appointed By: President Barack Obama
District Judge **Thomas O. Rice** . . . . (509) 458-2470
  Began Service: March 8, 2012
  Appointed By: President Barack Obama
District Judge **Stanley Allen Bastian** . . . . (414) 397-3372
  Began Service: May 1, 2014
  Appointed By: President Barack Obama

United States District Court for the Eastern District of Washington
continued

District Judge **Salvador Mendoza, Jr.** . . . . (509) 943-8160
  Began Service: June 19, 2014
  Appointed By: President Barack Obama
  825 Jadwin Avenue, Suite 190,
  Richland, WA 99352-3586
  E-mail: salvador_mendoza@waed.uscourts.gov
Senior Judge **Robert H. Whaley** . . . . (509) 458-5270
  Began Service: June 30, 1995
  Appointed By: President William J. Clinton
  E-mail: robert_whaley@waed.uscourts.gov
Senior Judge **Fred L. Van Sickle** . . . . (509) 458-5250
  Began Service: 1991
  Appointed By: President George H.W. Bush
Senior Judge **Justin L. Quackenbush** . . . . (509) 458-5280
  Began Service: 1980
  Appointed By: President Jimmy Carter
  E-mail: justin_quackenbush@waed.uscourts.gov
Senior Judge **Wm. Fremming Nielsen** . . . . (509) 458-5290
  Began Service: May 28, 1991
  Appointed By: President George H.W. Bush
  Thomas S. Foley U.S. Courthouse,
  920 West Riverside Avenue, Suite 904,
  Spokane, WA 99201
  E-mail: frem_nielsen@waed.uscourts.gov
Senior Judge **Edward F. Shea** . . . . (509) 943-8190
  Began Service: May 28, 1998
  Appointed By: President William J. Clinton
Senior Judge **Lonny R. Suko** . . . . (509) 573-6650
  Began Service: August 1, 2003
  Appointed By: President George W. Bush
  E-mail: lonny_suko@waed.uscourts.gov
Magistrate Judge **James P. Hutton** . . . . (509) 573-6670
  Began Service: January 2008
  E-mail: james_hutton@waed.uscourts.gov
Magistrate Judge **John T. Rodgers** . . . . (509) 458-5240

Court Staff

District Court Executive/Clerk of Court
  Sean F. McAvoy . . . . (509) 458-3400
Chief Probation Officer **Scott M. Morse** . . . . (509) 742-6300
  E-mail: scott_morse@waed.uscourts.gov

United States Bankruptcy Court for the Eastern District of Washington

U.S. Post Office Building, 904 West Riverside Avenue, Suite 304,
Spokane, WA 99201
P.O. Box 2164, Spokane, WA 99210-2164
402 East Yakima Avenue, Suite 200, Yakima, WA 98901 (Yakima Office)
Tel: (509) 458-5300 (Spokane Office)
Tel: (509) 576-6100 (Yakima Office)
Tel: (800) 519-2549 (Voice Case Information System VCIS)
Fax: (509) 458-2445
Internet: www.waeb.uscourts.gov

Number of Judgeships: 3

Judges

Chief Bankruptcy Judge **Frederick P. Corbit** . . . . (509) 458-5340
Bankruptcy Judge **Frank L. Kurtz** . . . . (509) 576-6122
  Began Service: 2005
  E-mail: frank_kurtz@waeb.uscourts.gov
Bankruptcy Judge (recalled) **John A. Rossmeissl** . . . . (509) 576-6122
  Began Service: 1987
  402 East Yakima Avenue, Suite 200,
  Yakima, WA 98901-5404

Court Staff

Clerk of the Court **Beverly A. Benka** . . . . (509) 458-5300

United States Bankruptcy Court for the Eastern District of Washington
continued

U.S. Attorney

Washington - Eastern District
Federal Courthouse, 920 West Riverside Avenue, Room 340,
Spokane, WA 99201
P.O. Box 1494, Spokane, WA 99210-1494
Tel: (509) 353-2767 Fax: (509) 353-2766

U.S. Attorney **Michael C. "Mike" Ormsby** . . . . (509) 353-2767

Federal Public Defender

Federal Defenders of Eastern Washington and Idaho
10 North Post Street, Suite 700, Spokane, WA 99201-0705
306 East Chestnut Street, Yakima, WA 98901
Tel: (509) 624-7606 (Spokane) Tel: (509) 248-8920 (Yakima)
Fax: (509) 747-3539 (Spokane) Fax: (509) 248-9118 (Yakima)

Federal Public Defender **Andrea George** . . . . (509) 624-7606
  E-mail: andrea.george@fd.org

United States District Court for the Western District of Washington

700 Stewart Street, Suite 2310, Seattle, WA 98101
Tel: (206) 370-8400 Tel: (206) 553-2288 (PACER)
Internet: www.wawd.uscourts.gov

Number of Judgeships: 7

Circuit: Ninth

Areas Covered: Counties of Clallam, Clark, Cowlitz, Grays Harbor, Island, Jefferson, King, Kitsap, Lewis, Mason, Pacific, Pierce, San Juan, Skagit, Skamania, Snohomish, Thurston, Wahkiakum and Whatcom

Judges

Chief Judge **Marsha J. Pechman** U.S. Courthouse,
  Room 14229 . . . . (206) 370-8820
  Began Service: October 4, 1999
  Appointed By: President William J. Clinton
  E-mail: Marsha_Pechman@wawd.uscourts.gov
District Judge **Robert S. Lasnik** Suite 15128 . . . . (206) 370-8810
  Began Service: December 2, 1998
  Appointed By: President William J. Clinton
  E-mail: robert_lasnik@wawd.uscourts.gov
District Judge **Ronald B. Leighton** . . . . (253) 882-3840
  Began Service: November 26, 2002
  Appointed By: President George W. Bush
  E-mail: ronald_leighton@wawd.uscourts.gov
District Judge **James L. Robart** Room 14134 . . . . (206) 370-8920
  Began Service: June 28, 2004
  Appointed By: President George W. Bush
  E-mail: james_robart@wawd.uscourts.gov
District Judge **Benjamin Hale Settle** . . . . (253) 882-3850
  Began Service: July 9, 2007
  Appointed By: President George W. Bush
  1717 Pacific Avenue, Room 3144,
  Tacoma, WA 98402
  E-mail: benjamin_settle@wawd.uscourts.gov
District Judge **Ricardo S. Martinez** Suite 13134 . . . . (206) 370-8880
  Began Service: June 2004
  Appointed By: President George W. Bush
  E-mail: ricardo_martinez@wawd.uscourts.gov
District Judge **Richard A. Jones** . . . . (206) 370-8870
  Began Service: October 29, 2007
  Appointed By: President George W. Bush
Senior Judge **Walter T. McGovern** Suite 13229 . . . . (206) 370-8860
  Began Service: May 14, 1971
  Appointed By: President Richard M. Nixon
  E-mail: walter_mcgovern@wawd.uscourts.gov

United States District Court for the Western District of Washington
continued

Senior Judge **Barbara Jacobs Rothstein** Suite 16128 . . . . (206) 370-8840
  Note: Judge Rothstein is currently assigned to the
  District of Columbia District Court as a visiting
  judge.
  Began Service: February 20, 1980
  Appointed By: President Jimmy Carter
  E-mail: barbara_rothstein@wawd.uscourts.gov
Senior Judge **Carolyn R. Dimmick** U.S. Courthouse,
  Suite 16134 . . . . (206) 370-8850
  Began Service: April 4, 1985
  Appointed By: President Ronald Reagan
  E-mail: carolyn_dimmick@wawd.uscourts.gov
Senior Judge **Robert J. Bryan** . . . . (253) 882-3870
  Began Service: 1986
  Appointed By: President Ronald Reagan
  1717 Pacific Avenue, Room 4427,
  Tacoma, WA 98402
  E-mail: robert_bryan@wawd.uscourts.gov
Senior Judge **Thomas S. Zilly** Suite 15229 . . . . (206) 370-8830
  Began Service: 1988
  Appointed By: President Ronald Reagan
  E-mail: thomas_zilly@wawd.uscourts.gov
Senior Judge **John C. Coughenour** Suite 16229 . . . . (206) 370-8800
  Began Service: 1981
  Appointed By: President Ronald Reagan
  E-mail: john_coughenour@wawd.uscourts.gov
Chief Magistrate Judge **James P. Donohue** . . . . (206) 370-8940
  Began Service: February 8, 2005
  E-mail: james_donohue@wawd.uscourts.gov
Magistrate Judge **Mary Alice Theiler** Suite 12141 . . . . (206) 370-8890
  Began Service: April 25, 2003
Magistrate Judge **Karen L. Strombom** . . . . (253) 882-3890
  Began Service: 2012
  E-mail: karen_strombom@wawd.uscourts.gov
Magistrate Judge **Brian Tsuchida** . . . . (206) 370-8930
  Began Service: May 13, 2008
  E-mail: brian_tsuchida@wawd.uscourts.gov
Magistrate Judge **J. Richard Creatura** . . . . (253) 882-3780
  Began Service: March 17, 2009
  Union Station Courthouse, 1717 Pacific Avenue,
  Room 3100, Tacoma, WA 98402-9800
Magistrate Judge **David W. Christel** . . . . (360) 993-4990
Magistrate Judge (Part-Time) **Dean Brett** . . . . (360) 733-0212
  Began Service: 2005
  Brett & Daugert, PLLC., 119 No. Commercial,
  Suite 110, Bellingham, WA 98227
  E-mail: dean_brett@wawd.uscourts.gov
Magistrate Judge (recalled) **John L. Weinberg** . . . . (206) 370-8910
  Began Service: October 1, 1973
  E-mail: john_weinberg@wawd.uscourts.gov
Magistrate Judge (recalled) **J. Kelley Arnold** . . . . (253) 882-3800
  Began Service: October 28, 1994
  E-mail: kelley_arnold@wawd.uscourts.gov

Court Staff
Clerk of Court **William McCool** . . . . (206) 370-8400
  E-mail: william_mccool@wawd.uscourts.gov
Chief Pretrial Services Officer **(Vacant)** . . . . (206) 370-8950
Chief Probation Officer **Connie Smith** . . . . (206) 370-8550

United States Bankruptcy Court for the Western District of Washington

U.S. Courthouse, 700 Stewart Street, Room 6301, Seattle, WA 98101-1271
Tel: (206) 370-5200 Tel: (800) 676-6856 (PACER)
Tel: (888) 409-4662 (Toll free Voice Case Information System VCIS)
Internet: www.wawb.uscourts.gov

Number of Judgeships: 5

Judges

Chief Bankruptcy Judge **Brian D. Lynch** . . . . (253) 882-3900
  Began Service: 2011
  1717 Pacific Avenue, Room 2100,
  Tacoma, WA 98402

Bankruptcy Judge **Paul B. Snyder** . . . . (253) 882-3950
  Began Service: November 1, 1996
  1717 Pacific Avenue, Suite 2209,
  Tacoma, WA 98402-3233
  E-mail: paul_snyder@wawb.uscourts.gov

Bankruptcy Judge **Karen A. Overstreet** . . . . (206) 370-5330
  Began Service: January 3, 1994
  700 Stewart Street, Room 7216,
  Seattle, WA 98101
  E-mail: karen_overstreet@wawb.uscourts.gov

Bankruptcy Judge **Marc Barreca** . . . . (206) 370-5310
  Began Service: 2010
  700 Stewart Street, Room 6301,
  Seattle, WA 98101
  E-mail: marc_barreca@wawb.uscourts.gov

Bankruptcy Judge **Timothy W. Dore** . . . . (206) 370-5300
  Began Service: April 4, 2011
  700 Stewart Street, Room 6301,
  Seattle, WA 98101

Bankruptcy Judge (recalled) **Philip H. Brandt** . . . . (206) 370-5320
  Began Service: October 11, 1991
  700 Stewart Street, Suite 8135,
  Seattle, WA 98101
  E-mail: philip_brandt@wawb.uscourts.gov

Court Staff

Clerk of the Court **Mark L. Hatcher** . . . . (206) 370-5205
  E-mail: mark_hatcher@wawb.uscourts.gov

U.S. Attorney

Washington - Western District
700 Stewart Street, Suite 5220, Seattle, WA 98101
Tel: (206) 553-7970 Fax: (206) 553-0882

U.S. Attorney (Interim) **Annette L. Hayes** . . . . (206) 553-7970

Federal Public Defender

Federal Public Defender for the Western District of Washington
Westlake Center Office Tower, 1601 Fifth Avenue, Room 700,
Seattle, WA 98101
Sound Credit Union Building, 1331 Broadway, Room 400,
Tacoma, WA 98402
Tel: (206) 553-1100 (Seattle) Tel: (253) 593-6710 (Tacoma)
Fax: (206) 553-0120 (Seattle) Fax: (253) 593-6714 (Tacoma)

Federal Public Defender **Michael Filipovic** . . . . (206) 553-1100
  E-mail: michael.filipovic@fd.org

United States District Court for the Northern District of West Virginia

U.S. Post Office / U.S. Courthouse, 1125 Chapline Street,
Suite 1000, Wheeling, WV 26301
P.O. Box 471, Wheeling, WV 26003
Tel: (304) 232-0011 Fax: (304) 233-2185 Fax: (304) 636-5746 (Elkins)
Internet: www.wvnd.uscourts.gov

Number of Judgeships: 3

Circuit: Fourth

Areas Covered: Counties of Barbour, Berkeley, Braxton, Brooke,
Calhoun, Doddridge, Gilmer, Grant, Hampshire, Hancock, Hardy,
Harrison, Jefferson, Lewis, Marion, Marshall, Mineral, Monongalia,
Morgan, Ohio, Pendleton, Pleasants, Pocahontas, Preston, Randolph,
Ritchie, Taylor, Tucker, Tyler, Upshur, Webster and Wetzel

Judges

Chief Judge **Gina Marie Groh** . . . . (304) 267-7027
  Began Service: March 20, 2012
  Appointed By: President Barack Obama

District Judge **John Preston Bailey** . . . . (304) 233-1492
  Began Service: March 22, 2007
  Appointed By: President George W. Bush

District Judge **Irene M. Keeley** . . . . (304) 624-5850
  Began Service: 1992
  Appointed By: President George H.W. Bush
  E-mail: Judge_Keeley@wvnd.uscourts.gov

Senior Judge **Frederick P. Stamp, Jr.** . . . . (304) 233-1120
  Began Service: July 30, 1990
  Appointed By: President George H.W. Bush

Magistrate Judge **James E. Seibert** . . . . (304) 233-1348
  Began Service: 1985

Magistrate Judge **John S. Kaull** . . . . (304) 623-7170
  Began Service: May 6, 1999

Magistrate Judge **Robert W. Trumble** . . . . (304) 267-5611
  Began Service: June 3, 2014
  217 West King Street, Room 207,
  Martinsburg, WV 25401

Court Staff

Clerk of Court **Cheryl Dean Riley** . . . . (304) 232-0011 ext. 228
  E-mail: cheryl_riley@wvnd.uscourts.gov

Chief Probation Officer **Terry Huffman** . . . . (304) 624-5504
  320 W. Pike St., Ste. 110, Clarksburg, WV 26302

United States Bankruptcy Court for the Northern District of West Virginia

Federal Building, 12th & Chapline Streets, Wheeling, WV 26003
P.O. Box 70, Wheeling, WV 26003
Tel: (304) 233-1655 Tel: (304) 233-2871 (PACER)
Tel: (304) 233-7318 (Voice Case Information System VCIS)
Fax: (304) 233-0185
Internet: www.wvnb.uscourts.gov

Number of Judgeships: 1

Judges

Chief Bankruptcy Judge **Patrick M. Flatley** . . . . (304) 233-1655
  Began Service: 2006

Court Staff

Clerk of the Court **Ryan Johnson** . . . . (304) 233-1655
  E-mail: ryan_johnson@wvnb.uscourts.gov

United States Bankruptcy Court for the Northern District of West Virginia *continued*

U.S. Attorney

West Virginia - Northern District
Federal Building, 1125 Chapline Street, Suite 3000, Wheeling, WV 26003
Tel: (304) 234-0100 Fax: (304) 234-0110 (Main)
Fax: (304) 234-0112 (Civil) Fax: (304) 234-0111 (Criminal)

U.S. Attorney **William J. Ihlenfeld II** . . . . (304) 234-0100

Federal Public Defender

Office of the Federal Public Defender for the Northern District of West Virginia
Huntinton National Bank Building, 230 West Pike Street, Room 360, Clarksburg, WV 26301-6301
651 Foxcroft Avenue, Room 202, Martinsburg, WV 26003
1125 Chapline Street, Room 228, Wheeling, WV 26003
Tel: (304) 622-3823 (Clarksburg) Tel: (304) 260-9421 (Martinsburg)
Tel: (304) 233-1217 (Wheeling) Fax: (304) 622-4631 (Clarksburg)
Fax: (304) 260-3716 (Martinsburg) Fax: (304) 233-1242 (Wheeling)

Federal Public Defender **Brian J. Kornbrath** . . . . (304) 622-3823
  E-mail: brian.kornbrath@fd.org

United States District Court for the Southern District of West Virginia

Robert C. Byrd U.S. Courthouse, 300 Virginia Street East,
Suite 7009, Charleston, WV 25301
Tel: (304) 347-3000 Fax: (304) 347-3007
Internet: www.wvsd.uscourts.gov

Number of Judgeships: 5

Circuit: Fourth

Areas Covered: Counties of Boone, Cabell, Clay, Fayette, Greenbrier, Jackson, Kanawha, Lincoln, Logan, Mason, McDowell, Mercer, Mingo, Monroe, Nicholas, Putnam, Raleigh, Roane, Summers, Wayne, Wirt, Wood and Wyoming

Judges

Chief Judge **Robert C. Chambers** . . . . (304) 528-7583
  Began Service: October 17, 1997
  Appointed By: President William J. Clinton
  E-mail: Judge_Chambers@wvsd.uscourts.gov
District Judge **Joseph Robert Goodwin** Suite 5009 . . . . . (304) 347-3192
  Began Service: May 15, 1995
  Appointed By: President William J. Clinton
  E-mail: joseph_goodwin@wvsd.uscourts.gov
District Judge **John T. Copenhaver, Jr.** . . . . (304) 347-3146
  Began Service: September 26, 1976
  Appointed By: President Gerald Ford
District Judge **Thomas E. Johnston** Room 6610 . . . . (304) 347-3217
  Began Service: April 17, 2006
  Appointed By: President George W. Bush
District Judge
  Irene Cornelia Berger . . . . (304) 347-3100 (Charleston Phone Number)
  Began Service: December 11, 2009   Tel: (304) 253-2438
  Appointed By: President Barack Obama
  110 North Heber Street, Room 336,
  Beckley, WV 25801
Senior Judge **David A. Faber** . . . . (304) 327-8144 (Bluefield Office)
  Began Service: December 27, 1991   Tel: (304) 347-3170
  Appointed By: President George H.W. Bush   (Charleston Office)
  601 Federal Street, Room 2303,
  Bluefield, WV 24701
Magistrate Judge **R. Clarke VanDervort** . . . . (304) 327-0376
  Began Service: December 2001   Tel: (304) 253-8516
                              (Beckley Chambers)

United States District Court for the Southern District of West Virginia *continued*

Magistrate Judge **Cheryl A. Eifert** . . . . (304) 529-5709
  Began Service: 2010
  845 Fifth Avenue, Room 109,
  Huntington, WV 25701
  E-mail: cheryl_eifert@wvsd.uscourts.gov
Magistrate Judge **Dwane L. Tinsley** Room 5408 . . . . (304) 347-3279
  E-mail: dwane_tinsley@wvsd.uscourts.gov

Court Staff

Clerk of Court **Teresa L. Deppner** . . . . (304) 347-3000
Chief Probation Officer **Keith Zutaut** . . . . (304) 347-3300
  E-mail: keith_zutaut@wvsd.uscourts.gov

United States Bankruptcy Court for the Southern District of West Virginia

3200 Robert C. Byrd U.S. Courthouse, 300 Virginia Street East,
Charleston, WV 25301
Tel: (304) 347-3003
Tel: (866) 222-8029 (Voice Case Information System VCIS)
Fax: (304) 347-3018
Internet: www.wvsb.uscourts.gov

Number of Judgeships: 1

Judges

Bankruptcy Judge **Ronald G. Pearson** . . . . (304) 347-3238
  Note: Until October 8, 2015.
  Began Service: 1983
  E-mail: ron_pearson@wvsb.uscourts.gov
Bankruptcy Judge **Frank W. Volk** . . . . (304) 347-3003
  Note: Effective October 8, 2015.

Court Staff

Clerk of the Court **Matthew J. Hayes** . . . . (304) 347-3003

U.S. Attorney

West Virginia - Southern District
300 Virginia Street East, Room 4000, Charleston, WV 25301
P.O. Box 1713, Charleston, WV 25326
Tel: (304) 345-2200 Fax: (304) 347-5104

U.S. Attorney **Robert Booth Goodwin II** . . . . (304) 345-2200
  E-mail: booth.goodwin@usdoj.gov

Federal Public Defender

Office of the Federal Public Defender for the Southern District of West Virginia
United States Courthouse, 300 Virginia Street East, Suite 3400, Charleston, WV 25301
Tel: (304) 347-3350 Fax: (304) 347-3356

Federal Public Defender **Christian M. Capece** . . . . (304) 347-3350
  E-mail: christian.capece@fd.org

United States District Court for the Eastern District of Wisconsin

362 U.S. Courthouse, 517 East Wisconsin Avenue, Milwaukee, WI 53202
125 South Jefferson Street, Room 102, Green Bay, WI 54305-2490 (Green Bay Divisional Office)
Tel: (414) 297-3372 Tel: (920) 884-3720 (Green Bay)
Fax: (414) 297-3203 Fax: (920) 884-3724 (Green Bay)
Internet: www.wied.uscourts.gov

Number of Judgeships: 5

Circuit: Seventh

Areas Covered: Counties of Brown, Calumet, Dodge, Door, Florence, Fond du Lac, Forest, Green Lake, Kenosha, Kewaunee, Langlade, Manitowoc, Marinette, Marquette, Menominee, Milwaukee, Oconto, Outagamie, Ozaukee, Racine, Shawano, Sheboygan, Walworth, Washington, Waukesha, Waupaca, Waushara and Winnebago

Judges

Chief Judge **William C. Griesbach** . . . . (920) 884-7775
  Began Service: May 17, 2002
  Appointed By: President George W. Bush
  Jefferson Court Building,
  125 South Jefferson Street, Room 203,
  Green Bay, WI 54301
  E-mail: william_griesbach@wied.uscourts.gov
District Judge **J. P. Stadtmueller** . . . .(414) 297-1122
  Began Service: 1987
  Appointed By: President Ronald Reagan
District Judge **Rudolph T. Randa** U.S. Courthouse,
  Room 310 . . . .(414) 297-3071
  Began Service: August 12, 1992
  Appointed By: President George H.W. Bush
  E-mail: rudolph_randa@wied.uscourts.gov
District Judge **Lynn Adelman** . . . . (414) 297-1285
  Began Service: December 9, 1997
  Appointed By: President William J. Clinton
  E-mail: lynn_adelman@wied.uscourts.gov
District Judge **Pamela Pepper** . . . . (414) 297-3335
  Appointed By: President Barack Obama
Senior Judge **Charles N. Clevert, Jr.** . . . .(414) 297-1585
  Began Service: July 31, 1996
  Appointed By: President William J. Clinton
Magistrate Judge **Patricia J. Gorence** . . . . (414) 297-4165
  Began Service: April 1, 1994
  E-mail: patricia_gorence@wied.uscourts.gov
Magistrate Judge **William E. Callahan, Jr.** U.S.
  Courthouse, Room 247 . . . .(414) 297-1664
  Began Service: August 1, 1995
  E-mail: William_Callahan@wied.uscourts.gov
Magistrate Judge **Nancy Joseph** U.S. Courthouse,
  Room 249 . . . .(414) 297-4167
  Began Service: 2010
Magistrate Judge **William E. Duffin** Room 296 . . . . (414) 297-3188
Magistrate Judge (Part-Time) **James R. Sickel** . . . .(920) 432-7716
  Began Service: December 1991
  125 South Jefferson Street, Suite 101,
  Green Bay, WI 54301
Magistrate Judge (recalled) **Aaron E. Goodstein** . . . .(414) 297-3963
  Began Service: November 1, 1979
  E-mail: aaron_goodstein@wied.uscourts.gov

Court Staff

Clerk of Court **Jon W. Sanfilippo** . . . .(414) 297-3372
  E-mail: jon_sanfilippo@wied.uscourts.gov
Chief Probation Officer **Michael Klug** . . . .(414) 297-1425

United States Bankruptcy Court for the Eastern District of Wisconsin

126 U.S. Courthouse, 517 East Wisconsin Avenue, Milwaukee, WI 53202
Tel: (414) 297-3291
Tel: (866) 222-8029 (Voice Case Information System VCIS)
Tel: (800) 676-6856 (PACER Registration) Fax: (414) 297-4040
Internet: www.wieb.uscourts.gov

Number of Judgeships: 4

Judges

Chief Bankruptcy Judge **Susan V. Kelley** . . . . (414) 290-2660
  Began Service: July 1, 2003
  E-mail: susan_v_kelley@wieb.uscourts.gov
Bankruptcy Judge **Margaret Dee McGarity** . . . .(414) 297-3291 ext. 3203
  Began Service: 1987
Bankruptcy Judge **G. Michael "Mike" Halfenger**
  Room 133 . . . .(414) 290-2680

Court Staff

Clerk of Court **Janet L. Medlock** . . . . (414) 297-3291
  E-mail: janet_medlock@wieb.uscourts.gov

U.S. Attorney

Wisconsin - Eastern District
Federal Courthouse, 517 East Wisconsin Avenue, Room 530,
Milwaukee, WI 53202
Tel: (414) 297-1700 Fax: (414) 297-1738

U.S. Attorney (Acting) **Gregory J. "Greg" Haanstad** . . . (414) 297-1700
  E-mail: greg.haanstad@usdoj.gov

Federal Public Defender

Federal Defender Services of Wisconsin, Inc.
517 East Wisconsin Avenue, Suite 182, Milwaukee, WI 53202
801 East Walnut Street, Second Floor, Green Bay, WI 54301-4401
222 West Washington Avenue, Room 300, Madison, WI 53703
Tel: (414) 221-9900 (Milwaukee) Tel: (920) 430-9900 (Green Bay)
Tel: (608) 260-9900 (Madison) Fax: (414) 221-9901 (Milwaukee)
Fax: (920) 430-9901 (Green Bay) Fax: (608) 260-9901 (Madison)

Federal Public Defender **Daniel Stiller** . . . . (414) 221-9900
  E-mail: daniel.stiller@fd.org

United States District Court for the Western District of Wisconsin

U.S. Courthouse, 120 North Henry Street, Room 320, Madison, WI 53703
Tel: (608) 264-5156 Tel: (608) 264-5914 (PACER)
Fax: (608) 264-5925
Internet: www.wiwd.uscourts.gov

Number of Judgeships: 2

Circuit: Seventh

Areas Covered: Counties of Adams, Ashland, Barron, Bayfield, Buffalo, Burnett, Chippewa, Clark, Columbia, Crawford, Dane, Douglas, Dunn, Eau Claire, Grant, Green, Iowa, Iron, Jackson, Jefferson, Juneau, La Crosse, Lafayette, Lincoln, Marathon, Monroe, Oneida, Pepin, Pierce, Polk, Portage, Price, Richland, Rock, Rusk, Sauk, Sawyer, St. Croix, Taylor, Trempealeau, Vernon, Vilas, Washburn and Wood

Judges

Chief Judge **William M. Conley** . . . . (608) 264-5156
  Began Service: March 30, 2010
  Appointed By: President Barack Obama
  E-mail: william_conley@wiwd.uscourts.gov

United States District Court for the Western District of Wisconsin
continued

District Judge **James D. Peterson** . . . .(608) 264-5156
  Began Service: 2014
  Appointed By: President Barack Obama
  E-mail: james_peterson@wiwd.uscourts.gov

Magistrate Judge **Stephen L. Crocker** . . . .(608) 264-5153
  Began Service: 1992
  E-mail: stephen_crocker@wiwd.uscourts.gov

Senior Judge **Barbara B. Crabb** . . . .(608) 264-5447
  Began Service: November 26, 1979
  Appointed By: President Jimmy Carter
  E-mail: barbara_crabb@wiwd.uscourts.gov

Court Staff
Fax: (608) 264-5925

Clerk of Court/Part Time Magistrate **Peter Oppeneer** . . . . (608) 261-5795
  E-mail: peter_oppeneer@wiwd.uscourts.gov

Chief Probation Officer **Paul Reed** . . . .(608) 261-5767
  E-mail: paul_reed@wiwp.uscourts.gov

United States Bankruptcy Court for the Western District of Wisconsin
U.S. Courthouse, 120 North Henry Street, Madison, WI 53703-0548
Tel: (608) 264-5178 Tel: (608) 264-5630 (PACER)
Tel: (800) 373-8708 (Toll Free PACER)
Tel: (608) 264-5035 (Voice Case Information System VCIS)
Tel: (800) 743-8247 (Toll Free Voice Case Information System VCIS)
Fax: (608) 264-5105
Internet: www.wiw.uscourts.gov/bankruptcy

Number of Judgeships: 2

Judges
Bankruptcy Judge **Robert D. Martin** . . . .(608) 264-5188
  Began Service: 1978

Bankruptcy Judge **Catherine J. Furay** . . . .(715) 839-2985

Court Staff
Clerk of Court **MG Marcia M. Anderson** . . . . (608) 264-5178

U.S. Attorney
Wisconsin - Western District
222 West Washington Avenue, Suite 700, Madison, WI 53703
Tel: (608) 264-5158 TTY: (608) 264-5006 Fax: (608) 264-5172

U.S. Attorney **John W. Vaudreuil** . . . .(608) 264-5158

Federal Public Defender
Federal Defender Services of Wisconsin, Inc.
517 East Wisconsin Avenue, Suite 182, Milwaukee, WI 53202
801 East Walnut Street, Second Floor, Green Bay, WI 54301-4401
222 West Washington Avenue, Room 300, Madison, WI 53703
Tel: (414) 221-9900 (Milwaukee) Tel: (920) 430-9900 (Green Bay)
Tel: (608) 260-9900 (Madison) Fax: (414) 221-9901 (Milwaukee)
Fax: (920) 430-9901 (Green Bay) Fax: (608) 260-9901 (Madison)

Federal Public Defender **Daniel Stiller** . . . . (414) 221-9900
  E-mail: daniel.stiller@fd.org

United States District Court for the District of Wyoming
2120 Capitol Avenue, Room 2131, Cheyenne, WY 82001
Tel: (307) 433-2120 Fax: (307) 433-2152
Internet: www.wyd.uscourts.gov

Number of Judgeships: 3

Circuit: Tenth

Judges
Chief Judge **Nancy D. Freudenthal** . . . . (307) 433-2190
  Began Service: June 1, 2010
  Appointed By: President Barack Obama
  E-mail: wyojudgendf@wyd.uscourts.gov

District Judge **Alan B. Johnson** Room2018 . . . .(307) 433-2170
  Began Service: 1986
  Appointed By: President Ronald Reagan
  E-mail: wyojudgeabj@wyd.uscourts.gov

District Judge **Scott W. Skavdahl** . . . .(307) 232-2600
  Began Service: December 8, 2011
  Appointed By: President Barack Obama
  111 South Wolcott, Suite 210,
  Casper, WY 82601

Magistrate Judge **Mark L. Carman** . . . . (307) 344-2569
  Began Service: 2013

Magistrate Judge **Kelly Harrison Rankin** . . . . (307) 433-2180
                                                     Tel: (307) 433-2180

Magistrate Judge (Part-Time) **Karen Marty** . . . .(307) 875-3235
  Began Service: 2003
  E-mail: karen_marty@wyd.uscourts.gov

Magistrate Judge (Part-Time) **R. Michael Shickich** . . . . . . (307) 266-5297
  Began Service: January 23, 2004
  111 West Second Street, Suite 500,
  Casper, WY 82601

Magistrate Judge (Part-Time) **Teresa M. McKee** . . . . (307) 332-9406
  Began Service: July 2006
  Appointed By: President George W. Bush
  E-mail: teresa_mckee@wyd.uscourts.gov

Court Staff
Clerk of the Court **Stephan Harris** . . . . (307) 433-2120
  E-mail: stephan_harris@wyd.uscourts.gov

Chief Probation Officer **Tambra Loyd** . . . .(307) 433-2300
  E-mail: tambra_loyd@wyp.uscourts.gov

United States Bankruptcy Court for the District of Wyoming
2120 Capitol Avenue, Suite 6004, Cheyenne, WY 82001-3633
Tel: (307) 433-2200
Tel: (307) 433-2238 (Voice Case Information System VCIS)
Tel: (888) 804-5537 (Toll Free Voice Case Information System VCIS)
Internet: www.wyb.uscourts.gov

Number of Judgeships: 1

Judges
Bankruptcy Judge **Michael E. Romero** . . . . (307) 433-2200
  Note: Judge Romero is currently serving the district
  of Wyoming on a temporary basis until a permanent
  replacement has been appointed.

Court Staff
Clerk of Court **Tim J. Ellis** . . . .(307) 433-2200

(continued on next page)

United States Bankruptcy Court for the District of Wyoming *continued*

U.S. Attorney

Wyoming District
J.C. O'Mahoney Federal Building, 2120 Capitol Avenue, Room 4002,
Cheyenne, WY 82001
P.O. Box 668, Cheyenne, WY 82003-0668
Tel: (307) 772-2124 Fax: (307) 772-2123

U.S. Attorney **Christopher A. "Kip" Crofts** . . . . (307) 772-2124

Federal Public Defender

Colorado and Wyoming Federal Public Defender
633 Seventeenth Street, Suite 1000, Denver, CO 80202
214 West Lincolnway, Suite 31A, Cheyenne, WY 82001
Tel: (303) 294-7002 (Denver) Tel: (307) 772-2781 (Cheyenne)
Fax: (303) 294-1192 (Denver) Fax: (307) 772-2788 (Cheyenne)

Federal Public Defender **Virginia L. Grady** . . . . (303) 294-7002
    E-mail: virginia.grady@fd.org

United States District Court for the District of Columbia

E. Barrett Prettyman U.S. Courthouse, 333 Constitution Avenue, NW,
Washington, DC 20001-2866
Tel: (202) 354-3000 Tel: (202) 273-0606 (PACER)
Fax: (202) 354-3023
Internet: www.dcd.uscourts.gov

Number of Judgeships: 15

Judges

Chief Judge **Richard W. Roberts** . . . . (202) 354-3400
    Began Service: July 31, 1998
    Appointed By: President William J. Clinton
    E-mail: roberts_chambers@dcd.uscourts.gov
District Judge **Emmet G. Sullivan** Room 4935 . . . . (202) 354-3260
    Began Service: June 15, 1994
    Appointed By: President William J. Clinton
    E-mail: sullivan_chambers@dcd.uscourts.gov
District Judge **Colleen Kollar-Kotelly** William Bryant
    Annex, Room 6939 . . . . (202) 354-3340
    Began Service: May 12, 1997
    Appointed By: President William J. Clinton
    E-mail: colleen_kollar-kotelly@dcd.uscourts.gov
District Judge **Reggie B. Walton** . . . . (202) 354-3290
    Began Service: October 29, 2001
    Appointed By: President George W. Bush
    E-mail: reggie_walton@dcd.uscourts.gov
District Judge **Richard J. Leon** . . . . (202) 354-3580
    Began Service: March 20, 2002
    Appointed By: President George W. Bush
    E-mail: richard_leon@dcd.uscourts.gov
District Judge **Rosemary M. Collyer** . . . . (202) 354-3560
    Began Service: January 2, 2003
    Appointed By: President George W. Bush
    333 Constitution Avenue, NW, Room 2428,
    Washington, DC 20001
    E-mail: rosemary_m_collyer@dcd.uscourts.gov
District Judge **Beryl A. Howell** Room 6600 . . . . (202) 354-3450
    Began Service: December 27, 2010
    Appointed By: President Barack Obama
    E-mail: howell_chambers@dcd.uscourts.gov
District Judge **James Emanuel Boasberg** Room 6321 . . . (202) 354-3300
    Began Service: April 1, 2011
    Appointed By: President Barack Obama
    E-mail: james_boasberg@dcd.uscourts.gov
District Judge **Amy Berman Jackson** . . . . (202) 354-3460
    Began Service: 2011
    Appointed By: President Barack Obama
    E-mail: amy_jackson@dcd.uscourts.gov

United States District Court for the District of Columbia *continued*

District Judge **Rudolph "Rudy" Contreras** . . . . (202) 354-3520
    Began Service: June 20, 2012
    Appointed By: President Barack Obama
    E-mail: rudolph_contreras@dcd.uscourts.gov
District Judge **Ketanji Brown Jackson** . . . . (202) 354-3350
    Began Service: May 10, 2013
    Appointed By: President Barack Obama
    E-mail: ketanji_jackson@dcd.uscourts.gov
District Judge **Christopher Reid "Casey" Cooper** . . . . . . (202) 354-3480
    Began Service: March 28, 2014
    Appointed By: President Barack Obama
    E-mail: christopher_r_cooper@dcd.uscourts.gov
District Judge **Tanya S. Chutkan** . . . . (202) 354-3390
    Began Service: June 5, 2014
    Appointed By: President Barack Obama
District Judge **Randolph D. Moss** . . . . (202) 354-3000
    Began Service: 2014
    Appointed By: President Barack Obama
District Judge **Amit Priyavadan Mehta** . . . . (202) 354-3000
    Began Service: January 22, 2015
    Appointed By: President Barack Obama
Senior Judge **Thomas F. Hogan** Room 4012 . . . . (202) 354-3420
    Began Service: October 4, 1982
    Appointed By: President Ronald Reagan
    E-mail: thomas_hogan@dcd.uscourts.gov
Senior Judge **Gladys Kessler** . . . . (202) 354-3440
    Began Service: 1994
    Appointed By: President William J. Clinton
    E-mail: gladys_kessler@dcd.uscourts.gov
Senior Judge **Paul L. Friedman** . . . . (202) 354-3490
    Began Service: August 1, 1994
    Appointed By: President William J. Clinton
    E. Barrett Prettyman U.S. Courthouse,
    333 Constitution Avenue, NW,
    William B. Bryant Annex, Room 6012,
    Washington, DC 20001-2866
    E-mail: friedman_chambers@dcd.uscourts.gov
Senior Judge **Barbara Jacobs Rothstein** . . . . (202) 354-3330
    Note: Judge Rothstein is currently assigned to the
    District of Columbia District Court as a visiting
    judge.
    Began Service: February 20, 1980
    Appointed By: President Jimmy Carter
    E-mail: barbara_rothstein@dcd.uscourts.gov
Senior Judge **Royce C. Lamberth** . . . . (202) 354-3380
    Began Service: November 16, 1987
    Appointed By: President Ronald Reagan
    E-mail: lamberth_chambers@dcd.uscourts.gov
Senior Judge **Ellen Segal Huvelle** . . . . (202) 354-3230
    Began Service: January 2000
    Appointed By: President William J. Clinton
    E-mail: ellen_segal_huvelle@dcd.uscourts.gov
Senior Judge **John D. Bates** . . . . (202) 354-3430
    Began Service: December 20, 2001
    Appointed By: President George W. Bush
    E-mail: bates_chambers@dcd.uscourts.gov
Magistrate Judge **Deborah A. Robinson** . . . . (202) 354-3070
    Began Service: July 1988
Magistrate Judge **Alan Kay** . . . . (202) 354-3030
    Began Service: 1991
    E. Barrett Prettyman U.S. Courthouse,
    333 Constitution Avenue NW, Room 2333,
    Washington, DC 20001-2866
    E-mail: alan_kay@dcd.uscourts.gov
Magistrate Judge **G. Michael Harvey** . . . . (202) 354-3130
    Began Service: February 12, 2015

Court Staff

Clerk of Court **Angela D. Caesar** . . . . (202) 354-3050
    E-mail: angela_caesar@dcd.uscourts.gov
Chief Probation Officer **Gennine Hagar** . . . . (202) 565-1302

United States Bankruptcy Court for the District of Columbia

E. Barrett Prettyman U.S. Courthouse, 333 Constitution Avenue, NW, 1st Floor, Room 1225, Washington, DC 20001-2866
Tel: (202) 354-3280 Tel: (800) 676-6856 (Toll Free PACER)
Tel: (866) 222-8029 (MCVCIS) Fax: (202) 354-3128
Internet: www.dcb.uscourts.gov

Number of Judgeships: 1

Judges
Bankruptcy Judge **S. Martin Teel, Jr.** . . . . (202) 354-3530
  Began Service: February 8, 1988

Court Staff
Clerk of the Court **Angela D. Caesar** . . . . (202) 354-3181

U.S. Attorney
District of Columbia District
555 Fourth Street, NW, Washington, DC 20530
Tel: (202) 252-7566 Fax: (202) 305-0266

U.S. Attorney (Acting) **Vincent H. Cohen, Jr.** . . . . (202) 252-6600
  E-mail: vincent.cohen@usdoj.gov

Federal Public Defender
Federal Public Defender for the District of Columbia
625 Indiana Avenue NW, Washington, DC 20004
Tel: (202) 208-7500 Fax: (202) 208-7515

Federal Public Defender **A. J. Kramer** . . . . (202) 208-7500
  E-mail: a._j._kramer@fd.org

United States District Court for the District of Guam

U.S. Courthouse, 520 West Soledad Avenue, 4th Floor,
Hagatna, GU 96910
Tel: (671) 473-9100 Fax: (671) 473-9152
Internet: www.gud.uscourts.gov

Number of Judgeships: 2
Circuit: Ninth

Judges
Chief Judge **Frances Tydingco-Gatewood** . . . . (671) 473-9200
  Began Service: October 2006
  Appointed By: President George W. Bush
Magistrate Judge **Joaquin V. E. Manibusan, Jr.** . . . . (671) 473-9180
  Began Service: February 9, 2004

Court Staff
Clerk of Court **Jeanne G. Quinata** . . . . (671) 473-9100
  E-mail: jeanne_quinata@gud.uscourts.gov

U.S. Attorney
Guam District - Northern Marianas District
108 Hernan Cortez, Suite 500, Agana, GU 96910
Tel: (671) 472-7332 Fax: (671) 472-7334

U.S. Attorney **Alicia Garrido Limtiaco** . . . . (671) 472-7332
  E-mail: alicia.limtiaco@usdoj.gov

United States District Court for the District of Guam *continued*
Federal Public Defender
Office of the Federal Public Defender
First Hawaiian Bank Building, 400 Route 8, Suite 501,
Mongmong, GU 96910
Tel: (671) 472-7111 Fax: (671) 472-7120

Federal Public Defender **John T. Gorman** . . . . (671) 472-7111
  E-mail: john_t_gorman@fd.org

United States District Court for the Northern Mariana Islands

Horiguchi Building, Beach Road Garapan, 2nd Floor, Saipan, MP 96950
P.O. Box 500687, Saipan, MP 96950-0687
Tel: (670) 237-1200 Fax: (670) 237-1201
Internet: www.nmid.uscourts.gov

Number of Judgeships: 1
Circuit: Ninth
Areas Covered: Commonwealth of the Northern Marianna Islands.

Judges
District Judge **Ramona Villagomez Manglona** . . . . (670) 237-1230
  Began Service: July 31, 2011
  Appointed By: President Barack Obama
  E-mail: usdcnmi@nmi.uscourts.gov
Senior Judge **Alex R. Munson** . . . . (670) 236-2900

Court Staff
Clerk of Court **Heather L. Kennedy** . . . . (670) 237-1210
  E-mail: heather_kennedy@nmid.uscourts.gov

U.S. Attorney
Guam District - Northern Marianas District
108 Hernan Cortez, Suite 500, Agana, GU 96910
Tel: (671) 472-7332 Fax: (671) 472-7334

U.S. Attorney **Alicia Garrido Limtiaco** . . . . (671) 472-7332
  E-mail: alicia.limtiaco@usdoj.gov

Federal Public Defender
Note: There is no federal public defender for the Northern Mariana Islands. Inquiries should be directed to the Federal Public Defender for the district of Guam at (671) 472-7111.

United States District Court for the District of Puerto Rico

Clemente Ruiz-Nazario Courthouse, 150 Carlos Chardon Avenue,
San Juan, PR 00918-1767
Tel: (787) 772-3000 Tel: (787) 766-5774 (Civil Cases PACER)
Fax: (787) 766-5693
Internet: www.prd.uscourts.gov

Number of Judgeships: 7

Circuit: First

Judges

Chief Judge **Aida M. Delgado-Colón** ....(787) 772-3195
  Began Service: March 20, 2006
  Appointed By: President George W. Bush
  Federico Degetau Federal Building,
  150 Carlos Chardon Avenue, Room 111,
  San Juan, PR 00918
  E-mail: Aida_Delgado-Colon@prd.uscourts.gov
District Judge **José Antonio Fusté** ....(787) 772-3120
  Began Service: 1985
  Appointed By: President Ronald Reagan
District Judge **Carmen Consuelo Cerezo** ....(787) 772-3110
  Began Service: 1980
  Appointed By: President Jimmy Carter
  E-mail: carmen_cerezo@prd.uscourts.gov
District Judge **Jay A. García-Gregory** ....(787) 772-3170
  Began Service: August 1, 2000
  Appointed By: President William J. Clinton
  E-mail: jay_garcia-gregory@prd.uscourts.gov
District Judge **Gustavo Antonio Gelpí, Jr.** ....(787) 772-3102
  Began Service: August 2006
  Appointed By: President George W. Bush
  150 Carlos Chardon Avenue, Suite CH-151,
  San Juan, PR 00918-0463
  E-mail: gustavo_gelpi@prd.uscourts.gov
District Judge **Francisco Augusto Besosa** Room 119 ....(787) 772-3241
  Began Service: October 2006
  Appointed By: President George W. Bush
  E-mail: francisco_besosa@prd.uscourts.gov
District Judge **Pedro A. Delgado Hernández** ....(787) 772-3133
  Began Service: 2014
  Appointed By: President Barack Obama
Senior Judge **Salvador E. Casellas** ....(787) 977-6060
  Began Service: November 1, 1994
  Appointed By: President William J. Clinton
  U.S. Courthouse, 300 Recinto Sur, Suite 342,
  San Juan, PR 00901
  E-mail: S._Casellas@prd.uscourts.gov
Senior Judge **Juan M. Pérez-Giménez** ....(787) 772-3140
  Began Service: 1979
  Appointed By: President Jimmy Carter
  Jose V. Toledo Building and U.S. Courthouse,
  300 Calle Vel Recinto Sur, Suite 129,
  San Juan, PR 00901
Senior Judge **Daniel R. Domínguez** ....(787) 772-3161
  Began Service: November 1, 1994
  Appointed By: President William J. Clinton
  E-mail: Daniel_Dominguez@prd.uscourts.gov
Magistrate Judge **Camille L. Velez-Rive** ....(787) 772-3188
  Began Service: March 22, 2004
Magistrate Judge **Bruce J. McGiverin** Federico Degetau
  Federal Building, Room 483 ....(787) 772-3341
  Began Service: January 2007
  E-mail: bruce_mcgiverin@prd.uscourts.gov
Magistrate Judge **Marcos E. Lopez** ....(787) 772-3350
  Began Service: 2007
  E-mail: marcos_lopez@prd.uscourts.gov
Magistrate Judge **Silvia Carreño-Coll** ....(787) 772-3190

Court Staff

Fax: (787) 766-5693

Clerk of Court **Frances Ríos De Morán** Room 150 ......(787) 772-3000
  E-mail: Frances_Moran@prd.uscourts.gov

United States District Court for the District of Puerto Rico *continued*

Chief of Pre-Trial
  Services/Chief
  Probation Officer
  Eustaquio Babilonia ... (787) 766-5647 ext. 5240 (Probation Services)
  E-mail: eustaquio_babilonia@prp.uscourts.gov   Tel: (787) 772-3300
                                                        (Pre-Trial Services)

United States Bankruptcy Court for the District of Puerto Rico

U.S. Post Office and Courthouse Building, 300 Recinto Sur Street,
Suite 109, Old San Juan, PR 00901
Tel: (787) 977-6000 Tel: (787) 977-6140 (PACER)
Tel: (800) 676-6856 ext. 225 (Toll Free Pacer) Fax: (787) 977-6008
Internet: www.prb.uscourts.gov

Number of Judgeships: 1

Judges

Chief Bankruptcy Judge **Enrique S. Lamoutte** Suite
  251 ....(787) 977-6030
  Began Service: November 1986
  E-mail: Enrique_S._Lamoutte@prb.uscourts.gov
Bankruptcy Judge **Brian K. Tester** ....(787) 977-6040
  Began Service: November 2006
  E-mail: brian_tester@prb.uscourts.gov
Bankruptcy Judge **Mildred Caban Flores** Jose
  V. Toledo Federal Building and U.S. Courthouse,
  Courtroom 3 ....(787) 977-6000
Bankruptcy Judge **Edward A. Godoy** ....(787) 290-6074

Court Staff

Clerk of the Court **María de los Angeles González**.....(787) 977-6015

U.S. Attorney

Puerto Rico District
350 Carlos Chardon Street, Torre Chardon, Suite 1201,
San Juan, PR 00918
Tel: (787) 766-5656 Fax: (787) 766-5632

U.S. Attorney **Rosa Emilia Rodriguez-Velez** ....(787) 766-5656
  E-mail: rosa.e.rodriguez@usdoj.gov

Federal Public Defender

Federal Public Defender for the District of Puerto Rico
Patio Gallery, 241 F.D. Roosevelt Avenue, Third Floor,
San Juan, PR 00918
Tel: (787) 281-4922 Fax: (787) 281-4899

Federal Public Defender **Eric A. Vos** ....(787) 281-4922
  E-mail: eric.vos@fd.org

United States District Court for the District of Virgin Islands

310 U.S. Courthouse, 5500 Veteran's Drive, Charlotte Amalie,
St. Thomas, VI 00802-6424
Tel: (340) 774-0640 Fax: (340) 774-1293
Internet: www.vid.uscourts.gov

Number of Judgeships: 2

Circuit: Third

Judges
Chief Judge **Wilma Antoinette Lewis** . . . . (340) 774-0640
  Began Service: July 28, 2011
  Appointed By: President Barack Obama
District Judge **Curtis V. Gomez** . . . .(340) 774-1800
  Began Service: January 3, 2005
  Appointed By: President George W. Bush
Magistrate Judge **George W. Cannon, Jr.** . . . . (340) 718-1601
  Began Service: April 12, 2012
  E-mail: cannon_chambers@vid.uscourts.gov
Magistrate Judge **Ruth Miller** Suite 345 . . . .(340) 774-5480
  Began Service: June 18, 2010
Magistrate Judge (recalled) **Geoffrey W. Barnard** . . . . (340) 774-5480
  Began Service: 2010
  5500 Veteran's Drive, Suite 342,
  St. Thomas, VI 00802-6424

Court Staff
Clerk of Court **Glenda L. Lake** . . . . (340) 718-1130
Chief Probation Officer **Larry T. Glenn** . . . .(340) 718-5515
  E-mail: larry_glenn@vid.uscourts.gov   Tel: (340) 718-5140
                                              (St. Croix)

United States Bankruptcy Court of the Virgin Islands

351 U.S. Courthouse, 5500 Veteran's Drive, St. Thomas, VI 00802-6424
Tel: (340) 774-8310 Fax: (340) 776-5615

Number of Judgeships: 1

Judges
Bankruptcy Judge **Mary F. Walrath** . . . .(302) 252-2929
  Note: Bankruptcy Judge Mary Walrath hears all
  bankruptcy cases filed in the Virgin Islands in the
  United States Bankruptcy Court for the District of
  Delaware.

Court Staff
Supervisor **Cicely B. Francis** . . . . (340) 774-8310
  E-mail: cicely_francis@vid.uscourts.gov

U.S. Attorney
Virgin Islands District
Ron DeLugo Federal Building and U.S. Courthouse, 5500 Veterans Drive,
Room 260, St. Thomas, VI 00802-6424
Tel: (340) 774-5757 Fax: (340) 776-3474

U.S. Attorney **Ronald W. Sharpe** . . . . (340) 773-3920
  E-mail: ronald.sharpe@usdoj.gov

United States Bankruptcy Court of the Virgin Islands *continued*
Federal Public Defender
Office of the Federal Public Defender for the District of Virgin Islands
Royal Strand Building, 1115 Strand Street, Second Floor,
St. Croix, VI 00822
P.O. Box 223450, St. Croix, VI 00822
51B Kongens Gade, Suite 1, St. Thomas, VI 00802
P.O. Box 1327, St. Thomas, VI 00804
Tel: (340) 773-3585 (St. Croix) Tel: (340) 774-4449 (St. Thomas)
Fax: (340) 773-3742 (St. Croix) Fax: (340) 776-7683 (St. Thomas)

Federal Public Defender **Edson A. Bostic** . . . .(302) 573-6010
  E-mail: edson.bostic@fd.org

Federal Districts - Divisions, Counties, and Court House Locations

Federal Districts - Divisions, Counties, and Court House Locations

Note: The following listing provides for each federal district, the counties in the district, and the places of holding court (civil session). For quick reference, the court website is included as is the court phone number for each place of holding court.

Alabama, Middle District
Internet: www.almd.uscourts.gov

Circuit: Eleventh

Counties in District: Northern Division: Counties of Autauga, Barbour, Bullock, Butler, Chilton, Coosa, Covington, Crenshaw, Elmore, Lowndes, Montgomery, and Pike.

Eastern Division: Counties of Chambers, Lee, Macon, Randolph, Russell, and Tallapoosa.

Southern Division: Counties of Coffee, Dale, Geneva, Henry, and Houston.

Places of Holding Court: Northern Division: Montgomery (334) 954-3600

Eastern Division: Opelika (334) 954-3600

Southern Division: Dothan (334) 954-3600

Alabama, Northern District
Internet: www.alnd.uscourts.gov

Circuit: Eleventh

Counties in District: Eastern Division: Counties of Calhoun, Clay, Cleburne, and Talladega.

Jasper Division: Counties of Fayette, Lamar, Marion, Walker, and Winston.

Middle Division: Counties of Cherokee, DeKalb, Etowah, Marshall, and St. Clair.

Northeastern Division: Counties of Cullman, Jackson, Lawrence, Limestone, Madison, and Morgan.

Northwestern Division: Counties of Colbert, Franklin, and Lauderdale.

Southern Division: Counties of Blount, Jefferson, and Shelby.

Western Division: Counties of Bibb, Greene, Pickens, Sumter, and Tuscaloosa.

Places of Holding Court: Eastern Division: Anniston (256) 236-4170

Jasper Division: Birmingham (205) 278-1700

Middle Division: Gadsden (256) 547-7301

Northeastern Division: Decatur (256) 584-7950 Huntsville (256) 534-6495

Northwestern Division: Florence (256) 760-8415

Southern Division: Birmingham (205) 278-1700

Western Division: Tuscaloosa (205) 561-1670

Alabama, Southern District
Internet: www.als.uscourts.gov

Circuit: Eleventh

Counties in District: Northern Division: Dallas, Hale, Marengo, Perry, and Wilcox.

Southern Division: Baldwin, Choctaw, Clarke, Conecuh, Escambia, Mobile, Monroe, and Washington.

Places of Holding Court: Northern Division: Selma (251 690-2371

Southern Division: Mobile (251) 690-2371

Alaska District
Internet: www.akd.uscourts.gov

Circuit: Ninth

Counties in District: The District comprises the entire State.

Places of Holding Court: Anchorage: (907) 677-6100

Fairbanks: (907) 451-5791

Juneau: (907) 586-7458

Ketchikan: (907) 228-8822

Nome: (907) 443-5216

Arizona District
Internet: www.azd.uscourts.gov

Circuit: Ninth

Counties in District: The District comprises the entire State.

Places of Holding Court: Flagstaff: (928) 774-2566

Phoenix: (602) 322-7200

Prescott: (928) 445-6598

Tucson: (520) 205-4200

Yuma: (928) 329-4766

Arkansas, Eastern District
Internet: www.are.uscourts.gov

Circuit: Eighth

Counties in District: Eastern Division: Counties of Cross, Lee, Monroe, Philips, Saint Francis, and Woodruff.

Western Division: Counties of Conway, Faulkner, Lonoke, Perry, Pope, Prairie, Pulaski, Saline, Van Buren, White, and Yell.

Pine Bluff Division: Counties of Arkansas, Chicot, Cleveland, Desha, Drew, Grant, Jefferson, and Lincoln.

Northern Division: Counties of Cleburne, Fulton, Independence, Izard, Jackson, Sharp, and Stone.

Jonesboro Division: Counties of Clay, Craighead, Crittenden, Greene, Lawrence, Mississippi, Poinsett, and Randolph.

Places of Holding Court: Eastern Division: Helena (501) 604-5300

Jonesboro Division: Jonesboro (870) 972-4610

Northern Division: Batesville (501) 604-5300

Pine Bluff Division: Pine Bluff (870) 536-1190

Western Division: Little Rock (501) 604-5300

Arkansas, Western District

Internet: www.arwd.uscourts.gov

Circuit: Eighth

Counties in District: El Dorado Division: Counties of Ashley, Bradley, Calhoun, Columbia, Ouachita, and Union.

Fayetteville Division: Counties of Benton, Madison, and Washington.

Fort Smith Division: Counties of Crawford, Franklin, Johnson, Logan, Polk, Scott, and Sebastian.

Harrison Division: Counties of Baxter, Boone, Carroll, Marion, Newton, and Searcy.

Hot Springs Division: Counties of Clark, Garland, Hot Springs, Montgomery, and Pike.

Texarkana Division: Counties of Hempstead, Howard, Lafayette, Little River, Miller, Nevada, and Sevier.

Places of Holding Court: El Dorado Division: El Dorado (870) 862-1202

Fayetteville Division: Fayetteville (479) 521-6980

Fort Smith Division: Fort Smith (479) 783-6833

Harrison Division: Harrison (479) 783-6833

Hot Springs Division: Hot Springs (501) 623-6411

Texarkana Division: (870) 773-3381

California, Central District

Internet: www.cacd.uscourts.gov

Circuit: Ninth

Counties in District: Counties of Los Angeles, Orange, Riverside, San Bernardino, San Luis Obispo, Santa Barbara, and Ventura.

Places of Holding Court: Eastern Division: Riverside (951) 328-4450

Southern Division: Santa Ana (714) 338-4750

Western Division: Los Angeles (213) 894-1565

California, Eastern District

Internet: www.caed.uscourts.gov

Circuit: Ninth

Counties in District: Counties of Alpine, Amador, Butte, Calaveras, Colusa, El Dorado, Fresno, Glenn, Inyo, Kern, Kings, Lassen, Madera, Mariposa, Merced, Modoc, Mono, Nevada, Placer, Plumas, Sacramento, San Joaquin, Shasta, Sierra, Siskiyou, Solano, Stanislaus, Sutter, Tehama, Trinity, Tulare, Tuolumne, Yolo, and Yuba.

Places of Holding Court: Bakersfield: (661) 326-6620

Fresno: (559) 499-5600

Redding: (530) 246-5416

Sacramento: (916) 930-4000

Yosemite: (209) 372-0320

California, Northern District

Internet: www.cand.uscourts.gov

Circuit: Ninth

Counties in District: Counties of Alameda, Contra Costa, Del Norte, Humboldt, Lake, Marin, Mendocino, Monterey, Napa, San Benito, San Francisco, San Mateo, Santa Clara, Santa Cruz, and Sonoma.

Places of Holding Court: Eureka: (707) 445-3612

Oakland: (510) 637-3530

San Francisco: (415) 522-2000

San Jose: (408) 535-5363

California, Southern District

Internet: www.casd.uscourts.gov

Circuit: Ninth

Counties in District: Counties of Imperial and San Diego.

Places of Holding Court: El Centro: (760) 339-4242

San Diego: (619) 557-5600

Colorado District

Internet: www.cod.uscourts.gov

Circuit: Tenth

Counties in District: The District comprises the entire State.

Places of Holding Court: Denver: (303) 844-3433

Connecticut District

Internet: www.ctd.uscourts.gov

Circuit: Second

Counties in District: The District comprises the entire State.

Places of Holding Court: Bridgeport: (203) 579-5861

Hartford: (860) 240-3200

New Haven: (203) 773-2140

Delaware District

Internet: www.ded.uscourts.gov

Circuit: Third

Counties in District: The District comprises the entire State.

Places of Holding Court: Wilmington: (302) 573-6170

District of Columbia District

Internet: www.dcd.uscourts.gov

Circuit: District of Columbia

Counties in District: The District comprises all of the District of Columbia.

Places of Holding Court: Washington: (202) 354-3080

Florida, Middle District
Internet: www.flmd.uscourts.gov

Circuit: Eleventh

Counties in District: Fort Myers Division: Counties of Charlotte, Collier, De Soto, Hendry, Glades, and Lee.

Jacksonville Division: Counties of Baker, Bradford, Clay, Columbia, Duval, Flagler, Hamilton, Nassau, Putnam, St. Johns, Suwannee, and Union.

Ocala Division: Counties of Citrus, Lake, Marion, and Sumter.

Orlando Division: Counties of Brevard, Orange, Osceola, Seminole, and Volusia.

Tampa Division: Counties of Hardee, Hernando, Hillsborough, Manatee, Pasco, Pinellas, Polk, and Sarasota.

Places of Holding Court: Fort Myers Division: Fort Myers (239) 461-2000

Jacksonville Division: Jacksonville (904) 549-1900

Ocala Division: Ocala (352) 369-4860

Orlando Division: Orlando (407) 835-4200

Tampa Division: Tampa (813) 301-5400

Florida, Northern District
Internet: www.flnd.uscourts.gov

Circuit: Eleventh

Counties in District: Gainesville Division: Counties of Alachua, Dixie, Gilchrist, Lafayette, and Levy.

Panama City Division: Counties of Bay, Calhoun, Gulf, Holmes, Jackson, and Washington.

Pensacola Division: Counties of Escambia, Okaloosa, Santa Rosa, and Walton.

Tallahassee Division: Counties of Franklin, Gadsden, Jefferson, Leon, Liberty, Madison, Taylor, Wakulla.

Places of Holding Court: Gainesville Division: Gainesville (352) 380-2400

Panama City Division: Panama City (850) 769-4556

Pensacola Division: Pensacola (850) 435-8440

Tallahassee Division: Tallahassee (850) 521-3501

Florida, Southern District
Internet: www.flsd.uscourts.gov

Circuit: Eleventh

Counties in District: Fort Lauderdale Division: County of Broward.

Fort Pierce Division: Counties of Highlands, Okeechobee, Indian River, St. Lucie, and Martin.

Key West Division: County of Monroe.

Miami Division: County of Dade.

West Palm Beach Division: County of Palm Beach.

Places of Holding Court: Fort Lauderdale Division: Fort Lauderdale (954) 769-5400

Fort Pierce Division: Fort Pierce (772) 467-2300

Key West Division: Key West (305) 295-8100

Miami Division: Miami (305) 523-5100

West Palm Beach Division: West Palm Beach (561) 803-3400

Georgia, Middle District
Internet: www.gamd.uscourts.gov

Circuit: Eleventh

Counties in District: Albany Division: Counties of Baker, Ben Hill, Calhoun, Crisp, Decatur, Dougherty, Early, Grady, Lee, Miller, Mitchell, Schley, Seminole, Sumter, Terrell, Turner, Webster, and Worth.

Athens Division: Counties of Clarke, Elbert, Franklin, Greene, Hart, Madison, Morgan, Oconee, Oglethorpe, and Walton.

Columbus Division: Counties of Chattahoochee, Clay, Harris, Marion, Muscogee, Quitman, Randolph, Stewart, Talbot, and Taylor.

Macon Division: Counties of Baldwin, Bibb, Bleckley, Butts, Crawford, Dooley, Hancock, Houston, Jasper, Jones, Lamar, Macon, Monroe, Peach, Pulaski, Putnam, Twiggs, Upson, Washington, Wilcox, and Wilkinson.

Valdosta Division: Counties of Berrien, Brooks, Clinch, Colquitt, Cook, Echols, Irwin, Lanier, Lowndes, Thomas, and Tift.

Places of Holding Court: Albany Division: Albany (229) 430-8432

Athens Division: Athens (706) 227-1094

Columbus Division: Columbus (706) 649-7816

Macon Division: Macon (478) 752-3497

Valdosta Division: Valdosta (229) 242-3616

Georgia, Northern District
Internet: www.gand.uscourts.gov

Circuit: Eleventh

Counties in District: Atlanta Division: Counties of Cherokee, Clayton, Cobb, DeKalb, Douglas, Fulton, Gwinnett, Henry, Newton, and Rockdale.

Gainesville Division: Counties of Banks, Barrow, Dawson, Fannin, Forsyth, Gilmer, Habersham, Hall, Jackson, Lumpkin, Pickens, Rabun, Stephens, Towns, Union, and White.

Newnan Division: Counties of Carroll, Coweta, Fayette, Haralson, Heard, Meriwether, Pike, Spalding, and Troup.

Rome Division: Counties of Bartow, Catoosa, Chattooga, Dade, Floyd, Gordon, Murray, Paulding, Polk, Walker, and Whitfield.

Places of Holding Court: Atlanta Division: Atlanta (404) 215-1660

Gainesville Division: Gainesville (678) 450-2760

Newnan Division: Newnan (678) 423-3060

Rome Division: Rome (706) 378-4060

Georgia, Southern District
Internet: www.gas.uscourts.gov

Circuit: Eleventh

Counties in District: Augusta Division: Counties of Burke, Columbia, Glascock, Jefferson, Lincoln, McDuffie, Richmond, Taliaferro, Warren, and Wilkes.

Brunswick Division: Counties of Appling, Camden, Glynn, Jeff Davis, Long, McIntosh, and Wayne.

Dublin Division: Counties of Johnson, Laurens, Montgomery, Telfair, Treutlen, and Wheeler.

Savannah Division: Counties of Bryan, Chatham, Effingham, and Liberty.

Statesboro Division: Counties of Bulloch, Candler, Emanuel, Evans, Jenkins, Screven, Tattnall and Toombs.

Waycross Division: Counties of Atkinson, Bacon, Brantley, Charlton, Coffee, Pierce, and Ware.

Places of Holding Court: Augusta Division: Augusta (706) 849-4400

Brunswick Division: Brunswick (912) 280-1330

Dublin Division: Dublin (478) 272-2121

Savannah Division: Savannah (912) 650-4020

Statesboro Division: Statesboro (912) 764-3276

Waycross Division: Waycross (912) 283-2870

Guam District
Internet: www.gud.uscourts.gov

Circuit: Ninth

Counties in District: The District comprise all of Guam.

Places of Holding Court: Hagatna: (671) 473-9100

Hawaii District
Internet: www.hid.uscourts.gov

Circuit: Ninth

Counties in District: This district includes the Hawaiian Islands, the Midway Islands, Wake Island, Johnston Island, San Island, Kingman Reef, Palmyra Island, Baker Island, Howland Island, Canton Island, Jarvis Island, and Enderbury Island.

Places of Holding Court: Honolulu: (808) 541-1300

Idaho District
Internet: www.id.uscourts.gov

Circuit: Ninth

Counties in District: Central Division: Counties of Clearwater, Idaho, Latah, Lewis, and Nez Perce.

Eastern Division: Counties of Bannock, Bear Lake, Bingham, Bonneville, Butte, Caribou, Cassia, Clark, Custer, Franklin, Fremont, Jefferson, Lemhi, Madison, Minidoka, Oneida, Power, and Teton.

Northern Division: Counties of Benewah, Bonner, Boundary, Kootenai, and Shoshone.

Southern Division: Counties of Ada, Adams, Blaine, Boise, Camas, Canyon, Elmore, Gem, Gooding, Jerome, Lincoln, Owyhee, Payette, Twin Falls, Valley, and Washington.

Places of Holding Court: Central Division: Moscow (208) 882-7612

Eastern Division: Pocatello (208) 478-4123

Northern Division: Coeur d'Alene (208) 665-6850

Southern Division: Boise (208) 334-1074

Illinois, Central District
Internet: www.ilcd.uscourts.gov

Circuit: Seventh

Counties in District: Peoria Division: Counties of Bureau, Fulton, Hancock, Knox, Livingston, Marshall, McDonough, McLean, Peoria, Putnam, Stark, Tazewell, and Woodford.

Rock Island Division: Counties of Henderson, Henry, Mercer, Rock Island, and Warren.

Springfield Division: Counties of Adams, Brown, Cass, Christian, DeWitt, Greene, Logan, Macoupin, Mason, Menard, Montgomery, Morgan, Pike, Sangamon, Schuyler, Scott, and Shelby.

Urbana Division: Counties of Champaign, Coles, Douglas, Edgar, Ford, Iroquois, Kankakee, Moultrie, Piatt, and Vermilion.

Places of Holding Court: Peoria Division: Peoria (309) 671-7117

Rock Island Division: Rock Island (309) 793-5778

Springfield Division: Springfield (217) 492-4020

Urbana Division: Urbana (217) 373-5830

Illinois, Northern District
Internet: www.ilnd.uscourts.gov

Circuit: Seventh

Counties in District: Eastern Division: Counties of Cook, Du Page, Grundy, Kane, Kendall, Lake, La Salle, and Will.

Western Division: Counties of Boone, Carroll, DeKalb, Jo Daviess, Lee, McHenry, Ogle, Stephenson, Whiteside, and Winnebago.

Places of Holding Court: Eastern Division: Chicago (312) 435-5670

Western Division: Rockford (815) 987-4354

Illinois, Southern District
Internet: www.ilsd.uscourts.gov

Circuit: Seventh

Counties in District: Benton Division: Counties of Alexander, Clark, Clay, Crawford, Cumberland, Edwards, Effingham, Franklin, Gallatin, Hamilton, Hardin, Jackson, Jasper, Jefferson, Johnson, Lawrence, Massac, Perry, Pope, Pulaski, Richland, Saline, Union, Wabash, Wayne, White, and Williamson.

East St. Louis Division: Counties of Bond, Calhoun, Clinton, Fayette, Jersey, Madison, Marion, Monroe, Randolph, St. Clair, and Washington.

Places of Holding Court: Benton Division: Benton (618) 439-7760

East St. Louis Division: East St. Louis (618) 482-9371

Indiana, Northern District
Internet: www.innd.uscourts.gov

Circuit: Seventh

Counties in District: Fort Wayne Division: Counties of Adams, Allen, Blackford, DeKalb, Grant, Huntington, Jay, LaGrange, Noble, Steuben, Wells, and Whitley.

Hammond Division: Counties of Lake and Porter.

Lafayette Division: Counties of Benton, Carroll, Jasper, Newton, Tippecanoe, Warren, and White.

South Bend Division: Counties Cass, Elkhart, Fulton, Kosciusko, LaPorte, Marshall, Miami, Pulaski, St. Joseph, Starke, and Wabash.

Places of Holding Court: Fort Wayne Division: Fort Wayne (260) 423-3000

Hammond Division: Hammond (219) 852-6500

Lafayette Division: Lafayette (765) 420-6250

South Bend Division: South Bend (574) 246-8000

Indiana, Southern District
Internet: www.insd.uscourts.gov

Circuit: Seventh

Counties in District: Evansville Division: Counties of Daviess, Dubois, Gibson, Martin, Perry, Pike, Posey, Spencer, Vanderburgh, and Warrick.

Indianapolis Division: Counties of Bartholomew, Boone, Brown, Clinton, Decatur, Delaware, Fayette, Fountain, Franklin, Hamilton, Hancock, Hendricks, Henry, Howard, Johnson, Madison, Marion, Monroe, Montgomery, Morgan, Randolph, Rush, Shelby, Tipton, Union, and Wayne.

New Albany Division: Counties of Clark, Crawford, Dearborn, Floyd, Harrison, Jackson, Jefferson, Jennings, Lawrence, Ohio, Orange, Ripley, Scott, Switzerland, and Washington.

Terre Haute Division: Counties of Clay, Greene, Knox, Owen, Parke, Putnam, Sullivan, Vermillion, and Vigo.

Places of Holding Court: Evansville Division: Evansville (812) 434-6410

Indianapolis Division: Indianapolis (317) 229-3700

New Albany Division: New Albany (812) 542-4510

Terre Haute Division: Terre Haute (812) 231-1840

Iowa, Northern District
Internet: www.iand.uscourts.gov

Circuit: Eighth

Business Description: Cedar Rapids Division: Counties of Benton, Cedar, Grundy, Hardin, Iowa, Jones, Linn, and Tama.

Central Division: Counties of Butler, Calhoun, Carroll, Cerro Gordo, Emmet, Franklin, Hamilton, Hancock, Humboldt, Kossuth, Palo Alto, Pocahontas, Webster, Winnebago, Worth, and Wright.

Eastern Division: Counties of Allamakee, Black Hawk, Bremer, Buchanan, Chickasaw, Clayton, Delaware, Dubuque, Fayette, Floyd, Howard, Jackson, Mitchell, and Winneshiek.

Western Division: Counties of Buena Vista, Cherokee, Clay, Crawford, Dickinson, Ida, Lyon, Monona, O'Brian, Osceola, Plymouth, Sac, Sioux, and Woodbury.

Places of Holding Court: Cedar Rapids: (319) 286-2300

Sioux City: (712) 233-3900

Iowa, Southern District
Internet: www.iasd.uscourts.gov

Circuit: Eighth

Counties in District: Central Division: Counties of Adair, Adams, Appanoose, Boone, Clarke, Dallas, Davis, Decatur, Greene, Guthrie, Jasper, Jefferson, Keokuk, Lucas, Madison, Mahaska, Marion, Marshall, Monroe, Polk, Poweshiek, Ringgold, Taylor, Story, Union, Wapello, Warren, and Wayne.

Eastern Division: Counties of Clinton, Des Moines, Henry, Johnson, Lee, Louisa, Muscatine, Scott, Van Buren, and Washington.

Western Division: Counties of Audubon, Cass, Fremont, Harrison, Mills, Montgomery, Page, Pottawattamie, and Shelby.

Places of Holding Court: Central Division: Des Moines (515) 284-6248

Eastern Division: Davenport (563) 884-7607

Western Division: Council Bluffs (712) 328-0283

Kansas District
Internet: www.ksd.uscourts.gov

Circuit: Tenth

Counties in District: The District comprises the entire State.

Places of Holding Court: Kansas City: (913) 735-2200

Topeka: (785) 338-5400

Wichita: (316) 315-4200

Kentucky, Eastern District
Internet: www.kyed.uscourts.gov

Circuit: Sixth

Counties in District: Counties of Anderson, Bath, Bell, Boone, Bourbon, Boyd, Boyle, Bracken, Breathitt, Campbell, Carroll, Carter, Clark, Clay, Elliott, Estill, Fayette, Fleming, Floyd, Franklin, Gallatin, Garrard, Grant, Greenup, Harlan, Harrison, Henry, Jackson, Jessamine, Johnson, Kenton, Knott, Knox, Laurel, Lawrence, Lee, Leslie, Letcher, Lewis, Lincoln, McCreary, Madison, Magoffin, Martin, Mason, Menifee, Mercer, Montgomery, Morgan, Nicholas, Owen, Owsley, Pendleton, Perry, Pike, Powell, Pulaski, Robertson, Rockcastle, Rowan, Scott, Shelby, Trimble, Wayne, Whitley, Wolfe, and Woodford.

Places of Holding Court: Ashland: (606) 329-2465

Covington: (859) 392-7925

Frankfort: (502) 223-5225

Lexington: (859) 233-2503

London: (606) 877-7910

Pikeville: (606) 437-6160

Kentucky, Western District
Internet: www.kywd.uscourts.gov

Circuit: Sixth

Counties in District: Counties of Adair, Allen, Ballard, Breckenridge, Bullitt, Butler, Caldwell, Calloway, Carlisle, Casey, Christian, Clinton, Crittenden, Cumberland, Daviess, Edmonson, Fulton, Graves, Grayson, Green, Hancock, Harding, Hart, Henderson, Hickman, Hopkins, Jefferson, Larue, Livingston, Logan, Lyon, McCracken, McClean, Marion, Marshall, Meade, Metcalfe, Monroe, Muhlenberg, Nelson, Ohio, Oldham, Russell, Simpson, Spencer, Taylor, Todd, Trigg, Union, Warren, Washington, and Webster.

Places of Holding Court: Bowling Green: (270) 393-2500

Louisville: (502) 625-3500

Owensboro: (270) 689-4400

Paducah: (270) 415-6400

Louisiana, Eastern District
Internet: www.laed.uscourts.gov

Circuit: Fifth

Counties in District: Parishes of Assumption, Jefferson, Lafourche, Orleans, Plaquemines, St. Bernard, St. Charles, St. James, St. John the Baptist, St. Tammany, Tangipahoa, Terrebonne, and Washington.

Places of Holding Court: New Orleans: (504) 589-7600

Louisiana, Middle District
Internet: www.lamd.uscourts.gov

Circuit: Fifth

Counties in District: Parishes of Ascension, East Baton Rouge, East Feliciana, Iberville, Livingston, Pointe Coupee, St. Helena, West Baton Rouge, and West Feliciana.

Places of Holding Court: Baton Rouge: (225) 389-3500

Louisiana, Western District
Internet: www.lawd.uscourts.gov

Circuit: Fifth

Counties in District: Alexandria Division: Parishes of Avoyelles, Catahoula, Concordia, Grant, LaSalle, Natchitoches, Rapides, and Winn.

Lafayette Division: Parishes of Acadia, Evangeline, Iberia, Lafayette, St. Martin, St. Mary, St. Landry, and Vermillion.

Lake Charles Division: Parishes of Allen, Beauregard, Calcasieu, Cameron, Jefferson Davis, and Vernon.

Monroe Division: Parishes of Caldwell, East Carroll, Franklin, Jackson, Lincoln, Madison, Morehouse, Ouachita, Richland, Tensas, Union, and West Carroll.

Shreveport Division: Parishes of Bienville, Bossier, Caddo, Claiborne, DeSoto, Red River, Sabine, and Webster.

Places of Holding Court: Alexandria Parishes: Alexandria (318) 473-7415

Lafayette Parishes: Lafayette (337) 593-5000

Lake Charles Parishes: Lake Charles (337) 437-3870

Monroe Parishes: Monroe (318) 322-6740

Shreveport Parishes: Shreveport (318) 676-4273

Maine District
Internet: www.med.uscourts.gov

Circuit: First

Counties in District: The District comprises the entire State.

Places of Holding Court: Bangor: (207) 945-0575

Portland: (207) 780-3356

Maryland District
Internet: www.mdd.uscourts.gov

Circuit: Fourth

Counties in District: The District comprises the entire State.

Places of Holding Court: Baltimore Division: Baltimore (410) 962-2600

Greenbelt Division: Greenbelt (301) 344-0660

Massachusetts District
Internet: www.mad.uscourts.gov

Circuit: First

Counties in District: The District comprises the entire State.

Places of Holding Court: Boston: (617) 748-9152

Springfield: (413) 785-6800

Worcester: (508) 929-9900

Michigan, Eastern District
Internet: www.mied.uscourts.gov

Circuit: Sixth

Counties in District: Northern Division: Counties of Alcona, Alpena, Arenac, Bay, Cheboygan, Clare, Crawford, Gladwin, Gratiot, Huron, Iosco, Isabella, Midland, Montmorency, Ogemaw, Oscoda, Otsego, Presque Isle, Roscommon, Saginaw, and Tuscola.

Southern Division: Counties of Genesee, Jackson, Lapeer, Lenawee, Livingston, Macomb, Monroe, Oakland, St. Clair, Sanilac, Shiawassee, Washtenaw, and Wayne.

Places of Holding Court: Northern Division: Bay City (989) 894-8800

Southern Division: Detroit (313) 234-5005; Flint (810) 341-7840

Michigan, Western District
Internet: www.miwd.uscourts.gov

Circuit: Sixth

Counties in District: Northern Division: Counties of Alger, Baraga, Chippewa, Delta, Dickinson, Gogebic, Houghton, Iron, Keweenaw, Luce, Mackinac, Marquette, Menominee, Ontonagon, and Schoolcraft.

Southern Division: Counties of Allegan, Antrim, Barry, Benzie, Berrien, Branch, Calhoun, Cass, Charlevoix, Clinton, Eaton, Emmet, Grand Traverse, Hillsdale, Ingham, Ionia, Kalamazoo, Kalkaska, Kent, Lake, Leelanau, Manistee, Mason, Mecosta, Missaukee, Montcalm, Muskegon, Newaygo, Oceana, Osceola, Ottawa, Saint Joseph, Van Buren, and Wexford.

Places of Holding Court: Northern Division: Marquette (906) 226-2021

Southern Division: Grand Rapids (616) 456-2381; Kalamazoo (269) 337-5706; Lansing (517) 377-1559

Minnesota District

Internet: www.mnd.uscourts.gov

Circuit: Eighth

Counties in District: Third Division: Counties of Chisago, Dakota, Dodge, Fillmore, Goodhue, Houston, Mower, Olmsted, Ramsey, Rice, Scott, Steele, Wabasha, Washington, and Winona.

Fourth Division: Counties of Anoka, Blue Earth, Brown, Carver, Chippewa, Cottonwood, Faribault, Freeborn, Hennepin, Isanti, Jackson, Kandiyohi, Lac Qui Parle, Le Sueur, Lincoln, Lyon, Marin, McLeod, Meeker, Murray, Nicollet, Nobles, Pipestone, Redwood, Renville, Rock, Sherburne, Sibley, Swift, Waseca, Watonwan, Wright, and Yellow Medicine.

Fifth Division: Counties of Aitkin, Benton, Carlton, Cass, Cook, Crow Wing, Itasca, Kanabec, Koochiching, Lake, Mille Lacs, Morrison, Pine, and St. Louis.

Sixth Divison: Counties of Becker, Beltrami, Big Stone, Clay, Clearwater, Douglas, Grant, Hubbard, Kittson, Lake of the Woods, Mahnomen, Marshall, Norman, Otter Tail, Pennington, Polk, Pope, Red Lake, Roseau, Stearns, Stevens, Todd, Traverse, Wadena, and Wilkin.

Places of Holding Court: Duluth: (218) 529-3500

Fergus Falls: (218) 739-5758

Minneapolis: (612) 664-5000

St. Paul: (651) 848-1100

Mississippi, Northern District

Internet: www.msnd.uscourts.gov

Circuit: Fifth

Counties in District: Aberdeen Division: Counties of Alcorn, Chickasaw, Choctaw, Clay, Itawamba, Lee, Lowndes, Monroe, Oktibbeha, Prentiss, Tishomingo, Webster, and Winston.

Greenville Division: Counties of Attala, Bolivar, Carroll, Coahoma, Grenada, Humphreys, Leflore, Montgomery, Sunflower, and Washington.

Oxford Division: Counties of Benton, Calhoun, DeSoto, Lafayette, Marshall, Panola, Pontotoc, Quitman, Tallahatchie, Tate, Tippah, Tunica, Union, and Yalobusha.

Places of Holding Court: Aberdeen Division: Aberdeen (662) 369-4952

Greenville Division: Greenville (662) 234-1971

Oxford Division: Oxford (662) 234-1971

Mississippi, Southern District

Internet: www.mssd.uscourts.gov

Circuit: Fifth

Counties in District: Eastern Division: Counties of Clarke, Covington, Forrest, Jasper, Jefferson Davis, Jones, Lamar, Lawrence, Marion, Perry, Walthall, and Wayne.

Northern Division: Counties of Copiah, Hinds, Holmes, Issaquena, Kember, Lauderdale, Leake, Madison, Neshoba, Newton, Noxubee, Rankin, Scott, Sharkey, Simpson, Smith, Warren, and Yazoo.

Southern Division: Counties of George, Greene, Hancock, Harrison, Jackson, Pearl River, and Stone.

Western Division: Counties of Adams, Amite, Claiborne, Franklin, Jefferson, Lincoln, Pike, and Wilkinson.

Places of Holding Court: Eastern Division: Hattiesburg (601) 583-2433

Northern Division: Jackson (601) 608-4000

Southern Division: Gulfport (228) 563-1700

Western Division: Natchez (601) 442-3006

Missouri, Eastern District

Internet: www.moed.uscourts.gov

Circuit: Eighth

Counties in District: Eastern Division: Counties of Crawford, Dent, Franklin, Gasconade, Jefferson, Lincoln, Maries, Phelps, St. Charles, St. Francois, St. Louis City, St. Louis County, Warren, and Washington.

Northern Division: Counties of Adair, Audrain, Chariton, Clark, Knox, Lewis, Linn, Macon, Marion, Monroe, Montgomery, Pike, Ralls, Randolph, Schuyler, Scotland, and Shelby.

Southeastern Division: Counties of Bollinger, Butler, Cape Girardeau, Carter, Dunklin, Iron, Madison, Mississippi, New Madrid, Pemiscot, Perry, Reynolds, Ripley, Scott, Shannon, Ste. Genevieve, Stoddard, and Wayne.

Places of Holding Court: Eastern Division: St. Louis (314) 244-7900

Northern Division: Hannibal (573) 221-0757

Southeastern Division: Cape Girardeau (573) 331-8800

Missouri, Western District

Internet: www.mow.uscourts.gov

Circuit: Eighth

Counties in District: Central Division: Counties of Benton, Boone, Callaway, Camden, Cole, Cooper, Hickory, Howard, Miller, Moniteau, Morgan, Osage, and Pettis.

Saint Joseph Division: Counties of Andrew, Atchison, Buchanan, Caldwell, Clinton, Daviess, De Kalb, Grundy, Harrison, Holt, Livingston, Mercer, Nodaway, Platte, Putnam, Sullivan, and Worth.

Southern Division: Counties of Cedar, Christian, Dade, Dallas, Douglas, Greene, Howell, Laclede, Oregon, Ozark, Polk, Pulaski, Taney, Texas, Webster, and Wright.

Southwestern Division: Counties of Barry, Barton, Jasper, Lawrence, McDonald, Newton, Stone, and Vernon.

Western Division: Counties of Bates, Carroll, Cass, Clay, Henry, Jackson, Johnson, Lafayette, Ray, Saline, and St. Clair.

Places of Holding Court: Jefferson City: (573) 636-4015

Kansas City: (816) 512-1800

Springfield: (417) 865-3869

Montana District

Internet: www.mtd.uscourts.gov

Circuit: Ninth

Counties in District: Billings Division: Counties of Big Horn, Carbon, Carter, Custer, Dawson, Fallon, Garfield, Golden Valley, McCone, Musselshell, Park, Petroleum, Powder River, Prairie, Richland, Rosebud, Stillwater, Sweetgrass, Treasure, Wheatland, Wibaux, and Yellowstone.

Butte Division: Counties of Beaverhead, Deer Lodge, Gallatin, Madison, and Silver Bow.

Great Falls Division: Counties of Blaine, Cascade, Chouteau, Daniels, Fergus, Glacier, Hill, Judith Basin, Liberty, Phillips, Pondera, Roosevelt, Sheridan, Teton, Toole, and Valley.

Helena Division: Counties of Broadwater, Jefferson, Lewis & Clark, Meagher, and Powell.

Missoula Division: Counties of Flathead, Granite, Lake, Lincoln, Mineral, Missoula, Ravalli, and Sanders.

Places of Holding Court: Billings Division: Billings (406) 247-7000

Butte Division: Butte (406) 497-1279

Great Falls Division: Great Falls (406) 727-1922

Helena Division: Helena (406) 441-1355

Missoula Division: Missoula (406) 542-7260

Nebraska District
Internet: www.ned.uscourts.gov

Circuit: Eighth

Counties in District: The District comprises the entire State.

Places of Holding Court: Lincoln: (402) 437-1900

Omaha: (402) 661-7350

Nevada District
Internet: www.nvd.uscourts.gov

Circuit: Ninth

Counties in District: The District comprises the entire State.

Places of Holding Court: Las Vegas: (702) 464-5400

Reno: (775) 686-5800

New Hampshire District
Internet: http://www.nhd.uscourts.gov

Circuit: First

Counties in District: The District comprises the entire State.

Places of Holding Court: Concord: (603) 225-1423

New Jersey District
Internet: www.njd.uscourts.gov

Circuit: Third

Counties in District: Camden Vicinage: Counties of Atlantic, Burlington, Camden, Cape May, Cumberland, Gloucester, and Salem.

Newark Vicinage: Counties of Bergen, Essex, Hudson, Morris, Northern-Middlesex, Passaic, Sussex, and Union.

Trenton Vicinage: Counties of Hunterdon, Mercer, Monmouth, Ocean, Somerset, Southern-Middlesex, and Warren.

Places of Holding Court: Camden: (856) 757-5021

Newark: (973) 645-3730

Trenton: (609) 989-2065

New York, Eastern District
Internet: www.nyed.uscourts.gov

Circuit: Second

Counties in District: Counties of Kings, Nassau, Queens, Richmond, and Suffolk.

Places of Holding Court: Brooklyn: (718) 613-2600

Central Islip: (631) 712-6000

New York, Northern District
Internet: www.nynd.uscourts.gov

Circuit: Second

Counties in District: Albany Division: Counties of Albany, Columbia, Greene, Rensselaer, Saratoga, Schenectady, Schoharie, Ulster, Warren, and Washington.

Binghamton Division: Counties of Broome, Chenango, Delaware, Otsego, and Tioga.

Malone/Plattsburgh Division: Counties of Clinton, Essex, and Franklin.

Syracuse Division: Counties of Cayuga, Cortland, Madison, Onondaga, Oswego, and Tompkins.

Utica Division: Counties of Fulton, Hamilton, Herkimer, Montgomery, and Oneida.

Watertown Division: Counties of Jefferson, Lewis, and St. Lawrence.

Places of Holding Court: Albany Division: Albany (518) 257-1800

Binghamton Division: Binghamton (607) 773-2893

Malone/Plattsburgh Division: Plattsburgh (518) 247-4501

Syracuse Division: Syracuse (315) 234-8500

Utica Division: Utica (315) 793-8151

New York, Southern District
Internet: www.nysd.uscourts.gov

Circuit: Second

Counties in District: Counties of Bronx, Dutchess, New York, Orange, Putnam, Rockland, Sullivan, and Westchester.

Places of Holding Court: Manhattan: (212) 805-0136

White Plains: (914) 390-4100

New York, Western District
Internet: www.nywd.uscourts.gov

Counties in District: Buffalo Division: Counties of Allegany, Cattaraugus, Chautauqua, Erie, Genesee, Niagara, Orleans, and Wyoming.

Rochester Division: Counties of Chemung, Livingston, Monroe, Ontario, Schuyler, Seneca, Steuben, Wayne, and Yates.

Places of Holding Court: Buffalo: (716) 551-1700

Rochester: (585) 613-4000

North Carolina, Eastern District
Internet: www.nced.uscourts.gov

Circuit: Fourth

Counties in District: Eastern Division: Counties of Beaufort, Carteret, Craven, Edgecombe, Greene, Halifax, Hyde, Jones, Lenoir, Martin, Pamlico, and Pitt.

Northern Division: Counties of Bertie, Camden, Chowan, Currituck, Dare, Gates, Hertford, Northampton, Pasquotank, Perquimans, Tyrrell, and Washington.

Southern Division: Counties of Bladen, Brunswick, Columbus, Duplin, New Hanover, Onslow, Pender, Robeson, and Sampson.

Western Division: Counties of Cumberland, Franklin, Granville, Harnett, Johnston, Nash, Vance, Wake, Wayne, Warren, and Wilson.

Places of Holding Court: Eastern Division: Greenville (252) 830-6009; New Bern (252) 638-8534

Southern Division: Wilmington (910) 815-4663

Western Division: Fayetteville (910) 483-9509; Raleigh (919) 645-1700

North Carolina, Middle District
Internet: www.ncmd.uscourts.gov

Circuit: Fourth

Counties in District: Counties of Alamance, Cabarrus, Caswell, Chatham, Davidson, Davie, Durham, Forsyth, Guilford, Hoke, Lee, Montgomery, Moore, Orange, Person, Randolph, Richmond, Rockingham, Rowan, Scotland, Stanly, Stokes, Surry, and Yadkin.

Places of Holding Court: Durham: (919) 425-8900

Greensboro: (336) 332-6000

Winston-Salem: (336) 734-2540

North Carolina, Western District
Internet: www.ncwd.uscourts.gov

Circuit: Fourth

Counties in District: Asheville Division: Counties of Avery, Buncombe, Burke, Cherokee, Clay, Cleveland, Graham, Haywood, Henderson, Jackson, Macon, Madison, McDowell, Mitchell, Polk, Rutherford, Swain, Transylvania, and Yancey.

Charlotte Division: Counties of Anson, Gaston, Mecklenburg, and Union.

Statesville Division: Counties of Alexander, Alleghany, Ashe, Caldwell, Catawba, Iredell, Lincoln, Watauga, and Wilkes.

Places of Holding Court: Asheville Division: Asheville (828) 771-7200

Charlotte Division: Charlotte (704) 350-7400

Statesville Division: Statesville (704) 883-1000

North Dakota District
Internet: www.ndd.uscourts.gov

Circuit: Eighth

Counties in District: Northeastern Division: Counties of Benson, Cavalier, Grand Forks, Nelson, Pembina, Ramsey, Traill, Towner, and Walsh.

Northwestern Division: Counties of Bottineau, Burke, Divide, McHenry, McKenzie, Mountrail, Pierce, Renville, Rolette, Sheridan, Ward, Wells, and Williams.

Southeastern Division: Counties of Barnes, Cass, Dickey, Eddy, Foster, Griggs, LaMoure, Ransom, Richland, Sargent, Steele, and Stutsman.

Southwestern Division: Counties of Adams, Billings, Bowman, Burleigh, Dunn, Emmons, Golden Valley, Grant, Hettinger, Kidder, Logan, McIntosh, McLean, Mercer, Morton, Oliver, Sioux, Slope, and Stark.

Places of Holding Court: Northeastern Division: Grand Forks (701) 297-7000

Northwestern Division: Minot (701) 530-2300

Southeastern Division: Fargo (701) 297-7000

Southwestern Division: Bismarck (701) 530-2300

Northern Mariana Islands District
Internet: www.nmid.uscourts.gov

Circuit: Ninth

Counties in District: The District comprises all of the Mariana Islands chain except for the island of Guam.

Places of Holding Court: Saipan: (670) 236-2902

Ohio, Northern District
Internet: www.ohnd.uscourts.gov

Circuit: Sixth

Counties in District: Eastern Division: Counties of Ashland, Ashtabula, Carroll, Columbiana, Crawford, Cuyahoga, Geauga, Holmes, Lake, Lorain, Mahoning, Medina, Portage, Richland, Stark, Summit, Trumbull, Tuscarawas, and Wayne.

Western Division: Counties of Allen, Auglaize, Defiance, Erie, Fulton, Hancock, Hardin, Henry, Huron, Lucas, Marion, Mercer, Ottawa, Paulding, Putnam, Sandusky, Seneca, Van Wert, Williams, Wood, and Wyandot.

Places of Holding Court: Eastern Division: Akron (330) 252-6000; Cleveland (216) 357-7000; Youngstown (330) 884-7400

Western Division: Toledo (419) 213-5500

Ohio, Southern District
Internet: www.ohsd.uscourts.gov

Circuit: Sixth

Counties in District: Eastern Division: Counties of Athens, Belmont, Coshocton, Delaware, Fairfield, Fayette, Franklin, Gallia, Guernsey, Harrison, Hocking, Jackson, Jefferson, Knox, Licking, Logan, Madison, Meigs, Monroe, Morgan, Morrow, Muskingum, Noble, Perry, Pickaway, Pike, Ross, Union, Vinton, and Washington.

Western Division: Counties of Adams, Brown, Butler, Champaign, Clark, Clermont, Clinton, Darke, Greene, Hamilton, Highland, Lawrence, Miami, Montgomery, Preble, Scioto, Shelby, and Warren.

Places of Holding Court: Eastern Division: Columbus (614) 719-3000

Western Division: Cincinnati (513) 564-7500; Dayton (937) 512-1400

Oklahoma, Eastern District
Internet: www.oked.uscourts.gov

Circuit: Tenth

Counties in District: Counties of Adair, Atoka, Bryan, Carter, Cherokee, Choctaw, Coal, Haskell, Hughes, Johnston, Latimer, Leflore, Love, McCurtain, McIntosh, Marshall, Murray, Muskogee, Okfuskee, Okmulgee, Pittsburg, Pontotoc, Pushmataha, Seminole, Sequoyah, and Wagoner.

Places of Holding Court: Muskogee: (918) 684-7920

Oklahoma, Northern District
Internet: www.oknd.uscourts.gov

Circuit: Tenth

Counties in District: Counties of Craig, Creek, Delaware, Mayes, Nowata, Osage, Ottawa, Pawnee, Rogers, Tulsa, and Washington.

Places of Holding Court: Tulsa: (918) 699-4700

Oklahoma, Western District
Internet: www.okwd.uscourts.gov

Circuit: Tenth

Counties in District: Counties of Alfalfa, Beaver, Beckham, Blaine, Caddo, Canadian, Cimarron, Cleveland, Comanche, Cotton, Custer, Dewey, Ellis, Garfield, Garvin, Grady, Grant, Greer, Harmon, Harper, Jackson, Jefferson, Kay, Kingfisher, Kiowa, Lincoln, Logan, Major, McClain, Noble, Oklahoma, Payne, Pottawatomie, Roger Mills, Stephens, Texas, Tillman, Washita, Wood, and Woodward.

Places of Holding Court: Oklahoma City: (405) 609-5000

Oregon District
Internet: www.ord.uscourts.gov

Circuit: Ninth

Counties in District: Eugene Division: Counties of Benton, Coos, Deschutes, Douglas, Lane, Lincoln, Linn, and Marion.

Medford Division: Counties of Curry, Jackson, Josephine, Klamath, and Lake.

Pendleton Division: Counties of Baker, Crook, Gilliam, Grant, Harney, Malheur, Morrow, Sherman, Umatilla, Union, Wallowa, and Wheeler.

Portland Division: Counties of Clackamas, Clatsop, Columbia, Hood River, Jefferson, Multnomah, Polk, Tillamook, Wasco, Washington, and Yamhill.

Places of Holding Court: Eugene: (541) 431-4100

Medford: (541) 608-8777

Portland (503) 326-8000

Pennsylvania, Eastern District
Internet: www.paed.uscourts.gov

Circuit: Third

Counties in District: Counties of Berks, Bucks, Chester, Delaware, Lancaster, Lehigh, Montgomery, Northampton, and Philadelphia.

Places of Holding Court: Allentown: (610) 434-3896

Philadelphia: (215) 597-7704

Pennsylvania, Middle District
Internet: www.pamd.uscourts.gov

Circuit: Third

Counties in District: Harrisburg Division: Counties of Adams, Cumberland, Dauphin, Franklin, Fulton, Huntingdon, Juanita, Lebanon, Mifflin, Perry, and York

Scranton Division: Counties of Bradford, Carbon, Lackawanna, Luzerne, Monroe, Pike, Schuylkill, Susquehanna, Wayne, and Wyoming.

Williamsport Division: Counties of Cameron, Centre, Clinton, Columbia, Lycoming, Montour, Northumberland, Potter, Snyder, Sullivan, Tioga, and Union.

Places of Holding Court: Harrisburg Division: Harrisburg (717) 221-3920

Scranton Division: Scranton (570) 207-5600

Williamsport Division: Williamsport (570) 323-6380

Pennsylvania, Western District
Internet: www.pawd.uscourts.gov

Circuit: Third

Counties in District: Erie Division: Counties of Crawford, Elk, Erie, Forest, McKean, Venango, and Warren.

Johnstown Division: Counties of Bedford, Blair, Cambria, Clearfield, and Somerset.

Pittsburgh Division: Counties of Allegheny, Armstrong, Beaver, Butler, Clarion, Fayette, Greene, Indiana, Jefferson, Lawrence, Mercer, Washington, and Westmoreland.

Places of Holding Court: Erie Division: Erie (814) 464-9600

Johnstown Division: Johnstown (814) 533-4504

Pittsburgh Division: Pittsburgh (412) 208-7500

Puerto Rico District
Internet: www.prd.uscourts.gov

Circuit: First

Counties in District: The District comprises the entire Commonwealth.

Places of Holding Court: San Juan: (787) 772-3000

Rhode Island District
Internet: www.rid.uscourts.gov

Circuit: First

Counties in District: The District comprises the entire State.

Places of Holding Court: Providence: (401) 752-7200

South Carolina District
Internet: www.scd.uscourts.gov

Circuit: Fourth

Counties in District: Aiken Division: Counties of Aiken, Allendale, and Barnwell.

Anderson Division: Counties of Anderson, Oconee, and Pickens.

Beaufort Division: Counties of Beaufort, Hampton, and Jasper.

Charleston Division: Counties of Berkeley, Charleston, Clarendon, Colleton, Dorchester, and Georgetown.

Columbia Division: Counties of Kershaw, Lee, Lexington, Richland, and Sumter.

Florence Division: Counties of Chesterfield, Carlington, Dillon, Florence, Horry, Marion, Marlboro, and Williamsburg.

Greenville Division: Counties of Greenville and Laurens. Greenwood Division: Abbeville, Edgefield, Greenwood, McCormick, Newberry, and Saluda.

Orangeburg Division: Counties of Bamberg, Calhoun, and Orangeburg.

Rock Hill Division: Counties of Chester, Fairfield, Lancaster, and York.

Spartanburg Division: Counties of Chrokee, Spartanburg, and Union.

Places of Holding Court: Aiken Division: Aiken (803) 648-6896

Anderson Division: Anderson (864) 241-2700

Beaufort Division: Beaufort (843) 521-2088

Charleston Division: Charleston (843) 579-1401

Columbia Division: Columbia (803) 765-5816

Florence Division: Florence (843) 676-3820

Greenville Division: Greenville (864) 241-2700

Greenwood Division: Greenville (864) 241-2700

Orangeburg Division: Aiken (803) 648-6896

Rock Hill Division: Columbia (803) 765-5816

Spartanburg Division: Greenville (864) 241-2700

South Dakota District

Internet: www.sdd.uscourts.gov

Circuit: Eighth

Counties in District: Central Division: Counties of Buffalo, Dewey, Faulk, Gregory, Haakon, Hand, Hughes, Hyde, Jerauld, Jones, Lyman, Mellette, Potter, Stanley, Sully, Todd, Tripp, and Ziebach.

Northern Division: Counties of Brown, Campbell, Clark, Codington, Corson, Day, Deuel, Edmunds, Grant, Hamlin, McPherson, Marshall, Roberts, Spink, and Walworth.

Southern Division: Counties of Aurora, Beadle, Bon Homme, Brookings, Brule, Charles Mix, Clay, Davison, Douglas, Hanson, Hutchinson, Kingsbury, Lake, Lincoln, McCook, Miner, Minnehaha, Moody, Sanborn, Turner, Union, and Yankton.

Western Division: Counties of Bennett, Butte, Custer, Fall River, Harding, Jackson, Lawrence, Meade, Pennington, Perkins, and Shannon.

Places of Holding Court: Central Division: Pierre (605) 945-4600

Northern Division: Aberdeen (605) 377-2600

Southern Division: Sioux City (605) 330-6600

Western Division: Rapid City (605) 399-6000

Tennessee, Eastern District

Internet: www.tned.uscourts.gov

Circuit: Sixth

Counties in District: Chattanooga Division: Counties of Bledsoe, Bradley, Hamilton, Marion, McMinn, Meigs, Polk, Rhea, and Sequatchie.

Greenville Division: Counties of Carter, Cocke, Greene, Hamblen, Hancock, Hawkins, Johnson, Sullivan, Unicoi, and Washington.

Knoxville Division: Counties of Anderson, Blount, Campbell, Claiborne, Grainger, Jefferson, Knox, Loudon, Monroe, Morgan, Roane, Scott, Sevier, and Union.

Winchester Division: Counties of Bedford, Coffee, Franklin, Grundy, Lincoln, Moore, Van Buren, and Warren.

Places of Holding Court: Chattanooga: (423) 752-5200

Greenville: (423) 639-3105

Knoxville: (865) 545-4228

Winchester: (931) 967-1444

Tennessee, Middle District

Internet: www.tnmd.uscourts.gov

Circuit: Sixth

Counties in District: Columbia Division: Counties of Giles, Hickman, Lawrence, Lewis, Marshall, Maury, and Wayne.

Nashville Division: Counties of Cannon, Cheatham, Davidson, Dickson, Houston, Humphreys, Montgomery, Robertson, Rutherford, Stewart, Sumner, Trousdale, Williamson, and Wilson.

Northeastern Division: Counties of Clay, Cumberland, DeKalb, Fentress, Jackson, Macon, Overton, Pickett, Putnam, Smith, and White.

Places of Holding Court: Columbia Division: (615) 736-5498

Nashville Division: (615) 736-5498

Northeastern Division: (615) 736-5498

Tennessee, Western District

Internet: www.tnwd.uscourts.gov

Circuit: Sixth

Counties in District: Eastern Division: Counties of Benton, Carroll, Chester, Crockett, Decatur, Dyer, Gibson, Hardeman, Hardin, Haywood, Henderson, Henry, Lake, McNairy, Madison, Obion, Perry, and Weakley.

Western Division: Counties of Fayette, Lauderdale, Shelby, and Tipton.

Places of Holding Court: Eastern Division: Jackson (731) 421-9200

Western Division: Memphis (901) 495-1200

Texas, Eastern District

Internet: www.txed.uscourts.gov

Circuit: Fifth

Counties in District: Beaumont Division: Counties of Hardin, Jasper, Jefferson, Liberty, Newton, and Orange.

Lufkin Division: Counties of Angelina, Houston, Nacogdoches, Polk, Sabine, Shelby, San Augustine, Trinity, and Tyler.

Marshall Division: Counties of Camp, Cass, Harrison, Marion, Morris, and Upshur.

Sherman Division: Counties of Collin, Cooke, Denton, Grayson, Delta, Fannin, Hopkins, and Lamar.

Texarkana Division: Counties of Bowie, Franklin, Titus, and Red River.

Tyler Division: Counties of Anderson, Cherokee, Gregg, Henderson, Panola, Rains, Rusk, Smith, Van Zandt, and Wood.

Places of Holding Court: Beaumont Division: Beaumont (409) 654-7000

Lufkin Division: Lufkin (936) 632-2739

Marshall Division: Marshall (903) 935-2912

Sherman Division: Sherman (903) 892-2921

Texarkana Division: Texarkana (903) 794-8561

Tyler Division: Tyler (903) 590-1000

Texas, Northern Division

Internet: www.txnd.uscourts.gov

Circuit: Fifth

Counties in District: Abilene Division: Counties of Callahan, Eastland, Fisher, Haskell, Howard, Jones, Mitchell, Nolan, Shackelford, Stephens, Stonewall, Taylor, and Throckmorton.

Amarillo Division: Counties of Armstrong, Briscoe, Carson, Castro, Childress, Collingsworth, Dallam, Deaf Smith, Donley, Gray, Hall, Hansford, Hartley, Hemphill, Hutchinson, Lipscomb, Moore, Ochiltree, Oldham, Parmer, Potter, Randall, Roberts, Sherman, Swisher, and Wheeler.

Dallas Division: Counties of Dallas, Ellis, Hunt, Johnson, Kaufman, Navarro, and Rockwall.

Fort Worth Division: Counties of Comanche, Erath, Hood, Jack, Palo Pinto, Parker, Tarrant, and Wise.

Lubbock Division: Counties of Bailey, Borden, Cochran, Crosby, Dawson, Dickens, Floyd, Gaines, Garza, Hale, Hockley, Kent, Lamb, Lubbock, Lynn, Motley, Scurry, Terry, and Yoakum.

San Angelo Division: Counties of Brown, Coke, Coleman, Concho, Crockett, Glasscock, Irion, Menard, Mills, Reagan, Runnels, Schleicher, Sterling, Sutton, and Tom Green.

Wichita Falls Division: Counties of Archer, Baylor, Clay, Cottle, Foard, Hardeman, King, Knox, Montague, Wichita, Wilbarger, and Young.

Places of Holding Court: Abilene Division: Abilene (325) 677-6311

Amarillo Division: Amarillo (806) 468-3800

Dallas Division: Dallas (214) 753-2200

Fort Worth Division: Fort Worth (817) 850-6600

Lubbock Division: Lubbock (806) 472-1900

San Angelo Division: San Angelo (325) 655-4506

Wichita Falls Division: Wichita Falls (940) 767-1902

Texas, Southern District

Internet: www.txs.uscourts.gov

Circuit: Fifth

Counties in District: Brownsville Division: Counties of Cameron and Willacy.

Corpus Christi Division: Counties of Aransas, Bee, Brooks, Duval, Jim Wells, Kenedy, Kleberg, Live Oak, Nueces, and San Patricio.

Galveston Division: Counties of Brazoria, Chambers, Galveston, and Matagorda.

Houston Division: Counties of Austin, Brazos, Colorado, Fayette, Fort Bend, Grimes, Harris, Madison, Montgomery, San Jacinto, Walker, Waller, and Wharton.

Laredo Division: Counties of Jim Hogg, La Salle, McMullen, Webb, and Zapata.

McAllen Division: Counties of Hidalgo and Starr.

Victoria Division: Counties of Calhoun, DeWitt, Goliad, Jackson, Lavaca, Refugio, and Victoria.

Places of Holding Court: Brownsville Division: Brownsville (956) 548-2500

Corpus Christi Division: Corpus Christi (361) 888-3142

Galveston Division: Galveston (409) 766-3530

Houston Division : Houston (713) 250-5500

Laredo Division: Laredo (956) 723-3542

McAllen Division: McAllen (956) 618-8065

Victoria Division: Victoria (361) 788-5000

Texas, Western District

Internet: www.txwd.uscourts.gov

Circuit: Fifth

Counties in District: Austin Division: Counties of Bastrop, Blanco, Burleson, Burnet, Caldwell, Gillespie, Hays, Kimble, Lampasas, Lee, Llano, Mason, McCulloch, San Saba, Travis, Washington, and Williamson.

Del Rio Division: Counties of Edwards, Kinney, Maverick, Terrell, Uvalde, Val Verde, and Zavala.

El Paso Division: Counties of El Paso and Hudspeth.

Midland-Odessa Division: Counties of Andrews, Crane, Ector, Martin, Midland, and Upton.

Pecos Division: Counties of Brewster, Culberson, Jeff Davis, Loving, Pecos, Presidio, Reeves, Ward, and Winkler.

San Antonio Division: Counties of Atascosa, Bandera, Bexar, Comal, Dimmit, Frio, Gonzales, Guadalupe, Kames, Kendall, Kerr, Medina, Real, and Wilson.

Waco Division: Counties of Bell, Bosque, Coryell, Falls, Freestone, Hamilton, Hill, Leon, Limestone, McLennan, Milam, Robertson, and Somervell.

Places of Holding Court: Austin Division: Austin (512) 916-5896

Del Rio Division: Del Rio (830) 703-2054

El Paso Division: El Paso (915) 534-6725

Midland-Odessa Division: Midland (432) 686-4001

Pecos Division: Pecos (432) 445-4228

San Antonio Division: San Antonio (210) 472-6550

Waco Division: Waco (254) 750-1501

Utah District

Internet: www.utd.uscourts.gov

Circuit: Tenth

Counties in District: Central Division: Counties of Beaver, Carbon, Daggett, Duchesne, Emery, Garfield, Grand, Iron, Juab, Kane, Millard, Piute, Salt Lake, San Juan, Sanpete, Sevier, Summit, Tooele, Uintah, Utah, Wasatch, Washington, and Wayne.

Northern Division: Counties of Box Elder, Cache, Davis, Morgan, Rich, and Weber.

Places of Holding Court: Salt Lake City: (801) 524-6100

Vermont District

Internet: www.vtd.uscourts.gov

Circuit: Second

Counties in District: The District comprises the entire State.

Places of Holding Court: Brattleboro: (802) 254-0250

Burlington: (802) 951-6301

Rutland: (802) 773-0245

Virgin Islands District

Internet: www.vid.uscourts.gov

Circuit: Third

Counties in District: The District comprises all of the Virgin Islands.

Places of Holding Court: St. Croix: (340) 718-1130

St. Thomas/St. John: (340) 774-0640

Virginia, Eastern District

Internet: www.vaed.uscourts.gov

Circuit: Fourth

Counties in District: Alexandria Division: Counties of Arlington, Fairfax, Fauquier, Loudoun, Prince William, and Stafford.

Newport News Division: Counties of Gloucester, James City, Matthews, and York.

Norfolk Division: Counties of Accomack, Isle of Wight, Northampton, and Southampton.

Richmond Division: Counties of Amelia, Brunswick, Caroline, Charles City, Chesterfield, Dinwiddie, Essex, Goochland, Greensville, Hanover, Henrico, King and Queen, King William, Lancaster, Lunenburg, Mecklenburg, Middlesex, New Kent, Northumberland, Nottoway, Powhatan, Prince Edward, Prince George, Richmond, Spotsylvania, Surry, Sussex, and Westmoreland.

Places of Holding Court: Alexandria Division: Alexandria (703) 299-2107

Newport News Division: Newport News (787) 247-0784

Norfolk Division: Norfolk (757) 222-7499

Richmond Division: Richmond (804) 916-2200

Virginia, Western District

Internet: www.vawd.uscourts.gov

Circuit: Fourth

Counties in District: Abingdon Division: Counties of Buchanan, Russell, Smyth, Tazewell, and Washington.

Big Stone Gap Division: Counties of Dickenson, Lee, Scott, and Wise.

Charlottesville Division: Counties of Albemarle, Culpeper, Fluvanna, Greene, Louisa, Madison, Nelson, Orange, and Rappahannock.

Danville Division: Counties of Charlotte, Halifax, Henry, Patrick, and Pittsylvania.

Harrisonburg Division: Counties of Augusta, Bath, Clarke, Frederick, Highland, Page, Rockingham, Shenandoah, and Warren.

Lynchburg Division: Counties of Amherst, Appomattox, Bedford, Buckingham, Campbell, Cumberland, and Rockbridge.

Roanoke Division: Counties of Alleghany, Bland, Botetourt, Carroll, Craig, Floud, Franklin, Giles, Grayson, Montgomery, Pulaski, Roanoke, and Wythe.

Places of Holding Court: Abingdon Division: Abingdon (276) 628-5116

Big Stone Gap Division: Big Stone Gap (276) 523-3557

Charlottesville Division: Charlottesville (434) 296-9284

Danville Division: Danville (434) 793-7147

Harrisonburg Division: Harrisonburg (540) 434-3181

Lynchburg Division: Lynchburg (434) 846-0842

Roanoke Division: Roanoke (540) 857-5180

Washington, Eastern District

Internet: www.waed.uscourts.gov

Circuit: Ninth

Counties in District: Richland Division: Counties of Benton, Franklin, and Walla Walla.

Spokane Division: Counties of Adams, Asotin, Chelan, Columbia, Douglas, Ferry, Garfield, Grant, Lincoln, Okanagan, Pend Oreille, Spokane, Stevens, and Whitman.

Yakima Division: Counties of Kittitas, Klickitat, and Yakima.

Places of Holding Court: Richland Division: Richland (509) 943-8170

Spokane Division: Spokane (509) 458-3400

Yakima Division: Yakima (509) 573-6600

Washington, Western District

Internet: www.wawd.uscourts.gov

Circuit: Ninth

Counties in District: Seattle Division: Counties of Island, King, San Juan, Skagit, Snohomish, and Whatcom.

Tacoma Division: Counties of Clallam, Clark, Cowlitz, Grays Harbor, Jefferson, Kitsap, Lewis, Mason, Pacific, Pierce, Skamania, Thurston, and Wahkiakum.

Places of Holding Court: Seattle Division: Seattle (206) 370-8400

Tacoma Division: Tacoma (253) 882-3800

West Virginia, Northern District

Internet: www.wvnd.uscourts.gov

Circuit: Fourth

Counties in District: Clarksburg Division: Counties of Braxton, Calhoun, Doddridge, Gilmer, Harrison, Marion, Monongalia, Pleasants, Preston, Ritchie, and Taylor.

Elkins Division: Counties of Barbour, Grant, Hardy, Lewis, Pendleton, Pocahontas, Randolph, Tucker, and Upshur.

Martinsburg Division: Counties of Berkeley, Hampshire, Jefferson, Mineral, and Morgan.

Wheeling Division: Counties of Brooke, Hancock, Marshall, Ohio, Tyler, and Wetzel.

Places of Holding Court: Clarksburg Division: Clarksburg (304) 622-8513

Elkins Division: Elkins (304) 636-1445

Martinsburg Division: Martinsburg (304) 267-8225

Wheeling Division: Wheeling (304) 232-0011

West Virginia, Southern Division
Internet: www.wvsd.uscourts.gov

Circuit: Fourth

Counties in District: Beckley Division: Counties of Greenbrier, Raleigh, Summer, and Wyoming.

Bluefield Division: Counties of Mercer, McDowell, and Monroe.

Charleston Division: Counties of Boone, Fayette, Kanawha, Logan, Mingo, Clay, Jackson, Lincoln, Nicholas, Roane, Wirt and Wood.

Huntington Division: Counties of Cabell, Mason, Putnam, and Wayne.

Places of Holding Court: Beckley Division: Beckley (304) 253-7481

Bluefield Division: Bluefield (304) 327-9798

Charleston Division: Charleston (304) 347-3000

Huntington Division: Huntington (304) 529-5588

Wisconsin, Eastern District
Internet: www.wied.uscourts.gov

Circuit: Seventh

Counties in District: Green Bay Division: Counties of Brown, Calumet, Door, Florence, Forest, Kewaunee, Langlade, Manitowoc, Marinette, Menominee, Oconto, Outagamie, Shawano, Waupaca, Waushara, and Winnebago.

Milwaukee Division: Counties of Fond de Lac, Green Lake, Kenosha, Marquette, Milwaukee, Ozaukee, Racine, Sheboygan, Walworth, Washington, and Waukesha.

Places of Holding Court: Green Bay Division: Green Bay (920) 884-3720

Milwaukee Division: Milwaukee (414) 297-3372

Wisconsin, Western District
Internet: www.wiwd.uscourts.gov

Circuit: Seventh

Counties in District: Counties of Adams, Ashland, Barron, Bayfield, Buffalo, Burnett, Chippewa, Clark, Columbia, Crawford, Dane, Douglas, Dunn, Eau Claire, Grant, Green, Iowa, Iron, Jackson, Jefferson, Juneau, La Crosse, Lafayette, Lincoln, Marathon, Monroe, Oneida, Pepin, Pierce, Polk, Portage, Price, Richland, Rock, Rusk, Sauk, St. Croix, Sawyer, Taylor, Trempealeau, Vernon, Vilas, Washburn, and Wood.

Places of Holding Court: Madison: (608) 264-5156

Wyoming District
Internet: www.wyd.uscourts.gov

Circuit: Tenth

Counties in District: The District comprises the entire State.

Places of Holding Court: Casper: (307) 232-2620

Cheyenne: (307) 433-2120

Jackson: (307) 733-4126

Mammoth: (307) 344-2569

U.S. (Bankruptcy) Trustees

United States (Bankruptcy) Trustees

United States Trustees, who operate nationwide, supervise the administration of bankruptcy cases, including Chapter 7 (liquidation), Chapter 11 (reorganization), Chapter 12 (family farmers), and Chapter 13 (wage earner plans). A listing of regional and field offices of the U.S. Trustee Program (28 USC 586) is given below.

There are 21 regional offices in the U.S. Trustee Program, each with a U.S. Trustee in charge and 66 field offices, most with an Assistant U.S. Trustee in charge. The U.S. Trustees job is to assist the court in bringing parties together, promoting full disclosure of relevant information, and watching for instances of impropriety or overreaching. U.S. Trustees are appointed for five-year terms by the U.S. Attorney General.

Executive Office for United States Trustees [EOUST]

441 G Street, NW, Suite 6150, Washington, DC 20530
Tel: (202) 307-1391 Fax: (202) 307-0672
Internet: www.justice.gov/ust

The United States Trustee Program is a component of the Department of Justice that seeks to promote the efficiency and protect the integrity of the Federal bankruptcy system. To further the public interest in the just, speedy and economical resolution of cases filed under the Bankruptcy Code, the Program monitors the conduct of bankruptcy parties and private estate trustees, oversees related administrative functions, and acts to ensure compliance with applicable laws and procedures. It also identifies and helps investigate bankruptcy fraud and abuse in coordination with United States Attorneys, the Federal Bureau of Investigation, and other law enforcement agencies.

National Bankruptcy Training Institute
National Advocacy Center, 1620 Pendleton Street, Columbia, SC 29201
Tel: (803) 705-5131 Fax: (803) 705-5305

Chief **Scott A. Farrow** .... (803) 705-5131
    E-mail: scott.a.farrow@usdoj.gov

Region 1
John W. McCormack Post Office and Courthouse, 5 Post Office Square, 10th Floor, Suite 1000, Boston, MA 02109
Tel: (617) 788-0400 Fax: (617) 565-6368
Internet: www.usdoj.gov/ust/r01/index.htm

Areas Covered: ME, MA, NH, RI

U.S. Trustee **William K. Harrington** .... (617) 788-0440
    E-mail: william.k.harrington@usdoj.gov

Boston (MA) Field Office
John W. McCormack Post Office and Courthouse, 5 Post Office Square, 10th Floor, Suite 1000, Boston, MA 02109
Tel: (617) 788-0400 Fax: (617) 565-6368

Assistant U.S. Trustee **John P. Fitzgerald III** .... (617) 788-0401
    E-mail: john.p.fitzgerald@usdoj.gov

Manchester (NH) Field Office
1000 Elm Street, Suite 605, Manchester, NH 03101
Tel: (603) 666-7908 Fax: (603) 666-7913

Assistant U.S. Trustee **Geraldine L. Karonis** .... (603) 666-7908
    E-mail: geraldine.l.karonis@usdoj.gov

Executive Office for United States Trustees [EOUST] *continued*

Portland (ME) Field Office
537 Congress Street, Room 303, Portland, ME 04101
Tel: (207) 780-3564 Fax: (207) 780-3568

Assistant U.S. Trustee **Stephen G. Morrell** ..... (207) 780-3564 ext. 205
    E-mail: stephen.g.morrell@usda.gov

Providence (RI) Field Office
One Exchange Terrace, Suite 431, Providence, RI 02903
Tel: (401) 528-5551 Fax: (401) 528-5163

Assistant U.S. Trustee **Gary L. Donahue** .... (401) 528-5551 ext. 100
    E-mail: gary.l.donahue@usdoj.gov

Worcester (MA) Field Office
446 Main Street, 14th Floor, Worcester, MA 01608
Tel: (508) 793-0555 Fax: (508) 793-0558

Assistant U.S. Trustee **Richard T. King** .... (508) 793-0555
    E-mail: richard.t.king@usdoj.gov

Region 2
201 Varick St, Suite 1006, New York, NY 10014
Tel: (212) 510-0500 Fax: (212) 668-2256 Fax: (212) 668-2255
Internet: www.usdoj.gov/ust/r02/index.htm

Areas Covered: CT, NY, VT

U.S. Trustee **William K. Harrington** .... (212) 510-0500 ext. 207
    E-mail: william.harrington@usdoj.gov

Albany (NY) District Office
74 Chapel Street, Suite 200, Albany, NY 12207
Tel: (518) 434-4553 Fax: (518) 434-4459

Assistant U.S. Trustee **Lisa M. Penpraze** .... (518) 434-4553
    E-mail: lisa.penpraze@usdoj.gov

Brooklyn (NY) District Office
201 Varick St, Room 1006, New York, NY 10014
Tel: (212) 510-0500 Fax: (212) 668-2255

Assistant U.S. Trustee **Alicia M. Leonhard** ..... (212) 510-0500 ext. 218
    E-mail: alicia.m.leonhard@usdoj.gov

Buffalo (NY) District Office
300 Pearl Street, Suite 401, Buffalo, NY 14202
Tel: (716) 551-5541 Fax: (716) 551-5560

Assistant U.S. Trustee **Joseph W. Allen** .... (716) 551-5541 ext. 231
    E-mail: joseph.w.allen@usdoj.gov

Central Islip (NY) District Office
560 Federal Plaza, Suite 560, Central Islip, NY 11722-4456
Tel: (631) 715-7800 Fax: (631) 715-7777

Assistant U.S. Trustee **Christine H. Black** ...... (631) 715-7800 ext. 228
    E-mail: christine.h.black@usdoj.gov

New Haven (CT) District Office
150 Court Street, Room 302, New Haven, CT 06510-2055
Tel: (203) 773-2210 Fax: (203) 773-2217

Assistant U.S. Trustee **Kim McCabe** .... (203) 773-2210 ext. 233
    E-mail: kim.mccabe@usdoj.gov

Manhattan (NY) District Office
201 Varick St, Suite 1006, New York, NY 10014
Tel: (212) 510-0500 Fax: (212) 668-2255

Assistant U.S. Trustee **Linda A. Riffkin** .... (212) 510-0500 ext. 233
    E-mail: linda.riffkin@usdoj.gov

(continued on next page)

Executive Office for United States Trustees [EOUST] *continued*

Rochester (NY) District Office
100 State Street, Room 609, Rochester, NY 14614
Tel: (585) 263-5812   Fax: (585) 263-5862

Assistant U.S. Trustee
  Kathleen Dunivin Schmitt . . . . (585) 263-5812 ext. 29
  E-mail: kathleen.d.schmitt@usdoj.gov

Utica (NY) District Office
10 Broad Street, Room 105, Utica, NY 13501
Tel: (315) 793-8191   Fax: (315) 793-8133

Assistant U.S. Trustee **Guy A. Van Baalen** . . . .(315) 793-8191
  E-mail: guy.a.vanbaalen@usdoj.gov

Region 3
833 Chestnut Street, Suite 500, Philadelphia, PA 19107
Tel: (215) 597-4411   Fax: (215) 597-5795
Internet: www.usdoj.gov/ust/r03/index.htm

Areas Covered: DE, NJ, PA

U.S. Trustee (Acting) **Andrew R. "Andy" Vara** . . . .(215) 597-4411
  E-mail: andy.vara@usdoj.gov

Harrisburg (PA) Field Office
228 Walnut Street, Suite 1190, Harrisburg, PA 17101
P.O. Box 969, Harrisburg, PA 17108-0969
Tel: (717) 221-4515   Fax: (717) 221-4554

Assistant U.S. Trustee **(Vacant)** . . . . (717) 221-4515

Newark (NJ) Field Office
One Newark Center, Suite 2100, Newark, NJ 07102
Tel: (973) 645-3014   Fax: (973) 645-5993

Assistant U.S. Trustee **Martha Hildebrandt** . . . . (973) 645-5912
  E-mail: martha.hildebrandt@usdoj.gov

Philadelphia (PA) Field Office
833 Chestnut Street, Suite 500, Philadelphia, PA 19107
Tel: (215) 597-4411   Fax: (215) 597-5795

Assistant U.S. Trustee **Frederic J. Baker** . . . .(215) 597-4411
  E-mail: frederic.j.baker@usdoj.gov

Pittsburgh (PA) Field Office
1001 Liberty Avenue, Suite 970, Pittsburgh, PA 15222
Tel: (412) 644-4756   Fax: (412) 644-4785

Assistant U.S. Trustee **Joseph S. Sisca** . . . . (412) 644-4756
  E-mail: joseph.s.sisca@usdoj.gov

Wilmington (DE) Field Office
844 King Street, Lockbox #35, Suite 2207, Wilmington, DE 19801
Tel: (302) 573-6491   Fax: (302) 573-6497

Assistant U.S. Trustee **Thomas Patrick Tinker** . . . .(302) 573-6493
  E-mail: thomas.p.tinker@usdoj.gov

Region 4
Strom Thurmond Federal Building, 1835 Assembly Street,
Suite 953, Columbia, SC 29201
Tel: (803) 765-5250   Fax: (803) 765-5260
Internet: www.usdoj.gov/ust/r04/index.htm

Areas Covered: DC, MD, SC, VA, WV

U.S. Trustee (Interim) **Judy A. Robbins** . . . .(713) 718-4650 ext. 243
  E-mail: judy.robbins@usdoj.gov

Executive Office for United States Trustees [EOUST] *continued*

Alexandria (VA) Field Office
115 South Union Street, Suite 210, Alexandria, VA 22314
Tel: (703) 557-7176   Fax: (703) 557-7279

Assistant U.S. Trustee **Joseph A. Guzinski** . . . . (703) 557-7274
  E-mail: joseph.a.guzinski@usdoj.gov

Baltimore (MD) Field Office
101 West Lombard Street, Suite 2625, Baltimore, MD 21201
Tel: (410) 962-4300   Fax: (410) 962-3537

Assistant U.S. Trustee **Gerard R. Vetter** . . . . (410) 962-4422
  E-mail: gerard.r.vetter@usdoj.gov

Charleston (WV) Field Office
300 Virginia Street East, Room 2025, Charleston, WV 25301
Tel: (304) 347-3400   Fax: (304) 347-3402

Assistant U.S. Trustee **Debra A. Wertman** . . . . (304) 347-3405
  E-mail: debra.a.wertman@usdoj.gov

Columbia (SC) Field Office
Strom Thurmond Federal Building, 1835 Assembly Street,
Suite 953, Columbia, SC 29201
Tel: (803) 765-5250   Fax: (803) 765-5260

Assistant U.S. Trustee **John Timothy Stack** . . . . (803) 765-5218
  E-mail: john.t.stack@usdoj.gov

Greenbelt (MD) Field Office
6305 Ivy Lane, Suite 600, Greenbelt, MD 20770
Tel: (301) 344-6216   Fax: (301) 344-8431

Assistant U.S. Trustee **Catherine M. Stavlas** . . . .(301) 344-6220
  E-mail: catherine.m.stavlas@usdoj.gov

Norfolk (VA) Field Office
200 Granby Street, Room 625, Norfolk, VA 23510
Tel: (757) 441-6012   Fax: (757) 441-3266

Assistant U.S. Trustee
  Kenneth N. Whitehurst III . . . .(757) 441-6012 ext. 101
  E-mail: kenneth.n.whitehurst@usdoj.gov

Richmond (VA) Field Office
701 East Broad Street, Suite 4304, Richmond, VA 23219
Tel: (804) 771-2310   Fax: (804) 771-2330

Assistant U.S. Trustee **Robert B. Van Arsdale** . . . .(804) 771-2327
  E-mail: robert.b.van.arsdale@usdoj.gov

Roanoke (VA) Field Office
First Campbell Square Building, 210 First Street, SW, Suite 505,
Roanoke, VA 24011
Tel: (540) 857-2806   Fax: (540) 857-2844

Assistant U.S. Trustee **Margaret K. Garber** . . . . (804) 771-2327
  E-mail: margaret.k.garber@usdoj.gov

Region 5
400 Poydras Street, Suite 2110, New Orleans, LA 70130
Tel: (504) 589-4018   Fax: (504) 589-4096
Internet: www.usdoj.gov/ust/r05/index.htm

Areas Covered: LA, MS

U.S. Trustee (Acting) **Henry G. Hobbs, Jr.** . . . . . (504) 589-4018 ext. 4080
  E-mail: henry.g.hobbs@usdoj.gov

Executive Office for United States Trustees [EOUST] *continued*

Jackson (MS) Field Office
501 East Court Street, Suite 6-430, Jackson, MS 39201
Tel: (601) 965-5241 Fax: (601) 965-5226

Assistant U.S. Trustee **Ronald H. McAlpin** . . . . (601) 965-5247
 E-mail: ronald.mcalpin@usdoj.gov

New Orleans (LA) Field Office
400 Poydras Street, Suite 2110, New Orleans, LA 70130
Tel: (504) 589-4018 Fax: (504) 589-4096

Assistant U.S. Trustee **Mary Langston** . . . . (504) 589-4093
 E-mail: mary.langston@usdoj.gov

Shreveport (LA) Field Office
300 Fannin Street, Suite 3196, Shreveport, LA 71101-3079
Tel: (318) 676-3456 Fax: (318) 676-3212

Assistant U.S. Trustee **Frances Hewitt** . . . . (318) 676-3554
 E-mail: frances.hewitt@usdoj.gov

Region 6
Earle Cabell Federal Building, 1100 Commerce Street, Room 976,
Dallas, TX 75242
Tel: (214) 767-8967 Fax: (214) 767-8971
E-mail: ustp.region06@usdoj.gov
Internet: www.usdoj.gov/ust/r06/template.htm

Areas Covered: TX (Northern & Eastern Judicial districts)

U.S. Trustee **William T. Neary** . . . . (214) 767-1070
 E-mail: william.neary@usdoj.gov
Assistant U.S. Trustee **Lisa L. Lambert** . . . . (214) 767-1080
 E-mail: lisa.l.lambert@usdoj.gov

Tyler (TX) Field Office
110 North College Avenue, Suite 300, Tyler, TX 75702
Tel: (903) 590-1450 Fax: (903) 590-1461

Assistant U.S. Trustee **Timothy W. O'Neal** . . . . . (903) 590-1450 ext. 215
 E-mail: timothy.w.o'neal@usdoj.gov

Region 7
515 Rusk Avenue, Suite 3516, Houston, TX 77002-2604
Tel: (713) 718-4650 Fax: (713) 718-4670
Internet: www.justice.gov/ust/r07

Areas Covered: TX (Southern & Western Judicial districts)

U.S. Trustee **Judy A. Robbins** . . . . (713) 718-4650 ext. 243
 E-mail: judy.robbins@usdoj.gov

Austin (TX) Field Office
903 San Jacinto Boulevard, Suite 230, Austin, TX 78701-2450
Tel: (512) 916-5328 Fax: (512) 916-5331

Assistant U.S. Trustee **Henry G. Hobbs, Jr.** . . . . (512) 916-5329
 E-mail: henry.g.hobbs@usdoj.gov

Corpus Christi (TX) Field Office
606 North Carancahua, Room 1107, Corpus Christi, TX 78476-1736
Tel: (361) 888-3261 Fax: (361) 888-3263

Assistant U.S. Trustee
 Diane Grittman Livingstone . . . . (713) 718-4650 ext. 23
 E-mail: diane.g.livingstone@usdoj.gov

Executive Office for United States Trustees [EOUST] *continued*

Houston (TX) Field Office
515 Rusk Avenue, Suite 3516, Houston, TX 77002-2604
Tel: (713) 718-4650 Fax: (713) 718-4680

Assistant U.S. Trustee
 Diane Grittman Livingstone . . . . (713) 718-4650 ext. 242
 E-mail: diane.g.livingstone@usdoj.gov

San Antonio (TX) Field Office
615 East Houston Street, Suite 533, San Antonio, TX 78205-2055
P.O. Box 1539, San Antonio, TX 78295-1539
Tel: (210) 472-4640 Fax: (210) 472-4649

Assistant U.S. Trustee **Nancy Ratchford** . . . . (210) 472-4647 ext. 223
 E-mail: nancy.ratchford@usdoj.gov

Region 8
One Memphis Place, 200 Jefferson Avenue, Suite 400,
Memphis, TN 38103
Tel: (901) 544-3251 Fax: (901) 544-4138
Internet: www.usdoj.gov/ust/r08/index.htm

Areas Covered: KY, TN

U.S. Trustee **Samuel K. Crocker** . . . . (901) 544-3251
 E-mail: sam.crocker@usdoj.gov

Chattanooga (TN) Field Office
Historic U.S. Courthouse, 31 East 11th Street, 4th Floor,
Chattanooga, TN 37402
Tel: (423) 752-5153 Fax: (423) 752-5161

Assistant U.S. Trustee **Kimberly C. Swafford** . . . . (423) 752-5153
 E-mail: kim.c.swafford@usdoj.gov

Knoxville (TN) Office
800 Market Street, Suite 114, Knoxville, TN 37902
Tel: (865) 545-4324 Fax: (865) 545-4325

Assistant U.S. Trustee (Acting) **Kimberly C. Swafford** . . . (865) 545-4324
 E-mail: kim.c.swafford@usdoj.gov

Lexington (KY) Field Office
100 East Vine Street, Suite 500, Lexington, KY 40507
Tel: (859) 233-2822 Fax: (859) 233-2834

Assistant U.S. Trustee **John L. Daugherty** . . . . . . (859) 233-2822 ext. 113
 E-mail: john.daugherty@usdoj.gov

Louisville (KY) Field Office
Gene Snyder Courthouse, 601 West Broadway, Room 512,
Louisville, KY 40202
Tel: (502) 582-6000 Fax: (502) 582-6147

Assistant U.S. Trustee **Charles Merrill** . . . . (502) 582-6000 ext. 234
 E-mail: charles.merrill@usdoj.gov

Memphis (TN) Field Office
One Memphis Place, 200 Jefferson Avenue, Suite 400,
Memphis, TN 38103
Tel: (901) 544-3251 Fax: (901) 544-4138

Assistant U.S. Trustee **Madalyn S. Greenwood** . . . (901) 544-3251 ext. 3
 E-mail: madalyn.s.greenwood@usdoj.gov

Nashville (TN) Field Office
701 Broadway, Suite 318, Nashville, TN 37203
Tel: (615) 736-2254 Fax: (615) 736-2260

Assistant U.S. Trustee **Beth Roberts Derrick** . . . . (615) 736-2254 ext. 232
 E-mail: beth.r.derrick@usdoj.gov

(continued on next page)

Region 9

Howard M. Mentzenbaum U.S. Courthouse, 201 Superior Avenue East, Suite 441, Cleveland, OH 44114-1240
Tel: (216) 522-7800 Fax: (216) 522-7193
Internet: www.usdoj.gov/ust/r09/region_9.htm

Areas Covered: MI, OH

U.S. Trustee **Daniel M. McDermott** . . . . (216) 522-7800 ext. 230
E-mail: daniel.m.mcdermott@usdoj.gov

Cincinnati (OH) Field Office
36 East Seventh Street, Suite 2030, Cincinnati, OH 45202
Tel: (513) 684-6988 Fax: (513) 684-6994

Areas Covered: Cincinnati

Assistant U.S. Trustee **Monica Kindt** . . . . (513) 684-6988 ext. 226
E-mail: monica.kindt@usdoj.gov

Cleveland (OH) Field Office
Howard M. Metzebbaum U.S. Courthouse, 201 Superior Avenue East, Suite 441, Cleveland, OH 44114-1240
Tel: (216) 522-7800 Fax: (216) 522-7193

Areas Covered: Northern OH

Assistant U.S. Trustee
Andrew R. "Andy" Vara . . . . (216) 522-7800 ext. 229
E-mail: andy.vara@usdoj.gov

Columbus (OH) Field Office
170 North High Street, Suite 200, Columbus, OH 43215-2403
Tel: (614) 469-7411 Fax: (614) 469-7448

Areas Covered: Southern OH (except Cincinnati)

Assistant U.S. Trustee **MaryAnne Wilsbacher** . . . (614) 469-7411 ext. 212
E-mail: maryanne.wilsbacher@usdoj.gov

Detroit (MI) Field Office
211 West Fort Street, Suite 700, Detroit, MI 48226
Tel: (313) 226-7999 Fax: (313) 226-7952

Areas Covered: Eastern MI

Assistant U.S. Trustee **Paul J. Randel** . . . . (313) 226-4531
E-mail: paul.randel@usdoj.gov

Grand Rapids (MI) Field Office
125 Ottawa Street, Suite 200R, Grand Rapids, MI 49503
Tel: (616) 456-2002 Fax: (616) 456-2550

Areas Covered: Western MI

Assistant U.S. Trustee **Matthew Cheney** . . . . (616) 456-2002 ext. 116
E-mail: matthew.cheney@usdoj.gov

Region 10

101 West Ohio Street, Suite 1000, Indianapolis, IN 46204
Tel: (317) 226-6101 Fax: (317) 226-6356
Internet: www.usdoj.gov/ust/r10/region10.htm

Areas Covered: IL (Northern, Southern, and Central Districts), IN

U.S. Trustee **Nancy J. Gargula** . . . . (317) 226-6101
E-mail: nancy.gargula@usdoj.gov

Indianapolis (IN) Field Office
101 West Ohio Street, Suite 1000, Indianapolis, IN 46204
Tel: (317) 226-6101 Fax: (317) 226-6356

Areas Covered: IN (Southern Judicial District)

Assistant U.S. Trustee **Ronald J. Moore** . . . . (317) 226-6101
E-mail: ronald.moore@usdoj.gov

Peoria (IL) Field Office
401 Main Street, Suite 1100, Peoria, IL 61602
Tel: (309) 671-7854 Fax: (309) 671-7857

Areas Covered: IL (Central and Southern Judicial Districts)

Assistant U.S. Trustee **Timothy E. Ruppel** . . . . (309) 671-7854
E-mail: tim.ruppel@usdoj.gov

South Bend (IN) Field Office
100 East Wayne Street, Room 555, South Bend, IN 46601-2349
Tel: (574) 236-8105 Fax: (574) 236-8163

Areas Covered: IN (Northern Judicial District)

Assistant U.S. Trustee **(Vacant)** . . . . (574) 236-8105

Region 11

219 South Dearborn Street, Room 873, Chicago, IL 60604
Tel: (312) 886-5785 Fax: (312) 886-5794
Internet: www.usdoj.gov/ust/r11/index_page.htm

Areas Covered: IL (Northern Judicial District), WI (Eastern and Western Judicial Districts)

U.S. Trustee **Patrick S. Layng** . . . . (312) 886-5785
E-mail: pat.s.layng@usdoj.gov

Chicago (IL) Field Office
219 South Dearborn Street, Room 873, Chicago, IL 60604
Tel: (312) 886-5785 Fax: (312) 886-5794

Assistant U.S. Trustee (Acting)
David Walter "Dave" Asbach . . . . (312) 886-5785
E-mail: dave.w.asbach@usdoj.gov

Madison (WI) Field Office
780 Regent Street, Suite 304, Madison, WI 53715
Tel: (608) 264-5522 Fax: (608) 264-5182

Assistant U.S. Trustee **Mary Jensen** . . . . (608) 264-5522
E-mail: mary.r.jensen@usdoj.gov

Milwaukee (WI) Field Office
Federal Courthouse, 517 East Wisconsin Avenue, Room 430, Milwaukee, WI 53202
Tel: (414) 297-4499 Fax: (414) 297-4478

Assistant U.S. Trustee **David Walter "Dave" Asbach** . . . . (414) 297-4499
E-mail: dave.w.asbach@usdoj.gov

Region 12

111 7th Avenue SE, Room 280, Cedar Rapids, IA 52401
Tel: (319) 364-2211 Fax: (319) 364-7370
Internet: www.usdoj.gov/ust/r12/index.htm

Areas Covered: IA, MN, ND, SD

U.S. Trustee **Daniel M. McDermott** . . . . (319) 364-2211 ext. 222
E-mail: daniel.m.mcdermott@usdoj.gov
Assistant U.S. Trustee **Janet G. Reasoner** . . . . . . (319) 364-2211 ext. 230
E-mail: janet.g.reasoner@usdoj.gov

Des Moines (IA) Field Office
Federal Building, 210 Walnut Street, Room 793, Des Moines, IA 50309
Tel: (515) 284-4982 Fax: (515) 284-4986

Assistant U.S. Trustee **James L. Snyder** . . . . (515) 284-4985
E-mail: james.l.snyder@usdoj.gov

Executive Office for United States Trustees [EOUST] *continued*

Minneapolis (MN) Field Office
1015 U.S. Courthouse, 300 South Fourth Street, Minneapolis, MN 55415
Tel: (612) 334-1350   Fax: (612) 335-4032

Assistant U.S. Trustee **Robert B. Raschke** . . . . (612) 664-5509
   E-mail: robert.raschke@usdoj.gov

Sioux Falls (SD) Field Office
314 South Main Street, Suite 303, Sioux Falls, SD 57104
Tel: (605) 330-4450   Fax: (605) 330-4456

Assistant U.S. Trustee (Acting) **James L. Snyder** . . . . (515) 284-4982
   E-mail: james.l.snyder@usdoj.gov

Region 13
Charles Evans Whittaker U.S. Courthouse, 400 East Ninth Street,
Suite 3440, Kansas City, MO 64106
Tel: (816) 512-1940   Fax: (816) 512-1967
Internet: www.usdoj.gov/ust/r13/Index.htm

Areas Covered: AR, MO, NE

U.S. Trustee (Acting) **Daniel J. Casamatta** . . . . (816) 512-1940
   E-mail: daniel.j.casamatta@usdoj.gov
Assistant U.S. Trustee **Daniel J. Casamatta** . . . . (816) 512-1943
   E-mail: daniel.j.casamatta@usdoj.gov

Little Rock (AR) Field Office
200 West Capitol, Suite 1200, Little Rock, AR 72201
Tel: (501) 324-7357   Fax: (501) 324-7388

Assistant U.S. Trustee **Charles W. Tucker** . . . . (501) 324-7357
   E-mail: charles.tucker@usdoj.gov

Omaha (NE) Field Office
111 South 18th Plaza, Room 1148, Omaha, NE 68102
Tel: (402) 221-4300   Fax: (402) 221-4383

Assistant U.S. Trustee **Patricia Dugan Fahey** . . . . (402) 221-4300
   E-mail: patricia.dugan@usdoj.gov

Saint Louis (MO) Field Office
111 South 10th Street, Room 6353, St. Louis, MO 63102
Tel: (314) 539-2976   Fax: (314) 539-2990

Assistant U.S. Trustee **Paul A. Randolph** . . . . (314) 539-2976
   E-mail: paul.a.randolph@usdoj.gov

Region 14
230 North First Avenue, Suite 204, Phoenix, AZ 85003-1706
Tel: (602) 682-2600   Fax: (602) 514-7270
Internet: www.usdoj.gov/ust/r14/index.htm

Areas Covered: AZ

U.S. Trustee **Ilene J. Lashinsky** . . . .(602) 682-2623
   E-mail: ilene.j.lashinsky@usdoj.gov
Assistant U.S. Trustee **Elizabeth C. Amorosi** . . . .(602) 682-2619
   E-mail: elizabeth.c.amorosi@usdoj.gov

Region 15
402 West Broadway, Suite 600, San Diego, CA 92101-8511
Tel: (619) 557-5013   Fax: (619) 557-5339
E-mail: ustp.region15@usdoj.gov
Internet: www.usdoj.gov/ust/r15

Areas Covered: CA (Southern Judicial District), GU, HI, Commonwealth
of the Northern Mariana Islands (CNMI)

U.S. Trustee (Acting) **Tiffany L. Carroll** . . . .(619) 557-5013
   E-mail: tiffany.l.carroll@usdoj.gov

Executive Office for United States Trustees [EOUST] *continued*

Hagatna (GU) Field Office
Sirena Plaza Building, 108 Hernan Cortes, Suite 131, Hagatna, GU 96932
Tel: (671) 472-7336   Fax: (671) 472-7344

Assistant U.S. Trustee **Curtis B. Ching** . . . . (808) 552-8154
   E-mail: curtis.b.ching@usdoj.gov

Honolulu (HI) Field Office
1132 Bishop Street, Suite 602, Honolulu, HI 96813-2830
Tel: (808) 522-8150   Fax: (808) 522-8156

Assistant U.S. Trustee **Curtis B. Ching** . . . . (808) 522-8154
   E-mail: curtis.b.ching@usdoj.gov

San Diego (CA) Field Office
402 West Broadway, Suite 600, San Diego, CA 92101-8511
Tel: (619) 557-5013   Fax: (619) 557-5339

Assistant U.S. Trustee (Acting) **Tiffany L. Carroll** . . . .(619) 557-5013
   E-mail: tiffany.l.carroll@usdoj.gov

Region 16
915 Wilshire Boulevard, Suite 1850, Los Angeles, CA 90017
Tel: (213) 894-6811   Fax: (213) 894-2603
Internet: www.justice.gov/ust/r16

Areas Covered: CA (Central Judicial District)

U.S. Trustee **Peter C. Anderson** . . . . (213) 894-0405
   E-mail: peter.c.anderson@usdoj.gov
Assistant U.S. Trustee **(Vacant)** . . . . (213) 894-3701

Riverside (CA) Field Office
3801 University Avenue, Suite 720, Riverside, CA 92501
Tel: (951) 276-6990   Fax: (951) 276-6973

Assistant U.S. Trustee **Abram S. Feuerstein** . . . . (951) 276-6975
   E-mail: abram.s.feuerstein@usdoj.gov

Santa Ana (CA) Field Office
411 West Fourth Street, Suite 9041, Santa Ana, CA 92701-8000
Tel: (714) 338-3400   Fax: (714) 338-3421

Assistant U.S. Trustee **Frank M. Cadigan** . . . . (714) 338-3405
   E-mail: frank.cadigan@usdoj.gov

Woodland Hills (CA) Field Office
21051 Warner Center Lane, Suite 115, Woodland Hills, CA 91367
Tel: (818) 716-8800   Fax: (818) 716-1576

Note: The Woodland Hills office staff work out of the Los Angeles office.

Assistant U.S. Trustee **Jennifer L. Braun** . . . . (213) 894-3240
   E-mail: jennifer.l.braun@usdoj.gov

Region 17
235 Pine Street, Suite 700, San Francisco, CA 94104
Tel: (415) 705-3300   Fax: (415) 705-3367
Internet: www.usdoj.gov/ust/r17/home.htm

Areas Covered: CA (Eastern & Northern Judicial Districts), NV

U.S. Trustee **Tracy Hope Davis** . . . . (415) 705-3300
   E-mail: tracy.davis2@usdoj.gov

Fresno (CA) Field Office
Office of U.S. Trustee, United States Courthouse, 2500 Tulare Street,
Fresno, CA 93721
Tel: (559) 487-5002   Fax: (559) 487-5030

Assistant U.S. Trustee **Gregory Powell** . . . . (559) 487-5002 ext. 225
   E-mail: greg.powell@usdoj.gov

(continued on next page)

Executive Office for United States Trustees [EOUST] *continued*

Las Vegas (NV) Field Office
300 Las Vegas Boulevard South, Suite 4300, Las Vegas, NV 89101
Tel: (702) 388-6600 Fax: (702) 388-6658

Assistant U.S. Trustee **Brian E. Goldberg** . . . . . . (702) 388-6600 ext. 235
  E-mail: brian.goldberg@usdoj.gov

Oakland (CA) Field Office
Federal Building, 1301 Clay Street, Suite 690N, Oakland, CA 94612-5202
Tel: (510) 637-3200 Fax: (510) 637-3220

Assistant U.S. Trustee (Acting) **Donna S. Tamanaha** . . . . (510) 637-3206
  E-mail: donna.s.tamanaha@usdoj.gov

Reno (NV) Field Office
300 Booth Street, Suite 3009, Reno, NV 89509
Tel: (775) 784-5335 Fax: (775) 784-5531

Assistant U.S. Trustee **Nicholas Strozza** . . . . (775) 784-5335
  E-mail: nick.strozza@usdoj.gov

Sacramento (CA) Field Office
501 I Street, Suite 7-500, Sacramento, CA 95814-2322
Tel: (916) 930-2100 Fax: (916) 930-2099

Assistant U.S. Trustee **Antonia G. Darling** . . . . (916) 930-2090
  E-mail: antonia.darling@usdoj.gov

San Francisco (CA) Field Office
235 Pine Street, Suite 700, San Francisco, CA 94104
Tel: (415) 705-3333 Fax: (415) 705-3379

Assistant U.S. Trustee **Donna S. Tamanaha** . . . . (415) 705-3341
  E-mail: donna.s.tamanaha@usdoj.gov

San Jose (CA) Field Office
280 South First Street, Suite 268, San Jose, CA 95113
Tel: (408) 535-5525 Fax: (408) 535-5532

Assistant U.S. Trustee **Edwina E. Dowell** . . . .(408) 535-5525 ext. 229
  E-mail: edwina.e.dowell@usdoj.gov

Region 18
700 Stewart Street, Suite 5103, Seattle, WA 98101-1271
Tel: (206) 553-2000 Fax: (206) 553-2566
Internet: www.usdoj.gov/ust/r18/r_default.htm

Areas Covered: AK, ID, MT, OR, WA

U.S. Trustee (Acting) **Gail B. Geiger** . . . . (206) 553-2000 ext. 261
  E-mail: gail.geiger@usdoj.gov

Anchorage (AK) Field Office
605 West Fourth Avenue, Suite 258, Anchorage, AK 99501
Tel: (907) 271-2600 Fax: (907) 271-2610

Assistant U.S. Trustee **Gail B. Geiger** . . . . (206) 553-2000
  E-mail: gail.geiger@usdoj.gov

Boise (ID) Field Office
720 Park Boulevard, Suite 220, Boise, ID 83712
Tel: (208) 334-1300 Fax: (208) 334-9756

Assistant U.S. Trustee **David W. Newman** . . . . .(208) 334-1300 ext. 2222
  E-mail: david.w.newman@usdoj.gov

Eugene (OR) Field Office
405 East Eighth Avenue, Room 1100, Eugene, OR 97401
Tel: (541) 465-6330 Fax: (541) 465-6335

Assistant U.S. Trustee (Acting) **Gary W. Dyer** . . . . (541) 465-6330
  E-mail: gary.w.dyer@usdoj.gov

Executive Office for United States Trustees [EOUST] *continued*

Great Falls (MT) Field Office
301 Central Avenue, Suite 204, Great Falls, MT 59401
Tel: (406) 761-8777 Fax: (406) 761-8895

Assistant U.S. Trustee **Neal G. Jensen** . . . .(406) 761-8777 ext. 104
  E-mail: neal.g.jensen@usdoj.gov

Portland (OR) Field Office
620 SW Main Avenue, Suite 213, Portland, OR 97205
Tel: (503) 326-4000 Fax: (503) 326-7658

Assistant U.S. Trustee **Pamela J. Griffith** . . . . (503) 326-4004
  E-mail: pamela.griffith@usdoj.gov

Seattle (WA) Field Office
700 Stewart Street, Suite 5103, Seattle, WA 98101-1271
Tel: (206) 553-2000 Fax: (206) 553-2566

Assistant U.S. Trustee **Thomas A. Buford III** . . . .(206) 553-2000 ext. 229
  E-mail: thomas.a.buford@usdoj.gov

Spokane (WA) Field Office
Federal Courthouse, 920 West Riverside Avenue, Room 593,
Spokane, WA 99201
Tel: (509) 353-2999 Fax: (509) 353-3124

Assistant U.S. Trustee **Gary W. Dyer** . . . . (509) 353-2999 ext. 110
  E-mail: gary.w.dyer@usdoj.gov

Region 19
Bryon G. Rogers Federal Building, 1961 Stout Street, Suite 12-200,
Denver, CO 80294
Tel: (303) 312-7230 Fax: (303) 312-7259
Internet: www.usdoj.gov/ust/r19/index.htm

Areas Covered: CO, UT, WY

U.S. Trustee (Interim) **Patrick S. Layng** . . . . (303) 312-7233
  E-mail: pat.s.layng@usdoj.gov

Cheyenne (WY) Field Office
308 West 21st Street, Room 203, Cheyenne, WY 82001
Tel: (307) 772-2790 Fax: (307) 772-2795

Assistant U.S. Trustee **Daniel J. Morse** . . . .(307) 772-2793
  E-mail: daniel.j.morse@usdoj.gov

Denver (CO) Field Office
999 - 18th Street, Suite 1551, Denver, CO 80202
Tel: (303) 312-7230 Fax: (303) 312-7259

Assistant U.S. Trustee **Gregory Garvin** . . . . (303) 312-7230
  E-mail: gregory.garvin@usdoj.gov

Salt Lake City (UT) Field Office
Ken Garff Building, 405 South Main Street, Suite 300,
Salt Lake City, UT 84111
Tel: (801) 524-5734 Fax: (801) 524-5628

Assistant U.S. Trustee **James "Vince" Cameron** . . . . (801) 524-5149
  E-mail: vince.cameron@usdoj.gov

Region 20
301 North Main, Suite 1150, Wichita, KS 67202
Tel: (316) 269-6637 Fax: (316) 269-6182

Areas Covered: KS, NM, OK

U.S. Trustee (Interim) **Samuel K. Crocker** . . . . (316) 269-6161
  E-mail: sam.crocker@usdoj.gov

Executive Office for United States Trustees [EOUST] *continued*

Albuquerque (NM) Field Office
421 Gold Avenue, SW, Room 112, Albuquerque, NM 87102
P.O. Box 608, Albuquerque, NM 87102
Tel: (505) 248-6544 Fax: (505) 248-6558

Assistant U.S. Trustee **Ronald E. "Ron" Andazola** . . . . . . (505) 248-6549
  E-mail: ronald.andazola@usdoj.gov

Oklahoma City (OK) Field Office
Old Postal Building, 215 Dean A. McGee Avenue, 4th Floor,
Oklahoma City, OK 73102
Tel: (405) 231-5950 Fax: (405) 231-5958

Assistant U.S. Trustee **Charles S. Glidewell** . . . . (405) 231-5950
  E-mail: charles.glidewell@usdoj.gov

Tulsa (OK) Field Office
224 South Boulder Avenue, Suite 225, Tulsa, OK 74103
Tel: (918) 581-6670 Fax: (918) 581-6674

Assistant U.S. Trustee **Katherine Vance** . . . . (918) 581-6686
  E-mail: katherine.vance@usdoj.gov

Wichita (KS) Field Office
301 North Main, Suite 1150, Wichita, KS 67202
Tel: (316) 269-6637 Fax: (316) 269-6182

Assistant U.S. Trustee **Jordan Sickman** . . . . (316) 269-6176
  E-mail: jordan.sickman@usdoj.gov

Region 21
Richard B. Russell Federal Building, 75 Spring Street, SW,
Suite 362, Atlanta, GA 30303
Tel: (404) 331-4437 Fax: (404) 331-4464
Internet: www.usdoj.gov/ust/r21/index.htm

Areas Covered: FL, GA, PR, VI

U.S. Trustee (Acting) **Guy G. Gebhardt** . . . . (404) 331-4437 ext. 120
  E-mail: guy.gebhardt@usdoj.gov

Atlanta (GA) Field Office
Richard B. Russell Federal Building, 75 Spring Street, SW,
Suite 362, Atlanta, GA 30303
Tel: (404) 331-4437 Fax: (404) 331-4464

Assistant U.S. Trustee **Guy G. Gebhardt** . . . . . . (404) 331-4437 ext. 120
  E-mail: guy.gebhardt@usdoj.gov

Macon (GA) Field Office
440 Martin L. King, Jr. Boulevard, Suite 302, Macon, GA 31201-7910
Tel: (478) 752-3544 Fax: (478) 752-3549

Assistant U.S. Trustee **Elizabeth A. Hardy** . . . . (478) 752-3401
  E-mail: elizabeth.a.hardy@usdoj.gov

Miami (FL) Field Office
Claude Pepper Federal Building, 51 SW First Avenue, Suite 1204,
Miami, FL 33130
Tel: (305) 536-7285 Fax: (305) 536-7360

Assistant U.S. Trustee **Steven R. Turner** . . . . (305) 536-7354
  E-mail: steve.r.turner@usdoj.gov

Orlando (FL) Field Office
400 West Washington Street, Suite 1101, Orlando, FL 32801-2440
Tel: (407) 648-6301 Fax: (407) 648-6323

Assistant U.S. Trustee **Charles R. Sterbach** . . . . . (407) 648-6301 ext. 121
  E-mail: charles.r.sterbach@usdoj.gov

Executive Office for United States Trustees [EOUST] *continued*

San Juan (PR) Field Office
Edificio Ochoa, 500 Tanca Street, Suite 301, San Juan, PR 00901-1922
Tel: (787) 729-7444 Fax: (787) 729-7449

Assistant U.S. Trustee **Monsita Lecaroz Arribas** . . . . (787) 729-7453
  E-mail: monsita.lecaroz@usdoj.gov

Savannah (GA) Field Office
Two East Bryan Street, Suite 725, Savannah, GA 31401
P.O. Box 10487, Savannah, GA 31412
Tel: (912) 652-4112 Fax: (912) 652-4123

Assistant U.S. Trustee **Matthew Mills** . . . . (912) 652-4117
  E-mail: matthew.mills@usdoj.gov

Tallahassee (FL) Field Office
110 East Park Avenue, Suite 128, Tallahassee, FL 32301
Tel: (850) 942-1660 Fax: (850) 942-1669

Assistant U.S. Trustee **Charles F. Edwards** . . . . (850) 942-1661
  E-mail: charles.edwards@usdoj.gov

Tampa (FL) Field Office
501 East Polk Street, Suite 1200, Tampa, FL 33602
Tel: (813) 228-2000 Fax: (813) 228-2303

Assistant U.S. Trustee
  Cynthia P. "Cindy" Burnette . . . . (813) 228-2000 ext. 229
  E-mail: cindy.p.burnette@usdoj.gov

Federal Administrative
Law Judges

Federal Administrative Law Judges

Federal Administrate Law Judges (FALJs), unlike federal judges who are appointed for life or specific terms, are employees of the U.S. Government, more specifically the executive departments and independent agencies for whom they conduct hearings and render decisions based on trial-type proceedings. In adjudicating cases before them, Federal Administrative Law Judges conduct formal trial-type hearings, make findings of fact and law, apply agency regulations, and issue either initial or recommended decisions. Appeals from FALJ decisions are generally to the U.S. Court of Appeals.

There are more than 1,600 Administrative Law Judges assigned across the federal government. The Social Security Administration is the agency employing the largest number of Federal Administrative law Judges, more than 1,150. Two other agencies employing large numbers of Federal Administrative Law Judges are the U.S. Department of Labor (50) and the National Labor Relations Board (60).

Federal Administrative Law Judges try cases falling into three broad categories: Regulatory cases, entitlement cases, and enforcement cases. Regulatory cases, such as those of the Federal Energy Regulatory Commission, involve economic regulation of rates and services provided by industries vital to the U.S. economy. Entitlement cases involve adjudication of claims by citizens to benefits provided by law. Enforcement cases involve adjudication of cases brought by various federal agencies against individuals or companies to enforce federal law and regulations. Judges assigned to a specific agency can be assigned to hear cases for another agency when caseloads warrant.

The following listing provides contact information for the Chief Federal Administrative Law Judges at major federal agencies.

Federal Communications Commission

Chief Administrative Law Judge **Richard L. Sippel** . . . . . . (202) 418-2280
445 - 12th Street, SW, Room 1-C768, Washington, DC 20554
E-mail: richard.sippel@fcc.gov

Federal Maritime Commission

Chief Administrative Law Judge **Clay G. Guthridge** . . . . . (202) 523-5750
800 North Capitol Street, NW, Room 1088,
Washington DC 20573-0001
E-mail: cguthridge@fmc.gov

Federal Mine Safety and Health Review Commission

Chief Administrative Law Judge **Robert J. Lesnick** . . . . . . (202) 434-9958
1331 Pennsylvania Avenue NW, Room 1414,
Washington, DC 20004-1710
E-mail: rlesnick@fmshrc.gov

Federal Trade Commission

Chief Administrative Law Judge **D. Michael Chappell** . . . . (202) 326-3637
600 Pennsylvania Avenue, NW, Room 106,
Washington, DC 20580
E-mail: mchappell@ftc.gov

National Labor Relations Board

Chief Administrative Law Judge **Robert A. Giannasi** . . . . . (202) 501-8800
1099 - 14th Street, NW, Room 5400, Washington, DC 20570
E-mail: robert.giannasi@nlrb.gov

National Transportation Safety Board

Chief Administrative Law Judge **Alfonso J. Montano** . . . . (202) 314-6150
490 L'Enfant Plaza East, SW, Washington, DC 20594
E-mail: alfonso.montano@ntsb.gov

Social Security Administration

Chief Administrative Law Judge **Debra Bice** . . . . (703) 605-8500
Skyline Towers, 5107 Leesburg Pike, Room 1608,
Falls Church, VA 22041
E-mail: debra.bice@ssa.gov

United States Department of Agriculture

Chief Administrative Law Judge (Acting)
Janice K. Bullard . . . . (202) 720-6383
South Agriculture Building,
1400 Independence Avenue, SW, Room 1049-S,
Washington, DC 20250
E-mail: janice.bullard@usda.gov

United States Department of Education

Director and Chief Administrative Law Judge
Frank J. Furey . . . . (202) 619-9713
470 L'Enfant Plaza East, SW, Room 2132,
Washington, DC 20202-4533
E-mail: frank.furey@ed.gov

United States Department of Energy

Chief Administrative Law Judge **Curtis L. Wagner Jr.** . . . . (202) 502-8500
888 First Street, NE, Room 11F-1, Washington, DC 20426
E-mail: curtis.wagner@ferc.gov

United States Department of Health and Human Services

Chief Administrative Law Judge **Nancy J. Griswold** . . . . . (703) 235-0635
1700 North Moore Street, Arlington, VA 22209-1912
E-mail: nancy.griswold@hhs.gov

United States Department of Homeland Security

Chief Administrative Law Judge (Acting)
Walter J. Brudzinski . . . . (202) 372-4440
2100 Second Street, SW, Room 6302, Mail Stop 7000,
Washington, DC 20593

United States Department of Housing and Urban Development

Chief Administrative Law Judge (Acting)
J. Jeremiah Mahoney . . . . (202) 254-0000
451 Seventh Street, SW, Room B133, Washington, DC 20410
E-mail: jeremiah.mahoney@hud.gov

United States Department of Justice

Chief Administrative Law Judge **John J. Mulrooney** . . . . . (202) 307-8686
1550 Crystal Drive, 9th Floor, Arlington, VA 22202

United States Department of Labor

Chief Administrative Law Judge
COL Stephen R. Henley, USA . . . . (202) 693-7542
TechWorld, 800 K Street, NW, Room 4148,
Washington, DC 20001-8002
E-mail: purcell.stephen@dol.gov

United States Department of the Interior

Supervisory Administrative Law Judge
Harvey C. Sweitzer . . . . (801) 524-5344
405 South Main Street, Suite 400, Salt Lake City, UT 84111
Chief Administrative Law Judge **Earl J. Waits** . . . . (505) 563-5330
1011 Indian School Road, NW, Room 322,
Albuquerque, NM 87104
E-mail: earl_waits@oha.doi.gov

United States Department of Transportation

Chief Administrative Law Judge **Ronnie A. Yoder** . . . . (202) 366-2137
1200 New Jersey Avenue, SE, Washington, DC 20590-9898
E-mail: ronnie.yoder@dot.gov

United States Environmental Protection Agency

Chief Administrative Law Judge **Susan L. Biro** . . . . (202) 564-6255
1099 14th Street, NW, Room 350-13,
Washington, DC 20005
E-mail: biro.susan@epa.gov

United States Federal Labor Relations Authority

Chief Administrative Law Judge **Charles Center** . . . . (202) 218-7950
1400 K Street, NW, Washington, DC 20424-0001
E-mail: ccenter@flra.gov

United States International Trade Commission

Chief Administrative Law Judge
Charles Edward Bullock . . . . (202) 205-2694
500 E Street, SW, Room 317-I, Washington, DC 20436
E-mail: charles.bullock@usitc.gov

United States Occupational Safety and Health Review Commission

Chief Administrative Law Judge **Covette Rooney** . . . . (202) 606-5405
One Lafayette Centre, 1120 20th Street, NW, 9th Floor,
Washington, DC 20036-3457

United States Postal Service

Chief Administrative Law Judge **James G. Gilbert** . . . . . . (703) 812-1909
Colonial Place I, 2101 Wilson Boulevard, Room 600,
Arlington, VA 22201-3078
E-mail: james.g.gilbert@usps.gov

United States Securities and Exchange Commission

Chief Administrative Law Judge **Brenda P. Murray** . . . . . . (202) 551-6030
100 F Street, NE, Room 2557, Washington, DC 20549
E-mail: murrayb@sec.gov

Alternative Dispute Resolution - Selected Organizations

Alternative Dispute Resolution — Selected Organizations

Alternative Dispute Resolution (ADR) refers to a broad range of mechanisms designed to assist individuals and companies in resolving disputes without having to resort to court litigation, the intention being to avoid the high costs and long delays often associated with litigation.

Court-related arbitration and mediation programs have proliferated in recent years in both federal and state courts. Added impetus has come from the Civil Justice Reform Act of 1990, which directed federal courts to consider litigation management and ADR techniques. Currently, a number of federal courts and nearly every state court have voluntary or mandatory ADR programs. A useful ADR website is the Mediation Information and Resource Center (www.mediate.com), which provides extensive background material on dispute resolution and includes an international directory of conflict resolvers as well as online mediators and arbitrators.

Listed below are selected organizations involved in dispute resolution or related services. In addition to these organizations, most state bar associations (and some local bar associations) have ADR programs.

American Arbitration Association [AAA]

120 Broadway, 21st Floor,
New York, NY 10271
Tel: (212) 716-5800 Fax: (212) 716-5905
Internet: www.adr.org

The American Bar Association Section of Dispute Resolution

1050 Connecticut, N.W., Suite 400, Washington, DC 20036
Tel: (202) 662-1680 Fax: (202) 662-1683
Internet: www.americanbar.org/dispute

Arbitration Forums, Inc.

3820 Northdale Boulevard, Suite 200A, Tampa, FL 33624
Tel: (866) 977-3434
E-mail: status@arbfile.org
Internet: www.arbfile.org

Association for Conflict Resolution [ACR]

1639 Bradly Park Drive, Suite 500-142, Columbus, GA 31904
Tel: (202) 780-5999
Internet: www.acrnet.org

International Institute for Conflict Prevention & Resolution, Inc. [CPR]

575 Lexington Avenue, 21st Floor, New York, NY 10022
Tel: (212) 949-6490 Fax: (212) 949-8859
E-mail: info@cpradr.org
Internet: www.cpradr.org

Council of Better Business Bureaus, Inc. [CBBB]

3303 Wilson Boulevard, Suite 600, Arlington, VA 22201
Tel: (703) 276-0100 Fax: (703) 525-8277
Internet: www.bbb.org

Federal Mediation and Conciliation Service [FMCS]

2100 K Street, NW, Washington, DC 20427
Tel: (202) 606-8080 (Public Information)
Tel: (202) 606-5460 (Personnel Locator)
Tel: (202) 606-3664 (Procurement Information)
Tel: (202) 606-5444 (Freedom of Information/Privacy Act)
Fax: (202) 606-4251
Internet: www.fmcs.gov

JAMS, The Resolution Experts

1920 Main Street, Suite 300, Irvine, CA 92614
Tel: (800) 352-5267 Tel: (949) 224-1810 Fax: (949) 224-1818
Internet: www.jamsadr.com

National Arbitration and Mediation [NAM]

990 Stewart Avenue, 1st Floor, Garden City, NY 11530
Tel: (800) 358-2550 Fax: (516) 794-8518
E-mail: customerservice@namadr.com
Internet: www.namadr.com

Federal and State Bar Associations

Federal and State Bar Associations

The website of the American Bar Association, listed below, includes resources for attorneys, students, and the general public.

This section also provides information on unified and voluntary state bar associations.

American Bar Association [ABA]

321 North Clark Street, Chicago, IL 60654
Tel: (312) 988-5000 Fax: (312) 988-6281
Email: info@americanbar.org
Internet: www.americanbar.org

Alabama State Bar

P.O. Box 671, Montgomery, AL 36101,
Tel: (334) 269-1515 Fax: (334) 261-6310
E-mail: information@alabar.org
Internet: www.alabar.org

Alaska Bar Association

P.O. Box 100279, Anchorage, AK 99510-0279
Tel: (907) 272-7469 Fax: (907) 272-2932
E-mail: info@alaskabar.org
Internet: www.alaskabar.org

State Bar of Arizona

270 North Church Avenue, Suite 100, Tucson, AZ, 85701-1113
Tel: (602) 252-4804 Fax: (602) 271-4930
Internet: www.azbar.org

Arkansas Bar Association

2224 Cottondale Lane, Little Rock, AR, 72202
Tel: (501) 375-4606 Fax: (501) 375-4901
E-mail: mglasgow@arkbar.com
Internet: www.arkbar.com

State Bar of California

180 Howard Street, San Francisco, CA 94105
Tel: (415) 538-2000
E-mail: feedback@calbar.ca.gov
Internet: www.calbar.ca.gov

Colorado Bar Association, CBA

1900 Grant St., 9th Floor, Denver, CO, 80203
Tel: (303) 860-1115 Fax: (303) 894-0821,
Internet: www.cobar.org

Connecticut Bar Association

30 Bank Street, New Britain, CT, 06050-0350
Tel: (860) 223-4400 Fax: (860) 223-4488
E-mail: msc@ctbar.org
Internet: www.ctbar.org

Delaware State Bar Association [DSBA]

405 North King Street, Suite 100, Wilmington, DE, 19801
Tel: (302) 658-5279 Fax: (302) 658-5212
Internet: www.dsba.org

The Bar Association of the District of Columbia [BADC]

1016 16th Street, NW, Suite 101, Washington, DC, 20036
Tel: (202) 223-6600 Fax: (202) 293-3388
E-mail: info@badc.org
Internet: www.badc.org

The District of Columbia Bar

1101 K Street, NW, Suite 200, Washington, DC, 20005
Tel: (202) 737-4700 Fax: (202) 626-3471
Internet: www.dcbar.org

The Florida Bar

651 East Jefferson Street, Tallahassee, FL, 32399-2300
Tel: (850) 561-5600
Internet: www.floridabar.org

State Bar of Georgia

104 Marietta Street, NW, Suite 100, Atlanta, GA, 30303-2702
Tel: (404) 527-8700 Fax: (404) 527-8717
Internet: www.gabar.org

Hawaii State Bar Association [HSBA]

1100 Alakea Street, Suite 1000, Honolulu, HI, 96813
Tel: (808) 537-1868 Fax: (808) 521-7936
E-mail: webinfo@hsba.org
Internet: www.hsba.org

Idaho State Bar [ISB]

P.O. Box 895, Boise, ID, 83701
Tel: (208) 334-4500 Fax: (208) 334-4515
Internet: www.isb.idaho.gov/

Illinois State Bar Association [ISBA]

20 South Clark Street, Suite 900, Chicago, IL, 60603-1802
Tel: (217) 525-1760
Internet: www.isba.org

Indiana State Bar Association [ISBA]

One Indiana Square, Suite 530, Indianapolis, IN, 46204
Tel: (317) 639-5465 Fax: (317) 266-2588
E-mail: isbaadmin@inbar.org
Internet: www.inbar.org

Iowa State Bar Association

625 East Court Avenue, Des Moines, IA, 50309
Tel: (515) 243-3179 Fax: (515) 243-2511
Internet: www.iabar.net

Kansas Bar Association [KBA]

1200 SW Harrison Street, Topeka, KS, 66612-1806
Tel: (785) 234-5696 Fax: (785) 234-3813
E-mail: info@ksbar.org
Internet: www.ksbar.org

Kentucky Bar Association

514 West Main Street, Frankfort, KY, 40601-1812
Tel: (502) 564-3795
E-mail: webmaster@kybar.org
Internet: www.kybar.org

Louisiana State Bar Association [LSBA]

601 St. Charles Avenue, New Orleans, LA, 70130-3404
Tel: (504) 566-1600 Fax: (504) 566-0930
Internet: www.lsba.org

Maine State Bar Association [MSBA]

124 State Street, Augusta, ME 04330
Tel: (207) 622-7523 Fax: (207) 623-0083
E-mail: info@mainebar.org
Internet: www.mainebar.org

Maryland State Bar Association, Inc. [MSBA]

520 W. Fayette St, Baltimore, MD, 21201
Tel: (410) 685-7878 Fax: (410) 685-1016
Internet: www.msba.org

Massachusetts Bar Association [MBA]

20 West Street, Boston, MA, 02111-1204
Tel: (617) 338-0500
Internet: www.massbar.org

State Bar of Michigan [SBM]

Michael Franck Building, 306 Townsend Street, Lansing, MI, 48933-2012
Tel: (517) 346-6300 Fax: (517) 482-6248
Internet: www.michbar.org

Minnesota State Bar Association [MSBA]

600 Nicollet Mall, Suite 380, Minneapolis, MN, 55402
Tel: (612) 333-1183
Internet: www.mnbar.org

The Mississippi Bar

P.O. Box 2168, Jackson, MS, 39225-2168
Tel: (601) 948-4471 Fax: (601) 355-8635
Internet: www.msbar.org

The Missouri Bar

P.O. Box 119, Jefferson City, MO, 65102
Tel: (573) 635-4128 Fax: (573) 635-2811
E-mail: mobar@mobar.org
Internet: www.mobar.org

State Bar of Montana

P.O. Box 577, Helena, MT, 59624
Tel: (406) 442-7660 Fax: (406) 442-7763
E-mail: mailbox@montanabar.com
Internet: www.montanabar.org

Nebraska State Bar Association

635 South 14th Street, Lincoln, NE, 68501
Tel: (402) 475-7091 Fax: (402) 475-7098
E-mail: webmaster@nebar.com
Internet: www.nebar.com

State Bar of Nevada

3100 West Charleston Boulevard, Las Vegas, NV 89102
Tel: (702) 382-2200 Fax: (702) 385-2878
Internet: www.nvbar.org

New Hampshire Bar Association

Two Pillsbury Street, Suite 300, Concord, NH, 03301
Tel: (603) 224-6942 Fax: (603) 224-2910
E-mail: nhbainfo@nhbar.org
Internet: www.nhbar.org

New Jersey State Bar Association [NJSBA]

New Jersey Law Center, One Constitution Square,
New Brunswick, NJ, 08901-1520
Tel: (732) 249-5000 Fax: (732) 249-2815
Internet: www.njsba.com

State Bar of New Mexico

P.O. Box 92860, Albuquerque, NM, 87199-2860
Tel: (505) 797-6000 Fax: (505) 828-3765
E-mail: sbnm@nmbar.org
Internet: www.nmbar.org

New York State Bar Association [NYSBA]

1 Elk Street, Albany, NY, 12207
Tel: (518) 463-3200 Fax: (518) 463-3200
Internet: www.nysba.org

North Carolina Bar Association [NCBA]

P.O. Box 3688, Cary, NC, 27519-3688
Tel: (919) 677-0561
E-mail: ncba@ncba.org
Internet: www.ncbar.org

The North Carolina State Bar
P.O. Box 25908, Raleigh, NC, 27611
Tel: (919) 828-4620
Internet: www.ncbar.com

State Bar Association of North Dakota [SBAND]
P.O. Box 2136, Bismarck, ND, 58502-2136
Tel: (701) 255-1404 Fax: (701) 224-1621
Internet: www.sband.org

Ohio State Bar Association [OSBA]
P.O. Box 16562, Columbus, OH, 43216-6562
Tel: (800) 282-6556 Fax: (614) 487-1008
E-mail: osba@ohiobar.org
Internet: www.ohiobar.org

Oklahoma Bar Association [OBA]
P.O. Box 53036, Oklahoma City, OK, 73152
Tel: (405) 416-7000 Fax: (405) 416-7001
E-mail: web@okbar.org
Internet: www.okbar.org

Oregon State Bar [OSB]
P.O. Box 231935, Tigard, OR, 97281-1935
Tel: (503) 620-0222 Fax: (503) 684-1366
E-mail: info@osbar.org
Internet: www.osbar.org

Pennsylvania Bar Association [PBA]
100 South Street, Harrisburg, PA, 17101
Tel: (717) 238-6715 Fax: (717) 238-7182
Internet: www.pabar.org

Bar Association of Puerto Rico
Colegio De Abogados De Puerto Rico,
P.O. Box 9021900, San Juan, PR, 00902-1900
Tel: (787) 721-3358 Fax: (787) 725-0330,
Internet: www.capr.org

Rhode Island Bar Association
41 Sharpe Drive, Cranston, RI 02920
Tel: (401) 421-5740 Fax: (401) 421-2703
E-mail: info@ribar.com
Internet: www.ribar.com

South Carolina Bar
950 Taylor Street, Columbia, SC, 29201
Tel: (803) 799-6653 Fax: (803) 799-4118
E-mail: scbar-info@scbar.org
Internet: www.scbar.org

State Bar of South Dakota
222 East Capitol Avenue, Pierre, SD, 57501-2596
Tel: (605) 224-7554 Fax: (605) 224-0282
Internet: www.sdbar.org

State Bar of Texas
Texas Law Center, 1414 Colorado Street, Austin, TX, 78701
Tel: (512) 427-1463 Fax: (512) 427-4100
Internet: www.texasbar.com

Tennessee Bar Association
221 Fourth Avenue North, Suite 400, Nashville, TN, 37219-2198
Tel: (615) 383-7421 Fax: (615) 297-8058
E-mail: email@tnbar.org
Internet: www.tba.org

Utah State Bar
645 South 200 East, Salt Lake City, UT, 84111
Tel: (801) 531-9077 Fax: (801) 531-0660
E-mail: info@utahbar.org
Internet: www.utahbar.org

Vermont Bar Association
P.O. Box 100, Montpelier, VT, 05601
Tel: (802) 223-2020 Fax: (802) 223-1573
E-mail: info@vtbar.org
Internet: www.vtbar.org

Virgin Islands Bar Association
P. O. Box 4108, Christiansted, VI, 00822-4108
Tel: (340) 778-7497 Fax: (340) 773-5060
E-mail: info@vibar.org
Internet: www.vibar.org

The Virginia Bar Association [VBA]
701 East Franklin Street, Suite 1120, Richmond, VA, 23219
Tel: (804) 644-0041 Fax: (804) 644-0052
E-mail: thevba@vba.org
Internet: www.vba.org/

Virginia State Bar [VSB]
1111 East Main Street, Suite 700, Richmond, VA 23219-0026
Tel: (804) 775-0500 Fax: (804) 775-0501
Internet: www.vsb.org

West Virginia Bar Association
P.O. Box 2162, Huntington, WV, 25722
Tel: (304) 522-2652 Fax: (304) 522-2795
Internet: www.wvbarassociation.org

The West Virginia State Bar

2000 Deitrick Boulevard, Charleston, WV, 25311
Tel: (304) 553-7220 Fax: (304) 558-2467
Internet: www.wvbar.org

State Bar of Wisconsin

P.O. Box 7158, Madison, WI, 53707-7158
Tel: (608) 257-3838 Fax: (608) 257-5502
E-mail: service@wisbar.org
Internet: www.wisbar.org

Wyoming State Bar

P.O. Box 109, Cheyenne, WY, 82003
Tel: (307) 632-9061 Fax: (307) 632-3737
Internet: www.wyomingbar.org

State Courts

ALABAMA

Chief Justice
Roy S. Moore
300 Dexter Avenue,
Montgomery, AL 36104-3741
(334) 229-0700

Justices of the Supreme Court
Michael F. Bolin
Tommy Elias Bryan
James Allen Main
Glenn Murdock
Tom Parker
Greg Shaw
Lyn Stuart
Alisa Kelli Wise

Clerk of the Supreme Court
Julia J. Weller
300 Dexter Avenue,
Montgomery, AL 36104-3741
(334) 229-0700

Court System Website
www.judicial.alabama.gov

Court Administration
Rich Hobson
Administrative Director of Courts
300 Dexter Avenue,
Montgomery, AL 36104-3741
(334) 954-5080

Governor
Robert Julian Bentley (R)
600 Dexter Avenue,
Montgomery, AL 36130
(334) 242-7210

State Website
www.alabama.gov

State Capitol Main Phone
(334) 242-7100

Attorney General
Luther J. Strange (R)
501 Washington Avenue,
Montgomery, AL 36130
(334) 242-7300

Secretary of State
John H. Merrill
P.O. Box 5616,
Montgomery, AL 36103-5616
(334) 242-7200

Vital Statistics
Cathy (Molchan) Donald
Director, Center for Health Statistics,
Alabama Department of Public Health
RSA Tower, 201 Monroe Street,
Suite 1168, Montgomery, AL 36104
(334) 206-5426
cathy.molchan@adph.state.al.us

Supreme Court
9 justices sit in 5-judge panels of 5 and en banc
Assigns cases to the Court of Civil Appeals

Jurisdiction:
- Appeal by right tort, contract, and real property, probate ($50,000 - no maximum), limited administrative agency.
- Appeal by permission criminal, civil, administrative agency. Interlocutory appeals in criminal, civil, administrative agency.
- Death penalty appeal by permission.
- Original proceeding writ application. Exclusive bar/judiciary, certified questions, advisory opinion.

Court of Civil Appeals
5 judges sit en banc

Jurisdiction:
- Appeal by right in civil ($0 - $50,000), administrative agency.
- Original proceeding writ application.

Court of Criminal Appeals
5 judges sit en banc

Jurisdiction:
- Appeal by right criminal, juvenile. Interlocutory appeals in criminal, juvenile.
- Death penalty appeal by right, writ application.
- Original proceeding writ application.

Circuit Court (41 circuits)
144 judges
Jury trials

Jurisdiction:
- Tort, contract, real property ($3,000 - no maximum). Exclusive civil appeals.
- Domestic relations.
- Felony, misdemeanor, and criminal appeals.
- Juvenile.

District Court (67 districts)
106 judges
No jury trials

Jurisdiction:
- Tort, contract, real property ($3,000 - $10,000). Exclusive small claims (up to $3,000).
- Paternity, custody, support, visitation, adoption.
- Preliminary hearings, misdemeanor.
- Juvenile.
- Traffic infractions.

Probate Court (68 courts)
68 judges
No jury trials

Jurisdiction:
- Exclusive mental health, probate/estate. Real Property.
- Adoption.

Municipal Court (273 courts)
279 judges
No jury trials

Jurisdiction:
- Misdemeanor.
- Exclusive ordinance violations. Traffic infractions, parking.

COURT OF LAST RESORT

INTERMEDIATE APPELLATE COURT

GENERAL JURISDICTION COURT

LIMITED JURISDICTION COURT

	Appellate level
	Trial level
↑	Route of appeal

Court structure as of Fiscal Year 2015.

ALASKA

Chief Justice
Craig F. Stowers
303 K Street,
Anchorage, AK 99501-2084
(907) 264-0612

Justices of the Supreme Court
Joel H. Bolger
Dana Fabe
Peter J. Maassen
Daniel E. Winfree

Clerk of the Supreme Court
Marilyn May
Boney Memorial Courthouse,
303 K Street,
Anchorage, AK 99501-2084
(907) 264-0608

Court System Website
www.courts.alaska.gov

Court Administration
Christine E. Johnson
Administrative Director
Boney Memorial Courthouse,
303 K Street,
Anchorage, AK 99501-2099
(907) 264-0547

Governor
William M. "Bill" Walker (I)
State Capitol, Third Floor,
Juneau, AK 99801
(907) 465-3500
bill.walker@alaska.gov

State Website
www.alaska.gov

State Capitol Main Phone
(907) 465-2111

Attorney General
Craig Richards
P.O. Box 110300
Juneau, AK 99811-0300
(907) 465-2133
craig.richards@alaska.gov

Lieutenant Governor
Byron I. Mallott
State Capitol Building, 3rd Floor,
Juneau, AK 99801
(907) 465-3520
byron.mallott@alaska.gov

Vital Statistics
Andrew Jessen
Bureau Chief, Bureau of Vital Statistics,
Division of Public Health
P.O. Box 110675, Juneau, AK 99811
(907) 465-8643
andrew.jessen@alaska.gov

Supreme Court
5 justices sit en banc

Jurisdiction:
- Exclusive appeal by right tort, contract, and real property, family, administrative agency.
- Appeal by permission criminal, civil. Interlocutory appeals in criminal, civil.
- Exclusive original proceeding bar/judiciary, certified question, advisory opinion.

COURT OF LAST RESORT

Court of Appeals
3 judges sit en banc

Jurisdiction:
- Appeal by right criminal, juvenile.
- Appeal by permission criminal, juvenile. Interlocutory appeals in criminal, juvenile.
- Exclusive original proceeding writ application.

INTERMEDIATE APPELLATE COURT

Superior Court (25 courts in 4 districts)
43 judges
Jury trials in most cases

Jurisdiction:
- Tort, contract. Exclusive real property, probate/estate, mental health, administrative agency appeals, civil appeals, miscellaneous civil.
- Exclusive domestic relations.
- Exclusive felony, criminal appeals.
- Juvenile.

GENERAL JURISDICTION COURT

District Court (44 locations in 4 districts)
23 judges, 51 magistrates
Jury trials in most cases

Jurisdiction:
- Tort, contract ($0 - $100,000), small claims (up to $10,000).
- Preliminary hearings, misdemeanor.
- Emergency juvenile.
- Exclusive traffic/other violations, except for uncontested parking violations (which are handled administratively).

LIMITED JURISDICTION COURT

Court structure as of Fiscal Year 2015.

☐ Appellate level
☐ Trial level
↑ Route of appeal

ARIZONA

Chief Justice
W. Scott Bales
Arizona State Courts Building,
1501 West Washington Street, Suite 434,
Phoenix, AZ 85007-3222
(602) 452-3534

Justices of the Supreme Court
Rebecca White Berch
Robert M. Brutinel
A. John Pelander
Ann Scott Timmer

Clerk of the Supreme Court
Janet Johnson
Arizona State Courts Building,
1501 West Washington Street,
Phoenix, AZ 85007
(602) 452-3396

Court System Website
www.azcourts.gov

Court Administration
David K. Byers
Administrative Director
Arizona State Courts Building,
1501 West Washington Street,
Phoenix, AZ 85007
(602) 452-3301

Governor
Douglas A. "Doug" Ducey (R)
State Capitol, Executive Tower,
1700 West Washington Street, 9th Floor,
Phoenix, AZ 85007
(602) 542-4331

State Website
www.az.gov

State Capitol Main Phone
(602) 542-4331

Attorney General
Mark Brnovich (R)
1275 West Washington,
Phoenix, AZ 85007
(602) 542-5025

Secretary of State
Michele Reagan
State Capitol, West Wing,
1700 West Washington Street, 7th Floor,
Phoenix, AZ 85007
(602) 542-0681

Vital Statistics
Krystal Colburn
Deputy Bureau Chief, Office of Vital
Records, Division of Public Health
Services
P.O. Box 3887, Phoenix, AZ 85030-3887
(602) 364-1225
krystal.colburn@azdhs.gov

COURT OF LAST RESORT

Supreme Court
5 justices sit en banc

Jurisdiction:
- Appeal by right criminal, tort, contract, and real property, probate, family.
- Appeal by permission criminal, civil, administrative agency. Interlocutory appeals in criminal, civil, administrative agency.
- Exclusive death penalty.
- Original proceeding writ application. Exclusive bar/judiciary, certified question.

INTERMEDIATE APPELLATE COURT

Court of Appeals
22 judges sit in panels

Jurisdiction:
- Appeal by right criminal, civil, limited administrative agency. Interlocutory appeals in criminal, civil, limited administrative agency.
- Appeal by permission administrative agency. Interlocutory appeals in administrative agency.
- Original proceeding writ application.

GENERAL JURISDICTION COURT

Superior Court (15 counties)
177 judges*
Jury trials

Jurisdiction:
- Tort, contract, real property ($5,000 to $10,000 - no maximum). Exclusive probate/estate, mental health, civil appeals, miscellaneous civil.
- Domestic relations.
- Exclusive felony, criminal appeals. Misdemeanor.
- Juvenile.

Tax Court
Superior court judge serves

Jurisdiction:
- Administrative agency appeals.

LIMITED JURISDICTION COURT

Justice of the Peace Court (88 precincts)
88 judges
Jury trials except in small claims

Jurisdiction:
- Tort, contract, real property ($0 - $5,000 to $10,000), non-domestic relations restraining order. Exclusive small claims (up to $2,500).
- Civil protection order.
- Preliminary hearings, misdemeanor.
- Traffic/other violations.

Municipal Court (84 courts)
154 judges
Jury trials

Jurisdiction:
- Non-domestic relations restraining order.
- Civil protection order.
- Misdemeanor.
- Traffic/other violations.

*There are also approximately 98 full- and part-time judges pro tempore, commissioners, and hearing officers in the Superior Court.

Court structure as of Fiscal Year 2015.

☐ Appellate level
☐ Trial level
↑ Route of appeal

ARKANSAS

Chief Justice
James R. "Jim" Hanna
Justice Building, 625 Marshall Street,
First Floor North,
Little Rock, AR 72201
(501) 682-6873

Justices of the Supreme Court
Karen R. Baker
Paul E. Danielson
Courtney Hudson (Henry) Goodson
Josephine Linker Hart
Rhonda Wood
Robin F. Wynne

Clerk of the Supreme Court
Stacy Pectol
Justice Building, 625 Marshall Street,
Little Rock, AR 72201
(501) 682-6849

Court System Website
courts.arkansas.gov

Court Administration
James D. Gingerich
Director, Arkansas Administrative Office
of the Courts
Justice Building, 625 Marshall Street,
Suite 1100, Little Rock, AR 72201-1020
(501) 682-9400

Governor
W. Asa Hutchinson (R)
State Capitol Building, Room 250,
Little Rock, AR 72201
(501) 682-2345

State Website
www.arkansas.gov

State Capitol Main Phone
(501) 682-3000

Attorney General
Leslie Rutledge (R)
323 Center Street, Suite 200,
Little Rock, AR 72201-2610
(501) 682-2007

Secretary of State
LTC J. Timothy "Tim" Griffin,
USAR (R)
State Capitol, Suite 270,
Little Rock, AR 72201
(501) 682-2144

Vital Statistics
Lynda Lehing
Branch Chief, Health Statistics Branch,
Arkansas Department of Health [ADH]
4815 West Markham Street,
Little Rock, AR 72205
(501) 661-2231
lynda.lehing@arkansas.gov

Supreme Court
7 justices sit en banc (1 chief justice, 6 associate justices)
Jurisdiction:
- Appeal by permission criminal, appeal by right criminal, civil, administrative agency.
- Exclusive revenue (tax). Interlocutory appeals in criminal, civil, administrative agency.
- Exclusive death penalty.
- Exlusice original proceeding writ application, bar/judiciary, certified question.

Court of Appeals
12 judges sit in 3-judge panels and en banc (1 chief judge, 11 judges)
Jurisdiction:
- Appeal by right criminal, civil, administrative agency.

Circuit Court (28 circuits)
121 judges
Jury trials
Jurisdiction:
- Tort, contract, real property ($100 - no maximum), miscellaneous civil. Exclusive probate/estate, mental health, civil appeals.
- Exclusive domestic relations.
- Exclusive felony, criminal appeals. Misdemeanor.
- Exclusive juvenile.

State District Court (16 courts)
67 departments
25 judges
No jury trials
Jurisdiction:
- Preliminary felony, misdemeanor.
- Civil cases involving contracts, property damage (up to $25,000).
- Small claims (up to $5,000).

Local District Court (77 courts)
178 departments
90 judges
No jury trials
Jurisdiction:
- Minor civil and criminal.
- Small claims (up to $5,000).

COURT OF LAST RESORT

INTERMEDIATE APPELLATE COURT

GENERAL JURISDICTION COURT

LIMITED JURISDICTION COURT

Court structure as of Fiscal Year 2015.

☐ Appellate level
☐ Trial level
↑ Route of appeal

CALIFORNIA

Chief Justice
Tani G. Cantil-Sakauye
350 McAllister Street,
San Francisco, CA 94102
(415) 865-7000

Justices of the Supreme Court
Ming W. Chin
Carol A. Corrigan
Mariano-Florentino "Tino" Cuéllar
Leondra R. Kruger
Goodwin Liu
Kathryn Mickle Werdegar

Clerk of the Supreme Court
Frank McGuire
Court Executive Officer
350 McAllister Street, Room 1295,
San Francisco, CA 94102
(415) 865-7000 ext. 57015

Court System Website
www.courtinfo.ca.gov

Court Administration
Martin A. Hoshino
Administrative Director of the Courts
455 Golden Gate Avenue,
San Francisco, CA 94102-3688
(415) 865-4200

Governor
Edmund Gerald "Jerry" Brown, Jr. (D)
State Capitol, Suite 1173,
Sacramento, CA 95814
(916) 445-2841

State Website
www.ca.gov

State Capitol Main Phone
(800) 807-6755

Attorney General
Kamala Devi Harris (D)
1300 I Street, Sacramento, CA 95814
(916) 324-5437

Secretary of State
Alejandro "Alex" Padilla (D)
1500 11th Street,
Sacramento, CA 95814
(916) 653-7244
alejandro.padilla@sausd.us

Vital Statistics
Tony Agurto
Vital Statistics State Registrar,
California Department of Public Health
[CDPH], Health and Human Services
Agency [CHHS]
P.O. Box 997377, MS 0500,
Sacramento, CA 95899-7377
(510) 620-3129
tony.agurto@cdph.ca.gov

Supreme Court
7 justices sit en banc

Jurisdiction:
- Appeal by permission criminal, civil, administrative agency.
- Exclusive death penalty.
- Original proceeding writ application. Exclusive bar/judiciary, certified question.

COURT OF LAST RESORT

Courts of Appeal (6 districts)
105 justices sit in panels

Jurisdiction:
- Appeal by right criminal, civil, administrative agency.
- Appeal by permission criminal, civil, administrative agency. Interlocutory appeals in criminal, civil, administrative agency.
- Original proceeding writ application.

INTERMEDIATE APPELLATE COURT

Superior Court (58 counties)
1,598 judges
Jury trials except in appeals, domestic relations, and juvenile cases

Jurisdiction:
- Tort, contract, real property ($25,000 - no maximum), miscellaneous civil. Exclusive small claims (up to $7,500), probate/estate, mental health, civil appeals. [Limited jurisdiction: tort, contract, real property ($0 - $25,000).]
- Exclusive domestic relations.
- Exclusive criminal.
- Exclusive juvenile.
- Exclusive traffic/other violations.

GENERAL JURISDICTION COURT

Court structure as of Fiscal Year 2015.

	Appellate level
	Trial level
↑	Route of appeal

COLORADO

Chief Justice
Nancy E. Rice
2 East Fourteenth Avenue,
Denver, CO 80203
(720) 625-5460

Justices of the Supreme Court
Brian Boatright
Nathan B. Coats
Allison H. Eid
Richard Lance Gabriel
Gregory J. Hobbs, Jr.
William W. Hood, III
Monica Marie Márquez

Clerk of the Supreme Court
Christopher T. Ryan
Ralph L. Carr Judicial Center,
2 East Fourteenth Avenue,
Denver, CO 80203
(303) 837-3790

Court System Website
www.courts.state.co.us

Court Administration
Gerald A. "Jerry" Marroney
State Court Administrator
1300 Broadway, Suite 1200,
Denver, CO 80203
(720) 625-5801

Governor
John W. Hickenlooper (D)
136 State Capitol,
Denver, CO 80203-1792
(303) 866-2471

State Website
www.colorado.gov

State Capitol Main Phone
(303) 866-5000

Attorney General
Cynthia H. Coffman (R)
1300 Broadway, 10th Floor,
Denver, CO 80203
(720) 508-6000

Secretary of State
Wayne W. Williams
1700 Broadway, 2nd Floor,
Denver, CO 80290
(303) 894-2200

Vital Statistics
Ronald S. Hyman
State Registrar, Center for Health
and Environmental Information and
Statistics, Colorado Department of
Public Health and Environment
4300 Cherry Creek Drive, South, HS-
VRD-VR-A1, Denver, CO 80246-1530
(303) 692-2164

Supreme Court
7 justices sit en banc

Jurisdiction:
- Appeal by right criminal, civil, administrative agency. Interlocutory appeals in criminal.
- Exclusive appeal by permission criminal, civil, administrative agency.
- Exclusive death penalty.
- Original proceeding certified question. Exclusive writ application, bar/judiciary, advisory opinion.

Court of Appeals
22 judges sit in 3-judge panels

Jurisdiction:
- Appeal by right criminal, civil, administrative agency.
- Original proceeding certified question (limited to interlocutory appeal from civil case).

District, Denver Juvenile, and Denver Probate Court
185 judges

District Court (22 districts)
174 judges
Jury trials except in appeals

Jurisdiction:
- Tort, contract, real property, probate/estate, civil appeals, mental health, miscellaneous civil.
- Exclusive domestic relations.
- Felony, criminal appeals.
- Exclusive juvenile.

Denver Juvenile Court
3 judges
Jury trials

Jurisdiction:
- Exclusive adoption, custody, support in Denver.
- Exclusive juvenile in Denver.

Denver Probate Court
1 judge
Jury trials

Jurisdiction:
- Exclusive probate/estate, mental health in Denver.

Water Court (7 courts)
District court judges serve
Jury trials

Jurisdiction:
- Real property.

County Court (64 counties)
114 judges
Jury trials except in small claims and appeals

Jurisdiction:
- Tort, contract, real property (0 - $15,000). Exclusive small claims (up to $7,500).
- Felony, preliminary hearings, misdemeanor, criminal appeals.
- Traffic infractions.

Municipal Court

Jury trials

Jurisdiction:
- DWI/DUI, domestic violence.
- Traffic infractions, parking, other violations. Exclusive ordinance violations.

COURT OF LAST RESORT

INTERMEDIATE APPELLATE COURT

GENERAL JURISDICTION COURT

LIMITED JURISDICTION COURT

Court structure as of Fiscal Year 2015.

☐ Appellate level
☐ Trial level
↑ Route of appeal

CONNECTICUT

Chief Justice
Chase Theodora Rogers
Supreme Court Building,
231 Capitol Avenue, Hartford, CT 06106
(860) 757-2200

Justices of the Supreme Court
Carmen Elisa Espinosa
Dennis G. Eveleigh
Andrew J. McDonald
Richard N. Palmer
Richard A. Robinson
Christine S. Vertefeuille
Peter T. Zarella

Clerk of the Supreme Court
Paul S. Hartan
Supreme Court Building,
231 Capitol Avenue, Hartford, CT 06106
(860) 757-2200

Court System Website
www.jud.ct.gov

Court Administration
Patrick L. Carroll, III
Chief Court Administrator
Supreme Court Building,
231 Capitol Avenue, Hartford, CT 06106
(860) 757-2100

Governor
Dannel P. "Dan" Malloy (D)
State Capitol, 210 Capitol Avenue,
Hartford, CT 06106
(860) 566-4840
governor.malloy@po.state.ct.us

State Website
www.ct.gov

State Capitol Main Phone
(800) 406-1527

Attorney General
George C. Jepsen (D)
55 Elm Street, Hartford, CT 06106
(860) 808-5318

Secretary of State
Denise W. Merrill (D)
State Capitol, 210 Capitol Avenue,
Room 104, Hartford, CT 06106
(860) 509-6200

Vital Statistics
Jane Purtill
Vital Records Director,
Population Health Statistics and
Surveillance Branch
410 Capitol Avenue, Mail Stop 11VRS,
Hartford, CT 06134
(860) 509-7895
jane.purtill@ct.gov

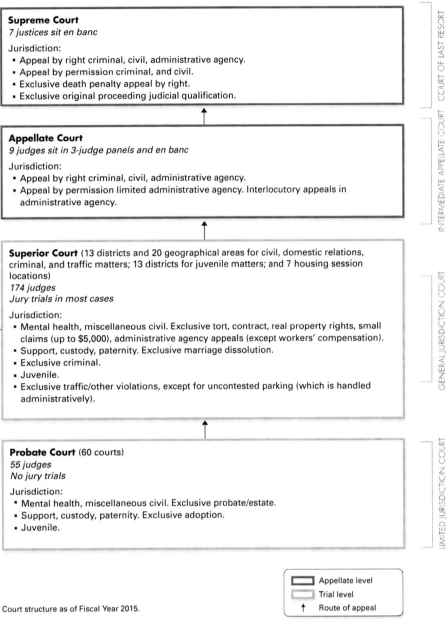

Court structure as of Fiscal Year 2015.

DELAWARE

Chief Justice
Leo E. Strine, Jr.
57 The Green, Dover, DE 19901-0476
(302) 651-3902

Justices of the Supreme Court
Randy J. Holland
Collins J. "C.J." Seitz
Karen Valihura
James T. Vaughn, Jr.

Clerk of the Supreme Court
Cathy L. Howard
Elbert N. Carvel State Office Building,
820 North French Street,
Wilmington, DE 19801
(302) 739-4155

Court System Website
www.courts.state.de.us

Court Administration
Patricia W. Griffin
State Court Administrator
1 South Race Street,
Georgetown, DE 19947
(302) 856-5406

Governor
Jack A. Markell (D)
Tatnall Building, 2nd Floor,
Dover, DE 19901
(302) 744-4101
jack.markell@state.de.us

State Website
www.delaware.gov

State Capitol Main Phone
(800) 464-4357

Attorney General
Matthew P. "Matt" Denn (D)
Carvel State Office Building,
820 North French Street,
Wilmington, DE 19801
(302) 577-8400
matthew.denn@state.de.us

Secretary of State
Jeffrey W. "Jeff" Bullock
401 Federal Street, Suite 3,
Dover, DE 19901
(302) 739-4111

Vital Statistics
Brenda (Abele) Conner
Vital Statistics Director, Division of
Public Health [DPH]
Jesse Cooper Building,
417 Federal Street, Dover, DE 19901
(302) 744-4748
brenda.conner@state.de.us

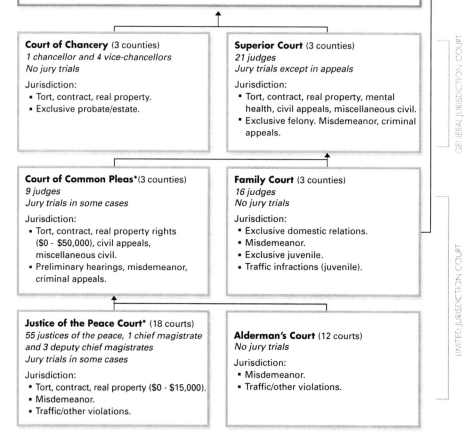

Supreme Court
5 justices sit in 3-judge panels and en banc
Jurisdiction:
- Exclusive appeal by right criminal, civil, administrative agency.
- Exclusive appeal by permission criminal, tort, contract, and real property, probate, family, administrative agency. Interlocutory appeals in criminal, tort, contract, and real property, probate, family, administrative agency.
- Exclusive death penalty.
- Exclusive original proceeding writ application, bar/matters, certified question, advisory opinion.

Court of Chancery (3 counties)
1 chancellor and 4 vice-chancellors
No jury trials
Jurisdiction:
- Tort, contract, real property.
- Exclusive probate/estate.

Superior Court (3 counties)
21 judges
Jury trials except in appeals
Jurisdiction:
- Tort, contract, real property, mental health, civil appeals, miscellaneous civil.
- Exclusive felony. Misdemeanor, criminal appeals.

Court of Common Pleas*(3 counties)
9 judges
Jury trials in some cases
Jurisdiction:
- Tort, contract, real property rights ($0 - $50,000), civil appeals, miscellaneous civil.
- Preliminary hearings, misdemeanor, criminal appeals.

Family Court (3 counties)
16 judges
No jury trials
Jurisdiction:
- Exclusive domestic relations.
- Misdemeanor.
- Exclusive juvenile.
- Traffic infractions (juvenile).

Justice of the Peace Court* (18 courts)
55 justices of the peace, 1 chief magistrate and 3 deputy chief magistrates
Jury trials in some cases
Jurisdiction:
- Tort, contract, real property ($0 - $15,000).
- Misdemeanor.
- Traffic/other violations.

Alderman's Court (12 courts)
No jury trials
Jurisdiction:
- Misdemeanor.
- Traffic/other violations.

COURT OF LAST RESORT

GENERAL JURISDICTION COURT

LIMITED JURISDICTION COURT

*The Municipal Court of Wilmington was eliminated effective May 1, 1998, and a new Justice of the Peace Court was created in Wilmington.

Appellate level
Trial level
↑   Route of appeal

Court structure as of Fiscal Year 2015.

DISTRICT OF COLUMBIA

Chief Judge — Court of Appeals
Eric T. Washington
Historic Courthouse, 430 E Street NW,
Room 319, Washington, DC 20001
(202) 879-2771

Appeals Court Associate Judges
Corinne Ann Beckwith
Anna Blackburne-Rigsby
John R. Fisher
Catharine "Kate" Friend Easterly
Stephen H. Glickman
Todd S. Kim (Designate)
Roy W. McLeese, III
Phyllis D. Thompson

Clerk of Court of Appeals
Julio A. Castillo
430 E Street NW,
Washington, DC 20001
(202) 879-2725

Court System Website
www.dcappeals.gov

Appeals Court Administration
Reginald Turner
Administration Director,
430 E Street NW,
Washington, DC 20001
(202) 879-2738

Mayor
Muriel Bowser (D)
John A. Wilson Building,
1350 Pennsylvania Avenue, NW,
Suite 316, Washington, DC 20004
(202) 727-6300

DC Website
www.dc.gov

DC Main Phone
(202) 737-4404

Attorney General
Karl A. Racine (D)
441 4th Street NW,
Washington, DC 20001
(202) 727-3400

Secretary of DC
Lauren C. Vaughan
1350 Pennsylvania Avenue, NW,
Room 419, Washington, DC 20004
(202) 727-6306

Vital Statistics
Terra Abrams
Vital Records Registrar, Center for
Policy, Planning and Evaluation, DOH
825 North Capitol Street, NE, 2nd Floor,
Washington, DC 20002
(202) 442-9029
terra.abrams@dc.gov

Court of Appeals
9 judges sit in 3-judge panels and en banc

Jurisdiction:
- Exclusive appeal by right criminal, civil, administrative agency. Interlocutory appeals in criminal, civil, administrative agency.
- Exclusive appeal by permission misdemeanor, small claims.
- Exclusive original proceeding writ application, bar/judiciary, certified question.

Superior Court
58 judges, 24 magistrates*
Jury trials

Jurisdiction:
- Exclusive civil ($5,001 - no maximum). Small claims (up to $5,000).
- Exclusive domestic relations.
- Exclusive criminal.
- Exclusive juvenile.
- Exclusive traffic/other violations, except for most parking cases (which are handled administratively).

*Does not include senior judges that serve on a part-time basis.

Court structure as of Fiscal Year 2015.

	Appellate level
	Trial level
↑	Route of appeal

COURT OF LAST RESORT

GENERAL JURISDICTION COURT

FLORIDA

Chief Justice
Jorge Labarga
Supreme Court Building, 500 South
Duval Street, Tallahassee, FL 32399
(850) 413-8371

Justices of the Supreme Court
Charles T. Canady
R. Fred Lewis
Barbara J. Pariente
James E. C. Perry
Ricky L. Polston
Peggy A. Quince

Clerk of the Supreme Court
John A. Tomasino
Supreme Court Building,
500 South Duval Street,
Tallahassee, FL 32399-1925
(850) 488-0125

Court System Website
ww.floridasupremecourt.org

Court Administration
Elisabeth H. Goodner
State Courts Administrator
Supreme Court Building,
500 South Duval Street,
Tallahassee, FL 32399-1900

Governor
Richard Lynn "Rick" Scott (R)
The Capitol,
Tallahassee, FL 32399-0001
(850) 488-7146

State Website
www.myflorida.com

State Capitol Main Phone
(850) 488-1234

Attorney General
Pamela J. Bondi (R)
The Capitol, Plaza Level One,
Tallahassee, FL 32399-1050
(850) 245-0140

Secretary of State
Kenneth W. "Ken" Detzner
500 South Bronough Street,
Tallahassee, FL 32399-0250
(850) 245-6524
secretaryofstate@dos.myflorida.com

Vital Statistics
Kenneth T. "Ken" Jones
Vital Statistics Administrator,
Department of Health
1217 Pearl Street,
Jacksonville, FL 32231
(904) 359-6900
vitalstats@doh.state.fl.us

Supreme Court
7 justices sit 5-judge panels and en banc
Jurisdiction:
- Appeal by right criminal, civil, administrative agency.
- Appeal by permission criminal, civil, administrative agency.
- Exclusive death penalty.
- Original proceeding writ application. Exclusive bar/judiciary, certified question, advisory opinion.

COURT OF LAST RESORT

District Courts of Appeal (5 courts)
61 judges sit in 3-judge panels
Jurisdiction:
- Appeal by right criminal, civil, administrative agency. Interlocutory appeals in criminal, civil, administrative agency.
- Appeal by permission criminal, civil, administrative agency.
- Original proceeding writ application.

INTERMEDIATE APPELLATE COURT

Circuit Court (20 circuits)
599 judges
Jury trials except in appeals
Jurisdiction:
- Tort, contract, real property ($15,001 - no maximum), miscellaneous civil. Exclusive mental health, probate/estate, civil appeals.
- Domestic relations.
- Felony, exclusive criminal appeals.
- Exclusive juvenile.

GENERAL JURISDICTION COURT

County Court (67 counties)
322 judges
Jury trials
Jurisdiction:
- Tort contract, real property ($5,001 - $15,000), miscellaneous civil. Exclusive small claims (up to $5,000).
- Dissolution/divorce.
- Preliminary hearings. Exclusive misdemeanor.
- Exclusive traffic/other violations, except parking (which is handled administratively).

LIMITED JURISDICTION COURT

Court structure as of Fiscal Year 2015.

☐ Appellate level
☐ Trial level
↑ Route of appeal

GEORGIA

Chief Justice
Hugh P. Thompson
State Judicial Building
40 Capitol Street, Room 507,
Atlanta, GA 30334-9003
(404) 656-3472

Justices of the Supreme Court
Robert Benham
Keith R. Blackwell
Carol W. Hunstein
P. Harris Hines
Harold D. Melton
David E. Nahmias

Clerk of the Supreme Court
Therese S. "Tee" Barnes
State Judicial Building,
244 Washington Street, SW, Room 572,
Atlanta, GA 30334
(404) 656-3470

Court System Website
www.gasupreme.us

Court Administration
Cynthia Hinrichs Clanton (Acting)
Director, Administrative Office of the
Georgia Courts
244 Washington Street, SW, Suite 300,
Atlanta, GA 30334
(404) 656-5171

Governor
Nathan Deal (R)
203 State Capitol, Atlanta, GA 30334
(404) 656-1776

State Website
www.georgia.gov

State Capitol Main Phone
(404) 656-2000

Attorney General
Samuel S. "Sam" Olens (R)
40 Capitol Square, SW,
Atlanta, GA 30334
(404) 483-2477

Secretary of State
Brian P. Kemp (R)
214 State Capitol, Atlanta, GA 30334
(404) 656-2881

Vital Statistics
Donna Moore
Vital Records Director,
Department of Public Health [DPH]
(404) 679-4702
donna.moore@dph.ga.gov

Supreme Court
7 justices sit en banc

Jurisdiction:
- Appeal by right criminal, civil, administrative agency.
- Appeal by permission criminal, civil, administrative agency. Interlocutory appeals in criminal, civil, administrative agency.
- Exclusive death penalty.
- Exclusive original proceeding habeas corpus writ, bar/judiciary, certified question, advisory opinion.

Capitol felonies; constitutional issues title to land; wills, equity and divorce

Court of Appeals (4 divisions)
12 judges sit in 3-judge panels

Jurisdiction:
- Appeal by right criminal, civil, administrative agency.
- Appeal by permission criminal, civil, administrative agency. Interlocutory appeals in criminal, civil, administrative agency.

Superior Court (159 counties, 49 circuits)
209 judges authorized
Jury trials

Jurisdiction:
- Tort, contract, probate/wills/intestate, civil appeals, miscellaneous civil. Exclusive real property.
- Exclusive domestic relations.
- Misdemeanor. Exclusive felony, criminal appeals.
- Traffic infractions, ordinance violations.

Only for counties with population over 96,000 where probate judge is attorney practicing at least 7 years.

Civil Court (Bibb and Richmond counties)
4 judges
Jury trials

Jurisdiction:
- Tort, contract [$0 - $25,000 (Bibb Co.); $0 - $45,000 (Richmond Co.)].
- Preliminary hearings, misdemeanor.

County Recorder's Court
(4 courts)
14 judges
No jury trials

Jurisdiction:
- Preliminary hearings, misdemeanors.
- Traffic/other violations.

Probate Court (159 circuits)
159 judges, 12 associate judges
Jury trials only in counties with populations greater than 96,000

Jurisdiction:
- Exclusive mental health, probate/estate. Preliminary hearings, misdemeanor.

State Court (70 courts)
123 judges
Jury trials

Jurisdiction:
- Tort, contract, civil appeals, miscellaneous civil.
- Preliminary hearings, misdemeanor.
- Traffic infractions.

Magistrate Court
(159 courts)
159 chief magistrates, and 333 magistrates
No jury trials

Jurisdiction:
- Small claims (up to $15,000).
- Preliminary hearings, misdemeanor.
- Ordinance violations.

Municipal Courts* (370 courts)
352 judges
No jury trials

Jurisdiction:
- Small claims (up to $15,000) in Columbus Co.
- Tort, contract ($0 - $25,000 Bibb Co.); ($0 - $45,000 Richmond Co.).
- Preliminary hearings, misdemeanor.
- Traffic/other violations.

Juvenile Court (159 courts)
138 judges
In Ogeechee circuit, 4 of the full-time judges are superior court judges who hear juvenile court cases.
No jury trials

Jurisdiction:
- Custody.
- Juvenile.
- Traffic infractions.

*A small number of special courts authorized by the Georgia constitution, have limited civil or criminal jurisdiction throughout a designated county.

COURT OF LAST RESORT
INTERMEDIATE APPELLATE COURT
GENERAL JURISDICTION COURT
LIMITED JURISDICTION COURT

Appellate level
Trial level
↑ Route of appeal

Court structure as of Fiscal Year 2015.

HAWAII

Chief Justice
Mark E. Recktenwald
Ali'iolani Hale, 417 South King Street,
Honolulu, HI 96813-2902
(808) 539-4735

Justices of the Supreme Court
Sabrina McKenna
Paula A. Nakayama
Richard W. Pollack
Michael D. Wilson

Clerk of the Supreme Court
Rochelle R. Hasuko
Ali'iolani Hale, 417 South King Street,
Room 103, Honolulu, HI 96813-2902
(808) 539-4919

Court System Website
www.courts.state.hi.us

Court Administration
Rodney A. Maile
Administrative Director of the Courts
Ali'iolani Hale, 417 South King Street,
Room 206A, Honolulu, HI 96813-2902
(808) 539-4900
rodney.a.maile@courts.hawaii.gov

Governor
David Y. Ige (D)
State Capitol, Honolulu, HI 96813
(808) 586-8201

State Website
www.hawaii.gov

State Capitol Main Phone
(808) 586-2211

Attorney General
David M. Louie
425 Queen Street, Honolulu, HI 96813
(808) 586-1282
david.m.louie@hawaii.gov

Lieutenant Governor
Shan S. Tsutsui (D)
State Capitol, Honolulu, HI 96813
(808) 586-0255
shan.tsutsui@hawaii.gov

Vital Statistics
Alvin Onaka, PhD
State Registrar and Chief, Office of
Health Status Monitoring [OHSM]
P.O. Box 3378, Honolulu, HI 96801
(808) 586-4600
alvino@hawaii.edu

Supreme Court
5 justices sit en banc

Jurisdiction:
- Appeal by right criminal, civil, administrative agency.
- Exclusive appeal by permission criminal, civil, administrative agency. Interlocutory appeals in criminal, civil, administrative agency.
- Original proceeding writ application, certified question. Exclusive bar/judiciary.

Intermediate Court of Appeals
6 judges sit in 3-judge panels

Jurisdiction:
- Appeal by right criminal, civil, administrative agency. Interlocutory in criminal, civil, administrative agency.
- Original proceeding writ application, certified question.

Circuit Court and Family Court (4 circuits)
32 circuit judges, 6 of which are designated Family Court judges, plus 17 District Family Court judges
Jury trials

Jurisdiction:
- Tort contract, real property ($10,000 - no maximum) [concurrent from $10,000 - $25,000], miscellaneous civil. Mental health, probate/estate, administrative agency appeals.
- Exclusive domestic relations.
- Juvenile.
- Traffic infractions.

District Court (4 circuits)
22 judges, 41 Per Diem Judges
No jury trials

Jurisdiction:
- Tort, contract, real property ($0 - $25,000) [concurrent from $10,000 - $25,000 (civil nonjury)], miscellaneous civil. Exclusive small claims up to ($5,000) unless residential security deposit case.
- Preliminary hearings, misdemeanor.
- Traffic infractions. Exclusive parking, ordinance violations.

COURT OF LAST RESORT

INTERMEDIATE APPELLATE COURT

GENERAL JURISDICTION COURT

LIMITED JURISDICTION COURT

Court structure as of Fiscal Year 2015.

☐ Appellate level
☐ Trial level
↑ Route of appeal

IDAHO

Chief Justice
Roger S. Burdick
P.O. Box 83720, Boise, ID 83720-0101
(208) 334-3464

Justices of the Supreme Court
Daniel T. Eismann
Joel D. Horton
Jim Jones
Warren E. Jones

Clerk of the Supreme Court
Stephen W. Kenyon
P.O. Box 83720, Boise, ID 83720-0101
(208) 334-2210

Court System Website
www.isc.idaho.gov

Court Administration
Linda Copple Trout
Administrative Director of the Courts
P.O. Box 83720, Boise, ID 83720-0101
(208) 334-2246

Governor
C. L. "Butch" Otter (R)
P. O. Box 83720, Boise, ID 83720
(208) 334-2100

State Website
www.idaho.gov

State Capitol Main Phone
(208) 334-2100

Attorney General
Lawrence G. Wasden (R)
P.O. Box 83720, Boise, ID 83720-0010
(208) 334-2400

Secretary of State
Lawerence E. Denney
P.O. Box 83720, Boise, ID 83720-0080
(208) 334-2300
ldenney@sos.idaho.gov

Vital Statistics
James Aydelotte
Health Policy and Vital Statistics
Bureau Chief, Public Health Division,
Department of Health and Welfare
450 West State Street,
Boise, ID 83720-0036
(208) 334-4969
aydelotj@dhw.idaho.gov

Supreme Court
5 justices sit en banc
Assigns cases to the Court of Appeals

Jurisdiction:
- Appeal by right criminal, civil. Exclusive administrative agency.
- Exclusive appeal by permission criminal, civil, administrative agency. Interlocutory appeals in criminal, civil, administrative agency.
- Exclusive death penalty.
- Original proceeding writ application. Exclusive bar discipline/eligibility, judicial qualification, certified question.

Court of Appeals
4 judges sit in 3-judge panels and en banc

Jurisdiction:
- Appeal by right criminal, civil.

District Court (7 districts)
44 district judges
Jury trials

Jurisdiction:
- Tort, contract, real property rights ($10,000 - no maximum), probate/estate, mental health, miscellaneous civil.
- Domestic relations.
- Exclusive felony and criminal appeals. Misdemeanor.
- Juvenile.

Magistrates Division
94 full-time magistrate judges
Jury trials

Jurisdiction:
- Tort, contract, real property rights ($0 - $10,000), small claims (up to $5,000), probate/estate, mental health, miscellaneous civil.
- Domestic relations.
- Preliminary hearings, misdemeanor.
- Juvenile.
- Exclusive traffic/other violations.

Notes: The Magistrates Division of the District Court functions as a limited jurisdiction court. There are an additional 44 senior judges that serve the judicial branch.

Court structure as of Fiscal Year 2015.

☐ Appellate level
☐ Trial level
↑ Route of appeal

ILLINOIS

Chief Justice
Rita B. Garman
1819 - 4th Avenue,
Rock Island, IL 61201
(309) 794-3608

Justices of the Supreme Court
Anne M. Burke
Charles E. Freeman
Lloyd A. Karmeier
Thomas L. Kilbride
Mary Jane Theis
Robert R. Thomas

Clerk of the Supreme Court
Carolyn Taft Grosboll
Supreme Court Building,
200 East Capitol Avenue,
Springfield, IL 62701
(217) 782-2035

Court System Website
www.state.il.us/court

Court Administration
Michael J. Tardy
Director, Administrative Office of the
Illinois Courts
222 North LaSalle Street, 13th Floor,
Chicago, IL 60601
(217) 558-4490

Governor
Bruce V. Rauner (R)
207 State Capitol Building,
Springfield, IL 62706
(217) 782-6830

State Website
www.illinois.gov

State Capitol Main Phone
(217) 782-2000

Attorney General
Lisa Madigan (D)
500 South Second Street,
Springfield, IL 62706
(217) 782-9000

Secretary of State
Jesse White (D)
213 State Capitol Building,
Springfield, IL 62756
(217) 782-2201

Vital Statistics
Joseph "Joe" Aiello
Division Chief, Division of Vital
Records, Illinois Department of Public
Health [IDPH]
925 East Ridgely Avenue,
Springfield, IL 62702
(217) 785-3163

Supreme Court
7 justices sit en banc

Jurisdiction:
- Appeal by right criminal, civil, administrative agency. Interlocutory appeals in criminal, civil, administrative agency.
- Appeal by permission in criminal, civil, administrative agency. Interlocutory appeals in criminal, civil, administrative agency.
- Exclusive death penalty.
- Original proceeding writ application. Exclusive bar admission, bar discipline/eligibility, certified question.

COURT OF LAST RESORT

Appellate Court (5 districts)
54 authorized judges, with 12 circuit court judges assigned to the appellate court, sit in 3-judge panels

Jurisdiction:
- Appeal by right criminal, civil, limited administrative agency. Interlocutory appeals in criminal, civil, limited administrative agency.
- Appeal by permission criminal, civil, limited administrative agency. Interlocutory appeals in criminal, civil, limited administrative agency.
- Original proceeding writ application.

INTERMEDIATE APPELLATE COURT

Circuit Court (23 circuits)
525 circuit judges, 382 associate judges
Jury trials permissible in most cases

Jurisdiction:
- Exclusive civil (including administrative agency appeals), small claims (up to $10,000).
- Exclusive domestic relations.
- Exclusive criminal.
- Exclusive juvenile.
- Exclusive traffic/other violations.

GENERAL JURISDICTION COURT

Court structure as of Fiscal Year 2015.

☐ Appellate level
☐ Trial level
↑ Route of appeal

INDIANA

Chief Justice
Loretta Hogan Rush
200 West Washington Street,
Indianapolis, IN 46204-3466
(317) 232-2540

Justices of the Supreme Court
Steven H. David
Brent E. Dickson
Mark S. Massa
Robert D. Rucker

Clerk of the Supreme Court
Kevin S. Smith
200 West Washington Street,
Indianapolis, IN 46204-2732
(317) 232-2540

Court System Website
www.courts.in.gov

Court Administration
Lilia G. Judson
Executive Director
30 South Meridian Street, Suite 500
Indianapolis, IN 46204-3568
(317) 232-2542

Governor
Mike Pence (R)
P.O. Box 1038, Anderson, IN 46015
(317) 232-4567

State Website
www.in.gov

State Capitol Main Phone
(317) 232-1000

Attorney General
Gregory F. "Greg" Zoeller (R)
302 West Washington Street, 5th Floor,
Indianapolis, IN 46204
(317) 232-6201

Secretary of State
Connie Lawson (R)
201 Statehouse, 200 West Washington
Street, Indianapolis, IN 46204-2790
(317) 232-6532
sos@sos.in.gov

Vital Statistics
Brian Carnes
State Registrar, Health Care Quality and
Regulatory Services Commission
P.O. Box 7125, Indianapolis, IN 46206
(317) 233-7523
bcarnes@isdh.in.gov

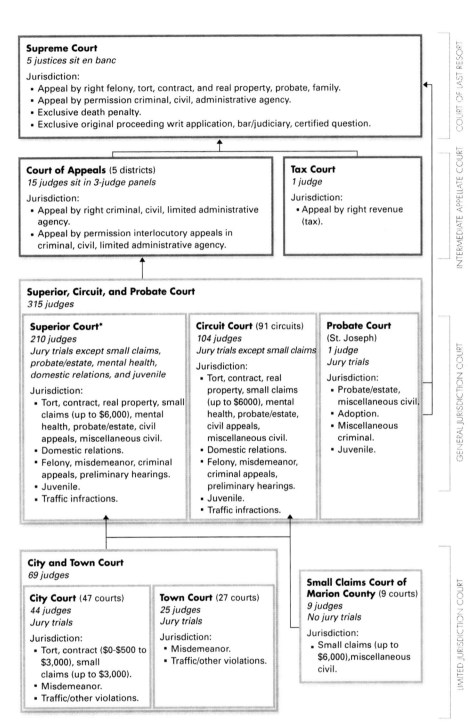

Supreme Court
5 justices sit en banc
Jurisdiction:
- Appeal by right felony, tort, contract, and real property, probate, family.
- Appeal by permission criminal, civil, administrative agency.
- Exclusive death penalty.
- Exclusive original proceeding writ application, bar/judiciary, certified question.

Court of Appeals (5 districts)
15 judges sit in 3-judge panels
Jurisdiction:
- Appeal by right criminal, civil, limited administrative agency.
- Appeal by permission interlocutory appeals in criminal, civil, limited administrative agency.

Tax Court
1 judge
Jurisdiction:
- Appeal by right revenue (tax).

Superior, Circuit, and Probate Court
315 judges

Superior Court*
210 judges
Jury trials except small claims, probate/estate, mental health, domestic relations, and juvenile
Jurisdiction:
- Tort, contract, real property, small claims (up to $6,000), mental health, probate/estate, civil appeals, miscellaneous civil.
- Domestic relations.
- Felony, misdemeanor, criminal appeals, preliminary hearings.
- Juvenile.
- Traffic infractions.

Circuit Court (91 circuits)
104 judges
Jury trials except small claims
Jurisdiction:
- Tort, contract, real property, small claims (up to $6000), mental health, probate/estate, civil appeals, miscellaneous civil.
- Domestic relations.
- Felony, misdemeanor, criminal appeals, preliminary hearings.
- Juvenile.
- Traffic infractions.

Probate Court
(St. Joseph)
1 judge
Jury trials
Jurisdiction:
- Probate/estate, miscellaneous civil.
- Adoption.
- Miscellaneous criminal.
- Juvenile.

City and Town Court
69 judges

City Court (47 courts)
44 judges
Jury trials
Jurisdiction:
- Tort, contract ($0-$500 to $3,000), small claims (up to $3,000).
- Misdemeanor.
- Traffic/other violations.

Town Court (27 courts)
25 judges
Jury trials
Jurisdiction:
- Misdemeanor.
- Traffic/other violations.

Small Claims Court of Marion County (9 courts)
9 judges
No jury trials
Jurisdiction:
- Small claims (up to $6,000), miscellaneous civil.

* Effective January 1, 1996, all Municipal Courts became Superior Court. Effective January 1, 2009, all County Courts merged with Superior Court.

COURT OF LAST RESORT

INTERMEDIATE APPELLATE COURT

GENERAL JURISDICTION COURT

LIMITED JURISDICTION COURT

Court structure as of Fiscal Year 2015.

☐ Appellate level
☐ Trial level
↑ Route of appeal

IOWA

Chief Justice
Mark S. Cady
P.O. Box 507, Fort Dodge, IA 50501
(515) 281-5911

Justices of the Supreme Court
Brent R. Appel
Daryl L. Hecht
Edward M. Mansfield
Thomas D. Waterman
David S. Wiggins
Bruce Zager

Clerk of the Supreme Court
Donna Humphal
Iowa Judicial Building,
1111 East Court Avenue,
Des Moines, IA 50319
(515) 281-5911

Court System Website
www.iowacourts.gov

Court Administration
David K. Boyd
State Court Administrator
Iowa Judicial Building,
1111 East Court Avenue,
Des Moines, IA 50319
(515) 281-5241

Governor
Terry E. Branstad (R)
1007 East Grand Avenue,
Des Moines, IA 50319
(515) 281-5211

State Website
www.iowa.gov

State Capitol Main Phone
(515) 281-5011

Attorney General
Thomas J. "Tom" Miller (D)
Hoover Building, 2nd Floor,
Des Moines, IA 50319
(515) 281-8373

Secretary of State
Paul D. Pate (R)
State Capitol, 1007 East Grand Avenue,
Room 105, Des Moines, IA 50319-0146
(515) 281-5204

Vital Statistics
Melissa R. Bird
Bureau Chief, Bureau of Health
Statistics, Iowa Department of Public
Health [IDPH]
Lucas State Office Building, 321 East
12th Street, Des Moines, IA 50319-0075
(515) 281-6762

Supreme Court
7 justices sit en banc
Assigns cases to the Court of Appeals

Jurisdiction:
- Appeal by right criminal, civil, administrative agency.
- Exclusive appeal by permission criminal, civil, administrative agency. Interlocutory appeals in criminal, civil, administrative agency.
- Original proceeding writ application. Exclusive bar/judiciary, certified question, advisory opinion.

Court of Appeals
9 judges sit in 3-panels and en banc

Jurisdiction:
- Appeal by right criminal, civil, administrative agency. Interlocutory appeals in criminal, civil, administrative agency.
- Original proceeding writ application.

District Court (8 districts in 99 counties)
114 authorized district judges, 69 district associate judges, 38 senior judges,
5 associate juvenile judges, 118 part-time magistrates, and 1 associate probate judge
Jury trials except in small claims, juvenile, equity cases, city and county ordinance
violations, mental health cases

Jurisdiction:
- Exclusive civil. Small claims (up to $5,000).
- Exclusive domestic relations.
- Exclusive criminal.
- Exclusive juvenile.
- Exclusive traffic/other violations, except for uncontested parking.

COURT OF LAST RESORT

INTERMEDIATE APPELLATE COURT

GENERAL JURISDICTION COURT

Court structure as of Fiscal Year 2015.

Appellate level
Trial level
↑   Route of appeal

KANSAS

Chief Justice
Lawton R. Nuss
389 Kansas Judicial Center,
301 SW Tenth Avenue,
Topeka, KS 66612-1507
(785) 296-4898

Justices of the Supreme Court
Carol A. Beier
William Daniel Biles
Lee Alan Johnson
Marla J. Luckert
Eric S. Rosen
Caleb Stegall

Clerk of the Supreme Court
Heather L. Smith
Clerk of the Appellate Courts
374 Kansas Judicial Center,
301 SW Tenth Avenue,
Topeka, KS 66612-1507
(785) 296-3229

Court System Website
www.kscourts.org

Court Administration
Nancy Maydew Dixon
Judicial Administrator
Kansas Judicial Center, 301 SW Tenth
Avenue, Topeka, KS 66612

Governor
Samuel Dale "Sam" Brownback (R)
State Capitol, 2nd Floor,
Topeka, KS 66612-1590
(785) 368-8500

State Website
www.kansas.gov

State Capitol Main Phone
(785) 296-5059

Attorney General
Derek Schmidt (R)
120 Southwest 10th Avenue, 2nd Floor,
Topeka, KS 66612-1597
(785) 296-2215

Secretary of State
Kris W. Kobach (R)
Memorial Hall, 120 S.W. 10th Avenue,
Topeka, KS 66612-1594
(785) 296-4575

Vital Statistics
Dr. Elizabeth "Lou" Saadi, PhD
State Registrar, Office of Vital
Statistics, Kansas Department of Health
and Environment [KDHE]
Curtis State Office Building,
1000 Southwest Jackson Street,
Suite 120, Topeka, KS 66612-2221
(785) 296-1400

Supreme Court
7 justices sit en banc

Jurisdiction:
- Appeal by right criminal, tort, contract, and real property, probate, family, administrative agency.
- Appeal by permission criminal, civil, administrative agency. Interlocutory appeals in criminal, civil, administrative agency.
- Exclusive death penalty.
- Original proceeding writ application. Exclusive bar/judiciary, certified question, advisory opinion.

Court of Appeals
14 judges

Jurisdiction:
- Appeal by right criminal, civil, limited administrative agency. Interlocutory appeals in criminal, limited administrative agency.
- Appeal by permission interlocutory appeals in tort, contract, and real property, probate, family.
- Original proceeding limited writ application.

District Court (31 districts)
244 judges (includes 73 magistrates)
Jury trials except in small claims

Jurisdiction:
- Exclusive civil (including civil appeals). Small claims (up to $4,000).
- Exclusive domestic relations.
- DWI/DUI. Exclusive felony, misdemeanor, criminal appeals.
- Exclusive juvenile.
- Traffic infractions.

Municipal Court (388 cities)
255 judges
No jury trials

Jurisdiction:
- DWI/DUI.
- Traffic infractions. Exclusive ordinance violations, parking.

Court structure as of Fiscal Year 2015.

Appellate level
Trial level
↑ Route of appeal

KENTUCKY

Chief Justice
John D. Minton, Jr.
231 State Capitol, 700 Capital Avenue,
Frankfort, KY 40601
(502) 564-4162

Justices of the Supreme Court
Lisabeth Hughes Abramson
David A. Barber
Bill Cunningham
Michelle M. Keller, RN
Mary C. Noble
Daniel J. Venters

Clerk of the Supreme Court
Susan Stokley Clary
Court Administrator, General Counsel
and Clerk of the Supreme Court
State Capitol Building, 700 Capital Ave,
Room 235, Frankfort, KY 40601
(502) 564-4176

Court System Website
www.kycourts.net

Court Administration
Laurie K. Dudgeon
Director, Kentucky Administrative
Office of the Courts
100 Millcreek Park,
Frankfort, KY 40601
(502) 573-2350

Governor
Steven L. "Steve" Beshear (D)
100 State Capitol, 700 Capital Avenue,
Suite 100, Frankfort, KY 40601
(502) 564-2611

State Website
www.kentucky.gov

State Capitol Main Phone
(502) 564-2500

Attorney General
Jack Conway (D)
State Capitol, 700 Capital Avenue,
Suite 118, Frankfort, KY 40601
(502) 696-5300

Secretary of State
Alison (Lundergan) Grimes (D)
P.O. Box 718, Frankfort, KY 40601
(502) 564-3490

Vital Statistics
Christina Stewart
Manager, Office of Vital Statistics,
Cabinet for Health and Family Services
275 East Main Street,
Frankfort, KY 40601
(502) 564-4212

Supreme Court
7 justices sit en banc

Jurisdiction:
- Appeal by right felony (limited to 20 yr+ sentence), workers' compensation. Interlocutory appeals in felony, workers' compensation.
- Appeal by permission criminal, civil, administrative agency. Interlocutory appeals in criminal, civil, administrative agency.
- Exclusive death penalty.
- Original proceeding writ application. Exclusive bar/judiciary, certified question, advisory opinion.

COURT OF LAST RESORT

Court of Appeals
14 judges sit in 3-judge panels, (sit en banc in a policy-making capacity)

Jurisdiction:
- Appeal by right criminal (limited to less than 20 year sentence), civil, limited administrative agency.
- Appeal by permission misdemeanor, civil, limited administrative agency. Interlocutory appeals in misdemeanor, civil, limited administrative agency.
- Original proceeding limited writ application.

INTERMEDIATE APPELLATE COURT

Circuit Court (57 judicial circuits)
102 judges plus domestic relations commissioners
Jury trials except in appeals

Jurisdiction:
- Tort, contract, real property ($4,001 - no maximum), interstate support, probate/estate. Exclusive civil appeals, miscellaneous civil.
- Domestic relations.
- Misdemeanor. Exclusive felony, criminal appeals.
- Juvenile.

Family Court (71 counties)
51 judges
Jury trials

Jurisdiction:
- Domestic relations.
- Domestic violence.
- Juvenile.
- Civil (contract, probate).

GENERAL JURISDICTION COURT

District Court (60 judicial districts)
116 judges plus trial commissioners
Jury trials in most cases

Jurisdiction:
- Tort, contract, real property ($0 - $4,000), probate/estate. Exclusive mental health, small claims (up to $1,500).
- Domestic relations.
- Preliminary hearings, misdemeanor.
- Juvenile.
- Exclusive traffic/other violations.

LIMITED JURISDICTION COURT

Note: There are also 60 senior status judges that can serve on any court except the Supreme Court.

Court structure as of Fiscal Year 2015.

- ▭ Appellate level
- ▭ Trial level
- ↑ Route of appeal

LOUISIANA

Chief Justice
Bernette Joshua Johnson
400 Royal Street,
New Orleans, LA 70130
(504) 310-2359

Justices of the Supreme Court
Marcus R. Clark
Greg Gerard Guidry
Jefferson D. Hughes, III
Jeannette Theriot Knoll
John L. Weimer

Clerk of the Supreme Court
John Tarlton Olivier
400 Royal Street, Suite 4200,
New Orleans, LA 70130-2104
(504) 310-2300

Court System Website
www.lasc.org

Court Administration
Sandra Vujnovich
Judicial Administrator
400 Royal Street, Suite 1190,
New Orleans, LA 70130
(504) 310-2550

Governor
Piyush "Bobby" Jindal (R)
P.O. Box 94004,
Baton Rouge, LA 70804-9004
(225) 342-7015

State Website
www.louisiana.gov

State Capitol Main Phone
(225) 342-6600

Attorney General
James D. "Buddy" Caldwell (R)
P.O. Box 94005,
Baton Rouge, LA 70804-9005
(225) 326-6708

Secretary of State
John Thomas "Tom" Schedler (R)
8585 Archives Avenue,
Baton Rouge, LA 70809
(225) 922-2880

Vital Statistics
Devin George
State Registrar and Center Director,
Center of State Registrar and Vital
Records, Department of Health and
Hospitals [DHH]
P.O. Box 60630,
New Orleans, LA 70160
(504) 593-5100

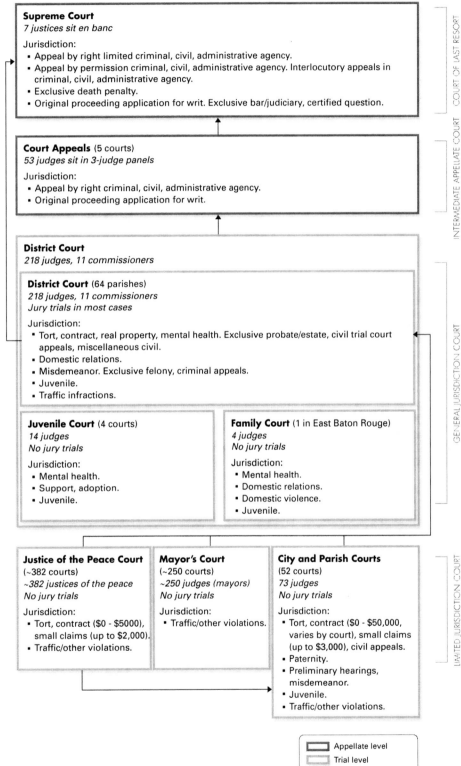

Court structure as of Fiscal Year 2015.

MAINE

Chief Justice
Leigh I. Saufley
Main Supreme Judicial Court,
205 Newbury Street, Room 139,
Portland, ME 04101-4125
(207) 822-4286

Justices of the Supreme Court
Donald G. Alexander
Ellen A. Gorman
Jeffrey L. Hjelm
Thomas E. Humphrey (Designate)
Joseph M. Jabar
Andrew M. Mead

Clerk of the Supreme Court
Matthew E. Pollack
Maine Supreme Judicial Court,
205 Newbury Street, Room 139,
Portland, ME 04101-4125
(207) 822-4146

Court System Website
www.courts.state.me.us

Court Administration
James T. Glessner
State Court Administrator
P.O. Box 4820,
Portland, ME 04112-4820
(207) 822-0710

Governor
Paul R. LePage (R)
One State House Station,
Augusta, ME 04333
(207) 287-3531

State Website
www.maine.gov

State Capitol Main Phone
(207) 264-9494

Attorney General
Janet T. Mills (D)
Six State House Station,
Augusta, ME 04333
(207) 626-8800

Secretary of State
Matthew Dunlap (D)
Nash Building, 148 State House Station,
2nd Floor, Augusta, ME 04333-0148
(207) 626-8400

Vital Statistics
Marty Henson
Data, Research & Vital Statistics Office
Director, Maine Center for Disease
Control and Prevention, Department of
Health and Human Services [DHHS]
244 Water Street, Augusta, ME 04330
(207) 287-3771

Supreme Judicial Court Sitting as Law Court
7 justices sit in 3-judge panels and en banc
Jurisdiction:
- Exclusive appeal by right criminal, civil, limited administrative agency. Interlocutory appeals in criminal, civil, administrative agency.
- Exclusive appeal by permission criminal (limited to extradition, 1 yr+ sentence), limited administrative agency.
- Exclusive original proceeding application for writ, bar/judiciary, certified question.

District Court (29 locations)
36 judges plus 8 family law magistrates
No jury trials
Jurisdiction:
- Tort, contract, real property rights ($0 - no maximum). Exclusive small claims (up to $4,500), mental health.
- Exclusive domestic relations (except for adoption).
- Felony, preliminary hearings, misdemeanor.
- Exclusive juvenile.
- Traffic infractions, ordinance violations. Exclusive parking.

Superior Court (19 locations)
17 justices
Jury trials in some cases
Jurisdiction:
- Tort, contract, real property, civil appeals, miscellaneous civil.
- Felony, misdemeanor, criminal appeals.

Probate Court (16 counties)
16 part-time judges
No jury trials
Jurisdiction:
- Exclusive probate/estate jurisdiction.
- Exclusive adoption.

Note: The Administrative Court was eliminated effective March 15, 2001, with the caseload absorbed by the District Court.

Court structure as of Fiscal Year 2015.

COURT OF LAST RESORT

GENERAL JURISDICTION COURT

LIMITED JURISDICTION COURT

⬜ Appellate level
⬜ Trial level
↑ Route of appeal

MARYLAND

Chief Judge — Court of Appeals
Mary Ellen Barbera
Judicial Center, 50 Maryland Avenue,
Rockville, MD 20850
(240) 777-9320

Judges of the Appeals Court
Sally D. Adkins
Lynne A. Battaglia
Clayton Greene, Jr.
Glenn T. Harrell, Jr.
Robert N. McDonald
Shirley M. Watts

Clerk of the Appeals Court
Bessie M. Decker
Robert C. Murphy Courts of Appeal
Building, 361 Rowe Boulevard,
Annapolis, MD 21401
(410) 260-1500

Court System Website
www.mdcourts.gov

Court Administration
Pamela Q. Harris
State Court Administrator
Maryland Judicial Ctr, 580 Taylor Ave,
Annapolis, MD 21401
(410) 260-1295

Governor
Lawrence J. "Larry" Hogan, Jr.
State Capitol, 100 State Circle,
Annapolis, MD 21401
(410) 974-3901

State Website
www.maryland.gov

State Capitol Main Phone
(410) 974-3901

Attorney General
Brian E. Frosh (D)
200 Saint Paul Place,
Baltimore, MD 21202-2021
(410) 576-6300

Secretary of State
John Casper Wobensmith
State House, 16 Francis Street,
Annapolis, MD 21401
(410) 974-5521

Vital Statistics
Geneva G. Sparks
Vital Records Deputy Director, Vital
Statistics Administration, Department of
Health and Mental Hygiene [DHMH]
6550 Reistertown Road,
Baltimore, MD 21215
(410) 764-3186

Court of Appeals
7 judges sit en banc

Jurisdiction:
- Limited appeal by right civil. Limited interlocutory appeals in civil.
- Appeal by permission criminal, civil, administrative agency. Interlocutory appeals in criminal, civil, administrative agency.
- Exclusive death penalty.
- Original proceeding writ application. Exclusive bar/judiciary, certified question.

Court of Special Appeals
13 judges sit in 3-judge panels and en banc

Jurisdiction:
- Appeal by right criminal, civil, administrative agency. Interlocutory appeals in criminal, civil, administrative agency.
- Appeal by permission criminal, civil.
- Original proceeding writ application.

Circuit Court (8 circuits in 24 counties)
161 judges
Jury trials in most cases

Jurisdiction:
- Tort, contract, real property ($5,000 - no maximum), probate/estate, miscellaneous civil. Exclusive mental health, civil appeals.
- Domestic relations.
- Felony, misdemeanor. Exclusive criminal appeals.
- Exclusive juvenile.

District Court (12 districts in 24 counties)
125 judges (plus 1 chief judge with administrative duties)
No jury trials

Jurisdiction:
- Tort, contract ($5,000 - $30,000), real property, miscellaneous civil. Exclusive small claims (up to $5,000).
- Civil protection/restraining orders.
- Felony, preliminary hearings, misdemeanor.
- Exclusive traffic/other violations.

Orphan's Court (23 counties)
68 judges
No jury trials

Jurisdiction:
- Probate/estate, except where such cases are handled by circuit court in Montgomery and Harford counties.

Court structure as of Fiscal Year 2015.

Appellate level
Trial level
↑ Route of appeal

MASSACHUSETTS

Chief Justice
Ralph D. Gants
One Pemberton Square,
Boston, MA 02108-1735
(617) 557-1020

Justices of the Supreme Court
Margot Botsford
Robert J. Cordy
Fernande R. V. "Nan" Duffly
Geraldine S. Hines
Barbara A. Lenk
Francis X. Spina

Clerk of the Supreme Court
Francis V. Kenneally
Clerk for the Commonwealth
One Pemberton Square, Suite 2500,
Boston, MA 02108-1750
(617) 557-1165

Court System Website
www.mass.gov/courts/sjc

Court Administration
Thomas Ambrosino
Executive Director
One Pemberton Square, Suite 2500,
Boston, MA 02108-1750
(617) 557-1194

Governor
Charles D. "Charlie" Baker, Jr. (R)
State House, Executive Office,
Room 360, Boston, MA 02133
(617) 725-4005

State Website
www.mass.gov

State Capitol Main Phone
(671) 725-4000

Attorney General
Maura Healey (D)
One Ashburton Place,
Boston, MA 02108-1518
(617) 727-2200

Secretary of the Commonwealth
William Francis Galvin (D)
McCormack Building,
One Ashburton Place, Room 1611,
Boston, MA 02108-1518
(617) 727-7030

Vital Statistics
Antonio "Tony" Sousa
Director, Bureau of Health
Information Research Statistics and
Evaluation, Department of Public Health
250 Washington Street, 6th Floor,
Boston, MA 02108
(617) 740-2617

COURT OF LAST RESORT

Supreme Judicial Court
7 justices sit in 5-judge panels and en banc*

Jurisdiction:
- Appeal by permission criminal, civil, administrative agency. Appeal by right criminal (limited to 1st degree murder). Interlocutory appeals in criminal, civil, administrative agency.
- Exclusive original proceeding application for writ, bar/judiciary, certified question, advisory opinion.

INTERMEDIATE APPELLATE COURT

Appeals Court
25 justices sit in 3-judge panels*

Jurisdiction:
- Appeal by right criminal, exclusive appeal by right, civil, administrative agency.
- Appeal by permission interlocutory appeals in criminal, civil, administrative agency.

GENERAL JURISDICTION COURT

Superior Court Department (14 divisions)
80 justices
Jury trials

Jurisdiction:
- Tort, contract, real property ($25,000 - no maximum), civil appeals, miscellaneous civil.
- Civil protection/restraining orders.
- Felony, misdemeanor.

LIMITED JURISDICTION COURT

District Court Department (62 divisions)
162 justices
Jury trials

Jurisdiction:
- Tort, contract, real property ($0 - $25,000), small claims (up to $7,000), mental health, civil appeals, miscellaneous civil.
- Civil protection/restraining orders.
- Felony, preliminary hearings, misdemeanor.
- Traffic/other violations.

Boston Municipal Court Department
(8 divisions)
30 justices
Jury trials

Jurisdiction:
- Tort, contract, real property rights ($0 - $25,000), small claims (up to $7,000), mental health, civil appeals, miscellaneous civil.
- Civil protection/restraining orders.
- Felony, preliminary hearings, misdemeanor.
- Traffic/other violations.

Juvenile Court Department
(11 divisions)
39 justices
Jury trials

Jurisdiction:
- Guardianship.
- Adoption.
- Juvenile.

Housing Court Department
(5 divisions)
10 justices
Jury trials except in small claims

Jurisdiction:
- Contract, small claims (up to $7,000).
- Preliminary hearings, misdemeanor.
- Ordinance violations.

Land Court Department
(1 statewide court)
7 justices
No jury trials

Jurisdiction:
- Mortgage foreclosure, real property.

Probate & Family Court Department
(14 divisions)
48 justices
No jury trials

Jurisdiction:
- Exclusive probate/estate, miscellaneous civil.
- Domestic relations. Exclusive divorce/ dissolution.
- Juvenile dependency.

Note: All departments (general and limited jurisdiction trial courts) make up the Trial Court of Massachusetts. The Administrative Office of the Trial Court reports caseload data by Department; thus, each Department is treated as a unique jurisdiction reporting unit.

*The justices also sit individually in the "single justice" side of the court, on a rotating basis.

Court structure as of Fiscal Year 2015.

▭ Appellate level
▭ Trial level
↑ Route of appeal

MICHIGAN

Chief Justice
Robert P. Young, Jr.
Cadillac Place,
3034 West Grand Boulevard,
Suite 8-500,
Detroit, MI 48202-6034
(313) 972-3250

Justices of the Supreme Court
Richard H. Bernstein
Stephen J. Markman
Bridget McCormack
David Viviano
Brian K. Zahra

Clerk of the Supreme Court
Larry Royster
P.O. Box 30052, Lansing, MI 48909
(517) 373-0120

Court System Website
www.courts.mi.gov

Court Administration
John A. Hohman, Jr.
State Court Administrator
P.O. Box 30048, Lansing, MI 48909
(517) 373-0128

Governor
Richard D. "Rick" Snyder (R)
P.O. Box 30013, Lansing, MI 48909
(517) 373-3400

State Website
www.michigan.gov

State Capitol Main Phone
(517) 373-1837

Attorney General
William D. "Bill" Schuette (R)
P.O. Box 30212, Lansing, MI 48909
(517) 373-1110

Secretary of State
Ruth Johnson (R)
Richard H. Austin Building,
430 West Allegan Street, 4th Floor,
Lansing, MI 48918-8900
(517) 373-2511

Vital Statistics
Glenn Copeland
Vital Records and Health Statistics State
Registrar, Public Health Administration
Chief Administrative Office, Department
of Community Health [MDCH]
201 Townsend Street,
Lansing, MI 48913
(517) 335-8677

Supreme Court
7 justices sit en banc
Jurisdiction:
- Appeal by permission criminal, civil, administrative agency. Interlocutory appeals in criminal, civil, administrative agency.
- Exclusive original proceeding bar/judiciary, certified question, advisory opinion.

Court of Appeals (4 districts)
28 judges sit in 3-judge panels
Jurisdiction:
- Exclusive appeal by right criminal, civil, administrative agency.
- Appeal by permission criminal, civil, administrative agency. Interlocutory appeals in criminal, civil, administrative agency.
- Exclusive original proceeding application for writ.

Court of Claims
(this is a function of the 30th Circuit Court)
4 judges
No jury trials
- Jurisdiction:
Administrative agency appeals involving claims against the state.

Circuit Court* (57 courts)**
233 judges
Jury trials except in domestic relations
Jurisdiction:
- Tort, contract, real property ($25,001 - no maximum), probate/estate, mental health, administrative agency appeals, miscellaneous civil. Exclusive civil trial court appeals.
- Exclusive domestic relations.
- Felony, criminal appeals.
- Juvenile.

District Court (90 Districts)
295 judges
Jury trials in most cases
Jurisdiction:
- Tort, contract, real property ($0 - $25,000), small claims (up to $3,000).
- Felony, preliminary hearings, misdemeanor.
- Ordinance violations.

Probate Court (73 courts)
132 judges
Jury trials in some cases
Jurisdiction:
- Probate/estate, mental health.

Municipal Court (4 courts)
4 judges
Jury trials in most cases
Jurisdiction:
- Tort, contract, real property ($0 - $1,500; $0 - $3,000 if approved by local funding unit), small claims (up to $100; up to $600 if approved).
- Preliminary hearings, misdemeanor.
- Traffic/other violations.

*The Recorder's Court of Detroit merged with the Circuit Court effective October 1, 1997.
**A Family Division of Circuit Court became operational on January 1, 1998.

Court structure as of Fiscal Year 2015.

MINNESOTA

Chief Justice
Lorie Skjerven Gildea
25 Rev. Dr. Martin Luther King, Jr. Blvd,
St. Paul, MN 55155
(651) 297-7650

Justices of the Supreme Court
G. Barry Anderson
Christopher J. Dietzen
David Lillehaug
Alan C. Page
David R. Stras
Wilhelmina M. Wright

Clerk of the Supreme Court
AnnMarie S. O'Neill
Clerk of the Appellate Courts and
Supreme Court Administrator
25 Rev. Dr. Martin Luther King, Jr. Blvd,
St. Paul, MN 5515
(651) 297-5529

Court System Website
www.mncourts.gov

Court Administration
Jeffrey "Jeff" Shorba
State Court Administrator
135 Minnesota Judicial Center,
25 Rev. Dr. Martin Luther King, Jr. Blvd,
St. Paul, MN 55155
(651) 296-2474

Governor
Mark Dayton (DFL)
130 State Capitol,
75 Rev. Dr. Martin Luther King, Jr. Blvd,
St. Paul, MN 55155
(651) 201-3400

State Website
www.mn.gov

State Capitol Main Phone
(651) 201-3400

Attorney General
Lori R. Swanson (DFL)
1400 Bremer Tower, 445 Minnesota
Street, St. Paul, MN 55101
(651) 296-6196

Secretary of State
Steve Simon (DFL)
180 State Office Building, 100 Rev. Dr.
Martin Luther King, Jr. Blvd,
St. Paul, MN 55155-1299
(651) 296-2803

Vital Statistics
Steven Elkins, State Registrar
P.O. Box 64499,
St. Paul, MN 55164-0499
(651) 201-5980

Supreme Court
7 justices sit en banc
Jurisdiction:
- Appeal by right felony, civil administrative agency.
- Appeal by permission criminal, civil, limited administrative agency.
- Original proceeding application for writ, certified question. Exclusive bar discipline/eligibility, advisory opinion.

Court of Appeals
19 judges sit in 3-judge panels en banc
Jurisdiction:
- Appeal by right criminal, civil, workers' compensation. Interlocutory appeals in criminal, civil, workers' compensation.
- Appeal by permission criminal, civil. Exclusive workers' compensation. Interlocutory appeals in criminal, civil, workers' compensation.
- Original proceeding application for writ, certified question.

District Court (10 districts)
289 judges
Jury trials except in small claims and non-extended juvenile jurisdiction cases
Jurisdiction:
- Exclusive civil (conciliation division: $0 - $7,500).
- Exclusive domestic relations.
- Exclusive criminal.
- Exclusive juvenile.
- Exclusive traffic/other violations.

COURT OF LAST RESORT

INTERMEDIATE APPELLATE COURT

GENERAL JURISDICTION COURT

Court structure as of Fiscal Year 2015.

Appellate level
Trial level
↑   Route of appeal

MISSISSIPPI

Chief Justice
William L. Waller, Jr.
P.O. Box 117, Jackson, MS 39205-0117
(601) 359-2139

Justices of the Supreme Court
David A. Chandler
Josiah D. Coleman
Jess H. Dickinson
Leslie D. King
James W. "Jim" Kitchens
Ann Hannaford Lamar
Randy G. "Bubba" Pierce
Michael K. Randolph

Clerk of the Supreme Court
Muriel Ellis
P.O. Box 117, Jackson, MS 39205
(601) 359-2175

Court System Website
www.mssc.state.ms.us

Court Administration
Hubbard T. "Hubby" Saunders, IV
Supreme Court Administrator
P.O. Box 117, Jackson, MS 39205
(601) 359-2182

Governor
Phil Bryant (R)
P.O. Box 139, Jackson, MS 39205
(601) 359-3150

State Website
www.mississippi.gov

State Capitol Main Phone
(601) 359-3100

Attorney General
James Matthew "Jim" Hood (D)
P.O. Box 220, Jackson, MS 39205
(601) 359-3680

Secretary of State
C. Delbert Hosemann, Jr. (R)
P.O. Box 136, Jackson, MS 39205-0136
(601) 359-6342
delbert.hosemann@sos.ms.gov

Vital Statistics
Judy Moulder
Director, Vital Records Office,
Office of Health Administration
570 East Woodrow Wilson,
Jackson, MS 39215-1700
(601) 576-7961
judy.moulder@msdh.state.ms.us

Supreme Court
9 justices sit in 3-judge panels and en banc
Assigns cases to the Court of Appeals

Jurisdiction:
- Appeal by right criminal, civil, administrative agency. Interlocutory appeals in criminal, civil, administrative agency.
- Exclusive appeal by permission criminal, civil, administrative agency. Interlocutory appeals in criminal, civil, administrative agency.
- Exclusive death penalty.
- Original proceeding application for writ. Exclusive bar/judiciary, certified question, advisory opinion.

COURT OF LAST RESORT

Court of Appeals (5 districts)
10 judges sit in 3-judge panels and en banc

Jurisdiction:
- Appeal by right criminal, civil, administrative agency. Interlocutory appeals in criminal, civil, administrative agency.
- Original proceeding application for writ.

INTERMEDIATE APPELLATE COURT

Circuit Court (22 districts)
53 judges
Jury trials

Jurisdiction:
- Tort, contract, real property ($201 - no maximum), civil law appeals.
- Criminal.

GENERAL JURISDICTION COURT

Chancery Court (20 districts)
49 judges
Jury trials (limited)

Jurisdiction:
- Tort, contract, real property ($0 - no maximum), probate/estate, mental health, civil equity appeals.
- Domestic relations.
- Juvenile (if no County Court).
- Appeals from Justice and Municipal Courts (if no County Court).

County Court (21 courts)
30 judges
Jury trials (limited)

Jurisdiction:
- Tort, contract, real property ($0 - $200,000), civil appeals. Probate/estate and mental health (as assigned by Chancery Court).
- Domestic relations (as assigned by Chancery Court).
- Preliminary hearings, misdemeanor.
- Juvenile.

Justice Court (82 courts)
197 judges
Jury trials

Jurisdiction:
- Small claims ($0 - $3,500).
- Preliminary hearings, misdemeanor.

Municipal Court (226 courts)
227 judges
No jury trials

Jurisdiction:
- Preliminary hearings, misdemeanor.
- Traffic/other violations.

LIMITED JURISDICTION COURT

The Family Court was abolished July 1, 1999 and merged into County Court.

Court structure as of Fiscal Year 2015.

Appellate level
Trial level
↑   Route of appeal

MISSOURI

Chief Justice
Mary Rhodes Russell
Supreme Court Building, 207 West High
Street, Jefferson City, MO 65101
(573) 751-6880

Justices of the Supreme Court
Patricia Breckenridge
George W. Draper, III
Zel Martin Fischer
Laura Denvir Stith
Richard B. Teitelman
Paul Wilson

Clerk of the Supreme Court
Bill L. Thompson
P.O. Box 150, Jefferson City, MO 65102
(573) 751-4144

Court System Website
www.courts.mo.gov

Court Administration
Kathy S. Lloyd
State Courts Administrator
P.O. Box 104480,
Jefferson City, MO 65110
(573) 526-8803

Governor
Jeremiah W. "Jay" Nixon (D)
P.O. Box 720, Jefferson City, MO 65102
(573) 751-3222

State Website
www.mo.gov

State Capitol Main Phone
(573) 751-2000

Attorney General
Chris Koster (D)
P.O. Box 899, Jefferson City, MO 65102
(573) 751-3321
attorney.general@ago.mo.gov

Secretary of State
Jason Kander (D)
P.O. Box 140252,
Kansas City, MO 64114
(573) 751-1880

Vital Statistics
Craig Ward
State Vital Records Registrar,
Epidemiology for Public Health Practice
Section, Department of Health and
Senior Services [DHSS]
P.O. Box 570, Jefferson City, MO 65102
(573) 526-0348

Supreme Court
7 judges

Jurisdiction:
- Appeal by right limited criminal, civil, administrative agency. Interlocutory appeals in criminal, civil, administrative agency.
- Appeal by permission criminal, civil, administrative agency. Interlocutory appeals in criminal, civil, administrative agency.
- Exclusive death penalty.
- Original proceeding application for writ. Exclusive bar/judiciary.

Court of Appeals (3 districts)
32 judges sit in 3-judge panels

Jurisdiction:
- Appeal by right criminal, civil, administrative agency. Interlocutory appeals in criminal, civil, administrative agency.
- Original proceeding application for writ.

Circuit Court (45 circuits)
141 circuit judges, 193 associate circuit judges, 32 commissioners and deputy commisioners
Jury trials in most cases

Jurisdiction:
- Exclusive civil (circuit division: $0 - $no maximum; associate division: $0 - $25,000), small claims (up to $3,000).
- Exclusive domestic relations.
- Exclusive criminal.
- Exclusive juvenile.
- Traffic/other violations.

Municipal Court (467 divisions)
476 municipal judges
Jury trials in Springfield Municipality only

Jurisdiction:
- Traffic/other violations.

COURT OF LAST RESORT

INTERMEDIATE APPELLATE COURT

GENERAL JURISDICTION COURT

LIMITED JURISDICTION COURT

Court structure as of Fiscal Year 2015.

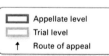

Appellate level
Trial level
↑ Route of appeal

MONTANA

Chief Justice
Mike McGrath
Justice Building,
215 North Sanders, Helena, MT 59620
(406) 444-5490

Justices of the Supreme Court
Beth Baker
Patricia Cotter
Laurie McKinnon
Jim Rice
James Jeremiah "Jim" Shea
Michael E. Wheat

Clerk of the Supreme Court
Ed Smith
P.O. Box 203003,
Helena, MT 59620-3001
(406) 444-3858

Court System Website
www.montanacourts.org

Court Administration
Beth McLaughlin
P.O. Box 203002,
Helena, MT 59620-3002
(406) 841-2966

Governor
Steve Bullock (D)
P.O. Box 200801,
Helena, MT 59620-0801
(406) 444-3111

State Website
www.mt.gov

State Capitol Main Phone
(406) 444-3111

Attorney General
Timothy C. "Tim" Fox (R)
P.O. Box 201401,
Helena, MT 59620-1401
(406) 444-2026

Secretary of State
Linda McCulloch (D)
P.O. Box 202801,
Helena, MT 59620-2801
(406) 444-4195

Vital Statistics
Karin Ferlicka
Vital Records State Registrar,
Department of Public Health and
Human Services [DPHHS]
111 North Sanders, Room 6,
Helena, MT 59604
(406) 444-4250
hhsvitalrecords@mt.gov

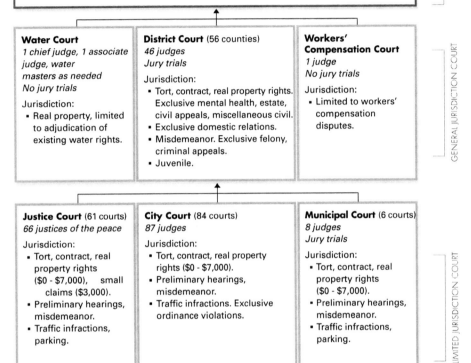

Supreme Court
7 justices sit in 5-judge panels and en banc

Jurisdiction:
- Exclusive appeal by right criminal, civil, administrative agency. Interlocutory appeals in criminal, civil, administrative agency.
- Exclusive death penalty.
- Exclusive original proceeding application for writ, certified question, advisory opinion.

Water Court
1 chief judge, 1 associate judge, water masters as needed
No jury trials

Jurisdiction:
- Real property, limited to adjudication of existing water rights.

District Court (56 counties)
46 judges
Jury trials

Jurisdiction:
- Tort, contract, real property rights. Exclusive mental health, estate, civil appeals, miscellaneous civil.
- Exclusive domestic relations.
- Misdemeanor. Exclusive felony, criminal appeals.
- Juvenile.

Workers' Compensation Court
1 judge
No jury trials

Jurisdiction:
- Limited to workers' compensation disputes.

Justice Court (61 courts)
66 justices of the peace

Jurisdiction:
- Tort, contract, real property rights ($0 - $7,000), small claims ($3,000).
- Preliminary hearings, misdemeanor.
- Traffic infractions, parking.

City Court (84 courts)
87 judges

Jurisdiction:
- Tort, contract, real property rights ($0 - $7,000).
- Preliminary hearings, misdemeanor.
- Traffic infractions. Exclusive ordinance violations.

Municipal Court (6 courts)
8 judges
Jury trials

Jurisdiction:
- Tort, contract, real property rights ($0 - $7,000).
- Preliminary hearings, misdemeanor.
- Traffic infractions, parking.

COURT OF LAST RESORT

GENERAL JURISDICTION COURT

LIMITED JURISDICTION COURT

Court structure as of Fiscal Year 2015.

- Appellate level
- Trial level
- ↑ Route of appeal

NEBRASKA

Chief Justice
Michael G. Heavican
P.O. Box 98910, Lincoln, NE 68509
(402) 471-3738

Justices of the Supreme Court
William B. Cassel
William M. Connolly
Michael McCormack
Lindsey Miller-Lerman
Kenneth C. Stephan
John F. Wright

Clerk of the Supreme Court
Teresa A. "Terri" Brown
Clerk of Supreme Court and
Court of Appeals
2413 State Capitol Building,
1445 K Street, Lincoln, NE 68509
(402) 471-3731

Court System Website
www.supremecourt.ne.gov

Court Administration
Corey R. Steel
State Court Administrator
P.O. Box 98910, Lincoln, NE 68509
(402) 471-3730

Governor
John Peter "Pete" Ricketts (R)
P.O. Box 94848,
Lincoln, NE 68509-4848
(402) 471-2244

State Website
www.nebraska.gov

State Capitol Main Phone
(402) 471-2311

Attorney General
Douglas J. "Doug" Peterson (R)
P. O. Box 98920, Lincoln, NE 98920
(402) 471-2682
jon.bruning@nebraska.gov

Secretary of State
John A. Gale (R)
2300 State Capitol, P.O. Box 94608,
Lincoln, NE 68509-4608
(402) 471-1572
john.gale@nebraska.gov

Vital Statistics
Stan Cooper
Vital Records Director,
Division of Public Health
1033 O Street, Suite 130,
Lincoln, NE 68508
(402) 471-0915
stan.cooper@nebraska.gov

Supreme Court
7 justices sit en banc

Jurisdiction:
- Appeal by right criminal, civil, administrative agency. Interlocutory appeals in criminal, civil, administrative agency.
- Exclusive appeal by permission criminal, civil, administrative agency. Interlocutory appeals in criminal, civil, administrative agency.
- Exclusive death penalty.
- Original proceeding application for writ, bar discipline/eligibility.

Court of Appeals
6 judges sit in 3-judge panels

Jurisdiction:
- Appeal by right criminal, civil, administrative agency. Interlocutory appeals in criminal, civil, administrative agency.

District Court (12 districts)
56 judges
Jury trials excpt in appeals

Jurisdiction:
- Tort, contract, real property ($52,001 - no maximum), civil appeals, miscellaneous civil. Exclusive mental health.
- Domestic relations.
- Misdemeanor. Exclusive felony, criminal appeals, miscellaneous criminal.

Separate Juvenile Court
(3 counties)
11 *judges*
No jury trials

Jurisdiction:
- Custody, support.
- Juvenile.

County Court (12 districts)
58 judges
Jury trials except in juvenile and small claims

Jurisdiction:
- Tort, contract, real property rights ($0 - $52,000), small claims ($3,500). Exclusive probate/estate.
- Exclusive adoption. Domestic relations.
- Preliminary hearings, misdemeanor.
- Juvenile.
- Traffic/other violations.

Workers' Compensation Court
7 judges
No jury trials

Jurisdiction:
- Administrative agency appeals.

COURT OF LAST RESORT

INTERMEDIATE APPELLATE COURT

GENERAL JURISDICTION COURT

LIMITED JURISDICTION COURT

Court structure as of Fiscal Year 2015.

Appellate level
Trial level
↑ Route of appeal

NEVADA

Chief Justice
James W. Hardesty
Supreme Court Building, 201 South
Carson Street, Carson City, NV 89701
(775) 684-1590

Justices of the Supreme Court
Michael A. Cherry
Michael L. Douglas
Mark Gibbons
Ronald Parraguirre
Kristina "Kris" Pickering
Nancy M. Saitta

Clerk of the Supreme Court
Tracie Lindeman
Supreme Court Building,
201 South Carson Street, Suite 201,
Carson City, NV 89701-4702
(775) 684-1600

Court System Website
www.nevadajudiciary.us

Court Administration
Robin Sweet
State Court Administrator
Supreme Court Building,
201 South Carson Street, Suite 250,
Carson City, NV 89701-4702
(775) 684-1717

Governor
Brian E. Sandoval (R)
101 North Carson Street,
Carson City, NV 89701
(775) 684-5670

State Website
www.nv.gov

State Capitol Main Phone
(775) 684-1000

Attorney General
Adam Paul Laxalt (R)
100 North Carson Street,
Carson City, NV 89701-4717
(775) 684-1100

Secretary of State
Barbara K. Cegavske (R)
State Capitol Bldg, 101 North Carson St,
Suite 3, Carson City, NV 89701-4786
(775) 684-5708

Vital Statistics
Steven "Steve" Gilbert
Vital Statistics Program Officer,
Health Division, Department of Health
and Human Services [DHHS]
4150 Technology Way,
Carson City, NV 89706
(775) 684-4242

Supreme Court
7 justices sit in 3-judge panels en banc

Jurisdiction:
- Exclusive appeal by right criminal, civil, administrative agency. Interlocutory appeals in criminal, civil, administrative agency.
- Exclusive death penalty.
- Exclusive original proceeding application for writ, bar admission, bar discipline/eligibility, certified questions.

COURT OF LAST RESORT

Court of Appeals
3 judges

Jurisdiction:
- Exclusive appeal by right criminal, civil, administrative agency. Interlocutory appeals in criminal, civil, administrative agency.
- Exclusive death penalty.
- Exclusive original proceeding application for writ, bar admission, bar discipline/eligibility, certified questions.

INTERMEDIATE APPELLATE COURT

District Court (10 districts)
82 judges
Jury trials in most cases

Jurisdiction:
- Tort, contract, real property ($10,001 - no maximum). Exclusive mental health, probate/estate, civil appeals, miscellaneous civil.
- Exclusive domestic relations.
- Felony, misdemeanor.*
- Exclusive criminal appeals.
- Exclusive juvenile.

GENERAL JURISDICTION COURT

Justice Court (43 towns)
75 justices of the peace
(8 of these also serve as Municipal Court judges)
Jury trials except in small claims, traffic and parking cases

Jurisdiction:
- Tort, contract, real property rights ($0 - $10,000), small claims up to $5,000).
- Preliminary hearings, misdemeanor.*
- Traffic infractions, parking.

Municipal Court
(17 incorporated cities/towns)
30 judges (8 of these also serve as Justice Court Judges)
Jury trials except in small claims, traffic, parking and ordinance violation cases

Jurisdiction:
- Small claims (up to $2,500).
- Misdemeanor.*
- Traffic infractions, parking. Exclusive ordinance violations.

LIMITED JURISDICTION COURT

*District Court hears gross misdemeanor anors cases; Justice & Municipal Courts hear misdemeanors with fines under $1,000 and/or sentence of less than six months.

Court structure as of Fiscal Year 2015.

☐ Appellate level
☐ Trial level
↑ Route of appeal

NEW HAMPSHIRE

Chief Justice
Linda S. Dalianis
One Charles Doe Drive,
Concord, NH 03301
(603) 271-2646

Justices of the Supreme Court
James P. "Jim" Bassett
Carol Ann Conboy
Gary E. Hicks
Robert J. Lynn

Clerk of the Supreme Court
Eileen Fox
Supreme Court Building,
One Charles Doe Drive,
Concord, NH 03301-6160
(603) 271-2646

Court System Website
www.courts.state.nh.us

Court Administration
Donald D. Goodnow, Esq.
Director, Administrative Office of the
Courts of New Hampshire
Two Charles Doe Drive,
Concord, NH 03301-6179
(603) 271-2521

Governor
Margaret Wood "Maggie" Hassan (D)
107 North Main Street,
Concord, NH 03301
(603) 271-2121

State Website
www.nh.gov

State Capitol Main Phone
(603) 271-1110

Attorney General
Joseph A. Foster (D)
33 Capitol Street,
Concord, NH 03301-639
(603) 271-1202

Secretary of State
William M. "Bill" Gardner (D)
State House, 107 North Main Street,
Room 204, Concord, NH 03301
(603) 271-3242

Vital Statistics
Stephen M. Wurtz
State Registrar, Division of Vital
Records Administration, Office of the
Secretary of State
71 South Fruit Street,
Concord, NH 03301
(603) 271-4655
stephen.wurtz@sos.nh.gov

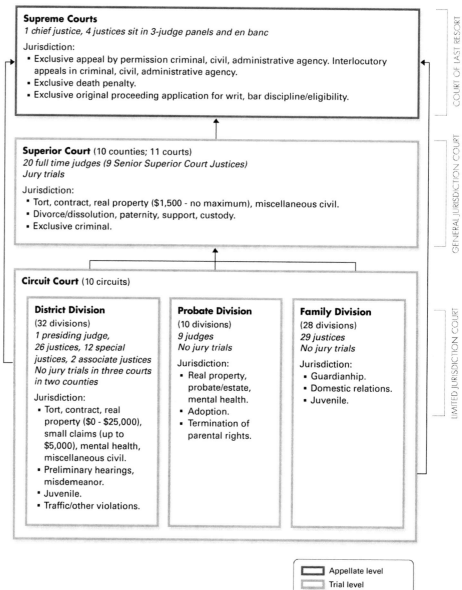

Supreme Courts
1 chief justice, 4 justices sit in 3-judge panels and en banc
Jurisdiction:
- Exclusive appeal by permission criminal, civil, administrative agency. Interlocutory appeals in criminal, civil, administrative agency.
- Exclusive death penalty.
- Exclusive original proceeding application for writ, bar discipline/eligibility.

COURT OF LAST RESORT

Superior Court (10 counties; 11 courts)
20 full time judges (9 Senior Superior Court Justices)
Jury trials
Jurisdiction:
- Tort, contract, real property ($1,500 - no maximum), miscellaneous civil.
- Divorce/dissolution, paternity, support, custody.
- Exclusive criminal.

GENERAL JURISDICTION COURT

Circuit Court (10 circuits)

District Division
(32 divisions)
*1 presiding judge,
26 justices, 12 special
justices, 2 associate justices
No jury trials in three courts
in two counties*
Jurisdiction:
- Tort, contract, real property ($0 - $25,000), small claims (up to $5,000), mental health, miscellaneous civil.
- Preliminary hearings, misdemeanor.
- Juvenile.
- Traffic/other violations.

Probate Division
(10 divisions)
*9 judges
No jury trials*
Jurisdiction:
- Real property, probate/estate, mental health.
- Adoption.
- Termination of parental rights.

Family Division
(28 divisions)
*29 justices
No jury trials*
Jurisdiction:
- Guardianhip.
- Domestic relations.
- Juvenile.

LIMITED JURISDICTION COURT

Court structure as of Fiscal Year 2015.

Appellate level
Trial level
↑ Route of appeal

NEW JERSEY

Chief Justice
Stuart Rabner
P.O. Box 023, Trenton, NJ 08625-0023
(609) 292-2448

Justices of the Supreme Court
Barry T. Albin
David Bauman (Designate)
Mary Catherine Cuff (Acting)
Faustino J. "F.J." Fernandez-Vina
Jaynee LaVecchia
Anne M. Patterson
Lee A. Solomon

Clerk of the Supreme Court
Mark Neary
P.O. Box 970, Trenton, NJ 08625-0970
(609) 292-4837

Court System Website
www.njcourts.com

Court Administration
Glenn A. Grant
Administrative Director (Acting)
P.O. Box 037, Trenton, NJ 08625-0037
(609) 984-0275

Governor
Christopher J. "Chris" Christie (R)
P.O. Box 001, Trenton, NJ 08625
(609) 292-6000

State Website
www.newjersey.gov

State Capitol Main Phone
(609) 292-2121

Attorney General
John Jay Hoffman
Attorney General (Acting)
P.O. Box 080, Justice Complex,
Trenton, NJ 08625
(609) 292-4930

Secretary of State
Kimberly A. "Kim" Guadagno
125 W. State Street, Trenton, NJ 08625
(609) 777-0884

Vital Statistics
Vincent Arrisi
Vital Statistics State Registrar,
Department of Health
P.O. Box 360, Trenton, NJ 08625-0360
(609) 292-4087

Supreme Court
7 justices sit en banc

Jurisdiction:
- Appeal by right criminal, civil, administrative agency. Interlocutory appeals in criminal, civil, administrative agency.
- Appeal by permission interlocutory appeals in criminal, civil, administrative agency.
- Exclusive original proceeding, bar/judiciary, certified question.

Appellate Division of Superior Court (8 parts)
32 judges sit in two- and three-judge panels

Jurisdiction:
- Appeal by right criminal, civil, administrative agency.
- Appeal by permission, interlocutory appeals in criminal, civil, administrative agency.

Superior Court (15 vicinages in 21 counties)
Approximately 360 judges
Jury trials in most cases

Jurisdiction:
- Exclusive civil ($0 - no maximum; special civil part: $0 - $15,000). Small claims (up to $3,000; up to $5,000 for security deposit demand cases).
- Exclusive domestic relations.
- Felony. Exclusive criminal appeals.
- Exclusive juvenile.

Municipal Court (539 courts, of which 21 are multi-municipal)
560 judges
No jury trials

Jurisdiction:
- Felony,* misdemeanor.
- Exclusive traffic/other violations.

Tax Court
12 judges
No jury trials

Jurisdiction:
- Administrative agency appeals, tax cases.

COURT OF LAST RESORT

INTERMEDIATE APPELLATE COURT

GENERAL JURISDICTION COURT

LIMITED JURISDICTION COURT

*Felony cases are handled on first appearance in the Municipal Courts and then are transferred through the county Prosecutor's office to the Superior Court.

Court structure as of Fiscal Year 2015.

Appellate level
Trial level
↑   Route of appeal

NEW MEXICO

Chief Justice
Barbara J. Vigil
P.O. Box 848, Santa Fe, NM 87504-0848
(505) 827-4883

Justices of the Supreme Court
Richard C. Bosson
Edward L. Chavez
Charles W. Daniels
Petra Jimenez Maes

Clerk of the Supreme Court
Joey Moya
P.O. Box 848, Santa Fe, NM 87504-0848
(505) 827-4860

Court System Website
www.nmcourts.com

Court Administration
Arthur W. Pepin
Administrative Office of the Courts
Director
Supreme Court Building,
237 Don Gaspar Avenue, Room 25,
Santa Fe, NM 87501
(505) 827-4800

Governor
Susana Martinez (R)
State Capitol Building,
490 Old Santa Fe Trail, Room 400,
Santa Fe, NM 87501
(505) 476-2200

State Website
www.newmexico.gov

State Capitol Main Phone
(800) 825-6639

Attorney General
Hector H. Balderas, CFE (D)
P.O. Drawer 1508,
Santa Fe, NM 87504-1508
(575) 770-7995

Secretary of State
Dianna J. Duran (R)
New Mexico State Capitol,
325 Don Gaspar, Suite 300,
Santa Fe, NM 87503
(505) 827-3600

Vital Statistics
Mark Kassouf
Vital Records and Health Statistics
Bureau Chief, Epidemiology and
Response Division
PO Box 25767, Albuquerque, NM 87125
(505) 827-0121

Supreme Court
5 justices sit en banc

Jurisdiction:
- Appeal by right felony, other criminal, limited administrative agency. Interlocutory appeals in felony, administrative agency.
- Appeal by permission criminal, civil, administrative agency. Interlocutory appeals in criminal, civil, administrative agency.
- Exclusive death penalty.
- Original proceeding application for writ. Exclusive bar discipline/eligibility, judicial qualification, certified question.

Court of Appeals
10 judges sit in 3-judge panels

Jurisdiction:
- Appeal by right criminal, limited administrative agency. Exclusive civil.
- Appeal by permission criminal, civil. Interlocutory appeals in criminal, civil.

District Court (13 districts)
94 judges
Jury trials

Jurisdiction:
- Tort, contract, real property, probate/estate. Exclusive mental health, civil appeals, miscellaneous civil.
- Exclusive domestic relations.
- Felony, misdemeanor. Exclusive criminal appeals.
- Exclusive juvenile.

Magistrate Court (54 courts)
67 judges
Jury trials in some cases

Jurisdiction:
- Small claims (up to $10,000).
- Preliminary hearings, misdemeanor.
- Traffic infractions.

Bernalillo County Metropolitan Court
19 judges
Jury trials in some cases

Jurisdiction:
- Small claims (up to $10,000).
- Preliminary hearings, misdemeanor.
- Traffic/other violation.

Municipal Court (80 courts)
82 judges
No jury trials

Jurisdiction:
- Misdemeanor.
- Traffic/other violations.

Probate Court (33 counties)
33 judges
No jury trials

Jurisdiction:
- Probate/estate (uncontested cases).

Court structure as of Fiscal Year 2015.

COURT OF LAST RESORT

INTERMEDIATE APPELLATE COURT

GENERAL JURISDICTION COURT

LIMITED JURISDICTION COURT

☐ Appellate level
☐ Trial level
↑ Route of appeal

© Leadership Directories, Inc.

NEW YORK

Chief Judge — Court of Appeals
Jonathan Lippman
Court of Appeals Hall, 20 Eagle Street,
Albany, NY 12207
(518) 455-7840

Judges of the Appeals Court
Sheila Abdus-Salaam
Eugene Fahey
Eugene F. Pigott, Jr.
Susan Phillips Read
Jenny Rivera
Leslie E. Stein

Clerk of the Appeals Court
Andrew W. Klein
Court of Appeals Hall, 20 Eagle Street,
Albany, NY 12207-1095
(518) 455-7700

Court System Website
www.nycourts.gov

Court Administration
Lawrence K. Marks
Chief Administrative Judge of the Courts
25 Beaver Street, New York, NY 10004
(212) 428-2120

Governor
Andrew Mark Cuomo (D)
State Capitol, Albany, NY 12224
(518) 474-8390

State Website
www.ny.gov

State Capitol Main Phone
(518) 474-8390

Attorney General
Eric T. Schneiderman (D)
120 Broadway,
New York, NY 10271-0332
(518) 474-7330

Secretary of State
Cesar A. Perales
One Commerce Plaza,
99 Washington Avenue,
Albany, NY 12231-0001
(518) 474-0050

Vital Statistics
Guy Warner
Vital Records Section Director,
Information Systems and Health
Statistics Group, New York State
Department of Health [NYSDOH]
P.O. Box 2602, Albany, NY 12220-2602
(518) 474-5245
vr@health.ny.gov

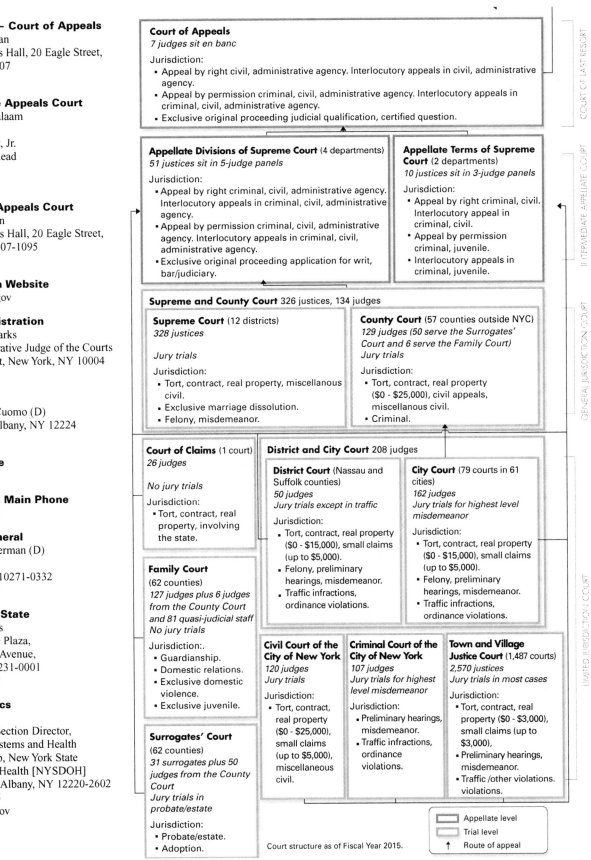

Court of Appeals
7 judges sit en banc
Jurisdiction:
- Appeal by right civil, administrative agency. Interlocutory appeals in civil, administrative agency.
- Appeal by permission criminal, civil, administrative agency. Interlocutory appeals in criminal, civil, administrative agency.
- Exclusive original proceeding judicial qualification, certified question.

Appellate Divisions of Supreme Court (4 departments)
51 justices sit in 5-judge panels
Jurisdiction:
- Appeal by right criminal, civil, administrative agency. Interlocutory appeals in criminal, civil, administrative agency.
- Appeal by permission criminal, civil, administrative agency. Interlocutory appeals in criminal, civil, administrative agency.
- Exclusive original proceeding application for writ, bar/judiciary.

Appellate Terms of Supreme Court (2 departments)
10 justices sit in 3-judge panels
Jurisdiction:
- Appeal by right criminal, civil. Interlocutory appeal in criminal, civil.
- Appeal by permission criminal, juvenile.
- Interlocutory appeals in criminal, juvenile.

Supreme and County Court 326 justices, 134 judges

Supreme Court (12 districts)
328 justices

Jury trials

Jurisdiction:
- Tort, contract, real property, miscellanous civil.
- Exclusive marriage dissolution.
- Felony, misdemeanor.

County Court (57 counties outside NYC)
129 judges (50 serve the Surrogates' Court and 6 serve the Family Court)
Jury trials

Jurisdiction:
- Tort, contract, real property ($0 - $25,000), civil appeals, miscellanous civil.
- Criminal.

Court of Claims (1 court)
26 judges

No jury trials
Jurisdiction:
- Tort, contract, real property, involving the state.

Family Court
(62 counties)
127 judges plus 6 judges from the County Court and 81 quasi-judicial staff
No jury trials
Jurisdiction:.
- Guardianship.
- Domestic relations.
- Exclusive domestic violence.
- Exclusive juvenile.

Surrogates' Court
(62 counties)
31 surrogates plus 50 judges from the County Court
Jury trials in probate/estate
Jurisdiction:
- Probate/estate.
- Adoption.

District and City Court 208 judges

District Court (Nassau and Suffolk counties)
50 judges
Jury trials except in traffic
Jurisdiction:
- Tort, contract, real property ($0 - $15,000), small claims (up to $5,000).
- Felony, preliminary hearings, misdemeanor.
- Traffic infractions, ordinance violations.

City Court (79 courts in 61 cities)
162 judges
Jury trials for highest level misdemeanor
Jurisdiction:
- Tort, contract, real property ($0 - $15,000), small claims (up to $5,000).
- Felony, preliminary hearings, misdemeanor.
- Traffic infractions, ordinance violations.

Civil Court of the City of New York
120 judges
Jury trials
Jurisdiction:
- Tort, contract, real property ($0 - $25,000), small claims (up to $5,000), miscellaneous civil.

Criminal Court of the City of New York
107 judges
Jury trials for highest level misdemeanor
Jurisdiction:
- Preliminary hearings, misdemeanor.
- Traffic infractions, ordinance violations.

Town and Village Justice Court (1,487 courts)
2,570 justices
Jury trials in most cases
Jurisdiction:
- Tort, contract, real property ($0 - $3,000), small claims (up to $3,000),
- Preliminary hearings, misdemeanor.
- Traffic /other violations. violations.

Court structure as of Fiscal Year 2015.

☐ Appellate level
☐ Trial level
↑ Route of appeal

COURT OF LAST RESORT
INTERMEDIATE APPELLATE COURT
GENERAL JURISDICTION COURT
LIMITED JURISDICTION COURT

NORTH CAROLINA

Chief Justice
Mark D. Martin
P.O. Box 1841, Raleigh, NC 27602
(919) 831-5712

Justices of the Supreme Court
Cheri Beasley
Robert H. Edmunds, Jr.
Sam J. "Jimmy" Ervin, IV
Robin E. Hudson
Barbara Jackson
Paul M. Newby

Clerk of the Supreme Court
Christie Speir Cameron Roeder
P.O. Box 1841, Raleigh, NC 27602
(919) 831-5700

Court System Website
www.nccourts.org

Court Administration
Marion Warren
Director, Administrative Office of the
Courts of North Carolina
P.O. Box 2448, Raleigh, NC 27602
(919) 890-1391

Governor
Patrick L. "Pat" McCrory (R)
20301 Mail Service Center,
Raleigh, NC 27699-0301
(919) 814-2000

State Website
www.nc.gov

State Capitol Main Phone
(919) 733-1110

Attorney General
Roy A. Cooper (D)
9001 Mail Service Center,
Raleigh, NC 27699-9001
(919) 716-6400

Secretary of State
Elaine Folk Marshall (D)
P.O. Box 29622,
Raleigh, NC 27626-0622
(919) 807-2008

Vital Statistics
Catherine Ryan
Vital Records Director and State
Registrar (Acting), Division of Public
Health, Department of Health and
Human Services [DHHS]
225 North McDowell Street,
Raleigh, NC 27603-1382
(919) 733-3526

Supreme Court
7 justices sit en banc

Jurisdiction:
- Appeal by right criminal, civil, administrative agency. Interlocutory appeals in criminal, civil, administrative agency.
- Appeal by permission criminal, civil, administrative agency. Interlocutory appeals in criminal, civil, administrative agency.
- Exclusive death penalty.
- Original proceeding application for writ, bar/judiciary. Exclusive advisory opinion.

COURT OF LAST RESORT

Court of Appeals
15 judges sit in 3-judge panels

Jurisdiction:
- Appeal by right criminal, civil, administrative agency.
- Appeal by permission criminal, civil, administrative agency. Interlocutory appeals in criminal, civil, administrative agency.
- Original proceeding application for writ, bar/judiciary.

INTERMEDIATE APPELLATE COURT

Superior Court (50 districts for administrative purposes; 65 districts for elective purposes)
112 judges (including 13 special judges) and 100 clerks serve as ex officio judges of probate with jurisdiction in estate cases and with certain other judicial authorities
Jury trials

Jurisdiction:
- Tort, contract, real property ($10,001 - no maximum), miscellaneous civil. Exclusive probate/estate, civil appeals.
- Criminal.

GENERAL JURISDICTION COURT

District Court (41 districts for administrative purposes; 40 districts for elective purposes)
270 judges and 654 magistrates
Jury trials in civil cases only

Jurisdiction:
- Tort, contract, real property ($0 - $10,000) miscellaneous civil. Exclusive small claims (up to $5,000), mental health.
- Exclusive domestic relations.
- Preliminary hearings, misdemeanor.
- Exclusive juvenile.
- Traffic/other violations.

LIMITED JURISDICTION COURT

Court structure as of Fiscal Year 2015.

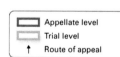

☐ Appellate level
☐ Trial level
↑ Route of appeal

NORTH DAKOTA

Chief Justice
Gerald W. VandeWalle
State Capitol, Judicial Wing,
Dept 180, 600 East Boulevard Avenue,
Bismarck, ND 58505-0530
(701) 328-2221

Justices of the Supreme Court
Daniel J. Crothers
Carol Ronning Kapsner
Lisa K. Fair McEvers
Dale V. Sandstrom

Clerk of the Supreme Court
Penny Miller
State Capitol, Judicial Wing,
600 East Boulevard Avenue, 1st Floor,
Bismarck, ND 58505-0530
(701) 328-2221

Court System Website
www.ndcourts.gov

Court Administration
Sally A. Holewa
State Court Administrator
State Capitol, Judicial Wing,
600 East Boulevard Avenue,
Bismarck, ND 58505-0530
(701) 328-4216

Governor
John S. "Jack" Dalrymple, III (R)
State Capitol, 600 East Boulevard Ave,
Department 101,
Bismarck, ND 58505-0001
(701) 328-2200

State Website
www.nd.gov

State Capitol Main Phone
(701) 328-2000

Attorney General
Wayne Stenehjem (R)
State Capitol, 600 East Boulevard Ave,
1st Floor, Department 125,
Bismarck, ND 58505-0040
(701) 328-2210

Secretary of State
Alvin A. "Al" Jaeger (R)
State Capitol, 600 East Boulevard Ave,
Dept 108, Bismarck, ND 58505-0500
(701) 328-2900

Vital Statistics
Darin J. Meschke
Vital Records Division Director, Dept
of Health, State of North Dakota
600 East Boulevard Avenue, Dept. 301,
Bismarck, ND 58505-0001
(701) 328-2360

Supreme Court
5 justices sit en banc
Assigns cases to the Temporary Court of Appeals

Jurisdiction:
- Appeal by right criminal, civil, administrative agency. Interlocutory appeals in criminal, civil, administrative agency.
- Original proceeding application for writ. Exclusive bar/judiciary, certified question, advisory opinion.

COURT OF LAST RESORT

Temporary Court of Appeals*
3 judges sit in panel

Jurisdiction:
- Appeal by right criminal, civil, administrative agency. Interlocutory appeals in criminal, civil, administrative agency.
- Original proceeding application for writ.

INTERMEDIATE APPELLATE COURT

District Court (8 judicial districts in 53 counties)
46 judges, 8 judicial referees
Jury trials in many cases

Jurisdiction:
- Exclusive civil.
- Exclusive domestic relations.
- Criminal.
- Exclusive juvenile.
- Traffic/other violations.

GENERAL JURISDICTION COURT

Municipal Court (104 municipalities)
74 judges
No jury trials

Jurisdiction:
- DWI/DUI.
- Traffic/other violations.

LIMITED JURISDICTION COURT

*Note: A temporary Court of Appeals was established July 1, 1987, to exercise appellate and original jurisdiction as delegated by the Supreme Court. Authorization for the Court of Appeals extends to January 1, 2017.

Court structure as of Fiscal Year 2015.

Appellate level
Trial level
↑ Route of appeal

OHIO

Chief Justice
Maureen O'Connor
65 South Front Street,
Columbus, OH 43215-3431
(614) 387-9060

Justices of the Supreme Court
Judith L. French
Sharon L. Kennedy
Judith Ann Lanzinger
Terrence O'Donnell
William O'Neill
Paul E. Pfeifer

Clerk of the Supreme Court
Sandra Grosko
65 South Front Street,
Columbus, OH 43215-3431
(614) 387-9530

Court System Website
www.supremecourtofohio.gov

Court Administration
Michael L. Buenger
Administrative Director
65 South Front Street,
Columbus, OH 43215-3431
(614) 387-9500

Governor
John Richard Kasich (R)
Vern Riffe Center, 77 South High Street,
30th Floor, Columbus, OH 43215-6123
(614) 466-3555

State Website
www.ohio.gov

State Capitol Main Phone
(614) 466-3357

Attorney General
Richard Michael "Mike" DeWine (R)
30 East Broad Street, 17th Floor,
Columbus, OH 43215-0421
(614) 466-4320

Secretary of State
Jon A. Husted (R)
180 East Broad Street, 16th Floor,
Columbus, OH 43215-3793
(614) 466-2655

Vital Statistics
Judith B. "Judy" Nagy
ital Statistics State Registrar,
Department of Health [ODH]
P.O. Box 15098,
Columbus, OH 43215-0098
(614) 466-0538
judy.nagy@odh.ohio.gov

COURT OF LAST RESORT

Supreme Court
7 justices sit en banc

Jurisdiction:
- Appeal by right criminal, civil, administrative agency.
- Exclusive appeal by permission criminal, civil, limited administrative agency. Interlocutory appeals in criminal, civil, administrative agency.
- Exclusive death penalty.
- Original proceeding application for writ. Exclusive bar/judiciary, certified question.

INTERMEDIATE APPELLATE COURT

Court of Appeals (12 courts)
69 judges sit in 3-judge panels

Jurisdiction:
- Appeal by right criminal, civil, administrative agency. Interlocutory appeals in criminal, civil, administrative agency.
- Original proceeding application for writ.

GENERAL JURISDICTION COURT

Court of Common Pleas (88 courts)
244 judges
Jury trials in most cases

Jurisdiction:
- Tort, contract, real property ($500 - no maximum), administrative agency appeals, miscellaneous civil. Exclusive mtal health, probate/estate.
- Exclusive domestic relations.
- Felony, misdemeanor.
- Exclusive juvenile.
- Traffic/other violations (juvenile only).

LIMITED JURISDICTION COURT

Municipal Court (126 courts)
215 judges
Jury trials in most cases

Jurisdiction:
- Tort, contract, real property ($0 - $15,000), small claims (up to $3,000), miscellaneous civil.
- Criminal.
- Traffic infractions, ordinance violations.

County Court (22 courts)
37 judges
Jury trials in most cases

Jurisdiction:
- Tort, contract, real property ($0 - $15,000), small claims (up to $3,000), miscellaneous civil.
- Criminal.
- Traffic infractions, ordinance violations.

Court of Claims
Judges assigned by the Chief Justice
Jury trials in some cases

Jurisdiction:
- Civil (actions against the state, victims of crime cases).

Mayors Court (310 courts)

No jury trials

Jurisdiction:
- DWI/DUI, other misdemeanors.
- Traffic/other violations.

Court structure as of Fiscal Year 2015.

Appellate level
Trial level
↑   Route of appeal

OKLAHOMA

Chief Justice
John F. Reif
State Capitol, 2300 North Lincoln Blvd,
Room 204, Oklahoma City, OK 73105
(405) 521-3843

Justices of the Supreme Court
Douglas L. Combs, Vice Chief Justice
Tom Colbert
James E. Edmondson
Noma Gurich
Yvonne Kauger
Steven W. Taylor
Joseph M. Watt
James Winchester

Clerk of the Supreme Court
Michael S. Richie
Oklahoma Judicial Center,
2100 North Lincoln Boulevard, Suite 2,
Oklahoma City, OK 73105-4907
(405) 556-9400

Court System Website
www.oscn.net

Court Administration
Michael D. Evans
Administrative Director
1915 North Stiles Avenue, Suite 305,
Oklahoma City, OK 73105
(405) 522-7878

Governor
Mary Fallin (R)
2300 North Lincoln Boulevard,
Suite 212, Oklahoma City, OK 73105
(405) 521-2342

State Website
www.ok.gov

State Capitol Main Phone
(405) 521-2011

Attorney General
E. Scott Pruitt (R)
313 Northeast 21st Street,
Oklahoma City, OK 73105
(405) 521-3921

Secretary of State
Chris Benge
101 State Capitol, 2300 North Lincoln
Blvd, Oklahoma City, OK 73105-4897
(405) 521-3912

Vital Statistics
Kelly Baker, MPH
State Registrar and Director, Center for
Health Statistics, OSDH
P.O. Box 53551,
Oklahoma City, OK 73152
(405) 271-2224

Supreme Court
9 justices sit en banc
Assigns cases to the Court of Civil Appeals
Jurisdiction:
- Appeal by right civil, administrative agency. Interlocutory appeals in civil, administrative agency.
- Appeal by permission civil, administrative agency. Interlocutory appeals in civil, administrative agency.
- Exclusive original proceeding bar/judiciary, certified question.

Court of Criminal Appeals
5 judges sit en banc
Jurisdiction:
- Exclusive appeal by right criminal, juvenile. Interlocutory appeals in criminal, juvenile.
- Exclusive appeal by permission criminal, juvenile. Interlocutory appeals in criminal, juvenile.
- Exclusive death penalty.
- Original proceeding application for writ.

Court of Civil Appeals (4 divisions)
12 judges sit in 3-judge panels
Jurisdiction:
- Appeal by right civil, administrative agency. Interlocutory appeals in civil, administrative agency.
- Original proceeding application for writ.

District Court (77 courts in 26 districts)
73 district, 77 associate district, and 89 special judges
Jury trials
Jurisdiction:
- Exclusive civil (except administrative agency appeals), small claims (up to $6,000).
- Exclusive domestic relations.
- Exclusive criminal.
- Exclusive juvenile.
- Traffic infractions, ordinance violations.

Court of Tax Review
3 District Court judges serve
No jury trials
Jurisdiction:
- Administrative agency appeals.

Municipal Court Not of Record (352 courts)
~360 full- and part-time judges
Jury trials
Jurisdiction:
- Traffic/other violations.

Municipal Criminal Court of Record (2 courts)
~7 full-time judges
Jury trials
Jurisdiction:
- Traffic/other violations.

Note: Oklahoma has a workers' compensation court, which hears complaints that are handled exclusively by administrative agencies in other states.

Court structure as of Fiscal Year 2015.

- Appellate level
- Trial level
- ↑ Route of appeal

COURT OF LAST RESORT

INTERMEDIATE APPELLATE COURT

GENERAL JURISDICTION COURT

LIMITED JURISDICTION COURT

OREGON

Chief Justice
Thomas A. "Tom" Balmer
State Supreme Court Building,
1163 State St, Salem, OR 97301-2563
(503) 986-5717

Justices of the Supreme Court
Richard C. Baldwin
David V. Brewer
Rives Kistler
Jack L. Landau
Virginia L. Linder
Martha L. Walters

Clerk of the Supreme Court
Rebecca J. "Becky" Osborne
Appellate Courts Records Administrator
Supreme Court Building, 1163 State St,
Salem, OR 97301-2563
(503) 986-5589

Court System Website
www.courts.oregon.gov/ojd

Court Administration
Kingsley W. Click
State Court Administrator
Supreme Court Building, 1163 State St,
Salem, OR 97301-2563
(503) 986-5500

Governor
Kate Brown (D)
160 State Capitol, 900 Court Street, NE,
Salem, OR 97301-4047
(503) 378-3111

State Website
www.oregon.gov

State Capitol Main Phone
(503) 378-3111

Attorney General
Ellen F. Rosenblum (D)
Justice Building, 1162 Court Street, NE,
Salem, OR 97301-4096
(503) 378-4400

Secretary of State
Jeanne Atkins (D)
136 State Capitol, Salem, OR 97310
(503) 986-1523

Vital Statistics
Jennifer A. Woodward
Section Manager/State Registrar, Vital
Records - Center for Health Statistics
800 Northeast Oregon Street,
Portland, OR 97232
(971) 673-1180
jennifer.a.woodward@state.or.us

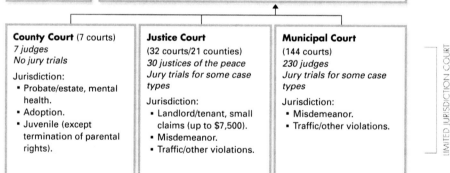

Supreme Court
7 justices sit en banc

Jurisdiction:
- Exclusive appeal by right revenue (tax).
- Exclusive appeal by permission criminal, civil, limited administrative agency.
- Exclusive death penalty.
- Exclusive original proceeding application for writ, bar/judiciary, certified question, advisory opinion.

Court of Appeals
13 judges sit in 3-judge panels and en banc

Jurisdiction:
- Exclusive appeal by right criminal, civil, limited administrative agency.

Tax Court
1 judge
No jury trials

Jurisdiction:
- Administrative agency appeals.

Circuit Court (27 judicial districts in 36 counties; 36 courts)
174 judges
Jury trials for most case types

Jurisdiction:
- Exclusive tort, contract, real property, probate/estate, civil appeals, civil miscellaneous. Small claims (up to $7,500), mental health.
- Exclusive domestic relations (except adoption).
- Exclusive felony, criminal appeals. Misdemeanor.
- Juvenile. Exclusive termination of parental rights.
- Traffic/other violations.

County Court (7 courts)
7 judges
No jury trials

Jurisdiction:
- Probate/estate, mental health.
- Adoption.
- Juvenile (except termination of parental rights).

Justice Court
(32 courts/21 counties)
30 justices of the peace
Jury trials for some case types

Jurisdiction:
- Landlord/tenant, small claims (up to $7,500).
- Misdemeanor.
- Traffic/other violations.

Municipal Court
(144 courts)
230 judges
Jury trials for some case types

Jurisdiction:
- Misdemeanor.
- Traffic/other violations.

COURT OF LAST RESORT

INTERMEDIATE APPELLATE COURT

GENERAL JURISDICTION COURT

LIMITED JURISDICTION COURT

Note: Effective January 15, 1998 all District Courts were eliminated and District judges became Circuit judges.

Court structure as of Fiscal Year 2015.

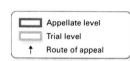

☐ Appellate level
☐ Trial level
↑ Route of appeal

© Leadership Directories, Inc.

Federal-State Court Directory

PENNSYLVANIA

Chief Justice
Thomas G. Saylor
200 North Third Street,
Harrisburg, PA 17101
(717) 772-1599

Justices of the Supreme Court
Max Baer
J. Michael Eakin
Correale F. Stevens
Debra Todd

Clerk of the Supreme Court
Irene Bizzoso
Prothonotary
P.O. Box 62575,
Harrisburg, PA 17106
(717) 787-6181

Court System Website
www.pacourts.us

Court Administration
Zygmont A. Pines
Court Administrator
1515 Market Street, Suite 1414,
Philadelphia, PA 19102
(215) 560-6300

Governor
Thomas W. "Tom" Wolf (D)
Main Capitol Building,
Harrisburg, PA 17120
(717) 787-2500

State Website
www.pa.gov

State Capitol Main Phone
(717) 787-2500

Attorney General
Kathleen Granahan Kane (D)
Strawberry Square, 16th Floor,
Harrisburg, PA 17120
(717) 787-3391

Secretary of State
Pedro A. Cortés
302 North Office Building,
Harrisburg, PA 17120
(717) 787-8727

Vital Statistics
Lana Adams
Health Statistics and Research State
Center Director, Department of Health
101 South Mercer Street,
New Castle, PA 16103
(717) 783-2548
lanadams@pa.gov

Supreme Court
7 justices sit en banc

Jurisdiction:
- Appeal by right criminal, civil, administrative agency. Interlocutory appeals in criminal, civil, administrative agency.
- Appeal by permission criminal, civil, administrative agency. Interlocutory appeals in criminal, civil, administrative agency.
- Exclusive death penalty.
- Original proceeding application for writ. Exclusive bar/judiciary, certified question.

COURT OF LAST RESORT

Commonwealth Court*
9 judges sit in 3-judge panels and en banc

Jurisdiction:
- Appeal by right criminal, civil, administrative agency. Interlocutory appeals in criminal, civil, administrative agency.
- Appeal by permission criminal, civil, limited administrative agency. Interlocutory appeals in criminal, civil, administrative agency.
- Original proceeding application for writ.

Superior Court
15 judges sit in 3-judge panels and en banc

Jurisdiction:
- Appeal by right criminal, civil. Interlocutory appeal in criminal, civil.
- Appeal by permission criminal, civil. Interlocutory appeal in criminal, civil.
- Original proceeding application for writ.

INTERMEDIATE APPELLATE COURT

Court of Common Pleas (60 districts in 67 counties)
545 judges
Jury trials in most cases

Jurisdiction:
- Tort, contract, real property, probate/estate, administrative agency appeals, miscellaneous civil.
- Domestic relations.
- Felony, miscellaneous criminal.
- Exclusive juvenile.

GENERAL JURISDICTION COURT

Philadelphia Municipal Court**
27 judges
No jury trials

Jurisdiction:
- Landlord/tenant, real property ($0 - $15,000), small claims (up to $10,000), miscellaneous civil.
- Felony, preliminary hearings, misdemeanor.
- Ordinance violations.

Magisterial District Judge Court***
(522 courts)
522 judges
No jury trials

Jurisdiction:
- Small claims (up to $8,000).
- Felony, preliminary hearings, misdemeanor.
- Traffic/other violations.

LIMITED JURISDICTION COURT

*Commonwealth Court hears cases brought by and against the Commonwealth.
**Effective 2013, the Philadelphia Traffic Court merged with the Philadelphia Municipal Court.
***Effective January 1, 2005, the Pittsburgh Municipal Court merged with the Allegheny County Magisterial District Judge Court.

Court structure as of Fiscal Year 2015.

Appellate level
Trial level
↑ Route of appeal

PUERTO RICO

Chief Justice
Liana Fiol Matta Hon
P.O. Box 9022392,
San Juan, PR 00902-2392
(787) 721-6625

Justices of the Supreme Court
Robert Cintron Feliberti
Luis Estrella Martinez
Eric V. Kolthoff Caraballo
Rafael L. Martinez Torres
Mildred G. Pabon Charneco
Edgardo Rivera Garcia
Maite Oronoz Rodriguez
Anabelle Rodriguez Rodriguez

Clerk of the Supreme Court
Aida Ileana Oquendo
P.O. Box 9022392,
San Juan, PR 00902-2392
(787) 641-6600 ext. 2072

Court System Website
www.ramajudicial.pr

Court Administration
Sonia Colon Velez Ivette
Administrative Director of the Courts
P.O. Box 9022392,
San Juan, PR 00902-2392
(787) 641-6600

Governor
Alejandro J. García Padilla (PDP)
403 Constitution Avenue,
San Juan, PR 00906
(787) 725-7234

State Website
www.pr.gov

State Capitol Main Phone
(787) 721-7000

Attorney General
César R. Miranda
P.O. Box 909192,
San Juan, PR 00902-9192
(787) 721-2900 ext. 2747

Secretary of State
Dr. David Bernier
P.O. Box 9023271,
San Juan, PR 00902-3271
(787) 722-2121

Vital Statistics
Wanda C. Llovet Diaz
Demographic Registry Director,
Health Department
P.O. Box 11854, San Juan, PR 00917
(787) 767-9120 ext. 2402

Supreme Court
1 presiding justice, 7 associate justices

Jurisdiction:
- Appeal by right criminal, civil, administrative agency.
- Appeal by permission criminal, civil, administrative agency. Interlocutory appeals in criminal, civil, administrative agency.
- Original proceeding application for writ. Exclusive bar/judiciary, certified questions.

Court of Appeals
38 judges sit in 3-judge panels

Jurisdiction:
- Appeal by right civil, administrative agency. Exclusive criminal.
- Appeal by permission criminal, civil, administrative agency. Interlocutory appeals in criminal, civil, administrative agency.
- Original proceeding application for writ.

Court of First Instance
13 regions, 337 judges

Superior Division
258 judges
Jury trials in felony cases

Jurisdiction:
- Tort, contract, real property, probate/estate, administrative agency appeals.
- Domestic relations.
- Exclusive felony. Preliminary hearings, misdemeanor.
- Juvenile.

Municipal Division
79 judges
No jury trials

Jurisdiction:
- Tort, contract, real property ($0 - $3,000), small claims (up to $5,000), miscellaneous civil.
- Non-criminal traffic (infraction), ordinance violations.

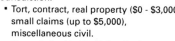

Note: The Judicial Law 2001, renamed the Judicial Reform Act of 1994, changed the name of the intermediate appellate court from the Circuit Court of Appeals to the Court of Appeals and abolished the District Division of the Court of First Instance. The District Division was abolished in 2002, and its functions were transferred to the Superior Division.

Court structure as of Fiscal Year 2015.

☐ Appellate level
☐ Trial level
↑ Route of appeal

RHODE ISLAND

Chief Justice
Paul A. Suttell
Frank Licht Judicial Complex,
250 Benefit Street, Providence, RI 02903
(401) 222-3943

Justices of the Supreme Court
Francis X. Flaherty
Maureen McKenna Goldberg
Gilbert V. Indeglia
William P. Robinson, III

Clerk of the Supreme Court
Debra Saunders
Frank Licht Judicial Complex,
250 Benefit Street, Providence, RI 02903
(401) 222-3272

Court System Website
www.courts.ri.gov

Court Administration
J. Joseph Baxter, Jr.
State Court Administrator
Frank Licht Judicial Complex,
250 Benefit Street, Providence, RI 02903
(401) 222-3266

Governor
Gina M. Raimondo (D)
222 State House, Providence, RI 02908
(401) 222-2080
gina.raimondo@governor.ri.gov

State Website
www.ri.gov

State Capitol Main Phone
(401) 222-2000

Attorney General
Peter F. Kilmartin (D)
150 South Main Street,
Providence, RI 02903
(401) 274-4400

Secretary of State
Nellie M. Gorbea (D)
State House, 82 Smith Street,
Room 217, Providence, RI 02903
(401) 222-2357
ngorbea@sos.ri.gov

Vital Statistics
Colleen Fontana
State Registrar Chief, Office of Vital
Records, Department of Health
Cannon Building, Three Capitol Hill,
Providence, RI 02908-5097
(401) 222-2812
colleen.fontana@health.ri.gov

Supreme Court
5 justices sit en banc

Jurisdiction:
- Exclusive appeal by right criminal, civil, administrative agency.
- Exclusive appeal by permission criminal, civil, administrative agency. Interlocutory appeals in criminal, civil, administrative agency.
- Exclusive original proceeding application for writ, bar/judiciary, certified question.

COURT OF LAST RESORT

Superior Court (4 counties)
22 justices, 5 magistrates
Jury trials

Jurisdiction:
- Tort, contract, real property ($5,000 - no maximum), civil appeals, miscellaneous civil.
- Felony. Exclusive criminal appeals.

GENERAL JURISDICTION COURT

Workers' Compensation Court
10 judges
No jury trials

Jurisdiction:
- All controversies regarding workers' compensation claims.

District Court (4 counties)
13 judges, 2 magistrates
No jury trials

Jurisdiction:
- Tort, contract, real property (no minimum - $10,000), administrative agency appeals. Exclusive small claims (up to $2,500), mental health.
- Exclusive, preliminary hearings, misdemeanor.

Family Court (4 counties)
12 justices, 9 magistrates
Jury trials

Jurisdiction:
- Exclusive domestic relations.
- Exclusive juvenile.

Traffic Tribunal*
3 judges , 5 magistrates
No jury trials

Jurisdiction:
- Traffic infractions, ordinance violations.

Municipal Court
(26 cities/towns)
28 judges, 1 magistrate
No jury trials

Jurisdiction:
- Ordinance violations. Exclusive parking.

Probate Court
(39 cities/towns)
39 judges
No jury trials

Jurisdiction:
- Exclusive probate/estate.

LIMITED JURISDICTION COURT

*This court was formerly known as the Rhode Island Administrative Adjudication Court.

Court structure as of Fiscal Year 2015.

▭	Appellate level
▭	Trial level
↑	Route of appeal

SOUTH CAROLINA

Chief Justice
Jean Hoefer Toal
P.O. Box 12456, Columbia, SC 29201
(803) 734-1584

Justices of the Supreme Court
Donald W. Beatty
Kaye G. Hearn
John W. Kittredge
Costa M. Pleicones

Clerk of the Supreme Court
Daniel E. Shearouse
P.O. Box 11330, Columbia, SC 29211
(803) 734-1080

Court System Website
www.judicial.state.sc.us

Court Administration
Rosalyn Woodson Frierson
Director, South Carolina Court
Administration
John C. Calhoun Building,
1015 Sumter Street, Suite 200,
Columbia, SC 29201
(803) 734-1800

Governor
Nimrata Randhawa "Nikki" Haley (R)
1205 Pendleton Street,
Columbia, SC 2920
(803) 734-2100

State Website
www.sc.gov

State Capitol Main Phone
(803) 896-0000

Attorney General
Alan McCrory Wilson (R)
P.O. Box 11549, Columbia, SC 29211
(803) 734-3970

Secretary of State
Mark Hammond (R)
Edgar Brown Building,
1205 Pendleton Street, Suite 525,
Columbia, SC 29201
(803) 734-2156

Vital Statistics
Angie Saleeby
Vital Records Division Director, Public
Health Statistics, Department of Health
and Environmental Control [DHEC]
2600 Bull Street, Columbia, SC 29201
(803) 898-3324

Supreme Court
5 justices sit en banc
Assigns cases to the Court of Appeals

Jurisdiction:
- Appeal by right criminal, civil. Interlocutory appeals in criminal, civil.
- Exclusive appeal by permission criminal, civil, administrative agency. Interlocutory appeals in criminal, civil, administrative agency.
- Exclusive death penalty.
- Exclusive original proceeding application for writ, bar/judiciary, certified question.

Court of Appeals
9 judges sit in 3-judge panels and en banc

Jurisdiction:
- Appeal by right criminal, civil. Exclusive administrative agency.

Circuit Court (16 circuits, 46 counties)
49 judges and 21 masters-in-equity
Jury trials except in appeals

Jurisdiction:
- Tort, contract, real property, miscellaneous civil. Exclusive civil appeals.
- Misdemeanor. Exclusive felony, criminal appeals.

Family Court (16 circuits, 46 counties)
58 judges
No jury trials

Jurisdiction:
- Exclusive domestic relations.
- Juvenile.
- Traffic/other violations (juvenile cases only).

Magistrate Court (46 counties)
317 magistrates
Jury trials

Jurisdiction:
- Small claims (up to $7,500).
- Preliminary hearings, misdemeanor.
- Traffic/other violations.

Probate Court (46 courts, 46 counties)
46 judges
No jury trials

Jurisdiction:
- Exclusive probate/estate, mental health.

Municipal Court (~200 courts)
329 judges
Jury trials

Jurisdiction:
- Preliminary hearings, misdemeanor.
- Traffic/other violations.

COURT OF LAST RESORT

INTERMEDIATE APPELLATE COURT

GENERAL JURISDICTION COURT

LIMITED JURISDICTION COURT

Court structure as of Fiscal Year 2015.

Appellate level
Trial level
↑ Route of appeal

SOUTH DAKOTA

Chief Justice
David Gilbertson
State Capitol Building,
500 East Capitol Avenue,
Pierre, SD 57501
(605) 773-4881

Justices of the Supreme Court
Janine Kern
Glen A. Severson
Lori S. Wilbur
Steven L. Zinter

Clerk of the Supreme Court
Shirley A. Jameson-Fergel
State Capitol Building,
500 East Capitol Avenue,
Pierre, SD 57501
(605) 773-3511

Court System Website
www.sdjudicial.com

Court Administration
Greg Sattizahn
State Court Administrator
State Capitol Building,
500 East Capitol Avenue,
Pierre, SD 57501-5070
(605) 773-3474

Governor
Dennis M. Daugaard (R)
500 East Capitol Avenue,
Pierre, SD 57501
(605) 773-3212

State Website
www.sd.gov

State Capitol Main Phone
(605) 773-3011

Attorney General
Martin J. "Marty" Jackley (R)
1302 East Highway 14,
Pierre, SD 57501-8501
(605) 773-3215

Secretary of State
Shantel Krebs (R)
500 East Capitol Avenue, Suite 204,
Pierre, SD 57501-5070
(605) 773-3537

Vital Statistics
Mariah Pokorny
State Registrar of Vital Records,
Department of Health
600 East Capitol Avenue,
Pierre, SD 57501-2536
(605) 773-4961
mariah.pokorny@state.sd.us

Supreme Court
5 justices sit en banc

Jurisdiction:
- Exclusive appeal by right criminal, civil, administrative agency.
- Exclusive appeal by permission criminal, civil, administrative agency. Interlocutory appeals in criminal, civil, administrative agency.
- Exclusive death penalty.
- Exclusive original proceeding application for writ, bar/judiciary, certified question, advisory opinion.

COURT OF LAST RESORT

Circuit Court (7 circuits)
41 judges
Jury trials except in small claims

Jurisdiction:
- Tort, contract, real property ($12,000 - no maximum), small claims (up to $12,000).
- Exclusive, domestic relations.
- Criminal.
- Exclusive juvenile.
- Exclusive traffic/other violations (except uncontested parking, which is handled administratively).

GENERAL JURISDICTION COURT

Magistrate Court (7 circuits)
13 magistrate judges
Jury trials

Jurisdiction:
- Tort, contract, real property ($0 - $10,000), small claims (up to $12,000).
- Preliminary hearings, misdemeanor.

LIMITED JURISDICTION COURT

Court structure as of Fiscal Year 2015.

- Appellate level
- Trial level
- ↑ Route of appeal

TENNESSEE

Chief Justice
Sharon Gail Lee
P.O. Box 444,
Knoxville, TN 37901-0444
(865) 594-6121

Justices of the Supreme Court
Jeffrey S. Bivins
Cornelia A. Clark
Holly M. Kirby
Gary R. Wade

Clerk of the Supreme Court
James M. Hivner
Supreme Court Building,
401 Seventh Avenue North,
Nashville, TN 37219-1407
(615) 253-1470

Court System Website
www.tncourts.gov

Court Administration
Deborah Taylor Tate
Administrative Director
600 Nashville City Center,
511 Union Street, Suite 600,
Nashville, TN 37219
(615) 741-2687

Governor
William Edward "Bill" Haslam (R)
State Capitol, First Floor,
Nashville, TN 37243
(615) 741-2001

State Website
www.tn.gov

State Capitol Main Phone
(615) 741-2001

Attorney General
Herbert H. Slatery, III
P.O. Box 20207, Nashville, TN 37202
(615) 741-3491

Secretary of State
Tré Hargett (R)
State Capitol, First Floor,
Nashville, TN 37243-0305
(615) 741-2819
tre.hargett@tn.gov

Vital Statistics
R. Benton McDonough
State Registrar and Vital Records Office
Director, Department of Health
Central Services Building,
421 Fifth Avenue North, Floor One,
Nashville, TN 37243
(615) 532-2600
r.benton.mcdonough@tn.gov

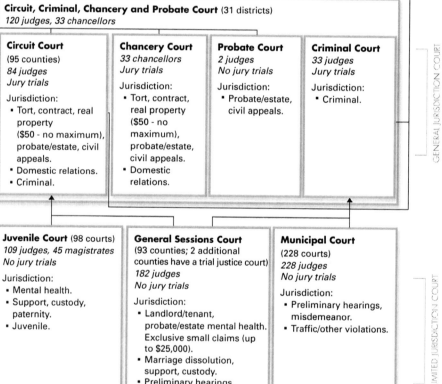

Supreme Court
5 justices sit en banc

Jurisdiction:
- Exclusive appeal by right workers' compensation.
- Appeal by permission criminal, civil, administrative agency. Interlocutory appeals in criminal, civil, administrative agency.
- Death penalty.
- Exclusive original proceeding bar admission, bar discipline/eligibility, certified question.

Court of Appeals (3 divisions)
12 judges sit in 3-judge panels

Jurisdiction:
- Exclusive appeal by right civil, limited administrative agency.
- Appeal by permission, civil, administrative agency. Interlocutory appeals in civil, administrative agency.

Court of Criminal Appeals (3 divisions)
12 judges sit in 3-judge panels

Jurisdiction:
- Exclusive appeal by right criminal.
- Appeal by permission criminal. Interlocutory appeals in criminal.
- Death penalty.
- Exclusive original proceeding limited application for writ.

Circuit, Criminal, Chancery and Probate Court (31 districts)
120 judges, 33 chancellors

Circuit Court
(95 counties)
84 judges
Jury trials

Jurisdiction:
- Tort, contract, real property ($50 - no maximum), probate/estate, civil appeals.
- Domestic relations.
- Criminal.

Chancery Court
33 chancellors
Jury trials

Jurisdiction:
- Tort, contract, real property ($50 - no maximum), probate/estate, civil appeals.
- Domestic relations.

Probate Court
2 judges
No jury trials

Jurisdiction:
- Probate/estate, civil appeals.

Criminal Court
33 judges
Jury trials

Jurisdiction:
- Criminal.

Juvenile Court (98 courts)
109 judges, 45 magistrates
No jury trials

Jurisdiction:
- Mental health.
- Support, custody, paternity.
- Juvenile.

General Sessions Court
(93 counties; 2 additional counties have a trial justice court)
182 judges
No jury trials

Jurisdiction:
- Landlord/tenant, probate/estate mental health. Exclusive small claims (up to $25,000).
- Marriage dissolution, support, custody.
- Preliminary hearings, misdemeanor.
- Juvenile.
- Traffic/other violations.

Municipal Court
(228 courts)
228 judges
No jury trials

Jurisdiction:
- Preliminary hearings, misdemeanor.
- Traffic/other violations.

COURT OF LAST RESORT

INTERMEDIATE APPELLATE COURT

GENERAL JURISDICTION COURT

LIMITED JURISDICTION COURT

Court structure as of Fiscal Year 2015.

Appellate level
Trial level
↑   Route of appeal

Federal-State Court Directory

TEXAS

Chief Justice
Nathan L. Hecht
P.O. Box 12248,
Capitol Station, Austin, TX 78711
(512) 463-1348

Justices of the Supreme Court
Jeffrey S. "Jeff" Boyd
Jeffrey V. "Jeff" Brown
John Devine
Paul W. Green
Eva M. Guzman
Phil Johnson
Debra H. Lehrmann
Don R. Willett

Clerk of the Supreme Court
Blake A. Hawthorne
P.O. Box 12248, Austin,
TX 78711-2248
(512) 463-1312

Court System Website
www.courts.state.tx.us

Court Administration
David Slayton
Administrative Director
P.O. Box 12066, Austin,
TX 78711-2066
(512) 463-1625

Governor
Greg Abbott (R)
P.O. Box 12428, Austin, TX 78711
(512) 463-2000

State Website
www.texas.gov

State Capitol Main Phone
(512) 463-2000

Attorney General
Ken Paxton (R)
P.O. Box 12548, Austin,
TX 78711-2548
(512) 463-2100

Secretary of State
Carlos H. Cascos, CPA, CGFM
State Capitol, P.O. Box 12697,
Austin, TX 78711
(512) 463-5770

Vital Statistics
Geraldine Harris
State Registrar, Center For Health
Statistics
P.O. Box 12040, Austin,
TX 78711-2040
(512) 776-2068
geraldine.harris@dshs.state.tx.us

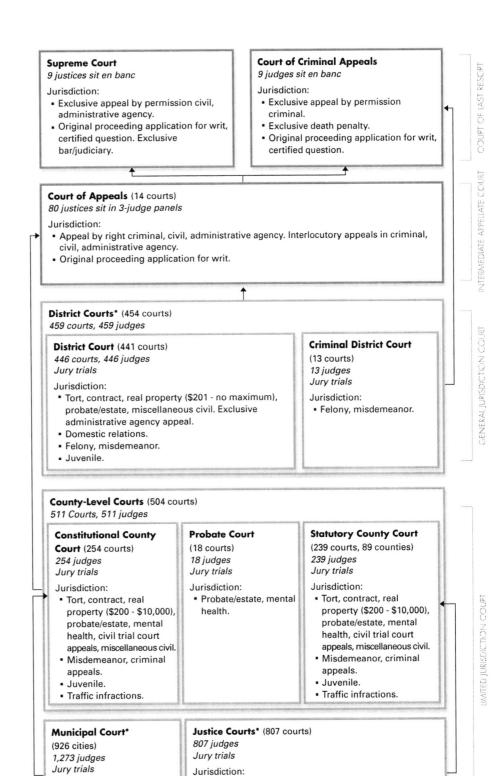

Supreme Court
9 justices sit en banc

Jurisdiction:
- Exclusive appeal by permission civil, administrative agency.
- Original proceeding application for writ, certified question. Exclusive bar/judiciary.

Court of Criminal Appeals
9 judges sit en banc

Jurisdiction:
- Exclusive appeal by permission criminal.
- Exclusive death penalty.
- Original proceeding application for writ, certified question.

Court of Appeals (14 courts)
80 justices sit in 3-judge panels

Jurisdiction:
- Appeal by right criminal, civil, administrative agency. Interlocutory appeals in criminal, civil, administrative agency.
- Original proceeding application for writ.

District Courts* (454 courts)
459 courts, 459 judges

District Court (441 courts)
446 courts, 446 judges
Jury trials

Jurisdiction:
- Tort, contract, real property ($201 - no maximum), probate/estate, miscellaneous civil. Exclusive administrative agency appeal.
- Domestic relations.
- Felony, misdemeanor.
- Juvenile.

Criminal District Court
(13 courts)
13 judges
Jury trials

Jurisdiction:
- Felony, misdemeanor.

County-Level Courts (504 courts)
511 Courts, 511 judges

Constitutional County Court (254 courts)
254 judges
Jury trials

Jurisdiction:
- Tort, contract, real property ($200 - $10,000), probate/estate, mental health, civil trial court appeals, miscellaneous civil.
- Misdemeanor, criminal appeals.
- Juvenile.
- Traffic infractions.

Probate Court
(18 courts)
18 judges
Jury trials

Jurisdiction:
- Probate/estate, mental health.

Statutory County Court
(239 courts, 89 counties)
239 judges
Jury trials

Jurisdiction:
- Tort, contract, real property ($200 - $10,000), probate/estate, mental health, civil trial court appeals, miscellaneous civil.
- Misdemeanor, criminal appeals.
- Juvenile.
- Traffic infractions.

Municipal Court*
(926 cities)
1,273 judges
Jury trials

Jurisdiction:
- Misdemeanor.
- Traffic infractions. Exclusive ordinance violations.

Justice Courts* (807 courts)
807 judges
Jury trials

Jurisdiction:
- Tort, contract, real property ($0 - $10,000), small claims (up to $10,000).
- Misdemeanor.
- Traffic infractions, parking.

*Some Municipal and Justice of the Peace courts may appeal to the District court.

Court structure as of Fiscal Year 2015.

COURT OF LAST RESORT

INTERMEDIATE APPELLATE COURT

GENERAL JURISDICTION COURT

LIMITED JURISDICTION COURT

☐ Appellate level
☐ Trial level
↑ Route of appeal

UTAH

Chief Justice
Matthew B. Durrant
P.O. Box 140210,
Salt Lake City, UT 84114-0210
(801) 238-7937

Justices of the Supreme Court
Christine M. Durham
Constandinos "Deno" Himonas
Thomas Rex "Tom" Lee
Jill N. Parrish

Clerk of the Supreme Court
Andrea Martinez
P.O. Box 140210,
Salt Lake City, UT 84114-0210
(801) 238-7974

Court System Website
www.utcourts.gov

Court Administration
Daniel J. "Dan" Becker
State Court Administrator
P.O. Box 140241,
Salt Lake City, UT 84114-0241
(801) 578-3806

Governor
Gary Richard Herbert (R)
P.O. Box 142220,
Salt Lake City, UT 84114-2220
(801) 538-1000

State Website
www.utah.gov

State Capitol Main Phone
(801) 538-3000

Attorney General
Sean D. Reyes
P.O. Box 142320,
Salt Lake City, UT 84114-2320
(801) 366-0260

Lieutenant Governor
Spencer J. Cox
Utah State Capitol, Suite 220,
Salt Lake City, UT 84114
(801) 538-1048

Vital Statistics
Janice Houston
State Registrar and Director, Office of
Vital Records, Center for Health Data
P.O. Box 141012,
Salt Lake City, UT 84114-1012
(801) 538-6262
jlhouston@utah.gov

Supreme Court
5 justices sit en banc

Jurisdiction:
- Appeal by right [criminal, civil, administrative agency.]
- Appeal by permission. Interlocutory appeals in criminal, civil, administrative agency.
- Exclusive death penalty.
- Original proceeding application for writ. Exclusive bar/judiciary, certified question, advisory opinion.

Court of Appeals
7 judges sit in 3-judge panels

Jurisdiction:
- Appeal by right criminal, civil, administrative agency.
- Appeal by permission interlocutory appeals in criminal, civil, administrative agency.
- Original proceeding application for writ.

District Court (8 districts in 29 counties)
71 judges

Jury trials in most cases

Jurisdiction:
- Exclusive tort, contract, real property, probate/estate, mental health, civil appeals, miscellaneous civil. Small claims (up to $10,000).
- Exclusive domestic relations.
- Felony, misdemeanor. Exclusive criminal appeals.
- Traffic/other violations.

Juvenile Court (8 districts in 29 counties)
29 judges
No jury trials

Jurisdiction:
- Exclusive juvenile.

Justice Court (134 courts)
108 judges
Jury trials in some case types

Jurisdiction:
- Small claims (up to $10,000).
- Misdemeanor.
- Traffic/other violations.

COURT OF LAST RESORT

INTERMEDIATE APPELLATE COURT

GENERAL JURISDICTION COURT

LIMITED JURISDICTION COURT

Court structure as of Fiscal Year 2015.

[ ] Appellate level
[ ] Trial level
↑ Route of appeal

VERMONT

Chief Justice
Paul L. Reiber
109 State Street,
Montpelier, VT 05609-0801
(802) 828-4784

Justices of the Supreme Court
John A. Dooley
Harold E. Eaton, Jr.
Beth Robinson
Marilyn S. Skoglund

Clerk of the Supreme Court
Patricia Gabel
Court Administrator and Clerk of Court
111 State Street,
Montpelier, VT 05609-0801
(802) 828-3278

Court System Website
www.vermontjudiciary.org

Court Administration
Patricia Gabel
Court Administrator and Clerk of Court
111 State Street,
Montpelier, VT 05609-0801
(802) 828-3278

Governor
Peter E. Shumlin (D)
Pavilion Office Building,
109 State Street, Fifth Floor,
Montpelier, VT 05609-0101
(802) 828-3333

State Website
www.vermont.gov

State Capitol Main Phone
(802) 828-1110

Attorney General
William H. "Bill" Sorrell (D)
Pavilion Office Building, 109 State St,
Montpelier, VT 05609-1001
(802) 828-3173
bsorrell@atg.state.vt.us

Secretary of State
James C. "Jim" Condos (D)
128 State Street, Montpelier, VT 05633
(802) 828-2148
secretary@sec.state.vt.us

Vital Statistics
Cynthia Hooley
Vital Records Section Chief, Health
Department, Agency of Human Services
PO Box 70, Burlington, VT 05402-0070
(802) 651-1636
cynthia.hooley@state.vt.us

Supreme Court
5 justices sit en banc

Jurisdiction:
- Exclusive appeal by right criminal, civil, administrative agency. Interlocutory appeals in criminal, civil, administrative agency.
- Exclusive appeal by permission criminal, civil, administrative agency. Interlocutory appeals in criminal, civil, administrative agency.
- Exclusive original proceeding bar admission, bar discipline/eligibility, certified question.

COURT OF LAST RESORT

Superior Court
34 superior judges, 14 probate judges, 5 magistrates, 28 assistant judges

Civil Division
14 counties, 32 superior judges, 5 magistrates, 28 assistant judges (shared)
Jury trials

Jurisdiction:
- Civil appeals, civil miscellaneous.

Criminal Division
14 counties, 32 superior judges, 5 magistrates, 28 assistant judges (shared)
Jury trials

Jurisdiction:
- Felonies and misdemeanors.
- Municipal appeals.
- License suspensions.

Family Division
14 counties, 32 superior judges, 5 magistrates, 28 assistant judges (shared)
No jury trials

Jurisdiction:
- Child support, visitation, protective services.
- Mental health.
- Divorce and annulment.

Environmental Division
Statewide, 2 superior judges
No jury trials

Jurisdiction:
- Administrative agency appeals.

Probate Division
14 counties, 14 judges
No jury trials

Jurisdiction:
- Wills, estates, trusts.
- Adoption and appointment of guardians.
- Certifications.
- Civil miscellaneous.

GENERAL JURISDICTION COURT

Vermont Judicial Bureau
2 hearing officers
No jury trials

Jurisdiction:
- Other civil violations.
- Traffic infractions, ordinance violations.

LIMITED JURISDICTION COURT

Note: On July 1, 2010 the courts of Vermont were unified into five divisions under the administrative control of the Supreme Court.

Court structure as of Fiscal Year 2015.

☐ Appellate level
☐ Trial level
↑ Route of appeal

VIRGINIA

Chief Justice
Donald W. Lemons
100 North Ninth Street,
Richmond, VA 23219
(804) 225-2183

Justices of the Supreme Court
S. Bernard Goodwyn
D. Arthur Kelsey
Elizabeth A. McClanahan
LeRoy F. Millette, Jr.
William C. "Bill" Mims
Cleo Elaine Powell
Lawrence L. Koontz, Jr., Senior Justice
Elizabeth B. Lacy, Senior Justice
Charles S. Russell, Senior Justice

Clerk of the Supreme Court
Patricia L. Harrington
100 North Ninth Street,
Richmond, VA 2321
(804) 786-2251

Court System Website
www.courts.state.va.us

Court Administration
Karl R. Hade
Executive Secretary
Supreme Court Bldg, 100 North Ninth
Street, 3rd Floor, Richmond, VA 23219
(804) 786-6455

Governor
Terence Richard "Terry" McAuliffe (D)
P.O. Box 1475, Richmond, VA 23218
(804) 786-2211

State Website
www.virginia.gov

State Capitol Main Phone
(804) 786-0000

Attorney General
Mark R. Herring (D)
900 East Main Street
Richmond, VA 23219
(804)786-2071

Secretary of the Commonwealth
Levar Stoney
P.O. Box 2454, Richmond, VA 23218
(804) 786-2441

Vital Statistics
Janet Rainey
Vital Records Division Director,
Department of Health [VDH], Health
and Human Resources Secretariat
2001 Maywill Street,
Richmond, VA 23230
(804) 662-6245

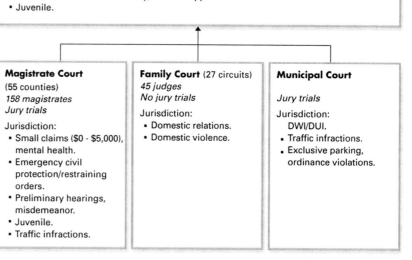

Supreme Court of Appeals
5 justices sit en banc
Jurisdiction:
- Exclusive appeal by permission criminal, civil, administrative agency. Interlocutory appeals in criminal, civil, administrative agency.
- Exclusive original proceeding application for writ, bar/judiciary, certified question.

Circuit Court (55 counties, 31 circuits)
70 judges
Jury trials
Jurisdiction:
- Tort, contract, real property ($300 - no maximum). Exclusive probate/estate, mental health, civil appeals.
- Domestic relations.
- Misdemeanor. Exclusive felony, criminal appeals.
- Juvenile.

Magistrate Court
(55 counties)
158 magistrates
Jury trials
Jurisdiction:
- Small claims ($0 - $5,000), mental health.
- Emergency civil protection/restraining orders.
- Preliminary hearings, misdemeanor.
- Juvenile.
- Traffic infractions.

Family Court (27 circuits)
45 judges
No jury trials
Jurisdiction:
- Domestic relations.
- Domestic violence.

Municipal Court

Jury trials
Jurisdiction:
DWI/DUI.
- Traffic infractions.
- Exclusive parking, ordinance violations.

COURT OF LAST RESORT

GENERAL JURISDICTION COURT

LIMITED JURISDICTION COURT

Court structure as of Fiscal Year 2015.

Appellate level
Trial level
↑ Route of appeal

WASHINGTON

Chief Justice
Barbara A. Madsen
P.O. Box 40929,
Olympia, WA 98504-0929
(360) 357-2037

Justices of the Supreme Court
Charles W. Johnson, Associate Chief
Justice
Mary E. Fairhurst
Steven C. González
Sheryl McCloud
Susan Owens
Debra L. Stephens
Charles K. Wiggins
Mary Yu

Clerk of the Supreme Court
Ronald R. Carpenter
P.O. Box 40929,
Olympia, WA 98504-0929
(360) 357-2077

Court System Website
www.courts.wa.gov

Court Administration
Callie T. Dietz
Administrator
P.O. Box 41170,
Olympia, WA 98504-1170
(360) 357-2121

Governor
Jay Robert Inslee (D)
P.O. Box 40002,
Olympia, WA 98504-0002
(360) 902-4111

State Website
www.access.wa.gov/

State Capitol Main Phone
(360) 753-5000

Attorney General
Robert W. "Bob" Ferguson (D)
P.O. Box 40100,
Olympia, WA 98504-0100
(360) 753-6200

Secretary of State
Kim Wyman, CERA (R)
PO Box 40220,
Olympia, WA 98504-0220
(360) 902-4499

Vital Statistics
Jennifer Tebaldi
Epidemiology, Health Statistics & Public
Health Laboratories Asst Sec, DOH
PO Box 47811,
Olympia, WA 98504-7811
(360) 236-4204

Supreme Court
9 justices sit en banc

Jurisdiction:
- Appeal by permission criminal, civil, administrative agency. Interlocutory appeals in criminal, civil, administrative agency.
- Exclusive death penalty.
- Original proceeding application for writ. Exclusive bar/judiciary, certified question.

Court of Appeals (3 courts/divisions)
22 judges sit in 3-judge panels

Jurisdiction:
- Exclusive appeal by right criminal, civil, administrative agency.
- Appeal by permission, interlocutory appeals in criminal, civil, administrative agency.
- Original proceeding application for writ.

Superior Court (32 districts in 39 counties)
185 judges (and 48 full-time court commissioners, 7.93 part-time commissioners) Jury trials

Jurisdiction:
- Tort, contract. Exclusive real property, probate/estate, mental health, civil appeals, miscellaneous civil.
- Exclusive domestic relations.
- Exclusive felony, criminal appeals.
- Exclusive juvenile.

Municipal Court (~81 courts)
111 judges (including 12 court commissioners and magistrates) Jury trials except in traffic infractions and parking violations

Jurisdiction:
- Misdemeanor.
- Traffic/other violations.

District Court* (~44 courts)
118 judges (including 10 court commissioners and magistrates) Jury trials except in traffic infractions and parking violations

Jurisdiction:
- Tort, contract ($0 - $75,000). Exclusive small claims (up to $5,000).
- Preliminary hearings, misdemeanor.
- Traffic/other violations.

*District Court provides services to municipalities that do not have a Municipal Court.

COURT OF LAST RESORT

INTERMEDIATE APPELLATE COURT

GENERAL JURISDICTION COURT

LIMITED JURISDICTION COURT

Court structure as of Fiscal Year 2015.

Appellate level
Trial level
↑   Route of appeal

WEST VIRGINIA

Chief Justice
Margaret L. Workman
State Capitol Complex,
Charleston, WV 25302
(304) 558-2606

Justices of the Supreme Court
Brent D. Benjamin
Robin Jean Davis
Menis E. Ketchum, II
Allen H. Loughry, II

Clerk of the Supreme Court
Rory L. Perry, II
Capitol Complex,
1900 Kanawha Blvdd East,
Room E-317, Charleston, WV 25305
(304) 558-2601

Court System Website
www.state.wv.us/wvsca

Court Administration
Steven D. Canterbury
Administrative Director
Capitol Complex,
1900 Kanawha Blvd East, Building 1,
Room E-100, Charleston, WV 25305
(304) 558-0145

Governor
Earl Ray Tomblin (D)
State Capitol Building, 1900 Kanawha
Boulevard East, Charleston, WV 25305
(304) 558-2000

State Website
www.wv.gov

State Capitol Main Phone
(304) 558-3456

Attorney General
Patrick Morrisey (R)
State Capitol Complex, Building 1,
Room E-26, Charleston, WV 25305
(304) 558-2021

Secretary of State
Natalie E. Tennant (D)
State Capitol Complex, Building One,
1900 Kanawha Blvd, East, Suite 157K,
Charleston, WV 25305-0770
(304) 558-6000

Vital Statistics
Gary L. Thompson
State Registrar and Assistant Director,
Health Statistics Center, Department of
Health and Human Resources [DHHR]
350 Capitol Street, Room 165,
Charleston, WV 25301
(304) 558-2931

Supreme Court of Appeals
5 justices sit en banc

Jurisdiction:
- Exclusive appeal by permission criminal, civil, administrative agency. Interlocutory appeals in criminal, civil, administrative agency.
- Exclusive original proceeding application for writ, bar/judiciary, certified question.

Circuit Court (55 counties, 31 circuits)
70 judges
Jury trials

Jurisdiction:
- Tort, contract, real property ($300 - no maximum). Exclusive probate/estate, mental health, civil appeals.
- Domestic relations.
- Misdemeanor. Exclusive felony, criminal appeals.
- Juvenile.

Magistrate Court
(55 counties)
158 magistrates
Jury trials

Jurisdiction:
- Small claims ($0 - $5,000), mental health.
- Emergency civil protection/restraining orders.
- Preliminary hearings, misdemeanor.
- Juvenile.
- Traffic infractions.

Family Court (27 circuits)
45 judges
No jury trials

Jurisdiction:
- Domestic relations.
- Domestic violence.

Municipal Court

Jury trials

Jurisdiction:
DWI/DUI.
- Traffic infractions.
- Exclusive parking, ordinance violations.

Court structure as of Fiscal Year 2015.

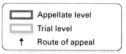

- Appellate level
- Trial level
- ↑ Route of appeal

© Leadership Directories, Inc.

Federal-State Court Directory

WISCONSIN

Chief Justice
Patience Drake Roggensack
P.O. Box 1688,
Madison, WI 53701-1688
(608) 266-1888

Justices of the Supreme Court
Shirley S. Abrahamson
Ann Walsh Bradley
N. Patrick Crooks
Michael J. Gableman
David T. Prosser
Annette Kingsland Ziegler

Clerk of the Supreme Court
Diane Fremgen
P.O. Box 1688,
Madison, WI 53701-1688
(608) 266-1880

Court System Website
www.wicourts.gov

Court Administration
J. Denis Moran
Director of State Courts (Interim)
P.O. Box 1688,
Madison, WI 53701-1688
(608) 266-6828

Governor
Scott K. Walker (R)
State Capitol, 115 East Capitol,
Madison, WI 53702
(608) 266-1212

State Website
www.wisconsin.gov

State Capitol Main Phone
(608) 266-1212

Attorney General
Brad Schimel (R)
P.O. Box 7857, Madison, WI 53707
(608) 266-1221

Secretary of State
Douglas La Follette (D)
P.O. Box 7848,
Madison, WI 53707-7848
(608) 266-8888

Vital Statistics
Rebecca Biel, Vital Records Section
Chief (Interim), Public Health Division,
Department of Health Services
P.O. Box 309, Madison, WI 53701-0309
(608) 267-9171
rebecca.biel@wisconsin.com

Supreme Court
7 justices sit en banc

Jurisdiction:
- Appeal by permission criminal, civil, administrative agency.
- Original proceeding application for writ. Exclusive bar/judiciary, certified question.

COURT OF LAST RESORT

Court of Appeals (4 districts)
16 judges sit in 3-judge panels

Jurisdiction:
- Exclusive appeal by right criminal, civil, administrative agency.
- Appeal by permission interlocutory appeals in criminal, civil, administrative agency.
- Original proceeding application for writ.

INTERMEDIATE APPELLATE COURT

Circuit Court (10 judicial districts/72 counties)
249 judges
Jury trials in most cases

Jurisdiction:
- Exclusive civil.
- Exclusive domestic relations.
- Exclusive criminal.
- Exclusive juvenile.
- Traffic/other violations.

GENERAL JURISDICTION COURT

Municipal Court (237 courts)
240 judges
No jury trials

Jurisdiction:
- Traffic/other violations.

LIMITED JURISDICTION COURT

Court structure as of Fiscal Year 2015.

Appellate level
Trial level
↑ Route of appeal

WYOMING

Chief Justice
E. James Burke
Supreme Court Building,
2301 Capitol Avenue,
Cheyenne, WY 82002
(307) 777-7557

Justices of the Supreme Court
Michael K. Davis
Catherine M. "Kate" Fox
William U. Hill
Keith G. Kautz
Marilyn S. Kite

Clerk of the Supreme Court
Carol Thompson
Supreme Court Building,
2301 Capital Avenue,
Cheyenne, WY 82002
(307) 777-6129

Court System Website
www.courts.state.wy.us

Court Administration
Lily Sharpe
Court Administrator
Supreme Court Building,
2301 Capital Avenue,
Cheyenne, WY 82002
(307) 777-7581

Governor
Matthew Hansen "Matt" Mead (R)
State Capitol, 200 West 24th Street,
Cheyenne, WY 82002-0010
(307) 777-7434

State Website
www.wyoming.gov

State Capitol Main Phone
(307) 777-7220

Attorney General
Peter K. Michael
Attorney General (Interim)
123 State Capitol, Cheyenne, WY 82002
(307) 777-7841

Secretary of State
Edward F. Murray, III (R)
State Capitol, 200 West 24th Street,
Room 106, Cheyenne, WY 82002-0020
(307) 777-7378

Vital Statistics
James M. "Jim" McBride
Vital Statistics Services Manager,
Wyoming Department of Health [WDH]
401 Hathaway Building, 2300 Capitol
Avenue, Cheyenne, WY 82002
(307) 777-6040

Supreme Court
5 justices sit en banc

Jurisdiction:
- Exclusive appeal by right criminal, civil, administrative agency. Interlocutory appeals in criminal, civil, administrative agency.
- Exclusive death penalty.
- Exclusive original proceeding application for writ, bar/judiciary, certified question, advisory opinion.

COURT OF LAST RESORT

District Court (9 districts)
23 judges
Jury trials

Jurisdiction:
- Tort, contract, real property ($7,001 - no maximum), civil miscellaneous. Exclusive probate/estate, mental health, civil appeals.
- Exclusive domestic relations.
- Exclusive felony, criminal appeals.
- Exclusive juvenile.

GENERAL JURISDICTION COURT

Circuit Court* (24 courts in 9 districts)
24 judges, 6 magistrates
Jury trials except in small claims

Jurisdiction:
- Tort, contract, real property ($0 - $7,000), small claims (up to $5,000), non-domestic relations restraining order.
- Civil protection/restraining order.
- Preliminary hearings.
- Traffic infractions.

Municipal Court

Jury trials

Jurisdiction:
- Traffic infractions, parking.
- Exclusive ordinance violations.

LIMITED JURISDICTION COURT

*In January 2003, Justice of the Peace courts were combined with County courts, and County Court was renamed Circuit Court.

Court structure as of Fiscal Year 2015.

☐ Appellate level
☐ Trial level
↑ Route of appeal

Indexes

Name Index

This index lists all individuals in the directory alphabetically by last name.